# Employee Training and Development

# Employee Training and Development

### Sixth Edition

### Raymond A. Noe
*The Ohio State University*

EMPLOYEE TRAINING AND DEVELOPMENT, SIXTH EDITION
International Edition 2013

10  09  08  07  06  05  04  03  02  01
20  15  14  13  12
CTP  MPM

When ordering this title, use ISBN 978-007-132638-4 or MHID 007-132638-3

Printed in Singapore

www.mhhe.com

This book is dedicated to John Weimeister, who excels at author relations. Thanks for all you have done to contribute to the development of textbooks that are fun to write and well received by professors and students!

# Preface

Traditionally, training and development were not viewed as activities that could help companies create "value" and successfully deal with competitive challenges. Today, that view has changed. Companies that use innovative training and development practices are likely to report better financial performance than their competitors that do not. Training and development also help a company meet competitive challenges. Current economic times have resulted in cuts in training and development budgets. However, many companies now recognize that learning through training, development, and knowledge management helps employees strengthen or increase their skills in order to improve or make new products, generate new and innovative ideas, and provide high-quality customer service. Also, development activities and career management are needed to prepare employees for managerial and leadership positions and to attract, motivate, and retain talented employees at all levels and in all jobs. An emphasis on learning through training, development, and knowledge management is no longer in the category of "nice to do"—they are a "must do" if companies want to gain a competitive advantage and meet employees' expectations.

Businesses today must compete in the global marketplace, and the diversity of the workforce continues to increase. As a result, companies need to train employees to work with persons from different cultures, both within the United States and abroad. New technologies, such as social media, and tablet computers, such as the iPad, reduce the costs associated with bringing employees to a central location for training. At the same time, the challenge is ensuring that these training methods include the necessary conditions (practice, feedback, self-pacing, etc.) for learning to occur. Also, through the blended learning approach, companies are seeking the best balance between private, self-paced, technology-based training (such as online learning), and methods that allow interpersonal interaction among trainees (such as classroom instruction or active learning).

The role of training has broadened beyond training program design. Effective instructional design remains important, but training managers, human resource experts, and trainers are increasingly being asked to create systems to motivate employees to learn, not only in programs but informally on the job; create knowledge; and share that knowledge with other employees in the company. Training has moved from an emphasis on a one-time event to the creation of conditions for learning that can occur through collaboration, online learning, traditional classroom training, or a combination of these methods. There is increased recognition that learning occurs informally, outside the boundaries of a formal training course.

Also, the employee-employer relationship has changed. Due to rapidly changing business environments and competition that can quickly cause profits to shrink and skill needs to change, companies are reluctant to provide job security to employees. At the same time, many employees are job-hopping to maximize the value that they can get for their skills in the job market, and not making a long-term commitment to any company. As a result, both employees and companies are concerned with developing future skills and managing careers. Companies want a workforce that is motivated and productive, has up-to-date skills, and can quickly learn new skills to meet changing customer and marketplace needs. Despite the prevalence of job-hopping, companies want to provide a work environment and training and development opportunities that will them the employer of choice for talented employees. Employees want to develop skills that not only are useful for their current jobs, but also are congruent with their personal interests and values. Given the increasing time demands of work, employees are also interested in maintaining balance between work and non-work interests.

The chapter coverage of *Employee Training and Development* reflects the traditional as well as the broadening role of training and development in organizations. Chapter One, "Introduction to Employee Training and Development," covers the role of training and development in companies. Chapter Two, "Strategic Training," discusses how training practices and the organization of the training function can support business goals. Because companies are interested in reducing costs, the amount of resources allocated to training is likely to be determined by the extent that training and development activities help the company reach business goals. Topics related to designing training programs are covered in Chapters Three through Six. Chapter Three, "Needs Assessment," discusses how to identify when training is appropriate. Chapter Four, "Learning and Transfer of Training," addresses the learning process and characteristics of a learning environment. The chapter also emphasizes what should be done in the design of training and the work environment to ensure that training is used on the job. Chapter Five, "Program Design," provides practical suggestions regarding what can be done to facilitate learning and transfer of training before, during, and after a course or program. The role of knowledge management in facilitating learning and transfer of training is also discussed. Chapter Six, "Training Evaluation," discusses how to evaluate training programs. Here, the student is introduced to the concepts of identifying cost-effective training, evaluating the return on investment of training and learning, and determining if training outcomes related to learning, behavior, or performance have been reached. Chapters Seven and Eight cover training methods. Chapter Seven, "Traditional Training Methods," discusses presentational methods (e.g., lecture), hands-on methods (e.g., on-the-job training and behavior modeling), and group methods (e.g., adventure learning). Chapter Eight, "Technology-Based Training Methods," introduces new technologies that are being used in training. These technology-based training methods include e-learning, mobile learning, social media, simulations, virtual worlds, and blended learning. Chapters Seven and Eight both conclude by comparing training methods on the basis of costs, benefits, and learning characteristics.

Chapter Nine, "Employee Development and Career Management," introduces developmental methods (assessment, relationships, job experiences, and formal courses). In addition, the use of development plans to help employees succeed in their self-directed or protean careers is highlighted. Topics such as succession planning and on boarding are discussed. Chapter Ten, "Social Responsibility: Legal Issues, Managing Diversity, and Career Challenges," emphasizes the role that training plays in helping companies improve the communities where they are located by increasing the skill level of the workforce, helping to provide jobs, and taking actions to help all employees grow and develop, regardless of their personal characteristics or career challenges. The chapter also discusses compliance with laws that affect training and development, training partnerships, managing diversity, cross-cultural preparation, and how companies can help employees deal with career challenges such as balancing work and life, coping with career breaks such as taking time off for family or required military service, job loss, and retirement. Finally, Chapter Eleven, "The Future of Training and Development," looks at how training and development might be different ten or twenty years from now.

*Employee Training and Development* is based on my more than twenty-five years of teaching training and development courses to both graduate and undergraduate students. From this experience, I have realized that managers, consultants, trainers, and faculty working in a variety of disciplines (including education, psychology, business, and industrial relations) have contributed to the research and practice of training and development. As a result, the book is based on research conducted in several disciplines, while offering a practical perspective. The book is appropriate for students in a number of programs. It suits both undergraduate and master's-level training courses in a variety of disciplines.

# DISTINCTIVE FEATURES

This book has several distinctive features. First, my teaching experience has taught me that students become frustrated if they do not see research and theory in practice. As a result, one distinctive feature of the book is that each chapter begins with a real-life vignette of a company practice that relates to the material covered in the chapter. Many examples of company practices are provided throughout the chapters. Each chapter ends with a real-life case and related questions that give students the opportunity to apply the chapter's content to an actual training or development issue.

A second distinctive feature of the book is its topical coverage. The chapters included in Part Two, "Designing Training," relate to training design (needs assessment, training methods, learning and transfer of training, and program design and evaluation). Instructional design is still the "meat and potatoes" of training. Part Three, "Training and Development Methods," covers the more exciting part of training and development—that is, training and development methods. But as the role of managers and trainers broadens, they are increasingly involved in helping all employees grow, develop, and cope with career challenges, as well as preparing high-potential employees for leadership positions. For example, managers and trainers need to understand generational differences in employees' career needs, career paths, cross-cultural training, diversity, outplacement, and succession planning—topics that fall outside the realm of instructional design. These topics are covered in Part Four, "Social Responsibility and the Future."

The book begins with a discussion of the context for training and development. Part One includes chapters that cover the economic and workplace factors that are influencing trends in the training profession. One of these trends is that companies are emphasizing learning through formal training and development, knowledge management, and informal learning. In addition, these chapters discuss the need for training, development, and learning to become strategic (i.e., to contribute to business strategy and organizational goals). Why? In successful, effective training, all aspects of training—including training objectives, methods, evaluation, and even who conducts the training—relate to the business strategy. More and more companies are demanding that the training function and training practices support business goals; otherwise, training may be outsourced or face funding cuts. Although students in business schools are exposed to strategic thinking, students in psychology and education who go on to become trainers need to understand the strategic perspective and how it relates to the organization of the training function and the type of training conducted.

Not only has technology changed the way we live and the way work is performed, but it also has influenced training practice. As a result, one chapter of the book is devoted entirely to the use of technologies for training delivery and instruction, such as online learning, social media, mobile learning, tablet computers, and virtual worlds.

The book reflects the latest "hot topics" in the area of training. Some of the new topics discussed in the book are corporate universities, outsourcing training, developing and measuring human capital, learning management systems, competencies, knowledge management, e-learning, mobile learning (using smartphones), iPads and other tablet computers, social media such as blogs, wikis, and social networks, and virtual worlds (such as Second Life) for training. Each chapter contains the most recent academic research findings and company practices.

# FEATURES DESIGNED TO AID LEARNING

*Employee Training and Development* provides several features to aid learning:

1. Each chapter lists objectives that highlight what the student is expected to learn in that chapter.
2. In-text examples and chapter openers feature companies from all industries, including service, manufacturing, retail, and nonprofit organizations.
3. Discussion questions at the end of each chapter help students learn the concepts presented in the chapter and understand potential applications of the material.
4. Important terms and concepts used in training and development are boldfaced in each chapter. Key terms are identified at the end of each chapter. These key terms are important to help the student understand the language of training.
5. Application assignments are useful for the students to put chapter content into practice. Most chapters include assignments that require the student to use the World Wide Web.
6. Cases at the end of each chapter and at the end of each of the four parts of the book help students apply what they have learned to training and development issues faced by actual companies.
7. Name and subject indexes at the end of the book help in finding key people and topics.

# WHAT'S NEW IN THE SIXTH EDITION

I want to personally thank all of you who have adopted this book! Based on the comments of the reviewers of the fifth edition and training research and practice, I have made several improvements. Some important changes in the sixth edition of *Employee Training and Development* stand out:

- Each chapter has been updated to include the most recent research findings and new best company practices. New examples have been added in each chapter's text.
- All the chapter opening vignettes are new. For example, the opening vignette for Chapter Eight highlights how Farmers Insurance is using a blended learning approach that includes face-to-face instruction, online learning, social networks, and iPads equipped with apps to deliver effective learning to its multigenerational and geographically dispersed workforce.

- This edition offers new and expanded coverage of such topics as informal learning, business-embedded training functions, knowledge management, learning management systems, intangible assets and human capital, implications of the multigenerational workforce for training and development, use of social media (including blogs, wikis, and social networks) in training, program design, and the important role of training partnerships with educational institutions, government agencies, unions, and nonprofits.

- Each chapter ends with application assignments, including new program design and updated web-based exercises. These assignments are also found on the book's website.

- Each chapter concludes with new or updated brief cases that illustrate a training, development, or learning issue faced by a company. The case questions ask students to consider issues and make recommendations based on the chapter content.

- To help students better understand the connections between topics, the book is organized into four different parts. Part One focuses on the context for training and development and includes a chapter devoted to strategic training. Part Two includes coverage related to the fundamentals of designing training programs. Chapters in Part Two focus on needs assessment, learning theories and transfer of training, program design, and training evaluation. Part Three focuses on training and development methods and includes chapters devoted to traditional training methods, e-learning, and the use of new training technologies such as social media and mobile learning. The chapters in Part Four cover employee development and career management and the role of training and learning in helping companies increase their social responsibility. This includes following laws and regulations that relate to training, as well as managing diversity and helping employees cope with career challenges such as balancing work and life, career breaks, identifying and moving along a career path, preparing for retirement, and coping with job loss. Finally, this part provides a look at the future of training and development.

- To ensure that students have a better understanding of program design and can leave the course with skills needed to design a course or program, an entire chapter, Chapter Five, is now devoted to program design.

- Chapter Nine now covers employee development and career management including an expanded discussion of succession planning (including use of the nine-box grid) and onboarding.

- Chapter Ten contains some new content and combines content from Chapters Ten, Eleven, and Twelve in the fifth edition. The emphasis of this chapter is training and learning's role in helping companies be socially responsible through legal training and development practices, training partnerships designed to improve the skills of and enhance employment opportunities for the local workforce, and help employees grow and develop through managing diversity and inclusion and deal with career challenges.

- The sixth edition includes eleven chapters, two fewer than the fifth edition, which can easily be covered in a semester course. This allows more time to be devoted to topics that the instructor wants to emphaisize in the course. Also, the new and combined chapters expose students to important content related to training, development, and career management.

# Acknowledgments

The author is only one of many important people involved in writing a textbook. The sixth edition of this book would not have been possible without the energy and expertise of several others from McGraw-Hill Irwin and S4Carlisle Publishing Services. Wendy Langerud, developmental editor, and project managers Jessica Portz and Shyam Ramasubramony, deserve my gratitude and thanks for their patience and expertise in following the insertions and changes I made, and for ensuring that my ideas made sense and my writing was clear, concise, and easy to understand.

I take full responsibility for any errors, omissions, or misstatements of fact in this book. However, regardless of your impression of the book, it would not have been this good had it not been for the manuscript reviewers. Special thanks to these people, who provided me with detailed comments that helped improve the sixth edition of the book for students and instructors. These reviewers include

**Wendy J. Casper**
*University of Texas at Arlington*

**Marilynn Cowgill**
*University of Colorado at Boulder*

**Sandra Lyn French**
*Radford University*

**Millicent J. Kelly**
*Barry University*

**John R. Knue**
*Baylor University*

**Gary Strood**
*Franklin University*

**Itoe Peter Valentine**
*Albany Technical College*

**Kostas Voutssas**
*Dickinson State University*

# About the Author

**Raymond A. Noe**    *The Ohio State University*

Raymond A. Noe is the Robert and Anne Hoyt Designated Professor of Management at The Ohio State University. He has taught for more than twenty-five years at Big Ten universities. Before joining the faculty at Ohio State, he was a professor in the Department of Management at Michigan State University and the Industrial Relations Center of the Carlson School of Management, University of Minnesota. He received a B.S. in psychology from The Ohio State University and M.A. and Ph.D. degrees in psychology from Michigan State University. Professor Noe conducts research and teaches all levels of students—from undergraduates to executives—in human resource management, managerial skills, quantitative methods, human resource information systems, training and development, and organizational behavior. He has published articles in the *Academy of Management Journal, Academy of Management Review, Journal of Applied Psychology, Journal of Vocational Behavior,* and *Personnel Psychology.* Professor Noe is currently on the editorial boards of several journals, including *Journal of Applied Psychology, Personnel Psychology,* and *Journal of Organizational Behavior.* Besides *Employee Training and Development,* he has co-authored two other textbooks: *Fundamentals of Human Resource Management* and *Human Resource Management: Gaining a Competitive Advantage,* both published by McGraw-Hill/Irwin. Professor Noe has received awards for his teaching and research excellence, including the Herbert G. Heneman Distinguished Teaching Award in 1991, the Ernest J. McCormick Award for Distinguished Early Career Contribution from the Society for Industrial and Organizational Psychology in 1993, and the ASTD Outstanding Research Article of the Year Award for 2001. He is also a fellow of the Society of Industrial and Organizational Psychology.

# Brief Contents

# Contents

## Chapter 11
## The Future of Training and Development   466

# ORGANIZATION OF THIS BOOK

This book is organized into five parts. Part One focuses on the context for training and development and includes this chapter, which offered a broad perspective on training and helped answer questions such as: What is training? Why is it important? Who is receiving training? How much money is spent on training? How should training be designed? Part One also includes Chapter Two, which discusses the strategic training and development process. In Chapter Two, you will see how a company's business strategy influences training practices and the organization of the training department. Chapters Three through Six make up Part Two. These chapters discuss the fundamentals of training design and address different aspects of the ISD model, the model used to guide the development of training (see Figure 1.1). Chapter Three deals with how to determine training needs. Chapter Four discusses the important issue of learning—specifically, the importance of learning and transfer of training. The chapter emphasizes what we learn, how we learn, and how to create an environment conducive to learning within a training session. The chapter also discusses what needs to be considered for transfer of training, i.e., ensuring that skills emphasized in training are used on the job. Chapter Five provides insights into the specific of how training programs should be designed to facilitate learning and transfer. The chapter covers the importance of room design, learning objectives, selecting and preparing trainers, and course planning for learning, as well as how managers, trainers, learners, and knowledge management can facilitate transfer of training. Chapter Six explains how to evaluate a training program. Part Three focuses on training and development methods. Chapter Seven looks at traditional training methods such as lecture, behavior modeling simulation, and role play. Chapter Eight examines e-learning and methods that have developed from applications of new technology, for example, web-based training, virtual reality, mobile learning and social collaboration.

Chapter Nine addresses the important issue of employee development and career management; it discusses four approaches used to develop employee assessments, assignments, relationships, courses, and formal programs. Part Five considers training's role in social responsibility and the future of training and development. Chapter Ten deals with legal issues and diversity. Topics covered include ethics and legal issues, managing diversity, cross-cultural training, and issues relevant to certain employee groups, such as coping with career breaks and melting the "glass ceiling." Chapter Eleven discusses how new technologies may influence training and how its role may change in the future.

Students should be aware of several important features of the book. Each chapter begins with chapter objectives. These objectives (1) highlight what the student should learn from each chapter and (2) preview the topics. Next comes an opening vignette—an example of a company practice related to the chapter topics. Company examples are liberally used throughout each chapter to help students see how theory and research in training are put into practice. Each chapter ends with key terms, discussion questions, application assignments, and a short case. Key terms are related to important concepts emphasized in the chapter. Discussion questions and application assignments can facilitate learning through interacting with other students and actually trying to develop and conduct various training applications. Many application assignments require the use of the web, a valuable source of information on training practices. Each of the parts concludes with a case that highlights a company's training and development practices. These cases include questions asking you to apply what you have learned in the chapters.

# The Context for Training and Development

Part One focuses on issues related to the context for training and development. Chapter One, "Introduction to Employee Training and Development," discusses why training and development are important to help companies successfully compete in today's business environment. The chapter provides an overview of training practices, the training profession, and how to design effective training (a topic that is covered in detail in Part Two, "Training Design"). Chapter Two, "Strategic Training," discusses the strategic training and development process, organizational characteristics that influence training, various models for organizing the training department, how to brand training and market it to the rest of the company, and the advantages and disadvantages of outsourcing training.

Part One concludes with a case that highlights how PricewaterhouseCoopers is using training to cope with competitive challenges, reach business goals, and expand learning beyond the classroom and boardroom.

1. Introduction to Employee Training and Development
2. Strategic Training

# Chapter **One**

# Introduction to Employee Training and Development

## Objectives

After reading this chapter, you should be able to

1. Discuss the forces influencing the workplace and learning, and explain how training can help companies deal with these forces.

2. Draw a figure or diagram and explain how training, development, informal learning, and knowledge management contribute to business success.

3. Discuss various aspects of the training design process.

4. Describe the amount and types of training occurring in U.S. companies.

5. Discuss the key roles for training professionals.

6. Identify appropriate resources (e.g., journals, websites) for learning about training research and practice.

## Forces Affecting the Workplace Make Training a Key Ingredient of Company Success

Customer service, productivity, safety, employee retention and growth, the uncertainty in the economy, coping with the retirement of skilled employees, the use of new technology—these are just some of the issues affecting companies in all industries and sizes and influencing training practices.

The examples presented below show how these concerns have affected companies in several different business sectors and how training has helped them succeed.

Many companies, recognizing that learning goes beyond typical face-to-face classes, are using technology to make it easier for employees in different locations to learn and share knowledge through formal courses, as well as through collaboration. For example, Jiffy Lube International is using training to prepare and retain employees and provide high-quality customer service. Car owners know that the oil in their cars has to be changed every 3,000 to 5,000 miles (fact or fiction? See below). Jiffy Lube International relies on training to prepare employees in more than 2,000 U.S. franchises to correctly change oil, provide consistent and accurate services, and satisfy its more than 2 million customers. All employees are required to complete specific certifications during their employment and can voluntarily complete others to prepare them for new jobs. These certifications are based on training courses that focus on customer service, management, technical procedures, and service standards. More than 150 hours of training are available to employees during their first year of employment. For example, within thirty days after they are hired, technicians must be certified in safety and product knowledge. Almost all of the certification training is available online and on-demand, i.e., any time employees want to take it. After completing a course, employees take online tests to demonstrate that they have mastered the knowledge emphasized in the course. Managers provide coaching to ensure that what was learned is correctly used on the job. Employees can access an online learning management system that uses a gas gauge to show them their progress toward completion of certification training. Store managers can download reports that show their employees' progress in meeting certification requirements. Training has helped the company succeed by reducing employee turnover (more than 50 percent in some locations) and improving customer perceptions about employee training. Also, employee training has helped the company change customer mindsets about oil changes and other services from one simply based on mileage to one based on auto manufacturer recommendations and customer driving conditions. Employees are better prepared to help customers select service that best fits their budget, vehicle, and driving conditions. Customer satisfaction is enhanced because they appreciate the employees' honesty and feel that they are in control of how their vehicle is serviced.

Blue Cross and Blue Shield of Michigan uses KnowIt and MISource to reach employees at forty different locations. KnowIt includes wikis, web courses, podcasts, discussion boards, and e-learning to provide information on more than eighty business topics. MISource gives claims and customer service employees access to information they need to better serve customers. Scotiabank Group, with operations in more than fifty companies, developed an internal social networking application, FaceForward, which includes user profiles, blogs, wikis, and social bookmarks.

Seattle City Light, the city's municipally owned electric company, expects more than a quarter of its workforce to retire within the next five years. Seattle City Light is using training courses and interactions with more experienced employees and mentors to help employees learn new and innovative technologies, as well as the electrical system's history, to prevent electrical demand from overloading aging dams and power tunnels. Final exams and hands-on field tests are administered after training to ensure that new employees have acquired the knowledge and skills needed to be successful operators. The company also uses apprenticeship programs to develop technical employees such as hydro machinists. They are rotated throughout the plant to ensure that they understand how their role and their interactions with other employees contribute to the effective and efficient operation of the utility.

U.S. Airways Group provides extensive training for flight attendants and pilots. Newly hired flight attendants receive five weeks of training, including an introduction to the aviation industry, and Airbus cabin simulators include "door trainers" to practice opening emergency exits under difficult evacuation conditions, such as total darkness and billowing smoke. Training also includes jumping into a pool and inflating a life raft and helping passengers into and out of a raft. Federal law requires annual classroom safety training for flight attendants, and performance drills every two years. Pilot training includes practicing skills in a simulator that presents many different scenarios, such as both engines failing, and re-creates the feelings and sounds experienced in flight, including turbulence. Forced landings and water ditchings are taught in the classroom. The payoff for this type of extensive training was most evident in the spectacularly safe landing of Flight 1549 and its 155 passengers and flight crew in the Hudson River in 2009. Based on their almost automatic responses developed through years of training, flight attendants were able to calm passengers, prepare them for a crash landing, and open doors and inflate life rafts to assist in the orderly but quick exit of the slowly sinking airplane. The cockpit crew followed the training they received in how to cope with engine failure and successfully conducted a water landing.

**Sources:** Based on J. Salopek, "Keeping learning well-oiled," *T+D* (October 2011), 32–35; Training Top 125, *training* (January/February 2011): 54–93. "Seattle's Strategy, Water Power and Dam Construction," *training* (February 29, 2009): 36; S. McCartney, "Crash Courses for the Crew," *The Wall Street Journal* (January 27, 2009): D1, D8.

# INTRODUCTION

The examples discussed in the chapter opening illustrate how training can contribute to companies' competitiveness. **Competitiveness** refers to a company's ability to maintain and gain market share in an industry. Although they are different types of businesses, these four companies have training practices that have helped them gain a **competitive advantage** in their markets. That is, the training practices have helped them grow the business and improve customer service by providing employees with the knowledge and skills they need to be successful.

Companies are experiencing great change due to new technologies, rapid development of knowledge, globalization of business, and development of e-commerce. Also, companies have to take steps to attract, retain, and motivate their workforces. Training is not a luxury; it is a necessity if companies are to participate in the global and electronic marketplaces by offering high-quality products and services. Training prepares employees to use new technologies, function in new work systems such as virtual teams, and communicate and cooperate with peers or customers who may be from different cultural backgrounds.

**Human resource management** refers to the policies, practices, and systems that influence employees' behavior, attitudes, and performance. Human resource practices play a key role in attracting, motivating, rewarding, and retaining employees. Other human resource management practices include recruiting employees, selecting employees, designing work, compensating employees, and developing good labor and employee relations. Chapter Two, "Strategic Training," details the importance placed on training in comparison to other human resource management practices. To be effective, training must play a strategic role in supporting the business.

Human resource management is one of several important functions in most companies. Other functions include accounting and finance, production and operations, research and development, and marketing. Keep in mind that although human resource management practices (such as training) can help companies gain a competitive advantage, the company needs to produce a product or provide a service that customers value. Without the financial resources and physical resources (e.g., equipment) needed to produce products or provide services, the company will not survive.

This chapter begins by defining training and development and discussing how the training function has evolved. Next, the forces that are shaping the workplace and learning are addressed. These forces influence the company's ability to successfully meet stakeholders' needs. The term **stakeholders** refers to shareholders, the community, customers, employees, and all the other parties that have an interest in seeing that the company succeeds. The discussion of the forces shaping the workplace (including technology, globalization, and attracting and winning talent) highlights the role of training in helping companies gain a competitive advantage.

The second part of the chapter focuses on current trends in the training area. This section also introduces you to the trainer's role in a business and how the training function is organized. This section should help you understand current training practices, the types of jobs that trainers may perform, and the competencies needed to be a successful trainer (or, if you are a manager, to identify a successful trainer). The chapter concludes with an overview of the topics covered in the book.

# TRAINING AND DEVELOPMENT: KEY COMPONENTS OF LEARNING

Our focus in this book is to help you understand the role of training and development in today's organizations. To do this, it is important for you to understand what training and development means in the broader business context. Figure 1.1 shows the role of training and development for the business. The overall goal of training and development is learning.

**FIGURE 1.1**
**The Business Role of Training and Development**

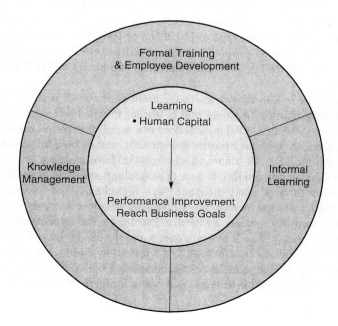

**Learning** refers to employees acquiring knowledge, skills, competencies, attitudes, or behaviors. But the focus of training and development is not just on employees learning for its own sake. Today, merely offering training programs is not enough to get support and funding from executives and to establish the credibility of the training and development function to managers and employees. Learning needs to demonstrate how it contributes to the company's competitive advantage through improving employee performance, supporting the business strategy (such as growing the business), and contributing positively to business outcomes such as quality, productivity, development of new products, and retaining key employees. From a company's perspective, what employees learn contributes to the development of intangible assets such as human capital. **Human capital** refers to knowledge (know what), advanced skills (know how), system understanding and creativity (know why), and motivation to deliver high-quality products and services (care why).[1] Human capital may be more valuable than physical capital (equipment or technology) or financial capital (monetary assets, cash) for providing a company with an advantage over its competitors, because it is difficult to imitate or purchase and it is unique to the company.

There are a number of different ways that learning occurs in a company. They are represented on the outside of the circle in Figure 1.1. **Training** refers to a planned effort by a company to facilitate learning of job-related competencies, knowledge, skills, and behaviors by employees. The goal of training is for employees to master the knowledge, skills, and behaviors emphasized in training and apply them to their day-to-day activities. Traditionally, companies have relied on formal training through a course, program, or "event" to teach employees the knowledge, skills, and behaviors they need to successfully perform their job. Development is similar to training, except that it tends to be more future-focused. **Development** refers to training as well as formal education, job experiences, relationship, and assessments of personality, skills, and abilities that help employees prepare for future jobs or positions. We will discuss development in more detail in Chapter Nine, "Employee Development and Careers." **Formal training and development** refers to training and development programs, courses, and events that are developed and organized by the company. Typically, employees are required to attend or complete these programs, which can include face-to-face training programs (such as instructor-led courses) as well as online programs. As you will see later in the chapter, U.S. companies invest billions of dollars in formal training.

Informal learning is also important for facilitating the development of human capital.[2] **Informal learning** refers to learning that is learner initiated, involves action and doing, is motivated by an intent to develop, and does not occur in a formal learning setting.[3] Informal learning occurs without a trainer or instructor, and its breadth, depth, and timing is controlled by the employee. It occurs on an as-needed basis and may involve an employee learning either alone or through face-to-face or technology-aided social interactions. Informal learning can occur through many different ways, including casual unplanned interactions with peers, e-mail, informal mentoring, or company-developed or publically available social networking websites such as Twitter or Facebook. The application of social media from a marketing strategy to a learning strategy and the availability of Web 2.0 technologies such as social networks, microblogs, and wikis allow employees easy access to social learning or learning through collaboration and sharing with one or two or more people.[4] One estimate is that informal learning may account for up to 75 percent of learning within organizations.

One reason why informal learning may be especially important is that it may lead to the effective development of *tacit* knowledge, which can be contrasted with *explicit* knowledge.[5] **Explicit knowledge** refers to knowledge which is well documented, easily articulated, and easily transferred from person-to-person. Examples of explicit knowledge include processes, checklists, flowcharts, formulas, and definitions. Explicit knowledge tends to be the primary focus of formal training and employee development. **Tacit knowledge** refers to personal knowledge based on individual experiences that is difficult to codify. The characteristics of formal training and development programs, such as the relatively short duration of classroom or online training and limited opportunities for practice, may limit the extent to which tacit knowledge can be acquired. Thus, informal learning is central to the development of tacit knowledge because it involves employee interactions in personal relationships with peers, colleagues, and experts through which tacit knowledge is shared. It is important to recognize, however, that informal learning cannot replace formal training and employee development. Formal training and development are still needed to prepare employees for their jobs and to help them advance to future positions. Informal learning complements training by helping employees gain tacit knowledge that formal training cannot provide.

**Knowledge management** refers to the process of enhancing company performance by designing and implementing tools, processes, systems, structures, and cultures to improve the creation, sharing, and use of knowledge.[6] Knowledge management contributes to informal learning. For example, Cerner Corporation, a global technology company in Kansas City, Missouri, developed uCern, a system that employees and clients can use to share their knowledge about solutions, projects, and professional interests.[7] Caterpillar Inc. moved toward becoming a continuous learning organization with the help of knowledge management.[8] Thirty years ago, Caterpillar Inc., a manufacturer of construction and mining equipment, engines, and gas turbines, had most of its value in its plant and equipment. Today, intangible assets account for most of the company's value. Caterpillar's web-based knowledge management system, known as Knowledge Network, has thousands of communities of practice. They range in size from small teams to hundreds of employees worldwide. The communities of practice are useful for employees to gain both explicit and tacit knowledge. They are used to distribute information, post questions, and provide space for reference materials. One community of practice focused on bolted joints and fasteners. This gives specialized engineers who generally work alone in manufacturing facilities the ability to ask other engineers questions or get second opinions on designs and problems. The community of practice has resulted in improved decision making, increased collaboration and teamwork, and better product design and development. For example, members of the Bolted Joints and Fastener community and the Dealer Service Training Community saved more than $1.5 million from online discussions.

Many companies who recognize the value of learning have taken steps to ensure that formal training and employee development is linked to strategic business objectives and goals, use an instructional design process to ensure that these programs are effective, and compares or benchmarks the company's programs against its competitors or other companies in the industry.[9]

Consider the role of learning at PricewaterhouseCoopers.[10] Its Learning and Education (L&E) team was restructured to better link it to the business goals related to value and impact. L&E works with the business to understand what it wants education to be. It ensures ongoing innovation in training delivery and instructional methods by evaluating emerging technologies and using them in small pilot projects. The chief learning officer in charge of L&E is a member of the company's leadership team, which gives that individual the opportunity to discuss ideas regarding training methods, delivery, and content with other top-level managers. L&E sponsors traditional and virtual classroom courses, self-study, team-based learning, action learning projects, coaching and mentoring, and conferences, and it has served more than 150,000 users each year, with over 6,000 courses, 12,000 classroom-based training sessions, and 19,000 web-based training sessions.

PricewaterhouseCoopers uses a learning management system to create a single access point for training activities. To help employees learn on an as-needed basis, the company's e-learning includes video and audio conferencing, virtual classrooms, and webcasting. To evaluate the success of training, L&E considers its influence on outcomes, such as retention of top people. Also, focus groups are used to determine whether trainees and managers are satisfied with the training. A program on sustainability was designed to help partners understand how to provide solutions for their clients. The company's investment in the program has paid off. The company believes that it has achieved a return on investment of more than 1,000 percent in new business sold and reputation gains in the marketplace. In the future, L&E plans to further strengthen the relationship between training, development, and the business by focusing on how it can make learning even more accessible and closer to the point where employees need it. L&E wants to integrate learning and knowledge to speed employees' development and improve their competencies.

This discussion is not meant to underestimate the importance of "traditional training" (a focus on acquisition of knowledge, skills, and abilities), but it should alert you that for many companies, training is evolving from a focus on skills to an emphasis on continuous learning and creating and sharing knowledge. This evolution of training is discussed in Chapter Two.

# DESIGNING EFFECTIVE TRAINING

The **training design process** refers to a systematic approach for developing training programs. Figure 1.2 presents the seven steps in this process. Step 1 is a needs assessment, which is necessary to identify whether training is needed. Step 2 is to ensure that employees have the motivation and basic skills necessary to master the training content. Step 3 is to create a learning environment that has the features necessary for learning to occur. Step 4 is to ensure that trainees apply the training content to their jobs. This step involves having the trainee understand how to manage skill improvement, as well as getting co-worker and manager support.

Step 5 is to develop an evaluation plan. Developing an evaluation plan includes identifying what types of outcomes training is expected to influence (for example, learning, behavior, or skills), choosing an evaluation design that allows you to determine the influence of training on these outcomes, and planning how to demonstrate how training affects the "bottom line" (that is, using a cost-benefit analysis to determine the monetary benefits resulting from training). Step 6 is to choose the training method based on the learning objectives and learning environment. This step may include a traditional training method of face-to-face interaction with a trainer or e-learning using CD-ROM or web-based training.

**FIGURE 1.2**  **Training Design Process**

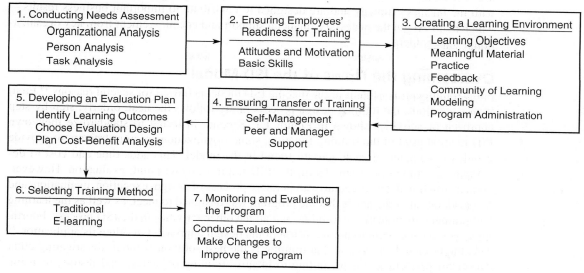

Step 7 is to evaluate the program and make changes in it or revisit any of the earlier steps in the process to improve the program so that learning, behavior, change, and other learning objectives are obtained.

The training design process shown in Figure 1.1 is based on principles of Instructional System Design. **Instructional System Design (ISD)** refers to a process for designing and developing training programs. There is not one universally accepted instructional systems development model. The training design process sometimes is referred to as the *ADDIE model* because it includes analysis, design, development, implementation, and evaluation.[11] In Figure 1.1, Step 1, conducting needs assessment, and Step 2, ensuring employees' readiness for training, are related to analysis. The next three steps—creating a learning environment, ensuring transfer of training, and developing an evaluation plan—are design issues. Step 6, selecting and using a training method, relates to implementation. Step 7, monitoring and evaluating the program, relates to evaluation. Regardless of the specific ISD approach used, all share the following assumptions:[12]

- Training design is effective only if it helps employees reach instructional or training goals and objectives.
- Measurable learning objectives should be identified before the training program begins.
- Evaluation plays an important part in planning and choosing a training method, monitoring the training program, and suggesting changes to the training design process.

American Infrastructure (AI), located in Worcester, Pennsylvania, uses the ADDIE model to design training for its employees involved in construction and mining.[13] Templates based on the ADDIE model are used to design and develop training and development programs. AI uses the templates to ensure that needs assessment is conducted and evaluation is considered as training and development programs are being designed. The use of the templates also helps to show that training and development programs are aligned with the business strategy and are designed to contribute to important business results—which helps AI get the necessary financial support and encouragement from key organizational stakeholders.

## Overcoming the Flows of the ISD Model

Some training professionals argue that the ISD model is flawed for several reasons.[14] First, in organizations, the training design process rarely follows the neat, orderly, step-by-step approach of activities shown in Figure 1.1. Second, in trying to standardize their own ISD method used in the training function, some organizations require trainers to provide detailed documents of each activity found in the model. This adds time and cost to developing a training program. Third, the ISD implies an end point: evaluation. However, good instructional design requires an iterative process of design, execution, evaluation, and reconsideration of the needs that the program was designed to meet, as well as the learning environment, the transfer of training, and all the other activities in the ISD process. Fourth, many companies claim to use an instructional design approach but dilute its application.[15] This might include assuming that training is the best solution without investigating other causes for performance gaps, failing to identify training objectives and results, focusing too much on the training method while ignoring the role of the work environment in transfer of training, and concentrating evaluation on whether trainees liked the program rather than on measuring the impact of training on job performance or business results. Despite these criticisms, use of the ISD process is the best way to help ensure the effectiveness of training and development.

The training design process should be systematic, yet flexible enough to adapt to business needs. Different steps may be completed simultaneously. Keep in mind that designing training unsystematically will reduce the benefits that can be realized. For example, choosing a training method before determining training needs or ensuring employees' readiness for training increases the risk that the method chosen will not be the most effective one for meeting training needs. Also, training may not even be necessary and may result in a waste of time and money. Employees may have the knowledge, skills, or behavior they need but simply not be motivated to use them.

The introduction of new technologies such as mobile learning (discussed in Chapter Eight) highlights a shift from trainees having to learn from an instructor in one location to trainees learning independently and not being bound to learn in the workplace. Still, good training design requires determining the trainees' needs, identifying resources so that trainees can learn what they need to know, and providing them with access to reference materials and knowledge bases when they encounter problems, issues, or questions on the job.[16]

The development of a web-based training program focused on teaching managers the skills needed to run effective business meetings provides a good example of the instructional design process. The first step of the process, needs assessment, involved determining that managers lacked skills for conducting effective meetings and helped to identify the type of meetings that managers were involved in. The needs assessment process involved interviewing managers and observing meetings. The needs assessment process also identified the most appropriate training method.

Because the managers were geographically dispersed and had easy access to computers, and because the company wanted a self-directed, self-paced program that the managers could complete during free time in their work schedule, the training designers and company management decided that web-based training was the appropriate method. Because training was going to be conducted over the web, the designers had to be sure that managers could access the web and were familiar with tools for using it (e.g., web browsers). This relates to determining the managers' readiness for training.

The next step was to create a positive learning environment on the web. Designers made sure that the program objectives were clearly stated to the trainees and provided opportunities within the program for exercises and feedback. For example, trainees were asked to prepare an outline for the steps they would take to conduct an effective meeting. The designers built into the program a feedback system that indicated to the managers which of the steps they outlined were correct and which needed to be changed. The designers also included assessment tests that allowed the trainees to receive feedback through the program and to skip ahead or return to earlier material based on their scores on the tests. The assessment included a test of meeting skills that the managers completed both prior to and after completing the program. The assessment tests were stored in a data bank that the company could use to evaluate whether trainees' meeting skills improved from pretraining levels.

# THE FORCES INFLUENCING WORKING AND LEARNING

Table 1.1 illustrates the forces that are influencing working and learning. Globalization of business, demographic changes, new technologies, and economic changes are several of the forces shown in Table 1.1 that influence all aspects of our lives: how we purchase products and services, how we learn, how we communicate with each other, and what we value in our lives and on the job.[17] These forces are affecting individuals, communities, businesses, and society. To survive, companies must address these forces—with training playing an important role.

The recession experienced in the United States between 2007 and the summer of 2009 was one of the worst ever, with the unemployment rate reaching over 10 percent in October 2009.[18] Although the recovery of the U.S. economy since 2009 can be characterized as slow and choppy, recent 2.5 percent growth in the gross domestic product (GDP), the total of all goods and services produced, and some positive job growth and small drop in the unemployment rate suggest that falling back into another recession is unlikely.[19] Dampening enthusiasm for an economic recovery, the labor force participation rate, which measures those who have jobs or are actively seeking work, was approximately 64 percent, its lowest point since the mid-1980s. Also, estimates suggest that 4.4 million people have been out

**TABLE 1.1**
**Forces Influencing Working and Learning**

Economic cycles
Globalization
Increased value placed on intangible assets and human capital
Focus on link to business strategy
Changing demographics and diversity of the workforce
Talent management
Customer service and quality emphasis
New technology
High-performance work systems

of work for over a year. Unemployment or underemployment is affecting all Americans, including recent college graduates. For example, 5.9 million Americans between the ages of 25 and 34 (about twenty-five percent of which have bachelor's degrees) are now living with their parents.[20] This means not only that parents are adding extra expenses, but that that some of those who are employed but have considered retirement can't afford it. This means that parents keep their jobs longer, crowding the younger generation out of the job market. Unfortunately, the economic recovery will likely remain slow for some time and could stop entirely or deteriorate if a solution is not found for the debt crisis in European countries such as Greece and Spain, as well as the huge budget deficit in the United States. Companies may be reluctant to increase their training budgets because of the economic uncertainty.[21] However, such economic times also provide an opportunity for companies to take a closer look at training and development to identify those activities that are critical for supporting the business strategy, as well as those mandated by law (such as safety training or sexual harassment training). Also, training technologies using iPads and online learning will likely receive more serious consideration to reduce training and development costs (such as travel and instructor costs) and increase employees' access to training. For example, Philips Electronics is cutting its training budget but will continue to offer its Inspire program for high-potential employees, emphasizing business strategy and personal leadership topics. Philips believes that investing in leadership development will help the company weather the recession and prepare for economic recovery. Likewise, Estée Lauder Companies, the cosmetics maker, has realized lower profits and sales, resulting in the elimination of over 2,000 jobs over the next two years. But Estée Lauder is continuing its leadership development programs, which will emphasize innovation and managing change in turbulent business conditions. Despite the recession, talent retention is still an important concern. Some companies are creating discretionary bonus pools to reward employees who may be recruited by other companies. To keep employees engaged, Best Buy uses online surveys to get employees' opinions and suggestions regarding how to cut costs.

## Globalization

Every business must be prepared to deal with the global economy. Global business expansion has been made easier by technology. The Internet allows data and information to be instantly accessible and sent around the world. The Internet, e-mail, and video conferencing enable business deals to be completed between companies thousands of miles apart.

Globalization is not limited to any particular sector of the economy, product market, or company size.[22] Companies without international operations may buy or use goods that have been produced overseas, hire employees with diverse backgrounds, or compete with foreign-owned companies operating within the United States. Globalization is also likely to increase as major opportunities to expand into new markets grow due to the increasing number of consumers overseas who have products and services and the income to buy them.

One estimate is that developing economies and emerging markets such as those found in the BRIC nations (Brazil, Russia, India, and China) will be responsible for 68 percent of the growth of the world's economy.[23] The importance of globalization is seen in recent hiring patterns of large U.S. multinational corporations who have increased their overseas workforce, particularly in Asia.[24] For example, Oracle, the business hardware and software developer, added twice as many workers overseas over the past five years in the United States; and 63 percent of its employees are outside the United States. Markets in Brazil,

China, and India have resulted in 60 percent of General Electric's business outside the United States, with 54 percent of employees being located overseas. Clothing retailer Gap Inc plans to open eleven stores in Hong Kong and China.[25] This will add to the four stores and e-business website that it opened in China in November 2010, and expands the Gap's Asian presence, which already included Gap and Banana Republic stores in Japan. Gap believes it needs to expand its international presence because the U.S. market is maturing and has many competitors. Yum! Brands, the parent company of KFC and Pizza Hut, has over 3,700 stores in China, contributing over 40 percent of its operating income in 2010.[26]

Global companies are struggling both to find and retain talented employees, especially in emerging markets. Companies are moving into China, India, Eastern Europe, the Middle East, Southeast Asia, and Latin America, but the demand for talented employees exceeds the supply. Also, companies often place successful U.S. managers in charge of overseas operations, but they lack the cultural understanding necessary to attract, motivate, and retain talented employees. To cope with these problems, companies are taking actions to better prepare their managers and their families for overseas assignments and to ensure that training and development opportunities are available for global employees. Cross-cultural training prepares employees and their families to understand the culture and norms of the country to which they are being relocated and assists in their return to their home country after the assignment. Cross-cultural training is discussed in Chapter Ten.

McDonalds opened 165 stores in China in 2010 and plans to open 1,000 more by the end of 2013.[27] To train future managers in store operations, leadership, and staff management skills that are needed for the expansion, McDonalds has built a new Hamburger University near Shanghai, China.

IBM obtains more than two-thirds of its revenue from outside the United States and is seeking to build team leadership in order to compete in emerging markets around the world. IBM's Corporate Service Program donates the time and services of about 600 employees for projects in countries such as Turkey, Romania, Ghana, Vietnam, the Phillipines, and Tanzania.[28] The goal of the program is to develop a leadership team to learn about the needs and the culture of these countries while at the same time providing valuable community service. For example, eight IBM employees from five countries traveled to Timisoara, Romania. Each employee was assigned to help a different company or nonprofit organization. One software-development manager helped GreenForest, a manufacturer of office, hotel, school, and industrial furniture, reach its goal of cutting costs and becoming more efficient by recommending the computer equipment and systems needed to increase production and exports to Western Europe. Another employee worked with a nonprofit organization that offers services to disabled adults. Besides benefiting the companies, the employees also found that the experience helped them understand cultural differences, improve their communication and teamwork skills, and gain insight into global marketing and strategy.

Globalization also means that employees working in the United States will come from other countries. One estimate is that immigrants, some of whom are illegal, will account for an additional million persons in the workforce.[28a] Immigrants provide scientific talent and also sometimes fill low-wage jobs. The impact of immigration will be especially large in certain areas of the United States, including the states on the Pacific Coast, where 70 percent of new entrants to the workforce are immigrants.[29] U.S. colleges cannot keep up with the demand for engineers. To find engineers, companies have to look overseas to

China, Japan, Korea, and India to hire them.[30] The H-1B visa program is for persons in highly skilled and technical occupations requiring completion of higher education. New visas are capped at 85,000 per year, 20,000 of which are reserved for employees with U.S. master's degrees. There is no cap on H-1Bs for employees working for the government, universities, and other nonprofit institutions. The largest number of H1-B visas are issued for computer-related occupations (43 percent). U.S.-based Microsoft and Cisco Systems are two of the top ten companies using H-1B visas, but most are used by Indian companies such as Infosys Technologies and Wipro Ltd.[31] Other visa programs are available for lower-skilled temporary or seasonal workers (H2-A, H2-B) with an annual cap of 66,000 nonagricultural workers. Many of these immigrants will have to be trained to understand the U.S. culture. U.S. employees will need skills to improve their ability to communicate with employees from different cultures. The terrorist attacks of 9/11 have not changed the use of immigrants but have raised security issues, resulting in more deliberate approval of visas (and longer waits for hiring to be approved).

Globalization also means that U.S. companies have to carefully consider the costs and benefits of moving jobs overseas or using foreign suppliers. **Offshoring** refers to the process of moving jobs from the United States to other locations in the world. One benefit of offshoring is that companies can realize lower labor costs because wage and benefits costs are lower. One disadvantage of offshoring is that employees may lack the skills needed to perform the jobs. Another potential disadvantage is that local standards for employee safety, health, and working conditions may be substantially lower than in the United States, resulting in negative publicity and turning off potential customers. Consider the decisions made by Whirlpool and Apple. Whirlpool decided to replace and build a new cooking appliance plant in Cleveland, Tennessee, rather than moving production to Mexico, where it has several factories.[32] The new plant, which will grow the size of its local workforce, will be Whirlpool's first U.S. factory since the mid-1990s. Although labor costs would be lower in Mexico, Whirlpool decided to build the new plant in the United States because it already has a trained workforce, it wouldn't have to pay layoff costs, it received tax breaks and incentives from state and local government, and shipping costs would be lower because most of its products are sold in the United States. Apple is known for introducing revolutionary and functional products such as the iPhone, Mac Air computers, and the iPad.[33]Apple relies on manufacturing partners in Asia to build its products. Apple Inc has been criticized by labor groups who have challenged how its manufacturing partners in Asia have treated their employees. Apple has taken these criticism seriously and is auditing its suppliers and manufacturing facilities to take steps to reduce, if not eliminate, illegal and poor treatment of workers who assemble or provide materials for any of its products. Apple is especially focused on ensuring that its partners don't hire underage workers, provide adequate training, and pay fair wages. In those cases in which Apple's recommendations based on its audits were not adopted, the company terminated its relationship with the supplier.

## Increased Value Placed on Intangible Assets and Human Capital

Training and development can help a company's competitiveness by directly increasing the company's value through contributing to intangible assets. A company's value includes three types of assets that are critical for the company to provide goods and services: financial

**TABLE 1.2**
**Examples of Intangible Assets**

Sources: Based on L. Weatherly, *Human Capital—The Elusive Asset* (Alexandria, VA: SHRM Research Quarterly, 2003); E. Holton and S. Naquin, "New Metrics for Employee Development," *Performance Improvement Quarterly* 17 (2004): 56–80; M. Huselid, B. Becker, and R. Beatty, *The Workforce Scorecard* (Boston: Harvard University Press, 2005).

**Human Capital**
- Tacit knowledge
- Education
- Work-related know-how
- Work-related competence

**Customer Capital**
- Customer relationships
- Brands
- Customer loyalty
- Distribution channels

**Social Capital**
- Corporate culture
- Management philosophy
- Management practices
- Informal networking systems
- Coaching/mentoring relationships

**Intellectual Capital**
- Patents
- Copyrights
- Trade secrets
- Intellectual property

assets (cash and securities), physical assets (property, plant, equipment), and intangible assets. Table 1.2 provides examples of intangible assets, which consist of human capital, customer capital, social capital, and intellectual capital. Human capital refers to the sum of the attributes, life experiences, knowledge, inventiveness, energy, and enthusiasm that the company's employees invest in their work.[34] **Intellectual capital** refers to the codified knowledge that exists in a company. **Social capital** refers to relationships in the company. **Customer capital** refers to the value of relationships with persons or other organizations outside the company for accomplishing the goals of the company (e.g., relationships with suppliers, customers, vendors, and government agencies). Intangible assets are equally as valuable as financial and physical assets, but they are not something that can be touched and they are nonmonetary.

Intangible assets have been shown to be responsible for a company's competitive advantage. A study by the American Society for Training and Development (ASTD) of more than 500 publicly traded, U.S.-based companies found that companies that invested the most in training and development had a shareholder return that was 86 percent higher than companies in the bottom half and 46 percent higher than the market average.[35] Training and development have a direct influence on human and social capital because they affect education, work-related know-how and competence, and work relationships. Training and development can have an indirect influence on customer and social capital by helping employees better serve customers and by providing them with the knowledge needed to create patents and intellectual property.

As mentioned earlier in the chapter, intangible assets such as human capital also contribute to a company's competitive advantage because they are difficult to duplicate or imitate.[36] For example, consider companies in the airline industry. Southwest Airlines is consistently profitable and ranks high in on-time arrivals and other indicators of airline success.[37] One of the distinctions between Southwest Airlines and its competitors is how it treats its employees. For example, Southwest has a policy of no layoffs and was able to maintain this record even during the difficult time for airlines following 9/11. Southwest also emphasizes training and development, which provide its employees with skills to perform multiple jobs. This benefit allows Southwest airplanes to be cleaned and serviced at airports quickly because employees have multiple skill sets that can be applied to various aspects of readying an aircraft for departure. As a result of these human resource policies, Southwest employees are loyal, productive, and flexible (which contributes to the success of the airline). Other airlines may have similar or greater levels of financial assets and may have physical assets that are comparable to Southwest's (e.g., same type of airplanes, similar gates), but what contributes to Southwest's success and gives the company a competitive advantage are its intangible assets in the form of human capital. American Airlines and United Airlines have similar (or greater!) financial and physical assets but have not been successful in competing with Southwest by offering flights on the same routes.

Consider the effort that Macy's is undertaking to develop human capital, social capital, and customer capital.[38] Almost half of customer complaints at Macy's department stores are focused on interactions with sales associates. To cut costs to survive during the recession, Macy's closed stores and invested in technology to improve efficiency, which diverted attention away from customer service. But now Macy's is making a considerable investment in training its sales associates to provide better customer service and to help the company to meet sales growth targets. The new training program requires new sales associates to attend a three-hour training session and includes refresher courses and coaching from managers when they are working on the sales floor. The "MAGIC Selling Program" ("MAGIC" stands for meet and make a connection, ask questions and listen, give options and advice, inspire to buy, and celebrate the purchase) is designed to help sales associates make more personal connections with shoppers. Positive interactions with sales associates contribute to the number of items that a customer purchases and can help enhance Macy's service reputation as customers share experiences on social network sites such as Twitter and Facebook.

Chapters Seven, Eight, and Nine discuss specific training and development activities that contribute to the development of human and social capital. How to measure human capital is explained in Chapter Six, "Training Evaluation." The value of intangible assets and human capital has three important implications:

1. A focus on knowledge workers,
2. Employee engagement, and
3. An increased emphasis on adapting to change and continuous learning.

### Focus on Knowledge Workers

One way that a company can increase its intangible assets, specifically human capital, is by focusing on attracting, developing, and retaining knowledge workers. **Knowledge workers** are employees who contribute to the company not through manual labor, but through what they know, perhaps about customers or a specialized body of knowledge. Employees cannot simply be ordered to perform tasks; they must share knowledge and collaborate on solutions. Knowledge workers contribute specialized knowledge that their managers may not have, such as information about customers, and managers depend on these knowledge workers to share that information. Knowledge workers have many job opportunities. If they choose, they can leave a company and take their knowledge to a competitor. Knowledge workers are in demand because of the growth of jobs requiring them.

### Employee Engagement

To fully benefit from employee knowledge requires a management style that focuses on engaging employees. **Employee engagement** refers to the degree to which employees are fully involved in their work and the strength of their commitment to their job and the company.[39] Employees who are engaged in their work and committed to their companies give those companies a competitive advantage, including higher productivity, better customer service, and lower turnover.

Perhaps the best way to understand engagement is to consider how companies measure employee engagement. Companies measure employees' engagement levels with attitude or opinion surveys. Although the types of questions asked on these surveys vary from company to company, research suggests the questions generally measure themes such as pride in the company, satisfaction with the job, prospects for future growth with the company, and opportunity to perform challenging work.[40] Many companies feeling significant pressure from the recession have not given much attention to employee engagement in recent years, but some survey results suggest that less than one-third of employees considered themselves engaged. Still, some companies have managed to sustain and improve engagement levels during the recession by systematically gathering feedback from employees, analyzing their responses, and implementing changes. In these companies, engagement measures are considered as important as customer service or financial data. For example, at Pitney Bowes, about 80 percent of its employees complete the survey each year, which gives them a chance to share their feelings and perceptions and help the company address problems.[41] The survey is also used to determine if the company is doing enough to help employees reach their career goals. Based on survey results, the company designed and is trying out a program that is supposed to help managers improve their skills in listening, managing change, and solving problems. Pitney Bowes managers are held accountable for helping employees with their careers, and this program ensures that they have the necessary skills for success. As you probably realize, employee engagement is influenced by most human resource management practices, including training and development. Training and development give employees an opportunity for personal growth within the company and help provide the company with the knowledge and skills it needs to gain a competitive advantage. At Hilton Worldwide, top performers are identified through manager and peer nomination programs.[42] Hilton's career management program provides employees with online access to information on roles within different departments and training programs for skill development. Hilton is also using surveys, town hall meetings, newsletters, and online videos, and asking executives to work "hands-on" in jobs at Hilton properties to help enhance employee engagement. Hilton believes that the key to retaining high-performing employees is that they need to feel they are fairly paid, have opportunities to learn and develop, and have fun in their jobs. At LifeGift, a Houston-based nonprofit that recovers human organs and tissues from recently deceased donors and matches them to transplant recipients across the United States, engagement means having employees who never give up on finding a donor. LifeGift's CEO, Samuel M. Holtzman, made employee engagement a priority and started measuring engagement annually starting in 2008. When engagement fell in the last survey, Holtzman required the company managers to hold quarterly one-on-one discussions with each of their employees, separate from annual evaluations. Results from the surveys and discussions ensure that employees receive the training, emotional support, and other resources needed to deal with the demands of the job. Most companies do not deal with life-or-death issues as LifeGift does, but focusing on employee engagement can ensure that employees are satisfied and productive.

### *Change and Continuous Learning*

In addition to acquiring and retaining knowledge workers, companies need to be able to adapt to change. **Change** refers to the adoption of a new idea or behavior by a company. Technological advances, changes in the workforce or government regulations, globalization, and new competitors are among the many factors that require companies to change. Change is inevitable in companies as products, companies, and entire industries experience shorter life cycles.[43] Consider how the National Aeronautics and Space Administration (NASA) is adapting to change. NASA's space shuttle program ended in 2011 after twenty-nine years.[44] Due to cuts in its budget, there was not enough money to pay for costs related to flying the space shuttle and operating the International Space Station. This development has affected the communities in which the space program is located, NASA employees, as well as employees from its contractors for space shuttle operations, such as Lockheed-Martin and United Space Alliance. NASA and contract engineers need to either seek other employment or put their skills to work on new space vehicles and new planetary missions such as to Mars. NASA must decide which employees and skills it needs and then use retirement, attrition, or layoffs to reduce headcount. To cope with the change, NASA is determining the skills they need for their next programs and how they relate to human resource requirements, and identify skill excesses and weaknesses in the current workforce as they relate to these new requirements. More than half of the 13,000 shuttle contractor employees lost their jobs as the program ended following the last flight in 2011. To help employees and contract workers cope with the change, NASA has improved communications to make sure that they know what training will be available for new skills. websites at Johnson and Kennedy space centers are used to provide information on the transition and help employees find positions that need their skills or help them transition to positions outside of NASA (such as with defense contractors). NASA and its subcontractors are also providing career planning, skill training, and counseling for employees to help them deal with the anxiety and grief associated with the ending of the shuttle program. The characteristics of an effective change process are discussed in Chapter Two, "Strategic Training."

A changing environment means that all employees must embrace a philosophy of learning. A **learning organization** embraces a culture of lifelong learning, enabling all employees to acquire and share knowledge continually. Improvements in product or service quality do not stop when formal training is completed.[45] Employees need to have the financial, time, and content resources (such as courses, experiences, and development opportunities) available to increase their knowledge. Managers take an active role in identifying training needs and helping to ensure that employees use training in their work. Also, employees are actively encouraged to share knowledge with colleagues and other work groups across the company using e-mail and the Internet.[46] At The Cheesecake Factory Inc, which operates about 160 restaurants in the United States, learning is less about formal programs and courses and more about being available on an as-needed basis, driven by employees.[47] The company is focused on fostering continuous learning related to guest satisfaction and perfect execution of the many dishes on its menu. To do so, the company is creating interactive learning content that employees access at work. Through the VideoCafe, employees can upload and share short videos on topics such as customer greetings and food preparation. The company plans to develop interactive games, including a simulation for building the perfect hamburger. Hands-on, employee-driven learning is supported by managers observing employees and providing coaching and feedback to help develop new skills and reinforce their use in the workplace. Chapter Five, "Program Design," discusses learning organizations and knowledge management in detail. For a learning organization to be successful, teams of employees must collaborate to meet customer needs. Managers need to empower employees to share knowledge, identify problems, and make decisions, which allows the company to experiment and improve continuously.

Social collaboration and social networking technology are helping employees share knowledge and contribute to the development of a learning organization.[48] CareSource uses wikis, websites with content created by users, and discussion boards to encourage employees to engage in critical thinking and learn from each other by sharing ideas about how to apply skills that they have acquired in formal training programs. Coldwell Banker encourages its real estate professionals to develop and share videos of the best sales techniques using the company's video portal. Coldwell Banker also uses communities of practice to encourage employees to share best practices and provide insights on how to best approach specific types of job assignments. inVentiv Health, Inc. uses tools on Facebook to help sales employees share information and update lessons learned.

## Focus on Links to Business Strategy

Given the important role that intangible assets and human capital play in a company's competitiveness, managers are beginning to see a more important role for training and development as a means to support a company's business strategy; that is, its plans for meeting broad goals such as profitability, market share, and quality. Managers expect training and development professionals to design and develop learning activities that will help the company successfully implement its strategy and reach business goals. Strategic training will be discussed in greater detail in Chapter Two.

## Changing Demographics and Diversity of the Workforce

Companies face several challenges as a result of increased demographics and diversity of the workforce. Population is the single most important factor in determining the size and composition of the labor force, which is composed of people who are either working or looking for work. The civilian labor force is projected to increase by 15.3 million between 2008 and 2018, reaching 166.2 million by 2018. The workforce will be older and more culturally diverse than at any time in the past 40 years.

### Increase in Ethnic and Racial Diversity

Between 2008 and 2018, the U.S. labor force will continue to grow more ethnically and racially diverse due to immigration, increased participation of minorities in the workforce, and higher minority fertility rates. Between 2008 and 2018, the projected annual growth rates for Hispanics (2.9 percent) and Asians (2.6 percent) are higher than for African Americans and other groups.[49] By 2018, the workforce is projected to be 79 percent white, 12 percent African American, and 9 percent Asian and other ethnic or cultural groups. The labor force participation rate of women in nearly all age groups is projected to increase. Not only must companies face the issues of race, gender, ethnicity, and nationality to provide a fair workplace, but they must also develop training programs to help immigrants acquire the technical and customer service skills required in a service economy.

### Aging Workforce

Figure 1.3 compares the projected distribution of the age of the workforce in 2008 and 2018. In 2018, baby boomers will be 57 to 70 years old, and this age group will grow significantly between 2008 and 2018. The labor force will continue to age. The 55-and-older age group is expected to grow by approximately 12 million to 40 million in 2018, representing a 43 percent increase between 2008 and 2018. This 12 million is nearly all of the 12.6 million workers who are projected to be added to the workforce by 2018.[50] The labor force participation of those 55 years and older is expected to grow because older individuals are leading healthier and longer lives than in the past, providing the opportunity to work more years. In addition, the high cost of health insurance and decrease in health benefits will cause many employees to keep working to maintain their employer-based insurance or will prompt them to return to work after retirement to obtain health insurance through their employer. Also, the trend toward pension plans based on individuals' contributions to them rather than on years of service, will provide yet another incentive for older employees to continue working.

**FIGURE 1.3**
**Comparison of the Age of the 2008 and 2018 Labor Force.**

Source: Based on M. Toossi, "Labor Force Projections to 2018: Older Workers Staying More Active," *Monthly Labor Review* (November 2009): 30–51.

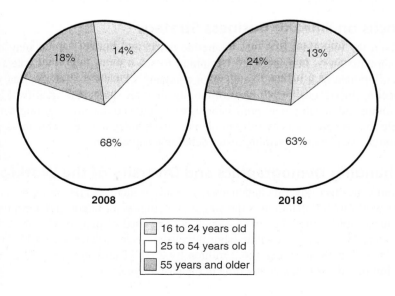

2008     2018

16 to 24 years old
25 to 54 years old
55 years and older

The aging population means that companies are likely to employ a growing share of older workers—many of them in their second or third careers. Older people want to work, and many say they plan a working retirement. Despite myths to the contrary, worker performance and learning in most jobs is not adversely affected by aging.[51] Older employees are willing and able to learn new technology. An emerging trend is for qualified older employees to ask to work part time, or for only a few months at a time, as a means of transitioning to retirement. Employees and companies are redefining what it means to be retired to include second careers, as well as part-time and temporary work assignments.

## Generational Differences

According to the U.S. Bureau of Labor Statistics, five generations will participate in the workforce in 2012, each one with unique and similar characteristics to the others. In Table 1.3, the year born, nicknames, and ages of each generation are shown. Consider some of the attributes that are believed to characterize each generation.[52] For example, millennials also known as Generation Y or Echo Boomers, grew up with access to computers at home and school and access to the Internet. They grew up with diversity in their schools and were coached, praised, and encouraged for participation rather than accomplishment by their baby boomer parents. Millennials are characterized as being optimistic, willing to work and learn, eager to please, technology literate, globally aware, and value diversity. They are also believed to have high levels of self-esteem, to the point of narcissism sometimes.

Generation Xers grew up during a time when the divorce rate doubled, the number of women working outside the home increased, and the personal computer was invented. They were often left to their own devices after school (latchkey kids). They value skepticism, informality, and practicality, seek work/life balance, and dislike close supervision. They tend to be impatient and cynical. They have experienced change in all of their lives (in terms of parents, homes, and cities).

Baby boomers, the "Me" generation, marched against the "establishment" for equal rights and an end to the Vietnam War. They value social conscientiousness and independence. They are competitive, hard-working, and concerned with the fair treatment of all employees. They are often considered to be workaholics and rigid in conforming to rules.

Traditionalists or the Silent Generation grew up during the Great Depression and lived during World War II. They tend to value frugality, are patriotic and loyal, adhere to rules, loyal to employers, and take responsibility and sacrifice for the good of the company.

**TABLE 1.3**
**Generations in the Workforce**

| Year Born | Generation | Ages |
|---|---|---|
| 1925–45 | Traditionalists Silent generation | 66–86 |
| 1946–64 | Baby boomers | 47–65 |
| 1965–80 | Generation X | 31–46 |
| 1981–95 | Millennials Generation Y Echo boomers | 16–30 |
| 1996– | Generation Z Digital natives | <16 |

It is important to note that although generation differences likely exist, members of the same generations are no more alike than members of the same gender or race. Research suggests that different generations of employees have similarities as well as differences.[53] Differences in work ethic have been found between baby boomers, Generation Xers, and millennials. However, millennial employees are more similar than different from other generations in their work beliefs, job values, and gender beliefs. Also, the lack of study of generational differences over time, the inability of most studies to separate generational effects from age or life stage, and possible differences across generation in how they interpret survey items used in studies means that you should be cautious inattributing differences in employee behaviors and attitudes to generational differences.[54] Also, treating employees differently based on their age, such as only inviting younger employees to attend training or development programs, may result in adverse legal consequences (e.g., employees forty years or older are covered by the Age Discrimination in Employment Act).

Nonetheless, members of each generation may have misperceptions of each other, causing tensions and misunderstanding in the workplace.[55] For example, millennials may think Generation X managers are bitter, jaded, abrasive, uninterested in them, and poor delegators. In turn, their Generation X managers consider millennials too needy for attention, demanding, and overly self-confident. Millennials might believe that baby boomers are too rigid and follow company rules too closely. They believe that employees in the older generations have been too slow to adopt social media tools and value tenure over knowledge and performance. Traditionalists and baby boomers believe that millennials don't have a strong work ethic because they are too concerned with work-life balance. Also, members of the younger generations may resent baby boomers and traditionalists who are working longer before retiring, thus blocking promotions and career moves for younger workers. We will discuss the potential implications of generational differences for training and development in Chapters Four and Five.

Companies can use increased diversity to gain a competitive advantage. A Society for Human Resource Management (SHRM) survey of its members showed that 68 percent have practices to address workplace diversity.[56] Important outcomes expected from diversity practices included improved public image of the company, improved financial bottom line, decreased complaints and litigation, and retention and recruitment of a diverse workforce.

Training plays a key role in ensuring that employees accept and work more effectively with each other. To successfully manage a diverse workforce, managers and employees must be trained in a new set of skills, including:

1. Communicating effectively with employees from a wide variety of backgrounds
2. Coaching, training, and developing employees of different ages, educational backgrounds, ethnicities, physical abilities, and races
3. Providing performance feedback that is free of values and stereotypes based on gender, ethnicity, or physical handicap
4. Training managers to recognize and respond to generational differences
5. Creating a work environment that allows employees of all backgrounds to be creative and innovative.[57]

Consider the programs that several companies are offering to capitalize on older employees' skills and accommodate their needs, provide development opportunities for a diverse workforce, and cope with generational differences.[58] Many of these programs are a part of companies' efforts to manage diversity, which we will discuss in more detail in Chapter Ten

S.C. Johnson offers retirees temporary work assignments, consulting and contract work, telecommuting, and part-time work. Centegra Health System's phased retirement program offers flexible scheduling, including part-time work, compressed workweeks, job sharing, summers off, and long-distance contract work.

CVS/pharmacy has stories in every climate and region in the United States. CVS created its Snowbirds Program to allow older employees to move among locations according to their preferences. This is especially important for older employees who spend winters in the southern states and summer in the northern states. More than 1,000 employees, including retail clerks, pharmacists, and managers, have participated in the program.

Johnson & Johnson's analysis of women's leadership programs showed that, although the company was not experiencing greater turnover of women, it had been ineffective in reaching multicultural women and women of color.[59] The company has since created a program, titled "Crossing the Finish Line," for high-performing, high-potential multicultural women and women of color. The program includes a two-and-a-half day project in which participants have open conversations with their managers and with executives, including the CEO and the vice chair of the company. The program helps Johnson & Johnson identify women who should be given new development opportunities, as well as help them understand that they must be visible, establish networks, and take the initiative to ask for development assignments. Also, the program educates managers about cultural differences and creates an awareness of how an employee's culture might affect his or her career.

A survey conducted at Ernst & Young LLC found that Generation Y (Gen-Y) employees want and ask for more frequent and candid feedback than baby boomers.[60] As a result, Ernst & Young developed an online "Feedback Zone," where employees can provide or ask for feedback at any time. Also, the company assigns every employee a mentor and offers training for managers on how to give effective feedback. To make sure that employees understand generational differences and how to connect and communicate with employees from different generations, Aflac, the insurance provider, offers a training program called "Connecting Generations."[61] Aflac believes that employees in all age groups are more effective if they understand how members of each generation approach their jobs. The program reviews the characteristics of each generation represented in the workplace. It also describes the effects of family and world events on each generation, analyzes their work styles and employment characteristics, and helps to show connections to bridging generation gaps.

## Talent Management

**Talent management** refers to the systematic, planned, and strategic effort by a company to use bundles of human resource management practices, including acquiring and assessing employees, learning and development, performance management, and compensation to attract, retain, develop, and motivate highly skilled employees and managers. Talent management is becoming increasingly more important because of changes in demand for certain occupations and jobs, skill requirements, the anticipated retirement of the baby boomer generation, and the need to develop managerial talent with leadership skills. Also, the results of surveys suggest that opportunities for career growth, learning, and development, and the performance of exciting and challenging work are some of the most important factors in determining employees' engagement and commitment to their current employer.[62] It is important to identify employees who want to develop their skills and seek promotions and to keep them growing through new job experiences and training. For example, WD-40 has a learning culture that supports the development of talent. Any employee who wants to be a leader can become one.[63] Employees can participate in a Leadership Academy, which requires them to teach classes and coach other employees for two years. Employees can also participate in its Leaders Coaching Leaders program. In this program, employees are matched with another employee who has the expertise in their area of interest. In the company's The Food 4 Thought training series, managers discuss workplace issues based on a scenario that they are given to review. Managers learn from each other by discussing and evaluating the scenario and agree on how to best handle it. All employees have access to the same coach used by the company CEO. If the coach notices employees reaching out to him for the same reasons, he provides this information to human resources so that they can create a course to address the issue or provide useful guidance.

U.S. employment is expected to increase from 150.9 million in 2008 to 166.2 million in 2018, adding 15.3 million jobs. Two service-providing sectors of the U.S. economy, professional and business services and health care and social assistant services, are expected to generate more than half the increase in total employment from 2008 to 2018.[64] As a result, most growth is projected for professional and service occupations. Service occupations are expected to increase 13.8 million, rising to 33.6 million jobs by 2018. Professional and related occupations are expected to grow 16.8 percent, resulting in 36.3 million jobs in 2018.[65] On the other hand, employment in production, farming, fishing, and forestry occupations is expected to decline. Keep in mind that there are likely some exceptions to these projected trends. Companies that require specialized labor to make industrial lathes, computer chips, and health care products requiring specialized skills, plan to expand and locate near towns and cities that have such an available workforce.[66] For example, Greatbatch Inc., which makes medical products, is expanding near Fort Wayne, Indiana, to take advantage of the local workforce's specialized skills.

Table 1.4 shows ten of the thirty fastest-growing occupations projected between 2008 and 2018. Of the thirty fastest-growing occupations, seventeen are in professional and related occupations (seven include healthcare practitioners and workers in technical occupations, such as physician assistants and biomedical engineers), ten are service occupations (such as fitness trainers, aerobics instructors, and occupational therapists), and three are management occupations (such as financial advisers and examiners). Many of the growing occupations are related to healthcare. This is because as the U.S. population ages, more in-patient and out-patient medical-related services are necessary. Also, technicians and assistants are providing many types of basic medical care, allowing more highly paid physicians, surgeons, and pharmacists to focus on more complex patient needs and treatments. Over two-thirds of the thirty fastest-growing occupations require education beyond high school, and slightly less than half require at least a bachelor's degree or higher as the most significant source of education and training. This is not surprising because occupations that involve a postsecondary award or degree will see faster employment growth than occupations requiring on-the-job training.

### Retirement of Baby Boomers

As the oldest baby boomers begin to retire in the next several years, the implications for the workforce could be enormous.[67] This could hinder prospects for economic growth and put a greater burden on those remaining in the workforce, perhaps forcing them to

**TABLE 1.4**  **Examples of the Fastest Growing Occupations**

| Occupation | Employment Change 2008–2018 | | Most Significant Education or Training |
|---|---|---|---|
| | Number (In Thousands) | Percent | |
| Biomedical engineers | 12 | 72 | Bachelor's degree |
| Network systems and data communicates analysts | 156 | 53 | Bachelor's degree |
| Home health aides | 461 | 50 | Short-term, on-the-job training |
| Personal and home care aides | 376 | 46 | Short-term, on-the-job training |
| Financial examiners | 11 | 41 | Bachelor's degree |
| Medical scientists, except epidemiologists | 44 | 40 | Doctoral degree |
| Physicians' assistants | 29 | 39 | Master's degree |
| Skin care specialists | 15 | 38 | Postsecondary vocational |
| Biochemists and biophysicists | 9 | 37 | Doctoral degree |
| Athletic trainers | 6 | 37 | Bachelor's degree |

Source: Based on T. Lacey and B. Wright, "Occupational Employment Projections to 2018," *Monthly Labor Review* (November 2009): 82–123.

work longer hours. Especially in occupations with functions less conducive to technology-driven productivity innovations—many jobs in health services and educational services, for example—quality of service may suffer and needs could go unmet unless older workers can be retained or other sources of workers can be found. Even in occupations in which technological innovations have produced relatively large productivity gains—many of the more complex machining jobs in manufacturing, for example—the learning curves often are steep, meaning that new workers need to enter these occupations soon, so they can become proficient in the necessary skills by the time the baby boomers begin leaving the labor force.

It is also important for companies to try to capture the valuable knowledge that is leaving.[68] Recognizing that many talented employees would soon be retiring and their knowledge would be lost or forgotten, LyondellBasell, a polymer manufacturer located in Clinton, Iowa, asked key employees to record what they had learned during their tenure, especially knowledge that they knew was not already documented. Employees were interviewed to better understand difficult tasks that lacked well-documented procedures. For example, an interview with a chemical specialist revealed that when a chemical reaches a specific fluidity and color, it is ready to use. That part of the interview was taped so that future employees would have a reference to the correct color of the solution.[69] Special People in Northeast, Inc, (SPIN), a nonprofit that provides services for persons with disabilities, uses electronic "How-to" manuals and flowcharts provided by key employees to ensure that current practices and procedures are available to employees with less experience who are replacing expert employees leaving the organization.[70]

### Skill Requirements

As the occupational structure of the U.S. economy has shifted, skill requirements have changed.[71] The demand for specific skills is being replaced by a need for cognitive skills—mathematical and verbal reasoning ability—and interpersonal skills related to being able to work in teams or to interact with "customers" in a service economy (e.g., patients, students, vendors, and suppliers). Cognitive and interpersonal skills are important because in the service-oriented economy, employees must take responsibility for the final product or service. Variety and customization require employees to be creative and good problem solvers. Continuous innovation requires the ability to learn. To offer novelty and entertainment value to customers, workers must be creative. Most companies relate these skills with educational attainment, so many firms use a college degree as a standard to screen prospective employees.

However, new entrants to the workplace, as well as the unemployed, lack these and other skills needed for companies to compete in the global economy. Several studies illustrate the skill deficit that U.S. companies are experiencing.[72] A study by the Business Roundtable found that 62 percent of employers report they are having difficulty finding qualified job applicants to fill job openings. More than half indicated that at least 16 percent of their workforce has a skill gap that adversely affects productivity. Similarly, a study by a consortium of SHRM, ASTD, The Conference Board, and Corporate Voices for Working Families found that regardless of their education level, only half of the companies surveyed rated new employees as adequately prepared for work. The greatest needs were in leadership and executive level skills, basic skills, professional or industry-specific skills, and managerial and supervisory skills. The greatest basic skills need was in reading, writing, and math. The major reasons for the skill gaps were that skills of the current workforce did not match changes in business strategy, goals, markets, or business models, and the lack of strength in the company's current and future leadership. Skill deficits are not just a problem facing U.S. companies. Due to migration, educational systems that have inconsistent quality, or declining birthrates, countries with developing economies such as India and Russia, as well as Japan and Western Europe, are experiencing difficulties in finding workers for the skilled trades, sales, technicians, engineers, and managers.[73]

Skill deficits are not limited to any one business sector, industry, or job. To cope with the need for qualified and skilled employees, companies such as Arcelor-Mittal and Aegis Sciences Corporation are either training or paying for training to prepare future employees.[74] Arcelor-Mittal has developed a program that pays U.S. high school graduates to participate in two-and-a-half years of training with the chance for a job that pays more than $17 per hour after they complete the program. Arcelor-Mittal started this program to fill job openings in mechanical and electrical trades created by retirements of older steelworkers. Aegis Sciences Corporation conducts drug-screening services and forensic testing has approximately 580 employees. Scientist and lab technician positions remain unfilled because the company cannot find enough experienced employees for those jobs. As a result, Aegis Sciences is hiring recent chemistry graduates who lack experience working at a professional lab with high standards for quality control and consistency. The graduates are trained in needed skills, such as how to extract materials from blood or urine and analyze the drug content of the samples. Aegis Sciences devotes about 5 percent of its revenues to training, which it expects to involve 21,000 hours in 2012.

IBM is making efforts to increase the skills of the workforce by investing in local secondary schools.[75] IBM's Transition to Teaching program allows employees to take leaves of absence to student-teach for three months. Eligible employees must meet certain requirements, such as ten years of service with IBM, a bachelor's degree in math or science or a higher degree in a related field, and some experience teaching, tutoring, or volunteering in schools. IBM hopes that many of its experienced employees with math and engineering backgrounds will take advantage of the program, providing high-quality math and science teachers for public schools.

### Developing Leadership

Companies report that the most important talent management challenges they face are identifying employees with managerial talent and training and developing them for managerial positions.[76] This is attributed to the aging of the workforce, globalization, and the need for managers to contribute to employee engagement. Executive, administrative, and managerial occupations will experience the greatest turnover due to death or retirement.[77] Also, many companies do not have employees with the necessary competencies to manage in a global economy.[78] To successfully manage in a global economy, managers need to be self-aware and be able to build international teams, create global management and marketing practices, and interact and manage employees from different cultural backgrounds. Managers contribute to employee engagement by performing basic management functions (planning, organizing, controlling, leading) but also through using good communication skills, helping employees develop, and working collaboratively with employees.

For example, consider the Schwan Food Company and Yum! Brands.[79] The Schwan Food Company, maker of frozen pizzas and pies, is selecting employees with leadership talent to attend programs involving management classes and coaching sessions. These employees, considered "high-potential" managers, also receive challenging job assignments that require them to capitalize on their skill strengths and develop new skill sets (such as helping to launch a new joint venture in Mexico). Yum! Brands, with more than 35,000 KFC, Pizza Hut, and Taco Bell restaurants worldwide, needs to develop a large number of managers to meet demands for new restaurants resulting from growth plans, such as opening two KFC restaurants a day in China. To support and sustain global growth in restaurant operations, Yum! is preparing new managers through identifying and assigning job experiences that involve food innovation, marketing, and the development of general management skills.

## Customer Service and Quality Emphasis

A company's customers judge its quality and performance. As a result, customer excellence requires attention to product and service features, as well as to interactions with customers. Customer-driven excellence includes understanding what the customer wants, anticipating future needs, reducing defects and errors, meeting specifications, and reducing complaints. How the company recovers from defects and errors is also important for retaining and attracting customers.

Due to increased availability of knowledge and competition, consumers are very knowledgeable and expect excellent service. This presents a challenge for employees who interact with customers. The way in which clerks, sales staff, front-desk personnel, and service providers interact with customers influences a company's reputation and financial performance. Employees need product knowledge and service skills, and they need to be clear about the types of decisions they can make when dealing with customers. Customer service as a strategic training and development initiative is discussed in Chapter Two.

To compete in today's economy, whether on a local or global level, companies need to provide a quality product or service. If companies do not adhere to quality standards, their ability to sell their product or service to vendors, suppliers, or customers will be restricted.

Some countries even have quality standards that companies must meet to conduct business there. **Total Quality Management (TQM)** is a companywide effort to continuously improve the ways people, machines, and systems accomplish work.[80] Core values of TQM include the following:[81]

- Methods and processes are designed to meet the needs of internal and external customers.
- Every employee in the company receives training in quality.
- Quality is built into a product or service so that errors are prevented from occurring rather than being detected and corrected.
- The company promotes cooperation with vendors, suppliers, and customers to improve quality and hold down costs.
- Managers measure progress with feedback based on data.

There is no universal definition of quality. The major differences in its various definitions relate to whether the customer, product, or manufacturing process is emphasized. For example, quality expert W. Edwards Deming emphasizes how well a product or service meets customer needs. Phillip Crosby's approach emphasizes how well the service or manufacturing process meets engineering standards.

The emphasis on quality is seen in the establishment of the **Malcolm Baldrige National Quality Award** and the **ISO 9000:2000** quality standards. The Baldrige award, created by public law, is the highest level of national recognition for quality that a U.S. company can receive. The award is given annually. To become eligible for the Baldrige, a company must complete a detailed application that consists of basic information about the firm and an in-depth presentation of how it addresses specific criteria related to quality improvement. The categories and point values for the Baldrige award are found in Table 1.5. The award is not given for specific products or services. Organizations can compete for the Baldrige award in one of six categories: manufacturing, service, small business, education, health care, and nonprofit. All applicants for the Baldrige Award undergo a rigorous examination process that takes from 300 to 1,000 hours. Applications are reviewed by an independent board of about 400 examiners who come primarily from the private sector. Each applicant receives a report citing company strengths and opportunities for improvement.

The Baldrige Award winners usually excel at human resource practices, including training and development. For example, consider Sharp HealthCare, an award winner in 2007.[82] Sharp is San Diego County's largest health care system, serving over 785,000 people each year. It is a not-for-profit organization that employs 14,000 staff members and 2,600 affiliated physicians, operates seven hospitals, three medical groups, and nineteen outpatient clinics, and manages its own health insurance plan. Sharp HealthCare meets and exceeds patients' expectations by providing high-quality care and services that are accessible, convenient, and cost effective. Sharp has made a considerable investment in its employees, including the use of yearly employee surveys to gauge the satisfaction and engagement of its workforce, action teams, performance improvement teams, and lean/Six Sigma teams (discussed later in this chapter) that encourage employee participation in creating change and increasing organizational effectiveness. Sharp's training expenditures per employee exceed those of the best-in-class companies (as identified by the ASTD). Sharp University offers training programs for developing current and future leaders. It provides each employee with a $1,000 fund to take advantage of educational opportunities offered outside the organization.

**TABLE 1.5**
Categories
and Point
Values for the
Malcolm
Baldrige
National Qual-
ity Award
Examination

Source: Based on
"2011–2012 Criteria
for Performance
Excellence" from
the website for the
National Institute
of Standards and
Technology,
www.nist/gov/
baldrige.

| | |
|---|---:|
| **Leadership**<br>The way senior executives create and sustain vision, values, and mission; promote legal and ethical behavior; create a sustainable company; and communicate with and engage the workforce | 120 |
| **Measurement, Analysis, and Knowledge Management**<br>The way the company selects, gathers, analyzes, manages, and improves its data, information, and knowledge assets | 90 |
| **Strategic Planning**<br>The way the company sets strategic direction, how it determines action plans, how it changes strategy and action plans if required, and how it measures progress | 85 |
| **Workforce Focus**<br>Company's efforts to develop and utilize the workforce to achieve high performance; how the company engages, manages, and develops the potential of the workforce in alignment with company goals | 85 |
| **Operations Focus**<br>Design, management, and improvement of work systems and work processes to deliver customer value and achieve company success and sustainability | 85 |
| **Results**<br>Company's performance and improvement in key business areas (product, service, and supply quality; productivity; and operational effectiveness and related financial indicators) | 450 |
| **Customer Focus**<br>Company's knowledge of the customer, customer service systems, current and potential customer concerns, customer satisfaction and engagement | 85 |
| **Total Points** | 1,000 |

The International Organization for Standardization (ISO), a network of national standards institutes that includes 160 countries and has a central governing body in Geneva, Switzerland, is the world's largest developer and publisher of international standards.[83] The ISO develops standards related to management as well as a wide variety of other areas, including education, music, ships, and even protecting children. ISO standards are voluntary, but countries may decide to adopt ISO standards in their regulations; and as a result, they may become a requirement to compete in the market. The ISO 9000 is a family of standards related to quality (ISO 9000, 9001, 9004, and 10011). The ISO 9000 quality standards address what the company does to meet regulatory requirements and the customer's quality requirements while striving to improve customer satisfaction and continuous improvement. The standards represent an international consensus on quality management practices. ISO 9000:2000 has been adopted as the quality standard in nearly 100 counties around the world, meaning that companies have to follow these standards to conduct business in those countries. The quality management standards of the ISO 9000 are based on eight quality management principles, including customer focus, leadership, people involvement, a process approach, a systems approach to management, continuous improvement, using facts to make decisions, and establishing mutually beneficial relationships with suppliers. ISO 9001:2008 is the most comprehensive standard because it provides a set of requirements for a quality management system for all organizations, both private and public. The ISO 9001:2008 has been implemented by more than 1 million organizations in 176 countries. ISO 9004 provides a guide for companies that want to improve.

Why are standards useful? Customers may want to check that the product they ordered from a supplier meets the purpose for which it is required. One of the most efficient ways to do this is when the specifications of the product have been defined in an international standard. That way, both supplier and customer are on the same wavelength, even if they are based in different countries, because they are both using the same references. Today, many products require testing for conformance with specifications, compliance with safety, or other regulations before they can be put on many markets. Even simpler products may require supporting technical documentation that includes test data. With so much trade taking place across borders, it is more practical for these activities to be carried out not by suppliers and customers, but by specialized third parties. In addition, national legislation may require such testing to be carried out by independent bodies, particularly when the products concerned have health or environmental implications. One example of an ISO standard is on the back cover of this book and nearly every other book. On the back cover is something called an International Standard Book Number (ISBN). Publishers and booksellers are very familiar with ISBN numbers, since these numbers are the method through which books are ordered and bought. Try buying a book on the Internet, and you will soon learn the value of the ISBN number—there is a unique number for the book you want. And it is based on an ISO standard.

In addition to competing for quality awards and seeking ISO certification, many companies are using the Six Sigma process. The **Six Sigma process** refers to a process of measuring, analyzing, improving, and then controlling processes once they have been brought within the narrow Six Sigma quality tolerances or standards. The objective of Six Sigma is to create a total business focus on serving the customer; that is, to deliver what customers really want when they want it. For example, at General Electric (GE), introducing the Six Sigma quality initiative meant going from approximately 35,000 defects per million operations—which is average for most companies, including GE—to fewer than 4 defects per million in every element of every process GE businesses perform—from manufacturing a locomotive part to servicing a credit card account to processing a mortgage application to answering a phone.[84] Training is an important component of the process. Six Sigma involves highly trained employees known as Champions, Master Black Belts, Black Belts, and Green Belts, who lead and teach teams that are focusing on an ever-growing number of quality projects. The quality projects focus on improving efficiency and reducing errors in products and services. The Six Sigma quality initiative has produced more than $2 billion in benefits for GE.

Training can help companies meet the quality challenge by teaching employees a concept known as "lean thinking." In the past three years, Cardinal Fastener & Specialty Co., Inc.'s sales to wind turbine manufacturers has grown more than 900 percent.[85] The growth of the Cleveland, Ohio–based company started over ten years ago, when under the leadership of the company's founder and president, Cardinal began using lean thinking, involving all employees in the process of what they referred to as "blowing up the company." The goal was to eliminate waste from the entire operation, including manufacturing, administration, and sales. As a result, manufacturing lead times went from six weeks to five days, productivity improvement increased 50 percent, and half of all sales now come from orders that are manufactured and shipped the same day the order is taken. Because of the company's reputation for fast turnaround of specialty manufactured fasteners, they received an order for a wind turbine project in Iowa. The company realized that there was an opportunity to expand into the global marketplace for renewable energy. **Lean thinking** is a way to do more with less effort, equipment, space, and time, but still provide customers with what they need and want. Part of lean thinking includes training workers in new skills or teaching them how to apply old skills in new ways so they can quickly take over new responsibilities or use new skills to help fill customer orders. As a result of lean thinking at Cardinal Fastener, machines were moved so that operators could make a complete bolt or fastener from start to finish, resulting in a decrease in the time it takes to make a finished product. Quality is near perfect, and inventory has been reduced 54 percent.

A group within the ISO has drafted a standard for employee training. **ISO 10015** is a quality management tool designed to ensure that training is linked to company needs and performance. ISO 10015 has two key features. First, companies have to determine the return on investment of training to company performance. Second, ISO 10015 requires companies to use appropriate design and effective learning processes. ISO 10015 defines training design as analyzing, planning, doing, and evaluating (recall the discussion of the Instructional System Design model earlier in this chapter). The first companies to have achieved ISO 10015 certification are in China and Switzerland, but U.S. companies are likely to attempt to achieve certification soon.[86]

## New Technology

Technology has reshaped the way we play, communicate, plan our lives, and work. Many companies' business models includes e-commerce, which allows consumers to purchase products and services online. The Internet is a global collection of computer networks that allows users to exchange data and information. Americans' use of the Internet has doubled over the last five years, with 48 percent reporting using the Internet more than one hour per day. A total of 60 percent of Americans visit Google during the week, and 43 percent have a Facebook page.[87] Using Facebook, Twitter, LinkedIn, and other social networking tools available on the Internet accessed through iPhones, Blackberries, or personal computers, company managers can connect with employees and employees can connect with friends, family, and coworkers.

### *Influence on Training*

Advances in sophisticated technology along with reduced costs for the technology are changing the delivery of training, making training more realistic, and giving employees the opportunity to choose where and when they will work. New technologies allow training to occur at any time and any place.[88]

Technological advances in electronics and communications software have made possible mobile technology such as personal digital assistants (PDAs), iPads, and iPods and enhanced the Internet through developing the capability for social networking. Social

**TABLE 1.6**    **Potential Uses of Social Networking for Training and Development**

| Issues | Uses |
|---|---|
| Loss of expert knowledge due to retirement | Knowledge sharing, capturing, and storing |
| Employee engagement | Collect employee opinions |
| Identify and promote employee expertise | Create online expert communities |
| Promote innovation and creativity | Encourage participation in online discussions |
| Reinforce learning | Share best practices, applications, learning, points, links to articles and webinars |
| Employees need coaching and mentoring | Interact with mentors and coaching peers |

Sources: Based on P. Brotherson, "Social Networks Enhance Employee Learning," *T+D* (April 2011): 18–19; T. Bingham and M. Connor, *The New Social Learning* (Alexandria, VA: American Society for Training & Development, 2010); M. Derven, "Social Networking: A Frame for Development," *T + D* (July 2009): 58–63; M. Weinstein, "Are You Linked In?" *training* (September/October 2010): 30–33.

networking refers to websites such as Facebook, Twitter, and LinkedIn, wikis, and blogs that facilitate interactions between people, usually around shared interests. Table 1.6 shows how social networks can be used for training and development.[89]

In general, social networking facilitates communications, decentralized decision making, and collaboration. Social networking can be useful for busy employees to share knowledge and ideas with their peers and managers, with whom they may not have much time to interact in person on a daily basis. Employees, especially young workers from the millennial or Gen-Y generations, have learned to use social networking tools such as Facebook throughout their lives and see them as valuable tools for both their work and personal lives.

Despite its potential advantages, many companies are uncertain as to whether they should embrace social networking.[90] They fear, perhaps correctly, that social networking will result in employees wasting time or offending or harassing their coworkers. But other companies believe that the benefits of using social networking for human resource practices and allowing employees to access social networks at work outweigh the risks. They trust employees to use social networking productively and are proactive in developing policies about personal use and training employees about privacy settings and social network etiquette. They realize that employees will likely check their Twitter, Facebook, or LinkedIn accounts, but they ignore it unless productivity is decreasing. In some ways, social networking has become the electronic substitute for daydreaming at one's desk or walking to the break room to socialize with coworkers.

Robotics, computer-assisted design, radio-frequency identification, and nanotechnology are transforming work.[91] Technology has also made it easier to monitor environmental conditions and operate equipment. For example, consider working a grader construction vehicle (which is used to smooth and level dirt on roadways and other construction projects). Older vehicle models required operating as many as fifteen levers in addition to a steering wheel and several foot pedals. As a result, working the grader usually left operators with sore backs and shoulders at the end of the day. Caterpillar's latest version of the grader includes redesigned controls that use only two joysticks and eliminate the physical demands of pushing pedals and turning a steering wheel. Besides reducing the physical demands, the redesign of the grader without a steering wheel resulted in operators having better visibility of the steel blade, and switches for lights, windshield wipers, and the parking brake could be grouped together in one place in the cab. A Japanese commercial farm,

Shinpuku Seika, relies on computer readings from monitors placed out in the fields that report temperature, soil, and moisture levels to the farmers.[92] Computer analysis of these data alerts farmers when to start planting or identifies specific crops that may grow best in each field. Farmers can use cameras in the fields to examine crops. Farm workers can also use their mobile phones to take pictures of potential diseased or infected crops that are uploaded to the computer for diagnosis by crop experts. The workers' phones also include a global positioning system, allowing the company to determine if workers are taking the most efficient routes between fields or slacking off on the job.

Technology has many advantages, including reduced travel costs, greater accessibility to training, consistent delivery, the ability to access experts and share learning with others, and the possibility of creating a learning environment with many positive features such as feedback, self-pacing, and practice exercises. While trainer-led classroom instruction remains the most popular way to deliver training, companies report that they plan on delivering a large portion of training through learning technologies such as intranets and iPods. For example, consider how training at Kinko's, the world's leading supplier of document solutions and business services with 1,100 locations in nine countries, has changed. Because Kinko's stores are geographically dispersed, the company has had to struggle with costly training programs offered in multiple locations to prepare employees for new products and services. Kinko's adopted a blended learning approach, including Internet instruction, job aids, virtual classroom training, and mentoring. Cost savings and greater efficiency occurred as a result of the blended approach. The approach has also resulted in increasing staff skills and reducing the time it takes to achieve competence and in increasing the speed with which new products and services can be brought to market.[93] Capital One, a financial services company, uses an audio learning program that allows employees to learn through their iPods at their own convenience.[94] The company has also developed a mobile audio learning channel. The channel supplements competency-based programs, leadership and management programs, and other existing company training courses. It is also used to ensure that employees receive information when they need it.

Technology is pushing the boundaries of artificial intelligence, speech synthesis, wireless communications, and networked virtual reality.[95] Realistic graphics, dialogue, and sensory cues can now be stored onto tiny, inexpensive computer chips. For example, Second Life is an online virtual world that allows members to develop fictional lives. In Second Life, members can run a business, take a date to a dance club, or visit a training center. Virtual sensations (vibrations and other sensory cues) are being incorporated into training applications. For example, in medical training, machines can replicate the feeling of pushing a needle into an artery and use sound and motion to simulate different situations such as a baby crying or a patient in pain.

### Flexibility in Where and When Work Is Performed

Advances in technology, including more powerful computer chips and increased processing power of PDAs, notebooks, and iPhones have the potential for freeing workers from going to a specific location to work and from traditional work schedules. One estimate is that 10 percent of the U.S. wage and salaried workforce work from home at least occasionally, and 55 percent of employers offer telecommuting, but only 10 percent offer it on a full-time basis.[96] Telecommuting has the potential to increase employee productivity, encourage family-friendly work arrangements, and help reduce traffic and air pollution.

But at the same time, technologies may result in employees being on call twenty-four hours a day, seven days a week. Many companies are taking steps to provide more flexible work schedules to protect employees' free time and to use employees' work time more productively. Amerisure Mutual Insurance in Farmington Hills, Michigan, built a work environment and provides flexible programs designed to increase employee retention and engagement.[97] A new computer system makes it easier for employees to work at home by giving them access to work files using their home computers. Employees meet with their managers to discuss the feasibility of working off-site and how their performance will be evaluated. Amerisure also allows employees to take days off each year for volunteer work and provides five paid days each year for family commitments related to medical care, such as ill grandparents and immediate family members. The company's turnover rate has dropped from 18 percent to 10 percent, and employee engagement survey scores have increased as a result.

At Delta Air Lines, more than 570 of the 5,000 agents work from home full time.[98] To strengthen their commitment and understanding of the company, each agent works in a call center for six months before working from home. While working at home, they can contact a team leader with questions. They also have monthly meetings. Delta spends $2,500 to purchase a computer and software for each reservation agent who works at home. The costs are offset by the lower hourly wage these agents receive compared to agents who work in the office. However, working at home reduces the agents' costs for gasoline and gives them more flexibility to balance their work and personal lives. The company has realized savings in rent and upkeep of office space, and the offsite agents have helped meet customer service demands due to bad weather by volunteering for more overtime than agents working in offices.

Technology also allows companies greater use of alternative work arrangements. **Alternative work arrangements** include independent contractors, on-call workers, temporary workers, and contract company workers. The Bureau of Labor Statistics estimates that alternative work arrangements make up 11 percent of total employment.[99] There are 10.3 million independent contractors, 2.5 million on-call workers, 1.2 million temporary help agency workers, and approximately 813,000 workers employed by contract firms. Use of alternative work arrangements allows companies to adjust staffing levels more easily based on economic conditions and product and service demand. And when a company downsizes by laying off workers, the damage to the morale of full-time employees is likely to be less severe. Alternative work arrangements also provide employees with flexibility for balancing work and life activities. For example, Verigy, a semiconductor manufacturer in California, employs only a small number of permanent employees, and nonessential jobs are outsourced. When demand for its products increases, engineers and other high-tech employees are hired through staffing companies or as independent contractors.[100] Also, the use of alternative work arrangements has resulted in the development of co-working sites where diverse workers such as designers, artists, freelancers, consultants, and other independent contractors pay a daily or monthly fee for a guaranteed work space.[101] The co-working site is equipped with desks and wireless Internet, and some provide access to copy machines, faxes, and conference rooms. Co-working sites help facilitate independent contractors, employees working at home, traveling, or telecommuting, combat their possible feelings of isolation, give them the ability to collaborate and interact, provide a more professional working atmosphere than coffee shops (and similar public locations where such employees often work off-site), and help to decrease traffic and pollution.

A key training issue that alternative work arrangements present is to prepare managers and employees to coordinate their efforts so that such work arrangements do not interfere with customer service or product quality. The increased use of alternative work arrangements means that managers need to understand how to motivate employees who may actually be employed by a third party such as a temporary employee service or leasing agency.

## High-Performance Models of Work Systems

New technology causes changes in skill requirements and work roles and often results in redesigned work structures (e.g., using work teams).[102] For example, computer-integrated manufacturing uses robots and computers to automate the manufacturing process. The computer allows the manufacture of different products simply by reprogramming the computer. As a result, laborer, material handler, operator/assembler, and maintenance jobs may be merged into one position. Computer-integrated manufacturing requires employees to monitor equipment and troubleshoot problems with sophisticated equipment, share information with other employees, and understand the relationships among all components of the manufacturing process.[103]

Through technology, the information needed to improve customer service and product quality becomes more accessible to employees. This means that employees are expected to take more responsibility for satisfying the customer and determining how they perform their jobs. One of the most popular methods for increasing employee responsibility and control is work teams. **Work teams** involve employees with various skills who interact to assemble a product or provide a service. Work teams may assume many of the activities usually reserved for managers, including selecting new team members, scheduling work, and coordinating activities with customers and other units in the company. To give teams maximum flexibility, cross training of team members occurs. **Cross training** refers to training employees in a wide range of skills so they can fill any of the roles needed to be performed on the team.

Consider the high-performance work system at the Global Engineering Manufacturing Alliance (GEMA) plant in Dundee, Michigan.[104] Compared to most engine plants, GEMA's plant is more automated and has fewer employees—275 compared to 600–2,000. The goal of the plant is to be the most productive engine plant in the world. The plant's hourly employees rotate jobs and shifts, giving the company greater flexibility. The plant's culture emphasizes problem solving and the philosophy that anyone can do anything, anytime, anywhere. Every employee is either a team member or a team leader. By rotating jobs, the plant keeps workers motivated and avoids injuries. Team leaders and engineers don't stay in their offices—they are expected to work on the shop floor as part of six-person teams. Contractors are also seen as part of the team, working alongside assembly workers and engineers and wearing the same uniforms. The GEMA plant gives employees access to technology that helps them monitor productivity. Large electronic screens hanging from the plant ceiling provide alerts of any machinery parts that are ending their lifespan and need to be replaced before they malfunction. A performance management system, available on personal computers as well as a display board, alerts employees to delays or breakdowns in productivity. This is different than in most engine plants, where only the managers have access to this information. The technology at the GEMA plant empowers all employees to fix problems—not just managers or engineers.

Use of new technology and work designs such as work teams needs to be supported by specific human resource management practices. These practices include the following actions:[105]

- Employees choose or select new employees or team members.
- Employees receive formal performance feedback and are involved in the performance improvement process.
- Ongoing training is emphasized and rewarded.
- Rewards and compensation are linked to company performance.
- Equipment and work processes encourage maximum flexibility and interaction between employees.
- Employees participate in planning changes in equipment, layout, and work methods.
- Employees understand how their jobs contribute to the finished product or service.

What role does training play? Employees need job-specific knowledge and basic skills to work with the equipment created by the new technology. Because technology is often used as a means to achieve product diversification and customization, employees must have the ability to listen and communicate with customers. Interpersonal skills, such as negotiation and conflict management, and problem-solving skills are more important than physical strength, coordination, and fine-motor skills—previous job requirements for many manufacturing and service jobs. Although technological advances have made it possible for employees to improve products and services, managers must empower employees to make changes.

Besides changing the way that products are built or services are provided within companies, technology has allowed companies to form partnerships with one or more other companies. **Virtual teams** refer to teams that are separated by time, geographic distance, culture, and/or organizational boundaries and that rely almost exclusively on technology (such as e-mail, Internet, and video conferencing) to interact and complete their projects. Virtual teams can be formed within one company, whose facilities are scattered throughout the country or the world. A company may also use virtual teams in partnerships with suppliers or competitors to pull together the necessary talent to complete a project or speed the delivery of a product to the marketplace. The success of virtual teams requires a clear mission, good communications skills, trust between members that they will meet deadlines and complete assignments, and an understanding of cultural differences (if the teams have global members).

At Nissan Motor Co.'s U.S. operations, sixteen teams, each with eight to sixteen salaried employees from different departments, meet weekly to discuss issues such as quality, diversity, or supply chain management.[106] The team members, chosen by management, are considered to be high performers who have demonstrated that they are receptive to new ideas. The teams are used to challenge the organization and propose new initiatives to make the company more creative and innovative. For example, as a result of one team's discussion of how to save money, a proposal for working at home was developed. A pilot study involving forty-one employees found that working at home resulted in reduced operating costs and improved morale, as well as productivity increases. As a result, a virtual office initiative is now in place at Nissan's North America headquarters in Franklin, Tennessee. The company's employees who analyze market trends and identify concepts for Nissan will now work from their homes in Los Angeles.

Software developers are positioning employees around the world; with clusters of three or four facilities six to eight hours apart, they are able to keep projects moving twenty-four hours a day.[107] Employees are able to focus continuously on projects by using highly talented engineers who can work in their own time zone and location without having to move to a different country or work inconvenient hours. The result is increased productivity and reduced project completion time. Also, globally distributed projects can draw on employees from many different cultures, backgrounds, and perspectives, helping to produce services and products that better meet the needs of global customers. The challenge is to organize the work so that teams in different locations and different work shifts can share tasks with minimum interaction.

Employees must be trained in principles of employee selection, quality, and customer service. They need to understand financial data so they can see the link between their performance and company performance.

# SNAPSHOT OF TRAINING PRACTICES

Training can play a key role in helping companies gain a competitive advantage and successfully deal with competitive challenges. Before you can learn how training can be used to help companies meet their business objectives, and before you can understand training design, training methods, and other topics covered in the text, you need to become familiar with the amount and type of training that occurs in the United States. Also, you must understand what trainers do. The next sections of this chapter present data regarding training practices (e.g., how much companies spend on training, what type of training is occurring, and who is being trained), as well as the skills and competencies needed to be a trainer.

## Training Facts and Figures

The snapshot of training practices provided in this section is based on data and collected from a number of sources, including surveys conducted by *Training* magazine and the ASTD.[108] For several reasons, these data should be viewed as reasonable estimates of practices rather than precise facts. One is that the samples may not be representative of all size or types of companies. For example, the *Training* survey was conducted by a research firm that e-mailed invitations to subscribers to participate in an online survey. The response rate ranged from 31 percent for large firms to 29 percent for small firms. The ASTD annual *State of the Industry Report* includes hundreds of organizations across all major industries grouped into three categories: companies who have received awards for training, ASTD BEST Award winners, Fortune Global 500 companies, and consolidated responses.

You may be asking yourself questions such as, "How much time and money do companies spend on training?" or "Is instructor-delivered training obsolete?" Table 1.7 provides a snapshot of trends in workplace learning. U.S. organizations continue to invest large amounts of money in learning initiatives. Here is an overview of some key trends in these investments:

- Direct expenditures, as a percentage of payroll and learning hours, have remained stable over the last several years.
- There is an increased demand for specialized learning that includes manager, professional, and industry-specific content.
- The use of technology-based learning delivery has increased from 11 percent in 2001 to 29 percent in 2010.

**TABLE 1.7**
**Questions and Answers about Training Practices**

Source: M. Green and E. McGill, "The 2011 State of the Industry," *T+D* (November 2011): 45–50; M. Green and E. McGill, *State of the Industry 2011* (Alexandria, VA: American Society for Training and Development, 2011); "2011 Training Industry Report," *training* (November/December 2011): 22–34.

**Investment and Distribution of Expenditures**
**Q:** How much do U.S. organizations spend on employee learning and development?
**A:** Approximately $171.5 billion
**Q:** How much is spent per employee?
**A:** $1,228
**Q:** What is the percentage of dollars spent on training and development as a percentage of payroll?
**A:** 2.7 percent
**Q:** How much is spent as a percentage of profit?
**A:** 5.3 percent
**Q:** How much time do employees spend in formal training each year?
**A:** 32 hours
**Q:** Who receives most of the training?
**A:** 41 percent of training budgets and dollars are spent on nonexempt employees, 25 percent on exempt employees, 24 percent on managers, and 10 percent on executives

**Efficiency**
**Q:** What percent of total expenses go to tuition reimbursement?
**A:** 12.9 percent
**Q:** How many training staff members are there for each employee?
**A:** 13 staff members for every 1,000 employees
**Q:** What is the average cost for providing one learning hour to one employee?
**A:** $72
**Q:** What is the average cost of producing one hour of formal training?
**A:** $1,415
**Q:** What is the ratio of learning hours used to learning hours available?
**A:** 52.9

**Delivery Methods**
**Q:** How is training delivered?
**A:** 42 percent by a instructor in a classroom, 24 percent via blended learning (including both face-to-face and technology delivery), 22 percent online, 1 percent via social network or mobile devices
**Q:** What percentage of direct learning expenditures are allocated to outside providers (i.e., outsourced)?
**A:** 23 percent

- Self-paced online learning is the most frequently used type of technology-based learning.
- Technology-based learning has helped improve learning efficiency, as shown by decrease in the reuse ration since 2003. (The "reuse ratio" is defined as how much learning content is used or received for every hour of content.) The reuse ratio dropped by 6 percent to almost 53 hours in 2010.This means that every hour of learning content available was received by about 53 employees. This decrease means that each hour of content was delivered fewer times.
- Technology-based learning has resulted in a larger employee–learning staff member ratio.
- The percentage of services distributed by external providers (e.g., consultants, workshops, and training programs) dropped from 29 percent in 2004 to 23 percent in 2010.

Of the $171 billion spent on training, 60 percent is for internal costs such as training-staff salaries and course development, and 40 percent is for services by external providers such as consultants, workshops, or training programs outside the company. Direct expenditures as a percentage of profit (5.3 percent) dropped from previous years (10.9 percent in 2009) due to smaller company profits and reduction in overall learning expenses, both likely resulting from the economic recession.

Figure 1.4 shows the different types of training provided by companies. Profession or industry-specific content, managerial and supervisory, and mandatory and compliance

**FIGURE 1.4**   **Different Types of Training Provided by Companies**

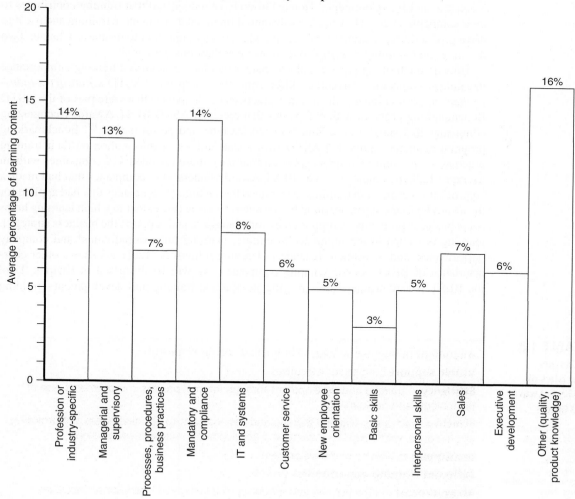

Note: Data from consolidated responses (companies that submitted their annual data as part of ASTD's benchmarking programs).
Source: Based on M. Green and E. McGill, "The 2011 State of the Industry," *T+ D* (November 2011): 45–50.

account for 41 percent of learning content. The least amount of learning content concerns basic skills.

## Training Investment Leaders

The chapter's opening vignette illustrates how training can be used by companies to gain a competitive advantage. Higher investment in training by companies in the United States is related to use of innovative training practices and high-performance work practices such as teams, employee stock ownership plans, incentive compensation systems (profit sharing), individual development plans, and employee involvement in business decisions. This spending (along with the use of high-performance work practices) has been shown to be related to improved profitability, customer and employee satisfaction, and the ability to retain employees. For example, companies including Grant Thornton LLP, Wipro Technologies, Steelcase, and InterContinental Hotels Group have recognized that training contributes to their competitiveness. They make a substantial financial investment in training and use it to drive productivity, customer service, and other results important to business. Chapter Two discusses how training can help companies meet their business goals.

How do the training practices of companies that have recognized training's importance in gaining a competitive advantage differ from other companies? ASTD's *State of the Industry Report, 2011* compares the training practices of companies that were part of the ASTD Benchmarking program with companies that received ASTD BEST Awards (recognizing companies that show a clear link between learning and performance).[109] Benchmarking program companies provided ASTD with a standard set of information on their training practices (e.g., number of hours spent on training); these included 412 companies with an average of 28,167 employees. The BEST Award winners were companies that had made a significant investment in training, determined by ranking all companies that had applied for the award on four criteria: learning has an enterprise role (the extent to which learning helps solve business problems, is supported by top managers, and supports the business strategy), learning is valued in the organization culture, learning links to individual and company performance, and investment is made in learning initiatives. Table 1.8 shows other characteristics of BEST Award–winning companies. As will be discussed in Chapter Two, the BEST Award winners are engaging in strategic training and development—training

**TABLE 1.8**

**Characteristics of BEST Award Winners**

Source: A. Paradise, *2008 State of the Industry Report* (Alexandria, VA: American Society for Training and Development, 2008).

**Alignment** of business strategy with training and development

**Visible support** from senior executives

**Efficiency** in training and development through internal process improvements, use of technology, and outsourcing

**Effective** practices by aligning training and development to business needs and providing all employees with access to training and development on an as-needed basis

**Investment** in training and development

**Different learning opportunities** provided

**Measurement** of effectiveness and efficiency of training and development activities

**Non-training solutions** for performance improvement used, including organization development and process improvement

**TABLE 1.9** Comparison of BEST Award Winners and Benchmark Companies

| | Benchmark Company | BEST Award Winner |
|---|---|---|
| Amount of training received per employee | 32 hours | 56 hours |
| Amount spent on training | | |
| • Percentage of payroll | 2.7% | 3.3% |
| • Per employee | $1,228 | $1,073 |
| Average percent of learning hours used via learning technology | 29% | 32% |
| Average percent of live, instructor-led training | 70% | 67% |

Source: M. Green and E. McGill, "The 2011 State of the Industry," *T+D* (November 2011): 45–50.

and development that supports the business's strategies and has measurable outcomes. The BEST Award winners included thirty-two companies with an average of 24,875 employees. Table 1.9 compares the BEST Award winners with the Benchmark companies. As the table shows, companies that were BEST Award winners used more learning technologies, such as internet-delivered training, and spent less time training in the classroom than Benchmark firms. Also, at BEST Award winning companies employees on average engaged in learning twenty-four more hours than employees at Benchmark companies.

What types of courses were purchased with training dollars? The learning content did not vary significantly between Benchmarking and BEST Award winners. For Benchmarking Forum companies, the top three learning content areas were managerial, profession- or industry-specific content; mandatory training and compliance; and processes, procedures, and business practices. For BEST Award winners, the top three content areas were profession- or industry-specific content, processes, procedures, and business practices, and managerial training.

## Roles, Competencies, and Positions of Training Professionals

Trainers can typically hold many jobs, such as instructional designer, technical trainer, or needs analyst. Each job has specific roles or functions. For example, one role of the needs analyst is to summarize data collected via interviews, observation, and even surveys to gain an understanding of training needs of a specific job or job family (a grouping of jobs). Special knowledge, skills, or behaviors—also called competencies—are needed to perform each role successfully. For example, the needs analyst must understand basic statistics and research methods to know what type of data to collect and to summarize data to determine training needs.

The most comprehensive study of training professionals has been conducted by the ASTD.[110] Figure 1.5 shows the ASTD competency model. The model describes what it takes for an individual to be successful in the training and development field. The top of the model shows the roles that training and development professionals can take. The learning strategist determines how workplace learning can be best used to help meet the company's business strategy. The business partner uses business and industry knowledge to create training that improves performance. The project manager plans, obtains, and monitors the effective delivery of learning and performance solutions to support the business. The professional specialist designs, develops, delivers, and evaluates learning and performance

**FIGURE 1.5** The 2011 ASTD Competency Model

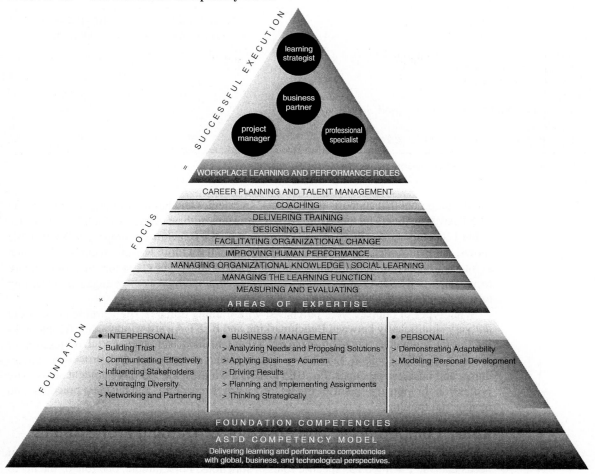

Source: Reprinted with permission from the American Society of Training and Development. From M. Allen and J. Naughton, "Social Learning: A Call to Action for Learning Professionals," *T+D* (August 2011): 50–55. Permission conveyed through Copyright Clearance Center, Inc.

solutions. These roles are included in jobs such as organizational change agent, career counselor, instructional designer, and classroom trainer. Training department managers devote considerable time to the roles of business partner and learning strategist. Training department managers may be involved in the project manager role but, because of their other responsibilities, they are involved to a lesser extent than are specialists who hold other jobs. Human resource or personnel managers may also be required to complete many of the training roles, although their primary responsibility is in overseeing the human resources functions of the company (e.g., staffing, recruiting, compensation, benefits).

The second tier of the model includes areas of expertise, which are the specific technical and professional skills and knowledge required for success (e.g., designing learning, delivering training, etc.). Although training professionals spend most of their time designing learning, delivering training, managing the learning function, and coaching, they do spend time in other areas as well. The model recognizes that social learning, which means learning with and from others using networking tools, is an important area of expertise.

The foundational competencies anchor the competency model. The foundational competencies include interpersonal competencies, business and management competencies, and personal competencies. The foundational competencies are important regardless of a trainer's area of expertise or role but are used to a different extent in each role or specialization.

Traditional narrow jobs in the training department focusing on one type of expertise (e.g., instructional designer and technical writer) are changing; having multiple areas of expertise becomes more necessary for training and development to contribute to the business. Project management requires the knowledge of new training technologies (e.g., web-delivered learning, CD-ROM, and knowledge management systems) and the ability to manage managers, engineers, scientists, and others who may have more experience, knowledge, or technical savvy than the trainer.

To provide you with an idea of the variety of responsibilities and expertise required for training professional jobs, Table 1.10 provides an example of a curriculum developer/instructional designer job that was posted on the ASTD website.

Table 1.11 shows median salaries for training professionals. Keep in mind that very rarely does anyone hold the highest-paying jobs (training manager, executive-level manager) without having developed competencies in a number of training roles.

## Who Provides Training?

In most companies, training and development activities are provided by trainers, managers, in-house consultants, and employee experts. However, as the snapshot of training practices suggests, training and development activities are also outsourced. **Outsourcing** means that training and development activities are provided by individuals outside the company. Training providers outside the company include colleges and universities, community and junior colleges, technical and vocational institutions, product suppliers, consultants and consulting firms, unions, trade and professional organizations, and government organizations. Outsourcing is discussed in greater detail in Chapter Two.

## Who Is in Charge of Training?

Training and development can be the responsibility of professionals in human resources, human resource development, or organizational development.[111] Companies may also have entire functions or departments called human resources, human resource development, talent management or development, or organizational development that provide training and development.

In small companies, training is the responsibility of the founder and all the employees. When organizations grow to 100 employees, typically someone within the company is in charge of human resources, either as part of that person's job or as his or her sole responsibility. At this point, training becomes one of the responsibilities of the employee in charge of human resources. In mid-sized to large organizations, training can be the responsibility of human resource professionals, or it can come from a separate function known as human resource development, talent management, development, learning, or organizational development.

**TABLE 1.10** **Example of Jobs Posted on the ASTD Website**

**Curriculum Developer/Instructional Designer**

**Role Overview:** You will work in a variety of content areas including soft-skills, technology, and business process training with a strong emphasis on practical application. As a member of this team, you will work hands-on with your projects from design through evaluation and collaborate closely with subject matter experts(s) and the Leadership Team on a regular basis.

**Responsibilities:**
- Develop new course content
- Update existing course content
- Facilitate course review and feedback sessions
- Promote continuous improvement Activities/Tasks
- Quickly and iteratively produce highly effective and engaging classroom and online training content based on business requirements through regular interactions with subject matter experts and executives
- Develop and maintain training deliverables including lecture, demonstrations, hands-on practice activities, role plays, identification of sample calls, job aids, knowledge checks, self-study materials, and more
- Develop representative role play/practice call scenarios and criteria to support Health Assistants learning how to handle client calls—including setup of supporting data in the CRM-based Training Environment
- Create content in order to support new hire and ongoing training activities based on adult learning theory and which support various learning styles ranging from 1 hour to several months in duration
- Work on multiple deliverables/courses concurrently
- Bring creative ideas into courseware
- Facilitate course design, build and review feedback sessions with course stakeholders—incorporate different inputs and feedback points into deliverables
- Regularly update existing course content based on business process or system changes in addition to general course enhancements
- Take course evaluation results along with other feedback and proactively identify course improvement opportunities

**Desired Qualifications and Experience:**
- Demonstrated ability to produce high-quality deliverables, on time, using a variety of delivery methods
- Proven ability to work in a fast-paced, ever changing environment
- Strong knowledge of Microsoft Office Suite
- Previous experience with CRM, call center, health insurance, and soft skills training is highly desirable

**Desired Personal Characteristics:**
- Effective communication skills—ability to work with individuals at all levels with varied backgrounds and personalities
- Ability to multitask, think on your feet, and creatively problem-solve issues
- Organized, dependable, and detail oriented
- Ability to manage own workload and competing priorities
- Strong communication skills

Source: From jobs posted at ASTD website, www.astd.org, accessed December 6, 2011.

**Human resource development** refers to the integrated use of training and development, organizational development, and career development to improve individual, group, and organizational effectiveness. Human resource development professionals might be involved in job and task analysis, instructional systems design, on-the-job training, and individual performance improvement. Organizational development professionals might

**TABLE 1.11**

**Average Salaries for Training Professionals**

Source: Based on "Training's 2011 Growth Spurt," *training* (November/December 2011): 36–41.

| | |
|---|---|
| Executive-Level Training/Human Resource Development Manager | $124,811 |
| Executive-Level Manager | 127,202 |
| Training Department Manager (1–5 trainers report to you) | 86,301 |
| Training Department Manager (more than 5 trainers report to you) | 98,614 |
| One-Person Training Department | 71,512 |
| Classroom Instructor/Trainer | 65,653 |
| Instructional Designer | 74,691 |
| CBT/Web/Multimedia Programmer Designer/Manager | 81,009 |
| Management/Career/Organization Development Specialist | 81,675 |
| Human Resource Manager/Specialist | 73,492 |

focus on training as well as team building, conflict avoidance, employee development, and change management. Talent management professionals might focus on identifying the top talent in the company and ensuring that they get the training and development needed to promote them or prepare them for new positions. Learning professionals might focus on formal training and development activities as well as ensuring that informal learning and knowledge sharing occurs through use of social networking tools. As you can see from these descriptions, training and development activities can be the responsibility of human resource management, human resource development, and organizational development professionals or departments. Keep in mind that regardless of what individual, department, or function is responsible, for training and development to succeed, employees, managers, training professionals, and top managers all have to take ownership for them. Throughout this book, the point is made that although training may be a formal responsibility of someone's job, employees at all levels of the company play a role in the success of training. Also, regardless of which function or department is responsible for training and development, it must be aligned with the business strategy and must support business needs. Professionals who are responsible for training and development may have specialized areas of expertise, such as change management for organizational development specialists, but they may also have training and development responsibilities. As shown in Figure 1.5, to perform workplace learning and performance roles successfully, professionals must understand the business and must master the competencies and areas of expertise.

As companies grow and/or recognize the important role of training for business success, they form an entire training or learning function (how training functions can be organized is discussed in Chapter Two). The training function may include instructional designers, instructors, technical training, and experts in instructional technology.

The reporting relationship between human resource management and the training function varies across companies.[112] Some organizations include training as part of the human resource function, believing that this provides strategic partnerships with other business functions and consistent companywide training. For example, at Life Care Centers of America, a Tennessee-based company that operates elder care facilities, training is included in the human resource department because the company believes that training is part of human resource expertise, including the ability to write training curriculum and evaluate learning. Being centrally located in the human resource department makes the best use of resources and helps communicate a common management culture.

Other companies separate training from the human resource function because it allows the training function to be decentralized to better respond to unique needs in different business units. The training and development department at A. G. Edwards has a learning center and develops training programs for its financial consultants and employees.[113] Representatives of the training department regularly meet with the company's management committee at corporate headquarters, as well as with regional officers and branch managers to help them understand how training can support business objectives. A new branch manager certification program succeeded because the branch managers were involved in identifying skill gaps and their suggestions were used in the program design. The branch managers took ownership of the program and helped develop the program proposal that they then presented to corporate managers to receive funding and approval for the program. Regardless of the organizational approach used for the training function, it must help meet the training needs of the business.

## Preparing to Work in Training

Everyone is a trainer at some point in his or her life. Consider the last time you had to teach some skill to a peer, sibling, spouse, friend, or even your boss. Although some people learn to train by trial and error, the best way is to take courses in training and development, or even choose an academic major related to training. For example, training and development courses are usually found in education, business and management, and psychology departments at colleges and universities. Business schools may offer undergraduate and graduate degrees in human resource management with courses in training and development, talent management, and organizational development. Education departments may have undergraduate and graduate degrees in human resource development and learning. Courses offered with such degrees include instructional design, curriculum development, adult learning, evaluation, and on-the-job training. Psychology departments offer courses in training and development as well. These courses can be part of a degree program in industrial and organizational psychology. If you are fortunate enough to be at a large university, you may have the opportunity to take courses from education, business/management, and the psychology departments that relate to training and development.

To be a successful training professional requires staying up-to-date on current research and training practices. The primary professional organizations for persons interested in training and development include the ASTD, the Academy of Human Resource Development (AHRD), the SHRM, the Society for Industrial and Organizational Psychology (SIOP), the Academy of Management (AOM), and the International Society for Performance Improvement (ISPI). The web addresses for these organizations are listed inside the front cover of this book. Articles about training practices can be found in the following journals: *Training, T + D, Training and Development, Chief Learning Officer, Workforce Management, HR Magazine, Academy of Management Executive,* and *Academy of Management Learning and Education.* Training and development research can be found in the following journals: *Human Resource Development Quarterly, Human Resource Development Review, Performance Improvement, Personnel Psychology, Journal of Applied Psychology, Academy of Management Journal,* and *Human Resource Management.*

## Key Terms

competitiveness, *6*

competitive advantage, *6*

human resource management, *6*

stakeholders, *7*

training, *8*

learning, *8*

development, *8*

formal training and development, *8*

informal learning, *8*

explicit knowledge, *9*

knowledge management, *9*

tacit knowledge, *9*

training design process, *10*

Instructional System Design (ISD), *11*

offshoring, *16*

human capital, *17*

intellectual capital, *17*

social capital, *17*

customer capital, *17*

knowledge workers, *18*

employee engagement, *19*

continuous learning, *20*

change, *20*

learning organization, *20*

talent management, *25*

Total Quality Management (TQM), *30*

Malcolm Baldrige National Quality Award, *30*

ISO 9000:2000, *30*

Six Sigma process, *32*

lean thinking, *33*

ISO 10015, *33*

alternative work arrangements, *36*

work teams, *37*

cross training, *37*

virtual teams, *38*

outsourcing, *45*

human resource development, *46*

## Discussion Questions

1. Describe the forces affecting the workplace and learning. How can training help companies deal with these forces?

2. Discuss the relationship between formal training and development, informal learning, and knowledge management. How are they related to learning and creating a learning organization?

3. What steps are included in the training design model? What step do you think is most important? Why?

4. What are intangible assets? How do they relate to training and development?

5. How is using training to benefit the company during difficult economic times?

6. Training professionals continue to debate whether the ISD model is flawed. Some argue that ISD should be treated as a project management approach rather than a step-by-step recipe for building training programs. Others suggest that ISD is too linear and rigid a process—that it is the primary reason training is expensive, and that it takes too long to develop. ISD focuses on inputs; management wants outputs. Businesses want results, not the use of a design technology. Do you believe that ISD is a useful process? Why or why not? Are there certain situations when it is a more (or less) effective way to design training?

7. Which of the training professionals' roles do you believe is most difficult to learn? Which is easiest?

8. How might technology influence the importance of training professionals' roles? Can technology reduce the importance of any of the roles? Can it result in additional roles?

9. Describe the training courses that you have taken. How have they helped you? Provide recommendations for improving the courses.

10. How does training differ between companies that are considered BEST Award winners and those that are not?

11. What are the implications of generational differences in the workforce? What strategies should companies consider from a training and development perspective to cope with generational differences and use them to benefit the company?

12. How has new technology improved training and development? What are some of the limitations of using iPhones or PDAs for training?

13. Explain how training relates to attracting new employees, employee retention, and motivation.

14. What is the relationship between talent management and employee engagement? What role can training and development practices play in keeping employee engagement high during poor economic times? Explain.

15. How can training, informal learning, and knowledge management benefit from the use of social collaboration tools like Twitter and Facebook? Identify the social collaboration tool and explain the potential benefits gained by using it.

## Application Assignments

1. Go to the American Society for Training and Development (ASTD) home page on the World Wide Web. The address is www.astd.org. Review the jobs found under "Featured Jobs." Choose a job that interests you and explain why. Based on the ASTD competency model presented in the chapter, discuss the roles, areas of expertise, and competencies needed in this job.

2. Go to www.quality.nist.gov, the website for the National Institute of Standards and Technology (NIST). The NIST oversees the Malcolm Baldrige Quality Award. Click on "2011–2012 Criteria for Performance Excellence." Download and review the award criteria. What questions are used to determine a company's education, training, and development focus?

3. NewBarista has created a barista skills training program. Go to www.newbarista.com. Click on "About Us" to learn about NewBarista. Next click on "Features," and watch the program overview. What technologies does this program use for training delivery and instruction? How do they contribute to helping baristas learn the skills needed to make a great cup of coffee?

4. Conduct a phone or personal interview with a manager or training manager. Ask this person to describe the role that training plays in his or her company; changes, if any, they have seen in training in the past five years; and how they believe it will change in the future.

5. In January 2012, *Training* identified the Top 125 companies for training. The top 10 ranked companies were:

   1. Verizon
   2. Farmers Insurance
   3. Miami Children's Hospital
   4. Mohawk Industries, Inc.
   5. McDonalds USA, LLC

6. The Economical Insurance Group
7. ABF Freight Systems, Inc.
8. BB&T Company
9. Coldwell Banker Real Estate
10. McCarthy Building Companies

Choose one of these companies to research. Visit the company's website, use a web search engine, or look for references to the company in publications such as *training, T + D, Workforce,* or *HR Magazine.* Prepare a report (not to exceed three pages) based on your research (a) describing why you believe the company was ranked in the top 10, and (b) explaining the relationship between training and the company's competitiveness, business goals, and objectives. Your instructor will advise you on whether the report should be submitted electronically or on hard copy. (*Hint:* Possible reasons a company might be ranked include the amount of money it devotes to training, the level of employee involvement in training, and the type of training used.)

## Case

# Zappos: *Facing Competitive Challenges*

Zappos, based in Las Vegas, is an online retailer. Its initial goal has been to be the best website for buying shoes, offering a wide variety of brands, styles, colors, sizes, and widths. The zappos.com brand has grown to offer shoes, handbags, eyewear, watches, and accessories for online purchase. Zappos's vision is that in the future, online sales will account for 30 percent of all retail sales in the United States, and Zappos will be the company with the best service and selection. As a result, Zappos believes that it can become the online service leader, drawing customers and expanding into selling other products. Zappos believes that the speed at which a customer receives an online purchase plays a critical role in how that customer thinks about shopping online again in the future, so it focuses on making sure that items get delivered to customers as quickly as possible.

In 2009, Zappos was acquired by the Amazon.com, Inc. family of companies, which share a strong passion for customer service. In 2010, Zappos had experienced tremendous growth, resulting in the need to restructure the company. Zappos was restructured into ten separate companies under the Zappos family umbrella, including Zappos.com, Inc. (the management company) and companies devoted to retail, gift cards, merchandising, and order fulfillment. Zappos has received many awards for its workplace culture and practices, including being recognized by *Fortune* magazine in 2011 as the #6 Best Company to Work For.

Zappos CEO Tony Heish has shaped the company's culture, brand, and business strategy around 10 core values:

1. Deliver WOW Through Service
2. Embrace and Drive Change
3. Create Fun and a Little Weirdness
4. Be Adventurous, Creative, and Open-Minded
5. Pursue Growth and Learning
6. Build Open and Honest Relationships with Communication
7. Build a Positive Team and Family Spirit
8. Do More with Less
9. Be Passionate and Determined
10. Be Humble

Deliver WOW Through Service means that call center employees need to provide excellent customer service. Call center employees encourage callers to order more than one size or color because shipping and return shipping are free. They are also encouraged to use their imaginations to meet customer needs.

Zappos's employment practices help to perpetuate its company culture. For example, the HR team uses unusual interview questions, such as "How weird are you?" and "What's your theme song?" to find employees who are creative and have strong individuality. Zappos provides free breakfast, lunch (cold cuts) and snacks, and a full-time life coach (employees have to sit on a red velvet throne to complain). Managers are encouraged to spend time with employees outside the office, and any employee can reward another employee a $50 dollar bonus for good performance. Most employees at Zappos are hourly. All new hires complete four weeks of training, including two weeks working the phones. New recruits are offered $2,000 to leave the company during training—an unusual practice designed to weed out individuals who will not be happy working at the company.

To reinforce the importance of the ten core values, Zappos performance management system asks managers to evaluate how well employee behavior demonstrates the core values, such as acting humble or expressing their personality. To evaluate task performance, managers are asked to provide employees with regular status reports on such things as how much time they spend on the telephone with customers. The status reports and evaluations of the core values are informational or used to identify training

needs. Zappos also believes in helping others understand what inspired the company culture. The company created the Zappos.com library, which provides a collection of books about creating a passion for customer service, products, and local communities. These books can be found in the front lobby of Zappos offices and are widely read and discussed by company employees.

Visit the Zappos website at www.zappos.com. Go to the bottom of the page under "About" and click on "about." Review the videos, the media kit, and the information provided about customer service, the family story, the culture, and the values.

*What challenges is Zappos facing that may derail its attempt to be the best online retailer? How can training and development help Zappos meet these challenges? Do you think that employees at Zappos have high levels of engagement? Why? Which of Zappos's ten core values do you believe training and development can influence the most? The least? Why?*

**Sources:** Based on the Zappos website, www.zappos.com; J. O'Brien, "Zappos Knows How to Kick It," *Fortune* (February 2, 2009): 55–66; M. Moskowitz, R. Levering, and C. Tkaczyk, "100 Best Companies to Work For," *Fortune* (February 7, 2011): 91–101; R. Pyrillis, "The reviews are in," *Workforce Management* (May 2011): 20–25.

## Endnotes

1. J. Quinn, P. Andersen, and S. Finkelstein, "Leveraging intellect," *Academy of Management Executive*, 10 (1996): 7–39.

2. J. Roy, "Transforming informal learning into a competitive advantage," *T+D* (October 2010): 23–25; P. Galagan, "Unformal, the new normal," *T+D* (September 2010): 29–31.

3. S. I. Tannenbaum, R. Beard, L. A. McNall, and E. Salas, "Informal Learning and Development in Organizations," In *Learning, Training, and Development in Organizations,* eds. S.W.J. Kozlowski and E. Salas (New York: Routledge, 2010); D. J. Bear, H. B. Tompson, C. L. Morrison, M. Vickers, A. Paradise, M. Czarnowsky, M. Soyars, and K. King, 2008. *Tapping the Potential of Informal Learning: An ASTD Research Study* (Alexandria, VA: American Society for Training and Development).

4. T. Bingham and M. Conner, *The New Social Learning* (Alexandria, VA: ASTD Press, 2010).

5. I. Nonaka and H. Takeuchi, *The Knowledge-Creating Company: How Japanese Companies Create the Dynamics of Innovation* (New York: Oxford University Press, 1995).

6. D. DeLong and L. Fahey, "Diagnosing cultural barriers to knowledge management," *Academy of Management Executive*, 14 (2000): 113–117; A. Rossett, "Knowledge management meets analysis," *Training and Development* (May 1999): 63–68.

7. "Training Top 125," *training* (January/February 2011): 57.

8. V. Powers, "Virtual communities at Caterpillar foster knowledge sharing," *T+D* (June 2004) : 40–45.

9. M. Green and E.McGill, *State of the Industry*, 2011 (Alexandria, VA: American Society for Training and Development, 2011); M. Weinstein, "Long-range learning plans," *training* (November/December 2010): 38–41.

10. L. Freifeld, "PWC does it again," *training* (February 2009): 24–28.

11. M. Molenda, "In search of the elusive ADDIE model," *Performance Improvement* (May/June 2003): 34–36; C. Allen (ed.), "ADDIE training system revisited," *Advances in Developing Human Resources* 8 (2006): 427–555.

12. G. Snelbecker, "Practical Ways for Using Theories and Innovations to Improve Training," in *The ASTD Handbook of Instructional Technology*, ed. G. Piskurich (Burr Ridge, IL: Irwin/McGraw-Hill, 1993): 19.3–19.26.

13. "American infrastructure: A cornerstone for learning," *T+D* (October 2008), 66–67.

14. R. Zemke and A. Rosett, "A hard look at ISD," *training* (February 2002): 26–34; R. Brinkerhoff and A. Apking, *High-Impact Learning*.(Perseus Publishing, 2001)

15. R. Chevalier, "When did ADDIE become addie?" *Performance Improvement* (July 2011):10–14.

16. H. Dolezalek, "Who has the time to design?" *training* (January 2006): 25–28.

17. F. Hansen, "Chief concern: Leaders," *Workforce Management* (July 20, 2009): 17–20; *SHRM's 2012 HR Trendbook, Special Supplement to HR Magazine* (December 2011): 51–99; K. Colteryahn and P. Davis, "8 trends you need to know now," *T+D* (January 2004): 29–36; M. Weinstein, "What does the future hold?" *training* (January 2006): 18–22; K. Tyler, "Training revs up," *HR Magazine* (April 2005): 58–63; B. Hall, "The top training priorities for 2005," *Training* (February 2005): 22–29; Society for Human Resource Management, "HR insight into the economy," *Workplace Visions* 4 (2008): 4; Society for Human Resource Management, "Workplace trends: An overview of the findings of the latest SHRM workplace forecast," *Workplace Visions* 3 (2008): 1–6.

18. J. Hagerty, "U.S. factories buck decline," *The Wall Street Journal* (January 19, 2011): A1–A2; J. Lahart, "Layoffs ease, but hiring is still slow," *The Wall Street Journal* (February 9, 2011): A2; Ian Katz and Bob Willis, "A CEO's dilemma: When is it safe to hire again?" *Bloomberg Business Week* (January 17–January 23, 2011): 22–24; Mark Hulbert (July 15, 2010). "It's dippy to fret about a double-dip recession," *The Wall Street Journal*; I. Wyatt and K. Byun, "The U.S. economy to 2018: From recession to recovery," *Monthly Labor Review* (November 2009): 11–29.

19. B. Casselman and J. Mitchell, "Jobless rate nears three-year low," *The Wall Street Journal,* (December 3–4, 2011): A1 and A5. S. Reddy and S. Murray, "Jobless rate falls further," *The Wall Street Journal* (March 5–6, 2011): A1,A2; R. Miller and V. Chen, "Hey, the U.S. economy does have a pulse," *Bloomberg Business Week* (October 17–23, 2011): 25–26; B. Cronin, "Slow recovery feels like a recession," *The Wall Street Journal* (October 31, 2011): A5; J. Mitchell and S. Murray, "Recession fears recede as economy grows 2.5%," *The Wall Street Journal* (October 28, 2011): A3; T. Keene, "2012: The crisis that won't go away," *Bloomberg Business Week* (November 7–November 13, 2011): 53–60.

20. J. Mitchell, "Grim job report sinks markets," *The Wall Street Journal* (June 2–3, 2011): A1, A6; J. Lublin, "The toll on parents when kids return home," *The Wall Street Journal* (November 10, 2011): B6.

21. J. McGregor, "Keeping talent in the fold," *BusinessWeek* (November 3, 2008): 51–52; D. Mattioli, "Despite cutbacks, firms invest in developing leaders," *The Wall Street Journal* (February 9, 2009): B4.

22. "Manufacturing: Engine of U.S. innovation," *National Association of Manufacturing* (October 4, 2006), available at website www.nam.org (January 21, 2009).

23. S. Kennedy, "U.S. won't dominate New World economy," *Columbus Dispatch* (January 16, 2011): G2.

24. D. Wessel, "Big U.S. firms shift hiring abroad," *The Wall Street Journal* (April 19, 2011): B1–B2.

25. M. Sanchanta, "Gap expands Japan push," *The Wall Street Journal* (March 2, 2011): B8.

26. M. Wei, "East meets west at Hamburger University," *Bloomberg Business Week* (January 31–February 6, 2011): 22–23.

27. Ibid.

28. C. Hymowitz, "IBM combines volunteer service, teamwork to cultivate emerging markets," *The Wall Street Journal* (August 4, 2008): B6.

28a. M. Horrigan, "Employment projections to 2012: Concepts and contexts," *Monthly Labor Review* 127 (February 2004): 3–22.

29. "The people problem," *Inc.* (May 29, 2001): 84–85.

30. "Manufacturing: Engine of U.S. innovation." *National Association of Manufacturing* (October 4, 2006), available at website www.nam.org (January 21, 2009).

31. R. Zeidner, "Does the United States need foreign workers?" *HR Magazine* (June 2009): 42–47; U.S. Department of Homeland Security, *Yearbook of Immigration Statistics: 2009.* Washington, D.C.: U.S. Department of Homeland Security, Office of Immigration Statistics, 2010.

32. J. Hagerty, "U.S. factories buck decline", *The Wall Street Journal* (January 19, 2011): A1–A2.

33. I. Sherr, "Apple says China partner made changes for workers," *The Wall Street Journal,* (February 15, 2011): B5.

34. L. Weatherly, *Human Capital—The Elusive Asset* (Alexandria, VA: SHRM Research Quarterly, 2003).

35. L. Bassi, J. Ludwig, D. McMurrer, and M. Van Buren, *Profiting from Learning: Do Firms' Investments in Education and Training Pay Off?* (Alexandria, VA: American Society for Training and Development, September 2000).

36. J. Barney, *Gaining and Sustaining Competitive Advantage* (Upper Saddle River, NJ: Prentice Hall, 2002).

37. W. Zeller, "Southwest: After Kelleher, more blue skies," *BusinessWeek* (April 2, 2001): 45; S. McCartney, "Southwest sets standards on costs," *The Wall Street Journal* (October 10, 2002): A2; S. Warren and M. Trottman, "Southwest's Dallas duel," *The Wall Street Journal* (May 10, 2005): B1, B4.

38. R. Dodes, "At Macy's, a makeover on service," *The Wall Street Journal,* April 11, 2011, B10.

39. R. Vance, *Employee Engagement and Commitment* (Alexandria, VA: Society for Human Resource Management (SHRM) Foundation, 2006).

40. Ibid.

41. G. Kranz, "Losing lifeblood," *Workforce Management* (June 2011): 24–28.

42. M. Ciccarelli, "Keeping the Keepers," *Human Resource Executive* (January/February 2011): 1-20–1-23.

43. J. Meister and K. Willyerd, *The 2020 Workplace* (New York: HarperCollins, 2010).

44. B. Testa, "New orbit," *Workforce Management* (August 17, 2009): 16–20.

45. D. Senge, "The learning organization made plain and simple," *Training and Development Journal* (October 1991): 37–44.

46. L. Thornburg, "Accounting for knowledge," *HR Magazine* (October 1994): 51–56.

47. G. Kranz, "More to learn," *Workforce Management* (January 2011): 27–30.

48. M. Weinstein, "Are you linked in?" *training* (September/October 2010): 30–33.

49. M. Toosi, "Labor force projections to 2018: Older workers staying more active" *Monthly Labor Review* (November 2009): 30–51.

50. Ibid.

51. N. Lockwood, *The Aging Workforce* (Alexandria, VA: Society for Human Resource Management, 2003).

52. S. Hewlett, L. Sherbin, and K. Sumberg, "How Gen Y and Boomers will reshape your agenda" *Harvard Business Review* (July–August 2009): 71–76; A. Fox, "Mixing it up," *HR Magazine* (May 2011): 22–27; K. Ball and G. Gotsill, *Surviving the Baby Boomer Exodus* (Boston: Cengage, 2011).

53. J. Meriac, D. Woehr, and C. Banister, "Generational differences in work ethic: An examination of measurement equivalence across three cohorts," *Journal of Business and Psychology*, 25 (2010): 315–324; K. Real, A. Mitnick, and W. Maloney, "More similar than different: Millennials in the U.S. building trades," *Journal of Business and Psychology*, 25 (2010): 303–313.

54. J. Deal, D. Altman, and S. Rogelberg, "Millennials at work: What we know and what we need to do (if anything)," *Journal of Business and Psychology*, 25 (2010): 191–199.

55. A. Fox, "Mixing it up," *HR Magazine* (May 2011): 22–27.

56. 2010 Society for Human Resource Management Workplace Diversity Practices study. Available at www.shrm.org, website for the Society for Human Resource Management.

57. M. Toosi, "Labor force projections to 2018: Older workers staying more active" *Monthly Labor Review* (November 2009): 30–51; M. Loden and J. B. Rosener, *Workforce America!* (Burr Ridge, IL: Business One Irwin, 1991); N. Lockwood, *The Aging Workforce* (Alexandria, VA: Society for Human Resource Management, 2003).

58. AARP website, www.aarp.org, "2009 AARP Best Employers for Workers Over 50," accessed May 6, 2011; S. Hewlett, L. Sherbin, and K. Sumberg, "How Gen Y and Boomers will reshape your agenda," *Harvard Business Review* (July–August 2009): 71–76.

59. J. Salopek, "Retaining women," *T+D* (September 2008): 24–27.

60. B. Hite, "Employers rethink how they give feedback," *The Wall Street Journal* (October 13, 2008): B5; E. White, "Age is as age does: Making the generation gap work for you," *The Wall Street Journal* (June 30, 2008): B3; P. Harris, "The work war," *T+D* (May 2005): 45–48; C. Hirshman, "Here they come," *HR Executive* (July 2006): 1, 22–26.

61. M. Rowh, "Older and wiser," *Human Resource Executive* (August 2008): 35–37.

62. M. O'Brien, "What's keeping you up now?" *Human Resource Executive* (September 2, 2011): 30–33. re:SEARCH, "Want to keep employees happy? Offer learning and development," *T+D* (April 2005): 18; P. Cappelli, "Talent management for the twenty-first century," *Harvard Business Review* (March 2008): 74–81.

63. A. Fox, "Achieving integration," *HR Magazine* (April 2011): 43–51.

64. R. Woods, "Industry output and employment projections to 2018" *Monthly Labor Review*, (November 2009): 52–81.

65. T. Lacey and B. Wright, "Occupational employment projections to 2018" *Monthly Labor Review* (November 2009): 82–123.

66. P. Wiseman, "U.S. a lean, mean factory machine," *Columbus Dispatch* (January 31, 2011): A3.

67. M. Toossi, "Labor force projections to 2014: Retiring boomers," *Monthly Labor Review* (November 2005): 25–44; N. Lockwood, *The Aging Workforce* (Alexandria, VA: Society for Human Resource Management, 2003).

68. J. Salopek, "The new brain drain," *T+D* (June 2005): 23–25; P. Harris, "Beware of the boomer brain drain!" *T+D* (January 2006): 30–33; M. McGraw, "Bye-bye boomers," *Human Resource Executive* (March 2, 2006): 34–37; J. Phillips, M. Pomerantz, and S. Gully, "Plugging the boomer drain," *HR Magazine* (December 2007): 54–58.

69. J. Thilmany, "Passing on knowledge," *HR Magazine* (June 2008): 100–104.

70. M. Weinstein, "Netting know-how," *Training* (September/October 2010): 26–29.

71. R. Davenport, "Eliminate the skills gap," *T+D* (February 2006): 26–34; M. Schoeff Jr., "Amid calls to bolster U.S. innovation, experts lament paucity of basic math skills," *Workforce Management* (March 2006): 46–49.

72. M. Schoeff Jr., "Companies report difficulty finding qualified employees," *Workforce Management* (October 19, 2009): 14; J. Casner-Lotto, E. Rosenblum, and M. Wright, "*The Ill-Prepared U.S. Workforce*" (New York: The Conference Board); P. Galagan, "Bridging the skills gap: New factors compound the growing skills shortage," *T+D* (February 2010): 44–49.

73. E. Krell, "The global talent mismatch," *HR Magazine* (June 2011): 68–73.

74. V. Chen and J. Berman, "Companies are hiring. Just not you," *Bloomberg Business Week* (August 15–August 28, 2011): 10–11; L. Weber, "Fine-tuning the perfect employee," *The Wall Street Journal* (December 5, 2011): B9. "IBMers pursue second careers in math and science education," from www.ibm.com/ibm/responsibility/teaching.shtml.

75. J. Barbian, "Get 'em while they're young," *training* (January 2004): 44–46; E. Frauenheim, "IBM urged to take tech skills to classrooms," *Workforce Management* (October 24, 2005): 8–9; K. Maher, "Skills shortage gives training programs new life," *The Wall Street Journal* (June 3, 2005): A2; "IBMers pursue second careers in math and science education," from www.ibm.com/ibm/responsibility/teaching.shtml.

76. Towers-Perrin, *Talent Management: The State of the Art* (Towers-Perrin, Chicago, IL, 2005).

77. A. Dohm, "Gauging the labor force effects of retiring babyboomers," *Monthly Labor Review* (July 2000): 17–25.

78. Society for Human Resource Management, *Workplace Visions* 5 (2000): 3–4.

79. E. White, "Manager shortage spurs small firms to grow their own," *The Wall Street Journal* (February 5, 2007): B1, B4; P. Galagan, "Talent management: What is it, who owns it, and why should you care?" *T+D* (May 2008): 40–44.

80. J. R. Jablonski, *Implementing Total Quality Management: An Overview* (San Diego: Pfeiffer, 1991).

81. R. Hodgetts, F. Luthans, and S. Lee, "New paradigm organizations: From total quality to learning to world-class," *Organizational Dynamics* (Winter 1994): 5–19.

82. "Malcolm Baldrige 2007 Award Recipient: Sharp HealthCare," Available at 2007 Baldrige Award recipients 2007 profiles at www.nist.gov, the website for the National Institute of Standards and Technology.

83. "ISO in One Page," "Quality Management Principles," "ISO 9000 Essentials," and "Management and Leadership Standards," from www.iso.org, accessed April 9, 2011.

84. General Electric 1999 Annual Report. Available at www.ge.com/annual99.

85. "Capitalizing on Opportunities," from *Smart Business* (February 16, 2011) accessed on April 9, 2011, from www.sbnonline.com website of *SmartBusiness;* D. Arnold, "Cardinal Fastener soars with lean thinking,"from www.cardinalfastener.com (accessed January 19, 2008).

86. L. Yiu and R. Saner, "Does it pay to train? ISO 10015 assures the quality and return on investment of training," *ISO Management Systems* (March–April 2005): 9–13.

87. L. Morales, "Nearly half of Americans are frequent Internet users," January 2, 2009, www.gallup.com; L. Morales, "Google and Facebook users, skew young, affluent, and educated," February 17, 2011, www.gallup.com.

88. D. Gayeski, "Goin' mobile," *T+D* (November 2004): 46–51; D. Hartley, "Pick up your PDA," *T+D* (February 2004): 22–24.

89. M. Derven, "Social networking: A frame for development," *T+D*, July 2009: 58–63; J. Arnold, "Twittering and Facebooking while they work," *HR Magazine* (December 2009): 53–55.

90. C. Goodman, "Employers wrestle with social-media policies," *The Columbus Dispatch*, (January 30, 2011): D3.

91. "Manufacturing: Engine of U.S. Innovation," *National Association of Manufacturing* (October 4, 2006). Available at www.nam.org (January 21, 2009).

92. D. Wakabayashi, "Japanese farms look to the 'cloud,'" *The Wall Street Journal* (January 18, 2011): B5.

93. B. Manville, "Organizing enterprise-wide e-learning and human capital management," *Chief Learning Officer* (May 2003): 50–55.

94. "Outstanding training initiatives: Capital One—Audio learning in stereo," *training* (March 2006): 64.

95. A. Weintraub, "High tech's future is in the toy chest," *BusinessWeek* (August 26, 2002): 124–126.

96. *2010 Employee Benefits Survey Report* (Alexandria, VA: Society for Human Resource Management, 2010).

97. Families and Work Institute, *2009 Guide to Bold Ideas for Making Work Work* (New York: Families and Work Institute, 2009); S. Shellenberger, "Time-zoned: Working round the clock workforce," *The Wall Street Journal* (February 15, 2007): D1.

98. D. Meinert, "Make telecommuting pay off," *HR Magazine* (June 2011): 32–37.

99. Bureau of Labor Statistics, "Contingent and Alternative Employment Arrangements, February 2005" from www.bls.gov, the website for the Bureau of Labor Statistics (accessed January 21, 2009).

100. R. Zeidner, "Heady debate," *HR Magazine* (February 2010): 28–33.

101. A. Fox, "At work in 2020," *HR Magazine* (January 2010): 18–23.

102. P. Choate and P. Linger, *The High-Flex Society* (New York: Knopf, 1986); P. B. Doeringer, *Turbulence in the American Workplace* (New York: Oxford University Press, 1991).

103. K. A. Miller, *Retraining the American Workforce* (Reading, MA: Addison-Wesley, 1989).

104. J. Marquez, "Engine of change," *Workforce Management* (July 17, 2006): 20–30. Also, based on Global Engineering Manufacturing Alliance website at www.gemaengine.com

105. J. Neal and C. Tromley, "From incremental change to retrofit: Creating high-performance work systems," *Academy of Management Executive* 9 (1995): 42–54; M. Huselid, "The impact of human resource

management practices on turnover, productivity, and corporate financial performance," *Academy of Management Journal* 38 (1995): 635–72.

106. J. Marquez, "Driving ideas forward at Nissan," *Workforce Management* (July 17, 2006): 28.

107. A. Gupta, "Expanding the 24-hour workplace," *The Wall Street Journal* (September 15–16, 2007): R9, R11.

108. M. Green and E. McGill, "The 2011 state of the industry," *T+D* (November 2011): 45–50; M. Green and E. McGill, *State of the Industry, 2011* (Alexandria, VA: American Society for Training and Development, 2011); 2011 Industry Report, *training* (November/December 2011): 22–34.

109. M. Green and E. McGill, "The 2011 state of the industry," *T+D* (November 2011): 45-–50.

110. P. Davis, J. Naughton, and W. Rothwell, "New roles and competencies for the profession," *T+D* (April 2004): 26–36; W. Rothwell and R. Wellins, "Mapping your future: Putting new competencies together to work for you," *T+D* (May 2004): 1–8.

111. W. Ruona and S. Gibson, "The making of twenty-first century HR: An analysis of the convergence of HRM, HRD, and OD," *Human Resource Management* (Spring 2004): 49–66.

112. J. Schettler, "Should HR control training?" *training* (July 2002): 32–38.

113. K. Ellis, "The mindset that matters most: Linking learning to the business," *training* (May 2005): 38–43.

# Strategic Training

## Objectives

After reading this chapter, you should be able to

1. Discuss how business strategy influences the type and amount of training in a company.
2. Describe the strategic training and development process.
3. Discuss how a company's staffing and human resource planning strategies influence training.
4. Explain the training needs created by concentration, internal growth, external growth, and disinvestment business strategies.
5. Discuss the advantages and disadvantages of centralizing the training function.
6. Discuss how to create a learning or training brand and why it is important.
7. Discuss the strengths of the business-embedded model for organizing the training function.
8. Explain a corporate university and its benefits.

## Soup Warms Our Hearts But Learning Raises the Profits

The Campbell Soup Company is a good example of a company that has embraced a continuous learning philosophy and where learning supports the business strategy. Campbell is the world's largest soup maker, but it is also growing business in healthy beverages (V8 brand) and baked snacks (Pepperidge Farms). Campbell's mission is to build the world's most extraordinary food company by nourishing people's lives everywhere, every day.

In 2000, Campbell lost about 50 percent of its market value in one year. Campbell was a legendary American company, but employee trust was low and product innovation and market development had stagnated. As a result, Doug Conant was hired as CEO. To help transform and revitalize the company, Conant created the "Campbell's Success Model." This model focuses on winning in the workplace, which will lead to winning in the marketplace, which in turn leads to winning in the community, creating shareholder value, and making a better world. Conant also established operating principles, one of which was the "Campbell Promise," which meant that the company needed to value its employees before they would value the company and its agenda. Conant also believed that for Campbell to be successful, it needs to have a culture that values learning.

Conant's learning agenda involved rebuilding training and development by creating a leadership development model. The leadership model includes inspiring trust, creating direction, driving organizational alignment, building organizational vitality, executing with excellence, and producing extraordinary results. Developing leaders is seen as strategically important because building an outstanding food company requires outstanding leaders. The CEO Institute was created to develop leadership skills of a cross section of high-performing, experienced and new managers. Campbell's University was created for the training and development of all employees. Campbell encourages all employees, from individual contributors to senior leaders, to learn and grow personally and professionally. Campbell's University includes classrooms and breakout rooms for training and development activities, as well as the opportunity to do virtual training at most of the company's locations around the world. Classes include finance, marketing, and other functional areas, as well as the business benefits of diversity and inclusion. Programs and initiatives include mentoring, 360 feedback tools, tuition assistance, and leadership development programs for manufacturing supervisors, general managers, and senior leaders. All employees have a training agenda. This fits the company's mission of building the world's most extraordinary food company by nourishing people's lives every day including those of its employees. Campbell believes that the more training and development opportunities are provided to employees, the more engaged in work they will become. Employee engagement leads to better performance in their roles and better performance for the company in the marketplace.

However, Conant believed that training and development involves more than just courses. It also needs to involve development planning. As a result, employees created a development plan with their managers that includes one or two development issues they want to work on. Conant personally spent time on development plans for Campbell's higher-level managers. This level of CEO involvement sent a message to all employees that development was important.

Conant retired from Campbell in July 2011. However, as a result of his emphasis on learning for all employees at Campbell for eight straight years, sales grew and employee engagement levels remained high. Conant has set Campbell on a positive course for achieving its mission.

**Sources:** T. Bingham and P. Galagan, "M'm M'm Good," *T+D*, March 2011, 36–43; N. Reardon, "Making Leadership Personal," *T+D*, March 2011, 44–48; www.campbellsoupcompany.com, website for Campbell Soup Company; A. Brown, "How Campbell's Soup went from stale to innovative," *Inc.*, September 14, 2011, accessed from www.inc.com, September 30, 2011.

# INTRODUCTION

As the chapter's opening vignette shows, training and development at Campbell Soup Company support the business strategy. Recognizing that learning is part of all employees' responsibilities, both managers and peers, along with training professionals, are actively involved in helping other employees gain new skills and perspectives. This helps to reinforce the value of learning and its importance for the business. Campbell recognizes that learning through training and development is critical for winning in the marketplace.

Why is the emphasis on strategic training important? Companies are in business to make money, and every business function is under pressure to show how it contributes to business success or else it faces spending cuts and even outsourcing. To contribute to a company's success, training activities should help the company achieve its business strategy. A **business strategy** is a plan that integrates the company's goals, policies, and actions.[1] The strategy influences how the company uses physical capital (e.g., plants, technology, and equipment), financial capital (e.g., assets and cash reserves), and human capital (employees). The business strategy helps direct the company's activities (production, finance, marketing, and human resources) to reach specific goals. The goals are what the company hopes to achieve in the medium- and long-term future. Most companies' goals include financial goals, such as to maximize shareholder wealth. But companies have other goals related to employee satisfaction, industry position, and community service.

There are both direct and indirect links between training and business strategy and goals. Training that helps employees develop the skills needed to perform their jobs directly affects the business. Giving employees opportunities to learn and develop creates a positive work environment, which supports the business strategy by attracting talented employees, as well as motivating and retaining current employees.

IBM is a company that reinvented itself in 2002.[2] Its business strategy reshaped its workforce to better meet clients' needs and expectations as IBM transformed itself from a high-tech industrial-age company to an information- and knowledge-driven company. This business strategy required a massive organizational culture change: Employees have had to accept the strategy and make it work. Dedication to clients is the core foundation of IBM's business strategy. To meet client needs, employees must be adaptable and constantly adjusting. As a result, IBM's training has shifted so that employees learn through work, on location, and based on client needs, rather than traveling to a different location for a training course, although formal training courses are still used to teach managers, executives, and salespeople new skills and product lines at critical moments in their careers. On-Demand Learning, as IBM has called it, requires that the learning teams that are responsible for designing the program understand the specific work being done by employees in different roles. IBM has defined more than 500 specific roles in the company and the expertise required for each role. The learning team has built learning opportunities into the work itself, a concept known as "work-embedded learning." Employees work via computer or access the company intranet on their phones to connect with experts, participate in an online community on a topic, or complete an online learning module. The amount of time spent on learning and training at IBM grew 32 percent through the expansion of work-embedded learning. The company has committed more than $700 million to its learning initiatives, which it believes are critical for achieving its business strategy.

Business strategy has a major impact on the type and amount of training that occurs and whether resources (money, trainers' time, and program development) should be devoted to training. Also, strategy influences the type, level, and mix of skills needed in the company. Strategy has a particularly strong influence on determining the following:

1. The amount of training devoted to current or future job skills
2. The extent to which training is customized for the particular needs of an employee or is developed based on the needs of a team, unit, or division

3. Whether training is restricted to specific groups of employees (such as persons identified as having managerial talent) or open to all employees

4. Whether training is planned and systematically administered, provided only when problems occur, or developed spontaneously as a reaction to what competitors are doing

5. The importance placed on training compared to other human resource management (HRM) practices such as selection and compensation[3]

This chapter begins with a discussion of how training is evolving. Traditionally, training has been seen as an event or program designed to develop specific, explicit knowledge and skills. But managers and trainers and human resource professionals have begun to recognize the potential contribution to business goals of knowledge that is based on experience, which is impossible to teach in a training program, and they have broadened the role of training to include learning and designing ways of creating and sharing knowledge. The chapter goes on to discuss the process of strategic training and development, including identifying business strategy, choosing strategic training and development initiatives that support the strategy, providing training and development activities that support the strategic initiatives, and identifying and collecting metrics to demonstrate the value of training. The chapter next describes organizational factors that influence how training relates to the business strategy. These include the roles of employees and managers, top management support for training, integration of business units, staffing and human resource planning strategy, degree of unionization, and manager, trainer, and employee involvement in training. The chapter addresses specific strategic types and their implications for training. Then the chapter emphasizes that for strategic learning, training, and development to be adopted, accepted and used by managers and employees, it is important to consider it from a change model and marketing perspective. The chapter ends with a description of several different ways of organizing the training function, emphasizing that the business-embedded and corporate university models are gaining in popularity as companies are aligning training activities with business goals.

## The Evolution of Training: From an Event to Learning

As more companies such as Campbell Soup Company recognize the importance of learning for meeting business challenges and providing a competitive advantage, the role of training in companies is changing.

Recall the discussion in Chapter One, "Introduction to Employee Training and Development," of the different ways that learning can occur in a company. Learning occurs through training, development, informal learning, and knowledge management. Training and development programs that are organized and created by the company, i.e., formal training and development programs, are one way to ensure that employees learn. In less strategic approaches, training involves a series of programs or events that employees are required to attend. After attending the training program, employees are responsible for using what they learned in training on the job, and any support they might receive is based on the whims of their manager. Also, training provides no information that would help employees understand the relationship between the training content and their job performance, development objectives, or business goals. This type of training usually fails to improve workplace performance and meet business needs. The role of training as a program or event will continue into the future because employees will always need to be taught specific knowledge and skills. This approach assumes that business conditions are predictable, they can be controlled by the company, and the company can control and anticipate the knowledge and skills that employees need in the future. These assumptions are true for certain skills, such as communication and conflict resolution. However, these training events or programs will need to be more closely tied to performance improvement and business needs to receive support from top management. The training design model, presented in Chapter One, and the different aspects of the model, discussed in Chapters Three though Eight, will help you understand how to design training programs that can improve employee performance and meet business needs.

# LEARNING AS A STRATEGIC FOCUS

## The Learning Organization

Many companies, recognizing the strategic importance of learning, have strived to become learning organizations. A **learning organization** is a company that has an enhanced capacity to learn, adapt, and change.[4] Training processes are carefully scrutinized and aligned with company goals. In a learning organization, training is seen as one part of a system designed to create human capital. King Arthur Flour Company encourages its 160 employees to learn about baking to motivate them to perform their jobs and to help customers better understand its product.[5] Employees are offered about fifteen "Brain Food" classes each year. In these classes, their peers teach topics ranging from how to bake whole-grain breads to how to read company financial statements and manage their personal finances. All employees are encouraged to attend the classes, which are voluntary and held during work hours. Employees can also attend classes the company offers for professional and home bakers.

The essential features of a learning organization appear in Table 2.1. Note that the learning organization emphasizes that learning occurs not only at the individual employee level

**TABLE 2.1**   **Key Features of a Learning Organization**

**Supportive Learning Environment**

- Employees feel safe expressing their thoughts about work, asking questions, disagreeing with managers, and admitting mistakes.
- Different functional and cultural perspectives are appreciated.
- Employees are encouraged to take risks, innovate, and explore the untested and unknown, such as trying new processes and developing new products and services.
- Thoughtful review of the company's processes is encouraged.

**Learning Processes and Practices**

- Knowledge creation, dissemination, sharing, and application are practiced.
- Systems are developed for creating, capturing, and sharing knowledge.

**Managers Reinforce Learning**

- Managers actively question and listen to employees, encouraging dialogue and debate.
- Managers are willing to consider alternative points of view.
- Time is devoted to problem identification, learning processes and practices, and post-performance audits.
- Learning is rewarded, promoted, and supported.

Sources: F. Gino and G. Pisano, "Why Leaders Don't Learn From Success," *Harvard Business Review* (April 2011): 68–74. Based on D. Garvin, A. Edmondson, and F. Gino, "Is Yours a Learning Organization?" *Harvard Business Review* (March 2008): 109–116; M. Gephart, V. Marsick, M. Van Buren, and M Spiro, "Learning Organizations Come Alive," *Training and Development* 50 (1996): 34–45.

(as we traditionally think of learning), but also at the group and organizational levels. The learning organization emphasizes knowledge management.

One of the most important aspects of a learning organization is the ability for employees to learn from failure and from successes. That is, learning includes understanding why things happen and why some choices lead to outcomes.[6] Both success and failure trigger investigation, which help employees revise assumptions, models, and theories. For example, Apple's Newton tablet failed miserably when it was introduced in 1990. However, the failure caused Apple to reexamine its theories about what makes successful products. As a result, Apple recognized that a touchphone would be accepted more easily by consumers because of the existing smartphone market. Subsequently, using what they learned about the iPhone helped develop a more successful tablet, the iPad. Pixar, which has created a number of successful and acclaimed animated films, still conducts reviews of the process used to make each of its films. For example, Pixar asks employees the top five things they would do and not do again. This is important to gain a better understanding of the reasons behind successful performance so they can be shared by others. To learn from failure and success requires providing employees with the opportunity to experiment with products and services similar to what happens in engineering and scientific research. Some of the conditions necessary for successful experimentation include that it involves genuine uncertainty, the cost of failure is small and contained, the risks of failure are understood and eliminated if possible, there is an understanding that failure still provides important information, success is defined, and the opportunity is significant.

At Walt Disney Company over the last ten years, training has evolved to include flexible learning delivery, customized learning experiences, and collaborative development with internal training customers.[7] Disney has moved from an instructor-led training approach to an approach that uses face-to-face instruction (either in a classroom or on the job) combined with online instruction (game simulation, e-learning). This suits Disney's business strategy, which has always emphasized matching the appropriate technology and methods to the audience regardless of whether the audience is a guest or an employee (cost member).

A single training event or program is not likely to give a company a competitive advantage because explicit knowledge is well known and programs designed to teach it can be easily developed and imitated. However, tacit knowledge developed through experience and shared through interactions between employees is impossible to imitate and can provide companies with a competitive advantage. Pixar's development of successful computer-animated films such as *WALL-E* (a robot love story set in a post-apocalyptic world of trash) and *Ratatouille* (a tale of a French rat who longs to be a chef) required the cooperation of a team of talented directors, writers, producers, and technology artists who were located in different buildings, have different priorities, and speak different technical languages.[8] Pixar follows three operating principles: (1) all employees must have the freedom to communicate with other employees, regardless of their position or department; (2) it must be safe for everyone to offer ideas; and (3) the company must maintain awareness of innovations occurring in the academic community. Pixar University offers a collection of in-house courses for training and cross-training employees within their specialty areas. But it also offers optional classes that provide opportunities for employees from different disciplines to meet and learn together. Screenplay writing, drawing, and sculpting are directly related to the business, while courses in Pilates and yoga are not. The courses are attended by employees with all levels of expertise—from novices to experts—which reinforces the idea that all employees are learning and it is fun to learn together.

## Implications of Learning for Human Capital Development

The emphasis on learning has several implications. First, there is a recognition that to be effective, learning has to be related to helping employee performance improve and the company achieve its business goals. This connection helps ensure that employees are motivated to learn and that the limited resources (time and money) for learning are focused in areas that will directly help the business succeed. Second, unpredictability in the business environment in which companies operate will continue to be the norm. Because problems cannot be predicted in advance, learning needs to occur on an as-needed basis. Companies need to move beyond the classroom and instead use job experiences, online learning, and mobile learning to help employees acquire knowledge and skills while they focus on business problems. Third, because tacit knowledge is difficult to acquire in training programs, companies need to support informal learning that occurs through mentoring, social networks, and job experiences. Fourth, learning has to be supported not only with physical and technical resources but also psychologically. The company work environment needs to support learning, and managers and peers need to encourage learning and help employees find ways to obtain learning on the job. Also, managers need to understand employees' interests and career goals to help them find suitable development activities that will prepare them to be successful in other positions in the company or deal with expansion of their current job. Chapter Five, "Program Design," discusses how to create a work environment that supports training and learning.

Creating and sharing knowledge refers to companies' development of human capital. As discussed in Chapter One, human capital includes cognitive knowledge (know what), advanced skills (know how), system understanding and creativity (know why), and self-motivated creativity (care why).[9] Traditionally, training has focused on cognitive and advanced skills. But the greatest value for the business may be created by having employees understand the manufacturing or service process and the interrelationships between departments and divisions (system understanding), as well as motivating them to deliver high-quality products and services (care why). To create and share knowledge, companies have to provide the physical space and technology (e-mail, websites, social networks) to encourage employee collaboration and knowledge sharing. Ford Motor Company has communities of practice organized around functions.[10] For example, all the painters in every Ford assembly plant around the world belong to the same community. At each plant, one of the painters serves as a "focal point." If a local painter discovers a better way to improve one of the sixty steps involved in painting, the focal person completes a template describing the improvement and its benefits. The template then is submitted electronically to a subject-matter expert located at Ford headquarters, who reviews the practice and decides whether it is worth sharing with other assembly plants. If so, the practice is approved and sent online to the other assembly plants. Ford has collected $1.3 billion in projected value for the company and has realized over $800 million of actual value from its communities of practice.

As companies recognize the value of training and development and view them as part of a broader learning strategy, seven key capabilities are needed, according to a survey by Accenture Learning.[11] These capabilities are:

1. Alignment of learning goals to business goals
2. Measurement of the overall business impact of the learning function
3. Movement of learning outside the company to include customers, vendors, and suppliers
4. A focus on developing competencies for the most critical jobs
5. Integration of learning with other human resource functions, such as knowledge management, performance support, and talent management
6. Delivery approaches that include classroom training as well as e-learning
7. Design and delivery of leadership development courses

These capabilities are part of the strategic training and development process, which is discussed next.

# THE STRATEGIC TRAINING AND DEVELOPMENT PROCESS

Now that you understand how training is evolving in companies and have been introduced to the concept of business strategy and how training can support a business strategy, you are ready to study the process of strategic training and development. Figure 2.1 shows a model of the strategic training and development process with examples of strategic initiatives, training activities, and metrics.

The model shows that the process begins with identifying the business strategy. Next, strategic training and development initiatives that support the strategy are chosen. Translating these strategic training and development initiatives into concrete training and development activities is the next step of the process. The final step involves identifying measures or metrics. These metrics are used to determine whether training has helped contribute to goals related to the business strategy. The following sections detail each step in the process.

**FIGURE 2.1**
**The Strategic Training and Development Process**

## Business Strategy Formulation and Identification

Five major components are part of developing a new business strategy or changing an existing one.[12] Figure 2.2 shows the components. The first component is the company **mission,** which is a statement of the company's reason for existing. Company missions vary, but they typically include information on the customers served, why the company exists, what the company does, the value received by the customers, and the technology used. The mission statement is often accompanied by a statement of the company's vision or values. The **vision** is the picture of the future the company wants to achieve, while **values** are what the company stands for. The second component is the company **goals,** which are what the company hopes to achieve in the medium to long term; they reflect how the mission will be carried out. Training can contribute to a number of different business goals, as shown in Table 2.2. Both for-profit and not-for-profit companies often include goals related to satisfying stakeholders. The term *stakeholders* refers to shareholders (if the company is publically traded and for-profit), the community, customers, employees, and all the other parties that have an interest in seeing that the company succeeds.

The third and fourth components, external and internal analysis, are combined to form what is called a SWOT analysis. A **SWOT analysis** consists of an internal analysis of strengths and weaknesses and an external analysis of opportunities and threats to the company that currently exist or are anticipated. **External analysis** involves examining the operating environment to identify opportunities and threats. The business challenges identified in Chapter One can represent opportunities (or threats) to the company. Examples of opportunities include customers and global markets who are not being served,

**FIGURE 2.2**
**Formulating the Business Strategy**

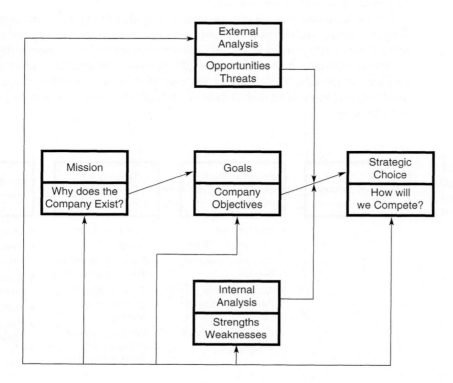

**TABLE 2.2**
**Possible Business Goals Influenced by Training**

Sources: Based on R. Rivera, "How to Demonstrate Value: Key Measures Every Learning Professional Should Know." In *WLP Scorecard: Why Learning Matters* (pp. 17–24). Alexandria: VA: ASTD Press.

Productivity
Reduced scrap and rework
Increased customer satisfaction
Reduced operational risks and accidents due to employee carelessness
Increased employee satisfaction and retention
Increased time and value-producing goods, such as increase in billable project time hours
Better management decisions
Increased development of human capital
Succession planning needed for competitive advantage and growth.

**TABLE 2.3**
**Decisions a Company Must Make About How to Compete to Reach Its Goals**

Source: "Strategy— Decisions About Competition." In R. Noe, J. Hollenbeck, B. Gerhart, and P. Wright, *Human Resource Management: Gaining a Competitive Advantage,* 8th ed. (Burr Ridge, IL: Irwin/McGraw-Hill, 2011): 77.

1. **Where to compete?**
   In what markets (industries, products, etc.) will we compete?
2. **How to compete?**
   On what outcome or differentiating characteristic will we compete? Cost? Quality? Reliability? Delivery? Innovativeness?
3. **With what will we compete?**
   What resources will allow us to beat the competition? How will we acquire, develop, and deploy those resources to compete?

technology that can help the company, and unused or underutilized potential sources of talented employees. Threats might include changes in the economy, talent and leadership shortages, new competitors, and changes in legislation that can adversely affect the company. **Internal analysis** attempts to identify the company's strength and weaknesses. It focuses on examining the available quantity and quality of financial, physical, and human capital. The last component is strategic choice. After completing the SWOT analysis, the company (usually managers involved in strategic planning) has all the information it needs to consider how to compete, generate several alternative business strategies and make a strategic choice. The decisions that a company has to make regarding how to compete are shown in Table 2.3. The possible alternative strategies are compared based on the ability to achieve the company goals. The **strategic choice** represents the strategy believed to be the best alternative to achieve the company goals.

Consider the role of SWOT analysis at CarMax, used car stores located across the United States with low, no haggle pricing, and DPR Construction.[13] Understanding the skills its employees need to succeed is an important part of the long-range strategy at CarMax. CarMax considers what skills employees need to both support its fundamental business principle of integrity as well as company performance. It emphasizes the importance of competencies that drive behavior and influence employee performance. CarMax training programs are based on both internal and external evaluations. Internal evaluations include input from managers about competency needs and gaps, as well as surveys of employees asking them what they need to improve their performance. External analysis includes monitoring trends and new practices in talent management, human resources, and broader society. For example, the emerging use of social networking technology convinced CarMax to incorporate it into its training programs.

DPR Construction's overall learning mission is "We create and provide learning opportunities to enhance the potential of our employees in support of our business objectives." At planning sessions for the next year that take place in the fall, DPRs global learning group meets. This group includes individuals from different offices and roles who focus on training initiatives, as well as company leaders. The global learning group discusses best practices, needs assessment data, and the business strategy. A summary of the meeting is presented to the Management Committee, which is responsible for operations across DPR. Subject matter experts are asked to help with the design and delivery of new training initiatives to meet identified training needs. Employee feedback is also taken into account when considering new training initiatives. For example, when DPR was interested in how new technology such as e-learning could be used in its training programs, they developed and administered an employee survey which included a list of courses and asked to choose which ones they preferred to be delivered in the classroom or via e-learning.

Although these decisions are equally important, companies often pay less attention to the "With what will we compete?" issue, resulting in failure to reach the goals. This decision includes figuring out how human, physical, and financial capital will be used. To use human capital to gain a competitive advantage requires linking the company's human resources practices (such as training and development) to the business strategy.

## Identify Strategic Training and Development Initiatives That Support the Strategy

**Strategic training and development initiatives** are learning-related actions that a company should take to help it achieve its business strategy.[14] The strategic training and development initiatives vary by company depending on a company's industry, goals, resources, and capabilities. The initiatives are based on the business environment, an understanding of the company's goals and resources, and insight regarding potential training and development options. They provide the company with a road map to guide specific training and development activities. They also show how the training function will help the company reach its goals (and in doing so, show how the training function will add value).

There is a tendency to have a disconnect between the strategy and execution of the strategy. To avoid this, learning professionals need to reach out to managers to ensure that the strategic training initiatives and training activities are aligned with the business strategy and that the necessary financial resources and support are provided to carry out the training activities.[15]

To contribute to a company's business strategy, it is important that the training function understand and support it and provide value to its customers. Linking training plans to business plans is important because business plans describe company priorities (plans or initiatives) and include descriptions of who will be involved, the context and how it might affect the plan, how the plan will be carried out (operations), and what decisions have to be made, including those involving training and development, to increase the likelihood that the plan will succeed. To help ensure that its training and development initiatives support the business strategy, CA, a software company, builds training plans and establishes priorities for separate business plans for nonmanagers, managers, and executives during the budget planning process each fiscal year.[16] Training plans include both the technical and interpersonal skills required for each group and how those skills will be developed. To ensure that the training plans help meet business needs, they are updated on a quarterly basis and monthly meetings are held that include both training staff and business leaders who review training needs and discuss future business plans. The training staff focuses on identifying the three to five initiatives that are most important to support the business strategy.

Table 2.4 shows strategic training and development initiatives and their implications for training practices. *Diversify the learning portfolio* means that companies may need to provide more learning opportunities than just traditional training programs. These learning opportunities include informal learning that occurs on the job through interactions with peers; new job experiences; personalized learning opportunities using mentors, coaches, and

**TABLE 2.4** **Strategic Training and Development Initiatives and Their Implications**

| Strategic Training and Development Initiatives | Implications |
| --- | --- |
| Diversify the Learning Portfolio | • Use technology, such as the Internet, for training<br>• Facilitate informal learning<br>• Provide more personalized learning opportunities |
| Expand Who Is Trained | • Train customers, suppliers, and employees<br>• Offer more learning opportunities to nonmanagerial employees |
| Accelerate the Pace of Employee Learning | • Quickly identify needs and provide a high-quality learning solution<br>• Reduce the time to develop training programs<br>• Facilitate access to learning resources on an as-needed basis |
| Improve Customer Service | • Ensure that employees have product and service knowledge<br>• Ensure that employees have skills needed to interact with customers<br>• Ensure that employees understand their roles and decision-making authority |
| Provide Development Opportunities and Communicate with Employees | • Ensure that employees have opportunities to develop<br>• Ensure that employees understand career opportunities and personal growth opportunities<br>• Ensure that training and development addresses employees' needs in current job as well as growth opportunities |
| Capture and Share Knowledge | • Capture insight and information from knowledgeable employees<br>• Organize and store information logically<br>• Provide methods to make information available (e.g., resource guides, websites) |
| Align Training and Development with the Company's Direction | • Identify needed knowledge, skills, abilities, or competencies<br>• Ensure that current training and development programs support the company's strategic needs |
| Ensure that the Work Environment Supports Learning and Transfer of Training | • Remove constraints to learning, such as lack of time, resources, and equipment<br>• Dedicate physical space to encourage teamwork, collaboration, creativity, and knowledge sharing<br>• Ensure that employees understand the importance of learning<br>• Ensure that managers and peers are supportive of training, development, and learning |

Source: Based on S. Tannenbaum, "A Strategic View of Organizational Training and Learning." In *Creating, Implementing, and Managing Effective Training and Development,* ed. K. Kraiger (San Francisco: Jossey-Bass, 2002): 10–52.

feedback customized to employee needs; and the use of technology (including web-based training). Such training is self-paced and available outside a formal classroom environment (these learning opportunities are discussed in Chapters Seven, Eight, and Nine).

Reliance Industries Ltd., an Indian company with businesses in energy and petrochemicals and polyester products, employs a wide variety of learning initiatives using different methods.[17] For example, to increase the opportunities for plant employees to train for emergencies and malfunctions, Reliance invested in simulator training at more than 185 facilities. To capture expert knowledge and make it available to other employees working anywhere in the company, a new technology-based solution was used. Experts can share their knowledge and experience using video lectures that are made available at any time to other employees on the company intranet. To help meet its needs for engineers, Reliance has partnered with educational institutions to create a curriculum that is supported by specific company assignments.

*Expand who is trained* refers to the recognition that because employees are often the customer's primary point of contact, they need as much if not more training than managers do. University Health System includes an inpatient hospital and seventeen care facilities located throughout Bexar County, Texas.[18] University Health System was challenged to provide opportunities for learning and skills development to its 1,500 remote employees. The learning department expanded opportunities by visiting clinics to develop curriculum and implement training. Education expos bring continuing education providers onsite so employees can see all the opportunities available to them at once. A website provides employees with access to colleges, universities, financial aid, and scholarship. The School at Work program helps employees in entry-level jobs get the skills and knowledge they need to move to new positions. The program covers topics including the math, reading, and communication skills needed to meet certification and degree program requirements. Employees work on the program on their own time using DVDs and online training. The learning department also created the Administrative Professionals Academy, designed to provide high-performing administrative professionals with the knowledge and skills to advance in their careers.

Also, to provide better customer service to suppliers, vendors, and consumers, companies need to distribute information about how to use the products and services they offer. Companies are beginning to train suppliers to ensure that the parts that suppliers provide will meet their customers' quality standards. To be successful, companies have to be able to deal with changes in technology, customer needs, and global markets. Training needs have to be identified quickly and effective training provided. That is, companies have to *accelerate the pace of employee learning.* Also, companies are relying on electronic performance support systems (EPSSs) that provide employees with immediate access to information, advice, and guidance (EPSSs are discussed in more detail in Chapter Five). EPSS can be accessed through personal computers, tablets, or mobile phones whenever they are needed. Because customers now have access to databases and websites and have a greater awareness of high-quality customer service, they are more knowledgeable, are better prepared, and have higher service expectations than ever before. Employees must be prepared to *improve customer service.* Employees have to be knowledgeable about the product or service, they need to have customer service skills, and they need to understand the types of decisions they can make (e.g., are they allowed to make an exception to the policy of no cash refunds?). *Providing development opportunities* and communicating them to employees is important to ensure that employees believe that they have opportunities to grow and learn new skills. Such opportunities are important for attracting and retaining talented employees. *Capturing and sharing knowledge* ensures that important knowledge about customers, products, or processes is not lost if employees leave the company. Also, giving employees access to knowledge that other employees have may quicken response times to customers and improve product and service quality. For example, rather than "reinventing the wheel," service personnel can tap into a database that allows them to search for problems and identify solutions that other service reps have developed.

AT&T uses social networks in three ways. "You Matter" allows employees to share ideas and blogs on a variety of topics, such as money management and wellness.[19] Using "tSpace," an internal company platform for blogs and wikis, employees create their own personal profiles and can join communities of practice organized around specific topics, which give employees the opportunity to learn through sharing ideas and asking questions. With Talent Optimization (TOP), managers can search companywide for employees with the skills they need to match employee talents with open positions. Managers can search companywide for employees who have the skills needed to fill open positions.

*Aligning training and development with the company's strategic direction* is important to ensure that training contributes to business needs. Companies need to identify what employee capabilities (e.g., knowledge, skills) are needed and whether training programs and services are helping to improve these capabilities. Finally, *a supportive work environment* is necessary for employees to be motivated to participate in training and learning activities, use what they learn on the job, and share their knowledge with others. Tangible support includes time and money for training and learning, as well as work areas that encourage employees to meet and discuss ideas. Psychological support from managers and peers for training and learning is also important. Types of tangible and psychological support for training are discussed in Chapter Five.

How might a company ensure that its training and development initiatives are linked to its business strategy? Table 2.5 shows the questions that a company needs to answer to identify and develop its strategic training and development initiatives. To help answer these questions,

**TABLE 2.5**
**Questions to Ask to Develop Strategic Training and Development Initiatives**

Source: Based on R. Hughes and K. Beatty, "Five Steps to Leading Strategically," *T+D* (December 2005): 46–48.

1. What is the vision and mission of the company? Identify the strategic drivers of the business strategy.
2. What capabilities does the company need as a result of the business strategy and business environment challenges?
3. What types of training and development will best attract, retain, and develop the talent needed for success?
4. Which competencies are critical for company success and the business strategy?
5. Does the company have a plan for making the link between training and development and the business strategy understood by executives, managers, and employees or customers?
6. Will the senior management team publicly support and champion training and development?
7. Does the company provide opportunities for training and developing not only individuals but also teams?

trainers need to read the annual reports, strategic plans, earnings releases, and analyst reports for their companies. To understand the business strategy and its implications for training, it may be useful to invite managers to attend training and development staff meetings and present information on the company's business strategy. Also, in companies with multiple divisions, it is important to understand each business, including how it measures effectiveness, how it monitors and reports performance, and what challenges it faces, such as supply chain management, new product development, competitive pressures, or service warranty issues.

## Provide Training and Development Activities Linked to Strategic Training and Development Initiatives

After a company chooses its strategic training and development initiatives related to its business strategy, it then identifies specific training and development activities that will enable these initiatives to be achieved. These activities include developing initiatives related to the use of new technology in training, increasing access to training programs for certain groups of employees, reducing development time, and developing new or expanded course offerings. For example, one of the strategic training and development initiatives for American Express Financial Advisors, located in Minneapolis, Minnesota, is to prepare employees to offer world-class service.[20] Training the company's customer service representatives is especially important because of the breadth of the job requirements. The customer service representatives have to be able to discuss the content of financial products, as well as handle transactions of these products over the phone with both customers and financial experts. Also, the representatives work in the securities industry, which is highly regulated, and some are required to have a license to sell securities. American Express's emphasis on training is related not only to the company's needs, but also to the basic business principle that it costs less to serve customers well and keep them than to try to replace them after they have left. Providing good customer service and maintaining customer loyalty depend on how well customer service representatives work the phones, take orders, offer assistance, and develop relationships with customers.

When new employees report for work in the customer services section of American Express, they begin an eight-week training program designed to help them succeed in building and solidifying the company's client base. First, they split their days into learning about American Express's investment products and practicing how they will work with the company's financial advisors and clients. After employees complete the initial training and begin to work on the phone with actual clients, they still receive at least two weeks of training each year. The ongoing training includes a mix of classroom and web-based training on subjects such as new financial products and changes in security regulations. Online training modules are used to teach computer skills, such as how to use a new software product or how to reduce the number of screens a representative must go through to retrieve a particular piece of information. American Express's training includes active participation by the trainees. Customer service trainees are given time to review material, ask questions, and practice on the computer systems they will be using.

## Identify and Collect Metrics to Show Training Success

How does a company determine whether training and development activities actually contribute to the business strategy and goals? This determination involves identifying and collecting **metrics,** business-level outcomes chosen to measure the overall value of training or learning initiatives. Examples of metrics include measures of employee retention, employee engagement, customer service, productivity, and quality. It is important to recognize the difference between training program outcomes and business metrics. Typically, training program evaluation involves measuring trainee satisfaction with the program, assessing improvements in trainee knowledge, skills, and abilities, or identifying if the program influenced business results such as productivity. Training evaluation, used for determining the effectiveness of training courses or programs, is discussed in more detail in Chapter Six, "Training Evaluation." In comparison to training evaluation outcomes, metrics focus on results rather than on other outcomes. They are strategic business-related measures. That is, they are not linked to one course or program but are chosen to represent the expected value of several programs or learning initiatives. For example, a fast-food company was interested in determining the overall strategic value of training. This meant the focus was on time and money spent in training across many fast-food stores, not on one or two programs within a store. The company found that training improved customer service, employee retention, and profits.[21]

The business-related outcomes should be directly linked to the business strategy and goals. For example, business-related outcomes could evaluate customer service, employee satisfaction or engagement, employee turnover, number of product defects, time spent in product development, number of patents, or time spent filling management positions. Some companies use the balanced scorecard as a process to evaluate all aspects of the business. The **balanced scorecard** is a means of performance measurement that provides managers with a chance to look at the overall company performance or the performance of departments or functions (such as training) from the perspective of internal and external customers, employees, and shareholders.[22] The balanced scorecard considers four different perspectives: customer, internal, innovation and learning, and financial. The emphasis and type of indicators used to measure each of these perspectives are based on the company's business strategy and goals. The four perspectives and examples of metrics used to measure them include:

- Customer (time, quality, performance, service, cost)
- Internal (processes that influence customer satisfaction)
- Innovation and learning (operating efficiency, employee satisfaction, continuous improvement)
- Financial (profitability, growth, shareholder value)

Metrics that might be used to assess training's contribution to the balanced scorecard include employees trained (employees trained divided by total number of employees), training costs (total training costs divided by number of employees trained), and training costs per hour (total training costs divided by total training hours). For example, EMC Corporation, a technology company, uses a balanced scorecard to track and measure learning.[23] Company performance is tracked quarterly with metrics measuring business alignment, workforce readiness, time-to-market, globalization, and effectiveness. The company has also implemented performance metrics that are directly linked to present and future business needs. Employees are given individual development plans that are based on an analysis of their jobs. Ingersoll Rand requires its business units to make strong business cases for new spending.[24] Following this model, Ingersoll Rand University (IRU) shows that learning makes a difference and contributes to the business strategy by using metrics such as expected benefits, one-time versus ongoing costs, shelf-life of learning products, and employee participation rates in its programs. Each year, IRU provides the company with an annual report communicating accomplishments, challenges, strategic directions, and operational efficiencies. For example, IRU has offered process improvement workshops related to Lean Six Sigma (a quality initiative), which is a business priority. IRU has been able to demonstrate that its workshops have saved the company hundreds of thousands of dollars by reducing vendor delivery costs by 76 percent. The process of identifying and collecting metrics is related to training evaluation, the final step in Figure 1.1 in Chapter One. Chapter Six discusses the different types of outcomes used to evaluate a training program's metrics in more detail. Of course, showing that training directly relates to the company "bottom line" (e.g., increased service, sales, or product quality) is the most convincing evidence of the value of training.

## Examples of the Strategic Training and Development Process

Consider the strategic training and development process in two very different companies: Barilla Group and Mike's Carwash. Barilla Group is a leader in the pasta business worldwide, in the pasta sauce business in continental Europe, in the bakery product business in Italy, and in the crisp bread business in Scandinavia.[25] Barilla's mission, vision, and values are shown in Table 2.6. Barilla's performance-based culture stresses competitiveness, engagement, and leadership. Barilla has 15,000 employees worldwide, including 420 at pasta-producing plants in Ames, Iowa, and Avon, New York.

At Barilla's North American operations, growth at these two plants is leading to expansion and an emphasis on learning. The importance of training and development to the business is emphasized by its organizational goals, which include to "strengthen competitive advantage through talent, performance, and culture," as well as achieving sales and financial goals. The division's learning organization designs, develops, and facilitates the annual strategic planning session. Corporate strategic goals influence the company's human resource strategic plans, which in turn affect learning priorities. The process includes one-to-one interviews between the director of learning and talent development and executives who work together to determine the objectives of the strategic planning session. The recent agenda of the strategic planning session included a focus on how to grow the

---

**TABLE 2.6**

**Barilla's Vision, Mission, and Values**

Source: From www .barillaus.com, the website for Barilla Group.

**Vision**
"We help people live better by bringing well-being and the joy of eating into their everyday lives."

**Mission**
- Since 1877, Barilla is the Italian Family Company that believes food is a joyful convivial experience, is taste, is a form of sharing and caring.
- Barilla offers delightful and safe products at a great value.
- Barilla believes in the Italian nutritional model that puts together superior-quality ingredients and simple recipes creating unique five-senses experiences.
- Sense of belonging, courage, and intellectual curiosity inspire our behaviors and characterize our people.
- Barilla has always linked its development to people's well-being and to the communities in which it operates.

**Values**
Passion, trust, intellectual curiosity, integrity, courage.

business by identifying key business indicators for the business teams, discussing the overall performance of the business teams, and allocating people, processes, and technology to help achieve the business strategy.

There are several strategic training and development initiatives and activities at the company's North American operations. First, to accelerate the pace of employee learning and development, individual development plans are matched to employee strengths and passions, using managers' input to determine if they are aligned. At the directorship level, each member of the leadership team provides input into the development plan. The learning organization plays a key role in change management. The learning organization was responsible for the successful implementation of the company's new resource planning system. Members of a small change management team were responsible for communicating directly with employees, allowing employees to see the conversion process for themselves. They held periodic meetings to solicit input from employees affected by the conversion and explain details of the conversion. A visual timeline gave employees monthly views of the transition to the new system, as well as progress updates and goals achieved. The timeline highlighted connections between the business strategy and daily work, including process change and team performance, from leaders and managers to line employees. To help diversify the learning opportunities and ensure that the necessary training was being conducted to support the business, the learning organization partnered with peers from the company's Italian headquarters to conduct a needs assessment. The needs assessment helped identify performance needs and which skills to develop by department, based on organizational goals, department goals, and skill gaps. Also, the needs assessment data was used to determine the learning methods and priorities of Barilla University.

Mike's Carwash, based in Indianapolis, Indiana, is a privately owned chain of car washes with thirty-seven locations and 650 employees in Indiana and Ohio.[26] Opened in 1948, the first Mike's was called "Mike's Minit Man Carwash," named after the type of equipment originally used. Figure 2.3 shows how Mike's Carwash links its business strategy to training and development.

Mike's business strategy is based on the reputation that it's known for: consistent and speedy service, return customers, and growing the business to four or five new locations

**FIGURE 2.3**
**How Mike's Carwash Links Training and Development to Business Strategy**

| Business Strategy | Strategic Training and Development Initiatives | Training and Development Activities | Metrics that Show the Value of Training |
|---|---|---|---|
| • Delight the customer | • Diversify the learning portfolio | • Orientation | • Return Customer |
| • Repeat Business | • Expand who is Trained | • Development Plan | • Revenue |
| • Consistent Service | • Improve Customer Service | • Internal Certification | • Customer Satisfaction |
| • Growth | • Provide Development Opportunities | • Online Training | • Mystery Shopper Scopes |
| | | • Manages Accountable for Employees Training and Provide Coaching to Improve Other Skills | • Ensure work Environments Supports Cleaning & Transfer |

each year. Mike's Carwashes are automated and feature equipment, systems, and technology developed by Mike's employees. Mike's credits some of its success to the Dahm family's business smarts but believes that most of its success comes from its employees and its hiring and training practices. Mike's original founders, Joe and Ed Dahm, were known to tell employees that the company was truly in the people business—it just happened to wash cars. Its mission is to provide friendly and fast service to the boss (i.e., customers) at a good value.

Customer satisfaction is very important to Mike's, with the emphasis placed on repeat business by serving customers so they will come back again. The biggest challenge that Mike's faces is providing a consistently enjoyable customer experience. Mike's is constantly trying to improve the customer experience through innovation and new ideas. If a new idea works, it is implemented in all locations. Mike's believes that the only way to provide a consistent customer experience is not only through finding great employees, but through training and development of those employees. The company website explains that it is "notoriously picky" when it comes to hiring. For every fifty people Mike's considers hiring, just one is hired. Mike's uses training and development to retain and engage its employees. Each employee has a development plan and receives performance appraisals twice each year. New employee training involves familiarizing them with best practices and how to help customers in different situations that they will encounter at the car wash. Before employees wait on their first customer, they receive two days of orientation and participate in workshops that focus on customer service, how to treat customers, how to recover from service errors and mistakes, and how to deal with difficult customers. Mike's also provides training to help employees advance in the company. The career path from hourly associate to supervisor to shift manager to assistant manager is well defined. Movement on the career path is possible through good performance and completing internal certifications that include up to twelve weeks of training and three exams requiring grades of at least 80 percent. Employee engagement and satisfaction are measured by semiannual surveys, as well as by gathering information from employees who are leaving Mike's. Employees play an important role in the choice and design of training and development activities. A fifteen- to twenty-person team consisting of members who have been nominated by their store manager serve a one-year term as subject-matter experts in helping to develop new and modify existing training programs. Team members also are the first trainees in new programs, providing feedback about needed changes and feedback on program effectiveness.

In addition to its regular training programs for new employees and certification programs for advancement, Mike's has developed programs to meet its emerging business needs. The recent economic recession resulted in a decrease in the volume of customers Mike's served, as well as in revenue. As a result, Mike's recognized the need to increase the spending of its customers by making sure that employees made them aware of value-added services such as underbody washes, tire treatments, and clearcoat application. To do this, Mike's developed an online training module and taught managers to encourage employees to complete their training and practice using their selling skills at monthly employee meetings.

Mike's recognizes the important role that managers play in helping employees learn. At Mike's, managers need to actively support and help deliver training. They are held accountable for training and developing employees in order to advance and succeed. In this program, managers were taught how to identify weaknesses in employees' service recommendations techniques and use weekly coaching sessions to enhance them. Managers were also encouraged to observe and document employees making service recommendations to customers and to provide them with feedback. The results of this program were positive: overall revenue, revenue per customer, customer satisfaction, and "mystery shopper" scores all increased.

# ORGANIZATIONAL CHARACTERISTICS THAT INFLUENCE TRAINING

The amount and type of training, as well as the organization of the training function in a company, are influenced by employee and manager roles; by top management support for training; by the company's degree of integration of business units; by its global presence; by its business conditions; by other HRM practices, including staffing strategies and human resource planning; by the company's extent of unionization; and by the extent of involvement in training and development by managers, employees, and human resource staff.[27]

## Roles of Employees and Managers

The roles that employees and managers have in a company influence the focus of training, development, and learning activity. Traditionally, employees' roles were to perform their jobs according to the managers' directions. Employees were not involved in improving the quality of the products or services. However, with the emphasis on the creation of intellectual capital and the movement toward high-performance work systems using teams, employees today are performing many roles once reserved for management (e.g., hiring, scheduling work, and interacting with customers, vendors, and suppliers).[28] If companies are using teams to manufacture goods and provide services, team members need training in interpersonal problem solving and team skills (e.g., how to resolve conflicts and give feedback). If employees are responsible for the quality of products and services, they need to be trained to use data to make decisions, which involves training in statistical process control techniques. As discussed in Chapter One, team members may also receive training in skills needed for all positions on the team (cross training), not just for the specific job they are doing. To encourage cross training, companies may adopt skill-based pay systems, which base employees' pay rates on the number of skills they are competent in rather than what skills they are using for their current jobs. Skill-based pay systems are discussed in Chapter Ten, "Social Responsibility, Legal Issues, Managing Diversity, and Career Challenges."

Research suggests that today's managers are expected to do the following:[29]

- *Manage individual and team performance.* Motivate employees to change performance, provide performance feedback, and monitor training activities. Clarify individual and team goals and ensure alignment with company goals.
- *Develop employees and encourage continuous learning.* Explain work assignments and provide technical expertise. Create environment that encourages learning.
- *Plan and allocate resources.* Translate strategic plans into work assignments and establish target dates for projects.
- *Coordinate activities and interdependent teams.* Persuade other units to provide products or resources needed by the work group, and understand the goals and plans of other units. Ensure that the team is meeting internal and external customer needs.

- *Manage group performance.* Define areas of responsibility, meet with other managers to discuss effects of changes in the work unit on their groups, facilitate change, and implement business strategy.
- *Facilitating decision-making process.* Facilitate team and individual decision making. Encourage the use of effective decision-making processes (dealing with conflict, statistical process control).
- *Creating and maintaining trust.* Ensure that each team member is responsible for his or her workload and customers. Treat all team members with respect. Listen and respond honestly to team ideas.
- *Represent one's work unit.* Develop relationships with other managers, communicate the needs of the work group to other units, and provide information on work group status to other groups.

Regardless of their level in the company (e.g., senior management), all managers are expected to serve as spokespersons to other work units, managers, and vendors (i.e., represent the work unit). Of course, the amount of time that managers devote to some of these roles is affected by their level. Line managers spend more time managing individual performance and developing employees than midlevel managers or executives do. The most important roles for midlevel managers and executives are planning and allocating resources, coordinating interdependent groups, and managing group performance (especially managing change). Executives also spend time monitoring the business environment by analyzing market trends, developing relationships with clients, and overseeing sales and marketing activities.

To manage successfully in a team environment, managers need to be trained in "people skills," including negotiation, sensitivity, coaching, conflict resolution, and communication skills. A lack of people skills has been shown to be related to managers' failure to advance in their careers.[30]

## Top Management Support

The CEO, the top manager in the company, plays a key role in determining the importance of training and learning in the company. The CEO is responsible for[31]

- Setting a clear direction for learning (vision)
- Encouragement, resources, and commitment for strategic learning (sponsor)
- Taking an active role in governing learning, including reviewing goals and objectives and providing insight on how to measure training effectiveness (governor)
- Developing new learning programs for the company (subject-matter expert)
- Teaching programs or providing resources online (faculty)
- Serving as a role model for learning for the entire company and demonstrating a willingness to learn constantly (learner)
- Promoting the company's commitment to learning by advocating it in speeches, annual reports, interviews, and other public relations tools (marketing agent)

For example, James Hackett, CEO of Steelcase, a company in the office furniture industry, declared publicly that learning is the core of Steelcase's strategy. The key, said Hackett, is for Steelcase to study space and help companies use it more efficiently and effectively.[32]

At Ingersoll Rand, to ensure that top managers understand and support the role that training and development can play in the company, a "ladder of engagement" model has been created.[33] Top managers are engaged in training and development in many different ways, including providing input into learning program development, serving as trainers or co-trainers, visiting courses as executive speakers, or serving as advisory council members for Ingersoll Rand's corporate university.

## Integration of Business Units

The degree to which a company's units or businesses are integrated affects the kind of training that takes place. In a highly integrated business, employees need to understand other units, services, and products in the company. Training likely includes rotating employees between jobs in different businesses so they can gain an understanding of the whole business.

## Global Presence

As noted in Chapter One, the development of global product and service markets is an important challenge for U.S. companies. For companies with global operations, training is used to prepare employees for temporary or long-term overseas assignments. Also, because employees are geographically dispersed outside the United States, companies need to determine whether training will be conducted and coordinated from a central U.S. facility or will be the responsibility of satellite installations located near overseas facilities.

Consider how globalization has affected the training practices of KLA-Tencor, a manufacturer of equipment and systems for semiconductor manufacturers.[34] KLA-Tencor has factories in China, Taiwan, Singapore, and India in order to better serve its customers that also have global locations, such as Intel. At KLA-Tencor, employees are trained in installing and servicing machine tools in its global operations. Employees also need to know how to adjust the machines to maximize productivity so they can educate customers on how to use them more effectively. Technology training is provided regionally because trainees need hands-on experience with the machines. KLA-Tencor finds local instructors who are qualified to teach in the local language. The local instructors are trained in how to deliver the technical training and use the machines. Before teaching courses on their own, the local instructors co-teach a class with another trainer to ensure that they are comfortable and proficient in delivering training. Network Appliances, a data storage technology company, is headquartered in the United States but has locations in the Middle East, Asia, and Africa. NetApp University provides training to account managers, systems engineers, technical support employees, customers, and maintenance suppliers. NetApp training centers in overseas locations provide training that is delivered in English. Some courses, such as customer training, are available in twenty-three different languages.

At Intel, a semiconductor and microprocessor manufacturer, providing for the company's global strategic needs begins with a needs assessment.[35] Regardless of whether employees are in China or Arizona, they are going to receive the same training content. Intel's programs are delivered by local instructors (subject-matter experts, not full-time trainers) who tailor the training content to meet the needs of the learners at each location. Intel uses local instructors to ensure that the training content is not too generic or U.S.-focused. Typically, the content is 80 to 90 percent consistent across the company, but instructors have the flexibility to use examples that are relevant to the geographic location and/or the business-unit.

## Business Conditions

When unemployment is low and/or businesses are growing at a high rate and need more employees, companies often find it difficult to attract new employees, find employees with necessary skills, and retain current employees.[36] Companies may find themselves in the position of hiring employees who might not be qualified for the job. Also, in these types of business conditions, companies need to retain talented employees. In a knowledge-based economy (including the information technology and pharmaceuticals areas), product development depends on employees' specialized skills. Losing a key employee may cause a project to be delayed or hinder a company's taking on new projects. Training plays a key role in preparing employees to be productive, as well as motivating and retaining current employees. Studies of what factors influence employee retention suggest that employees rate working with good colleagues, having challenging job assignments, and getting opportunities for career growth and development as top reasons for staying with a company. Across all industries, from high-tech to retailing, companies are increasingly relying on training and development to attract new employees and retain current ones. For example, companies such as Eli Lilly (a pharmaceutical company) and Microsoft are successful in terms of financial returns. They are typically found on lists of great places to work (for example, they regularly appear on *Fortune* magazine's annual list of "Best Companies to Work For"). They are quite successful in attracting and retaining employees. Not only do they provide employees with very competitive pay and benefits, but they also are committed to training and development. Retailers such as Macy's and Nordstroms cannot generate sales unless they have enough skilled employees.[37] For example, Macy's begins its employee retention strategy by starting with executives. Executives are accountable for retaining the employees who report to them. Managers have been trained to run meetings and conduct performance evaluations (skills that influence employees' perceptions of how they are treated, which ultimately affects whether they remain with Macy's). Macy's has also provided training programs and courses for employees.

For companies in an unstable or recessionary business environment—one characterized by mergers, acquisitions, or disinvestment of businesses—training may be abandoned, be left to the discretion of managers, or become more short-term (such as offering training courses only to correct skill deficiencies rather than to prepare staff for new assignments). These programs emphasize the development of skills and characteristics needed (e.g., how to deal with change), regardless of the structure the company takes. Training may not even occur as the result of a planned effort. Employees who remain with a company following a merger, acquisition, or disinvestment usually find that their job now has different responsibilities requiring new skills. For employees in companies experiencing growth—that is, an increased demand for their products and services—there may be many new opportunities for lateral job moves and promotions resulting from the expansion of sales, marketing, and manufacturing operations or from the start-up of new business units. These employees are usually excited about participating in development activities because new positions often offer higher salaries and more challenging tasks.

During periods when companies are trying to revitalize and redirect their business, earnings are often flat. As a result, fewer incentives for participation in training—such as promotions and salary increases—may be available. In many cases, companies downsize their workforces as a way of cutting costs. Training activities under these conditions focus on ensuring that employees are available to fill the positions vacated by retirement or turnover. Training also involves helping employees avoid skill obsolescence. (Strategies to help employees avoid skill obsolescence are discussed in Chapter Ten.)

## Other HRM Practices

**Human resource management (HRM) practices** consist of the management activities related to investments (time, effort, and money) in staffing (determining how many employees are needed, and recruiting and selecting employees), performance management, training, and compensation and benefits. Companies that adopt state-of-the-art HRM practices that contribute to business strategy tend to demonstrate higher level of performance than firms that do not.[38] These HRM practices contribute to the attraction, motivation, and retention of human capital (the knowledge, skills, and abilities embedded in people), which can help a company gain a competitive advantage. Training, along with selection, performance management, and compensation influence attraction motivation and retention of human capital. Training helps develop company-specific skills, which can contribute to productivity and ultimately company performance. Also, training helps provide the skills that employees need to move to new jobs in the company, therefore increasing their satisfaction and engagement. The type of training and the resources devoted to training are influenced by staffing strategy, the strategic value of jobs and employee uniqueness, and human resource planning.

### Staffing Strategy

**Staffing strategy** refers to the company's decisions regarding where to find employees, how to select them, and the desired mix of employee skills and statuses (temporary, full-time, etc.). It is important for you to recognize that training and development and learning opportunities can vary across companies because of differences in companies' evaluation of the labor market, their staffing strategy, or the strategic value and uniqueness of jobs or positions. For example, one staffing decision a company has to make is how much to rely on the internal labor market (within the company) or external labor market (outside the company) to fill vacancies. Two aspects of a company's staffing strategy influence training: the criteria used to make promotion and assignment decisions (assignment flow) and the places where the company prefers to obtain the human resources to fill open positions (supply flow).[39]

Companies vary in terms of the extent to which they make promotion and job assignment decisions based on individual performance or group or business-unit performance. They also vary in terms of the extent to which their staffing needs are met by relying on current employees (internal labor market) or employees from competitors and recent entrants into the labor market, such as college graduates (external labor market). Figure 2.4 displays the two dimensions of staffing strategy. The interaction between assignment flow and supply flow results in four distinct types of companies: fortresses, baseball teams, clubs, and academies. Each company type places a different emphasis on training activities. For example, some companies (such as medical research companies) emphasize innovation and creativity. These types of companies are labeled "baseball teams." "Because it may be difficult to train skills related to innovation and creativity, they tend to handle staffing needs by luring employees away from competitors or by hiring graduating students with specialized skills. "Academies" tend to be companies such as Proctor & Gamble (P&G), dominant in their industry or markets, which rely primarily

**FIGURE 2.4**
**Implications of Staffing Strategy for Training**

Source: Adapted from J. A. Sonnenfeld and M. A. Peiperl, "Staffing policy as a strategic response: A typology of career systems," *Academy of Management Review* 13 (1988): 588–600.

External Labor Market

**Fortress**

*Development*
- Focuses on avoiding obsolescence
- No systematic development

*Key Strategic Characteristics*
- Survival
- Struggle for resources

*Industries*
- Natural resources

**Baseball Team**

*Development*
- Use of job experiences
- No development related to succession planning

*Key Strategic Characteristics*
- Innovation
- Creativity

*Industries*
- Advertising, consulting firms, biomedical research

Supply Flow

**Club**

*Development*
- Job rotation
- Special assignments with career paths

*Key Strategic Characteristics*
- Monopoly
- Highly regulated

*Industries*
- Utilities, nursing homes, public sector

**Academy**

*Development*
- Assessment and sponsorship
- Use of upward, lateral, and downward moves within and across functions

*Key Strategic Characteristic*
- Dominant in market

*Industries*
- Consumer products, pharmaceuticals

Internal Labor Market

Group Contribution          Assignment Flow          Individual Contribution

on training and developing their current employees (i.e., the internal labor market) to fill new positions and managerial roles. "Clubs" tend to be companies in highly regulated industries such as energy or health care that also rely on developing talent from their internal labor market but rely on team or department performance to determine promotions or opportunities to obtain important development activities or assignments. "Fortresses" include companies in industries that are undergoing significant change and struggling for survival. In "Fortresses" financial and other resources are not available for development so companies tend to rely on hiring talent from outside, i.e., from the external labor market, on an "as-needed" basis. Figure 2.4 can be used to identify development activities that support a specific staffing strategy. For example, if a company wants to reward individual employee contributions and promote from within (the bottom-right quadrant of Figure 2.4), it needs to use lateral, upward, and downward moves within and across functions to support the staffing strategy.

## Strategic Value of Jobs and Employee Uniqueness

Another strategic consideration affecting how companies invest its training and development resources is based on different types of employees. One distinction that some companies make is in training and development activities for managers and individual contributors. Managers may receive development opportunities such as job experiences and international assignments that individual contributors do not because they are being evaluated and prepared for leadership positions in the company. Another way different types of employees can be identified is based on their strategic value and uniqueness to the company.[40] **Uniqueness** refers to the extent to which employees are rare and specialized and not highly available in the labor market. **Strategic value** refers to employee potential to improve company effectiveness and efficiency. This results in four types of employees: knowledge-based workers (high value and uniqueness), job-based employees (high value and low uniqueness), contract employees (low value and low uniqueness), and alliance/ partnerships (high uniqueness and low value).

Consider a pharmaceutical company which includes many different employee groups including scientists (knowledge-based workers), lab technicians (job-based workers), secretarial and administrative staff (contract employees), and legal advisers (alliance/ partnerships). Because knowledge-based employees posses valuable and unique skills, the company is expected to invest heavily in training and developing them, especially in developing skills specific to the company's needs. Job-based employees are likely to receive less training than knowledge-based employees because although they create value for the firm, they are not unique. If they receive training, it would tend to focus on skills that they need to perform their jobs. Their development opportunities will be limited unless they have been identified as outstanding performers. The training for contractual workers likely would be limited to ensuring that they comply with company policies and legal or industry-based licensure and certification requirements. Because they are not full-time employees of the company but provide valued services, training for alliance/partnership employees tends to focus on encouraging them to share their knowledge and using team training and experiential exercises designed to develop their trust and relationships with job-based and knowledge-based employees.

### Human Resource Planning

**Human resource planning** includes the identification, analysis, forecasting, and planning of changes needed in the human resource area to help the company meet changing business conditions.[41] Human resource planning allows the company to anticipate the movement of human resources in the company because of turnover, transfers, retirements, or promotions. Human resource plans can help identify where employees with certain types of skills are needed in the company. Training can be used to prepare employees for increased responsibilities in their current job, promotions, lateral moves, transfers, and downward moves or demotions that are predicted by the human resource plan.

## Extent of Unionization

Unions' interest in training has resulted in joint union-management programs designed to help employees prepare for new jobs. When companies begin retraining and productivity-improvement efforts without involving unions, the efforts are likely to fail. The unions may see the programs as just another attempt to make employees work harder without sharing the productivity gains. Joint union-management programs (detailed in Chapter Ten) ensure that all parties (unions, management, employees) understand the development goals and are committed to making the changes necessary for the company to make profits and for employees to both keep their jobs and share in any increased profits.

## Staff Involvement in Training and Development

How often and how well a company's training program is used are affected by the degree to which managers, employees, and specialized development staff are involved in the process. If managers are not involved in the training process (e.g., determining training needs, being used as trainers), training may be unrelated to business needs. Managers also may not be committed to ensuring that training is effective (e.g., giving trainees feedback on the job). As a result, training's potential impact on helping the company reach its goals may be limited because managers may feel that training is a "necessary evil" forced on them by the training department rather than a means of helping them to accomplish business goals.

If line managers are aware of what development activity can achieve, such as reducing the time it takes to fill open positions, they will be more willing to become involved in it. They will also become more involved in the training process if they are rewarded for participating. Constellation Energy, located in Baltimore, Maryland, links employee learning to individual and organizational performance.[42] Each year, the company is involved in a business planning process from the summertime until December, involving monitoring, reviewing, and making changes to its a comprehensive five-year plan detailing organizational and business goals and objectives. The human resources plan, which includes learning, ensures that employee development strategies are aligned with business strategies. Individual development plans and goals jointly established between employees and their managers are established based on the company's business goals and objectives and human resource needs. Managers are held accountable for developing employees. One of the competencies they are evaluated on is human capital management, which includes employee engagement, talent management, and diversity. Part of each manager's bonus is based on the evaluation he or she receives on this competency.

Today, companies expect employees to initiate the training process.[43] Companies with a greater acceptance of a continuous learning philosophy require more development planning. Companies will support training and development activities (such as tuition reimbursement and the offering of courses, seminars, and workshops) but will give employees the responsibility for planning their own development. Training and development planning involve identifying needs, choosing the expected outcome (e.g., behavior change, greater knowledge), identifying the actions that should be taken, deciding how progress toward goal attainment will be measured, and creating a timetable for improvement. To identify strengths and weaknesses and training needs, employees need to analyze what they want to do, what they can do, how others perceive them, and what others expect of them. A need can result from gaps between current capabilities and interests and the type of work or position the employee wants in the future. The needs assessment process is discussed in greater detail in Chapter Three, "Needs Assessment."

# TRAINING NEEDS IN DIFFERENT STRATEGIES

Table 2.7 describes four business strategies—concentration, internal growth, external growth, and disinvestment—and highlights the implications of each for training practices.[44] Each strategy differs based on the goal of the business. A **concentration strategy** focuses on increasing market share, reducing costs, or creating and maintaining a market niche for products and services. For many years, Southwest Airlines has had a concentration strategy

**TABLE 2.7** **Implications of Business Strategy for Training**

| Strategy | Emphasis | How Achieved | Key Issues | Training Implications |
|---|---|---|---|---|
| Concentration | • Increased market share<br>• Reduced operating costs<br>• Market niche created or maintained | • Improve product quality<br>• Improve productivity or innovate technical processes<br>• Customize products or services | • Skill currency<br>• Development of existing workforce | • Team building<br>• Cross training<br>• Specialized programs<br>• Interpersonal skill training<br>• On-the-job training |
| Internal Growth | • Market development<br>• Product development<br>• Innovation<br>• Joint ventures<br>• Mergers<br>• Globalization | • Market existing products/add distribution channels<br>• Expand global market<br>• Modify existing products<br>• Create new or different products<br>• Expand through joint ownership<br>• Identify and develop managers | • Creation of new jobs and tasks<br>• Innovation<br>• Talent Management | • High-quality communication of product value<br>• Cultural training<br>• Development of organizational culture that values creative thinking and analysis<br>• Technical competence in jobs<br>• Manager training in feedback and communication<br>• Conflict negotiation skills |
| External Growth (Acquisition) | • Horizontal integration<br>• Vertical integration<br>• Concentric diversification | • Acquire firms operating at same stage in product market chain (new market access)<br>• Acquire business that can supply or buy products<br>• Acquire firms that have nothing in common with acquiring firm | • Integration<br>• Redundancy<br>• Restructuring | • Determination of capabilities of employees in acquired firms<br>• Integration of training systems<br>• Methods and procedures of combined firms<br>• Team building<br>• Development of shared culture |
| Disinvestment | • Retrenchment<br>• Turnaround<br>• Divestiture<br>• Liquidation | • Reduce costs<br>• Reduce assets<br>• Generate revenue<br>• Redefine goals<br>• Sell off all assets | • Efficiency | • Motivation, goal setting, time management, stress management, cross training<br>• Leadership training<br>• Interpersonal communications<br>• Outplacement assistance<br>• Job-search skills training |

(although it recently purchased Airteam). It focuses on providing short-haul, low-fare, high-frequency air transportation. It utilizes one type of aircraft (the Boeing 737), has no reserved seating, and serves no meals. This concentration strategy has enabled Southwest to keep costs low and revenues high. An **internal growth strategy** focuses on new market and product development, innovation, and joint ventures. For example, the merger between Continental and United Airlines created the world's largest airline. An **external growth strategy** emphasizes acquiring vendors and suppliers or buying businesses that allow the company to expand into new markets. For example, General Electric, a manufacturer of lighting products and jet engines, acquired the National Broadcasting Corporation (NBC), a television and communications company. A **disinvestment strategy** emphasizes liquidation and divestiture of businesses. For example, Citigroup, which took over the financially troubled music company EMI, sold it to Universal and Sony.

Preliminary research suggests a link between business strategy and amount and type of training.[45] Table 2.7 shows that training issues vary greatly from one strategy to another. Divesting companies need to train employees in job-search skills and to focus on cross-training remaining employees who may find themselves in jobs with expanding responsibilities. Companies focusing on a market niche (a concentration strategy) need to emphasize skill currency and development of their existing workforce. New companies formed from a merger or acquisition need to ensure that employees have the skills needed to help the company reach its new strategic goals. Also, for mergers and acquisitions to be successful, employees need to learn about the new, merged organization and its culture.[46] The organization must provide training in systems, such as instruction on how the phone, e-mail, and company intranet work. Managers need to be educated on how to make the new merger successful (e.g., dealing with resistance to change). Consider the role of the learning function at Ciena during an acquisition.[47] Ciena specializes in optical transport, optical switching, and Ethernet technologies, which helps it deliver equipment, software, and services that improve networks for clients around the world. To compete with larger companies, Ciena needs to be more agile, more innovative, and faster. Ciena emphasizes establishing trust with its customers through developing strong relationships and collaborating with them. Trust is necessary for its customers to feel that the equipment and services they purchase from Ciena provide an added value for their business. When Ciena acquired Nortel's Metro Ethernet Networks business, the company size doubled and it gained access to new global markets. To integrate Nortel's employees successfully into Ciena, Ciena's learning function provided the training that employees needed to understand the products, systems, and process requirements. This was important to ensure that the business strategy was consistent across the company. Also, Ciena took steps to ensure that it recognized the strengths and weaknesses of the cultures of both companies and worked to create a new culture. For example, Ciena's Emerging Leaders Program was used to integrate high-potential managers from both companies and have them work on creating a new list of values that would guide the new, integrated company.

Compaines with an internal growth and strategy face the challenge of identifying and developing talent, especially managers.

Eric Wiseman, the CEO of VF Corporation, a global clothing business including The North Face, Nautica, Lee, and Wrangler, understands that he needs strong finances, winning brands, and talent to drive business growth.[48] The focus is on developing the top management group of 1,500 people. The company conducts senior talent assessment review two times each year. These reviews include meeting with the company's operating committee, the vice president for human resources, business leaders, and the head of human resources for each business unit. Top managers are each individually reviewed, discussing their strengths and weaknesses, how they can improve, and their possibilities for career advancement. This is critical for the company to prepare and have ready the necessary management talent necessary to meet two key growth drivers for the company: global expansion and aggressive acquisitions of other businesses. Also, the vice president for human resources plays a key role in developing the time frame for expansion and preparing managers for international positions. In addition, the vice president for human resources plays an important role in helping to understand the available talent in companies targeted for acquisition, as well as taking steps to retain talented employees in the acquired company needed to support the brand. The vice president for human resources also is responsible for gathering information about changes in business expectations and growth projects from the vice presidents for human resources at the business unit level and communicating that information to the CEO.

Despite the dismal financial picture for automobile companies, instead of cutting worker hours or downsizing, Toyota Motor Corporation is known for retaining employees at its plants and encouraging them to participate in training programs designed to improve their job skills and find more efficient and effective methods of assembling vehicles.[49] Based on their union contracts, employees at GM, Ford, and Chrysler are paid for not working when their assembly lines are shut down. If a plant is shut down temporarily, employees receive most of their pay but don't have to show up for work. At its Princeton, New Jersey plant, Toyota used downtime to improve employees' quality control and productivity skills, keeping good on its pledge never to lay off any of its full-time non-union employees. The training resulted in continuous improvements (also known as *kaizen*). One example is a Teflon ring that was designed by an assembly line employee that helps prevent paint damage when an electrical switch is installed on the edge of a vehicle's door.

A disinvestment strategy resulted in Edwards Life Sciences Corporation being spun off from another company.[50] The new company's management team developed a new strategic plan that described goals for sales growth, new product development, customer loyalty, and employee commitment and satisfaction. The company realized that it had to prepare leaders who could help the company meet its strategic goals. A review of leadership talent showed that leadership development was needed, and a leadership program was created in response. The program included twenty participants from different functions and company locations. Part of the weeklong program is devoted to a simulation in which teams of managers run their own business and take responsibility for marketing, manufacturing, and financials. The sessions also include classes taught by company executives, who speak about important topics such as the company's business strategy.

# MODELS OF ORGANIZING THE TRAINING DEPARTMENT

The business-embedded model and the corporate university model (or a blended model that includes both) are the models that companies are moving to in order to ensure that training is used to help the company achieve its business objectives. These models are also being adopted as companies begin to value human capital and view training as part of a learning system designed to create and share knowledge. This review of these structures should help you to understand that the organization of the training department has important consequences for how the training department (and trainers employed in the department) contributes (or fails to contribute) to the business strategy. Keep in mind that—particularly with large, decentralized companies—there may be multiple separate training functions, each organized using a different model.

One of the important decisions that companies have to consider in choosing how to organize the training department (or learning function) is the extent to which training and learning is centralized. Typically, companies do not choose to centralize or decentralize training and learning completely. Rather, they choose a model for organizing the training department that best fits the needs of the business. Many companies, including Boeing, Cingular Wireless, and Harley-Davidson, have centralized their training departments.[51] **Centralized training** means that training and development programs, resources, and professionals are primarily housed in one location and that decisions about training investment, programs, and delivery methods are made from that department. Training at Boeing used to be decentralized because of the company's many geographic locations. Boeing and other companies have found several advantages to centralized training, including the ownership of training to one organization and the elimination of course and program variation and duplication in the training system. Wyeth, a global leader in pharmaceuticals and consumer and animal health care products, uses a centralized training function to ensure that selling skills are adopted across the company. Instead of the four different selling models that were being used, Wyeth businesses in more than 140 countries are now using a consistent selling model.

Also, a centralized training function helps drive stronger alignment with business strategy, allows development of a common set of metrics or scorecards to measure and report rates of quality and delivery, helps to streamline processes, and gives the company a cost advantage in purchasing training from vendors and consultants because of the number of trainees who will be involved. Finally, a centralized training function helps companies better integrate programs for developing leaders and managing talent with training and learning during times of change. At both Cingular Wireless and Harley-Davidson, a centralized training function allows selection of a common technology for delivery of training programs.[52] This policy helps reduce the chances that functional groups will adopt different technologies, for which some training programs and their features, such as video, will work and others will not. The key to the success of a centralized approach is that top managers must believe they are in control of the training function and that the training function is aligned with the business strategy. That is, the business objectives have to be communicated and understood, and training and development have to help drive that strategy. At the same time, centralized training functions must be in touch with the unique needs of the functions and divisions they serve. At ETS, employee education is the responsibility of the learning and development (L&D) unit of strategic workforce solutions.[53] The 50 L&D employees are organized around "people processes," including learning and knowledge management. The director and executive director work with the chief learning officer to ensure that training and development and learning strategies are related to ETS's business strategy.

## The Corporate University Model (Corporate Training Universities)

To gain the advantages of centralized training, many companies use the corporate university model, as shown in Figure 2.5. The **corporate university model** differs from other models in that the client group includes not only employees and managers, but also stakeholders

**FIGURE 2.5**
**The Corporate University Model**

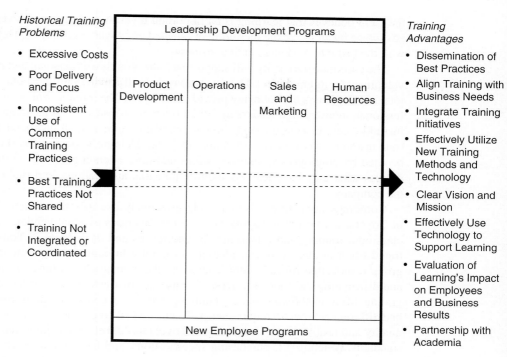

*Historical Training Problems*

- Excessive Costs
- Poor Delivery and Focus
- Inconsistent Use of Common Training Practices
- Best Training Practices Not Shared
- Training Not Integrated or Coordinated

Leadership Development Programs

| Product Development | Operations | Sales and Marketing | Human Resources |

New Employee Programs

*Training Advantages*

- Dissemination of Best Practices
- Align Training with Business Needs
- Integrate Training Initiatives
- Effectively Utilize New Training Methods and Technology
- Clear Vision and Mission
- Effectively Use Technology to Support Learning
- Evaluation of Learning's Impact on Employees and Business Results
- Partnership with Academia

outside the company, including community colleges, universities, high schools, and grade schools. Corporate universities can provide significant advantages for a company's learning efforts by helping to overcome many of the historical problems that have plagued training departments (see the left side of Figure 2.5). A corporate university can help make learning more strategic by providing a clear mission and vision for learning, and ensuring that it is aligned with business needs. It can also help companies who have a strong business culture and values ensure that they are emphasized in the learning curriculum. Also, the corporate university can control costs and maximize the benefits of learning. This occurs through providing consistent training activities, disseminating best learning practices throughout the company, effectively using technology to support learning, evaluating learning's impact on employees and business results, and establishing partnerships with academia and other company stakeholders (community) to develop custom training and degree programs.[54] Consider the benefits that several different companies have realized from their corporate universities.

Deloitte LLP is investing $300 million in building a corporate university in Westlake, Texas.[55] The corporate university will include state-of-the-art learning technology, 800 sleeping rooms, and even a ballroom. Such an investment runs counter to the cost savings and efficiencies resulting from instructional solutions such as mobile learning, virtual reality, and e-learning that require only that learners have access to a personal computer, iPhone, or iPad, eliminating the need to travel to a physical training site. Deloitte conducted extensive research before investing in a physical campus for its corporate university. The results suggested that its partners were supportive and most Generation Y (Gen-Y) employees wanted a physical location where they could meet and learn face to face. Also, the CEO believes that learning is an important investment that can provide a competitive advantage by aiding in the recruiting of talented employees and helping Deloitte LLP cope with the fast rate of change in the business.

The corporate university will support Deloitte's culture of personal and professional development for its employees. Deloitte University will provide 1 million hours of the 3 million total training hours the company provides each year. The training will cover technical, professional, industry, and leadership skills. Interactive instructional techniques will be used, including case discussions and simulations that require a small instructor-to-student ratio (one instructor to every five students). D Street, Deloitte's social networking system, will be used by employees to interact before and after attending courses at the university to discuss what they have learned, explore potential applications, and find expertise across the company.

Corporate universities also can help effectively use new technology. The University of Toyota, a division of Toyota Motor Sales, oversees external vendors' development of classroom training and e-learning for employees and dealerships.[56] Trainees were frustrated because there was considerable variability in course navigation and quality. The group responsible for uploading courses to the company's learning management system and distributing the courses to learners was also frustrated because it had difficulties integrating different software and explaining to users why courses coming from the university had different bandwidth requirements. To ensure that courses meet minimum standards for quality and usability, the University of Toyota has developed a single set of development standards, benchmarks, purchasing specifications, and best practices. The information is housed on e-Source, the university's website. Vendors are required to visit e-Source to bid on any e-learning projects for the University of Toyota. Courses that do not meet the specifications are revised at the vendor's expense. E-mail bulletins are sent to course owners and developers to notify them of any content additions or changes to the website.

Both large and small companies have started their own universities to train new employees and to retain and update the skills and knowledge of current employees. Caterpillar University comprises six colleges: leadership, marketing and distribution, technology, business and business processes, Six Sigma, and product support.[57] The deans of the colleges report to the president of the university. Caterpillar's CEO, vice presidents, and two group presidents provide policy guidance, approve budgets, and identify priorities for the university. One priority was to support new business growth goals through the development of leaders who are willing to collaborate with others, have a global mindset, and understand the financial aspects of the business. The College of Marketing and Distribution focuses on providing a comprehensive curriculum for sales professionals and sales marketing managers. It includes product knowledge, sales skills, and management skills. All learning goals are tied to business goals. The College of Product Support focuses on training dealer employees to meet certification standards. Caterpillar University staff members help the business units deal with their learning needs. Lead learning managers in each unit have a reporting relationship both to the university and to the unit's human resource manager. The learning managers work with the business unit managers to set up learning plans.

Hamburger University, the corporate university for McDonald's, is charged with continuing to teach the core values that founder Ray Kroc believed were the key to success: quality, service, cleanliness, and value.[58] Hamburger University is one of the oldest and most effective corporate universities. Founded in 1961, it is estimated that approximately 5,000

McDonalds employees attend the U.S.-based Hamburger University each year, and more than 90,000 managers and owner-operators have graduated from it. Hamburger University is a global center for operations training and leadership development for McDonalds. It also gives employees the opportunity to get a college degree. McDonalds has a university in Oakbrook, Illinois, six global universities, and twenty-two regional training centers. To promote learning, the facilities and programs offered at Hamburger University are reviewed and revised. As a result, Hamburger University has transitioned away from teaching courses with a lecture format and is moving toward fewer large group sessions and more interactive learning in classes of twenty-five to thirty-five students, which are then further divided into small groups for discussion and exercises. McDonalds changed its learning format to accommodate how most of its students (who would be considered Gen-Y) learn. The typical education level of frontline service workers has influenced curriculum design through the development of more easily understandable coursework. E-learning is used to deliver the basics of restaurant operations or management training, and classroom instruction and simulations are used to help the learner apply the basics on the job. Recently, new audiovisual equipment was installed, a cybercafe was added, and large auditorium classroom spaces were converted into smaller spaces that facilitate collaboration and interaction. Virtual classrooms were also built to connect instructors with McDonalds employees around the world. Learners are provided with headphones that connect them to translators who provide instruction in the learner's native language during class. McDonalds is planning to add connectivity to classrooms that will allow learning using mobile devices and social networking.

Besides classroom instruction, Hamburger University includes a simulated kitchen and drive-through window. Despite having learners at the university who are already familiar with behind-the-counter operations, everyone takes part in the simulation, making real food and filling orders just as they would at a real McDonalds restaurant. Learners have performance goals to meet, and they receive feedback from fellow learners and trainers. Managers can support and track earner development by accessing online course completion reports of their scores on tests of their knowledge and behavior. All of McDonalds restaurant management and middle manager courses are accredited, meaning that participants can receive college credit. The credits for these courses represent half of the credits required to earn an associate's degree at a two-year college and a large number of the credits needed to receive a bachelor's degree in business administration or management at a four-year college or university. The curriculum for department managers now allows them to test content they already know, and training time has been reduced from one-and-a-half years to two years to four to six months.

Are corporate universities effective? Corporate University Xchange surveyed corporate universities at 170 different companies.[59] The top five organizational goals of corporate universities were to improve customer service and retention, improve productivity, reduce costs, retain talented employees, and increase revenue. The survey found that measuring business impact was a high priority; 70 percent of the companies measured business impact through product and service quality and customer service, and more than 50 percent measured reductions in operating costs and increased revenues.

For example, the Ritz-Carlton Hotels company manages fifty-eight luxury hotels worldwide.[60] The Ritz-Carlton hotels and resorts are renowned for indulgent luxury. Beautiful surroundings and legendary award-winning service are provided to every guest. The

Ritz-Carlton Leadership Center is designed to support the growth and expansion of the company's products and services. The Leadership Center includes the School of Performance Excellence, which houses all the training and development for hourly employees; the School of Leadership and Business Excellence, which trains leaders; and the School of Service Excellence, which helps ensure high customer service. Programs at the School of Service Excellence are offered to other companies, which has resulted in yearly revenues for Ritz-Carlton of more than $1 million. These revenues help offset the costs of training and development for employees. For example, a new customized training certification system for housekeeping staff uses CD-ROM and web-based training. The training is linked to the results of room inspections that highlight defects for the day, week, and year. The housekeeper can then identify the correct processes that are needed to remedy the defects. This just-in-time training has helped increase customer satisfaction scores at Ritz-Carlton. One hotel increased its satisfaction score with cleanliness from 82 percent to 92 percent in six months.

Steelcase's business is making workspace more effective to facilitate innovation, productivity, efficiency, and creativity. To highlight Steelcase's capabilities for effective workspace design and to facilitate learning, creativity, and collaboration, the Steelcase University Learning Center was developed.[61] The university created a new curriculum called "Think." Many organizations visit annually to benchmark the university, the social network capabilities, and the learning tools. Also, the Steelcase University Learning Center has centralized all the company's training and development efforts—reducing redundancies, facilitating consistency, and ensuring knowledge sharing. The learning center includes 70 percent formal and 30 percent informal learning space, putting into practice research results regarding how learning and social networking occur. The learning center provides a flexible, informal space that allows employees to meet privately, as well as interacting in groups, facilitating cooperation and collaboration. Nine classrooms and ten breakout areas include flexible furniture and the newest technology. Each room and area can be changed to fit the specific needs of the users. The learning center is also the gathering place for cross-functional teams. Activities held in the learning center include town hall meetings, lunch-and-learn sessions, and virtual teaching sessions. The learning center is also known as the place for employee leadership development. The company's global leadership teams can use the center to meet both physically and virtually. The investment in Steelcase University has paid off as a result of the Think curriculum and other courses. Designers created a new classroom chain called Node, which allowed flexibility in classroom arrangement. Sales representatives surpassed their first-year sales goals by 30 percent.

## Creating a Corporate University

Creating a corporate university from scratch involves several steps.[62] First senior managers and business managers form a governing body with the responsibility of developing a vision for the university. (This group answers questions such as "What are the university's policies, systems, and procedures?" and "What are the key functional areas for which training courses will be developed?") Second, this vision is fleshed out, and the vision statement is linked to the business strategy. For example, Ingersoll Rand has a business goal of obtaining 38 percent of its revenue from new product innovation.[63] As a result, most of the programs and courses offered through Ingersoll Rand University discuss how to get close to the customer, innovation, and strategic marketing. The programs are designed for teams working on real business issues. Subject matter experts and managers teach these programs, which are scheduled based on key product launch dates. Third, the company decides how to fund the university. The university can be funded by charging fees to business units and/or by monies allocated directly from the corporate budget. Fourth, the company determines the degree to which all training will be centralized. Many universities centralize the development of a learning philosophy, core curriculum design, and policies and procedures related to registration, administration, measurement, marketing, and distance learning. Local and regional on-site delivery and specialized business-unit curriculum are developed by business units. Fifth, it is important to identify the needs of university "customers," including employees, managers, suppliers, and external customers. Sixth, products and services are developed. The Bank of Montreal uses a service team that includes a client-relationship manager, a subject-matter expert, and a learning manager. The client-relationship manager works with the business units to identify their needs. The subject-matter expert identifies the skill requirements for meeting those needs. The learning manager recommends the best mix of learning, including classroom training and training based on, say, the web or CD-ROM. Seventh, the company chooses learning partners, including suppliers, consultants, colleges, and companies specializing in education. Eighth, the company develops a strategy for using technology to train more employees and do so more frequently and more cost-effectively than instructor-led training. Ninth, learning that occurs as a result of a corporate university is linked to performance improvement. This involves identifying how performance improvement will be measured (tests, sales data, etc.). For example, Sprint's corporate university, the University of Excellence, developed the Standard Training Equivalent (STE) unit, an evaluation tool for its customers who are internal business units.[64] The STE unit is equal to one hour of the traditional instructor-led classroom time that would be required to deliver a course to a group of employees at a central location. An STE unit consisting of a one-hour course over the company intranet is worth much more than the same amount of time spent in the classroom. The STE program helps the University of Excellence demonstrate its value to Sprint's business units, who fund the university. Finally, the value of the corporate university is communicated to potential "customers." Questions about the types of programs offered, how learning will occur, and how employees will enroll are addressed.

## Business-Embedded Model

Many companies are organizing their training function so that they can better control their training costs and ensure that training is aligned with the business strategy, but at the same time respond quickly to client needs and provide high-quality services.[65] The **business-embedded (BE) model** is characterized by five competencies: strategic direction, product design, structural versatility, product delivery, and accountability for results. Strategic direction includes a clearly described goal and direction to the department, as well as a customer focus that includes customizing training to meet customer needs and continuously improving programs. A BE training function not only views trainees as customers, but also views managers as customers who make decisions to send employees to training, and senior-level managers as customers who allocate money for training. Table 2.8 shows the features of a training function organized by the BE model with a traditional training department. BE function is customer-focused. It takes more responsibility for learning and evaluating training effectiveness, provides customized training solutions based

**TABLE 2.8**
**Features of a Training Function Organized by the BE Model**

Source: S. S. McIntosh, "Envisioning Virtual Training Organization," *Training and Development* (May 1995): 47.

**Strategic Direction**
Broadly disseminates a clearly articulated mission
Recognizes that its customer base is segmented
Provides customized solutions to its clients' needs
Understands product life cycles
Organizes its offerings by competencies
Competes for internal customers

**Product Design**
Uses benchmarking and other innovative design
Implements strategies to develop products quickly
Involves suppliers strategically

**Structural Versatility**
Employs professionals who serve as product and classroom instructors, managers, and internal consultants
Uses resources from many areas
Involves line managers in determining the direction of the department's offerings and content

**Product Delivery**
Offers a menu of learning options
Delivers training at the work site

**Accountability for Results**
Believes that individual employees must take responsibility for their personal growth
Provides follow-up on the job to ensure that learning takes place
Considers the manager the key player in supporting learning
Evaluates the strategic effects of training and it's bottom-line results
Guarantees that training will improve performance

on customer needs, and determines when and how to deliver training based on customer needs. To ensure that EMC's business strategy is supported by training, the company uses learning councils and development frameworks.[66] Every business unit, including the sales, technical, and engineering units, has education and development performance consultants who serve on the unit's learning council. The consultants report to EMC's central training organization, thus ensuring that the needs of the business units are discussed when training delivery or design is discussed. EMC uses a consistent training design framework, which makes it easier for managers and employees in all business units to understand how training leads to skill development and career advancement.

The most noticeable feature of a BE function is its structure.[67] In BE training functions, all persons who are involved in the training process communicate and share resources. Trainers—who are responsible for developing training materials, delivering instruction, and supporting trainees—work together to ensure that learning occurs. For example, access to project managers and subject-matter experts can be provided by developers to instructors who usually do not have contact with these groups. The number of trainers in BE training functions varies according to the demand for products and services. The trainers not only have specialized competencies (e.g., instructional design) but can also serve as internal consultants and provide a wide range of services (e.g., needs assessment, content improvement, customization of programs, and results measurement).

### *Current Practice: The BE Model with Centralized Training*

Because many companies are recognizing training's critical role in contributing to the business strategy, there is an increasing trend for the training function, especially in companies that have separate business units, to be organized by a blend of the BE model with centralized training that often includes a corporate university. This approach allows the company to gain the benefits of centralized training but at the same time ensure that training can provide programs, content, and delivery methods that meet the needs of specific businesses.

At Carter & Burgess, a professional services company, every learning program is aligned with the business strategy.[68] Because the company has federal contracts, employees must complete yearly compliance training and professional education courses to maintain their licenses. Other learning programs are determined based on an annual needs analysis, exit interviews, and information from focus groups and stakeholders. The training and development team lets offices determine their training needs based on their business needs. Office managers review the training programs and decide which ones they want to invest in. The training and development team monitors the usage of training and consults with the office on strategy and delivery. Allowing customization based on office needs, while at the same time centralizing strategy and training delivery, has helped to decrease costs. A company-wide commitment to a single external vendor of training practices has resulted in a savings of more than 34 percent in the first year.

At General Mills, innovation is a core company value.[69] As a result, learning and development is aligned with the business strategy and its internal customers. Each of the company's functional teams develops short- and long-term strategies. For example, the marketing function holds an annual planning process (Plan to Win) to ensure that learning and development activities support the business strategy and help to build the brand. This translates into specific learning programs, such as Brand Champions, which provides brand marketing knowledge to junior marketers. Company leaders also recognize and support the relationship between business success and employee growth and development. Senior leaders sponsor learning activities, ensure that they are aligned with the business, and teach programs. Annual employee surveys include items asking employees about learning and development (such as "I believe I have opportunity for personal growth and development"). Trends in responses to these items are evaluated and considered in designing new learning initiatives, as well as assessing the capabilities and health of the business.

## Learning, Training, and Development from a Change Model Perspective

As was discussed in Chapter One, change involves the adoption of a new behavior or idea by a company. There are many reasons why companies are forced to change, including the introduction of new technology, the need to better take advantage of employee skills and capitalize on a diverse workforce, or the desire to enter global markets. For training and development programs and learning initiatives to contribute to the business strategy, they must be successfully implemented, accepted, and used by customers (including managers, executives, and employees).

Four conditions are necessary for change to occur: (1) Employees must understand the reasons for change and agree with those reasons; (2) employees must have the skills needed to implement the change; (3) employees must see that managers and other employees in powerful positions support the change; and (4) organizational structures, such as compensation and performance management systems, must support the change.[70] For managers and employees, change is not easy. Even when employees know that a practice or program could be better, they have learned to adapt to its inadequacies. Therefore, resistance to new training and development practices is likely. Prior to implementing a new training or development practice, trainers should consider how they can increase the likelihood of its acceptance.

Figure 2.6 provides a model of change. The process of change is based on the interaction among four components of the organization: task, employees, formal organizational arrangements (structures, processes, and systems), and informal organization (communication patterns, values, and norms).[71] As shown in the figure, different types of change-related problems occur depending on the organizational component that is influenced by the change. For example, introducing new technology for training into a company (such as multimedia training using the Internet) might cause changes in the organization's power structure. With the new technology, managers may have less control over access to training programs than they had with traditional methods of training. The result is tension related to the power imbalance created by the new system. If these issues are not dealt with, managers will not accept the new technology or provide support for transfer of training.

The four change-related problems that need to be addressed before implementation of any new training practice are resistance to change, loss of control, power imbalance, and

**FIGURE 2.6**
**A Change Model**

Sources: David A. Nadler and Michael L. Tushman, "A Congruence Model for Diagnosing Organizational Behavior." In *Organizational Psychology: A Book of Readings,* ed. D. Rabin and J. McIntyre (Englewood Cliffs, NJ: Prentice Hall, 1979), as reprinted in David A. Nadler, "Concepts for the Management of Organizational Change," in *Readings in the Management of Innovation,* 2d ed., ed. M. L. Tushman and N. Moore (Cambridge, MA: Ballinger Publishing Co., 1988): 722.

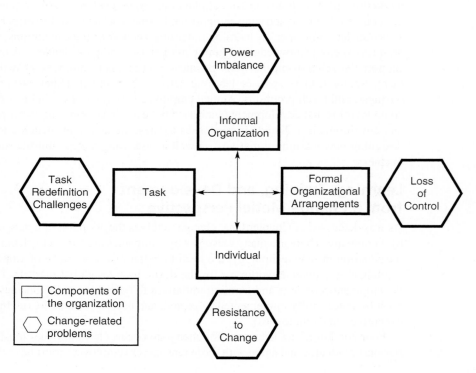

task redefinition. **Resistance to change** refers to managers' and employees' unwillingness to change. Managers and employees may be anxious about change, feel that they will be unable to cope, value the current training practice, or do not understand the value of the new practice. **Control** relates change to managers' and employees' ability to obtain and distribute valuable resources such as data, information, or money. Changes can cause managers and employees to have less control over resources. Change can also give managers and employees control over processes that they have not previously been involved in (e.g., choosing which training programs to attend). **Power** refers to the ability to influence others. Managers may lose the ability to influence employees as employees gain access to databases and other information, thus getting more autonomy to deliver products and services. Employees may be held accountable for learning in self-directed training. Web-based training methods, such as **task redefinition,** create changes in managers' and employees' roles and job responsibilities. Employees may be asked not only to participate in training, but also to consider how to improve its quality. Managers may be asked to become facilitators and coaches.

Senior managers often make three important mistakes in trying to implement change, which can result in failure to produce the desired results.[72] These include telling or issuing communications for employees to "buy in" to the changes, believing that they know enough about the company to understand the impact of change on individuals and how the change should be managed to achieve the desired results, and ignoring or not giving enough consideration to barriers that may slow down or cause change initiatives to fail. Training departments are often in the best position to help senior company leaders implement change, especially if they play a strategic role in the company, because they interact and have the opportunity to hear from business leaders and employees about problems, challenges, and needs they are facing. For example, The Economical Insurance Group (TEIG) restructured its Learning and Development unit into Learning and Education and Organizational Development, consisting of four areas: Leadership, Organizational Culture, Learning Culture, and Learning Transformation.[73] Organizational Development helps in shaping and creating organizational change through assessing the current state of the organization against its future needs, and reduces the gaps between the two through action planning and development. The goal of Learning and Organization Development is to use assessment data, development tools, change interventions, and learning opportunities to promote a culture of excellence and help achieve TEIG's mission, vision, and goals.

Table 2.9 shows seven key steps that training professionals can take to help senior managers effectively manage a change initiative.

# MARKETING TRAINING AND CREATING A BRAND

Despite the increased recognition of the importance of training and learning to achieving business goals, many managers and employees may not recognize the value of training. Internal marketing involves making employees and managers excited about training and learning. Internal marketing is especially important for trainers who act as internal consultants to business units. For internal consultants to survive, they must generate fees for their services. Some, if not all, of their operating expenses come from fees paid for their services. Marketing is also important for the successful adoption of new training programs

**TABLE 2.9**

**Steps in a Change Process**

Sources: Based on C. McAllaster, "Leading Change by Effectively Utilizing Leverage Points Within an Organization," *Organizational Dynamics* 33 (2004): 318; L. Freifeld, "Changes with Penguins," *training* (June 2008): 24–28, N. Miller, "Brave New World," *T+D* (June 2010): 54–58.

1. **Clarify the request for change.** Is the stated reason for change an important issue? How does the change fit into the company's business strategy? Why are you making the change? How many people does this affect, and how does it affect them? What are the outcomes of the change?

2. **Make the vision clear.** Identify the reason for the change, what will be achieved, and how the change will be achieved.

3. **Design the solution.** What is the best mix of performance measures and feedback, support tools, learning plans, formal training, and job processes? Review the potential risks and benefits of different approaches.

4. **Communicate and market for buy-in.** Connect with other groups that will be involved, including communications, finance, and operations, to consider the impact of the change and develop an internal marketing plan. Employees need to know what is occurring. Use briefings, newsletters, discussion boards, websites, and informational meetings. Senior managers need to be visible and involved in communicating about the change.

5. **Choose and announce the action as soon as possible.** Employees affected by the change must hear about it as soon as possible. Employees need to know why and how the final action was selected, how the process has progressed, and what is going to happen in the next days and months. Communicating logic and reasoning can help overcome resistance to change. Provide short previews to employees so they know what changes are coming.

6. **Execute and create short-term wins.** Success requires management attention and the desire to do it right. Managers and change leaders must model new behavior and become enthusiastic supporters for the process. Leaders should involve employees and provide them with the necessary training and resources. If a pilot test or beta program is used, employees should be kept informed on its progress and asked for their opinions. Learning should occur from any mistakes.

7. **Follow up, reevaluate, and modify.** Be flexible and make changes if they are needed. Share information about mistakes or issues, and work with the employees affected to fix them.

by helping to overcome resistance to change, especially misconceptions about the value of training. Here are some successful internal marketing tactics:[74]

- Involve the target audience in developing the training or learning effort.
- Demonstrate how a training and development program can be used to solve specific business needs.
- Showcase an example of how training has been used within the company to solve specific business needs.
- Identify a "champion" (e.g., a top-level manager) who actively supports training.
- Listen and act on feedback received from clients, managers, and employees.
- Advertise on e-mail, on company websites, and in employee break areas.
- Designate someone in the training function as an account representative who will interact between the training designer or team and the business unit, which is the customer.

- Determine what financial numbers—such as return on assets, cash flow from operations, or net profit or loss—top-level executives are concerned with and show how training and development will help improve those numbers.
- Speak in terms that employees and managers understand. Don't use jargon.

It is also important to develop and communicate the training brand. A **brand** includes the look and feeling of the training function that is used to create expectations for its customers.[75] The brand is used to acquire and retain customers. To build a training brand, follow the suggestions shown in Table 2.10. The training function also needs to develop its own strategy and communicate it to its customers.[76] The strategy should include what products and services it plans to offer, how training requests will be handled and by whom, how it will demonstrate partnerships with other departments and business units in the company, and the service level that it intends to provide to customers. Service before, during, and after training, development, or other learning initiatives needs to be considered. The training function strategy should be aligned with and contribute to the business strategy.

For example, at IKON Office Solutions, the learning and development group publishes a strategic document each year that demonstrates what it has delivered, how its efforts align with the company business strategy, and what the group plans to do to help business leaders achieve their future goals.[77] At the end of each year, the document is used to measure the learning and development group's successes, and this information is shared with senior management to make a case for continued investment in training.

The training department at Booz Allen Hamilton, a consulting firm in McLean, Virginia, develops a marketing plan every year that includes a branding strategy (how the department will be recognized, including logos and slogans); overall marketing objectives; techniques for communications with employees, managers, and all internal customers; and plans for launching all new learning programs.[78] One marketing objective is to increase awareness of the company's Center for Performance Excellence and to make it a tool

**TABLE 2.10**
**How to Build a Training Brand**

Source: Based on A. Hand, "How to enhance your training brand," *T+D* (February 2011): 76–77.

- Ask current "customers" of training, including managers who purchase or ask for training and employees who participate in training what their perceptions are of the brand. For example, what emotions describe how they feel about the training brand? What words summarize their feelings? What conclusions have they made about doing business with you? Answers to these questions provide information regarding the strength of the training brand and if it is being perceived positively or as intended.
- Define how you want to be perceived by current and future customers.
- Identify factors that influence your customer's perceptions of the training function.
- Review each of the factors to determine if it is supporting and communicating the brand to your customers in a way that you intended.
- Make changes so that each factor is supporting the brand.
- Get customers feedback at each step of this process (define the brand, identify factors, suggest changes, etc.).
- When interacting with customers, create an experience that supports and identifies the brand.

for employee recruitment and retention. The marketing effort communicates the message that training programs will help workers in their jobs and their careers. Also, Booz Allen's accomplishments, such as appearing on *training* magazine's list of top 100 training companies, are communicated to prospective hires to show them that the company takes training and development seriously.

Training functions are beginning to become profit centers by selling training courses or seats in training courses to other companies.[79] Companies sell training services for a number of reasons. Some businesses are so good at a particular aspect of their operations that other companies are asking for their expertise. Other companies aim training at their own customers or dealers. In some cases, the training department sells unused seats in training programs or e-learning courses. For example, Walt Disney Company sells training on customer service and organizational creativity at the Disney Institute in Florida. The institute gives employees from other companies the opportunity to understand how Disney developed its business strengths, including leadership development, service, customer loyalty, and team building. Dell Educational Services, a division of Dell Computer, sells basic training to product users and sells professional training to software engineers, developers, systems administrators, and dealership salespeople. Courses are delivered via traditional classroom instruction, on CDs, and online in self-paced and virtual classrooms. When Ohio Savings Bank has extra seats in its team dynamics or time management courses, the training function recovers costs by selling the seats to other companies. For example, Sherwin-Williams, the Cleveland, Ohio–based paint company, sent its information technology employees through a team-building program with bank employees. Randstad sells online training to its customers, who employ Randstad's workers in customer service call centers.[80] Although Randstad makes revenue by selling the training, its greater benefit is realized from building relationships with its clients. Within a one-year period, Randstad was able to show that $45 million in company business was influenced by providing training to clients who chose the company (or stayed with the company).

# OUTSOURCING TRAINING

**Outsourcing** refers to the use of an outside company (an external services firm) that takes complete responsibility and control of some training or development activities or that takes over all or most of a company's training, including administration, design, delivery, and development.[81] **Business process outsourcing** refers to the outsourcing of any business process, such as HRM, production, or training. Survey results suggest that slightly more than half of all companies outsource instruction.[82] Approximately 47 percent outsource some or all of the responsibility for developing customized training content and courses. Training experts predict that within 10 years, half of all trainers will work for outsourcing providers. Why would companies outsource training? Some of the reasons are cost savings; time savings that allow a company to focus on business strategy; improvements in compliance and accuracy in training mandated to comply with federal, state, or local rules (e.g., safety training); the lack of capability within the company to meet learning demands; and the desire to access best training practices. Some companies choose a comprehensive approach, outsourcing all training activities. For example, consider the outsource provider Accenture Learning Business Process Outsourcing.[83] Accenture Learning operates Avaya University for Avaya, a global leader in communication systems, applications, and services.[84] Accenture helped Telstra, Australia's leading telecommunications and information services company, develop self-paced e-learning, as well as virtual instructor-led training and podcasting to provide learning opportunities to its geographically diverse workforce. Although some companies are beginning to outsource and the trend appears to be growing, most companies outsource only smaller projects, not the complete training and development function. Two reasons that companies do not outsource their training are (1) the inability of outsourcing providers to meet company needs and (2) companies' desire to maintain control over all aspects of training and development, especially delivery and learning content. Table 2.11 shows some of the questions that should be considered when a company is deciding whether to outsource. Any decision to outsource training is complex. Training functions that do not add any value to the company are likely candidates for outsourcing (see Table 2.11, Questions 1–4 and 9). Many companies have training functions that add value to the business but still may not be capable of meeting all training needs. For example, a company that has a strong skilled training function, values training, and views it as important to the business strategy probably doesn't need to outsource its entire training function. However, that company may turn to outsourcing providers for special training needs beyond staff capabilities or for certain training content that changes rapidly. Consider the case of Texas Instruments (TI).[85] TI contracts General Physics, a training outsource provider, to conduct all its open-enrollment courses for professional development and technical training. These courses are offered often by TI in areas in which knowledge changes quickly. As a result, these courses were seen as the best candidates for outsourcing, and TI wanted to achieve cost savings by outsourcing them. TI is still in charge of its customized professional development offerings. In the outsourcing agreement, TI was careful to include contract language that allowed it to raise and lower the amount of training that it was buying as needed. Given the cyclical nature of the semiconductor business, the ability to raise and lower the amount of training, yet still keep customized programs that add significant value to the business, was an important reason that TI decided to outsource some of its training programs. Research suggests that company satisfaction with the outsourcing of training and development depends on company-supplier trust

**TABLE 2.11**

**Questions to Ask When Considering Outsourcing**

Sources: Based on G. Johnson, "To Outsource or Not to Outsource . . . That Is the Question," *Training* (August 2004): 26–29; K. Tyler, "Carve Out Training?" *HR Magazine* (February 2004): 52–57.

1. What are the capabilities of your in-house training function? Does the staff know enough that you can grow the training skills you need, or do you need to hire training skills from the outside?
2. Can your in-house training function take on additional training responsibilities?
3. Is training key to your company's strategy? Is it proprietary?
4. Does your company value its training organization?
5. Does the training content change rapidly?
6. Are outsourced trainers viewed as experts, or are they viewed with cynicism?
7. Do you understand the strengths and weaknesses of your current training programs?
8. Do you want to outsource the entire training function?
9. Are executive trying to minimize training's impact on your company? Does your company accept responsibility for building skills and talent?
10. Is a combination of internal and external training the best solution?

(e.g., managers of both the company and the outsource provider are loyal to each other and look out for each other's interests) and the specificity of the contract (e.g., whether the contract clearly outlines responsibilities).[86]

**Summary**

For training to help a company gain a competitive advantage, it must help the company reach business goals and objectives. This chapter emphasized how changes in work roles, organizational factors, and the role of training influence the amount and type of training, as well as the organization of the training functions. The process of strategic training and development was discussed. The chapter explained how different strategies (such as concentration, internal growth, external growth, and disinvestment) influence the goals of the business and create different training needs. The chapter included a discussion of different models of the training function. Because training makes a greater contribution to the achievement of business strategies and goals, the business-embedded and corporate university models will become more prevalent. Because learning, training, and development involve change, the chapter discusses the conditions necessary for managers and employees to accept and benefit from new programs. The chapter concluded with information about marketing and outsourcing the training function.

## Key Terms

business strategy, *60*
learning organization, *62*
goals, *66*
mission, *66*
vision, *66*
values, *66*
SWOT analysis, *66*
external analysis, *66*
internal analysis, *67*
strategic choice, *67*
strategic training and development initiatives, *68*
metrics, *72*

balanced scorecard, *73*
human resource management (HRM) practices, *81*
staffing strategy, *81*
human resource planning, *83*
uniqueness, *83*
strategic value, *83*
concentration strategy, *84*
internal growth strategy, *86*
external growth strategy, *86*
disinvestment strategy, *86*
centralized training, *88*

corporate university model, *88*
business-embedded (BE) model, *93*
resistance to change, *97*
control, *97*
power, *97*
task redefinition, *97*
brand, *99*
outsourcing, *100*
business process outsourcing, *100*

## Discussion Questions

1. How would you expect the training activities of a company that is dominant in its product market to differ from those of a company that emphasizes research and development?

2. What do you think is the most important organizational characteristic that influences training? Why?

3. Why could the business-embedded model be considered the best way to organize the training function?

4. Schering-Plough HealthCare Products Inc. decided several years ago to expand its product line by developing pocket-size sticks and sprays of Coppertone sunblock,

previously only available as lotions packaged in squeeze bottles. The company placed a strategic emphasis on developing markets for this product. The company knew from market research studies that its Coppertone customers were already using the product in its original squeeze container at the beach. Due to increased awareness of the dangers of excessive skin exposure, consumers who had not previously used sunblock except when at the beach were looking for a daily sunblock product. Company managers reasoned that their market could be expanded significantly if the product were repackaged to fit conveniently in consumers' pockets, purses, and gym bags. Identify the business strategy. What training needs result from this strategy? What are the training implications of this decision for (1) manufacturing and (2) the sales force?

5. Which strategic training and development initiatives do you think all companies should support regardless of economic conditions? Why?

6. Are any of the strategic training and development initiatives more important for small business? Explain.

7. How can a training function support a business strategy?

8. How does the strategic value of jobs and their uniqueness influences how training and learning resources are invested?

9. What is human capital? How is human capital influencing the changing role of training from skill and knowledge acquisition to creating and sharing knowledge?

10. How could SWOT analysis be used to align training activities with business strategies and goals?

11. What are the training implications of the increased use of teams to manufacture products or provide services?

12. How would you design a corporate university? Explain each step you would take.

13. What are the advantages and disadvantages of a centralized training function?

14. What factors should a company consider in deciding whether to outsource its entire training function? Are the considerations different if the company wants to outsource a training program? Explain.

15. What is a training "brand"? Why is it important? How does it relate to marketing the training or learning function in an organization?

16. What does "change" have to do with training and learning? What four change-related problems need to be addressed for a new training program to be accepted by employees?

## Application Assignments

1. Go to www.mcdonalds.com, the website for McDonalds. Review "Our Company." Next, click on "careers," then click on "training and education" and "Hamburger University." Watch the video on "college credit connections." Answer the following questions:

   a. Does Hamburger University support the company's business? Explain why or why not.

   b. Identify the learning resources available at Hamburger University and how they contribute to the business strategy.

2. Find a company's annual report by using the Internet or visiting a library. Using the annual report, do the following:

   a. Identify the company's mission, values, and goals.

   b. Find any information provided in the report regarding the company's training practices and how they relate to the goals and strategies. Be prepared to give a brief presentation of your research to the class.

3. Go to www.orkin.com, the website for Orkin, a company committed to providing the world's best pest and termite control. Click on "Orkin Careers" at the bottom of the page. Investigate the company by clicking on "Who We Are," "Culture," "Opportunities," and "Community Involvement." Click on Orkin University. Does the university support the company culture and business strategy? What type of training does Orkin offer employees? Is training strategic? Why or why not? How does Orkin use training to contribute to the company's competitive advantage?

4. Go to www.corpu.com, the website for Corporate University Xchange, a corporate education and research and consulting firm that is an expert on corporate universities. What kind of information about corporate universities is available on this site? Why is it useful?

5. Go to www.adayanaauto.com, the website for Adayana Automotive, an outsourcing company that specializes in training for the automotive industry. What services does Adayana Automotive provide? If you worked as a human resource professional in the automotive industry, what would be the advantages and disadvantages of outsourcing training to Adayana Automotive?

---

# Case: *Using Training and Development to Spice up Business Results*

You may know McCormick & Company from its flavorings and spices that enhance the taste of appetizers, main dishes, and desserts (who doesn't appreciate the great aroma of just-baked chocolate chip cookies?). You should also know that training and development play a strategic role at McCormick & Company. Learning is driven by the company strategy. The company's main strategies include growing sales, fostering innovation, managing the cost base, and planning for succession.

To ensure that training and development are strategic, the director of learning and development has positioned the training department as a team of performance consultants who serve the needs of the business. Also, McCormick & Company has emphasized teaching at all levels of the organization, with the goal of making the company more agile and able to adapt to change and cope with the loss of expertise due to the retirement of baby boomers. Teachers include trainers and all employees with supervisory responsibility, regardless of their level.

McCormick & Company's board of directors will provide additional funding for training and development initiatives if a business case is made for additional financial resources.

If you were the Vice President of Learning, what types of training and development initiatives would you create? What metrics would you collect to measure to determine the effectiveness of your initiatives? Does having employees (who are not training or learning experts) teach—contribute to making training and learning more strategic? Explain your answer.

**Sources:** T. Bingham and P. Galagan, "Growing Talent and Sales at McCormick," *T+D* (July 2007): 30–34; R. Frattali, "The Company That Teaches Together Performs Together," *T+D* (July 2007): 36–39. Also, go to www.mccormick.com, the website for McCormick & Company.

# Endnotes

1. J. Meister, "The CEO-Driven Learning Culture," *Training and Development* (June 2000): 52–70.
2. R. Davenport, "A New Shade of Big Blue," *T+D* (May 2005): 35–40.
3. R. S. Schuler and S. F. Jackson, "Linking Competitive Strategies with Human Resource Management Practices," *Academy of Management Executive* 1 (1987): 207–219.
4. U. Sessa and M. London, *Continuous Learning in Organizations* (Mahwah, NJ: Erlbaum, 2006); J.C. Meister and K. Willyerd, *The 2020 Workplace* (New York: HarperCollins, 2010); D. Garvin, A. Edmondson, and E. Gino, "Is Yours a Learning Organization," *Harvard Business Review* (March 2008): 109–116.
5. *The Wall Street Journal* (October 13, 2008): R6; K Spors, "Top Small Workplaces 2008; King Arthur Flour Company.
6. F. Gino and G. Pisano, "Why leaders don't learn from success," *Harvard Business Review* (April 2011): 68–74; R. McGrath, "Failing by design," *Harvard Business Review* (April 2011): 77–83.
7. M. Weinstein, "Managing the Magic," *Training* (July/August 2008): 20–22.
8. E. Catmull, "How Pixar Fosters Collective Creativity," *Harvard Business Review* (September 2008): 64–72.
9. J. B. Quinn, P. Andersen, and S. Finkelstein, "Leveraging Intellect," *Academy of Management Executive* 10 (1996): 7–39
10. K. Ellis, "Share Best Practices Globally," *Training* (July 2001): 32–38.
11. R. Hughes and K. Beatty, "Five Steps to Leading Strategically," *T+D* (December 2005): 46–48.
12. R. Noe, J. Hollenbeck, B. Gerhart, and P. Wright. *Human Resource Management: Gaining a Competitive Advantage* (New York: McGraw-Hill-Irwin, 2011); K. Golden and V. Ramanujam, "Between a dream and a nightmare," *Human Resource Management* 24 (1985): 429–451; C. Hill and G. Jones, *Strategic Management Theory: An Integrated Approach* (Boston: Houghton Mifflin, 1989).
13. M. Weinstein, "Look ahead: Long-range learning plans," *training* (November/December 2010): 38–41.
14. S. Tannenbaum, "A Strategic View of Organizational Training and Learning." In *Creating, Implementing, and Managing Effective Training and Development*, ed. K. Kriger (San Francisco: Jossey-Boss, 2002): 10–52.
15. M. Lippitt, "Fix the Disconnect between Strategy and Execution," *T+D* (August 2007): 54–56.
16. M. Bolch, "Training gets down to business," *training* (March/April 2010): 31–33.
17. Reliance Industries Ltd., Group Manufacturing Services, *T+D* (October 2011): 80.
18. P. Harris, "Instilling competencies from top to bottom," *T+D* (October 2011): 65–66.
19. D. Zielinski, "In-house connections," *HR Magazine* (August 2011): 65.
20. F. Jossi, "Lesson Plans," *HR Magazine* (February 2003): 72–76.
21. C. Van Iddekinge, G. Ferris, P. Perrewe, A. Perryman, F. Blass, and T. Heetderks, "Effects of selection and training on unit-level performance over time: A latent growth modeling approach," *Journal of Applied Psychology*, 94 (2009): 829–843.
22. R. Kaplan and D. Norton, "The Balanced Scorecard—Measures That Drive Performance," *Harvard Business Review* (January–February 1992): 71–79; R. Kaplan and D. Norton, "Putting the Balanced Scorecard to Work," *Harvard Business Review* (September–October 1993): 134–147.
23. J. Salopek, "Best 2005: EMC Corporation," *T+D* (October 2005): 42–43.
24. R. Smith, "Aligning Learning with Business Strategy," *T+D* (November 2008): 40–43.
25. "A high-touch, low-tech approach to training," *T+D* (October 2009): 60–62; www.barillaus.com, website for Barilla America.
26. J. Salopek, "Learning-assisted service," *T+D*, October 2010, 40–42; website for Mike's Carwash at www.mikescarwash.com; T. Jones, "Inner Strength," *Modern Car Magazine*, April 2008, 48–53.
27. R. J. Campbell, "HR Development Strategies." In *Developing Human Resources*, ed. K. N. Wexley (Washington, D.C.: BNA Books, 1991): 5-1–5-34; J. K. Berry, "Linking Management Development to Business Strategy," *Training and Development* (August 1990): 20–22.
28. D. F. Van Eynde, "High-Impact Team Building Made Easy," *HR Horizons* (Spring 1992): 37–41; J. R. Hackman, ed., *Groups That Work and Those That Don't: Creating Conditions for Effective Teamwork* (San Francisco: Jossey-Bass, 1990); D. McCann and C. Margerison, "Managing High-Performance Teams," *Training and Development* (November 1989): 53–60.

29. A. I. Kraut, P. R. Pedigo, D. D. McKenna, and M. D. Dunnette, "The Role of the Manager: What's Really Important in Different Managerial Jobs," *Academy of Management Executive* 4 (1988): 36–48; F. Luthans, "Successful versus Effective Real Managers," *Academy of Management Executive* 2 (1988): 127–32; H. Mintzberg, *The Nature of Managerial Work* (New York: Harper and Row, 1973); S. W. Floyd and B. Wooldridge, "Dinosaurs or Dynamos? Recognizing Middle Management's Strategic Role," *Academy of Management Executive* 8 (1994): 47–57.

30. P. Kizilos, "Fixing Fatal Flaws," *Training* (September 1991): 66–70; F. S. Hall, "Dysfunctional Managers: The Next Human Resource Challenge," *Organizational Dynamics* (August 1991): 48–57.

31. J. Meister, "The CEO-Driven Learning Culture," *Training and Development* (June 2000): 52–70.

32. T. Bingham and P. Galagan, "At C Level: A Conversation with James P. Hackett," *T+D* (April 2005): 22–26.

33. R. Smith, "Aligning Learning with Business Strategy," *T+D* (November 2008): 40–43.

34. H. Dolezalek, "It's a Small World," *Training* (January 2008): 22–26.

35. M. Weinstein, "Taking the Global Initiative," *Training* (January 2009): 28–31.

36. K. Dobbs, "Winning the Retention Game," *Training* (September 1999): 50–56.

37. N. Breuer, "Shelf Life," *Workforce* (August 2000): 28–32.

38. J. Barney, "Firm resources and sustained competitive advantage," *Journal of Management*, 17 (1991): 99–120; P. Wright, B. Dunford, and S. Snell, " Human resources and the resource-based view of the firm," *Journal of Management* 27 (2001): 701–721; R. Ployart, J. Weekley, and K. Baughman, "The structure and function of human capital emergence: A multilevel examination of the attraction-selection-attrition model," *Academy of Management Journal* 49 (2006): 661–677; T. Crook, S. Todd, J. Combs, D. Woehr, and D. Ketchen, "Does human capital matter? A meta-analysis of the relationship between human capital and firm performance," *Journal of Applied Psychology* 96 (2011): 443–456.

39. J. A. Sonnenfeld and M. A. Peiperl, "Staffing policy as a strategic response: A typology of career systems," *Academy of Management Review* 13 (1988): 588–600.

40. D. Lepak and S. Snell, "Examining the human resource architecture: The relationships among human capital, employment, and human resource configurations," *Journal of Management* 28 (2002): 517–543.

41. V. R. Ceriello and C. Freeman, *Human Resource Management Systems: Strategies, Tactics, and Techniques* (Lexington, MA: Lexington Books, 1991).

42. Constellation Energy, "Shining stars," *T+D* (October 2008): 35–36.

43. D. T. Jaffe and C. D. Scott, "Career Development for Empowerment in a Changing Work World." In *New Directions in Career Planning and the Workplace,* ed. J. M. Kummerow (Palo Alto, CA: Consulting Psychologist Press, 1991): 33–60; L. Summers, "A logical approach to development planning," *Training and Development* 48 (1994): 22–31; D. B. Peterson and M. D. Hicks, *Development First* (Minneapolis, MN: Personnel Decisions, 1995).

44. A. P. Carnevale, L. J. Gainer, and J. Villet, *Training in America* (San Francisco: Jossey-Bass, 1990); L. J. Gainer, "Making the competitive connection: Strategic management and training," *Training and Development* (September 1989): s1–s30.

45. S. Raghuram and R. D. Arvey, "Business strategy links with staffing and training practices," *Human Resource Planning* 17 (1994): 55–73.

46. K. Featherly, "Culture shock," *Training* (November 2005): 24–29.

47. J. Caprara, "Ciena's hybrid learning solutions engine," *T+D* (May 2011): 40–43; T. Bingham and P. Galagan, "Learning linked to success," *T+D* (May 2011): 34–39.

48. F. Hansen, "Chief concern: Leaders," *Workforce Management*, July 20, 2009: 17–20.

49. K. Linebaugh, "Idle workers busy at Toyota," *The Wall Street Journal* (October 13, 2008): B1, B3.

50. K. Ellis, "The mindset that matters: Linking learning to the business," *Training* (May 2005): 38–43.

52. K. Oakes, "Grand Central Training, Part 2," *T+D* (July 2005): 22–25.

53. ETS: Princeton, New Jersey, "A tested commitment to learning," *T+D* (October 2008): 38–40.

54. J. Li and A. Abei, "Prioritizing and maximizing the impact of corporate universities," *T+D* (May 2011): 54–57.

55. P. Galagan, "Back to bricks and mortar," *T+D* (March 2011): 30–31.

56. M. Morrison, "Leaner e-learning," *Training* (January 2008): 16–18.

57. "Identify needs, meet them," *T+D* (October 2005): 30–32.

58. M. Weinstein, "Getting McSmart," *Training* (May 2008): 44–47.

59. "Training Today: Update on corporate universities," *Training* (April 2005): 8.

60. "Ritz-Carlton: #9," *Training* (March 2005): 45–46.

61. G. Wolfe, "Leveraging the learning space," *T+D* (July 2007): 40–44.

62. J. Meister, "Ten steps to creating a corporate university," *Training and Development* (November 1998): 38–43.

63. L. Freifeld, "CU there," *Training* (May 2008): 48–49.

64. G. Johnson, "Nine tactics to take your corporate university from good to great," *Training* (July/August 2003) 38–42. "Professional and career development," from Sprint website. *http://careers.sprint.com/work .html,* accessed December 21, 2001.

65. S. S. McIntosh, "Envisioning virtual training organization," *Training and Development* (May 1995): 46–49.

66. H. Dolezalek, "EMC's competitive advantage," *Training* (February 2009): 42–46.

67. B. Mosher, "How 'siloed' is your training organization?" *Chief Learning Officer* (July 2003): 13.

68. "Carter & Burgess," *T+D* (October 2008): 55–56.

69. N. Morera, "A 'brand' new way of learning," *Chief Learning Officer* (May 30, 2011) accessed at http:// clomedia.com, September 28, 2011.

70. E. Lowsen and C. Prive, "The psychology of change management," *The McKinsey Quarterly 2* (2003).

71. D. A. Nadler, "Concepts for the Management of Organizational Change." In *Readings in the Management of Innovation,* 2d ed, M. L. Tushman and N. L.Moore (Cambridge, MA: Ballenger): 722.

72. N. Miller, "Brave new role," *T+D* (June 2010): 54–58.

73. L. Freifeld, "TEIG locks in on leadership," *training* (January/February 2012): 34–39.

74. W. Webb, "Who moved my training?" *Training* (January 2003): 22–26; T. Seagraves, "The inside pitch," *T+D* (February 2005): 40–45; K. Oakes, "Over the top or on the money," *T+D* (November 2005): 20–22; H. Dolezalek, "Building buzz," *training* (March/April 2010): 36–38.

75. A. Hand, "How to enhance your training brand," *T+D* (February 2011): 76–77.

76. R. Cooperman, "Value over profit," *T+D* (May 2010): 58–62.

77. S. Boehle, "Get your message out," *Training* (February 2005): 36–41.

78. *Ibid.*

79. J. Gordon, "Selling it on the side," *Training* (December 2005): 34–39.

80. D. Sussman, "What HPLOs know," *T+D* (August 2005); 35–39.

81. N. DeViney and B. Sugrue, "Learning outsourcing: A reality check," *T+D* (December 2004): 40–45.

81. G. Johnson, "To outsource or not to outsource . . . That is the question," *Training* (August 2004): 26–29.

82. "2011 Training Industry Report," *Training* (November/December 2011) 33–35.

83. P. Harris, "Outsourced training begins to find its niche," *T+D* (November 2004); DeViney and Sugrue, "Learning outsourcing."

84. Harris, "Outsourced training begins." "Learning BPO Client Successes," from www.accenture.com, website for Accenture, accessed December 21, 2011.

85. C. Cornell, "Changing the supply chain," *Human Resource Executive* (March 2, 2005): 32–35.

86. T. Gainey and B. Klass, "The outsourcing of training and development: Factors affecting client satisfaction," *Journal of Management* 29(2): 207–229 (2003).

## PricewaterhouseCoopers Tests Partners by Sending Them to Work in Poor Nations

PriceWaterhouseCoopers (PwC), a 2011 inductee into *Training* magazine's Top 10 Hall of Fame has been transforming its curriculum into a blended learning experience that includes formal education, informal learning, and technology-based programs. Accounting and consulting giant PwC tapped partner Tahir Ayub for a consulting gig unlike anything he had done before. His job: helping village leaders in the Namibian outback grapple with their community's growing AIDS crisis. Faced with language barriers, cultural differences, and scant access to electricity, Ayub, thirty-nine, and two colleagues had to scrap their Microsoft PowerPoint presentations in favor of a lower-tech approach: face-to-face discussion. The village chiefs learned that they needed to garner community support for programs to combat the disease, and Ayub learned an important lesson as well: Technology isn't always the answer. "You better put your beliefs and biases to one side and figure out new ways to look at things," he said.

Ayub may never encounter as extreme a cultural disconnect at PwC as he did in Namibia. But for the next generation of partners, overcoming barriers and forging a connection with clients the world over will be a crucial part of their jobs. It's those skills that PwC hopes to foster in partners who take part in the Ulysses Program, which sends top mid-career talent to the developing world for eight-week service projects. For a fairly modest investment—$15,000 per person, plus salaries—Ulysses both tests the talent and expands the worldview of the accounting firm's future leaders.

While results are hard to quantify, PwC is convinced that the program works. All two dozen graduates are still working at the company. Half of them have been promoted, and most have new responsibilities. Just as important, all twenty-four people say they have a stronger commitment to PwC—in part because of the commitment the firm made to them and in part because of their new vision of the firm's values. Says global managing partner Willem Bröcker: "We get better partners from this exercise."

The Ulysses Program is PwC's answer to one of the biggest challenges confronting professional services companies: identifying and training up-and-coming leaders who can find unconventional answers to intractable problems. By tradition and necessity, new PwC leaders are nurtured from within. But with thousands of partners, identifying those with the necessary business savvy and relationship-building skills isn't easy. Just as the program gives partners a new view of PwC, it also gives PwC a new view of them, particularly their ability to hold up under pressure.

For mid-career partners who were weaned on e-mail and the Blackberry, this was no walk in the park. They had become accustomed to a world of wireless phones, sleek offices, and Chinese takeout, so the rigors of the developing world came as quite a shock. One mergers and acquisitions expert from PwC's Boston office, who had never been to a developing country before his stint in Belize, where he encountered dirt-floored houses, sick children, and grinding poverty.

For more than 15 years, companies have used social-responsibility initiatives to develop leaders. But PwC takes the concept to a new level. Participants spend eight weeks in developing countries lending their business skills to local aid groups, from an ecotourism collective in Belize to small organic farmers in Zambia to AIDS groups in Namibia. Ulysses also presents participants with the challenge of collaborating across cultures with local clients, as well as with PwC colleagues from other global regions. Ayub, for example, was paired with partners from Mexico and the Netherlands.

PwC also gets interns involved in poor nations to improve their leadership skills and motivate them to better serve their home communities. One intern in Belize working with the Ministry of Education helped students to understand how to budget, apply for university scholarships, and grasp the idea of college credit.

# BEYOND ACCOUNTING

The PWC program gives participants a broad, international perspective that's crucial for a company that does business around the world. Ulysses helps prepare participants for challenges that go beyond the strict confines of accounting or consulting and instills values such as community involvement that are fundamental to its corporate culture.

Ulysses is also a chance for partners to learn what they can accomplish without their usual resources to lean on. The program forces them to take on projects well outside their expertise. For example, the mergers and acquisitions expert developed a business plan for an ecotourism group in Belize. The experience was an eye-opener.

PwC partners say that they've already adapted their experiences to the task of managing people and clients. A Malaysian partner says that her team noticed a shift in her managerial style after the Belize trip. She listened more and became more flexible. Ayub manages twenty partners. He says he favors face-to-face conversations over e-mail because the low-tech approach builds trust. "It made the difference in Namibia," he says.

If insights like those ripple out across the firm, Ulysses will be more than a voyage of personal discovery for a handful of partners. It could help build leaders capable of confronting the challenges of an increasingly global business. And that, says PwC, is the whole point.

## Questions

1. What competitive challenges motivated PwC to develop the Ulysses Program?

2. Do you think the Ulysses Program contributes to PwC's business strategy and goals? Explain.

3. How would you determine if the Ulysses Program was effective? What metrics or outcomes would you collect? Why?

4. What are the advantages and disadvantages of the Ulysses Program compared to more traditional ways of training leaders such as formal courses (e.g., an MBA program) or giving them more increased job responsibility?

**Source:** J. Hempel and S. Porges, "It Takes a Village—and a Consultant: PricewaterhouseCoopers Tests Partners by Sending Them to Work in Poor Nations," *Business Week* (September 6, 2004), retrieved from www.businessweek.com on February 23, 2009, www.pwc.com, PwC inducted into *Training* magazine's Top 10 Hall of Fame, from PwC website accessed December 21, 2011, www.pwc.com, "Project Belize participants share their stories."

# Designing Training

Part Two focuses on how to systematically design effective training. Chapter Three, "Needs Assessment," discusses the process used to determine whether training is necessary. Needs assessment includes analyzing the organization, people, and tasks involved. Chapter Four, "Learning and Transfer of Training," discusses learning and transfer of training theories and their implications for creating an environment that will help trainees learn the desired outcomes from training and use them on their jobs. Chapter Five, "Program Design" reviews practical issues in training program design, including developing training courses and programs, how to choose and prepare a training site, choosing a consultant or vendor, and how to create a work environment that maximizes learning and transfer of training, including manager and peer support. The role of knowledge management in transfer of training is also discussed. Chapter Six, "Training Evaluation," provides an overview of how to evaluate training programs, including the types of outcomes that need to be measured and the types of evaluation designs available.

Part Two concludes with a case on the use of on-the-job video gaming for the purpose of training.

# Needs Assessment

## Objectives

After reading this chapter, you should be able to

1. Discuss the role of organization analysis, person analysis, and task analysis in needs assessment.

2. Identify different methods used in needs assessment and identify the advantages and disadvantages of each method.

3. Discuss the concerns of upper- and mid-level managers and trainers in needs assessment.

4. Explain how personal characteristics, input, output, consequences, and feedback influence performance and learning.

5. Create conditions to ensure that employees are receptive to training.

6. Discuss the steps involved in conducting a task analysis.

7. Analyze task analysis data to determine the tasks for which people need to be trained.

8. Explain competency models and the process used to develop them.

## Needs Assessment at B&W Pantex and NetApp

Needs assessment is a critical first step in designing new and revising current training courses. Consider how needs assessment was used at B&W Pantex and Network Appliances (NetApp).

The B&W Pantex plant, located near Amarillo, Texas, is charged with maintaining the safety, security, and reliability of the nation's nuclear weapons stockpile. The facility is managed and operated by B&W Pantex for the U.S. Department of Energy/National Nuclear Security Administration. The nuclear weapons industry is highly regulated and most training is focused on mandatory safety and compliance. However, B&W Pantex also offers technical training and management development courses, and every employee has an individual development plan. Training and development at B&W Pantex is of high quality and delivers business results: the company was recognized by the American Society for Training and Development (ASTD) as a 2010 Best Award winner. The mission of the technical training department is to provide quality training that is necessary, precise, timely, and behavior- or ability-changing. Recently, the technical training program was reviewed to help improve its efficiency and effectiveness. The review found that training required a great time commitment by employees to be away from their jobs, and 20 percent of the courses accounted for 8 percent of the training hours. As a result, the technical training department reexamined its course offerings by considering if the training was still necessary, if the training objectives were still relevant, if the course provided redundant information, and if the target audience for the course had changed. This analysis led the technical training department to consolidate or remove more than 700 courses, and many courses were redesigned to reduce the time of completion by more than half. Many classroom sessions were replaced with computer-based training or informal meetings between employees and their manager. As a result, training efficiency has improved by 49 percent, and employees now participate in 5.5 hours of training each month. NetApp creates innovative storage and data management solutions that help customers accelerate business breakthroughs and achieve outstanding cost efficiency. NetApp is one of the fastest-growing storage and data management providers, with over 8,000 employees in 130 offices around the world. NetApp was rated the sixth-best workplaces in 2012 in *Fortune* magazine's "100 Best Companies to Work For" annual report. Since 2006 it has consistently been ranked as one of the top fifteen best workplaces. NetApp is known for several of its training and development programs, including its "Training On All Special Things" (TOAST), a new-hire orientation program with top-level NetApp executives, and NetApp University.

As a result of company growth, NetApp needed to develop recently hired support engineers in order to provide world-class services. Existing training programs were inadequate. NetApp needed training that would cover troubleshooting skills for all aspects of support, including process, systems, operations, and soft skills needed to ensure that newly hired support engineers would competently meet demands for the company's services. To conduct a needs assessment, NetApp asked its best performers to participate in focus groups. These groups were asked to consider what types of support engineers needed to know to perform their jobs. From the focus groups, more than 1,400 tasks were identified. The tasks were ranked according to difficulty, frequency, and importance. A total of 500 tasks were identified as being critical for support engineers to perform within their first year on the job. To address these tasks, a new-hire training program was developed. It includes self-paced e-learning, hands-on work in the classroom, and cases based on the company's computerized support system or initiated by customers on the Web.

**Sources:** Based on J. Salopek, "Keeping Knowledge Safe and Sound," *T+D* (October 2010): 64–66; www.pantex.com, the website for B&W Pantex. S. Varman and B. Collins, "On Ramp to Success at Network Appliances," *T+D* (July 2007); 58-61; www.netapp.com.

# INTRODUCTION

As discussed in Chapter One, "Introduction to Employee Training and Development," effective training practices involve the use of a training design process. The design process begins with a needs assessment. Subsequent steps in the process include ensuring that employees have the motivation and basic skills necessary to learn, creating a positive learning environment, making sure that trainees use learned skills on the job, choosing the training method, and evaluating whether training has achieved the desired outcomes. As the NetApp example highlights, before you choose a training method, it is important to determine what type of training is necessary and whether trainees are willing to learn. **Needs assessment** refers to the process used to determine whether training is necessary.

Needs assessment typically involves organizational analysis, person analysis, and task analysis.[1] An organizational analysis considers the context in which training will occur. That is, **organizational analysis** involves determining the appropriateness of training, given the company's business strategy, its resources available for training, and support by managers and peers for training activities. You are already familiar with one aspect of organizational analysis. Chapter Two, "Strategic Training," discussed the role of the company's business strategy in determining the frequency and type of training.

Person analysis helps to identify who needs training. **Person analysis** involves (1) determining whether performance deficiencies result from a lack of knowledge, skill, or ability (a training issue) or from a motivational or work-design problem; (2) identifying who needs training; and (3) determining employee readiness for training. **Task analysis** identifies the important tasks and knowledge, skills, and behaviors that need to be emphasized in training for employees to complete their tasks.

# WHY IS NEEDS ASSESSMENT NECESSARY?

Needs assessment is important because a manager or other client asking for training (which focuses on closing skill gaps resulting from a lack of knowledge or skill) could really be asking for or need something else, such as employee motivation, changing perspectives or attitudes, or redesign workflow.[2] If a manager requests training for a performance problem, what he or she is looking for is a solution to a problem that may (or may not involve training). In conducting a needs assessment, your role is to determine if training is the appropriate solution.

Needs assessment is the first step in the instructional design process, and if it is not properly conducted, any one or more of the following situations could occur:

- Training may be incorrectly used as a solution to a performance problem (when the solution should deal with employee motivation, job design, or a better communication of performance expectations).
- Training programs may have the wrong content, objectives, or methods.
- Trainees may be sent to training programs for which they do not have the basic skills, prerequisite skills, or confidence needed to learn.
- Training will not deliver the expected learning, behavior change, or financial results that the company expects.
- Money will be spent on training programs that are unnecessary because they are unrelated to the company's business strategy.

Figure 3.1 shows the three types of analysis involved in needs assessment and the causes and outcomes that result. There are many different causes or "pressure points" that suggest that training is necessary. These pressure points include performance problems, new technology, internal or external customer requests for training, job redesign, new legislation, changes in customer preferences, new products, or employees' lack of basic skills.

**FIGURE 3.1**   **Causes and Outcomes of Needs Assessment**

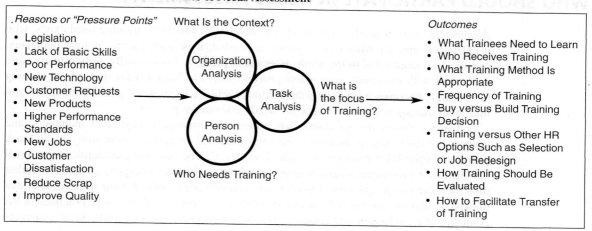

*.Reasons or "Pressure Points"*

- Legislation
- Lack of Basic Skills
- Poor Performance
- New Technology
- Customer Requests
- New Products
- Higher Performance
  Standards
- New Jobs
- Customer
  Dissatisfaction
- Reduce Scrap
- Improve Quality

What Is the Context?

Organization Analysis

Task Analysis

Person Analysis

What is the focus of Training?

Who Needs Training?

*Outcomes*

- What Trainees Need to Learn
- Who Receives Training
- What Training Method Is
  Appropriate
- Frequency of Training
- Buy versus Build Training
  Decision
- Training versus Other HR
  Options Such as Selection
  or Job Redesign
- How Training Should Be
  Evaluated
- How to Facilitate Transfer
  of Training

Note that these pressure points do not automatically mean that training is the correct solution. For example, consider, a delivery truck driver whose job is to deliver anesthetic gases to medical facilities. The driver mistakenly hooks up the supply line of a mild anesthetic to the supply line of a hospital's oxygen system, contaminating the hospital's oxygen supply. Why did the driver make this mistake, which is clearly a performance problem? The driver may have made this mistake because of a lack of knowledge about the appropriate line hookup for the anesthetic, because of anger over a requested salary increase that the driver's manager recently denied, or because of mislabeled valves for connecting the gas supply. Only the lack of knowledge can be addressed by training. The other pressure points require reviewing and making decisions related to the the driver's anger-motivated behavior (fire the driver) or the design of the work environment (remind supervisor and drivers to check to insure that valves and hook-up lines are properly labeled at all work sites).

What outcomes result from a needs assessment? Needs assessment provides important input into most of the remaining steps in the training design. As shown in Figure 3.1, the needs assessment process results in information related to who needs training and what trainees need to learn, including the tasks in which they need to be trained, plus knowledge, skill, behavior, or other job requirements. Needs assessment helps to determine whether the company will outsource its training (that is, purchase training from a vendor or consultant, or develop training through internal resources). Determining exactly what trainees need to learn is critical for the next step in the instructional design process: identifying learning outcomes and objectives. Chapter Four, "Learning and Transfer of Training," explores identifying learning outcomes and learning objectives and creating a training environment so that learning occurs and is used on the job. Through identifying the learning outcomes and resources available for training, the needs assessment also provides information that helps the company choose the appropriate training or development method (discussed in Part Three of this book). Needs assessment also provides information regarding the outcomes that should be collected to evaluate training effectiveness. The process of evaluating training is discussed in Chapter Six, "Training Evaluation."

# WHO SHOULD PARTICIPATE IN NEEDS ASSESSMENT?

Because the goal of needs assessment is to determine whether a training need exists, who it exists for, and for what tasks training is needed, it is important to include managers, trainers, and employees in the needs assessment process. Traditionally, only trainers were concerned with the needs assessment process. But, as Chapter Two showed, as training increasingly becomes used to help the company achieve its strategic goals, both upper- and mid-level managers are involved in the needs assessment process.

Table 3.1 shows the questions that upper-level managers, mid-level managers, and trainers are interested in answering for organizational analysis, person analysis, and task analysis. Upper-level managers include directors, CEOs, and vice presidents. Upper-level managers view the needs assessment process from the broader company perspective rather than focusing on specific jobs. Upper-level managers are involved in the needs assessment process to identify the role of training in relation to other human resource practices in the company (e.g., selection and compensation of employees). That is, upper-level managers help to determine if training is related to the company's business strategy, and if so, what type of training is required. Upper-level managers are also involved in identifying what business functions or units need training (person analysis) and in determining if the company has the knowledge, skills, and abilities in the workforce that are necessary to meet its strategy and be competitive in the marketplace. Mid-level managers are more concerned

**TABLE 3.1**   **Key Concerns of Upper- and Mid-Level Managers and Trainers in Needs Assessment**

|  | **Upper-Level Managers** | **Mid-Level Managers** | **Trainers** |
|---|---|---|---|
| Organizational Analysis | Is training important to achieve our business objectives? How does training support our business strategy? | Do I want to spend money on training? How much? | Do I have the budget to buy training services? Will managers support training? |
|  | What are the threats to our talent base? | How will training and development help meet my business goals? Are we retaining top talent? |  |
| Person Analysis | Do employees in specific functions or business units need training? | Who should be trained? Managers? Professionals? Core employees? | How will I identify which employees need training? |
|  | What do employees need to do to accomplish our business objectives? |  |  |
| Task Analysis | Does the company have people with the knowledge, skills, and abilities or competencies needed to compete in the marketplace? | For what jobs can training make the biggest difference in product quality or customer service? | For what tasks should employees be trained? What knowledge, skills, ability, or other characteristics are necessary? |

with how training may affect the attainment of financial goals for the particular units they supervise. As a result, for mid-level managers, organizational analysis focuses on identifying (1) how much of their budgets they want to devote to training; (2) the types of employees who should receive training (e.g., engineers, or core employees who are directly involved in producing goods or providing services); and (3) for what jobs training can make a difference in terms of improving products or customer service.

At DPR Construction, a national building company with regional offices throughout the United States including Atlanta, Georgia, San Francisco, California, and Washington, D.C., an annual training summit is held with key people from across the company to discuss training needs related to business objectives.[3] This helps ensure that the necessary training is in place to help reach the business objectives. Each business team has a sponsor from the company's learning group to help implement business strategies. For example, one important business strategy relates to sustainability (i.e., environmentally friendly building methods such as using rooftop gardens to help reduce storm water runoff). Also, the learning groups has helped develop a software application known as "greenBook," which provides a database of green products and services and helps determine costs of different levels of energy efficiency.

As discussed in Chapter Two, trainers (including training managers and instructional designers) need to consider whether training is aligned with the business strategy. However, trainers are primarily interested in needs assessment to provide them with information that they need to administer, develop, and support training programs. This information includes determining if training should be purchased or developed in-house, identifying the tasks for which employees need to be trained, and determining upper- and mid-level managers' interest in and support for training.

Upper-level managers are usually involved in determining whether training meets the company's strategy and then providing the appropriate financial resources. Upper-level managers are not usually involved in identifying which employees need training, the tasks for which training is needed, or the knowledge, skills, abilities, and other characteristics needed to complete those tasks. This is the role of subject-matter experts (SMEs). **Subject-matter experts (SMEs)** are employees, academics, managers, technical experts, trainers, and even customers or suppliers who are knowledgeable with regard to (1) training issues, including tasks to be performed; (2) the knowledge, skills, and abilities required for successful task performance; (3) the necessary equipment; and (4) the conditions under which the tasks have to be performed. A key issue with SMEs is making sure that they are knowledgeable about the content that training must cover, as well as realistic enough to be able to prioritize what content is critical to cover in the time allotted for the subject in the training curriculum. SMEs also must have information that is relevant to the company's business and have an understanding of the company's language, tools, and products. There is no rule regarding how many types of employees should be represented in the group conducting the needs assessment. Still, it is important to get a sample of **job incumbents** (employees who are currently performing the job) involved in the process because they tend to be most knowledgeable about the job and can be a great hindrance to the training process if they do not feel they have had input into the needs assessment.

For example, Fallon Clinic, a multilocation, specialty group medical practice with 1,700 employees including doctors, nurses, therapists, and clerical support personnel, conducts needs assessment on an ongoing basis to determine where training would have the most value.[4] The learning and organization development department conducts an annual companywide needs assessment that includes the use of employee surveys and face-to-face meetings with managers and employees.

# METHODS USED IN NEEDS ASSESSMENT

Several methods are used to conduct needs assessment, including observing employees performing the job, using online technology, reading technical manuals and other documentation, interviewing SMEs, conducting focus groups with SMEs, and asking SMEs to complete questionnaires designed to identify the tasks and knowledge, skills, abilities, and other characteristics required for a job. Table 3.2 presents the advantages and disadvantages

**TABLE 3.2** Advantages and Disadvantages of Needs Assessment Techniquesg

| Technique | Advantages | Disadvantages |
|---|---|---|
| Observation | • Generates data relevant to work environment <br> • Minimizes interruption of work | • Needs skilled observers <br> • Employees' behavior may be affected by being observed |
| Questionnaires | • Inexpensive <br> • Can collect data from a large number of persons <br> • Data easily summarized | • Requires time <br> • Possible low return rates, inappropriate responses <br> • Lacks detail <br> • Only provides information directly related to questions asked |
| Interviews | • Good at uncovering details of training needs, as well as causes of and solutions to problems <br> • Can explore unanticipated issues that come up <br> • Questions can be modified | • Time-consuming <br> • Difficult to analyze <br> • Needs skilled interviewers <br> • Can be threatening to SMEs <br> • Difficult to schedule <br> • SMEs provide only information they think you want to hear |
| Focus groups and collaboration tools | • Useful with complex or controversial issues that one person may be unable or unwilling to explore <br> • Questions can be modified to explore unanticipated issues | • Time-consuming to organize <br> • Group members provide only information they think you want to hear |
| Documentation (technical manuals, records) | • Good source of information on procedure <br> • Objective <br> • Good source of task information for new jobs and jobs in the process of being created | • You may be unable to understand technical language <br> • Materials may be obsolete |
| Online technology (software) | • Objective <br> • Minimizes interruption of work <br> • Requires limited human involvement | • May threaten employees <br> • Manager may use information to punish rather than train <br> • Limited to jobs requiring interaction with customers via computer or phone |
| Historical data reviews | • Provides data related to performance and practices | • Available data may be inaccurate, incomplete, or not fully represent performance |

Sources: Based on S. V. Steadham, "Learning to Select a Needs Assessment Strategy," *Training and Development Journal* (January 1980): 56–61; R. J. Mirabile, "Everything You Wanted to Know About Competency Modeling," *Training and Development* (August 1997): 74; K. Gupta, *A Practical Guide to Needs Assessment* (San Francisco: Jossey-Bass, 1999); M. Casey and D. Doverspike, "Training Needs Analysis and Evaluation for New Technologies Through the Use of Problem-Based Inquiry," *Performance Improvement Quarterly* 18(1) (2005): 110–124.

of each method. For example, Texas Instruments (TI) was trying to determine how to train engineering experts to become trainers for new engineers.[5] All the engineers had technical expertise. The problem was that their level of instructional expertise varied. Some had no experience teaching, whereas others taught courses at local colleges. When new engineers became inexperienced instructors, both the trainees and the instructors were frustrated. In assessing the engineers' training needs, training and development specialists used five of the six methods shown in Table 3.2. They collected information that was useful for organization and task analysis. Training course listings and mission statements were used to identify the engineering department mission, and current and previous course offerings were used to develop engineers. Competency studies and project checklists were used to identify relevant tasks. Classroom observation of new and experienced instructors was used to identify the strengths and weaknesses of instructors' presentations (person analysis). Both instructors and noninstructors were interviewed to validate the information gathered through the written documentation and surveys. Another example is Boeing, which uses a process borrowed from the field of artificial intelligence. Experts are observed and interviewed to identify their thinking processes for solving problems, dealing with uncertainty, and minimizing risks. The expert practices that are uncovered are then included in the training curriculum.[6]

For newly created jobs, trainers often do not have job incumbents to rely on for this information. Rather, technical diagrams, simulations, and equipment designers can provide information regarding the training requirements, tasks, and conditions under which the job is performed. Historical data review involves collecting performance data from electronic or paper records. It provides information regarding current performance levels, which is useful for identifying gaps between actual and desired performance. For example, a needs assessment conducted at a hospital to determine the causes of a high number of errors in radiology orders (e.g., x-rays) from physicians collected historical data on errors, including incorrect exams, examination of the wrong side of the patient's body, use of incorrect diagnosis codes, and duplicate orders.[7] The historical data was used along with semistructured interviews and observations to identify the causes for the errors and interventions to reduce them. Another source of information for companies that have introduced a new technology is the help desk that companies often set up to deal with calls regarding problems, deficiencies in training, or deficiencies in documentation, software, or systems.[8] Help desk management software can categorize and track calls and questions by application, by caller, or by vendor. Report creation capability built into the software makes it easy to generate documents on user problems and identify themes among calls. Analyzing these calls is practical for identifying gaps in training. For example, common types of call problems can be analyzed to determine if they are due to inadequate coverage in the training program and/or inadequate written documentation and job aids used by trainees.

Online technology is available to monitor and track employee performance. This information is useful for identifying training needs and providing employees with feedback regarding their skill strengths and weaknesses. In call centers, for example, technology provides an ongoing assessment of performance.[9] An employee who triggers the online system by failing to meet a defined standard, such as receiving more than five callbacks on an unresolved issue, is automatically referred to the appropriate job aid or training event. As shown in Table 3.2, online technology has several advantages: It provides an objective report of behaviors, the data can be quickly summarized into reports, it does not require a trainer or SME to observe or interview employees, and it minimizes work interruptions. However, the use of online technology in needs assessment is best suited for only a small number of jobs requiring interactions with customers through the use of a computer or telephone.[10] Also, for online technology to be effective, managers need to ensure that the information is used to train employees, not to punish them. Otherwise, employees will feel threatened, which will contribute to employee dissatisfaction and turnover.

Because no single method of conducting needs assessment is superior to the others, multiple methods are usually used. The methods vary in the type of information, as well as the level of detail provided. The advantage of questionnaires is that information can be collected from a large number of persons. Also, questionnaires allow many employees to participate in the needs assessment process. However, when using questionnaires, it is difficult to collect detailed information regarding training needs. Face-to-face and telephone interviews are time consuming, but more detailed information regarding training needs can be collected. **Focus groups** are a type of SME interview that involves a face-to-face meeting with groups of SMEs in which the questions that are asked relate to specific training needs. Crowdsourcing can also be used for needs assessment. In this context, **crowdsourcing** refers to asking a large group of employees (i.e., the crowd) to help provide information for needs assessment that they are not traditionally asked to do. Computer Services Corporation uses "Ideation," a web-based tool for collaboration and crowdsourcing to help identify training needs.[11] The process requires a review team to filter, sort, and build on the best ideas. The process allows the learning department to get a larger number of employees involved in the needs assessment process rather than relying only on interviews with SMEs. It is important to verify the results of interviews and observations because what employees and managers say they do and what they really do may differ. At Brown-Forman Corporation, producer and marketer of beverages and alcohol brands such as Jack Daniel's Tennessee Whiskey, training needs are identified in a number of different ways, including monitoring employee development and performance management data, trends in the beverage alcohol industry, and issues raised by the company's operating groups who pay for training services.[12] Yapi Kredi Academy was established to provide learning and development for Yapi ve Kredi Bank's headquartered in Istanbul, Turkey.[13] The bank's executive committee (including the CEO, executive vice presidents, and an advisory committee with senior managers and individuals from outside the bank who identify trends, challenges, and opportunities in the industry) provides the strategic direction and vision for the academy. The bank's needs assessment process includes branch visits, surveys, and focus groups, as well as meetings with business units. The academy surveyed more than 3,000 branch employees about their satisfaction with the training they received, and their experiences with individual development plans and training offerings. The results are used to determine how to meet learning and development needs.

With the increasing emphasis on Total Quality Management (TQM), many companies are also using information about other companies' training practices (a process known as **benchmarking**) to help determine the appropriate type, level, and frequency of training.[14] For example, Chevron, Federal Express, GTE, Xerox, and several other companies are members of the ASTD benchmarking forum. A common survey instrument is completed by each company. The survey includes questions on training costs, staff size, administration, design, program development, and delivery. The information is summarized and shared with the participating companies.

# THE NEEDS ASSESSMENT PROCESS

This section examines the three elements of needs assessment: organizational analysis, person analysis, and task analysis. Figure 3.2 illustrates the needs assessment process. In practice, organizational analysis, person analysis, and task analysis are not conducted in any order. The question of whether time and money are devoted to training is contingent on the results of organizational, person, and task analyses. While any one analysis can indicate the need for training, companies need to consider the information from all three types of analysis before the decision is made to devote time and money to training. Because organizational analysis is concerned with identifying whether training suits the company's strategic objectives and whether the company has the budget, time, and expertise for training (the context for training), it is usually conducted first. Person analysis and task analysis are often conducted at the same time because it is difficult to determine whether performance deficiencies are a training problem without understanding the tasks and the work environment. An initial organizational analysis may suggest that a company does not want to spend financial resources on training. However, if person analysis reveals that a large number of employees lack a skill in an important area that is related to the company's business objectives (such as customer service), upper-level managers may decide to reallocate financial resources for training.

**FIGURE 3.2**  **The Needs Assessment Process**

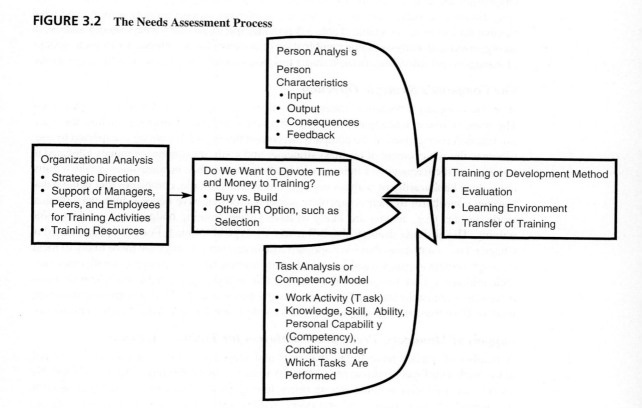

**TABLE 3.3** Questions to Ask in an Organizational Analysis

How might the training content affect our employees' relationship with our customers?

What might suppliers, customers, or partners need to know about the training program?

How does this program align with the strategic needs of the business?

Should organizational resources be devoted to this program?

What do we need from managers and peers for this training to succeed?

What features of the work environment might interfere with training (e.g., lack of equipment, no time to use new skills)?

Do we have experts who can help us develop the program content and ensure that we understand the needs of the business as we develop the program?

Will employees perceive the training program as an opportunity? Reward? Punishment? Waste of time?

Which persons or groups (e.g., employees, managers, vendors, suppliers, and program developers) have an interest in seeing training succeed? Whose support do we need?

Sources: Based on F. Nickols, "Why a Stakeholder Approach to Evaluating Training?" *Advances in Developing Human Resources* (February 2005): 121–134; S. Tannenbaum, "A Strategic View of Organizational Training and Learning." In *Creating, Implementing, and Managing Effective Training and Development*, ed. K. Kraiger (San Francisco: Jossey-Bass, 2002): 10–52.

## Organizational Analysis

Organizational analysis involves identifying whether training supports the company's strategic direction; whether managers, peers, and employees support training activity; and what training resources are available. Table 3.3 provides questions that trainers should address in an organizational analysis. Some combination of documentation, interviews, or focus groups of managers and individuals in the training function should be used to answer these questions.

### *The Company's Strategic Direction*

How the company's business strategy influences training was discussed in Chapter Two. The strategic role of training influences the frequency and type of training and how the training function is organized in the company. In companies in which training is expected to contribute to the achievement of business strategies and goals, the amount of money allocated to training and the frequency of training will likely be higher than in companies in which training is done haphazardly or with no strategic intent. For example, companies that believe that learning contributes to their competitive advantage or that have adopted high-performance work systems (e.g., teams) are likely to have greater training budgets and conduct more training. The business strategy also influences the type of training. For example, as noted in Chapter Two, companies that have adopted a disinvestment strategy are more likely to focus on outplacement assistance and job search skills training than are companies with other strategic initiatives. Last, the greater the strategic role of training, the more likely that the company will organize the training function using the business-embedded or corporate university models. Both these models emphasize that training is used to help solve business problems.

### *Support of Managers, Peers, and Employees for Training Activities*

A number of studies have found that peer and manager support for training is critical, along with employee enthusiasm and motivation to attend training. The key factors for success are a positive attitude among peers, managers, and employees about participation in training activities; managers' and peers' willingness to provide information to trainees about how they can use the knowledge, skill, or behaviors learned in training to perform their jobs more effectively; and opportunities for trainees to use training content in their jobs.[15] If peers' and managers' attitudes and behaviors are not supportive, employees are not likely to apply training content to their jobs.

### Training Resources

It is necessary to identify whether the company has the budget, time, and expertise for training. One of the questions that the company must answer is whether it has the resources (i.e., time, money, and expertise) to build or develop training programs itself or whether it should buy them from a vendor or consulting firm. This is known as the "buy versus build" decision. For example, if the company is installing computer-based manufacturing equipment in one of its plants, it has three possible strategies for dealing with the need to have computer-literate employees. First, the company can decide that, given its staff expertise and budget, it can use internal consultants to train all affected employees. Second, the company may decide that it is more cost effective to identify employees who are computer literate by using tests and work samples. Employees who fail the test or perform below standards on the work sample can be reassigned to other jobs. Choosing this strategy suggests that the company has decided to devote resources to selection and placement rather than training. Third, because it lacks time or expertise, the company may decide to buy training from a consultant. We will discuss how to identify and choose a high-quality vendor or consultant to provide training services in Chapter Five, "Program Design."

One way to identify training resources is for companies that have similar operations or departments located across the country or the world to share practices.[16] For example, Pfizer Pharmaceuticals has created a "virtual learning team" to promote the sharing of "best practices" in technical training among its U.S. manufacturing sites. Training managers from New York, New Jersey, Missouri, Nebraska, Indiana, Puerto Rico, and Belgium serve on the team. The team members meet face to face once every business quarter and also have a regular conference call every six weeks. The objectives of the team are to (1) provide a centralized focus to Pfizer's training strategies, (2) enable training managers to mentor peers and exchange training practices, and (3) establish training standards for each of the manufacturing sites. The team has made some valuable contributions, including the development of a new operator training standard, a 10-step method for teaching and evaluating the skills of employees who make drug products or operate machinery. The team based the standard on an existing practice at one of the manufacturing sites. Another accomplishment was that the New York and Puerto Rico team representatives found that they had similar work areas in their plants, so they decided to each create one module of a new training plan and transfer the module to the other location.

## Person Analysis

Person analysis helps to identify employees who need training; that is, whether employees' current performance or expected performance indicates a need for training. The need for training may result from the pressure points in Figure 3.1, including performance problems, changes in the job, or use of new technology. Person analysis also helps determining employees' readiness for training. **Readiness for training** refers to whether (1) employees have the personal characteristics (ability, attitudes, beliefs, and motivation) necessary to learn program content and apply it on the job, and (2) the work environment will facilitate learning and not interfere with performance. This process includes evaluating person characteristics, input, output, consequences, and feedback.[17]

A major pressure point for training is poor or substandard performance. Poor performance is indicated by customer complaints, low performance ratings, or on-the-job incidents such as accidents and unsafe behavior. Another potential indicator of the need for training is if the job changes such that current levels of performance need to be improved or employees must be able to complete new tasks.

### The Process for Person Analysis

Figure 3.3 shows a process for analyzing the factors that influence performance and learning. **Person characteristics** refer to employee knowledge, skill, ability, and attitudes. **Input** relates to the instructions that tell employees what, how, and when to perform. Input also refers to the resources that the employees are given to help them perform. These resources may include equipment, time, or budget. **Output** refers to the job's performance

**FIGURE 3.3**

**The Process for Analyzing the Factors That Influence Employee Performance and Learning**

Sources: G. Rummler, "In Search of the Holy Performance Grail," *Training and Development* (April 1996): 26–31; C. Reinhart, "How to Leap over Barriers to Performance," *Training and Development* (January 2000): 20–24; G. Rummler and K. Morrill, "The Results Chain," *T+D* (February 2005): 27–35.

*Person Characteristics*
- Basic Skills
  - Cognitive Ability
  - Reading Level
- Self-efficacy
- Awareness of Training Needs, Career Interests, Goals
- Age & Generation

+

*Input*
- Understand What, How, When to Perform
- Situational Constraints
- Social Support
- Opportunity to Perform

+

*Output*
- Expectations for Learning and Performance

+

*Consequences*
- Norms
- Benefits
- Rewards

+

*Feedback*
- Frequency
- Specificity
- Detail

Motivation to Learn
Learning
Job Performance

standards. **Consequences** refer to the type of incentives that employees receive for performing well. **Feedback** refers to the information that employees receive while they are performing.

Interviews or questionnaires can be used to measure personal characteristics, input, output, consequences, and feedback. For example, a package delivery company believed that lead drivers were valuable for providing on-the-job training for new employees.[18] The company employed 110 lead drivers, and the job involved driving, delivery, and bookkeeping duties. The lead drivers benefited from training because coaching and training made their jobs more interesting, and the company benefited because on-the-job training was relatively inexpensive and effective. Lead drivers often quickly spotted and corrected performance problems with new trainees, and they knew the technical aspects of the delivery job quite well. Although many of the lead drivers were good trainers and coaches, the company believed that they needed to learn how to coach and train the new drivers. The company used interviews to identify what type of coaching and training skills the lead drivers needed. Interviews were conducted with fourteen lead drivers, six supervisors, and two regional vice presidents. The interview for the lead drivers consisted of questions such as the following:

- What types of situations call for coaching on your part?
- What keeps you from being a good coach on the job?
- How do you encourage or motivate other lead drivers? Do you use incentives or rewards? Do you try other things (compliments, personal attention)?
- What common types of performance problems do new hires have?
- What were the biggest problems you encountered as a new coach and trainer? What mistakes did you make? What lessons have you learned over time?
- Tell me about a successful coaching experience and an unsuccessful coaching experience.

Recurring trends in the interview data were noted and categorized. For example, interview questions on obstacles to coaching related to three themes: lack of time to coach, the physical environment (no privacy), and reluctance to coach peers. These three topics were covered in the coaching course.

Person characteristics, input, output, consequences, and feedback influence the motivation to learn. **Motivation to learn** is trainees' desire to learn the content of training programs.[19] Consider how your motivation to learn may be influenced by personal characteristics and the environment. You may have no problem understanding and comprehending the contents of this textbook. But your learning may be inhibited because of your attitude toward the course. That is, perhaps you do not believe that the course will be important for your career. Maybe you are taking the course only because it fits your schedule or is required in your degree program. Learning may also be inhibited by the environment. For example, maybe you want to learn, but your study environment prevents you from doing so. Every time you are prepared to read and review your notes and the textbook, your roommates could be having a party. Even if you do not join them, the music may be so loud that you cannot concentrate.

Marriott International, the hotel and restaurant chain, found that personal characteristics were having a significant influence on the success rate of the company's welfare-to-work program.[20] This program involved training welfare recipients for jobs in the company's hotels and restaurants. (These types of programs are discussed in greater detail in Chapter Ten,

"Social Responsibility: Legal Issues, Managing Diversity, and Career Challenges.") Many trainees were unable to complete the training program because of poor attendance due to unreliable child care, drug problems, or abusive partners As a result, Marriott has instituted strict standards for selecting welfare recipients for the training program. These standards include requiring trainees to have child care, transportation, and housing arrangements. Also, Marriott added an additional drug test during training.

A number of research studies have shown that motivation to learn is related to knowledge gained, behavior changes, or skill acquisition resulting from training.[21] Besides considering the factors of personal characteristics, input, output, consequences, and feedback in determining whether training is the best solution to a performance problem, managers should also take them into account when selecting which employees will attend a training program. These factors relate to the employees' motivation to learn. The following sections describe each of these factors and its relationship to performance and learning.

## *Personal Characteristics*

Personal characteristics include basic skills, cognitive ability, language skills, and other traits that employees need to perform their jobs or learn in training and development programs effectively. Personal characteristics also include employees' age or generation, which might affect how they prefer to learn. As mentioned in Chapter One, recent forecasts of workforce skill levels and survey results suggest that companies are experiencing a skills gap. That is, companies are having difficulty finding employees who have the right knowledge, skills, or abilities to fill open positions or succeed in training to prepare them for today's jobs.

## Basic Skills

**Basic skills** refer to skills that are necessary for employees to perform on the job and learn the content of training programs successfully. Basic skills include cognitive ability and reading and writing skills. For example, one assumption that your professor is making in this course is that you have the necessary reading level to comprehend this textbook and the other course materials such as overhead transparencies, videos, or readings. If you lacked the necessary reading level, you likely would not learn much about training in this course. As Chapter One discussed, recent forecasts of skill levels of the U.S. workforce indicate that managers will likely have to work with employees who lack basic skills. A literacy audit can be used to determine employees' basic skill levels. Table 3.4 shows the activities involved in conducting a literacy audit.

It is important to note that possession of a high school diploma or a college degree is no guarantee that an employee has basic skills. If participants do not have the fundamental reading, writing, and math skills to understand the training, they will not be able to learn, they will not apply their training to the job (a process known as transfer, which is discussed in Chapter Four, and the company will have wasted money on training that does not work. Trainers need to evaluate the strengths and weaknesses of trainees before designing a training program. The skill weaknesses that are identified can be used to determine prerequisites that trainees need or must acquire before entering a training program. How do trainers identify skills gaps?[22] First, trainers collect general information through position-specific training materials and job descriptions. They also observe the job to become familiar with the necessary skills. Next, trainers meet with SMEs, including employees, managers, engineers, or others who are familiar with the job. With the help of these SMEs, trainers

**TABLE 3.4**

**Steps in Performing a Literacy Audit**

Sources: U.S. Department of Education, U.S. Department of Labor, *The Bottom Line: Basic Skills in the Workplace* (Washington, DC: 1988): 14–15.

| Step 1: | Observe employees to determine the basic skills that they need to be successful in their job. Note the materials the employee uses on the job, the tasks performed, and the reading, writing, and computations completed. |
|---|---|
| Step 2: | Collect all materials that are written and read on the job and identify the computations that must be performed to determine the necessary level of basic skill proficiency. Materials include bills, memos, and forms such as inventory lists and requisition sheets. |
| Step 3: | Interview employees to determine the basic skills that they believe are needed to do the job. Consider the basic skill requirements of the job yourself. |
| Step 4: | Determine whether employees have the basic skills needed to perform the job successfully. Combine the information gathered by observing and interviewing employees and evaluating materials they use on their job. Write a description of each job in terms of the reading, writing, and computation skills needed to perform the job successfully. |
| Step 5: | Develop or buy tests that ask questions relating specifically to the employees' job. Ask employees to complete the tests. |
| Step 6: | Compare test results (from step 5) with the description of the basic skills required for the job (from step 4). If the level of the employees' reading, writing, and computation skills does not match the basic skills required by the job, then a basic skills problem exists. |

identify a list of regularly performed activities and prioritize the list according to importance. Finally, trainers identify the skills and skill levels that are needed to perform the activities or job tasks. For example, nurses must watch for changes in patient conditions, reactions, and comfort levels; they need to identify and recall details when observing patients. These activities require good observation skills, and the trainer needs to find or create a test to measure those skills. Once the skills analysis is complete, trainers conduct a basic (or pretraining) skills evaluation to identify skills gaps that need to be addressed prior to enrolling employees in a training session.

### Cognitive Ability

Research shows that cognitive ability influences learning and job performance. **Cognitive ability** includes three dimensions: verbal comprehension, quantitative ability, and reasoning ability.[23] *Verbal comprehension* refers to the person's capacity to understand and use written and spoken language. *Quantitative ability* refers to how fast and accurately a person can solve math problems. *Reasoning ability* refers to the person's capacity to invent solutions to problems. Research shows that cognitive ability is related to successful performance in all jobs.[24] The importance of cognitive ability for job success increases as the job becomes more complex.

For example, a supermarket cashier needs low to moderate levels of all three dimensions of cognitive ability to perform that job successfully. An emergency room physician needs higher levels of verbal comprehension, quantitative ability, and reasoning ability than the cashier. The supermarket cashier needs to understand the different denominations of bills and coins to give customers the correct amount of change. The cashier also needs to invent solutions to problems. (For example, how does the cashier deal with items that are not priced that the customer wants to purchase?) The cashier also needs to be able to understand and communicate with customers (verbal comprehension). The physician also needs quantitative ability, but at a higher level. For example, when dealing with an infant experiencing seizures in an emergency situation, the physician needs to be able to calculate the correct dosage of medicine (based on an adult dosage) to stop the seizures after considering the child's weight. The physician has to be able to diagnose the situation quickly and determine what actions (blood tests, x-rays, respiratory therapy, etc.) are necessary. In this case, the physician also needs to communicate clearly to the patient's parents the treatment and recovery process.

Trainees' level of cognitive ability also can influence how well they can learn in training programs.[25] Trainees with low levels of cognitive ability are more likely to fail to complete training or (at the end of training) receive lower grades on tests that measure how much they have learned.

To identify employees without the cognitive ability to succeed on the job or in training programs, companies use paper-and-pencil cognitive ability tests. For example, consider the actions taken by the Federal Aviation Administration (FAA) to identify potential air traffic controllers who will complete training successfully.[26] Air traffic control work requires quick analytical thinking and strong communications skills. These skills are emphasized and further developed in air traffic controller training. In addition to classroom training, air traffic controllers receive training through computer-based simulations of airport towers and en route centers, which direct planes between airports. The FAA estimates that in the past, it spent $10 million per year on unsuccessful trainees, which resulted in a doubling of training costs. To reduce its training costs and increase the number of new controllers who will be successful, the FAA uses an eight-hour test of cognitive skills that identifies whether applicants can think spatially, have good short- and long-term memory, and can work well under pressure—skills that are needed by successful air traffic controllers. Determining a job's cognitive ability requirement is part of the task analysis process, discussed later in this chapter.

### Reading Ability

**Readability** refers to the difficulty level of written materials.[27] Lack of the appropriate reading level can impede performance and learning in training programs. Material used in training should be evaluated to ensure that its reading level does not exceed that required by the job. A readability assessment usually involves analysis of sentence length and word difficulty.

If trainees' reading level does not match the level needed for the training materials, four options are available. First, trainers can determine whether it is feasible to lower the reading level of training materials or use video or on-the-job training, which involves learning by watching and practicing rather than by reading. Second, employees without the necessary reading level could be identified through reading tests and reassigned to other positions more congruent with their skill levels. Third, again using reading tests, trainers can identify employees who lack the necessary reading skills and provide them with remedial training. Fourth, trainers can consider whether the job can be redesigned to accommodate employees' reading levels. The fourth option is certainly the most costly and least practical. Therefore, alternative training methods need to be considered, or managers can elect a nontraining option. Nontraining options include selecting employees for jobs and training opportunities on the basis of reading, computation, writing, and other basic skill requirements.

To develop basic skills or close the skills gap, many companies are engaging in skills assessment, training, or a combination of the two. They are working to identify and close skill gaps, either alone or in partnerships with state government agencies.[28] For example, to help ensure that employees have the necessary basic skills needed to succeed in training, Georgia-Pacific, a paper manufacturer, used skills assessment in combination with a training program. For employees to be eligible to attend training programs, they had to take reading and math skills tests and score at or above a ninth-grade level. Those who scored below ninth-grade level were advised to attend basic skills training. Test results were communicated confidentially and were not part of employees' personnel files. This was done to alleviate employees' fears that their lack of literacy would cost them their jobs and to establish trust needed to motivate them to attend the basic skills training. A local community college provided the basic training at sites close to Georgia-Pacific plants to make it easy for employees to attend classes before or after work. As a result of the assessment and training, the current workforce has reached the basic skills standard established by the company. To ensure that new employees met the basic skill standards, Georgia-Pacific changed its hiring qualifications. New job applicants are required to have completed (or met the requirements for) a specific eighteen-month schedule of courses at the local community college. Delta Wire, a small manufacturing company in Mississippi, developed a basic skills training program to help employees understand how to record, interpret, and communicate information on a statistical control chart. That helped reduce product defects from 7 percent to 2 percent. McCain Foods Limited, a multinational producer of frozen foods (you may have enjoyed their French fries), was challenged to teach its leadership model to top-performing employees with managerial potential whose first language was not English. A needs assessment showed that there were gaps in these employees' ability to understand and participate in leadership development sessions. Also, these employees were having difficulties communicating in English in e-mails, reports, and meetings. As a result, McCain Foods offered English as a Second Language (ESL) training to these employees in thirty-six countries where the company had plants and operations. Employees who participated in the ESL program completed almost forty hours of training. After training, it was estimated that as a result of time savings on e-mails, presentations, and meetings due to improved English skills, the productivity gained had an estimated value of over $500,000.

The state of Illinois awarded Caterpillar Inc. a $500,000 training grant to upgrade the skills of 2,200 employees from 350 of its preferred suppliers. The training focused on skills in design, assembly, blueprint reading, metal casting and forging, statistics, and computer training. The purpose of the grant was part of a strategy to create economic growth and create jobs throughout the state. The state of Indiana is working with companies to develop training programs designed to raise the skill levels of workers. Indiana estimates that about one-third of employees have workplace literacy skills below the standards needed for employment in a knowledge-based economy. In response to a shortage of engineers with UNIX and Oracle skills needed at its operations in South Carolina, Computer Sciences Corporation (CSC) jointly sponsored an apprenticeship program in information technology with a local technical college. The program combined on-the-job learning and job-related classroom instruction. CSC was able to put more than forty people to work on client accounts as a result of the training they received as apprentices. Also, the joint effort helped to reduce the information technology skills gap in South Carolina, which is partly responsible for the state's 12 percent unemployment rate.

## Self-Efficacy

**Self-efficacy** is employees' belief that they can perform their job or learn the content of the training program successfully. The job environment can be threatening to too many employees who may not have been successful performers in the past. For example, as you will see in Chapter Ten, people who are hired through a welfare-to-work program—a program designed to help find jobs for welfare recipients—may lack self-efficacy. The training environment can also be threatening to people who have not received training or formal education for some length of time, lack education, or are not experienced in the training program's subject matter. For example, training employees to use equipment for computer-based manufacturing may represent a potential threat, especially if they are intimidated by new technology and lack confidence in their ability to master the skills needed to use a computer. Research has demonstrated that self-efficacy is related to performance in training programs.[29] Employees' self-efficacy level can be increased by

1. Letting employees know that the purpose of training is to try to improve performance rather than to identify areas in which employees are incompetent.
2. Providing as much information as possible about the training program and the purpose of training prior to the actual training.
3. Showing employees the training success of their peers who are now in similar jobs.
4. Providing employees with feedback that learning is under their control and they have the ability and the responsibility to overcome any learning difficulties they experience in the program.

## Awareness of Training Needs, Career Interests, and Goals

To be motivated to learn in training programs, employees must be aware of their skill strengths and weaknesses and of the link between the training program and improvement of their weaknesses.[30] Managers should make sure that employees understand why they have been asked to attend training programs, and they should communicate the link between training and improvement of skill weaknesses or knowledge deficiencies. This can be accomplished by sharing performance feedback with employees, holding career development discussions, or having employees complete a self-evaluation of their skill strengths and weaknesses as well as career interests and goals. For example, Reynolds and Reynolds, an Ohio-based information services company, uses surveys to obtain sales employees' opinions about what kinds of training they want.[31] The survey asks questions about what additional training the company could provide to improve sales effectiveness and productivity and how employees want to receive training. In response, 60 percent of the employees felt that they needed more training on how to create and present credible estimates of return on investments for each solution they offer customers. Time management training, working in a virtual environment, problem-solving decision making, and listening skills were personal development areas identified by the employees as needing improvement. Most employees preferred classroom training, but they also mentioned webcasts, on-the-job training, or DVDs. The internal training director shares the results with the sales leadership teams, including vice presidents and service directors. The results are being used as part of the process for setting goals for the training department.

If possible, employees need to be given a choice of what programs to attend and must understand how actual training assignments are made to maximize motivation to learn. Several studies have suggested that giving trainees a choice regarding which programs to attend and then honoring those choices maximizes motivation to learn. Giving employees choices but not necessarily honoring them can undermine motivation to learn.[32]

## Age and Generation

There is biological evidence that certain mental capacities decrease from age twenty to age seventy.[33] Short-term memory and the speed at which people process information decline as we age. However, with age comes experience, which can compensate for the loss of memory and mental quickness. Although mental quickness and memory losses diminish at a steady pace, at older ages, memory loss is much greater because mental resources are more depleted than at earlier ages.

Chapter One discussed some of the differences (and similarities) of employees from different generations. The terms *millenniums* and *Generation Y* refer to people born after 1980. They are optimistic, willing to work and learn, and technology-literate; they appreciate diversity. The term *Gen Xers* refers to people born from 1965 to 1980. Gen Xers need feedback and flexibility; they dislike close supervision. They have experienced change all their lives (in terms of parents, homes, and cities). Gen Xers value a balance between their work and nonwork lives. *Baby boomers* are people born between 1946 and 1964. They are competitive, hardworking, and concerned that all employees be fairly treated. *Traditionalists* are people born between 1925 and 1945. They are patriotic and loyal, and they have a great deal of knowledge of the history of organizations and work life. Each generation may have specific preferences for the arrangement of the learning environment, type of instruction, and learning activities.[34] For example, traditionalists prefer a stable, orderly training environment and expect the instructor to provide expertise. But Gen Xers prefer more of a self-directed training environment in which they can experiment and receive feedback. As a result, it is important to consider the learners' ages and generations as part of the person analysis. We will discuss these preferences and their implications for training design in Chapter Five.

### *Input*

Employees' perceptions of two characteristics of the work environment—situational constraints and social support—are determinants of performance and motivation to learn. **Situational constraints** include lack of proper tools and equipment, materials and supplies, budgetary support, and time. **Social support** refers to managers' and peers' willingness to provide feedback and reinforcement.[35] If employees have the knowledge, skills, attitudes, and behavior needed to perform but do not have the proper tools and equipment needed, their performance will be inadequate.

To ensure that the work environment enhances trainees' motivation to learn, managers should take the following steps:

1. Provide materials, time, job-related information, and other work aids necessary for employees to use new skills or behavior before participating in training programs.
2. Speak positively about the company's training programs to employees.
3. Let employees know they are doing a good job when they are using training content in their work.

4. Encourage work-group members to involve each other in trying to use new skills on the job by soliciting feedback and sharing training experiences and situations in which training content has been helpful.

5. Provide employees with time and opportunities to practice and apply new skills or behaviors to their work.

### Output

Poor or substandard performance can occur on the job because employees do not know at what level they are expected to perform. For example, they may not be aware of quality standards related to speed or the degree of personalization of service that is expected. Employees may have the knowledge, skill, and attitudes necessary to perform and yet fail to perform because they are not aware of the performance standards. Lack of awareness of the performance standards is a communications problem, but it is not a problem that training can "fix."

Understanding the need to perform is important for learning. Trainees need to understand what specifically they are expected to learn in the training program. To ensure that trainees master training content at the appropriate level, trainees in training programs also need to understand the level of proficiency that is expected of them. For example, for tasks, level of proficiency relates to how well employees are to perform a task. For knowledge, level of proficiency may relate to a score on a written test. The standards or the level of performance is part of the learning objectives (discussed in Chapter Four).

### Consequences

If employees do not believe that rewards or incentives for performance are adequate, they will be unlikely to meet performance standards even if they have the necessary knowledge, behavior, skill, or attitudes. Also, work-group norms may encourage employees not to meet performance standards. **Norms** refer to accepted standards of behavior for work-group members. For example, during labor contract negotiations, baggage handlers for Northwest Airlines worked slowly loading and unloading baggage from airplanes. As a result, many passenger departures and arrivals were delayed. The baggage handlers had the knowledge, skills, and behaviors necessary to unload the planes more quickly, but they worked slowly because they were trying to send a message to management that the airlines could not perform effectively if their contract demands were not met.

Consequences also affect learning in training programs. Incentive systems, such as providing gift cards redeemable for food, clothes, or movies or accumulating points that can be used toward paying for enrollment in future courses, may be useful for motivating some employees to attend and complete training courses.[36] However, one of the most powerful ways to motivate employees to attend and learn from training is to communicate the personal value of the training. For example, how will it help them improve their skills, career, or deal with problems they encounter on the job? It is important that the communication from the manager about potential benefits be realistic. Unmet expectations about training programs can hinder the motivation to learn.[37]

### Feedback

Performance problems can result when employees do not receive feedback regarding the extent to which they are meeting performance standards. Training may not be the best solution to this type of problem if employees know what they are supposed to do (output) but do not understand how close their performance is to the standard. Employees need to be given specific, detailed feedback of effective and ineffective performance. For employees to perform to standard, feedback needs to be given frequently, not just during a yearly performance evaluation.

In Chapter Four, the role of feedback in learning is discussed in detail. Keep in mind that feedback is critical for shaping trainees' behaviors and skills.

## Determining Whether Training Is the Best Solution

To determine whether training is needed to solve a performance problem, managers need to analyze characteristics of the performer, input, output, consequences, and feedback. How might this be done?[38] Managers should assess the following:

1. Is the performance problem important? Does it have the potential to cost the company a significant amount of money from lost productivity or customers?
2. Do employees know how to perform effectively? Perhaps they received little or no previous training, or the training was ineffective. (This problem is a characteristic of the person.)
3. Can employees demonstrate the correct knowledge or behavior? Perhaps employees were trained but they infrequently or never used the training content (knowledge, skills, etc.) on the job. (This is an input problem.)
4. Were performance expectations clear (input)? Were there any obstacles to performance, such as faulty tools or equipment?
5. Were positive consequences offered for good performance? Was good performance not rewarded? For example, if employees are dissatisfied with their compensation, their peers or a union may encourage them to slow down their pace of work. (This involves consequences.)
6. Did employees receive timely, relevant, accurate, constructive, and specific feedback about their performance (a feedback issue)?
7. Were other solutions—such as job redesign or transferring employees to other jobs— too expensive or unrealistic?

If employees lack the knowledge and skill to perform a job and the other factors are satisfactory, training is needed. If employees have the knowledge and skill to perform but input, output, consequences, or feedback is inadequate, training may not be the best solution. For example, if poor performance results from faulty equipment, training cannot solve this problem, but repairing the equipment will. If poor performance results from lack of feedback, then employees may not need training, but their managers may need training on how to give performance feedback.

It is also important to consider the relationships among a critical job issue (a problem or opportunity that is critical to the success of a job within the company), a critical process issue (a problem or opportunity that is critical to the success of a business process), and a critical business issue (a problem or opportunity that is critical to the success of the company).[39] If the critical job issue, process issue, and business issue are related, training should be a top priority because it will have a greater effect on business outcomes and results and will likely receive greater management support. Table 3.5 shows the relationships among the critical job, process, and business issues for a sales representative. This analysis resulted from a request from a top manager who suggested that sales representatives needed more training because incomplete sales orders were being submitted to production.

Consider how a global retailer of rugged, athletic, casual, and stylish clothes for kids and young adults identifies whether a performance need should be addressed by training or other solutions. Figure 3.4 shows how this retailer determines the type of need, who is

**TABLE 3.5    Example of the Relationships Among a Critical Job Issue, a Critical Process Issue, and a Critical Business Issue**

| Critical Job Issue | Critical Process Issue | Critical Business Issue |
|---|---|---|
| *Desired Results*<br>No incomplete order forms<br>100% accurate orders | *Desired Results*<br>Order cycle time of three days | *Desired Results*<br>Market share of 60% |
| *Current Results*<br>10% incomplete order forms<br>83% accurate orders | *Current Results*<br>Order cycle time of thirty days | *Current Results*<br>Market Share of 48% |

Source: Based on G. A. Rummler and K. Morrill, "The Results Chain," *T+D* (February 2005): 27–35.

**FIGURE 3.4**
**Identifying How to Solve Performance Issues**

# 1. WHAT?
DETERMINE THE TYPE OF NEED:

| PROBLEM | IMPROVEMENT | FUTURE PLANNING |

# 2. WHO?
DETERMINE THE LEVEL OF THE ORGANIZATION IMPACTED:

| ENTIRE ORGANIZATION | DIVISION | DEPARTMENT | INDIVIDUAL | JOB |

# 3. HOW?
DETERMINE THE CORRECTIVE STRATEGY:

IS THERE A SYSTEMS PROBLEM?

ARE THERE PROPER SYSTEMS AND RESOURCES AVAILABLE FOR PERFORMANCE TO IMPROVE?

ARE WE RECRUITING THE RIGHT PEOPLE?

ARE OUR RECRUITING EFFORTS TARGETED TO ATTRACT EMPLOYEES WHO START OUT WITH THE BASIC COMPETENCIES TO DO THE JOB?

IS COACHING NEEDED?

DOES INFORMAL TRAINING OR PASSING OF INFORMATION EXIST? IS IT SUPPORTED? ARE THERE RESOURCES FOR ASSOCIATES BUILT INTO THEIR ROLES?

IS THERE AN ORGANIZATIONAL DEVELOPMENT PROBLEM?

ARE THERE POLICY ROADBLOCKS TO PERFORMANCE? DO INCENTIVES MATCH PERFORMANCE?

IS PLACEMENT AN ISSUE?

IS THE WRONG ASSOCIATE IN THE JOB? HAVE YOU EXPLORED THE BEHAVIORAL TENDENCIES OF ASSOCIATES? DO THEY MATCH THEIR JOB REQUIREMENTS?

IS THERE A TRAINING NEED?

DO ASSOCIATES HAVE THE POTENTIAL TO PERFORM JOB FUNCTIONS? IS THERE A KNOWLEDGE GAP THAT NEEDS TO BE FILLED? ARE MANAGERS AND SUPERVISORS CREATING A SUPPORTIVE ENVIRONMENT THAT ENCOURAGES PERFORMANCE?

affected, and the corrective strategy. As you can see from Figure 3.4, training and development is only one of several possible solutions and addresses issues related specifically to knowledge gaps, sharing knowledge and skills, informal learning, and manager and supervisor support.

## Task Analysis

Task analysis results in a description of work activities, including tasks performed by the employee and the knowledge, skills, and abilities required to complete the tasks. A **job** is a specific position requiring the completion of certain tasks. (The job exemplified in Table 3.6 is that of an electrical maintenance worker.) A **task** is the employee's work activity in a specific job. Table 3.6 shows several tasks for the electrical maintenance worker job. These tasks include replacing lightbulbs, electrical outlets, and light switches. To complete tasks, employees must have specific levels of knowledge, skill, ability, and other considerations (KSAOs). **Knowledge** includes facts or procedures (e.g., the chemical properties of gold). **Skill** indicates competency in performing a task (e.g., negotiation skill, a skill in getting another person to agree to take a certain course of action). **Ability** includes the physical and mental capacities to perform a task (e.g., spatial ability, the ability to see the relationship between objects in physical space). **Other** refers to the conditions under which tasks are performed. These conditions include identifying the equipment and environment that the employee works in (e.g., the need to wear an oxygen mask, work in extremely hot conditions), time constraints for a task (e.g., deadlines), safety considerations, or performance standards.

Task analysis should be undertaken only after the organizational analysis has determined that the company wants to devote time and money for training. Why? Task analysis is a time-consuming, tedious process that involves a large time commitment to gather and summarize data from many different persons in the company, including managers, job incumbents, and trainers.

**TABLE 3.6**  Sample Items from Task Analysis Questionnaires for the Electrical Maintenance Job

| | | Job: Electrical Maintenance Worker | | |
|---|---|---|---|---|
| | | Task Performance Ratings | | |
| Task # | Task Description | Frequency of Performance | Importance | Difficulty |
| 199–264 | Replace a light bulb | 0 1 2 3 4 5 | 0 1 2 3 4 5 | 0 1 2 3 4 5 |
| 199–265 | Replace an electrical outlet | 0 1 2 3 4 5 | 0 1 2 3 4 5 | 0 1 2 3 4 5 |
| 199–266 | Install a light fixture | 0 1 2 3 4 5 | 0 1 2 3 4 5 | 0 1 2 3 4 5 |
| 199–267 | Replace a light switch | 0 1 2 3 4 5 | 0 1 2 3 4 5 | 0 1 2 3 4 5 |
| 199–268 | Install a new circuit breaker | 0 1 2 3 4 5 | 0 1 2 3 4 5 | 0 1 2 3 4 5 |
| | | Frequency of Performance | Importance | Difficulty |
| | | 0 = Never | 1 = Negligible | 1 = Easiest |
| | | 5 = Often | 5 = Extremely high | 5 = Most difficult |

Source: E. F. Holton III and C. Bailey, "Top to Bottom Curriculum Redesign," *Training and Development* (March 1995): 40–44.

### Steps in a Task Analysis

A task analysis involves four steps:[40]

1. Select the job or jobs to be analyzed.
2. Develop a preliminary list of tasks performed on the job by (1) interviewing and observing expert employees and their managers and (2) talking with others who have performed a task analysis.
3. Validate or confirm the preliminary list of tasks. This step involves having a group of SMEs (job incumbents, managers, etc.) answer in a meeting or on a written survey several questions regarding the tasks. The types of questions that may be asked include the following: How frequently is the task performed? How much time is spent performing each task? How important or critical is the task for successful performance of the job? How difficult is the task to learn? Is performance of the task expected of entry-level employees?

   Table 3.7 presents a sample task analysis questionnaire. This information is used to determine which tasks will be focused on in the training program. The person or committee conducting the needs assessment must decide the level of ratings across dimensions that will determine that a task should be included in the training program. Tasks that are important, frequently performed, and of moderate-to-high level of difficulty are tasks for which training should be provided. Tasks that are not important and are infrequently performed should not involve training. It is difficult for managers and trainers to decide if tasks that are important but are performed infrequently and require minimal difficulty should be included in training. Managers and trainers must determine whether or not important tasks—regardless of how frequently they are performed or their level of difficulty—will be included in training.

4. Once the tasks have been identified, it is important to identify the knowledge, skills, or abilities necessary to perform each task successfully. This information can be collected through interviews and questionnaires. Recall this chapter's discussion of how ability influences learning. Information concerning basic skill and cognitive ability requirements is critical for determining if certain levels of knowledge, skills, and abilities will be prerequisites for entrance to the training program (or job) or if supplementary training in underlying skills is needed. For training purposes, information concerning how difficult it is to learn the knowledge, skill, or ability is important—as is whether the knowledge, skill, or ability is expected to be acquired by the employee before taking the job.[41]

Table 3.8 summarizes key points to remember regarding task analysis.

### Example of a Task Analysis

Each of the four steps of a task analysis can be seen in this example from a utility company. Trainers were given the job of developing a training system in six months.[42] The purpose of the program was to identify tasks and KSAOs that would serve as the basis for training program objectives and lesson plans.

The first phase of the project involved identifying potential tasks for each job in the utility's electrical maintenance area. Procedures, equipment lists, and information provided by SMEs were used to generate the tasks. SMEs included managers, instructors, and senior technicians. The tasks were incorporated into a questionnaire administered to all technicians in the electrical maintenance department. The questionnaire included 550 tasks. Table 3.6 shows sample items from the questionnaire for the electrical maintenance job. Technicians

**TABLE 3.7**  **Sample Task Statement Questionnaire**

| Name | Date |
|---|---|

Position

Please rate each of the task statements according to three factors: (1) the *importance* of the task for effective performance, (2) how *frequently* the task is performed, and (3) the degree of *difficulty* required to become effective in the task. Use the following scales in making your ratings.

*Importance*

4 = Task is critical for effective performance.
3 = Task is important but not critical for effective performance.
2 = Task is of some importance for effective performance.
1 = Task is of no importance for effective performance.
0 = Task is not performed.

*Frequency*

4 = Task is performed once a day.
3 = Task is performed once a week.
2 = Task is performed once every few months.
1 = Task is performed once or twice a year.
0 = Task is not performed.

*Difficulty*

4 = Effective performance of the task requires extensive prior experience and/or training (12–18 months or longer).
3 = Effective performance of the task requires minimal prior experience and training (6–12 months).
2 = Effective performance of the task requires a brief period of prior training and experience (1–6 months).
1 = Effective performance of the task does not require specific prior training and/or experience.
0 = This task is not performed.

| Task | Importance | Frequency | Difficulty |
|---|---|---|---|
| 1. Ensuring maintenance on equipment, tools, and safety controls | | | |
| 2. Monitoring employee performance | | | |
| 3. Scheduling employees | | | |
| 4. Using statistical software on the computer | | | |
| 5. Monitoring changes made in processes using statistical methods | | | |

**TABLE 3.8**
**Key Points to Remember When Conducting a Task Analysis**

Source: Adapted from A. P. Carnevale, L. J. Gainer, and A. S. Meltzer, *Workplace Basics Training Manual* (San Francisco: Jossey-Bass, 1990).

A task analysis should identify both what employees are actually doing and what they should be doing on the job.
Task analysis begins by breaking the job into duties and tasks.
Use more than two methods for collecting task information to increase the validity of the analysis.
For task analysis to be useful, information needs to be collected from SMEs, including job incumbents, managers, and employees familiar with the job.
In deciding how to evaluate tasks, the focus should be on tasks necessary to accomplish the company's goals and objectives. These may not be the tasks that are the most difficult or take the most time.

were asked to rate each task on importance, difficulty, and frequency of performance. The rating scale for frequency included zero. A zero rating indicated that the technician rating the task had never performed the task. Technicians who rated a task zero were asked not to evaluate the task's difficulty and importance.

Customized software was used to analyze the ratings collected via the questionnaire. The primary requirement used to determine whether a task required training was its importance rating. A task rated "very important" was identified as one requiring training regardless of its frequency or difficulty. If a task was rated moderately important but difficult, it also was designated for training. Tasks rated as unimportant, not difficult, or done infrequently were not designated for training.

The list of tasks designated for training was reviewed by the SMEs to determine if it accurately described job tasks. The result was a list of 487 tasks. For each of the 487 tasks, two SMEs identified the necessary KSAOs required for performance. This included information on working conditions, cues that initiate the task's start and end, performance standards, safety considerations, and necessary tools and equipment. All data were reviewed by plant technicians and members of the training department. More than 14,000 KSAOs were grouped into common areas and assigned an identification code. These groups were then combined into clusters that represented qualification areas. That is, the task clusters were related to linked tasks that the employees must be certified in to perform the job. The clusters were used to identify training lesson plans and course objectives. Trainers also reviewed the clusters to identify prerequisite skills for each cluster.

# COMPETENCY MODELS

In today's global and competitive business environment, many companies are finding that it is difficult to determine whether employees have the capabilities needed for success. The necessary capabilities may vary from one business unit to another, and even across roles, within a business unit. As a result, many companies are using competency models to help them identify the knowledge, skills, and personal characteristics (attitudes, personality) needed for successful performance in a job. Competency models are also useful for ensuring that training and development systems are contributing to the development of such knowledge, skills, and personal characteristics.

Traditionally, needs assessment has involved identifying knowledge, skills, abilities, and tasks. However, a current trend in training is for needs assessment to focus on competencies, especially for managerial positions. **Competencies** are sets of skills, knowledge, abilities, and personal characteristics that enable employees to perform their jobs successfully.[43]

A **competency model** identifies the competencies necessary for each job. Competency models provide descriptions of competencies that are common for an entire occupation, organization, job family, or specific job. Competency models can be used for performance management. However, one of the strengths of competency models is that they are useful for a variety of human resource (HR) practices, including recruiting, selection, training, and development. Competency models can be used to help identify the best employees to fill open positions and to serve as the foundation for development plans that allow employees and their manager to target specific strengths and development areas. The competencies included in competency models vary according to the company's business strategy and goals. They can include sales, leadership, interpersonal, technical, and other types

**TABLE 3.9  Competencies from a Competency Model**

| Technical Cluster | Proficiency Ratings |
|---|---|
| **Systems Architecture**<br>Ability to design complex software applications, establish protocols, and create prototypes. | **0**—Is not able to perform basic tasks.<br>**1**—Understands basic principles; can perform tasks with assistance or direction.<br>**2**—Performs routine tasks with reliable results; works with minimal supervision.<br>**3**—Performs complex and multiple tasks; can coach or teach others.<br>**4**—Considered an expert in this task; can describe, teach, and lead others. |
| **Data Migration**<br>Ability to establish the necessary platform requirements to efficiently and completely coordinate data transfer. | **0**—Is not able to perform basic tasks.<br>**1**—Understands basic principles; can perform tasks with assistance or direction.<br>**2**—Performs routine tasks with reliable results; works with minimal supervision.<br>**3**—Performs complex and multiple tasks; can coach or teach others.<br>**4**—Considered an expert in this task; can describe, teach, and lead others. |
| **Documentation**<br>Ability to prepare comprehensive and complete documentation including specifications, flow diagrams, process control, and budgets. | **0**—Is not able to perform basic tasks.<br>**1**—Understands basic principles; can perform tasks with assistance or direction.<br>**2**—Performs routine tasks with reliable results; works with minimal supervision.<br>**3**—Performs complex and multiple tasks; can coach or teach others.<br>**4**—Considered an expert in this task; can describe, teach, and lead others. |

Source: R. J. Mirabile, "Everything You Wanted to Know About Competency Modeling," *Training and Development* (August 1997): 73–77.

of competencies. Competency models typically included the name of each competency, the behaviors that represent proficiency in the competency, and levels that include descriptions representing demonstrated levels of mastery or proficiency. Table 3.9 shows the technical cluster of competencies from a competency model for a systems engineer. The left side of the table lists technical competencies within the technical cluster (such as systems architecture, data migration, and documentation). The right side shows behaviors that might be used to determine a systems engineer's level of proficiency for each competency.

One way to understand competency models is to compare them to job analysis. As you may recall from other classes or experiences, **job analysis** refers to the process of developing a description of the job (tasks, duties, and responsibilities) and the specifications (knowledge, skills, and abilities) that an employee must have to perform it. How does job analysis compare to competency models? Job analysis is more work- and task-focused (what is accomplished), whereas competency modeling is worker-focused (how objectives are met or how work is accomplished). Focusing on "how" versus "what" provides valuable information for training and development. A recent study asked competency modeling experts (consultants, HR practitioners, academics, and industrial psychologists) to compare and contrast competency modeling and job analysis.[44] The study found several differences between job analysis and competency models. Competency models are more likely to link competencies and the company's business goals. Competency models provide descriptions of competencies that are common for an entire occupational group, level of jobs, or an entire organization. Job analysis describes what is different across jobs, occupational groups, or organization levels. Finally, job analysis generates specific knowledge, skills, and abilities for particular jobs. It is used to generate specific requirements to be used for employee selection. The competencies generated by competency modeling are more general and believed to have greater application to a wider variety of purposes, including selection, training, employee development, and performance management.

Another way to think about competency models is by considering performance management.[45] Unfortunately, many performance management systems suffer from a lack of agreement on what outcomes should be used to evaluate performance. Manager-employee discussions about performance deficiencies tend to lack specificity. By identifying the areas of personal capability that enable employees to perform their jobs successfully, competency models ensure an evaluation of what gets done and how it gets done. Performance feedback can be directed toward specific concrete examples of behavior; and knowledge, skills, ability, and other characteristics that are necessary for success are clearly described.

How are competencies identified and competency models developed? Figure 3.5 shows the process used to develop a competency model. First, the business strategy is identified. The implications of business strategy for training were discussed in Chapter Two. The business strategy helps identify what types of competencies are needed to ensure that business goals are met and the company's strategy is supported. Changes in the business strategy might cause new competencies to be needed or old competencies to be altered. Second, the job or position to be analyzed is identified. Third, effective and ineffective performers are identified. Fourth, the competencies responsible for effective and ineffective performance are identified. There are several approaches for identifying competencies. These include analyzing one or several "star" performers, surveying persons who are familiar with the job (SMEs), and investigating benchmark data of good performers in other companies.[46] Fifth, the model is validated. That is, a determination is made as to whether the competencies included in the model truly are related to effective performance. In the example of the technical competencies for the systems engineer shown in Table 3.9, it is important to verify that (1) these three competencies are necessary for job success, and (2) the level of proficiency of the competency is appropriate.

Following the development process outlined in Figure 3.5 will ensure that competencies and competency models are valid. However, trainers, employees, managers, and other experts should be trained (especially inexperienced raters) in how to determine accurate competency ratings. Training should ensure that raters understand each competency and the differences between them and can distinguish between low, medium, and high levels of proficiency.[47]

**FIGURE 3.5**   **The Process Used in Developing a Competency Model**

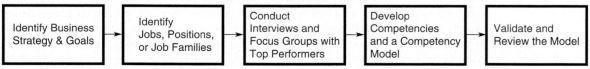

Competency models are useful for training and development in several ways:[48]

- They identify behaviors needed for effective job performance. These models ensure that feedback given to employees as part of a development program (such as 360-degree feedback) relate specifically to individual and organizational success.
- They provide a tool for determining what skills are necessary to meet today's needs, as well as the company's future skill needs. They can be used to evaluate the relationship between the company's current training programs and present needs. That is, they help align training and development activities with the company's business goals. They can be used to evaluate how well the offerings relate to anticipated future skill needs.
- They help to determine what skills are needed at different career points.
- They provide a framework for ongoing coaching and feedback to develop employees for current and future roles. By comparing their current personal competencies to those required for a job, employees can identify competencies that need development and choose actions to develop those competencies. These actions may include courses, job experiences, and other types of development. (Development methods are detailed in Chapter Nine, "Employee Development and Career Management.")
- They create a "road map" for identifying and developing employees who may be candidates for managerial positions (succession planning).
- They provide a common set of criteria that are used for identifying appropriate development training and learning activities for employees, as well as for evaluating and rewarding them. This helps integrate and align the company's HR systems and practices.

For example, at American Express, competency models are used to help managers lead their own teams by providing a framework that their employees can use to capitalize on strengths and improve weaknesses.[49] At the company level, competencies are used to determine the talent level of the entire company, including capabilities, strengths, and opportunities. This information is provided to managers who use the data to identify key needs and plan actions to ensure that current and future competencies are developed in employees.

Table 3.10 shows the competency model that Luxottica Retail, known for premium, luxury, and sports eyewear sold through LensCrafters, Sunglass Hut, and Pearle Vision, developed for its associates in field and store positions.[50] The competency model includes leadership and managerial, functional, and foundational competencies. The goal was to define and identify competencies that managers could use for hiring, performance management, and training. Also, competencies would help associates identify and develop the skills they needed to apply for different jobs. To use competency models effectively for performance evaluation, they must be up to date, drive business performance, job-related (valid), relevant (or customized) for all of the company's business units, and provide sufficient detail to make an accurate assessment of employees performance. At Luxottica Retail, developing competencies started with meeting with business leaders to understand their current and future business strategies. Business drivers were identified and questionnaires, focus groups, and meetings with managers and associates were used to identify important competencies and examples of behaviors related to each. Competencies across business units and brands are reviewed every four or five years, or whenever a major change in jobs or business strategy occurs to ensure they are relevant. Also, the weighting given to each set of competencies in the performance evaluation is reviewed to ensure

**TABLE 3.10**
Luxottica
Retail's
Competency
Model

Source: From
C. Spicer, "Building a
Competency Model,"
*HR Magazine,*
April 2009, 34–36.

**Leadership and Managerial**
Leadership
Coach and Develop Others
Motivate Others
Foster Teamwork
Think Strategically
**Functional**
Global Perspective
Financial Acumen
Business Key Performance Indicators
**Foundational**
Critical Thinking
Foster Open Communications
Build Relationships and Interpersonal Skills
Develop and Manage Oneself
Adaptability and Flexibility
Customer Focus
Act with Integrity
Diversity and Multiculturalism
Drive and Commitment

that they are appropriate (e.g., what weights should be given to the functional skills?). Depending on their relevance for a specific job, various combinations of these competencies are used for evaluating associates' performance. Associates are rated on a 1–5 scale for each competency, with 5 meaning "far exceeds expectations." HR, training and development and operations teams worked together to define the levels of each competency. That is, what does it mean and what does the competency look like when an employee is rated "meets expectations" versus "below expectations"? This was necessary to ensure that managers are using a similar frame of reference when they evaluate associates using the competencies.

# SCOPE OF NEEDS ASSESSMENT

Up to this point, the chapter has discussed the various aspects of needs assessment, including organizational, person, and task analyses. This involves interviews, observations, and potentially even surveying employees. You might be saying to yourself, "This sounds good, but it appears to be a very elaborate process that takes time. What happens if I don't have time to conduct a thorough needs assessment? Should I abandon the process?"

Needs assessment is often skipped for several reasons based on assumptions such as training is always the issue or is mandated; it's too costly, takes too long, and is too complex; and managers will not cooperate. Despite the constraints to conducting a needs assessment, it is necessary to determine if a problem or pressure point exists and to identify the best solution, which could be training.

However, even if managers demand a training course right now, needs assessment should still be conducted. There are several ways to conduct a rapid needs assessment. A **rapid needs assessment** refers to a needs assessment that is done quickly and accurately, but without sacrificing the quality of the process or the outcomes.[51] The key to conducting a rapid needs assessment is choosing the needs assessment methods that will provide the results you can have the greatest confidences in while using the fewest resources (time, money, SMEs). There are several ways to conduct a rapid needs assessment. First, the scope of needs assessment depends on the size of the potential pressure point. If the pressure point seems to be local and has a potentially small impact on the business, then the information-gathering part of needs assessment could consist of only a few interviews with managers or job incumbents. If the pressure point will have a large impact on the business, then more information gathering should be conducted. If, after interviewing SMEs and job incumbents, you can tell that you are not learning anything new about the job, then interviewing could be stopped. Second, consider using already available data collected for other purposes. For example, error data, sales data, customer complaints, and exit interviews might provide valuable clues as to the source of performance and survey problems. The web may be a useful source for quickly conducting interviews and surveys with SMEs in different locations. Finally, if you are attuned to the business problems, technological developments, and other issues facing the organization, you will be able to anticipate training needs. For example, if the company is opening sales offices in an international location and introducing new technology in the manufacturing plants, cross-cultural training and training designed to help employees use the new technology undoubtedly will be needed. Be prepared by understanding the business.

## Needs Assessment in Practice

The manufacturing operations of the Owens-Corning insulation business were interested in increasing the productivity, product quality, and safety performance of the business. This was consistent with the companywide strategy of trying to increase shareholder value, ensure individual dignity, and deliver customer service. To help meet the strategic goals, plant-based specialists in human resources, training, organization development, and project management created a group to direct training activities. The first priority of this group was to establish supervisor training. At that time, there was no formal training for manufacturing supervisors. Therefore, the group worked on developing such a program. Interviews with plant HR managers and trainers suggested that creation of a generic training program would not be effective. As a result, the group developed a survey that was administered to employees in all the plants. The survey asked specific questions about the supervisors' skill needs—for example, "The supervisor actively listens to individuals or teams to check for understanding" and "The supervisor meets all deadlines on projects, action items, and special requests." The data collected from the survey indicated that supervisors' greatest skill deficiencies included two-way communications, active listening skills, setting performance expectations, providing feedback, handling conflict, and time management. The design of each plant supervisor training program was based on these needs, taking into account the uniqueness of the facility and its culture.

This example illustrates several aspects of the needs assessment process. First, training was viewed as critical for helping the company meet its strategic objectives. As a result, resources and time were allocated for needs assessment and training. Second, the person analysis consisted of a survey of supervisor skills. This information was used to identify overall skill deficiencies across the plants. Third, training programs were developed to improve the identified skill deficiencies through methods that were congruent with the plant environment and culture. For example, one plant used a three-day skills workshop, a one-day quarterly leadership skills conference (which updates and refreshes supervisors' skills), and an informal, once-per-month leadership discussion.

## Summary

The first step in a successful training effort is to determine that a training need exists through a process known as needs assessment. Needs assessment involves three steps: organizational analysis, person analysis, and task analysis. Various methods—including observation, interviews, and surveys or questionnaires—are used to conduct a needs assessment. Each has advantages and disadvantages. Organizational analysis involves determining (1) the extent to which training is congruent with the company's business strategy and resources and (2) if peers and managers are likely to provide the support needed for trainees to use training content in the work setting.

Person analysis focuses on identifying whether there is evidence that training is the solution, who needs training, and whether employees have the prerequisite skills, attitudes, and beliefs needed to ensure that they master the content of training programs. Because performance problems are one of the major reasons that companies consider training for employees, it is important to investigate how personal characteristics, input, output, consequences, and feedback relate to performance and learning. Managers and trainers need to be concerned about employees' basic skill levels, attitudes, age and generation, and the work environment in determining if performance problems can be solved using training and how training should be designed.

Training is likely the best solution to a performance problem if employees don't know how to perform. If employees have not received feedback about their performance, if they lack the equipment needed to perform the job, if the consequences for good performance are negative, or if they are unaware of an expected standard for performance, then training is not likely to be the best solution.

To maximize employees' motivation to learn in training programs, managers and trainers need to understand these factors prior to sending employees to training. For example, lack of basic skills or reading skills can inhibit both job performance and learning.

A task analysis involves identifying the task and the training that employees will require in terms of knowledge, skills, and abilities. Competency modeling is a new approach to needs assessment that focuses on identifying personal capabilities, including knowledge, skills, attitudes, values, and personal characteristics.

## Key Terms

needs assessment, *114*
organizational
analysis, *114*
person analysis, *114*
task analysis, *114*
subject-matter experts
(SMEs), *117*
job incumbent, *117*
focus groups, *120*

crowdsourcing, *120*
benchmarking, *120*
readiness for training, *123*
person characteristics, *124*
input, *124*
output, *124*
consequences, *125*
feedback, *125*
motivation to learn, *125*

basic skills, *126*
cognitive ability, *127*
readability, *128*
self-efficacy, *130*
situational constraints, *131*
social support, *131*
norms, *132*
job, *135*
task, *135*

knowledge, *135*              other, *135*                    job analysis, *139*
skill, *135*                  competencies, *138*            rapid needs
ability, *135*                competency model, *138*        assessment, *142*

## Discussion Questions

1. Which of the factors that influence performance and learning do you think is most important? Which is least important?
2. If you had to conduct a needs assessment for a new job at a new plant, describe the method you would use.
3. If you were going to use online technology to identify training needs for customer service representatives for a web-based clothing company, what steps would you take to ensure that the technology was not threatening to employees?
4. Needs assessment involves organization, person, and task analyses. Which one of these analyses do you believe is most important? Which is least important? Why?
5. Why should upper-level managers be included in the needs assessment process?
6. Explain how you would determine if employees had the reading level necessary to succeed in a training program. How would you determine if employees had the necessary computer skills needed to use a web-based training program?
7. What conditions would suggest that a company should buy a training program from an outside vendor? Which would suggest that the firm should develop the program itself?
8. Assume that you have to prepare older employees with little computer experience to attend a training course on how to use the Internet. How will you ensure that they have high levels of readiness for training? How will you determine their readiness for training?
9. Review the accompanying sample tasks and task ratings for the electronic technician's job. What tasks do you believe should be emphasized in the training program? Why?
10. Explain the process you would use to determine the cause of a performance problem. Draw a picture showing the process.

| Task | Importance | Frequency | Learning Difficulty |
|------|------------|-----------|---------------------|
| 1. Replaces components | 1 | 2 | 1 |
| 2. Repairs equipment | 2 | 5 | 5 |
| 3. Interprets instrument readings | 1 | 4 | 5 |
| 4. Uses small tools | 2 | 5 | 1 |

Explanation of ratings:
Frequency: 1 = very infrequently to 5 = very frequently
Importance: 1 = very important to 5 = very unimportant
Learning difficulty: 1 = easy to 5 = very difficult

11. Why would we consider age and generational differences as part of needs assessment? Is this important? Explain. Discuss the types of evidence that you would look for to determine whether a needs analysis has been conducted improperly.
12. How is competency modeling similar to traditional needs assessment? How does it differ?
13. What is a rapid needs assessment? How would you conduct a rapid needs assessment so that it is valuable and accurately identifies training needs?

## Application Assignments

1. Develop a competency model for a job held by a friend, spouse, or roommate (someone other than yourself). Use the process discussed in this chapter to develop your model. Note the most difficult part of developing the model. How could the model be used?

2. The Department of Social Services represents a large portion of your county's budget and total number of employees. The job of eligibility technician is responsible for all client contact, policy interpretation, and financial decisions related to several forms of public aid (e.g., food stamps, aid to families with dependent children). Eligibility technicians must read a large number of memos and announcements of new and revised policies and procedures. Eligibility technicians were complaining that they had difficulty reading and responding to this correspondence. The county decided to send the employees to a speed reading program costing $250 per person. The county has 200 eligibility technicians.

   Preliminary evaluation of the speed reading program was that trainees liked it. Two months after the training was conducted, the technicians told their managers that they were not using the speed reading course in their jobs, but were using it in leisure reading at home. When their managers asked why they weren't using it on the job, the typical response was, "I never read those memos and policy announcements anyway."

   a. Evaluate the needs assessment process used to determine that speed reading was necessary. What was good about it? Where was it faulty?

   b. How would you have conducted the needs assessment? Be realistic.

3. Consider the interview questions for the lead drivers that are shown on page 000. Write questions that could be used to interview the six lead driver supervisors and the two regional vice presidents. How do these questions differ from those for the lead drivers? How are they similar?

4. Several companies are known for linking their values and HR practices in ways that have led to business success as well as employee satisfaction. These companies include Southwest Airlines (*www.iflyswa.com*), Cisco Systems (*www.cisco.com*), SAS Institute (*www.sas.com*), Men's Wearhouse (*www.menswearhouse.com*), Intel (*www.intel.com*), Steelcase (*www.steelcase.com*), Whole Foods (*www.wholefoods.com*), and TELUS (*http://abouttelus.com*). Choose one of these companies' websites and perform an organizational needs analysis. Read about the company's values and vision; look for statements about the importance of training and personal development. Is training important in the company? Why or why not? Provide supporting evidence from the website.

5. Go to *www.careeronestop.org/CompetencyModel*, the website for CareerOneStop, sponsored by the U.S. Department of Labor, Employment and Training Administration to help job seekers, students, businesses, and career professionals. Choose and review one of the industry competency models. How might these competency models be useful for training and development for companies within the industry you selected? For their employees? For individuals such as students or the unemployed interested in working in the industry?

## Case:

# Determining Training Needs at Summit Credit Union

Summit Credit Union, located in Madison, Wisconsin, is a small company with 366 employees. A merger in 2008 doubled the size of the company and made it necessary to build a new corporate culture. Summit's mission is to improve credit members' financial lives to help them achieve their dreams. Summit has invested in creating a world-class learning function, which includes a team of seven professionals who are able to design and deliver instructor-led training as well as e-learning. Summit has shifted away from generic off-the-shelf training to develop online and face-to-face programs customized to employee needs and the company's goals and initiatives. For example, the learning function is expected to play a key role in dealing with business issues such as efficiency, loan growth, and increased sales. All learning staff members are expected to contribute to new company initiatives, such as new products and services, systems, or regulations. Summit has recently identified a problem with its new lenders. They were starting to perform their jobs without the necessary skills, information, and knowledge that they needed. One potential reason for this is how the lending training curriculum is organized. New lenders attend a course on different types of loans and the lending system, start their jobs, and then later return for a course on lending guidelines, underwriting, and sales skills.

*How would you conduct a needs assessment to determine if new lenders are starting their jobs without the necessary knowledge and skills to perform well, and if the organization of the training curriculum (or another training issue) is responsible for this problem? Who would be involved in the needs assessment?*

Source: Based on J. Salopek, "Investing in learning," *T+D* (October 2011): 56–58.

## Endnotes

1. I. L. Goldstein, E. P. Braverman, and H. Goldstein, "Needs Assessment," In *Developing Human Resources*, ed. K. N. Wexley (Washington, DC: Bureau of National Affairs, 1991): 5–35 to 5–75.
2. K. Tyler, "The strongest link,"*HR Magazine* (January 2011): 51–53; S. Villachica, D. Stepich, and S. Rist, "Surviving troubled times: Five best practices for training solutions," *Performance Improvement*, 50 (March 2011): 9–15.
3. A. Khanzode, C. Williams, and T. Van Derlinden, "Life on the cutting edge of learning," *T+D* (October 2009): 53–54.
4. R. Nichols, D. Segal, and D. Kessler, "Linking training to care," *T+D* (October 2009): 64–66.
5. J. Wircenski, R. Sullivan, and P. Moore, "Assessing Training Needs at Texas Instruments," *Training and Development* (April 1989): 61–63.
6. L. Overmyer-Day and G. Benson, "Training Success Stories," *Training and Development* (June 1996): 24–29.
7. B. Durman, S. Chyung, S. Villachica and D. Winiecki, "Root causes of errant ordered radiology exams: Results of a needs assessment,"*Performance Improvement*, 50 (January 2011): 17–24.
8. M. Casey and D. Doverspike, "Training needs analysis and evaluation for new technologies through the use of problem-based inquiry," *Performance Improvement Quarterly* 18(1) (2005): 110–24.
9. K. Ellis, "The right track," *training* (September 2004): 40–45.
10. K. Mahler, "Big Employer is watching," *The Wall Street Journal* (November 4, 2003): B1 and B6.
11. G. Siekierka, H. Huntley, and M. Johnson, "Learning is center stage at CSC," *T+D* (October 2009): 48–50.
12. P. Schamore, "Spirited learning," *T+D* (October 2009): 56–58.

13. J. Salopek, "From learning department to learning partner," *T+D* (October 2010): 48–50.

14. L. E. Day, "Benchmarking training," *Training and Development* (November 1995): 27–30.

15. J. Rouiller and I. Goldstein, "The relationship between organizational transfer climate and positive transfer of training," *Human Resource Development Quarterly* 4 (1993): 377–90. R. Noe and J. Colquitt, "Planning for Training Impact." In *Creating, Implementing, and Managing Effective Training and Development*, ed. K. Kraiger (San Francisco: Jossey-Bass, 2002): 53–79.

16. D. Zielinski, "Have you shared a bright idea today?" *training* (July 2000): 65–68.

17. G. Rummler, "In search of the Holy Performance Grail," *Training and Development* (April 1996): 26–31; D. G. Langdon, "Selecting interventions," *Performance Improvement* 36 (1997): 11–15.

18. K. Gupta, *A Practical Guide to Needs Assessment* (San Francisco: Jossey-Bass/Pfeiffer, 1999).

19. R. A. Noe, "Trainee attributes and attitudes: Neglected influences on training effectiveness," *Academy of Management Review* 11 (1986): 736–49. R. Noe and J. Colquitt, "Planning for Training Impact." In *Creating, Implementing, and Managing Effective Training and Development*, ed. K. Kraiger (San Francisco: Jossey-Bass, 2002): 53–79.

20. D. Milibank, "Marriott tightens job program screening," *The Wall Street Journal* (July 15, 1997): A1, A12.

21. T. T. Baldwin, R. T. Magjuka, and B. T. Loher, "The perils of participation: Effects of choice on trainee motivation and learning," *Personnel Psychology* 44 (1991): 51–66; S. I. Tannenbaum, J. E. Mathieu, E. Salas, and J. A. Cannon-Bowers, "Meeting trainees' expectations: The influence of training fulfillment on the development of commitment, self-efficacy, and motivation," *Journal of Applied Psychology* 76 (1991): 759–769; J. Colquitt, J. LePine, and R. Noe, "Toward an integrative theory of training motivation: A meta-analytic path analysis of 20 years of research," *Journal of Applied Psychology* 85 (2000): 678–707.

22. M. Eisenstein, "Test, then train," *T+D* (May 2005): 26–27.

23. J. Nunally, *Psychometric Theory* (New York: McGraw-Hill, 1978).

24. L. Gottsfredson, "The G factor in employment," *Journal of Vocational Behavior* 19 (1986): 293–296.

25. M. J. Ree and J. A. Earles, "Predicting training success: Not much more than G," *Personnel Psychology* 44 (1991): 321–332.

26. S. McCartney, "The air-traffic cops go to school," *The Wall Street Journal* (March 29, 2005): D1, D7.

27. D. R. Torrence and J. A. Torrence, "Training in the face of illiteracy," *Training and Development Journal* (August 1987): 44–49.

28. American Society for Training and Development, *Bridging the Skills Gap* (Alexandria, VA: American Society for Training and Development, 2009); R. Davenport, "Eliminate the skills gap," *T+D* (February 2006): 26–31; R. Zamora, "Developing your team members' basic skills," *Wenatchee Business Journal* (August 2005): C8; M. Davis, "Getting workers back to basics," *Training and Development* (October1997): 14–15.

29. M. E. Gist, C. Schwoerer, and B. Rosen, "Effects of alternative training methods on self-efficacy and performance in computer software training," *Journal of Applied Psychology* 74 (1990): 884–891; J. Martocchio and J. Dulebohn, "Performance feedback effects in training: The role of perceived controllability," *Personnel Psychology* 47 (1994): 357–373; J. Martocchio, "Ability conceptions and learning," *Journal of Applied Psychology* 79 (1994): 819–825.

30. R. A. Noe and N. Schmitt, "The influence of trainee attitudes on training effectiveness: Test of a model," *Personnel Psychology* 39 (1986): 497–523.

31. H. Johnson, "The Whole Picture," *training* (July 2004): 30–34.

32. M. A. Quinones, "Pretraining context effects: Training assignments as feedback," *Journal of Applied Psychology* 80 (1995): 226–38; Baldwin, Magjuka, and Loher, "The perils of participation," *Personnel Psychology* 44 (1991): 51–66.

33. R. Boyd, "Steady drop in brain process starts in 20s," *Columbus Dispatch*, November 17, 2000; A5.

34. C. Houck, "Multigenerational and virtual: How do we build a mentoring program for today's workforce?" *Performance Improvement*, 50 (February 2011): 25–30; K. Ball and G. Gotsill, *Surviving the Baby Boom Exodus* (Boston: Cengage Learning, 2011); R. Zemke, C. Raines, and B. Filipezak, "Generation gaps in the classroom," *Training* (November 2000): 48–54; J. Salopek, "The young and the rest of us," *Training and Development* (February 2000): 26–30.

35. L. H. Peters, E. J. O'Connor, and J. R. Eulberg, "Situational Constraints: Sources, Consequences, and Future Considerations." In *Research in Personnel and Human Resource Management,* ed. K. M. Rowland and G. R. Ferris (Greenwich, CT: JAI Press,1985), 79–114; E. J. O'Connor, L. H. Peters, A. Pooyan, J. Weekley, B. Frank, and B. Erenkranz, "Situational constraints effects on performance, affective reactions, and turnover: A field replication and extension," *Journal of Applied Psychology* 69 (1984): 663–672; D. J. Cohen, "What motivates trainees?" *Training and Development Journal* (November 1990): 91–93; J. S. Russell, J. R. Terborg, and M. L. Power, "Organizational performance and organizational level training and support," *Personnel Psychology* 38 (1985): 849–863.

36. L. Freifeld, "Why cash doesn't motivate…," *training* (July/August 2011): 16–20.

37. W. D. Hicks and R. J. Klimoski, "Entry into training programs and its effects on training outcomes: A field experiment," *Academy of Management Journal* 30 (1987): 542–552.

38. R. F. Mager and P. Pipe, *Analyzing Performance Problems: Or You Really Oughta Wanna,* 2d ed. (Belmont, CA: Pittman Learning, 1984); Carnevale, Gainer, and Meltzer, *Workplace Basics Training Manual* (San Francisco: Jossey-Bass, 1990); Rummler, "In Search of the Holy Performance Grail," *Training and Development* (April 1996): 26–31; C. Reinhart, "How to leap over barriers to performance," *Training Development* (January 2000): 46–49.

39. G. A. Rummler and K. Morrill, "The results chain," *T+D* (February 2005): 27–35; D. LaFleur, K. Smalley, and J. Austin, "Improving performance in a nuclear cardiology department," *Performance Improvement Quarterly* 18(1) (2005): 83–109.

40. C. E. Schneier, J. P. Guthrie, and J. D. Olian, "A practical approach to conducting and using training needs assessment," *Public Personnel Management* (Summer 1988): 191–205; J. Annett and N. Stanton, "Task Analysis." In G. Hodgkinson and J. Ford, *International Review of Industrial and Organizational Psychology* 21 (John Wiley and Sons, 2006): 45–74.

41. I. Goldstein, "Training in Organizations." In *Handbook of Industrial/Organizational Psychology,* 2d ed., ed. M. D. Dunnette and L. M. Hough (Palo Alto, CA: Consulting Psychologists Press, 1991): 507–619.

42. E. F. Holton III and C. Bailey, "Top-to-bottom curriculum redesign," *Training and Development* (March 1995): 40–44.

43. M. Campion et al., "Doing competencies well: Best practices in competency modeling," *Personnel Psychology,* 64 (2011): 225–262; J. Shippmann et al., "The practice of competency modeling," *Personnel Psychology* 53 (2000): 703–740; A. Lucia and R. Lepsinger, *The Art and Science of Competency Models* (San Francisco: Jossey-Bass,1999).

44. J. S. Shippmann et al., "The practice of competency modeling," *Personnel Psychology* 53 (2000): 703–740.

45. A. Lucia and R. Lepsinger, *The Art and Science of Competency Models* (San Francisco: Jossey-Bass, 1999).

46. J. Kochanski, "Competency-based management," *Training and Development* (October 1997): 41–44; D. Dubois and W. Rothwell, "Competency-based or a traditional approach to training," *T+D* (April 2004): 46–57; E. Kahane, "Competency management: Cracking the code," *T+D* (May 2008): 71–76.

47. F. Morgeson, K. Delaney-Klinger, M. Mayfield, P. Ferrara, and M. Campion, "Self-presentation processes in job analysis: A field experiment investigating inflation in abilities, tasks, and competencies," *Journal of Applied Psychology* 89 (2004): 674–686; F. Lievens and J. Sanchez, "Can training improve the quality of inferences made by raters in competency modeling? A quasi-experiment," *Journal of Applied Psychology* 92 (2007): 812–819; F. Lievens, J. Sanchez, and W. DeCorte, "Easing the inferential leap in competency modeling: The effects of task-related information and subject matter expertise," *Personnel Psychology* 57 (2004): 881–904.

48. A. Lucia and R. Lepsinger, *The Art and Science of Competency Models* (San Francisco: Jossey-Bass, 1999); M. Derven, "Lessons Learned," *T+D* (December 2008) 68–73. M. Campion, A. Fink, B. Ruggerberg, L. Carr, G. Phillips, & R. Odman, "Doing Competencies Well: Best Practices in Competency Modeling," *Personnel Psychology,* 64 (2011): 225–262.

49. M. Derven, "Lessons learned," *T+D* (December 2008): 68–73.

50. C. Spicer, "Building a competency model," *HR Magazine* (April 2009): 34–36.

51. K. Gupta, *A Practical Guide to Needs Assessment* (San Francisco: Jossey-Bass, 1999); R. Zemke, "How to do a needs assessment when you don't have the time," *Training* (March 1998): 38–44; G. Piskurich, *Rapid Instructional Design* (San Francisco, CA: Pfeiffer, 2006).

# Chapter **Four**

# Learning and Transfer of Training

## Objectives

After reading this chapter, you should be able to

1. Discuss the five types of learner outcomes.
2. Explain the implications of learning theory for instructional design.
3. Incorporate adult learning theory into the design of a training program.
4. Describe how learners receive, process, store, retrieve, and act upon information.
5. Discuss the internal conditions (within the learner) and external conditions (learning environment) necessary for the trainee to learn each type of capability.
6. Discuss the implications of open and closed skills and near and far transfer for designing training programs.
7. Explain the features of instruction and the work environment that are necessary for learning and transfer of training.

## Energizing Training Means Better Learning and Transfer of Training

Boring lectures, lack of meaningful content in e-learning, training that doesn't give employees the opportunity to practice and receive feedback—all these methods demotivate trainees and make it difficult for them to learn and use what they learned on the job. However, many companies are using innovative instructional methods to make training more interesting and to help trainees learn and apply it to their work.

Verizon relies on instructor-led virtual classrooms to bring training to many of its employees who are geographically dispersed. Recognizing the importance of keeping learners actively involved with each other and the training content, Verizon has implemented a number of new learning strategies. The training that supports its business customer service billing process combines leader-led discussions with interactive assignments that participants complete in groups in virtual breakout rooms. Webinars include online polling to keep learners engaged. Its information technology classes include labs and simulated technical equipment for practice and instruction. For retail training, Verizon's Virtual Trainer (VT) brings the trainer to the retail store virtually, with initial training provided by VT. VT is then supported by a document completed by the learner and used as a job aid to reinforce training, a discussion guide used by managers to discuss examples, ideas, content, and activities, and a scenario and coaching form that gives the learner the opportunity to apply skills after training.

At PNC Financial Services Group, PNC University provided web-based training to all its employees to aid in the conversion to a new HR system. The training was customized to the employee role and organization within the company to ensure that it was relevant and meaningful. An online help feature allowed employees to use their preferred method of learning through one of four approaches: "See it!" "Try it!" "Do it!" or "Print it!." "See it!" provided a short instructional video showing how a task is completed. "Try it!" let employees practice entering transactions with coaching, in a simulated version of the system. "Do it!" allowed employees to enter transactions in the live system with a Help coaching tool, going through the task step by step. "Print it!" allowed employees to print step-by-step procedures for completing transactions.

The training offered to truck technicians at ArvinMeritor (now Meritor, Inc.) was revised to get learners more involved and to see how they can use what they learned to repair trucks. Technicians complete online prework that helps them learn about rear drive axle components, operations, and preventative maintenance. Next, in-person class time is used for hands-on work, such as disassembling and reassembling drive axle parts and making adjustments to drive axles. After training, learners complete post-work, which reviews the concepts covered in the hands-on sessions. Every four to six months, learners are asked to go online to practice using simulation technology that allows them to select tools from their toolbox to measure, adjust, or otherwise work with drive axle components using their computer mouse.

Colorado Springs Utilities, a community-owned utility, provides natural gas, water, and electric services to more than 600,000 customers. All the company executives issue public statements in support of learning, participate in learning events as instructors or speakers, and include the purpose and expected outcome of training activities (learning objectives) as part of their performance goals. Every training program begins with a brainstorming session to identify themes and activities; this beginning engages trainees and helps them enjoy training and retain more of what they have learned. In a safety training class, students experience a simulated emergency and have to respond using skills they have learned along with their knowledge of an evacuation plan. The trainees perform different roles and activities in response to a power shutdown. Afterward, the trainer critiques their performance, and trainees discuss what they have learned (or still need to learn). Trainees complete a written exam and review to ensure their knowledge retention.

**Sources:** Based on J. Salopek, "Colorado Springs Utilities: 2005 BEST Award Winner," *T+D* (October 2005): 38–40; M. Weinstein, "Wake-up Call," *Training* (June 2007): 48–50; M. Weinstein, "Verizon connects to success," *training*, January/February 2011: 40–42; M. Weinstein, "PNC invests in excellence," *training,* January/February 2011: 48–50.

# INTRODUCTION

Although they use different methods, the purpose of the training at the four companies just described is to help employees learn so they can perform their jobs successfully. Regardless of the training method, certain conditions must be present for learning to occur and employees to use what they learned on their jobs. These include (1) providing opportunities for trainees to practice and receive feedback, i.e., information about how well people are meeting the training objectives, (2) offering meaningful training content, (3) identifying any prerequisites that trainees need to complete the program successfully, and (4) allowing trainees to learn through observation and experience and ensuring that the work environment, including managers and peers, support learning and use of skills on the job. For example, feedback from trainers and coaches is provided at Colorado Springs Utilities. The meaningfulness of training content is enhanced at both Colorado Springs Utilities and ArvinMeritor by having trainees perform tasks and work on problems that are identical to those they will encounter on the job. Recognizing that employees may have preferences regarding how they want to learn, PNC allowed employees to choose how they wanted to learn about the new HR system. To help ensure that managers support training and trainees have the opportunity to apply what they have learned in their jobs, Verizon provides managers with a guide that can help them coach and motivate trainees to use and further develop skills emphasized in training.

As you may have recognized by now, this chapter emphasizes not only what has to occur during training sessions for learning to occur, but also how to ensure that trainees use what they have learned in their jobs. That is, this chapter discusses both learning and transfer of training. **Learning** refers to a relatively permanent change in human capabilities that can include knowledge, skills, attitudes, behaviors, and competencies that are not the result of growth processes.[1] A key part of learning is that trainees commit to memory (i.e., remember) what they have learned and can recall it. **Transfer of training** refers to trainees effectively and continually applying what they have learned in training to their jobs.[2] As the organizations in the chapter opener illustrate, trainee characteristics, the design of the training program (or what occurs during training), and the work environment influence whether trainees learn and use or apply what they have learned to their jobs. Figure 4.1 presents a model of learning and transfer of training. As the model shows, transfer of training

**FIGURE 4.1**
**A Model of Learning and Transfer of Training**

Source: Adapted from T. T. Baldwin and J. K. Ford, "Transfer of Training: A Review and Directions for Future Research," *Personnel Psychology* 41 (1988): 63–103.

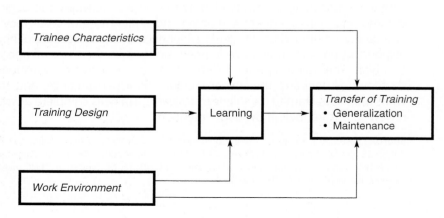

includes both the generalization of training to the job and maintenance of learned material. **Generalization** refers to a trainee's ability to apply what they learned to on-the job work problems and situations that are similar but not necessarily identical to those problems and situations encountered in the learning environment; i.e., the training program. **Maintenance** refers to the process of trainees continuing to use what they learned over time.

It is important to realize that for training to be effective, both learning and transfer of training are needed. Trainees can fail or incorrectly apply training content (what was emphasized in training) to their jobs, either because the training was not conducive to learning, the work environment provides them with the opportunity to use training content or supports its correct use, or both. Also, it is a mistake to consider transfer of training as something to be concerned about after training because it deals with the use of training content on the job. Instead, transfer of training should be considered during the design or purchase of training. If you wait until after training to consider transfer of training, it is likely too late. Trainees' perceptions of the work environment and its support for training have likely influenced their motivation to learn and what, if anything, they have learned (recall the discussion of motivation to learn in Chapter Three, "Needs Assessment").

This chapter coverage is based on the model shown in Figure 4.1. First, we discuss learning. We begin by identifying what is to be learned—that is, to identify learning outcomes. Learning outcomes should be related to what is required to perform the job successfully. As the chapter opener illustrates, this may include repairing trucks, selling products, providing services, operating systems—or even climbing a utility pole to make repairs! As a student, you are familiar with one type of learning outcome: intellectual skills. We also discuss how trainees' learning style may influence the way they prefer to learn. The influence of other trainee characteristics, such as basic skills, cognitive ability, self-efficacy, age and generation, and interests on motivation to learn and learning, was discussed in Chapter Three.

Next, we consider training design. Training design includes consideration of how to create a learning environment to help the trainee acquire the learning outcomes. We discuss various learning and transfer of training theories. Last, we look at how these theories are used to create a learning environment and supportive work environment designed to help the trainee learn the desired outcomes and apply them on the job.

# WHAT IS LEARNING? WHAT IS LEARNED?

Understanding learning outcomes is crucial because they influence the characteristics of the training environment that are necessary for learning to occur. For example, if trainees are to master motor skills such as climbing a pole, they must have opportunities to practice climbing and receive feedback about their climbing skills. Learning outcomes are presented in Table 4.1.

**Verbal information** includes names or labels, facts, and bodies of knowledge. Verbal information includes specialized knowledge that employees need in their jobs. For example, a manager must know the names of different types of equipment as well as the body of knowledge related to Total Quality Management (TQM).

**Intellectual skills** include concepts and rules, which are critical to solve problems, serve customers, and create products. For example, a manager must know the steps in the performance appraisal process (e.g., gather data, summarize data, or prepare for an appraisal interview with an employee) in order to conduct an employee appraisal.

**TABLE 4.1**   **Learning Outcomes**

| Type of Learning Outcome | Description of Capability | Example |
|---|---|---|
| Verbal information | State, tell, or describe previously stored information. | State three reasons for following company safety procedures. |
| Intellectual skills | Apply generalizable concepts and rules to solve problems and generate novel products. | Design and code a computer program that meets customer requirements. |
| Motor skills | Execute a physical action with precision and timing. | Shoot a gun and consistently hit a small moving target. |
| Attitudes | Choose a personal course of action. | Choose to respond to all incoming mail within 24 hours. |
| Cognitive strategies | Manage one's own thinking and learning processes. | Use three different strategies selectively to diagnose engine malfunctions. |

Source: R. Gagne and K. Medsker, *The Conditions of Learning* (New York: Harcourt-Brace, 1996).

**Motor skills** include coordination of physical movements. For example, a telephone repair person must have the coordination and dexterity required to climb ladders and telephone poles.

**Attitudes** are a combination of beliefs and feelings that predispose a person to behave a certain way. Attitudes include a cognitive component (beliefs), an affective component (feeling), and an intentional component (the way a person intends to behave with regard to the focus of the attitude). Important work-related attitudes include job satisfaction, commitment to the organization, and job involvement. Suppose you say that an employee has a "positive attitude" toward her work. This means the person likes her job (the affective component). She may like her job because it is challenging and provides an opportunity to meet people (the cognitive component). Because she likes her job, she intends to stay with the company and do her best at work (the intentional component). Training programs may be used to develop or change attitudes because attitudes have been shown to be related to physical and mental withdrawal from work, turnover, and behaviors that affect the well-being of the company (e.g., helping new employees).

**Cognitive strategies** regulate the processes of learning. They relate to the learner's decision regarding what information to attend to (i.e., pay attention to), how to remember, and how to solve problems. For example, a physicist recalls the colors of the light spectrum through remembering the name "Roy G. Biv" (red, orange, yellow, green, blue, indigo, violet).

As this chapter points out, each learning outcome requires a different set of conditions for learning to occur. Before this chapter investigates the learning process in detail, it looks at the theories that help explain how people learn.

# LEARNING THEORIES

Each theory about how people learn relates to different aspects of the learning process. Many of the theories also relate to trainees' motivation to learn, which was discussed in Chapter Three. The application of these theories for instruction and program design are discussed later in this chapter and in Chapter Five, "Program Design."

## Reinforcement Theory

**Reinforcement theory** emphasizes that people are motivated to perform or avoid certain behaviors because of past outcomes that have resulted from those behaviors.[3] There are several processes in reinforcement theory. *Positive reinforcement* is a pleasurable outcome resulting from a behavior. *Negative reinforcement* is the removal of an unpleasant outcome. For example, consider a machine that makes screeching and grinding noises unless the operator holds levers in a certain position. The operator will learn to hold the levers in that position to avoid the noises. The process of withdrawing positive or negative reinforcers to eliminate a behavior is known as *extinction*. Punishment is presenting an unpleasant outcome after a behavior, leading to a decrease in that behavior. For example, if a manager yells at employees when they are late, they may avoid the yelling by being on time (but they may also call in sick, quit, or fool the boss into not noticing when they arrive late).

From a training perspective, reinforcement theory suggests that for learners to acquire knowledge, change behavior, or modify skills, the trainer needs to identify what outcomes the learner finds most positive (and negative). Trainers then need to link these outcomes to learners' acquiring knowledge or skills or changing behaviors. As was mentioned in Chapter Three, learners can obtain several types of benefits from participating in training programs. The benefits may include learning an easier or more interesting way to perform their job (job-related), meeting other employees who can serve as resources when problems occur (personal), or increasing opportunities to consider new positions in the company (career-related). According to reinforcement theory, trainers can withhold or provide these benefits to learners who master program content. The effectiveness of learning depends on the pattern or schedule for providing these reinforcers or benefits. Similarly, managers can provide these benefits to help ensure transfer of training.

Behavior modification is a training method that is primarily based on reinforcement theory. For example, a training program in a bakery focused on eliminating unsafe behaviors such as climbing over conveyor belts (rather than walking around them) and sticking hands into equipment to dislodge jammed materials without turning off the equipment.[4] Employees were shown slides depicting safe and unsafe work behaviors. After viewing the slides, employees were shown a graph of the number of times that safe behaviors were observed during past weeks. Employees were encouraged to increase the number of safe behaviors they demonstrated on the job. They were given several reasons for doing so: for their own protection, to decrease costs for the company, and to help their plant get out of last place in the safety rankings of the company's plants. Immediately after the training, safety reminders were posted in employees' work areas. Data about the number of safe behaviors performed by employees continued to be collected and displayed on the graph in the work area following the training. Employees' supervisors were also instructed to recognize workers whenever they saw them performing a safe work behavior. In this example, the data of safe behavior posted in the work areas and supervisors' recognition of safe work behavior represent positive reinforcers.

## Social Learning Theory

**Social learning theory** emphasizes that people learn by observing other persons (models) whom they believe are credible and knowledgeable.[5] Social learning theory also recognizes that behavior that is reinforced or rewarded tends to be repeated. The models' behavior or skill that is rewarded is adopted by the observer. According to social learning theory, learning new skills or behaviors comes from (1) directly experiencing the consequences of using that behavior or skill, or (2) the process of observing others and seeing the consequences of their behavior.[6]

According to social learning theory, learning also is influenced by a person's self-efficacy. **Self-efficacy** is a person's judgment about whether he or she can successfully learn knowledge and skills. Chapter Three emphasizes self-efficacy as an important factor to consider in the person analysis phase of needs assessment. Why? Self-efficacy is one determinant of readiness to learn. A trainee with high self-efficacy will make efforts to learn in a training program and will be most likely to persist in learning even if an environment is not conducive to learning (e.g., a noisy training room). In contrast, a person with low self-efficacy will have self-doubts about mastering the content of a training program and is more likely to withdraw psychologically and/or physically (e.g., daydream or fail to attend the program). These persons believe that they are unable to learn, and regardless of their effort level, they will be unable to learn.

A person's self-efficacy can be increased using several methods: verbal persuasion, logical verification, observation of others (modeling), and past accomplishments.[7] **Verbal persuasion** means offering words of encouragement to convince others they can learn. **Logical verification** involves perceiving a relationship between a new task and a task already mastered. Trainers and managers can remind employees when they encounter learning difficulties that they have been successful at learning similar tasks. **Modeling** involves having employees who already have mastered the learning outcomes demonstrate them for trainees. As a result, employees are likely to be motivated by the confidence and success of their peers. **Past accomplishments** refers to allowing employees to build a history of successful accomplishments. Managers can place employees in situations where they are likely to succeed and provide training so that employees know what to do and how to do it.

Social learning theory suggests that four processes are involved in learning: attention, retention, motor reproduction, and motivational processes (see Figure 4.2).

*Attention* suggests that persons cannot learn by observation unless they are aware of the important aspects of a model's performance. Attention is influenced by characteristics of the model and the learner. Learners must be aware of the skills or behavior they are supposed to observe. The model must be clearly identified and credible. The learner must have the physical capability (sensory capability) to observe the model. Also, a learner who has successfully learned other skills or behavior by observing the model is more likely to attend to the model.

Learners must remember the behaviors or skills that they observe. This is the role of *retention*. Learners have to code the observed behavior and skills in memory in an organized

**FIGURE 4.2**    **Processes of Social Learning Theory**

Sources: Based on A. Bandura, *Social Foundations of Thoughts and Actions* (Englewood Cliffs, NJ: Prentice Hall, 1986); P. Taylor, D. Russ-Eft, and D. Chan, "A meta-analytic review of behavior modeling training," *Journal of Applied Psychology,* 90 (2005): 692–709.

manner so they can recall them for the appropriate situation. Behaviors or skills can be coded as visual images (symbols) or verbal statements.

*Motor reproduction* involves trying out the observed behaviors to see if they result in the same reinforcement that the model received. The ability to reproduce the behaviors or skills depends on the extent to which the learner can recall the skills or behavior. The learner must also have the physical capability to perform the behavior or exhibit the skill. For example, a firefighter can learn the behaviors necessary to carry a person away from a dangerous situation, but he may be unable to demonstrate the behavior because he lacks upper body strength. Note that performance of behavior is usually not perfect on the first attempt. Learners must have the opportunity to practice and receive feedback to modify their behavior to be similar to the model behavior.

Learners are more likely to adopt a modeled behavior if it results in positive outcomes. Social learning theory emphasizes that behaviors that are reinforced (a *motivational process*) will be repeated in the future. For example, a major source of conflict and stress for managers often relates to the performance appraisal interview. A manager may, through observing successful managers, learn behaviors that allow employees to be more participative in a performance appraisal interview (e.g., give employees the opportunity to voice their concerns). If the manager uses this behavior in the performance appraisal interview and the behavior is rewarded by employees (e.g., they make comments such as, "I really felt the feedback meeting was the best we have ever had") or the new behavior leads to reduced conflicts with employees (e.g., negative reinforcement), the manager will more likely use this behavior in subsequent appraisal interviews.

As you will see in the discussion of training methods in Chapters Seven and Eight, social learning theory is the primary basis for behavior modeling training and has influenced how models are used in videos, which can be part of face-to-face, online, or mobile training programs. For example, in the training program developed by Zenger Miller called "Getting Your Ideas Across," trainees are first presented with five key behaviors for getting their ideas across: (1) state the point and purpose of the message, (2) present points to aid understanding, (3) check the audience for reactions and understanding, (4) handle reactions from the audience to what was presented, and (5) summarize the main point. The trainer provides a rationale for each key behavior. Next, trainees view a video of a business meeting in which a manager is having difficulty getting subordinates to accept his ideas regarding how to manage an impending office move. The manager, who is the model, is ineffective in getting his ideas across to his subordinates. As a result, the video shows that the subordinates are dissatisfied with the manager and his ideas. The video is turned off and the trainer leads the trainees in a discussion of what the manager did wrong in trying to get his ideas across. Trainees again view the video. But this time the manager, in the same situation, is shown using the key behaviors. As a result, subordinates react quite positively to their boss (the model). Following this video segment, the trainer leads a discussion of how the model used the key behaviors to get his ideas across.

After observing the model and discussing the key behaviors, each trainee is paired with another trainee for practice. Each group is given a situation and a message to communicate. The trainees take turns trying to get their ideas across to each other using the key behaviors. Each trainee is expected to provide feedback regarding the partner's use of the key behaviors. The trainer also observes and provides feedback to each group. Before leaving training, the trainees are given a pocket-size card with the key behaviors, which they take back with them to their jobs. Also, they complete a planning guide in which they describe a situation where they want to use the key behaviors and how they plan to use them.

## Goal Theories

### Goal Setting Theory

**Goal setting theory** assumes that behavior results from a person's conscious goals and intentions.[8] Goals influence a person's behavior by directing energy and attention, sustaining effort over time, and motivating the person to develop strategies for goal attainment.[9] Research suggests that specific, challenging goals result in better performance than vague, unchallenging goals.[10] Goals have been shown to lead to high performance only if people are committed to the goal. Employees are less likely to be committed to a goal if they believe that it is too difficult.

An example of how goal setting theory influences training methods is seen in a program designed to improve pizza deliverers' driving practices.[11] The majority of pizza deliverers are young (ages 18–24) and inexperienced drivers, who are compensated based on the number of pizzas they can deliver. This creates a situation in which deliverers are rewarded for fast but unsafe driving practices—for example, not wearing a safety belt, failing to use turn signals, and not coming to complete stops at intersections. These unsafe practices have resulted in a high driving accident rate.

Prior to goal setting, pizza deliverers were observed by their managers leaving the store and then returning from deliveries. The managers observed the number of complete stops at intersections over a one-week period. In the training session, managers and trainers presented the deliverers with a series of questions for discussion. Here are examples: In what situations should you come to a complete stop? What are the reasons for coming to a complete stop? What are the reasons for not coming to a complete stop?

After the discussion, pizza deliverers were asked to agree on the need to come to a complete stop at intersections. Following the deliverers' agreement, the managers shared the data they collected regarding the number of complete stops at intersections they had observed the previous week. (Complete stops were made 55 percent of the time.) The trainer asked the pizza deliverers to set a goal for complete stopping over the next month. They decided on a goal of 75 percent complete stops.

After the goal setting session, managers at each store continued observing their drivers' intersection stops. The following month in the work area, a poster showed the percentages of complete stops for every four-day period. The current percentage of total complete stops was also displayed.

Goal setting theory also is used in training program design. Goal setting theory suggests that learning can be facilitated by providing trainees with specific challenging goals and objectives. Specifically, the influence of goal setting theory can be seen in the development of training lesson plans. Lesson plans begin with specific goals providing information regarding the expected action that the learner will demonstrate, conditions under which learning will occur, and the level of performance that will be judged acceptable. Goals can also be part of action plans or application assignments that are used to motivate trainees to transfer training.

### Goal Orientation

**Goal orientation** refers to the goals held by a trainee in a learning situation. Goal orientation can include a learning orientation or a performance orientation. **Learning orientation** relates to trying to increase ability or competence in a task. People with a learning orientation believe that training success is defined as showing improvement and making progress, prefer trainers who are more interested in how trainees are learning than in how they are performing, and view errors and mistakes as part of the learning process. **Performance orientation** refers to learners who focus on task performance and how they compare to others. Persons with a performance orientation define success as high performance relative to others, value high ability more than learning, and find that errors and mistakes cause anxiety and want to avoid them.

Goal orientation is believed to affect the amount of effort that a trainee will expend in learning (motivation to learn). Learners with a high learning orientation will direct greater attention to the task and learn for the sake of learning, as opposed to learners with a performance orientation. Learners with a performance orientation will direct more attention to performing well and less effort to learning. Research has shown that trainees with a learning orientation exert greater effort to learn and use more complex learning strategies than do trainees with a performance orientation.[12] There are several ways to create a learning orientation in trainees.[13] These include setting goals around learning and experimenting with new ways of having trainees perform trained tasks rather than emphasizing trained-task performance, deemphasizing competition among trainees, creating a community of learning (discussed later in the chapter), and allowing trainees to make errors and to experiment with new knowledge, skills, and behaviors during training.

## Need Theories

Need theories help to explain the value that a person places on certain outcomes. A **need** is a deficiency that a person is experiencing at any point in time. A need motivates a person to behave in a manner that satisfies the deficiency. Abraham Maslow's and Clayton Alderfer's need theories focused on physiological needs, relatedness needs (needs to interact with other persons), and growth needs (self-esteem and self-actualization).[14] Both Maslow and Alderfer believed that persons start by trying to satisfy needs at the lowest level, then progress up the hierarchy as lower-level needs are satisfied. That is, if physiological needs are not met, a person's behavior will focus on satisfying these needs before relatedness or growth needs receive attention. The major difference between Alderfer's and Maslow's hierarchies of needs is that Alderfer allows the possibility that if higher-level needs are not satisfied, employees will refocus on lower-level needs.

David McClelland's need theory focused primarily on needs for achievement, affiliation, and power.[15] According to McClelland, these needs can be learned. The need for achievement relates to a concern for attaining and maintaining self-set standards of excellence. The need for affiliation involves concern for building and maintaining relationships with other people and for being accepted by others. The need for power is a concern for obtaining responsibility, influence, and reputation.

Need theories suggest that to motivate learning, trainers should identify trainees' needs and communicate how training program content relates to fulfilling these needs. Also, if certain basic needs of trainees (e.g., physiological and safety needs) are not met, they are unlikely to be motivated to learn. For example, consider a word processing training class for secretaries in a downsizing company. It is doubtful that even the best-designed training class will result in learning if employees believe that their job security is threatened (unmet need for security) by the company's downsizing strategy. Also, it is unlikely the secretaries will be motivated to learn if they believe that word processing skills emphasized in the program will not help them keep their current employment or increase their chances of finding another job inside (or even outside) the company.

Another implication of need theory relates to providing employees with a choice of training programs to attend. As Chapter Three mentioned, giving employees a choice of which training course to attend can increase their motivation to learn. This occurs because trainees are able to choose programs that best match their needs.

## Expectancy Theory

Expectancy theory suggests that a person's behavior is based on three factors: expectancy, instrumentality, and valence.[16] Beliefs about the link between trying to perform a behavior and actually performing well are called **expectancies.** Expectancy is similar to self-efficacy. In expectancy theory, a belief that performing a given behavior (e.g., attending a training program) is associated with a particular outcome (e.g., being able to better perform your job) is called **instrumentality. Valence** is the value that a person places on an outcome (e.g., how important it is to perform better on the job).

According to expectancy theory, various choices of behavior are evaluated according to their expectancy, instrumentality, and valence. Figure 4.3 shows how behavior is determined based on finding the mathematical product of expectancy, instrumentality, and valence. People choose the behavior with the highest value.

From a training perspective, expectancy theory suggests that learning is most likely to occur when employees believe that they can learn the content of the program (expectancy). Also, learning and transfer of training are enhanced when they are linked to outcomes such as better job performance, a salary increase, or peer recognition (instrumentality), and when employees value these outcomes (valence).

## Adult Learning Theory

Adult learning theory was developed out of a need for a specific theory of how adults learn. Most educational theories, as well as formal educational institutions, have been developed exclusively to educate children and youths. Pedagogy, the art and science of teaching children, has dominated educational theory. Pedagogy gives the instructor the major responsibility for making decisions about learning content, method, and evaluation. Students are generally seen as (1) being passive recipients of directions and content and (2) bringing few experiences that may serve as resources to the learning environment.[17]

**FIGURE 4.3** **Expectancy Theory of Motivation**

Educational psychologists, recognizing the limitations of formal education theories, developed **andragogy,** the theory of adult learning. Malcolm Knowles is most frequently associated with adult learning theory. Knowles's model is based on several assumptions:[18]

1. Adults have the need to know why they are learning something.
2. Adults have a need to be self-directed.
3. Adults bring more work-related experiences into the learning situation.
4. Adults enter a learning experience with a problem-centered approach to learning.
5. Adults are motivated to learn by both extrinsic and intrinsic motivators.

Adult learning theory is especially important to consider in developing training programs because the audience for many such programs tends to be adults, most of whom have not spent a majority of their time in a formal education setting. Table 4.2 shows implications of adult learning theory for learning. Consider how adult learning theory is incorporated into training programs.[19] Yapi ve Kredi Bank's program to help managers improve their skills in motivating and coaching their employees includes classroom sessions in which trainers reviewed common case studies of common situations in coaching and provided students with online readings and videos. Senior managers reviewed coaching and development techniques, and program participants were given coaching assignments with their peers to complete. The first-line manager course at B&W Pantex focuses on soft skills as well as human resource (HR) policies, discipline, and supervision using instructor-led training with video presentations and role playing. The course includes real-life scenarios based on actual situations that have occurred in its facilities. The program also includes on-the-job training in which trained and qualified subject matter experts (SMEs) teach tasks and procedures. Brown-Forman, one of the largest companies in the global wine and spirits industry (its brands include Jack Daniel's Tennessee Whiskey, Southern Comfort, Findlandia vodka, and Herradura tequila) created a two-and-a-half day training program focused on helping the company's marketing professionals build the brand. The company's chief marketing officer visits the class to explain the importance of its content and why the course was developed. In the course, participants work in teams to develop a brand campaign for a sample brand. This includes making presentations and completing exercises. Representatives from Brown-Forman's creative agencies attend the program, part of which involves interacting with consumers to identify their drinking patterns and preferences. At the end of the program, participant teams present their final project to a panel of senior marketing executives who serve as judges.

**TABLE 4.2**
**Implications of Adult Learning Theory for Training**

Source: Based on M. Knowles, *The Adult Learner,* 4th ed. (Houston, TX: Gulf Publishing, 1990).

| Design Issue | Implications |
|---|---|
| Self-concept | Mutual planning and collaboration in instruction |
| Experience | Use learner experience as basis for examples and applications |
| Readiness | Develop instruction based on the learner's interests and competencies |
| Time perspective | Immediate application of content |
| Orientation to learning | Problem-centered instead of subject-centered |

## Information Processing Theory

Compared to other learning theories, information processing theories give more emphasis to the internal processes that occur when training content is learned and retained. Figure 4.4 shows a model of information processing. Information processing theories propose that information or messages taken in by the learner undergo several transformations in the human brain.[20] Information processing begins when a message or stimulus (which could be a sound, smell, touch, or picture) from the environment is received by receptors (i.e., ears, nose, skin, and eyes). The message is registered in the senses and stored in short-term memory, and then it is transformed or coded for storage in long-term memory. A search process occurs in memory, during which time a response to the message or stimulus is organized. The response generator organizes the learner's response and tells the effectors (muscles) what to do. The "what to do" instruction relates to one of the five learning outcomes: verbal information, cognitive skills, motor skills, intellectual skills, or attitudes. The final link in the model is feedback from the environment. This feedback provides the learner with an evaluation of the response given. This information can come from another person or the learner's observation of the results of his or her own action. A positive evaluation of the response provides reinforcement that the behavior is desirable and should be stored in long-term memory for use in similar situations.

Besides emphasizing the internal processes needed to capture, store, retrieve, and respond to messages, the information processing model highlights how external events influence learning. These events include:[21]

1. Changes in the intensity or frequency of the stimulus that affect attention.
2. Informing the learner of the objectives to establish an expectation.
3. Enhancing perceptual features of the material (stimulus), drawing the attention of the learner to certain features.
4. Verbal instructions, pictures, diagrams, and maps suggesting ways to code the training content so that it can be stored in memory.
5. Meaningful learning context (examples, problems) creating cues that facilitate coding.
6. Demonstration or verbal instructions helping to organize the learner's response, as well as facilitating the selection of the correct response.

**FIGURE 4.4**
**A Model of Human Information Processing**

Source: Adapted from R. Gagne, "Learning processes and instruction," *Training Research Journal,* 1 (1995/96):17–28.

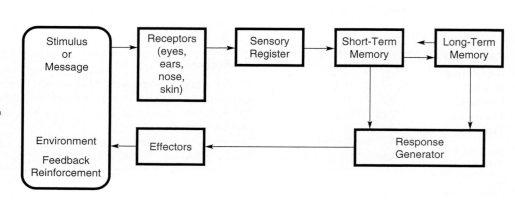

# TRANSFER OF TRAINING THEORY

Transfer of training is more likely to occur when the trainee works on tasks during training (e.g., knowledge, equipment, or processes) that are very similar, if not identical, to the work environment (near transfer). Transfer of training is more difficult when tasks during training are different from the work environment, i.e., far transfer, such as applying customer service principles to interaction with an angry customer in front of a long line of customers at a cash register. The tasks that are used during training relate to the training objectives.

**Closed skills** refer to training objectives that are linked to learning specific skills that are to be identically produced by the trainee on their job. In contrast, **open skills** are linked to more general learning principles. For example, customer service skills are examples of open skills. There is not a single correct way to perform and the learner is given some general principles to follow. For example a sales clerk is likely trained on general principles or process for how to interact with an angry customer but has the freedom to choose how to interact with them because their intentions and responses are not entirely predictable.[22] Open skills are more difficult to train than closed skills because they require the trainee to not only acquire and recall general principles, but also to consider how they can be adapted and used to fit a wide range of circumstances, many of which cannot be practiced during training. Also, manager and peer support on the job is important for giving the trainee the opportunity to learn by seeing how experienced employees use the skills and to get feedback when they have the chance to apply them. Later in this chapter, we discuss the implications of transfer of training theories for designing training. In Chapter Five, we will discuss how specific training program design features can facilitate learning and transfer of both open and closed skills.

Consider the transfer of training issues that Continental Airlines currently faces in preparing its pilots to fly the new 787 Dreamliner airplane.[23] First, Continental will fly the airplane on its U.S. routes to familiarize flight and ground crew staff with it. Continental plans to train approximately twenty-four pilots for each plane that is delivered. The 787 flight deck is similar but not identical to the 777 airplane that Continental's pilots are currently flying. Training includes use of a flight simulator of the 787 and computer-based courses. One of the most difficult tasks for pilots is to become familiar with a display that drops down in front of them, providing important flight information. The purpose of the display is to improve visibility during difficult flying conditions. Pilots like the display but find that it takes time to get used to it because it requires them to adjust their depth perception.

Three theories of transfer of training have implications for training design (the learning environment): the theory of identical elements, the stimulus generalization approach, and the cognitive theory of transfer.[24] Table 4.3 shows each theory's primary emphasis and the conditions that it is most appropriate to consider.

## Theory of Identical Elements

The **theory of identical elements** proposes that transfer of training occurs when what is being learned in the training session is identical to what the trainee has to perform on the job.[25] Transfer will be maximized to the degree that the tasks, materials, equipment, and

**TABLE 4.3**
**Transfer of Training Theories**

| Theory | Emphasis | Appropriate Conditions | Type of Transfer |
|---|---|---|---|
| Identical elements | Training environment is identical to work environment. | Training focuses on closed skills Work environment features are predictable and stable. *Example:* Training to use equipment. | Near |
| Stimulus generalization | General principles are applicable to many different work situations. | Training focuses on open skills. Work environment is unpredictable and highly variable. *Example:* Training in interpersonal skills. | Far |
| Cognitive theory | Meaningful material and coding schemes enhance storage and recall of training content. | All types of training and environments. | Near and far |

other characteristics of the learning environment are similar to those encountered in the work environment.

The use of identical elements theory is shown in the hostage training simulation used by the Baltimore Police Department. The Baltimore Police Department needed to teach police sergeants the skills to handle hostage-barricade situations in which lives are at stake—skills such as negotiating with a troubled husband holding his wife and/or children hostage. The first hour of a hostage situation is critical. The sergeant must organize resources quickly to achieve a successful end to the situation, with minimal or no injuries. A simulation was chosen because it provides a model of reality, a mock-up of a real situation without the danger. Multiple scenarios can be incorporated into the simulation, allowing the sergeants to practice the exact skills that they will need when facing a hostage crisis.

The simulation begins by having the trainees briefed on the hostage situation. Then they are directed to take charge of resolving the incident in the presence of an instructor who has personally been involved in similar real-life incidents. Each trainee supervises one difficult and one easy scenario. The simulation is designed to emphasize the importance of clear thinking and decision making in a situation in which time is critical. It is essential that the trainees take actions according to a set of priorities that place the greatest value on minimizing the risks to the hostages and isolating the suspects before communicating with them. The simulation scenarios include elements of many actual hostage incidents, such as forced entry, taking persons against their will, the presence of a weapon, and threats. As trainees work in the simulation, their actions are evaluated by the instructor. The instructor provides feedback to the trainees in writing after they complete the simulation, or the instructor can correct mistakes as they happen.

The training simulation mirrors the exact circumstances of actual hostage situations encountered by police officers. Also, the checklist of activities and behaviors that the sergeants are provided in training is the exact checklist used in hostage situations that occur on the street. Evidence of generalization is provided by police sergeants who have successfully dealt with a bank-hostage situation by using the skills emphasized in the simulation. The Baltimore Police Department is also concerned with maintenance. At the conclusion of the simulation, officers may be able to demonstrate how to free hostages successfully. However, the incidence of hostage situations is fairly low compared to other tasks that police officers perform (e.g., issuing traffic citations or investigating burglaries). As a result, the police department is concerned that officers may forget what they learned in training and therefore have difficulties in hostage situations. To ensure that officers have opportunities to practice these infrequently used but important skills, the training department occasionally schedules mock hostage situations.[26]

Another application of the theory of identical elements is found in the use of simulators for training airline pilots. Pilots are trained in a simulator that looks exactly like the cockpit of a commercial aircraft. All aspects of the cockpit in the simulator (e.g., gauges, dials, and lights) are the same as in a real aircraft. In psychological terms, the learning environment has complete fidelity with the work environment. **Fidelity** refers to the extent to which the training environment is similar to the work environment. If skills in flying, taking off, landing, and dealing with emergency situations are learned in the simulator, they will be transferred to the work setting (commercial aircraft).

The identical elements approach has also been used to develop instruments that are designed to measure the similarity of jobs.[27] Job similarity can be used as one measure of the extent to which training in the knowledge and skills required for one job prepares an employee to perform a different job.

The theory of identical elements has been applied to many training programs, particularly those that deal with the use of equipment or that involve specific procedures that must be learned. Identical elements theory is particularly relevant in making sure that near transfer occurs. **Near transfer** refers to trainees' ability to apply learned capabilities exactly to the work situation.

Identical elements theory does not encourage transfer where the learning environment and the training environment are not necessarily identical. This situation arises particularly in interpersonal skills training. For example, a person's behavior in a conflict situation is not easily predictable. Therefore, trainees must learn general principles of conflict resolution that they can apply to a wide variety of situations as circumstances dictate (e.g., an irate customer versus a customer who lacks product knowledge).

## Stimulus Generalization Approach

The **stimulus generalization approach** suggests that the way to understand the transfer of training issue is to construct training so that the most important features or general principles are emphasized. It is also important to identify the range of work situations in which these general principles can be applied. The stimulus generalization approach emphasizes far transfer. **Far transfer** refers to the trainee's ability to apply learned capabilities to the work environment, even though the work environment (equipment, problems, and tasks) is not identical to that of the training session.

The stimulus generalization approach can be seen in the design of some skill training programs, which are based on social learning theory. Recall from the discussion of social learning theory that modeling, practice, feedback, and reinforcement play key roles in learning. One step in developing effective interpersonal skill training programs is to identify key behaviors that are needed to be successful in a situation. **Key behaviors** refer to behaviors that can be used successfully in a wide variety of situations. The model demonstrates these key behaviors in a video, and trainees have opportunities to practice them. The key behaviors are believed to be applicable to a wide variety of situations. In fact, the practice sessions in this type of training requires the trainee to use the behaviors in a variety of situations that are not identical.

## Cognitive Theory of Transfer

The cognitive theory of transfer is based on the information processing theory of learning discussed earlier in the chapter. Recall that the storage and retrieval of information are key aspects of this model of learning. According to the **cognitive theory of transfer,** the likelihood of transfer depends on the trainees' ability to retrieve learned capabilities. This theory suggests that the likelihood of transfer is increased by providing trainees with meaningful material that enhances the chances that they will link what they encounter in the work environment to the learned capability. Also important is providing the trainee with cognitive strategies for coding the learned capabilities in memory so that they are easily retrievable.

The influence of cognitive theory is seen in training design that encourages trainees, as part of the program, to consider potential applications of the training content to their jobs. Many training programs include having trainees identify a work problem or situation and discuss the potential application of training content.

# THE LEARNING PROCESS

Now that you have reviewed the learning and transfer of training theories, you are ready to address three questions: What are the physical and mental processes involved in learning? How does learning and transfer occur? Do trainees have different learning styles?

## Mental and Physical Processes

Table 4.4 shows the learning processes, which include expectancy, perception, working storage, semantic encoding, long-term storage, retrieval, generalizing, and gratification.[28] Table 4.4 emphasizes that learning depends on the learner's cognitive processes, including attending to what is to be learned (learning content), organizing the learning content into a mental representation, and relating the learning content to existing knowledge from long-term memory.[29] **Expectancy** refers to the mental state that the learner brings to the instructional process. This includes factors such as readiness for training (motivation to learn, basic skills) as well as an understanding of the purpose of the instruction and the likely benefits that may result from learning and using the learned capabilities on the job. **Perception** refers to the ability to organize the message from the environment so that it can be processed and acted upon. Both working storage and semantic encoding relate to short-term memory. In **working storage,** rehearsal and repetition of information occur, allowing material to be coded for memory.

Working storage is limited by the amount of material that can be processed at any one time. Research suggests that not more than five messages can be prepared for storage at the same time. **Semantic encoding** refers to the actual coding process of incoming messages.

**TABLE 4.4** **The Relationship Among Learning Processes, Instructional Events, and Forms of Instruction**

| Processes of Learning | External Instructional Events | Forms of Instruction |
|---|---|---|
| 1. Expectancy | 1. Informing the learner of the lesson objective | 1a. Demonstrate the expected performance.<br>1b. Indicate the kind of verbal question to be answered. |
| 2. Perception | 2. Presenting stimuli with distinctive features | 2a. Emphasize the features of the subject to be perceived.<br>2b. Use formatting and figures in text to emphasize features. |
| 3. Working storage | 3. Limiting the amount to be learned | 3a. Arrange lengthier material in chunks.<br>3b. Provide a visual image of material to be learned.<br>3c. Provide practice and overlearning to aid the attainment of automaticity. |
| 4. Semantic encoding | 4. Providing learning guidance | 4a. Provide verbal cues to the proper combining sequence.<br>4b. Provide verbal links to a larger meaningful context.<br>4c. Use diagrams and models to show relationships among concepts. |
| 5. Long-term storage | 5. Elaborating the amount to be learned | 5a. Vary the context and setting for presentation and recall of material.<br>5b. Relate newly learned material to previously learned information.<br>5c. Provide a variety of contexts and situations during practice. |
| 6. Retrieval | 6. Providing cues that are used in recall | 6a. Suggest cues that elicit the recall of material.<br>6b. Use familiar sounds or rhymes as cues. |
| 7. Generalizing | 7. Enhancing retention and learning transfer | 7a. Design the learning situation to share elements with the situation to which learning applies.<br>7b. Provide verbal links to additional complexes of information. |
| 8. Gratifying | 8. Providing feedback about performance correctness | 8a. Provide feedback on degree of accuracy and timing of performance.<br>8b. Confirm whether original expectancies were met. |

Source: R. Gagne, "Learning processes and instruction," *Training Research Journal,* 1 (1995/96): 17–28.

Different learning strategies influence how training content is coded. Learning strategies include rehearsal, organizing, and elaboration.[30] **Rehearsal,** the simplest learning strategy, focuses on learning through repetition (memorization). **Organizing** requires the learner to find similarities and themes in the training material. **Elaboration** requires the trainee to relate the training material to other, more familiar knowledge, skills, or behaviors. Trainees use a combination of these strategies to learn. The "best" strategy depends on the learning outcome. For knowledge outcomes, rehearsal and organization are most appropriate. For skill application, elaboration is necessary. After messages have been attended to, rehearsed, and coded, they are ready for storage in long-term memory.

To use learned material (e.g., cognitive skills or verbal information), it must be retrieved. **Retrieval** involves identifying learned material in long-term memory and using it to influence performance. An important part of the learning process is not only being able to reproduce exactly what was learned, but also being able to adapt the learning for use in similar but not identical situations. This is known as **generalizing.** Finally, **gratifying** refers to the feedback that the learner receives as a result of using learning content. Feedback is necessary to allow the learner to adapt responses so they are more appropriate. Feedback also provides information about the incentives or reinforcers that may result from performance.

## The Learning Cycle

Learning can be considered a dynamic cycle that involves four stages: concrete experience, reflective observation, abstract conceptualization, and active experimentation.[31] First, a trainee encounters a concrete experience (e.g., a work problem). This is followed by thinking (reflective observation) about the problem, which leads to generation of ideas of how to solve the problem (abstract conceptualization) and finally to implementation of the ideas directly to the problem (active experimentation). Implementing the ideas provides feedback as to their effectiveness, so the learner can see the results and start the learning process over again. Trainees continually develop concepts, translate them into ideas, implement them, and adapt them as a result of their personal observations about their experiences.

Researchers have developed questionnaires to measure trainees' weak and strong points in the learning cycle. Some people have a tendency to overemphasize or underemphasize one stage of the learning cycle, or to avoid certain stages altogether. The key to effective learning is to be competent in each of the four stages. Four fundamental learning styles are believed to exist. These learning styles combine elements of each of the four stages of the learning cycle.

Table 4.5 shows the characteristics and dominant learning stage of individuals in each style, called Divergers, Assimilators, Convergers, and Accommodators.[32] Keep in mind

**TABLE 4.5**   **Learning Styles**

| Learning Style Type | Dominant Learning Abilities | Learning Characteristics |
|---|---|---|
| *Diverger* | • Concrete experience<br>• Reflective observation | • Is good at generating ideas, seeing a situation from multiple perspectives, and being aware of meaning and value<br>• Tends to be interested in people, culture, and the arts |
| *Assimilator* | • Abstract conceptualization<br>• Reflective observation | • Is good at inductive reasoning, creating theoretical models, and combining disparate observations into an integrated explanation<br>• Tends to be less concerned with people than with ideas and abstract concepts |
| *Converger* | • Abstract conceptualization<br>• Active experimentation | • Is good at decisiveness, practical application of ideas, and hypothetical deductive reasoning<br>• Prefers dealing with technical tasks rather than interpersonal issues |
| *Accommodator* | • Concrete experience<br>• Active experimentation | • Is good at implementing decisions, carrying out plans, and getting involved in new experiences<br>• Tends to be at ease with people but may be seen as impatient or pushy |

Source: Based on D. Kolb, *Learning Style Inventory, Version 3.1* (Boston: Hay/McBer Training Resources Group, 2005).

that although researchers agree that we have learning styles and preferences, there is disagreement about how to measure them.

In trying to match instruction to learning preferences, it is important that instructional or training strategies should be determined first by *what* is being taught or the learning outcomes. Then, learning styles should be considered to adjust the training or instructional strategy.[33]

For example, AmeriCredit, an auto finance company located in Fort Worth, Texas, is trying to modify training to better match its employees' learning styles.[34] The company has created a database to identify and track each employee's learning style. Also, employees' learning styles are being considered in course design. In a new e-learning class, employees who prefer learning by action will receive information in bullet points and will complete activities that help them learn. Employees who prefer thought and reasoning will receive more conceptual material during the course and be involved in fewer experiences. The company plans to compare the new e-learning class that takes into account learning styles with one that does not, so it can determine whether the adaptation to learning styles makes a difference in trainee satisfaction and learning.

## Implications of the Learning Process and Transfer of Training for Instruction

**Instruction** refers to the trainer's manipulation of the environment in order to help trainees learn.[35] The right side of Table 4.4 shows the forms of instruction that support learning. To provide trainees with the best chance to learn, it is important to ensure that these forms of instruction are included in training. Table 4.6 summarizes the features of good instruction that facilitate the learning process. The features of a positive learning environment and transfer of training need to be designed into training courses, programs, or specific training methods that might be used, whether in the form of lectures, e-learning, or on-the-job training. Here, as well as later in the chapter, we discuss these features.

### *Employees Need to Know the Objectives*

Employees learn best when they understand the objective of the training program. The **objective** refers to the purpose and expected outcome of training activities. There may be objectives for each training session, as well as overall objectives for the program. Recall the discussion of goal setting theory earlier in the chapter. Because objectives can serve as goals, trainees need to understand, accept, and be committed to achieving the training objectives for learning to occur. Training objectives based on the training needs analysis help employees understand why they need training and what they need to learn. Objectives

| |
|---|
| **TABLE 4.6** <br> **Features of Instruction and the Work Environment That Facilitate Learning and Transfer of Training** |

- Objectives
- Meaningful content
- Opportunities to practice
- Methods for committing training content to memory
- Feedback
- Observation, experience, and social interaction
- Proper coordination and arrangement of the training program
- Encourage trainee responsibility and self-management
- Ensure that the work environment supports learning and transfer

are also useful for identifying the types of training outcomes that should be measured to evaluate a training program's effectiveness.

A training objective has three components:[36]

1. A statement of what the employee is expected to do (performance or outcome)
2. A statement of the quality or level of performance that is acceptable (criterion)
3. A statement of the conditions under which the trainee is expected to perform the desired outcome (conditions)

The objective should not describe performance that cannot be observed, such as "understand" or "know." Table 4.7 shows verbs that can be used for cognitive, affective, and psychomotor (physical abilities and skills) outcomes. For example, a training objective for a customer-service training program for retail salespeople might be "After training, the employee will be able to express concern [performance] to all irate customers by a brief (fewer than 10-word) apology, only after the customer has stopped talking [criteria] and no matter how upset the customer is [conditions]." Table 4.8 shows the characteristics of good training objectives.

Some of the most common problems with objectives include that they are unclear, incomplete, or unspecific.[37] Table 4.9 provides some example of learning objectives. As you review each objective, identify if it includes each of the three components (performance, criteria, condition). Are these good objectives? How can they be improved?

### Employees Need Meaningful Training Content

Employees are most likely to learn when the training is linked to their current job experiences and tasks—that is, when it is meaningful to them.[38] To enhance the meaningfulness of training content, the message should be presented using concepts, terms, and examples

**TABLE 4.7** Examples of Performance or Outcomes for Objectives

| Domain | Performance |
|---|---|
| Knowledge (recall of information) | Arrange, define, label, list, recall, repeat |
| Comprehension (interpret in own words) | Classify, discuss, explain, review, translate |
| Application (apply to new situation) | Apply, choose, demonstrate, illustrate, prepare |
| Analysis (break down into parts and show relationships) | Analyze, categorize, compare, diagram, test |
| Synthesis (bring together to form a whole) | Arrange, collect, assemble, propose, set up |
| Evaluation (judgments based on criteria) | Appraise, attack, argue, choose, compare |
| Receiving (pay attention) | Listen to, perceive, be alert to |
| Responding (minimal participation) | Reply, answer, approve, obey |
| Valuing (preferences) | Attain, assume, support, participate |
| Organization (development of values) | Judge, decide, identify with, select |
| Characterization (total philosophy of life) | Believe, practice, carry out |
| Reflexes (involuntary movement) | Stiffen, extend, flex |
| Fundamental movements (simple movements) | Crawl, walk, run, reach |
| Perception (response to stimuli) | Turn, bend, balance, crawl |
| Physical abilities (psychomotor movements) | Move heavy objects; make quick motions |
| Skilled movements (advanced learned movements) | Play an instrument; use a hand tool |

Sources: Based on H. Sredl and W. Rothwell, "Setting Instructional Objectives," Chapter 16 in *The ASTD Reference Guide to Professional Training Roles and Competencies, Vol. II* (New York: Random House, 1987); and R. Mager, *Preparing Instructional Objectives*, 3d ed. (Atlanta: Center for Effective Performance, 1997).

**TABLE 4.8**
**Characteristics of Good Training Objectives**

- Provide a clear idea of what the trainee is expected to be able to do at the end of training.
- Include standards of performance that can be measured or evaluated.
- State the specific resources (e.g., tools and equipment) that the trainee needs to perform the action or behavior specified.
- Describe the conditions under which performance of the objective is expected to occur (e.g., the physical work environment, such as at night or in high temperatures; mental stresses, such as angry customers; or equipment failure, such as malfunctioning computer equipment).

**TABLE 4.9**
**Examples of Learning Objectives**

- Develop a diverse multifunctional team that can compete in a challenging environment to produce outcomes that will enhance results.
- Use conflict management skills when faced with a conflict.
- Smile at all customers, even when exhausted, unless the customer is irate.
- Reduce product defects from 10 percent to 7 percent.
- List all of the nodes of a DC-3 multi-switch correctly, without using a reference manual.
- Use the software 100 percent accurately, given access to the quick reference guide.

familiar to trainees. Also, the training context should mirror the work environment. The **training context** refers to the physical, intellectual, and emotional environment in which training occurs. For example, in a retail salesperson customer-service program, the meaningfulness of the material will be increased by using scenarios of unhappy customers actually encountered by salespersons in stores. Some useful techniques for convincing trainees that the training program content is meaningful include:[39]

- Telling stories about others' success in applying training content, especially former trainees
- Relating training content to what trainees already know about their jobs
- Showing how training relates to company goals and strategy
- Showing how trainees can use training content ideas at work
- Discussing examples or cases that remind trainees of the good and poor work they have seen
- Repeating the application of ideas in different contexts
- Presenting evidence that what they will learn during training is what high-performing employees use in their jobs
- Showing how the conditions that trainees face in training are similar to those on the job
- Providing practice or application activities that can be used on the job
- Providing hard copies or electronic access to well-organized materials so trainees can refer to them on the job or use them to teach others
- Allowing trainees to choose their practice strategy and how they want training content presented (e.g., verbally, visually, problem-based, or a combination of approaches)

### Employees Need Opportunities to Practice

**Practice** refers to the physical or mental rehearsal of a task, knowledge, or skill to achieve proficiency in performing the task or skill or demonstrating the knowledge. Practice involves having the employee demonstrate the learned capability (e.g., cognitive strategy, verbal information) emphasized in the training objectives under conditions and performance standards specified by the objectives. For practice to be effective, it needs to involve the trainee actively, include overlearning (repeated practice), take the appropriate amount of time, and include the appropriate unit of learning (amount of material). Practice also needs to be relevant to the training objectives. It is best to include a combination of examples and practice, rather than all practice.[40] This helps to avoid overloading trainees' memory so they can engage in the cognitive processes needed for learning to occur (selecting, organizing, and integrating content). Viewing examples helps learners develop a new mental model of skills, which they can then use in practice. Some examples of ways to practice include case studies, simulations, role plays, games, and oral and written questions.

### Pre-practice Conditions

Trainers need to focus not just on training content, but also on how to enable trainees to process information in a way that will facilitate learning and the use of training on the job. There are several steps that trainers can take within the training course prior to practice to enhance trainees' motivation to learn and facilitate retention of training content. Before practice, trainers can[41]

1. Provide information about the process or strategy that will result in the greatest learning. For example, let trainees in a customer service class know about the types of calls they will receive (irate customer, request for information on a product, challenge of a bill), how to recognize such calls, and how to complete the calls.

2. Encourage trainees to develop a strategy (metacognition) to reflect on their own learning process. **Metacognition** refers to individual control over one's thinking. Two ways that individuals engage in metacognition are monitoring and control.[42] Research shows that metacognition, including self-regulation, promotes learning.[43] **Self-regulation** refers to the learner's involvement with the training material and assessing their progress toward learning. Learners who engage in self-regulation likely learn more effectively because they are able to monitor their progress, identify areas needing improvement, and adjust their learning. Self-regulation may be especially important for online training courses, in which learners have control over the learning experience such that they can decide to drop out of courses and decide how much effort, if any, they want to exert to learn the training content. Table 4.10 shows how trainers can encourage self-regulation.

3. Provide **advance organizers**—outlines, texts, diagrams, and graphs that help trainees organize the information that will be presented and practiced.

4. Help trainees set challenging mastery or learning goals.

5. Create realistic expectations for trainees by communicating what will occur in training.

6. When training employees in teams, communicate performance expectations and clarify the roles and responsibilities of team members.

**TABLE 4.10**

**Examples of Questions That Encourage Self-Regulation**

Source: From T. Sitzmann, "Self-regulating online course engagement," *T+D* (March 2010): 26.

- Am I concentrating on the training material?
- Do I understand the key points?
- Am I setting goals to help me remember the material after I finish the course?
- Are the study tactics I have been using effective for learning the training material?
- Would I do better on the test if I studied more?
- Have I spent enough time reviewing to remember the information after I finish the course?

## Practice Involves Experience

Learning will not occur if employees practice only by talking about what they are expected to do. For example, using the objective for the customer service course previously discussed, practice would involve having trainees participate in role playing with unhappy customers (customers upset with poor service, poor merchandise, or unsatisfactory exchange policies). Training should involve an active learning approach in which trainees must explore and experiment to determine the rules, principles, and strategies for effective performance.[44] Trainees need to continue to practice even if they have been able to perform the objective several times (known as **overlearning**). Overlearning helps the trainee become more comfortable using new knowledge and skills and increases the length of time the trainee will retain the knowledge, skill, or behavior.

Conventional wisdom is that we all learn the most from our errors. However, most people feel that errors are frustrating and lead to anger and despair. Research suggests that from a training perspective, errors can be useful.[45] **Error management training** refers to giving trainees opportunities to make errors during training. In error management training, trainees are instructed that errors can help learning, and they are encouraged to make errors and learn from them. Trainees may actually commit more errors and may take longer to complete training that incorporates error management training. However, error management training helps improve employee use of learned skills on the job; i.e., transfer of training.

Error management training is effective because it provides the opportunity for trainees to engage in metacognition (i.e., to plan how to use training content, to monitor use of training content, and to evaluate how training content was used). This results in a deeper level of cognitive processing, leading to better memory and recall of training. Trainers should consider using error management training in the training program along with traditional approaches by giving trainees the opportunity to make errors when they work alone on difficult problems and tasks while encouraging them to use errors as a way to learn.

It is important to note that allowing trainees simply to make errors does not help learning. For errors to have a positive influence on learning, trainees need to be taught to use errors as a chance to learn. Error management training may be particularly useful whenever the training content to be learned cannot be completely covered during a training session. As a result, trainees have to discover on their own what to do when confronted with new tasks or problems.

## Massed versus Spaced Practice

The frequency of practice has been shown to influence learning, depending on the type of task being trained.[46] **Massed practice** conditions are those in which individuals practice a task continuously, without resting. Massed practice also involves having trainees complete practice exercises at one time within a lesson or class rather than distributing the exercises within the lesson. In **spaced practice** conditions, individuals are given rest intervals within practice sessions. Spaced practice is superior to massed practice in general. However, the difference in effectiveness of massed versus spaced practice varies by the characteristics of the task. Task characteristics include overall task complexity, mental requirements, and physical requirements. **Overall task complexity** refers to the degree to which a task requires a number of distinct behaviors, the number of choices involved in performing the task, and the degree of uncertainty in performing the task. **Mental requirements** refers to the degree to which the task requires the subject to use or demonstrate mental skills or cognitive skills or abilities to perform the task. **Physical requirements** refers to the degree to which the task requires the person to use or demonstrate physical skills and abilities to perform and complete the task.  Table 4.11 shows how tasks can differ.

For more complex tasks (including those that are representative of training settings, such as web-based instruction, lecture, and distance learning), relatively long rest periods appear to be beneficial for task learning.

After practice, trainees need specific feedback to enhance learning. This includes feedback from the task or job itself, trainers, managers, and peers.

### Whole versus Part Practice

A final issue related to practice is how much of the training should be practiced at one time. One option is that all tasks or objectives should be practiced at the same time (**whole practice**). Another option is that an objective or task should be practiced individually as soon as each is introduced in the training program (**part practice**). It is probably best to employ both whole and part practice in a training session. Trainees should have the opportunity to practice individual skills or behaviors. If the skills or behaviors introduced in training are related to one another, the trainee should demonstrate all of them in a practice session after they have been practiced individually.

**TABLE 4.11   Mental and Physical Requirements and Overall Complexity for Tasks**

| Mental Requirements | Overall Complexity | Physical Requirements | Tasks |
|---|---|---|---|
| Low | Low | High | Rotary pursuit, typing, ball toss, ladder climb, peg reversal, bilateral transfer, crank turning |
| High | Average | Low | Free recall task, video games, foreign language, slide-bar task, voice recognition, classroom lecture, sound localization, word processing, stoop task, verbal discrimination, maze learning, connecting numbers, upside-down alphabet printing, distance learning, web training |
| Low | High | High | Gymnastic skills, balancing task |
| High | High | High | Air traffic controller simulation, milk pasteurization simulation, airplane control simulation, hand movement memorization, puzzle box task, music memorization and performance |

Source: J. Donovan and D. Radosevich, "A meta-analytic review of the distribution of practice effect: Now you see it, now you don't," *Journal of Applied Psychology*, 84 (1999):795–805.

For example, one objective of the customer service training for retail salespeople is learning how to deal with an unhappy customer. Salespeople are likely to have to learn three key behaviors: (1) greeting disgruntled customers, (2) understanding their complaints, and then (3) identifying and taking appropriate action. Practice sessions should be held for each of the three behaviors (part practice). Then another practice session should be held so that trainees can practice all three skills together (whole practice). If trainees are only given the opportunity to practice the behaviors individually, it is unlikely that they will be able to deal with an unhappy customer.

### Effective Practice Conditions

For practice to be relevant to the training objectives, several conditions must be met.[47] Practice must involve the actions emphasized in the training objectives, be completed under the conditions specified in the training objectives, help trainees perform to meet the criteria or standard that was set, provide some means to evaluate the extent to which trainees' performance meets the standards, and allow trainees to correct their mistakes.

Practice must be related to the training objectives. The trainer should identify what trainees will be doing when practicing the objectives (performance), the criteria for attainment of the objective, and the conditions under which they may perform. These conditions should be present in the practice session. Next, the trainer needs to consider the adequacy of the trainees' performance. That is, how will trainees know whether their performance meets performance standards? Will they see a model of desired performance? Will they be provided with a checklist or description of desired performance? Can the trainees decide if their performance meets standards, or will the trainer or a piece of equipment compare their performance with standards?

The trainer must also decide—if trainees' performance does not meet standards—whether trainees will be able to understand what is wrong and how to fix it. That is, trainers need to consider whether trainees will be able to diagnose their performance and take corrective action, or if they will need help from the trainer or a fellow trainee.

### Employees Need to Commit Training Content to Memory

Memory works by processing stimuli we perceive through our senses into short-term memory. If the information is determined to be "important," it moves to long-term memory, where new interconnections are made between neurons or electrical connections in the brain. There are several ways that trainers can help employees store knowledge, skills, behavior, and other training in long-term memory.[48] One way is to make trainees aware of how they are creating, processing, and accessing memory. It is important for trainees to understand how they learn. A presentation of learning styles (discussed earlier in this chapter) can be a useful way to determine how trainees prefer to learn.

To create long-term memory, training programs must be explicit on content and elaborate on details. There are several ways to create long-term memory. One approach that trainers use is to create a concept map to show relationships among ideas. Another is to use multiple forms of review including writing, drawings, and role playing to access memory through multiple methods. Teaching key words, a procedure, or a sequence, or providing a visual image gives trainees another way to retrieve information. Reminding trainees of knowledge, behavior, and skills that they already know that are relevant to the current training content creates a link to long-term memory that provides a framework for recalling the new training content. External retrieval cues can also be useful. Consider a time when you misplaced your keys or wallet. In trying to remember, we often review all the information we can recall that was close in time to the event or preceded the loss. We often go to the place where we were when we last saw the item because the environment can provide cues that aid in recall.

Research suggests that no more than four or five items can be attended to at one time. If a lengthy process or procedure is to be taught, instruction needs to be delivered in relatively small chunks or short sessions in order to not exceed memory limits.[49] Long-term memory is also enhanced by going beyond one-trial learning. That is, once trainees correctly demonstrate a behavior or skill or correctly recall knowledge, it is often assumed that they have learned it, but this is not always true. Making trainees review and practice over multiple days (overlearning) can help them retain information in long-term memory. Overlearning also helps to automize a task.

**Automatization** refers to making performance of a task, recall of knowledge, or demonstration of a skill so automatic that it requires little thought or attention. Automatization also helps reduce memory demands. The more that automatization occurs, the more that memory is freed up to concentrate on other learning and thinking. The more active a trainee is in rehearsal and practice, the greater the amount of information retained in long-term memory and the less memory decay occurs over time.

Another way to avoid overwhelming trainees with complex material is to give them pretraining work that can be completed online or using workbooks.[50] For example, trainees can become familiar with the "basics" such as names, definitions, principles, and characteristics of components before they are trained in how the principles are applied (e.g., dealing with angry customers) or how a process works (e.g., testing for pathogens in a blood sample, changing a car's water pump).

### Employees Need Feedback

**Feedback** is information about how well people are meeting the training objectives. To be effective, feedback should focus on specific behaviors and be provided as soon as possible after the trainees' behavior.[51] Also, positive trainee behavior should be verbally praised or reinforced. Videotape is a powerful tool for giving feedback. Trainers should view the videotape with trainees, provide specific information about how behaviors need to be modified, and praise trainee behaviors that meet objectives. Feedback can also come from tests and quizzes, on-the-job observation, performance data, a mentor or coach, written communications, or interpersonal interactions.

The specificity of the level of feedback provided to trainees needs to vary if trainees are expected to understand what leads to poor performance as well as good performance.[52] For example, employees may need to learn how to respond when equipment is malfunctioning as well as when it is working properly; therefore, feedback provided during training should not be so specific that it leads only to employee knowledge about equipment that is working properly. Less specific feedback can cause trainees to make errors that lead to equipment problems, providing trainees with opportunities to learn which behaviors lead to equipment problems and how to fix those problems. Difficulties encountered during practice as a result of errors or reduced frequency of feedback can help trainees engage more in exploration and information processing to identify correct responses.

### Employees Learn Through Observation, Experience, and Interaction

As mentioned earlier in the chapter, one way employees learn is through observing and imitating the actions of models. For the model to be effective, the desired behaviors or skills need to be clearly specified and the model should have characteristics (e.g., age or position) similar to the target audience.[53] After observing the model, trainees should have the opportunity in practice sessions to reproduce the skills or behavior shown by the model. According to adult learning theory, employees also learn best if they learn by doing,[54] which involves giving employees hands-on experiences or putting them with more experienced employees and providing them with the tools and materials needed to manage their knowledge gaps.

Employees also learn best through interaction interacting with training content, with other learners, and with the trainer or instructor.[55] Table 4.12 shows the three ways that employees learn through interaction and when to use them. **Learner-content interaction** means that the learner interacts with the training content. Learner-content interaction includes reading text on the web or in books, listening to multimedia modules, performing activities that require the manipulation of tools or objects (such as writing), completing case studies and worksheets, or creating new content based on learned information.

**Learner-instructor interaction** refers to interaction between the learner and the expert (trainer). Trainers can facilitate learning by presenting, demonstrating, and reinforcing content. Also, trainers provide support, encouragement, and feedback that are valued by most learners. Learner-instructor discussions can be useful for helping learners understand content, enhance learners' self-awareness and self-assessment, gain an appreciation for different opinions, and implement ideas on the job. To maximize learners' critical thinking and analysis skills, discussion should go beyond instructors asking questions and learners providing answers.

**Learner-learner interaction** refers to interaction between learners, with or without an instructor. Learner-learner interaction, including observing and sharing experience with peers, may be especially useful for training interpersonal skills (such as communications), acquiring personal knowledge based on experience (such as tacit knowledge about how to close a sale or resolve a conflict), context-specific knowledge (such as managing in an international location), and learning to cope with uncertainty or new situations (such as marketing a new product or service).[56]

**TABLE 4.12**
**Three Types of Instructional Interaction**

| Type | When to Use |
|---|---|
| Learner-content | Requires mastering a task that is completed alone. Learn process of studying information and acting on it in a team context |
| Learner-learner | Requires mastering a task that is completed in a group. Learners will gain new knowledge or validate their understanding by discussing content with peers. |
| Learner-instructor | Best for in-depth topic exploration and to develop strengths in critical analysis and thinking. Discussion may be limited when large amounts of material need to be presented in a short timespan. |

Sources: Based on H. Nuriddin, "Building the right interaction," *T+D* (March 2010): 32–35; D. Leonard and W. Swap, "Deep Smarts," *Harvard Business Review* (September 2004): 88–97.

**Communities of practice (COPs)** refers to groups of employees who work together, learn from each other, and develop a common understanding of how to get work accomplished.[57] COPs can involve face-to-face or electronic interaction. The idea of COPs suggests that learning occurs on the job as a result of social interaction. Every company has naturally occurring COPs that arise as a result of relationships that employees develop to accomplish work, and as a result of the design of the work environment. For example, at Siemens Power Transmission in Wendell, North Carolina, managers were wondering how to stop employees from gathering in the employee cafeteria for informal discussions.[58] But that was before the managers discovered that the informal discussions actually encouraged learning. In the discussions, employees were developing problem-solving strategies, sharing product and procedural information, and providing career counseling to each other. Now Siemens is placing pads of paper and overhead projectors in the lunchroom as aids for these informal meetings. Managers who were previously focused on keeping workers on the job are now encouraging employees by providing essential tools and information and giving employees the freedom to meet.

COPs also take the form of social networks, discussion boards, list servers, or other forms of computer-mediated communication in which employees communicate electronically. In doing so, each employee's knowledge can be accessed in a relatively quick manner. It is as if employees are having a conversation with a group of experts. Wyeth Pharmaceuticals has 11 COPs that focus on maintaining shop floor excellence.[59] The COPs make it easy for employees to share best practices, learn from one another, and improve business processes. The maintenance function used its COP to deliver more than 600 hours of training on new technology and maintenance processes. This has resulted in more reliable equipment and higher productivity, such as increasing equipment use in one manufacturing plant from 72 to 92 percent.

COPs are most effective for learning and improving work performance when managers and employees believe they contribute to the core operating processes of the company, such as engineering or quality.[60] Despite the benefits of improved communication, a drawback to these communities is that participation is often voluntary, so some employees may not share their knowledge unless the organizational culture supports participation. That is, employees may be reluctant to participate without an incentive or may be fearful that if they share their knowledge with others, they will give away their personal advantage in salary and promotion decisions.[61] Another potential drawback is information overload. Employees may receive so much information that they fail to process it, which may cause them to withdraw from the COP.

### Employees Need the Training Program To Be Properly Coordinated and Arranged

Training coordination is one of several aspects of training administration. **Training administration** refers to coordinating activities before, during, and after the program.[62] Training administration involves:

1. Communicating courses and programs to employees
2. Enrolling employees in courses and programs
3. Preparing and processing any pretraining materials, such as readings or tests
4. Preparing materials that will be used in instruction (e.g., copies of overheads, cases)
5. Arranging for the training facility and room
6. Testing equipment that will be used in instruction

7. Having backup equipment (e.g., paper copy of slides or an extra overhead projector bulb) should equipment fail
8. Providing support during instruction
9. Distributing evaluation materials (e.g., tests, reaction measures, surveys)
10. Facilitating communications between trainer and trainees during and after training (e.g., coordinating exchange of e-mail addresses)
11. Recording course completion in the trainees' training records or personnel files

Good coordination ensures that trainees are not distracted by events (such as an uncomfortable room or poorly organized materials) that could interfere with learning. Activities before the program include communicating to trainees the purpose of the program, the place it will be held, the name of a person to contact if they have questions, and any preprogram work they are supposed to complete. Books, speakers, handouts, and videotapes need to be prepared. Any necessary arrangements to secure rooms and equipment (such as DVD players) should be made. The physical arrangement of the training room should complement the training technique. For example, it would be difficult for a team-building session to be effective if the seats could not be moved for group activities. If visual aids will be used, all trainees should be able to see them. Make sure that the room is physically comfortable with adequate lighting and ventilation. Trainees should be informed of starting and finishing times, break times, and location of bathrooms. Minimize distractions such as phone messages; request that trainees turn off cell phones and pagers. If trainees will be asked to evaluate the program or take tests to determine what they have learned, allot time for this activity at the end of the program. Following the program, any credits or recording of the names of trainees who completed the program should be done. Handouts and other training materials should be stored or returned to the consultant. The end of the program is also a good time to consider how the program could be improved if it will be offered again. Practical issues in selecting and preparing a training site and designing a program are discussed in more detail in Chapter Five.

### Encourage Trainee Responsibility and Self-Management

Trainees need to take responsibility for learning and transfer,[63] which includes preparing for training, being involved and engaged during training, and using training content back on the job. Before training, trainees need to consider why they are attending training and set specific learning goals (either alone or, preferably, in a discussion with their manager) as part of completing an action plan (action plans are discussed in more detail later in this chapter). Also, trainees need to complete any assigned pretraining assignments. During training, trainees need to be involved. That is, they need to participate and share experiences in discussions, to practice, and to ask questions if they are confused. After training, trainees need to review and work toward reaching the goals established in their action plan. They need to be willing to change (e.g., try new behaviors or apply new knowledge) and ask peers and managers for help if they need it.

**Self-management** refers to a person's attempt to control certain aspects of decision making and behavior. Training programs should prepare employees to self-manage their use of new skills and behaviors on the job. Self-management involves:

1. Determining the degree of support and negative consequences in the work setting for using newly acquired capabilities
2. Setting goals for using learned capabilities

3. Applying learned capabilities to the job

4. Monitoring use of learned capabilities on the job

5. Engaging in self-reinforcement[64]

Research suggests that trainees exposed to self-management strategies exhibit higher levels of transfer of behavior and skills than do trainees who are not provided with self-management strategies.[65]

### Ensure That the Work Environment Supports Learning and Transfer

There is no magic "formula" for ensuring that transfer of training occurs. Effective strategies for transfer of training include ensuring that trainees are motivated and managers and coworkers support learning and transfer.[66] These strategies are especially important when training open skills; that is, trainees have more choice about what and how to apply trained principles. Closed skills include prescribed behaviors that likely are less influenced by managers, peers, and the work environment. Also, designing training to increase knowledge and self-efficacy has a positive relationship with transfer of training.

Table 4.13 shows a list of obstacles in the work environment that can inhibit learning and transfer of training. They include (1) lack of support from peers and managers and (2) factors related to the work itself (e.g., time pressure). Given the restructuring, downsizing, and cost cutting occurring in many companies, these obstacles are often a reality for trainees.

For example, new technologies allow employees to gain access to resources and product demonstrations using the World Wide Web or personal computers equipped with DVD

**TABLE 4.13** **Examples of Obstacles in the Work Environment That Inhibit Transfer of Training**

| Obstacle Work Conditions | Description of Influence |
|---|---|
| Time pressures<br>Inadequate equipment<br>Few opportunities to use skills<br>Inadequate budget | Trainee has difficulty using new knowledge, skills, or behavior. |
| **Lack of Peer Support**<br>Peers discourage use of new knowledge and skills on the job.<br>Peers are unwilling to provide feedback.<br>Peers see training as waste of time. | Peers do not support use of new knowledge, skills, or behavior. |
| **Lack of Management Support**<br>Management does not accept ideas or suggestions that are learned in training.<br>Management does not discuss training opportunities.<br>Management opposes use of skills learned in training.<br>Management communicates that training is a waste of time.<br>Management is unwilling to provide reinforcement, feedback, and encouragement needed for trainees to use training content. | Managers do not reinforce training or provide opportunities to use new knowledge, skills, or behavior |

Sources: Based on J. Tracey and M. Tews, "Construct validity of a general training climate scale," *Organizational Research Methods*, 8 (2005): 353–374; R. D. Marx, "Self-managed skill retention," *Training and Development Journal* (January 1986): 54–57.

drives. But while employees are being trained to use these resources with state-of-the-art technology, they often become frustrated because comparable technology is not available to them at their work site. Employees' computers may lack sufficient memory or links to the World Wide Web for them to use what they have learned.

These obstacles inhibit transfer because they cause lapses. **Lapses** take place when the trainee uses previously learned, less effective capabilities instead of trying to apply the capability emphasized in the training program. Lapses into old behavior and skill patterns are common. Trainees should try to avoid a consistent pattern of slipping back or using old, ineffective learned capabilities (e.g., knowledge, skills, behaviors, and strategies). Also, trainees should understand that lapses are common and be prepared to cope with them. Trainees who are unprepared for lapses may give up trying to use new capabilities—especially trainees with low self-efficacy and/or self-confidence.

One way to ensure that learning and transfer of training occurs is to ensure that the climate for transfer is positive. **Climate for transfer** refers to trainees' perceptions about a wide variety of characteristics of the work environment that facilitate or inhibit the use of trained skills or behavior. These characteristics include manager and peer support, the opportunity to use skills, and the consequences of using learned capabilities.[67] Table 4.14 shows characteristics of a positive climate for transfer of training. Research has shown that transfer of training climate is significantly related to positive changes in managers' administrative and interpersonal behaviors following training. To support the transfer of financial training emphasizing Southwest Airlines's key business metrics, cost checklists explaining how employees can contribute to the company's bottom line are distributed companywide

**TABLE 4.14**   **Characteristics of a Positive Climate for Learning Transfer of Training**

| Characteristic | Example |
|---|---|
| Supervisors and coworkers encourage and set goals for trainees to use new skills and behaviors acquired in training. | Newly trained managers discuss how to apply their training on the job with their supervisors and other managers. |
| *Task cues:* Characteristics of a trainee's job prompt or remind him or her to use new skills and behaviors acquired in training. | The job of a newly trained manager is designed in such a way as to allow him or her to use the skills taught in training. |
| *Feedback consequences:* Supervisors support the application of new skills and behaviors acquired in training. | Supervisors notice newly trained managers who use their training. |
| *Lack of punishment:* Trainees are not openly discouraged from using new skills and behaviors acquired in training. | When newly trained managers fail to use their training, they are not reprimanded. |
| *Extrinsic reinforcement consequences:* Trainees receive extrinsic rewards for using new skills and behaviors acquired in training. | Newly trained managers who successfully use their training will receive a salary increase. |
| *Intrinsic reinforcement consequences:* Trainees receive intrinsic rewards for using new skills and behaviors acquired in training. | Supervisors and other managers appreciate newly trained managers who perform their job as taught in training. |

Source: Adapted from J. B. Tracey, S. I. Tannenbaum, and M. J. Kavanagh, "Applying trained skills on the job: The importance of the work environment," *Journal of Applied Psychology,* 80(1995): 235–52; E. Holton, "What's *Really* Wrong: Diagnosis for Learning Transfer System Change." In *Improving Learning Transfer in Organizations,* ed. E. Holton and T. Baldwin (San Fransisco: Jossey-Bass, 2003): 59–79.

following training.[68] Flip charts showing highlights from manager-employee question-and-answer sessions are posted in work areas. All managers receive large posters displaying the company's four "magic numbers" (net income, unit cost measure, net margin, and invested capital). The posters include blank columns that managers are expected to complete and regularly update to show the past year's performance, the current year's goals, year-to-date numbers, and quarterly results.

Consider how the work environment at Vanderbilt University Medical Center (VUMC) supports transfer of training. VUMC's team training program is designed to teach participants about patient safety mistakes and ways to avoid them, team building, cross-checking and communications, decision making, and performance feedback.[69] Several steps are taken to ensure that transfer of training occurs. Before the training starts, VUMC leaders are prepared to help the training succeed. Senior administrators, medical directors, and nursing staff attend a boot camp that highlights the team training program. A safety climate survey is conducted to determine how each department perceives the VUMC attitudes toward safety practices and patient safety issues. Then, each department is reviewed to find built-in errors that are system problems and to evaluate how the team communicates and deals with conflict. After the training, medical supervisors provide observation, coaching, and feedback. Checklists are provided for certain procedures, such as patient handoffs, medication administration, and briefing and debriefing sessions. These checklists help participants use the strategies emphasized in training to improve patient safety and the quality of patient care. Patients also help ensure safety. VUMC has created a video that patients are asked to watch when they are admitted to the hospital. The video emphasizes the importance of asking questions about medications and medical procedures.

An interesting example that illustrates many of the features of good instruction that have just been explained can be found in the training programs of the Culinary Institute of America (CIA), located in the rolling hills of the Hudson River Valley, a 90-minute drive from New York City. The CIA, the world's finest training facility for chefs, has approximately 2,000 full-time students in its degree programs. CIA graduates are chefs in some of the best restaurants in the world and in prestigious private dining rooms (such as the White House), and they direct food service operations for large hotel chains such as the Marriott, Hyatt, Radisson, and Hilton. Besides offering degree programs, the CIA also hosts more than 6,000 trainees from a wide variety of companies that have food service operations.

Whether an instructor is teaching meat-cutting or sautéing techniques, the programs' learning environments are basically the same. A lecture is followed by demonstration and several hours of guided hands-on practice. The trainee then receives feedback from the instructor. The trainer moves from a show-and-tell approach to become a coach over the course of the training session. Videos are produced for every class that a student will take. They can be viewed from residence halls or can be seen at the video learning center where students can review the tapes at their own pace; the students control what they see.

CIA programs deal not only with cognitive learning, but also with physical and emotional learning. In addition to cooking and baking courses, students are required to study psychology, TQM, languages, marketing, communications, restaurant management, and team supervision. Physical fitness and stress management are required parts of the curriculum. Why? Running a commercial kitchen involves long hours and high levels of stress—it is very physically demanding. Thanks to the learning environment created at CIA, the institute is recognized as the world leader in gastronomic training, providing a foundation of basic knowledge for chefs from around the world.[70]

# INSTRUCTIONAL EMPHASIS FOR LEARNING OUTCOMES

The discussion of the implications of the learning process for instruction provide general principles regarding how to facilitate learning. However, you should understand the relationship between these general principles and the learning process. Different internal and external conditions are necessary for learning each outcome. **Internal conditions** refer to processes within the learner that must be present for learning to occur. These processes include how information is registered, stored in memory, and recalled. **External conditions** refer to processes in the learning environment that facilitate learning. These conditions include the physical learning environment, as well as opportunities to practice and receive feedback and reinforcement. The external conditions should directly influence the design or form of instruction. Table 4.15 shows what is needed during instruction at each step of the learning process. For example, during the process of committing training content to memory, verbal cues, verbal links to a meaningful context, and diagrams and models are necessary. If training content is not coded (or is incorrectly coded), learning will be inhibited.

**TABLE 4.15**  **Internal and External Conditions Necessary for Learning Outcomes**

| Learning Outcome | Internal Conditions | External Conditions |
|---|---|---|
| **Verbal Information** | | |
| Labels, facts, and propositions | Previously learned knowledge and verbal information<br>Strategies for coding information into memory | Repeated practice<br>Meaningful chunks<br>Advance organizers<br>Recall cues |
| **Intellectual Skills** | | |
| Knowing how | | Link between new and previously learned knowledge |
| **Cognitive Strategies** | | |
| Process of thinking and learning | Recall of prerequisites, similar tasks, and strategies | Verbal description of strategy<br>Strategy demonstration<br>Practice with feedback<br>Variety of tasks that provide opportunity to apply strategy |
| **Attitudes** | | |
| Choice of personal action | Mastery of prerequisites<br>Identification with model<br>Cognitive dissonance | Demonstration by a model<br>Positive learning environment<br>Strong message from credible source<br>Reinforcement |
| **Motor Skills** | | |
| Muscular actions | Recall of part skills<br>Coordination program | Practice<br>Demonstration<br>Gradual decrease of external feedback |

Source: Based on R. M. Gagne and K. L. Medsker, *The Conditions of Learning* (Fort Worth, TX: Harcourt-Brace College Publishers, 1996).

## Summary

Learning and transfer of learning must occur for training to be effective. This chapter began by defining learning and transfer of learning and identifying the capabilities that can be learned: verbal information, intellectual skills, motor skills, attitudes, and cognitive strategies. To explain how these capabilities can be learned, the chapter discussed several theories of learning: reinforcement theory, social learning theory, goal setting theory, need theories, expectancy theory, adult learning theory, and information processing theory. To understand how to ensure that what is learned is applied to the job, three transfer of training theories were discussed: identical elements, stimulus generalization, and cognitive theory. Next, the chapter investigated the learning process and its implications about how people learn. The section on learning process emphasized that internal processes (expectancy, storage, and retrieval), as well as external processes (gratifying), influence learning. The potential influence of learning styles in learning was examined. The chapter then discussed the relationship between the implications of the learning process, transfer of training, and the design of instruction. Important design elements include providing learners with an understanding of why they should learn, meaningful content, practice opportunities, feedback, opportunities for interaction and a coordinated program. Also, the training design should encourage learners to self-manage and ensure that the learners' work environment supports learning and transfer.

## Key Terms

learning, *152*
transfer of training, *152*
generalization, *153*
maintenance, *153*
verbal information, *153*
intellectual skills, *153*
motor skills, *154*
attitudes, *154*
cognitive strategies, *154*
reinforcement theory, *155*
social learning theory, *155*
self-efficacy, *156*
verbal persuasion, *156*
logical verification, *156*
modeling, *156*
past accomplishments, *156*
goal setting theory, *158*
goal orientation, *158*
learning orientation, *158*
performance orientation, *159*
need, *159*
expectancies, *160*
instrumentality, *160*
valence, *160*

andragogy, *161*
open skills, *163*
closed skills, *163*
theory of identical
elements, *163*
fidelity, *165*
far transfer, 165
near transfer, *165*
stimulus generalization
approach, *165*
key behaviors, *166*
cognitive theory
of transfer, *166*
expectancy, *166*
perception, *166*
working storage, *166*
semantic encoding, *166*
rehearsal, *167*
organizing, *167*
elaboration, *167*
retrieval, *167*
generalizing, *168*
gratifying, *168*
instruction, *169*

objective, *169*
training context, *171*
practice, *172*
metacognition, *172*
self-regulation, *172*
advance organizers, *172*
overlearning, *173*
error management
training, *173*
massed practice, *173*
spaced practice, *174*
overall task complexity, *174*
mental requirements, *174*
physical requirements, *174*
whole practice, *174*
part practice, *174*
automatization, *176*
feedback, *176*
learner-learner
interaction, *177*
learner-instructor
interaction, *177*
learner-content
interaction, *177*

## Discussion Questions

1. Compare and contrast any two of the following learning theories: expectancy theory, social learning theory, reinforcement theory, information processing theory.

2. What learning condition do you think is most necessary for learning to occur? Which is least critical? Why?

3. Are learning and transfer of training related? Explain why or why not.

4. How do instructional objectives help learning to occur?

5. Assume that you are training an employee to diagnose and repair a loose wire in an electrical socket. After demonstrating the procedure to follow, you let the trainee show you how to do it. The trainee correctly demonstrates the process and repairs the connection on the first attempt. Has learning occurred? Justify your answer.

6. Your boss says, "Why do I need to tell you what type of learning capability I'm interested in? I just want a training program to teach employees how to give good customer service!" Explain to the boss how "good customer service" can be translated into different learning outcomes.

7. How does practice help learning? What could a trainer do in a training session to ensure that trainees engage in self-regulation?

8. Can allowing trainees to make errors in training be useful? Explain.

9. What learning conditions are necessary for short- and long-term retention of training content to occur?

10. What is near transfer? Far transfer? What are their implications for training design?

11. How can employees learn through interaction? Are some types of interaction best for learning in some situations but not others? Explain.

12. How can the work environment inhibit learning and transfer of training? Explain. What work environment characteristics do you believe have the largest influence on transfer of training? Justify your answer.

13. You have a one-day classroom experience in which you need to help a group of engineers and software programmers learn to become project managers. After training, they will have to manage some significant projects. Discuss the instructional characteristics and activities you will use to ensure that the engineers and software programmers learn project management.

## Application Assignments

1. Using any source possible (magazines, journals, personal conversation with a trainer, etc.), find a description of a training program. Consider the learning process and the implications of the learning process for instruction discussed in the chapter. Evaluate the degree to which the program facilitates learning. Provide suggestions for improving the program.

2. You are the training director of a hotel chain, Noe Suites. Each Noe Suites hotel has 100 to 150 rooms, a small indoor pool, and a restaurant. Hotels are strategically located near exit ramps of major highways in college towns such as East Lansing, Michigan, and Columbus, Ohio. You receive the following e-mail message from the vice president of operations. Prepare an answer.

   To: You, Training Director

   From: Vice President of Operations, Noe Suites

   As you are probably aware, one of the most important aspects of quality service is known as "recovery"—that is, the employee's ability to respond effectively to customer complaints. There are three possible outcomes to a customer complaint: The customer complains and is satisfied by the response; the customer complains and is dissatisfied with the response; and the customer does not complain but remains dissatisfied. Many dissatisfied customers do not complain because they want to avoid confrontation, there is no convenient way to complain, or they do not believe that complaining will do much good.

   I have decided that to improve our level of customer service, we need to train our hotel staff in the "recovery" aspect of customer service. My decision is based on the results of recent focus groups we held with customers. One theme that emerged from these focus groups was that we had some weaknesses in the recovery area. For example, last month in one of the restaurants, a waiter dropped the last available piece of blueberry pie on a customer as he was serving her. The waiter did not know how to correct the problem other than offer an apology.

   I have decided to hire two well-known consultants in the service industry to discuss recovery, as well as to provide an overview of different aspects of quality customer service. These consultants have worked in service industries and manufacturing industries.

   I have scheduled the consultants to deliver a presentation in three training sessions. Each session will last three hours. There will be one session for each shift of employees (day, afternoon, and midnight shift).

   The sessions will consist of a presentation and question-and-answer session. The presentation will last one and a half hours, and the question-and-answer session approximately 45 minutes. There will be a half-hour break.

   My expectations are that following this training, the service staff will be able to recover successfully from service problems.

   Because you are an expert on training, I want your feedback on the training session. Specifically, I am interested in your opinion regarding whether our employees will learn about service recovery from attending this program. Will they be able to recover from service problems in their interactions with customers? What recommendations do you have for improving the program?

3. Identify what is wrong with each of the following training objectives. Then rewrite it.
   a. To be aware of the safety rules for operating the ribbon-cutting machine in three minutes.
   b. Given a personal computer, a table, and a chair, enter the data into a Microsoft Excel spreadsheet.
   c. Use the World Wide Web to learn about training practices.

    d. Given a street address in the city of Dublin, Ohio, be able to drive the ambulance from the station to the address in less than 10 minutes.

4. Go to *www.nwlink.com/~donclark/hrd/sat.html,* Big Dog's Instructional System Design (ISD) page. This website is an excellent resource that describes all aspects of the ISD model. Click on "Learning" and scroll to the concept map or list of terms under the map. Click on "Learning Styles" and take the Visual, Auditory, and Kinesthetic (VAK) survey. What are the implications of your learning style for how you best learn? What type of learning environment is best suited for your style? Be as specific as possible.

5. Go to *cs.gmu.edu/cne/modules/dau/algebra/algebra_frm.html,* the website for an interactive tutorial that provides a refresher on algebra. Choose a topic (such as Fractions), and review the module for the topic. What does the module include that can help make the learning process effective? Why?

6. Go to *http://agelesslearner.com/intros/adultlearning.html,* a site created by Marcia L. Conner about how adults learn. Under "How adults learn," click on "learning styles." Next, on this page, click on "Learning Style Assessment" and complete it. What are the assessment's implications for the way that you learn best?

7. Go to *www.schneider.com,* the website for Schneider National, a transportation management company that provides logistics and trucking services. Click on "Jobs." Under "Company Drivers," click on "Driving School Programs." Watch the video *Schneider, Truck Driving School Graduates.* What types of learning outcomes are emphasized in training? Considering the features of good instruction discussed in the chapter, identify the features of Schneider's training program that contribute to learning and transfer of training. Explain how each feature you identify contributes to learning.

## Case:

# Plastics Make Perfect

A small group of U.S. plastics companies have enacted the Global Standards for Plastic Certification (GSPC) training program. The program is modeled after a series of globally recognized protocols to make certain workers have an in-depth knowledge of manufacturing, safety, quality, and other elements of a business. GSPC is the sole structured certification program in the world for the plastics sector. It is available for numerous processing strategies and has three levels of certification. Level 1 concentrates on general knowledge of a company, with limited processing instruction. Level II focuses more on the manufacturing procedures and the ability to track and maintain product quality. Finally, Level III focuses on advanced knowledge of injection molding and the ability to use this information on the manufacturing floor. Every level mandates a larger comprehension of and responsibility for the business's specific procedure and the facility overall, and to move on to the next level, a worker must pass an oral, standardized test.

*Describe the different types of instructional characteristics that you believe each level of this program should have for learning to occur and workers to pass the oral standardized test.*

**Source:** Based on P. Katen and D. Snyder, "U.S. manufacturers adopt training program," *Plastics News* (July 14, 2008): 7.

# Endnotes

1. R. M. Gagne and K. L. Medsker, *The Conditions of Learning* (Fort Worth, TX: Harcourt-Brace, 1996).

2. M. L. Broad and J. W. Newstrom, *Transfer of Training* (Reading, MA: Addison-Wesley, 1992).

3. B. F. Skinner, *Science and Human Behavior* (New York: Macmillan, 1953).

4. J. Komaki, K. D. Barwick, and L. R. Scott, "A behavioral approach to occupational safety: Pinpointing and reinforcing safe performance in a food manufacturing plant," *Journal of Applied Psychology,* 63 (1978): 434–445.

5. A. Bandura, *Social Foundations of Thought and Action* (Englewood Cliffs, NJ: Prentice Hall, 1986); A. Bandura, "Self-efficacy mechanisms in human behavior," *American Psychologist* 37 (1982): 122–147.

6. Bandura, *Social Foundations of Thought and Action.*

7. M. E. Gist and T. R. Mitchell, "Self-efficacy: A theoretical analysis of its determinants and malleability," *Academy of Management Review,* 17 (1992): 183–221.

8. E. A. Locke and G. D. Latham, *A Theory of Goal Setting and Task Performance* (Englewood Cliffs, NJ: Prentice Hall, 1990).

9. Ibid.

10. E. A. Locke et al., "Goal setting and task performance," *Psychological Bulletin,* 90 (1981): 125–152.

11. T. D. Ludwig and E. S. Geller, "Assigned versus participative goal setting and response generalization: Managing injury control among professional pizza drivers," *Journal of Applied Psychology,* 82 (1997): 253–261.

12. S. Fisher and J. Ford, "Differential effects of learner effort and goal orientation on two learning outcomes," *Personnel Psychology,* 51 (1998): 397–420.

13. D. VandeWalle, D. W. Cron, and J. Slocum, "The role of goal orientation following performance feedback," *Journal of Applied Psychology,* 86 (2001): 629–640; R. Noe and J. Colquitt, "Planning for Impact Training: Principles of Training Effectiveness," in *Creating, Implementing, and Managing Effective Training and Development,* ed. K. Kraiger (San Francisco: Jossey-Bass, 2002): 53–79; A. Schmidt and J. Ford, "Learning within a learner control training environment: The interactive effects of goal orientation and metacognitive instruction on learning outcomes," *Personnel Psychology,* 56 (2003): 405–429.

14. A. H. Maslow, "A theory of human motivation," *Psychological Reports,* 50 (1943): 370–396; C. P. Alderfer, "An empirical test of a new theory of human needs," *Organizational Behavior and Human Performance,* 4 (1969): 142–175.

15. D. McClelland, "Managing motivation to expand human freedom," *American Psychologist,* 33 (1978): 201–210.

16. V. H. Vroom, *Work and Motivation* (New York: John Wiley, 1964).

17. M. S. Knowles, "Adult Learning." In *The ASTD Training and Development Handbook,* ed. R. L. Craig (New York: McGraw-Hill): 253–265.

18. M. Knowles, *The Adult Learner,* 4th ed. (Houston: Gulf Publishing, 1990).

19. "Spirited learning," *T+D,* October 2009, 56–58; J. Salopek, "From learning department to learning partner," *T+D,* October 2010, 48–50; J. Salopek, "Keeping knowledge safe and sound," *T+D,* October 2010, 64–66.

20. R. M. Gagne and K. L. Medsker, *The Conditions of Learning* (Fort Worth, TX: Harcourt-Brace, 1996); W. C. Howell and N. J. Cooke, "Training the Human Information Processor: A Review of Cognitive Models," in *Training and Development in Organizations,* ed. I. L. Goldstein and Associates (San Francisco: Jossey-Bass, 1991): 121–182.

21. R. M. Gagne, "Learning processes and instruction," *Training Research Journal,* 1 (1995/96): 17–28.

22. S. L. Yelonand, and J. K. Ford, "Pursuing a multidimensional view of transfer," *Performance Improvement Quarterly, 12,* 58–78 (1999); K. Kapp, "Matching the right design strategy to the right content," *T+D* (July 2011): 48–52.

23. D. Cameron, "Dreamliner's here: Now learn to fly it," *Wall Street Journal* (November 1, 2011): B3.

24. J. M. Royer, "Theories of the transfer of learning," *Educational Psychologist,* 14 (1979): 53–69.

25. E. L. Thorndike and R. S. Woodworth, "The influence of improvement of one mental function upon the efficiency of other functions," *Psychological Review,* 8 (1901): 247–261.

26. J. F. Reintzell, "When training saves lives," *Training and Development,* 51 (1997): 41–42.

27. J. A. Sparrow, "The measurement of job profile similarity for the prediction of transfer of learning," *Journal of Occupational Psychology,* 62 (1989): 337–341.

28. R. M. Gagne, "Learning processes and instruction," *Training Research Journal,* 1 (1995/96): 17–28.

29. R. Mayer, "Applying the science of learning: Evidence-based principles for the design of multimedia instruction," *American Psychologist* (November 2008): 760–769; R. Clark and R. Mayer, "Learning by viewing versus learning by doing: Evidence-based guidelines for principled learning environments," *Performance Improvement* 47 (2008): 5–13.

30. "Cognitive Strategies," Chapter 6 in Gagne and Medsker, *The Conditions of Learning* (Fort Worth, TX: Harcourt-Brace, 1996); M. Gist, "Training Design and Pedagogy: Implications for Skill Acquisition, Maintenance, and Generalization." In *Training for a Rapidly Changing Workplace,* ed. R. Quinches and A. Ehrenstein (Washington, D.C.: American Psychological Association, 1997): 201–222.

31. D. Kolb, "Management and the learning process," *California Management Review,* 18 (1996): 21–31.

32. D. Kolb, I. Rubin, and J. McIntyre, *Organizational Psychology: An Experimental Approach,* 3d ed. (Englewood Cliffs, NJ: Prentice Hall, 1984): 27–54; M. Delahousaye, "The perfect learner: An expert debate on learning styles," *Training* (March 2002): 28–36.

33. D. Merrill, "Instructional Strategies and Learning Styles: Which takes Precedence?" In *Trends and Issues in Instructional Technology,* R. Reiser and J. Dempsey, eds. (Englewood Cliffs, NJ: Prentice Hall, 2000).

34. H. Dolezalek, "AmeriCredit," *Training* (March 2003): 46–47.

35. R. M. Gagne, "Learning processes and instruction," *Training Research Journal,* 1 (1995/96): 17–28.

36. B. Mager, *Preparing Instructional Objectives,* 5th ed. (Belmont, CA: Lake Publishing, 1997); B. J. Smith and B. L. Delahaye, *How to Be an Effective Trainer,* 2d ed. (New York: John Wiley and Sons, 1987); S. Moore, J. Ellsworth, and R. Kaufman, "Objectives—are they useful? A quick assessment," *Performance Improvement Quarterly,* 47 (2008): 41–47.

37. J. Phillips and P. Phillips, "The power of objectives: Moving beyond learning objectives,"*Performance Improvement* (July 2010): 17–24.

38. K. A. Smith-Jentsch et al., "Can pre-training experiences explain individual differences in learning?" *Journal of Applied Psychology,* 81 (1996): 110–116; S. Caudron, "Learners speak out. What actual learners think about actual training, *Training and Development* (April 2000): 52–27.

39. J. K. Ford et al., "Relationship of goal orientation, metacognitive activity, and practice strategies with learning outcomes and transfer," *Journal of Applied Psychology,* 83 (1998): 218–33; A. Schmidt and J. Ford, "Learning within a learner control training environment: The interactive effects of goal orientation and metacognitive instruction on learning outcomes," *Personnel Psychology,* 56 (2003): 405–429; S. Yelon, L. Sheppard, and J. Ford, "Intention to transfer: How do autonomous professionals become motivated to use new ideas?" *Performance Improvement Quarterly,* 17(2) (2004): 82–103; M. Hequet, "Training no one wants," *Training* (January 2004): 22–28.

40. R. Clark and R. Mayer, "Learning by viewing versus learning by doing: Evidence-based guidelines for principled learning environments," *Performance Improvement,* 47 (2008): 5–13; T. Katz-Navon, E. Naveh, and Z. Stren, "Active learning: When is more better? The case of resident physicians' medical errors" *Journal of Applied Psychology,* 94 (2009): 1200–1209.

41. J. Cannon-Bowers et al., "A framework for understanding pre-practice conditions and their impact on learning," *Personnel Psychology,* 51 (1998): 291–320.

42. A. Schmidt and J. Ford, "Learning within a learner control training environment: The interactive effects of goal orientation and metacognitive instruction on learning outcomes," *Personnel Psychology,* 56 (2003): 405–429.

43. T. Sitzmann et al., "A multilevel analysis of the effect of prompting self-regulation in technology driven instruction," *Personnel Psychology,* 62 (2009): 697–734; T. Sitzmann and K. Ely, "Sometimes you need a reminder: The effects of prompting self-regulation on regulatory processes, learning, and attrition," *Journal of Applied Psychology,* 95 (2010): 132–144.

44. B. S. Bell and S. W. J. Kozlowski, "Active learning: Effects of core training design elements on self-regulatory processes, learning, and adaptability," *Journal of Applied Psychology,* 93 (2008): 296–316.

45. D. Heimbeck et al., "Integrating errors into the training process: The function of error management instructions and the role of goal orientation," *Personnel Psychology,* 56 (2003): 333–61; N. Keith and

M. Frese, "Self-regulation in error management training: Emotion control and metacognition as mediators of performance effects," *Journal of Applied Psychology,* 90 (2005): 677–91; N. Keith and M. Frese, "Effectiveness of error management training: A meta-analysis," *Journal of Applied Psychology,* 93 (2008): 59–69.

46. J. Donovan and D. Radosevich, "A meta-analytic review of the distribution of practice effect: Now you see it, now you don't," *Journal of Applied Psychology,* 84 (1999): 795–805.

47. R. M. Mager, *Making Instruction Work* (Belmont, CA: David Lake, 1988).

48. R. Weiss, "Memory and learning," *Training and Development* (October 2000): 46–50; R. Zemke, "Toward a science of training," *Training* (July 1999): 32–36.

49. J. C. Naylor and G. D. Briggs, "The effects of task complexity and task organization on the relative efficiency of part and whole training methods," *Journal of Experimental Psychology,* 65 (1963): 217–224.

50. R. Mayer, "Applying the science of learning: Evidence-based principles for the design of multimedia instruction," *American Psychologist* (November 2008): 760–769.

51. R. M. Gagne and K. L. Medsker, *The Conditions of Learning* (Fort Worth, TX: Harcourt-Brace, 1996).

52. J. Goodman and R. Wood, "Feedback specificity, learning opportunities, and learning," *Journal of Applied Psychology,* 89 (2004): 809–821.

53. P. J. Decker and B. R. Nathan, *Behavior Modeling Training: Principles and Applications* (New York: Praeger, 1985); M. Merril, "First principles of instruction," *Educational Technology Research and Development,* 50 (2002): 43–59; K. Kapp, "Matching the right design strategy to the right content," *T+D* (July 2011): 48–52.

54. S. Caudron, "Learners Speak Out. What actual learners think about actual training."

55. B. Bell and S. W. J. Kozlowski, "Active learning: Effects of core training design elements on self–regulatory processes, learning, and adaptability," *Journal of Applied Psychology,* 93 (2008): 296–316; H. Nuriddin, "Building the right interaction," *T+D* (March 2010): 32–35.

56. D. Leonard and W. Swap, "Deep smarts," *Harvard Business Review* (September 2004): 88–97.

57. D. Stamps, "Communities of practice," *Training* (February 1997): 35–42.

58. D. Goldwasser, "Me, a trainer," *Training* (April 2001): 61–66.

59. M. Weinstein, "Rx for excellence," *Training* (February 2009): 48–52.

60. B. Kirkman et al., "Managing a new collaborative entity in business organizations: Understanding organizational communities of practice effectiveness., *Journal of Applied Psychology,* 96 (2011): 1234–1245.

61. R. Williams and J. Cothrel, "Four smart ways to run on-line communities," *Sloan Management Review* (Summer, 2000): 81–91.

62. B. J. Smith and B. L. Delahaye, *How to Be an Effective Trainer,* 2d ed. (New York: John Wiley and Sons, 1987); M. Van Wa, N. J Cayer, and S. Cook, *Handbook of Training and Development for the Public Sector* (San Francisco: Jossey-Bass, 1993).

63. J. Barbazette, *Managing the Training Function for Bottom-Line Results* (San Francisco: Pfeiffer, 2008).

64. C. A. Frayne and J. M. Geringer, "Self-management training for joint venture general managers," *Human Resource Planning* 15 (1993); 69–85; L. Burke and T. Baldwin, "Workforce training transfer: A study of the effect of relapse prevention training and transfer climate." *Human Resource Management* (Fall 1999): 227–242; C. Frayne and J. Geringer, "Self-management training for improving job performance: A field experiment involving salespeople," *Journal of Applied Psychology* (2000): 361–372.

65. A. Tziner, R. R. Haccoun, and A. Kadish, "Personal and situational characteristics influencing the effectiveness of transfer of training strategies," *Journal of Occupational Pyschology* 64 (1991): 167–177; R. A. Noe, J. A. Sears, and A. M. Fullenkamp, "'Release training: Does it influence trainees' post-training behavior and cognitive strategies?" *Journal of Business and Psychology* 4 (1990): 317–328; M. E. Gist, C. K. Stevens, and A. G. Bavetta, "Effects of self-efficacy and post-training intervention on the acquisition and maintenance of complete interpersonal skills," *Personal Psychology* 44 (1991): 837–861; M. J. Tews and J. B. Tracey, "An empirical examination of post training on-the-job supplements for enhancing the effectiveness of interpersonal skills training," *Personnel Psychology,* 61 (2008): 375–401.

66. B. Bell and S. W. J. Kozlowski, "Active learning: Effects of core training design elements on self–regulatory processes, learning, and adaptability," *Journal of Applied Psychology,* 93 (2008): 296–316; H. Nuriddin, "Building the right interaction," *T+D* (March 2010): 32–35.

67. J. B. Tracey, S. I. Tannenbaum, and M. J. Kavanaugh, "Applying trained skills on the job: The importance of the work environment," *Journal of Applied Psychology*, 80 (1995): 239–252; P. E Tesluk et al., "Generalization of employee involvement training to the job setting: Individual and situations effects," *Personnel Psychology*, 48 (1995): 607–632; J. K. Ford et al., "Factors affecting the opportunity to perform trained tasks on the job," *Personnel Psychology*, 45 (1992): 511–527; E. Holton, R. Bates, and W. Ruona, "Development of a generalized learning transfer system inventory," *Human Resource Development Quarterly*, 11 (2001): 333–360; K. Bunch, "Training failure as a consequence of organizational culture," *Human Resource Development Review*, 6 (2007): 142–163.

68. S. Boehle, "Dollars and sense," *Training* (June 2007): 42–45.

69. P. Keller, "Soaring to new safety heights," *T+D* (January 2006): 51–54

70. R. Zemke, "Cooking up world-class training," *Training* 34 (1997): 52–58.

# Chapter **Five**

# Program Design

## Objectives

After reading this chapter, you should be able to:

1. Be able to choose and prepare a training site based on how trainees will be involved and interact with the content and each other in the course.
2. Prepare for instruction using a curriculum road map, lesson plan, design document, and concept map.
3. Explain how trainees' age, generational differences, and personality might influence how programs are designed.
4. Prepare a request for proposal (RFP) and a list of questions to evaluate training consultants and suppliers.
5. Explain the program design elements that should be included to ensure near and far transfer of training.
6. Develop a self-management module for a training program.
7. Design application assignments and action plans to enhance learning and transfer of training.
8. Make recommendations about what managers can do before, during, and after training to facilitate learning and transfer.
9. Identify different ways to manage knowledge and the conditions necessary for employees to share knowledge.

## Program Redesign Reduces Costs and Satisfies Learners

Autodesk, Inc., is a leader in three-dimensional design, engineering, and entertainment software for customers in manufacturing, architecture, building, construction, and the entertainment industries. (In fact, the last sixteen Academy Award winners for Best Visual Effects used Autodesk software.)

Traditionally, Autodesk used to hold two annual training events for its partners in the United States and Canada. These events were attended by more than 300 salespeople, who learned about new product features and the customer base, and more than 700 engineers, who learned how to support the products. The high cost, planning demands, and logistical support needed for the annual training events motivated Autodesk to redesign the training.

Autodesk decided to convert the face-to-face, instructor-led training event to a virtual, instructor-led training event. To develop the virtual classroom, the program's core content (which included Microsoft PowerPoint presentations and product demonstrations) was reviewed. Quality content was kept and other materials were either revised or eliminated from the program. To make the content more engaging, interactive, and to keep participants motivated, polls, questions and answers, and quizzes were developed. Questions, exercises, and polls kept learners' attention and provided insight into whether learning was occurring. The instructional designers created "rooms" in which each class was held. They also developed pods that delivered a specific learning activity, such as conducting an exercise. Session maps were created for instructors to use as outlines for their presentations. This helped the instructors organize content, plan interactions, and identify necessary technical support. All roles and responsibilities for the virtual learning event were carefully defined. To help facilitate the instruction and aid the instructor, each event had a producer, host, and moderator. The producer facilitated the learning event, loaded files for sharing, was responsible for rehearsing, and kept the session running on time. The host presented an overview of the session, reviewed tools, and providing closing comments. The moderator was responsible for answering learner questions and solving technical issues. The entire crew held practice sessions to help the instructor become comfortable with giving the class and keep the pace fast to maintain the learners' interest.

As the result of the conversion, Autodesk reduced its carbon footprint and travel expenses by $1 million. The highly interactive, virtual, instructor-led training led to satisfied learners who had increased their product knowledge to increase sales and improve customer service.

**Sources:** S. Hall, "Virtual instructor-led training: Powerful, not PowerPoint," *T+D* (July 2010): 72–73; *www.autodesk.com* website for Autodesk.

# INTRODUCTION

As emphasized in Chapter Four, "Learning and Transfer of Training," for learning and transfer of training to occur, training programs need to include meaningful material, clear objectives, opportunities for practice and feedback, learner interaction, and a supportive work environment. However, these features are not enough to create an effective training program. An effective training program also needs a high-quality program design to maximize trainee learning and transfer of training. **Program design** refers to the organization and coordination of the training program. For example, the chapter opener showed how Autodesk redesigned its training program to ensure that content was appropriate, instructors were organized and prepared, and learners were motivated and interacted with the content and each other.

It is important to take a broad perspective when designing training, regardless of whether it is an online or a face-to-face training program, class, or course. Employees have to be motivated to attend training events, use what they learned on their job, share their knowledge and skills with others, and continue to shape and modify the knowledge and skills acquired to meet changing business and job demands. This means that program design should include not only what goes on during training based on course and lesson plans, but also creating conditions before the training event to ensure that trainees are willing, ready,

**FIGURE 5.1**

**The program design process**

Sources: Based on J. Zenger, J. Folkman, and K. Sherwin, "The promise of phase 3," *T+D* (January 2005): 31–34; C. Wick, R. Pollock, and A. Jefferson, "A new finish line for learning," *T+D* (July 2009): 64–69; J. Halsey, "How to ENGAGE and bring out the brilliance in everyone," From *www .trainingmag.com,* the website for *Training* magazine, accessed August 3, 2011.

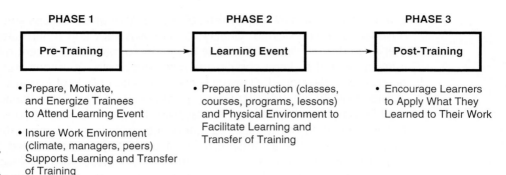

| PHASE 1 | PHASE 2 | PHASE 3 |
|---|---|---|
| **Pre-Training** | **Learning Event** | **Post-Training** |
| • Prepare, Motivate, and Energize Trainees to Attend Learning Event<br><br>• Insure Work Environment (climate, managers, peers) Supports Learning and Transfer of Training | • Prepare Instruction (classes, courses, programs, lessons) and Physical Environment to Facilitate Learning and Transfer of Training | • Encourage Learners to Apply What They Learned to Their Work |

and motivated to learn knowledge and skills. In addition, program design should include taking steps to ensure that after training, the acquired knowledge and skills are used on the job and shared with other employees.

Figure 5.1 shows the three phases of the program design process: pretraining, the learning event, and post-training. As discussed in Chapter Three, "Needs Assessment," information collected during the needs assessment is important in identifying appropriate pretraining activities, designing the learning event, and helping to ensure that transfer of training occurs after training ends. Phase 1, pretraining, involves preparing, motivating, and energizing trainees to attend the learning event. Phase 1 also involves ensuring that the work environment (i. e., climate, managers, and peers) supports learning and transfer. Phase 2, the learning event, involves preparing instruction (classes, the overall program) and the physical environment to facilitate learning. Phase 2 focuses on creating a positive learning environment, including planning the activities that occur during training, selecting a high-quality instructor or trainer, choosing a training room and creating positive interaction with learners, and having a proper program design. Phase 3, post-training, refers to transfer of training, or getting learners to apply what they have learned to their work. Typically, most effort, attention, and financial resources tend to be devoted to designing and choosing the learning event itself. However, what happens before the learning event (pretraining) and after the learning event (post-training) may be equally, if not more, important in determining if learners are motivated to learn, acquire new knowledge and skills, and apply, share, and use what they have learned.

This chapter discusses important program design issues that relate to the three phases of the instructional process. It begins by discussing important considerations in effective program design, including selecting and preparing the training site, identifying and choosing the best trainers, and how trainers can arrange the training site and create an instructional environment that is conducive to learning. Next, the chapter introduces you to curricula, courses, and lessons and shows how to use design documents and lesson plans. Because many companies do not have the staff, resources, or expertise needed to design training programs, this section of the chapter ends with a discussion of how to identify and choose a vendor or consultant for training services. The chapter concludes by discussing important post-training issues related to transfer of training, including how to create a supportive work environment, provide trainees with self-management skills, and gain manager and peer support. The important role of knowledge management in facilitating learning and transfer of training is also discussed.

# CONSIDERATIONS IN DESIGNING EFFECTIVE PROGRAMS

## Selecting and Preparing the Training Site

The **training site** refers to the room where training will be conducted. A good training site offers the following features:[1]

1. It is comfortable and accessible.
2. It is quiet, private, and free from interruptions.
3. It has sufficient space for trainees to move around easily, offers enough room for trainees to have adequate work space, and has good visibility for trainees to see each other, the trainer, and any visual displays or examples that will be used (e.g., videos, product samples, charts, and slides).

### *Details to Be Considered in the Training Room*

Table 5.1 presents characteristics of the meeting room that a trainer, program designer, or manager should use to evaluate a training site. Keep in mind that many times, trainers do not have the luxury of choosing the "perfect" training site. Rather, they use their evaluation

**TABLE 5.1**
**Details to Consider When Evaluating a Training Room**

Source: Based on C. L. Finkel, "Meeting Facilities," in the *ASTD Training and Development Handbook*, 3d ed., ed. R. L. Craig (New York: McGraw-Hill, 1996): 978–989.

*Noise.* Check for noise from heating and air conditioning systems, adjacent rooms and corridors, and outside the building.

*Colors.* Pastel hues such as oranges, greens, blues, and yellows are warm colors. Variations of white are cold and sterile. Blacks and brown shades will close the room in psychologically and become fatiguing.

*Room structure.* Use rooms that are somewhat square in shape. Are the rooms and seating tiered? Long, narrow rooms make it difficult for trainees to see, hear, and participate in the discussion. Check for availability and proximity of breakout or case rooms if needed.

*Lighting.* The main source of lighting should be fluorescent lights. Incandescent lighting should be spread throughout the room and used with dimmers when projection is required.

*Wall and floor covering.* Carpeting should be placed in the meeting area. Solid colors are preferable because they are not distracting. Only meeting-related materials should be on the walls.

*Meeting room chairs.* Chairs should have wheels, swivels, and backs that provide support for the lower lumbar region.

*Glare.* Check and eliminate glare from metal surfaces, TV monitors, and mirrors.

*Ceiling.* Ten-foot-high ceilings are preferable.

*Electrical outlets.* Outlets should be available every six feet around the room. A telephone jack should be next to the outlets. Outlets for the trainer should be available as well. Make sure that outlets are available for trainees to plug in their laptops, if necessary.

*Acoustics.* Check the bounce or absorption of sound from the walls, ceiling, floor, and furniture. Try voice checks with three or four different people, monitoring voice clarity and level.

*Technology.* Check that the room has permanent screens and a computer with Internet access for the trainer (and for trainees if needed).

of the training site to familiarize themselves with the site's strengths and weaknesses in order to adjust the training program and/or physical arrangements of the site (e.g., re-arrange the trainer's position so it is closer to electrical outlets needed to run equipment).

Recognizing that trainee learning can be facilitated though both mental and physical involvement, it is important to consider this when choosing, designing, or deciding how to use a training space. For example, Blue Cross Blue Shield of Michigan has transitioned to classrooms with spaces that can be configured as needed.[2] Because training classes might involve online learning, teamwork, physical movement, and quiet contemplation, spaces need flexible furniture and equipment that can be moved within the class (or moved out altogether to make more space). The key is to have a classroom that is able to accommodate a wide variety of activities and instructor-learner, learner-learner, and learner-content interactions. For example, in a sales course, learners work with a partner. They physically walk through the sales process using a map on the floor outlining the steps in the process. The physical movement through the steps has helped learners better recall the sales process. When choosing training spaces, whether on-site or off-site at a conference site or hotel, trainers at The Economical Insurance Group (TEIG) consider the size of the room needed for the number of trainees attending, and ensure that the physical space is engaging to the learner and promotes a sense of community between the facilitator and the instructor. They make certain that the training space can incorporate a blend of technology-based (such as graphics, multimedia, flash technology, and immediate feedback tools) with face-to-face training methods (such as roundtable discussions among small groups of trainees). Also, for courses such as leadership training, the environment outside the classroom needs to be comfortable (e.g., quiet areas, gardens, and lounge chairs) to encourage networking, creativity, and innovation. Sometimes, trainers may find themselves having to work in a training space that is not ideal. At Century 21 Real Estate LLC, trainers make sure that they get a look at the space before the training course to consider its strengths and limitations and how to use it to best maximize learning. For example, at one training session held at a local hotel, trainers had to work around banquet tables. As a result, they decided to get trainees energized and involved by using a team exercise that trainees seated at each table could work on. Steelcase modified its classrooms so that content is projected from different sides of the room, not just the front, so learners look over one another.[3] Instructors can be anywhere in the room because they can use a switcher to project content from any student's or instructor's laptop to any or all screens in the room. Also, in addition to classrooms, Steelcase also has cafes, booths, and small rooms to encourage collaboration and knowledge sharing, as well as areas for quiet, individual work.

***Seating Arrangements*** Seating arrangements at the training site should be based on an understanding of the desired type of trainee interaction and trainee-trainer interaction.[4] Figure 5.2 shows several types of seating arrangements.

Fan-type seating is conducive to allowing trainees to see from any point in the room. Trainees can easily switch from listening to a presentation to practicing in groups, and trainees can communicate easily with everyone in the room. Fan-type seating is also effective for training that includes trainees working in groups and teams to analyze problems and synthesize information.

If the training primarily involves knowledge acquisition, with lecture and audiovisual presentation being the primary training method, traditional classroom–type seating is appropriate. Traditional classroom instruction allows trainee interaction with the trainer, but

**FIGURE 5.2**
**Examples
of seating
arrangements**
Source: Based on
F. H. Margolis and
C. R. Bell, *Managing
the Learning Process*
(Minneapolis,
MN: Lakewood
Publications, 1984).

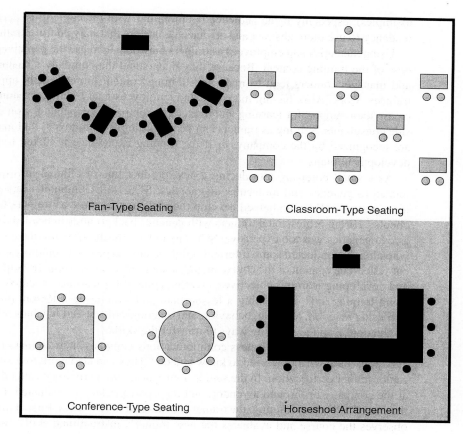

Fan-Type Seating

Classroom-Type Seating

Conference-Type Seating

Horseshoe Arrangement

it also makes it difficult for trainees to work in teams (particularly if the seats are not movable to other locations in the room).

If training emphasizes total-group discussion with limited presentation and no small-group interaction, a conference-type arrangement may be most effective. If the training requires both presentation and total-group instruction, the horseshoe arrangement is useful.

## Choosing Trainers

Selecting professional trainers or consultants is one obvious possibility for companies. Trainers, whether from inside or outside the company, should have expertise in the topic and experience in training.[5] Train-the-trainer programs are necessary for managers, employees, and "experts" who may have content knowledge but need to improve presentation and communications skills, gain an understanding of the key components of the learning process (e.g., feedback, practice), or learn to develop lesson plans. This may involve having employees and managers earn a certificate verifying that they have the skills needed to be effective trainers. To increase their chances of success in their first courses, new trainers should be observed and should receive coaching and feedback from more experienced trainers. When companies use in-house experts for training, it is important to emphasize that these experts convey training content in as concrete a manner as possible (e.g., use examples), especially if the audience is unfamiliar with the content. Experts may have a tendency to use more abstract and advanced concepts that may confuse trainees.[6]

Using managers and employees as trainers may help increase the perceived meaningfulness of the training content. Because they understand the company's business, employee and manager trainers tend to make the training content more directly applicable to the trainees' work. Also, having managers and employees lead training sessions can help increase their support for learning and reduce the company's dependency on expensive outside consultants. Serving as trainers can be rewarding for employees and managers if they are recognized by the company, or if the training experience is linked to their personal development plans.

As a small company introducing a new product line of clinical information systems related to genetics and molecular diagnostics, SCC Soft Computer needed subject matter experts (SMEs) who helped develop the tools to also serve as trainers for its staff and clients.[7] Hiring professional trainers with genetics backgrounds in needed disciplines such as cytogenetics was too expensive. SCC created a train-the-trainer course for non-trainers who already conducted some informal training, such as product demonstrations during client visits. The content of the course included applying adult learning principles, identifying and developing learning objectives, creating content for learning objectives, creating and using training aids, developing a lesson plan and structuring a lesson, planning evaluation using reaction, learning, behavior, and outcomes (discussed in Chapter Six, "Training Evaluation"), and identifying ways to transfer the skills.

At Alltel Wireless, a wireless communications company, new trainers take a series of classes to learn what they need to know and do.[8] They can also work toward a higher-level senior trainer certification. In the senior trainer program, participants attend training either at the company or through a vendor, and their performance is evaluated. For example, at the end of call center training, the trainer is evaluated in two ways. First, a training manager observes the course and evaluates the new trainer's instructional skills. Second, the new trainer is evaluated based on the number of trainees who pass the test, certifying they have the skills needed to work in a call center.

## How Trainers Can Make the Training Site and Instruction Conducive to Learning

As a trainer, you can take several steps before and during training to make the room and instruction conducive to learning.[9]

### *Creating a Learning Setting*

Before choosing a training room, consider how the trainees are expected to learn. That is, determine the extent to which trainees decide when, where, and how they will learn (self-direction), and whether learning will occur by interaction with others (collaboration).[10] Table 5.2 describes the types of training rooms that are appropriate for the amount of self-direction and collaboration necessary for learning. For example, a classroom with easy-to-move furniture supports high collaboration but low self-direction; this classroom can be used for lectures, presentations, discussions, and small groups. A distance learning room that includes computers, cameras, and data equipment supports learning that requires low collaboration but high self-direction. Self-directed learning that requires little collaboration is best suited for labs equipped with computers and software that support online learning,

**TABLE 5.2**
**Matching Training Rooms with Learning Requirements**

Sources: Based on "Workplace Issues: One in a Series. Learning Environments for the Information Age," available from the Steelcase website, **www.steelcase.com** (accessed March 1, 2006), and "Rethinking Higher Education Spaces," available at www.steelcase.com (accessed June 12, 2012).

| For Learning That Requires | Suggested Training Rooms |
| --- | --- |
| High collaboration, low self-direction | Classroom with breakout rooms |
| | Lecture hall with breakout rooms |
| High collaboration, high self-direction | Breakout rooms |
| | Project room |
| | Conference room |
| Low collaboration, low self-direction | Classroom |
| | Computer classroom |
| | Lecture hall |
| Low collaboration, high self-direction | Distance learning room |
| | Media lab |
| | Computer lab |

computer-based training, or software instruction. Of course, a dedicated training space may not be necessary for these learning requirements because trainees can work from their own personal computers, at home or at work. The advantages and disadvantages of online learning are discussed in Chapter Eight, "Technology-Based Training Methods," but be aware that employees may not like the lack of face-to-face collaboration that occurs in online learning programs.

Think about the physical requirements of the training room. Do trainees need to be able to concentrate and write? Do they need to be able to see detailed visuals? Choose a room that is large enough to meet your purpose, not just to accommodate a certain number of trainees. Avoid putting 25 people in a room that can seat 250. A small number of trainees in a large room makes it impersonal and leaves people feeling insignificant. Consider the room design well in advance of the session, and work with the training site coordinator to design a setting that meets your learning needs.

### Preparation of Materials

You need to know your content very well. Use mental and physical rehearsals to help build your confidence and to evaluate the pace and timing of material. Observe master trainers to get new ideas. Design the training from the audience's perspective—ask "So what?" about everything you plan to do. If you are using computers, CD-ROMs, the Internet, distance learning, or other technologies, make sure you know how to work the equipment and have backup materials in case the technology fails. Make sure that your visuals are available in at least two formats (e.g., PowerPoint slides and overheads). Arrive at the training room at least 15 minutes early to make sure the room is set up correctly, materials are available, and technology is functioning. Greet the trainees as they enter the room.

### Know the Audience: Age, Generation, and Personality Differences

To be an effective trainer, you need to stay in touch with pop culture and world events, be familiar with relevant studies and surveys, and know your audience.[11] Trainers need to be aware of the shared values of the learners that may be based around age, personality, or other characteristics such as geography or profession. This will help you use language, examples, stories, illustrations, and references in training that the learners can relate to based on their experiences.

***Age and Generational Differences***   Traditionalists prefer a standard training room with a stable, orderly learning environment. They do not like to be put on the spot in front of other trainees. They value direct presentation of information and training materials that are organized logically. They like trainers to ask them to share their experiences or anecdotes; but they also look to the trainer to provide expertise.

Baby boomers prefer classroom learning. Baby boomers respond well to interactive training activities—they like group activities and well-organized training materials with an overview of the information and an easy way to access more detailed information. Compared to the other groups, they are especially motivated to learn if they believe that training content will benefit them personally. Baby boomers need to work on translating the knowledge they have into skills.

Members of Generation X (Gen Xers) prefer a self-directed learning environment that includes technology-delivered methods. They respond best to training methods that allow them to work at their own pace: CD-ROMs and web-based training, for instance. Gen Xers are highly motivated learners who view training as a way to increase their employability. They like to learn by doing, through experimentation and feedback. They respond best to training materials that provide visual stimulation with relatively few words.

Although they are techno-savvy, millenniums like to learn by working alone and helping others to learn. They prefer a blended learning approach that involves self-paced online learning for acquiring basic concepts, ideas, and knowledge, followed by group activities and hands-on practice in which they work with others on questions, cases, and role playing.[12] They are motivated to learn skills and acquire knowledge that will help make their working lives less stressful and increase their employability. They place a high value on money so linking training to monetary incentives may facilitate learning. Nexters (like Gen Xers) prefer entertaining training activities. Training needs to be interactive and to use music, art, and games. UPS was experiencing much higher than normal failure rates among its millennium drivers. The initial idea was to train millenniums using video games and simulations. However, needs assessment found that while these employees wanted to use technology in their training, they also wanted hands-on training in the skills needed to be successful drivers. As a result, UPS's new Integrad learning facility for driver trainees in Maryland includes online learning, podcasts, and videos, along with classroom training and simulations involving driving delivery trucks and delivering packages on the streets of a fictitious town named Clarksville.[13]

The potential for generational differences to affect learning suggests that an awareness of the learners' ages and generations is important because it can help trainers try to create a learning environment and develop materials that meet learner preferences. Recent research summarizing the findings of studies on the influence of age on performance in training found that self-paced training had the largest influence on the training performance of trainees over 40 years of age.[14] Self-pacing gives older trainees time to assume responsibility for their learning, to focus on what is required to learn, and to understand the training and its importance. Also, training that occurred in small groups was advantageous for older trainees. Most training groups probably have a mix of generations. Employees can learn much from cross-generation interaction if it is managed well. Trainees of all age groups need to feel that participation in the session through questioning, providing answers, and discussing issues is valued and rewarded. If a group of trainees includes all generations, the training must take a blended approach—use examples that include people from different generations and use different training approaches (such as experts, audience involvement, group work, self-directed learning activities, and online learning).

*Personality* In addition to understanding trainees' learning styles, which was discussed in Chapter Four, some companies are using other assessment tools to help instructors better understand the preferences and characteristics of learners who will be in their courses and programs. The Learning and Development Group within PricewaterhouseCoopers (PwC) is using the Myers-Briggs Type Indicator (MBTI) as a tool for instructors to understand learner needs and styles.[15] The MBTI focuses on how we gather information and how we make decisions. It is an assessment tool designed to help individuals understand their personality and how to use their personality preferences at work and in their lives. MBTI theory suggests that personalities differ on four dimensions. We gather information with an emphasis on either facts and details (Sensing or S) or on abstract patterns and possibilities (Intuition). We make decisions based on logical analysis (Thinking or T) or on personal values (Feeling). Also, we differ in our orientation toward and how we deal with the environment. Individuals with an Extroversion (E) gain energy from interpersonal interactions, while those with an Introversion (I) preference draw energy from within themselves. Individuals with a preference for Judging (J) desire structure and closure, while those with a Perceiving (P) preference prefer to have many decision options. The MBTI assessment provides a four-letter personality type that is related to each of the four personality dimensions. The dimensions combine to form sixteen personality types (e.g., an individual can be an ISTJ, an ENFP, or an INFP).

Instructors can have learners complete the assessment prior to attending training courses. Then, instructors can use this information about learners' personality types to help design training that the learners will find interesting, increasing their motivation to learn. For example, if an instructor has a course with trainees who are high on Sensing, this means they tend to receive and process information through a linear approach involving the five senses. As a result, the instructor would want to be sure that they included training methods that involved multiple senses. Logic and analysis appeal to Thinking learners, while Feeling learners needs a personal reason for learning. For Thinking learners, instructors can emphasize the logic of an approach, while for Feeling learners, personal needs, beliefs, values, and experiences should be emphasized. The extent to which learners are extraverts or introverts can help an instructor decide whether to use a structured or flexible learning environment.

If you can't assess trainees' learning styles or personality type in advance, you can still ensure that at least some parts of training appeal to most learners. At American Fidelity Assurance Company, training emphasizes a learner-centered approach to reach employees with different learning styles. This means that in each course, company trainers are encouraged to include multiple activities and create a learning environment that includes toys, music, vivid figures, charts, and graphs, and exercises that require working in pairs to stimulate interaction.

### Pretraining: Enhance Motivation to Learn Through Communications, Prework, and Manager Involvement

The important role of motivation in learning was discussed in Chapter Four. To enhance trainee motivation to learn, it is important to communicate to trainees before they attend training the purpose of the course, learning objectives, course prerequisites, and who else will be attending. It is important to also communicate how the course will be meaningful and useful. One way to do this is by sharing testimonials or examples of how other trainees have benefited from the course. Prework or pretraining assignments such as readings, cases, or asking trainees to e-mail trainers or bring to class work-related problems or issues that will be used as examples or discussed during class also increase the meaningfulness of the course and motivation to learn, and help trainees come to the course or program with a sense of purpose and focus.

Trainee motivation to learn and use training content on the job can also be enhanced by getting their managers to communicate and reinforce the importance of training, provide trainees with the opportunity to attend, and discussing with them their expectations for using training content in their work (or even teaching others to use what they learned). Later in the chapter, it is discussed in detail how to get a manager's support for training.

### *Provide an Overview of the Course*

When beginning a course or workshop, it is important to give learners an idea of the "big picture" (i.e., what will be covered), including the objectives, timeline, activities, assignments, and other relevant information.[16] The overall concept, usefulness of the course, the objective, and its relevance to the job should be presented first, followed by an explanation of how the course structure to achieve its objectives. This is important to get learners into the appropriate mental state for learning and allow them to understand the personal and work-related meaningfulness and relevance of course content (recall the discussion of meaningfulness in Chapter Four). Using a flowchart or course outline, you should present the general topics first, followed by more specific subtopics. A concept map can also be used for organizing and presenting knowledge. Such a map includes concepts shown in boxes, with the relationships between the concepts indicated by connecting lines. At the start of each part, you can present the appropriate part of the outline and flowchart. This helps the learner organize the content in memory. Also, you can return to the entire flowchart or outline during the course to show how the content covered fits into the course and its relationship to the next topic. Figure 5.3 shows a concept map for a course on conducting an effective performance review.

***Help Trainees Retain and Recall Training Content***   Mnemonics and metaphors can be useful for recalling important ideas. They help relate concepts, behaviors, and knowledge to be learned to concepts that the learner already knows. This makes it easier to retrieve the information from memory. *Mnemonics* are acronyms in which the first letter of the word represents a term or step in the process. For example, in a course emphasizing a method for protecting new ideas in meetings, the acronym PIN is used to help learners remember to identify the positive aspects of the idea (P), present interesting or important implications of the ideas (I), and only after they have considered the value of the idea do they criticize it (N).[17] The instructor may give each learner a small safety pin as a souvenir and symbol to help them recall how to protect ideas in meetings, or demonstrate idea killing by popping balloons with a pin and then introduce the metaphor of the safety pin as a way to remember how easy it is to suppress and squelch new ideas.

Another way to help trainees recall what they have learned is to have them consider how they can use what they are learning in training. Application assignments increase the likelihood that trainees will recall the training content and apply it to their work setting when they encounter the appropriate cues (problems and work situations) in the environment. **Application assignments** refer to assignments in which trainees are asked to identify work

**FIGURE 5.3**
**A Concept Map for a Course on Conducting an Effective Performance Review**

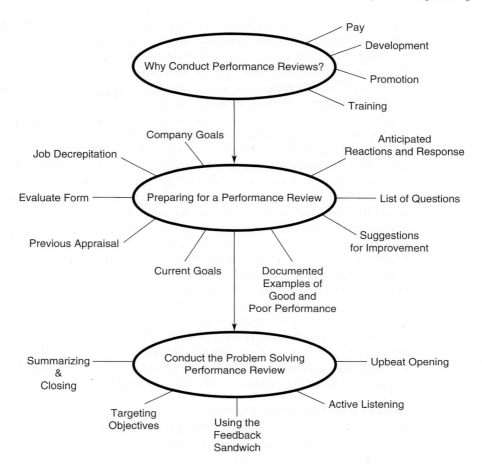

problems or situations and to apply training content to solve them. The use of application assignments in training helps trainees understand the link between the learned capabilities and real-world application, which makes it easier to recall the capability when needed.

### *Classroom Management*

Monitor the room for extra chairs, overflowing trash cans, and piles of materials left over from previous training sessions. A messy, disorganized, uninviting training room creates learning distractions. Give trainees frequent breaks so they can leave the room and return ready to start learning again.

### *Interacting with Trainees*

As a trainer, you carry the responsibility for the trainees' learning experience. You need to communicate the topics that will be covered, the learning approach that will be used, and the expectations for trainees. You need to be dramatic to draw attention to important points. Research suggests that trainees have the best recall of training content when the trainer is enthusiastic and avoids vocal distractions (e. g., use of "er" and "um").[18] Also, you should use a relaxed style and make learners comfortable.[19] As a trainer, you should recognize that your expectations for trainees' learning and your stereotypes can result in learners confirming those expectations (i.e., a self-fulfilling prophecy).[20] Negative expectations held by instructors can lead to learners' negative evaluation of the training and the trainer.[21]

How you should engage trainees is based on both the size of the room and the number of trainees. The larger the room, the more your gestures and movements must be exaggerated to get the audience's attention. To create intimacy with the training group, you must move close to them. Standing in the front of the room is a way to establish authority. One of the best ways to gain trainees' attention is to facilitate discussion from different places in the room. Strive to lead the instruction, but focus on the trainees. Help trainees develop their own answers, apply tools and techniques, and use reference materials to reach solutions that are effective in training and on the job. Use questions that lead trainees to answers or points that you want to make. Strive continually for interaction with trainees—trainees may have more real-life experiences with, exposure to, or applications related to training topics than you do. Create a training environment where trainees can learn from each other. Listen to trainees, summarize learning points, and provide feedback. Consider how Edward Jones, a financial services company based in St. Louis, Missouri, encourages learning by combining a training course with ongoing coaching and feedback. Also, typical class sizes are no more than twelve learners, often including SMEs and an instructor. The training sessions are based on an interactive question-and-answer format, which engages learners. Edward Jones also distributes surveys during the course that asks learners how difficult they found the lessons and whether they think they are learning. This allows instructors to change lesson plans during the session to better facilitate learning. Table 5.3 provides examples of how to get trainees involved in a training session.

### Dealing with Disruptive Trainees

How can you deal with employees who don't want to be trained despite being informed in advance of the course and how it relates to the business?[22] First, take charge of the session immediately, communicate your credentials, and in a friendly but assertive way tell employees why the training is important and how it will help them. Then let them vent their frustrations. Useful methods for this activity are to have trainees describe what they would be doing if they were not in the program, have trainees draw pictures of how the person next to them feels about attending the training, or have trainees break into groups and then ask some groups to make a list of the top 10 reasons not to be in the class and the

---

**TABLE 5.3**
**Examples of How to Get Trainees Involved**

Source: Based on J. Curtis, "Engage Me, Please!" *T+D* (November 2008): 68–73.

- Prepare and distribute content-related, open-ended questions to be discussed in breakout groups.
- Use creative activities or games that relate to the training content.
- Use assessment or measures that allow the trainees to learn about themselves and each other.
- Incorporate role playing.
- Conclude the training session by asking trainees, either individually or in teams from the same company or work group, to consider the following questions: "As a result of this session, what do you plan to start, stop, or continue doing? On what topic would you like to have more information?"

other groups to list 10 reasons to be in the class. Reassemble the class and discuss first the reasons not to be in the class, and then end with the reasons to be in the class. For trainees who disrupt, sleep through, or constantly interrupt the training sessions, consider using activities that get them moving, engaged, and energized. Ask disruptive trainees to leave the session only as a last resort when all other options discussed here have failed.

### Managing Group Dynamics

To ensure an even distribution of knowledge or expertise in groups, ask trainees to indicate whether they consider themselves novice, experienced, or expert in terms of knowledge about a topic. Arrange the groups so that they contain a mix of novice, experienced, and expert trainees. Group dynamics can be altered by changing learners' positions in the room. Pay attention to group dynamics by wandering through the room and noticing which groups are frustrated or stalled, who is withdrawn, and who is dominating the group. Your role is to make sure that everyone in a group has an opportunity to contribute. Seating arrangements such as rectangular tables often give trainees authority based on where they are seated. For example, the end of a rectangular table is the position of authority. Putting a quiet person in the "power seat" creates an opportunity for that person to assume a leadership role within the group.

## Curriculum Course and Lesson Design

Keep in mind that although the responsibility for designing the training program may belong to the instructional designer, human resource professional, or manager, the "clients" of the program should also be involved in program design. As already discussed in Chapter Three, managers and employees should be involved in the needs assessment process. In addition, their role may include reviewing prototypes of the program, providing examples and program content, and participating in the program as instructors.[23]

A **curriculum** refers to an organized program of study designed to meet a complex learning objective, such as preparing a learner to become a salesperson, certified computer network technician, licensed nurse, or manager.[24] A curriculum usually includes several courses, and it usually focuses on developing a set of competencies needed to perform a job. Because these competencies are often expected to be developed over time, curricula and the courses within the curricula are completed over an extended time period.

In comparison to a curriculum, a **course** or **program** usually covers more specific learning objectives and addresses a more limited number of competencies or skills. For example, courses can address topics such as negotiations, talent management, customer service, and (as you are learning) even training and development. A course typically includes units or lessons that are smaller sections or modules covering different topics. The time frame for courses can range from one to several hours, a half-day, a full day, or even weeks.

Although curricula, courses, and lessons all use learning objectives, they tend to vary in specificity. Learning objectives for curricula tend to be broader and less measurable than objectives for courses or lessons.[25] For example, for a project management course within a curriculum, an objective might be "Describe the four stages of the project life cycle using text and graphs." However, one of the objectives for a project management curriculum might include "Apply decision-aiding models when selecting a project." This objective is much broader than the course objectives because it describes the general knowledge, skills, and abilities developed throughout the curriculum and is likely emphasized in several courses.

## Curriculum Road Map

A **curriculum road map** refers to a figure showing all of the courses in a curriculum, the paths that learners can take through it, and the sequences in which courses have to be completed (e.g., identify prerequisite courses). Figure 5.4 shows an example of a curriculum road map for a security management training program. For each course, information that can be used to help develop and design detailed courses is provided. This includes[26]:

1. A brief statement of the course purpose, including why the course is important.
2. Prerequisite skills needed for the course.
3. Learning objectives or competencies covered by the course and a supporting or enabling objective(i.e., an objective that has to be reached in order for the learning objective to be accomplished).
4. The format of the content and course expectations. Expectations might relate to the type of content to be covered, how the content will be presented, and the structure of the content.
5. Delivery method for the content (e.g., online, classroom, blended learning).

### *Design Document*

A design document can be used to guide the development of training and to explain the training to managers, SMEs, reviewers, or other trainers. Table 5.4 shows a design document template.[27] Information for the design document is based on the information obtained from the needs assessment discussed in Chapter Three.

The level of detail in the design document can vary. *Scope of project* includes the goals, outcomes, or achievement expectations for trainees; a description of the trainees; a description of how long it will take to develop the course and the checkpoints or tasks that need to be completed as the course is developed; and the length of the course. The length of a course is determined by considering trainees' abilities and their availability for training, the resources needed for training, whether the course is part of a larger curriculum or is a stand-alone course, and the need to develop modules in order to provide an opportunity for trainees to practice concepts and skills to avoid being overwhelmed.

*Delivery* includes what the course will cover, how it will be delivered (e.g., face-to-face or online), an estimate of the training time, and the identification of any special conditions

**FIGURE 5.4**
**An Example of a Curriculum Road Map for a Security Management Training Curriculum**

Source: Based on SANS Security Management Training Curriculum, from *http://www.suns.org/ security-training/ curriculums/ management*.

**TABLE 5.4**
**Design**
**Document**
**Template**

Source: Based on
G. Piskurich, *Rapid
Instructional Design*
(San Francisco:
Pfeiffer, 2006).

**Scope of Project**

- Goal
- Audience
- Design time and checkpoints
- Length of the course

**Delivery**

- Content
- Method
- Training time
- Problems and opportunities

**Objectives**

- Resources
- Who is involved
- Topical outline
- Administration and evaluation
- Links to other programs

**TABLE 5.5**
**Design**
**Document**

*Purpose:* To prepare managers to conduct effective performance review sessions with their direct reports

*Goals:* Managers will be able to conduct a performance review session using the problem-solving approach

*Target audience:* Managers

*Training time:* 1 day

*Method:* Lecture, video, role plays

*Number of participants per session:* 20–25

*Locations:* Various

*Prerequisites:* None

*Problems and opportunities:* New performance appraisal system introduced; manager dislikes conducting feedback sessions

*Instructor:* Caroline O'Connell and facilitators

or issues that may affect the course (e.g., problems getting equipment for video role plays and providing feedback).

*Objectives* refers to the course or program objectives. Those are broader summary statements of the purpose of the program.

*Resources* refers to the materials—cases, DVDs, videos, models, process maps, podcasts, lesson plans, or guides for use by the facilitator or participants—that need to be purchased or developed for the course. *Who is involved* includes trainers, program designers, and individuals who will be involved in the design, delivery, and evaluation of the program. The *topical outline* includes a brief outline of the topics that will be covered in the program. *Administration and evaluation* refers to who will be in charge of course scheduling, how trainees will enroll, how the course will be evaluated, and who will review and update the course. *Links to other programs* refers to any other needs, such as a train-the-trainer program or manager introduction or kickoff for the program. Table 5.5 shows a simple design document for the performance appraisal review course designed to increase managers' effectiveness in conducting performance appraisal reviews. Performance appraisal review sessions are meetings between a manager and employee, during which the strengths and weaknesses of the employee's performance are discussed and improvement goals agreed upon.

**TABLE 5.6**
**Sample of a**
**Detailed**
**Lesson Plan**

*Course title:* Conducting an Effective Performance Review Session

*Lesson title:* Using the problem-solving style in the performance review

*Lesson length:* Full day

*Learning objectives:*

1. Explain the purpose of performance reviews.
2. Describe steps in preparing for a performance review.
3. Describe the behaviors used in the problem-solving style of giving appraisal feedback without error.
4. Demonstrate the behaviors in an appraisal feedback role play without error.

*Target audience:* Managers

*Prerequisites:*

   *Trainee:* None
   *Instructor:* Familiarity with the tell-and-sell, tell-and-listen, and problem-solving approaches used in performance appraisal feedback interviews

*Room arrangement:* Fan-type

*Materials and equipment needed:* VCR, overhead projector, pens, transparencies, VCR tape titled "Performance Appraisal Interviews," role-play exercises

*Evaluation and assignments:* Role playing; read article titled, "Conducting Effective Appraisal Interviews"

*Comment:* Article needs to be distributed two weeks prior to session.

| Lesson Outline | Instructor Activity | Trainee Activity | Time |
|---|---|---|---|
| Introduction and why conduct reviews | Presentation | Listening | 8–8:50 A.M. |
| Discussion of how to prepare and steps in conducting the review | Questioning | Participation | 8:50–10 A.M. |
| Break | | | 10–10:20 A.M. |
| View videos of three styles | Discussion of strengths and weaknesses of each | Watching | 10:20–11:20 A.M. |
| Lunch | | | 11:30 A.M.–1 P.M. |
| Presentation and video of eight key behaviors of problem-solving style | Presentation | Listening | 1–2 P.M. |
| Role plays | Watch exercise | Practice using key behaviors | 2–3 P.M. |
| Wrap-up | Answer questions | Ask questions | 3–3:15 P.M. |

### Course or Lesson Plan

Lesson plans are typically more detailed than the design document. They include the specific steps involved in the lesson, instructor and trainee activities, and the time allocated to each topic included in the lesson.

Lesson plans can be designed for programs lasting a day, a week, or several hours. If training takes place over several days, a separate lesson plan is prepared for each day.

The **detailed lesson plan** translated the content and sequence of training activities into a guide that is used by the trainer to help deliver the training. That is, lesson plans include the sequence of activities that will be conducted in the training session and identify the administrative details. Table 5.6 shows a lesson plan. The lesson plan provides a table of contents for the training activity, which helps to ensure that training activities are consistent regardless of the trainer. Lesson plans also help ensure that both the trainee and the trainer are aware of the course and program objectives. Most training departments have written lesson plans that are stored in notebooks or in an electronic database. Because lesson plans are documented, they can be shared with customers of the training department (i.e., managers who pay for training services) to provide them with detailed information regarding program activities and objectives.

Table 5.7 shows the features of an effective lesson plan. The lesson plan includes the learning objectives, topics to be covered, target audience, time of session, lesson outline, the activity involved, any required preparation or prerequisites, how learning will be evaluated, and steps to ensure transfer of training.[28]

**TABLE 5.7** **Features of an Effective Lesson Plan**

| Feature | |
|---|---|
| Learning objectives or outcomes | What is the lesson designed to accomplish? What is the standard for successful learning? |
| Target audience | Who is attending the lesson? What are the characteristics of the audience? |
| Prerequisites (trainees and instructor) | What will trainees need to be able to do before they can benefit from the course? Who is qualified to be in the program? Who is qualified to be an instructor? |
| Time | How much time is devoted to each part of the lesson? |
| Lesson outline | What topics will be covered? In what sequence? |
| Activity | What will trainees' and instructor's role be during each topic covered? |
| Support materials | What materials and/or equipment is needed for delivery of instruction or to facilitate instruction? |
| Physical environment | Is a certain size or arrangement of room necessary? |
| Preparation | Do the trainees have homework that needs to be completed before the lesson? What does the instructor need to do? |
| Lesson topic | What topic is the lesson going to cover? |
| Evaluation | How will learning be evaluated (e.g., tests, role plays)? |
| Transfer and retention | What will be done to ensure that training content is used on the job? |

Sources: Based on R. Vaughn, *The Professional Trainer* (Euclid, OH: Williams Custom Publishing, 2000); R. F. Mager, *Making Instruction Work,* 2d ed. (Atlanta, GA: Center for Effective Performance, 1997); L. Nadler and Z. Nadler, *Designing Training Programs,* 2d ed. (Houston, TX: Gulf Publishing, 1992); Big Dog's Human Resource Development website, *www. nwlink.com/donclark/hrd.html.*

In developing the lesson outline, trainers need to consider the proper sequencing of topics. Trainers must answer questions such as, "What knowledge and skills need to be learned first?" "In what order should the knowledge, skills, and behavior be taught?" "What order will make sense to the trainees?" It is also important to consider the target audience. Any information about their training and experience, their motivation for taking the course, and their interests, learning styles, and background (e.g., education and work experience) will be useful for choosing meaningful examples, determining program content, deciding on support materials, and building the credibility of the training. Information about the target audience should be available from the person analysis of the needs assessment (see Chapter Three). Additional information can be collected by talking to the "clients" (e.g., managers) who requested the training program and to past program participants, if available. Support materials include any equipment needed for delivery of instruction, such as computers, overhead projectors, or DVD players. Trainers should arrange for the purchase of any whiteboards, flip charts, or markers that may be used in instruction. Any exercises needed for trainees' practice or preparation, such as readings, role-play exercises, assessments, or pretests, need to be ordered or reproduced (after copyright permission is obtained). In considering instructor and trainee activity, the focus should be on ensuring that the lesson has as many features of a positive learning process as possible, including communication of objectives, feedback, opportunities for practice, opportunities for trainees to share experiences and ask questions, and modeling or demonstration. Transfer and retention strategies might include chat rooms, follow-up meetings with the manager, and action planning. Transfer and retention strategies are discussed later in this chapter.

The four learning objectives for the course, "Conducting an Effective Performance Review Session," are shown in Table 5.6. The eight key behaviors referred to in the "Learning Objectives" section are as follows: (1) explain the purpose of the meeting; (2) ask the employee to describe what he or she has done to deserve recognition; (3) ask the employee to describe what to stop doing, start doing, or do differently; (4) ask the employee for areas in which you can provide assistance; (5) give the employee your opinion of his or her performance; (6) ask for and listen to the employee's concerns about your evaluation; (7) agree on steps/actions to be taken by each of you; and (8) agree to a follow-up date.[29]

The prerequisites include (1) arrangement of the training site, equipment, and materials needed; (2) instructor preparation; and (3) trainee prerequisites. In the example, the trainer needs a computer with a DVD player to show a video of performance appraisal feedback styles. The trainer also needs an overhead projector to record points made by the trainees during the planned discussion of the strengths and weaknesses of the appraisal styles presented on the video. The room needs to be fan-shaped, so trainees can see the trainer and each other. Also, the fan arrangement is good for role-play exercises that involve trainees working in groups of two or three.

Trainee prerequisites refer to any preparation, basic skills, or knowledge that the trainee needs prior to participating in the program. Recall our discussion of basic skills in Chapter Three. Trainee prerequisites may include basic math and reading skills, completion of prior training sessions, or successful completion of tests or certificate or degree programs. Instructor prerequisites indicate what the instructor needs to do to prepare for the session (e.g., rent equipment or review the previous day's training session) and any educational qualifications the instructor needs. Lesson plans also may cover how the lesson will be evaluated and any assignments that the trainees need to complete. In the example,

**TABLE 5.8**
Sample Lesson
Overview

| 8–8:50 A.M. | Introduction, and why conduct performance reviews? |
|---|---|
| 8–8:50 A.M. | Introduction: Why conduct performance reviews? |
| 10–10:00 A.M. | Discussion of how to prepare, and steps in the problem-solving review |
| 10:00–10:20 A.M. | Break |
| 10:20–11:30 A.M. | Watch videos of three styles of appraisal feedback. Discussion of strengths and weaknesses of each style |
| 11:30 A.M.–1 P.M. | Lunch |
| 1–2 P.M. | Presentation and video of eight key behaviors of the problem-solving approach |
| 2–3 P.M. | Role plays |
| 3–3:15 P.M. | Wrap-up (questions and answers) |

trainees are required to read an article on effective performance appraisal feedback interviews. The instructor needs to be familiar with the purpose for performance review, how to prepare for a performance review, and the behaviors for conducting problem-solving appraisal feedback interviews.

### Lesson Plan Overview

The **lesson plan overview** matches major activities of the training program and specific times or time intervals.[30] Table 5.8 provides an example of a lesson plan overview for the performance appraisal feedback training.

Completing a lesson plan overview helps the trainer determine the amount of time that needs to be allocated for each topic covered in the program. The lesson plan overview is also useful in determining when trainers are needed during a program; time demands on trainees; program breaks for snacks, lunch, and dinner; and opportunities for practice and feedback. For the performance appraisal feedback training, the lesson plan shows that approximately half the training time is devoted to active learning by the trainees (discussion, role plays, question-and-answer session).

The experience of Health Partners, which administers Medicaid and Medicare coverage for patients in and around Philadelphia, Pennsylvania, illustrates the importance of lesson planning and program design.[31] The company installed a major upgrade to its data processing system, but the upgrade was unfamiliar to most employees. To conduct the training, Health Partners identified employees who were familiar with the program and asked them to be part-time instructors. Instead of providing daylong classes that would likely be boring and overwhelming, the company's training staff broke the training into a series of 45-minute sessions that employees could fit easily into their work schedules. The curriculum was organized by department rather than by tasks, and staff from other departments were invited to attend the program so they could understand how the entire company used the system. Portions of the training time were devoted to discussing with employees the stress of change in the workplace and the benefits of the new system. The management teams also met periodically with the instructors to keep them up to date on the types of problems that employees faced in working with the new system so that those issues could be incorporated into the training.

## How to Choose a Vendor or Consultant for Training Services

If a company decides to purchase a training program from a consultant or vendor rather than build the program in-house, it is important to choose a high-quality provider. Training providers may include individual consultants, consulting firms, companies that specialize in designing and selling training programs or academic institutions. Many companies identify vendors and consultants who can provide training services by using requests for proposals.[32] A **request for proposal (RFP)** is a document that outlines for potential vendors and consultants the type of service the company is seeking, the type and number of references needed, the number of employees who need to be trained, funding for the project, the follow-up process used to determined level of satisfaction and service, the expected date of completion of the project, and the date when proposals must be received by the company. The RFP may be mailed to potential consultants and vendors or posted on the company's website. The RFP is valuable because it provides a standard set of criteria against which all consultants will be evaluated. The RFP also helps eliminate the need to evaluate outside vendors that cannot provide the needed services.

Usually, the RFP helps to identify several vendors who meet the criteria. The next step is to choose the preferred provider. Table 5.9 provides examples of questions to ask vendors. Managers and trainers should check every vendor's reputation by contacting prior clients and professional organizations such as the American Society for Training and Development (ASTD). The consultant's experience should be evaluated. (For example, in what industry has the vendor worked?) Managers should carefully consider the services, materials, and fees outlined in the consulting contract. For example, it is not uncommon for training materials such as manuals and handouts to remain the property of the consultant. If the company wants to use the consultant's materials for training at a later date, it would have to pay additional fees to the consultant.

When using a consultant or other outside vendor to provide training services, it is also important to consider the extent to which the training program will be customized based on the company's needs or whether the consultant is going to provide training services based on a generic framework that it applies to many different organizations. For example, Towers Perrin, a well-known, successful New York consulting firm, told several clients that it would study their companies in detail and provide a customized diversity training program to fit their needs. However, six companies (including Nissan North America, Thompson

| | |
|---|---|
| **TABLE 5.9**<br>Questions<br>to Ask<br>Vendors and<br>Consultants | How much and what type of experience does your company have in designing and delivering training?<br>What are the qualifications and experiences of your staff?<br>Can you provide demonstrations or examples of training programs you have developed?<br>Can you provide references of clients for whom you have worked?<br>What evidence do you have that your programs work?<br>What instructional design methods do you use?<br>How do your products or services fit our needs?<br>What about recurring costs, such as costs related to administering, updating, and maintaining the training program? Do you provide technical support? |

Sources: Based on R. Zemke and J. Armstrong, "Evaluating Multimedia Developers," *Training* (November 1996): 33–38; B. Chapman, "How to Create the Ideal RFP," *Training* (January 2004): 40–43; M. Weinstein, "What Vendors Wished You Knew," *Training* (February 2010): 122–125.

Consumer Electronics, and Harris Bank) were given the exact same 18 recommendations (e.g., separate the concept of affirmative action from that of managing diversity).[33]

How long should it take a vendor or consultant to develop a training program? The answer is, "It depends."[34] Some consultants estimate that development time ranges from 10 to 20 hours for each hour of instruction. Highly technical content, that may require more frequent meetings with SMEs, can add up to 50 percent more time. For online, mobile, or virtual reality training programs, development time can range from 300 to 1,000 hours per hour of program time, depending on how much animation, graphics, video, and audio are included; how much new content needs to be developed; the number of practice exercises and the type of feedback to be provided to trainees; and the amount of "branches" to different instructional sequences.

## Program Design Implications of Transfer of Training

Recall the discussion of identical elements and near transfer and stimulus generalization and far transfer in Chapter Four. One of the important decisions that trainers have to make is to determine whether the learning environment and learning conditions should perfectly match the job environment, or if it should emphasize general principles that can be applied to many different work situations. Also, to facilitate transfer of training, instructors need to consider encouraging trainees to self-manage the use of learned skills, how to ensure that managers and peers provide trainees with opportunities to use training content, support training, and provide electronic performance support.

### *Determine if Focus is on Near or Far Transfer*

The degree of flexibility and variability in the skills and knowledge that the learner needs for successful performance is important to consider in determining the extent to which the learning environment and learning conditions should match the job and working conditions.[35] For example, if the tasks emphasized in training involves responding to predictable situations with standardized responses, then training should be designed with an emphasis on identical elements and near transfer. This is often the case when the focus is on procedural knowledge, or when a series of steps must be followed in a specific way to complete a task successfully. Examples of procedures that company employees often must follow to that level of exactness include answering the phone, securing offices and buildings, handling client questions, logging into computers, and using software. In these cases, instruction should emphasize near transfer. Near transfer means the need to apply learned capabilities exactly in a work situation. Programs that emphasizes near transfer should include the following:[36]

- Trainees need to follow standardized procedures, processes, and checklists.
- Trainees should be given an explanation as to any differences between training and work tasks.
- Trainees should be encouraged to focus only on important differences between training tasks and work tasks (e.g., speed of completion) rather than unimportant differences (e.g., equipment with the same features but a different model).
- Trainees should be provided with an explanation of why as well as how the procedure should be performed to help them understand the concepts behind the procedure.
- Behaviors or skills that trainees learn in the program should contribute to effective performance.

For example, consider the importance of carefully following these principles in designing training for police officers. In police officer training, new hires (cadets) practice shooting targets. During practice sessions, cadets fire a round of shells, empty the cartridges into their hands, and dispose of the empty cartridges into the nearest garbage can. This process is repeated several times. After graduation from the police academy, one new officer was involved in a shooting. He fired his gun, emptied the cartridges into his hand, and proceeded to look for a garbage can for the empty cartridges. As a result, he was seen by the gunman, shot, and killed!

In contrast, if the tasks emphasized in training involve more variable interactions with people or equipment and unpredictable responses, then instruction should emphasize learning more general principles and knowing when and why to pursue a course of action. That is, instruction should emphasize far transfer. This is the case when teaching learners how to deal with novel situations involving original thinking to develop a solution, create a new product, or solve a difficult problem. Programs that emphasize far transfer should include the following:[37]

- Teach general concepts, broad principles, or key behaviors.
- General principles that might apply to a greater set of contexts than those presented in the training session.
- Provide a list of prompts or questions to help trigger thoughts and question sets, such as "How is this similar to problems I have encountered before?" and "Have I identified the real problem?" This helps trainees see connections among strategies that have been effective in different situations.

### Encourage Self-Management

One way to prepare trainees to deal with the obstacles that they may face in work environments (such as lack of opportunity to use skills or an unsupportive manager) is to provide instruction in self-management techniques at the end of the training program. Table 5.10 shows an example of self-management instruction. The module begins with a discussion of lapses, emphasizing that lapses are not evidence of personal inadequacy; rather, they result

**TABLE 5.10**  Content of a Sample Self-Management Module

| | |
|---|---|
| **1. Discuss lapses.**<br> • Note evidence of inadequacy<br> • Provide direction for improvement | **4. Discuss coping skills and strategies.**<br> • Time management<br> • Setting priorities<br> • Self-monitoring<br> • Self-rewards<br> • Creating a personal support network |
| **2. Identify skills targeted for transfer.**<br> • Specify the skills<br> • Make them measurable and countable | **5. Identify when lapses are likely.**<br> • Situations<br> • Actions to deal with lapses |
| **3. Identify personal or environment factors contributing to lapses.**<br> • Low self-efficacy<br> • Time pressure<br> • Lack of manager or peer support | **6. Discuss resources to ensure transfer of skills.**<br> • Manager<br> • Trainer<br> • Other trainees |

Sources: Adapted from R. D. Marx, "Improving Management Development Through Relapse Prevention Strategies," *Journal of Management Development* 5 (1986): 27–40; M. L. Broad and J. W. Newstrom, *Transfer of Training* (Reading, MA: Addison-Wesley, 1992); R. D. Marx and L. A. Burke, "Transfer Is Personal." In *Improving Learning Transfer in Organizations*, ed. E. Holton and T. Baldwin (San Francisco: Jossey-Bass, 2003): 227–242.

from habits of usage of knowledge and skill that have developed over time. Lapses provide information necessary for improvement. They help identify the circumstances that will have the most negative influence on transfer of training. Next, a specific behavior, skill, or strategy is targeted for transfer. The skill should be measurable and countable. Then, obstacles that inhibit transfer of training are identified; these can include both work environment character-istics and personal characteristics (such as low self-efficacy). Trainees are then provided with an overview of coping skills or strategies that they can use to deal with these obstacles. These skills and strategies include time management, creating a personal support network (persons to talk with about how to transfer skills to the work setting), and self-monitoring to identify successes in transferring skills to the job. Next, to deal with lapses, trainees are instructed to be aware of where the situations are most likely to occur. The final part of the module deals with the use of resources to aid transfer of training. These resources may include communica-tions with the trainer or fellow trainees via e-mail and discussions with their boss.

For example, a manager may have attended a training program designed to increase her leadership skills. After a discussion of lapses, the manager identifies a target skill (say, participative decision making—that is, discussing problems and potential solutions with subordinates before making decisions that will affect the work group). The manager defines the skill and how to measure it: "Discussing problems and solutions with my subordinates at least two times each week." Next, the manager identifies factors that may contribute to a lapse. One factor may be the manager's lack of confidence in being able to deal with subor-dinates who disagree with her view. Potential coping strategies that the manager identifies may include (1) scheduling time on the calendar to meet with subordinates (time manage-ment), (2) communicating to the boss the transfer goal and asking for help (create a support group), and (3) taking an assertiveness training course. In what situation may the manager be especially likely to experience a lapse? The manager identifies that she may be most likely to lapse back into an autocratic style when faced with a short time frame for making a decision (time pressure being an obstacle). The manager recognizes that it may be inap-propriate to try to gain consensus for a decision when time constraints are severe and subor-dinates lack expertise. In the last step of the module, the manager suggests that she will (1) meet with her mentor to review her progress, (2) talk with other managers about how they use participative decision making effectively, and (3) resolve to communicate with other managers who attended the training session with her. The manager also commits to moni-toring her use of participative decision making, noting successes and failures in a diary.

### Encourage Manager Support for Training

**Manager support** refers to the degree to which trainees' managers (1) emphasize the importance of attending training programs, (2) stress the application of training content to the job, and (3) provide opportunities for trainees to use what they have learned on the job. Managers can communicate expectations to trainees, as well as provide the encouragement and resources needed to apply training on the job. One company asked trainees and their bosses to prepare and send memos to each other. The memos described what the other person should "start to do," "continue to do," "do less," or "stop doing" to improve learning transfer.[38]

Managers can provide different levels of support for training activities, as illustrated in Figure 5.5.[39] The greater the level of support, the more likely that transfer of training will occur. Managers should be actively involved in the design and delivery of training programs. The basic level of support that a manager can provide is acceptance (allowing

**FIGURE 5.5**

**Levels of management support for training**

| Level | | Description |
|---|---|---|
| | HIGH SUPPORT | |
| Teaching in program | | Participate as trainer |
| Practice skills | | Allow trainees opportunity to practice |
| Reinforcement | | Discuss progress with trainees; Ask how to support trainees' use of new capabilities |
| Participation | | Attend session |
| Encouragement | | Accommodate attendance at training through rearranging work schedule; endorse employees' attending training |
| Acceptance | LOW SUPPORT | Permit employees to attend training; acknowledge importance of training |

trainees to attend training). The greatest level of support is to participate in training as an instructor (teaching in the program). Managers who serve as instructors are more likely to provide many of the lower-level support functions, such as reinforcing use of newly learned capabilities, discussing progress with trainees, and providing opportunities to practice. To maximize transfer of training, trainers need to achieve the highest level of support possible. Managers can also facilitate transfer through reinforcement (use of action plans). An **action plan** is a written document that includes the steps that the trainee and manager will take to ensure that training transfers to the job (see the sample action plan shown in Figure 5.6). The action plan includes (1) a goal identifying what training content will be used and how it will be used (project, problem); (2) strategies for reaching the goal (including what the trainee will do differently, resources needed, and type of support from managers and peers); (3) strategies for receiving feedback; and (4) expected results. The action plan also provides a progress check schedule, with specific dates and times when the manager and trainee agree to meet to discuss the progress being made in using learned capabilities on the job. The action planning process should start by identifying a goal and the strategies for reaching that goal. Once those are determined, strategies for obtaining feedback and identifying what the accomplishment of the goal will look like are completed. To complete their action plans, trainees may need additional technical support, such as access to experts who can answer questions or reference materials. Trainers or project managers can help trainees get the resources that they need to complete their action plans through either face-to-face or electronic meetings.

Table 5.11 presents a checklist that can be used to determine the level of manager support before, during, and after training. The more statements that managers agree with, the greater their level of support for the training program. There are several ways to gain managers' support for training.[40] First, managers need to be briefed on the purpose of the program and its relationship to business objectives and the business strategy. Managers should be given the schedule of topics and a checklist of what they should do after the training to ensure that transfer occurs. Second, trainees should be encouraged to bring to the training session work problems and situations they face on the job. These can be used as practice exercises or put into action plans. Trainees should jointly identify the problems and situations with their managers. Third, information regarding the benefits of the course collected from past

**FIGURE 5.6**
**A Sample**
**Action Plan**

**Training Topic** _____
**Goal** *Include training content (knowledge, skill, behavior, competency, etc.) and application (project, problem, etc.)*
_____
_____
_____
_____

**Strategies for Reaching Goal**
*Modifying behavior (What will I do differently?)*
_____
_____
_____

*Resources needed (Equipment, financial)*
_____
_____
_____

*Support from peers and manager (Be as specific as possible.)*
_____
_____
_____

**Strategies for Receiving Feedback About My Progress** *(Include meetings with peers and managers, self-monitoring of progress, customer reactions, etc.)*
_____
_____
_____

**Expected Results** *(When I reach the goal, what will be different? Who will notice the difference? What will they notice?)*

*What will be different?*
_____
_____
_____

*Who will notice?*
_____
_____
_____

*What will they notice?*
_____
_____

**Progress Date Checks** _____   _____   _____

participants should be shared with managers. Fourth, trainers can assign trainees to complete action plans with their managers. Fifth, if possible, use managers as trainers. That is, train the managers first, and then give them the responsibility of training their subordinates.

Mac's Convenience Stores in Toronto, Ontario, Canada, wanted market managers to provide more business consulting to its stores, as well as to make sure the stores looked

**TABLE 5.11**   **Checklist for Determining a Manager's Level of Support for Training**

| |
|---|
| **Please read each statement and check all that apply to you:** |
| _____ I have discussed the course and set learning objectives for employees. |
| _____ I understand the purpose of training. |
| _____ I know how training matches what the employee needs to learn. |
| _____ I know enough about the training to support employees use of what they learn when they return. |
| _____ The employee has completed action plans or other types of learning contracts designed to help apply learning on the job. |
| _____ I have communicated my expectations regarding training. |
| _____ I encourage employees to share what they have learning after the course or program. |
| _____ I encourage employees attending training to prevent distractions using phone forwarding and Out of Office e-mail notices. |
| _____ I allow employees to attend training. |
| _____ After training, I will debrief employees on the learning objectives and discuss how to apply them. |
| _____ After training, I will meet with employees to hear their ideas of how to apply what they learned. |
| _____ I will provide opportunities to share what they learned with other employees. |
| _____ I recognize and reward learning that is demonstrated on the job. |

Source: Based on R. Saunderson, "ROI for recognition," *training* (November/December 2010): 52–54; A. Rossett, "That was a great class, but . . . " *Training & Development* (July 1997): 21.

good, the employees were wearing clean uniforms, good customer service was being provided, and health and safety information was being posted.[41] Financial understanding was made a key competency for the position, and market managers were trained. To help ensure transfer of training, working with store operators to build sales was made an important job requirement, as well as a part of market managers' performance evaluation and pay level. Also, market managers were held accountable for providing financial training to store operators. The training has resulted in profitability increases and a reduction in costs related to employee theft and shoplifting throughout Ontario.

At a minimum, special sessions should be scheduled with managers to explain the purpose of the training and to set expectations that they will encourage attendance at the training session, provide practice opportunities, reinforce use of training, and follow up with trainees to determine the progress in using newly acquired capabilities.

Alltel Wireless, discussed at the beginning of this chapter, uses managers as trainers.[42] When changes in systems, products, or policies occur, managers are the primary trainers for employees. Alltel uses a series of monthly teleconferences to educate managers in the field about new marketing strategies, new rate plans, new wireless or data services, and new offerings in products such as telephone headsets. The emphasis in the sessions is not only on communicating changes, but also on teaching managers to use learning principles effectively to train employees. For example, the teleconferences might have managers participate in a role play designed to teach salespeople how to talk to customers about an equipment upgrade.

KLA-Tencor, a supplier of process control solutions for the semiconductor industry, values training and development, invests in training and development, and ties it to the company's business strategy. Because of its high level of investment in training, KLA-Tencor takes several steps with employees and managers to ensure that training is taken seriously and is used on the job.[43]

One of the company's concerns was that too many employees viewed training as a vacation from their job. To deal with this concern, KLA-Tencor has incorporated a pass/fail policy into its training curriculum. If an employee fails any section within a training course, management action is immediately taken. The employee is removed from the course, and a performance improvement plan is developed that requires the employee to retake the course. The pass/fail policy has resulted in improved employee competency levels, a reduction in marginally performing employees, and savings of $1.4 million. But the most important result has been that the policy has changed employees' view of training. Instead of leaving quickly when a training session has ended, trainees are staying late and forming study groups to complete homework and assignments. The class tardiness rate has dropped from 20 percent to zero. The pass/fail policy has also boosted the morale of the technical instructors because they can see that students are actually learning from and are interested in the courses.

Managers pay attention to the development of their staff because part of their incentive plan is based on training and development. The incentive plan comprises fiscal, productivity, and strategic goals. Training and development is considered a strategic goal. Typically, 10 percent to 30 percent of a manager's bonus pay is based on development. For some managers, as much as 75 percent of their bonus pay can be based on staff development, as measured by employee training and certification levels. The percentage varies depending on how critical the training is for business operations. The incentive plans also help employees receive bonuses, which are tied to productivity goals. Only employees who maintain training and certification levels are eligible for productivity bonuses. For some jobs, such as service engineer, bonuses can range from 10 percent to 15 percent. This incentive plan makes training the responsibility of not only managers, but each employee as well.

### Peer Support

Transfer of training can also be enhanced by a support network among the trainees.[44] A **support network** is a group of two or more trainees who agree to meet and discuss their progress in using learned capabilities on the job. This may involve face-to-face meetings, communications via e-mail, or interactions on an electronic social network similar to Facebook. Trainees may share successful experiences in using training content on the job. They also might discuss how they obtained resources needed to use training content or how they coped with a work environment that interfered with the use of training content. One company in the U.S. Midwest scheduled a series of meetings with each training group between two and twelve weeks after their training session.[45] The more peer meetings that trainees attended, especially trainees who felt there was weak management support for training, the more learning was transferred to the workplace.

Trainers also might use a newsletter to show how trainees are dealing with transfer of training issues. Distributed to all trainees, the newsletter might feature interviews with trainees who have been successful in using new skills. Trainers may also provide trainees with a mentor—a more experienced employee, or even a peer who previously attended the same training program. The mentor can provide advice and support related to transfer of training issues (e.g., how to find opportunities to use the learned capabilities).

### *Opportunity to Use Learned Capabilities*

Opportunity to use learned capabilities (**opportunity to perform**) refers to the extent to which the trainee is provided with or actively seeks experiences that allow application of the newly learned knowledge, skill, and behaviors from the training program. Opportunity to perform is influenced by both the work environment and trainee motivation. One way that trainees have the opportunity to use learned capabilities is through assigned work experiences (e. g., problems or tasks) that require their use. The trainees' manager usually plays a key role in determining work assignments. Opportunity to perform is also influenced by the degree to which trainees take personal responsibility to seek out assignments actively that allow them to use newly acquired capabilities.

Opportunity to perform is determined by breadth, activity level, and task type.[46] *Breadth* includes the number of trained tasks performed on the job. *Activity level* is the number of times or the frequency with which trained tasks are performed on the job. *Task type* refers to the difficulty or critical nature of the trained tasks that are actually performed on the job. Trainees who are given opportunities to use training content on the job are more likely to maintain learned capabilities than trainees given few opportunities.[47]

Opportunity to perform can be measured by asking former trainees to indicate (1) whether they perform a task, (2) how many times they perform the task, and (3) the extent to which they perform difficult and challenging tasks. Individuals who report low levels of opportunity to perform may be prime candidates for "refresher courses" (courses designed to let trainees practice and review training content). Refresher courses are necessary because these persons have likely experienced a decay in learned capabilities because they have not had opportunities to perform. Low levels of opportunity to perform may also indicate that the work environment is interfering with using new skills. For example, the manager may not support training activities or give the employee the opportunity to perform tasks using skills emphasized in training. Finally, low levels of opportunity to perform may indicate that training content is not important for the employee's job.

### *Technological Support*

An **electronic performance support system (EPSS)** is a computer application that can provide skills training, information access, and expert advice, as requested.[48] An EPSS may be used to enhance transfer of training by providing trainees with an electronic information source that they can refer to on an as-needed basis while they attempt to apply learned capabilities on the job. The use of EPSS in training is discussed in detail in Chapter Eight.

Cagle's, an Atlanta-based poultry processor, uses EPSS for employees who maintain the chicken-processing machines.[49] Because the machines that measure and cut chickens are constantly increasing in sophistication, it is impossible to train technicians continually so that they know the equipment's details. However, technicians are trained on the basic procedures that they need to know to maintain these types of machines. When the machines encounter a problem, the technicians rely on what they have learned in training, as well as the EPSS, which provides more detailed instructions about the repairs. The EPSS also tells technicians the availability of parts and where in inventory to find replacement parts. The EPSS consists of a postage stamp–size computer monitor attached to a visor that magnifies the screen. The monitor is attached to a three-pound computer that is about half the size of a portable CD player. Attached to the visor is a microphone that the technician uses to give verbal commands to the computer. The EPSS helps employees diagnose and fix the machines very quickly. This speed is important, given that the plant processes more than 100,000 chickens a day, and chicken is a perishable food product.

Trainers also can monitor trainees' use of EPSS, which provides the trainer with valuable information about the transfer of training problems that trainees are encountering. These problems might relate to the training design (e.g., lack of understanding of process or procedure) or work environment (e.g., trainees either not having or not being able to find resources or equipment needed to complete an assignment).

## Using Knowledge Management for Learning and Transfer of Training

Recall from Chapter Two, "Strategic Training," that the term *knowledge* refers to what individuals or teams of employees know or know how to do (human and social knowledge), as well as a company's rules, processes, tools, and routines (structured knowledge). Knowledge is either tacit knowledge or explicit knowledge. Tacit knowledge is personal knowledge based on individual experience and influenced by perceptions and values. The communication of tacit knowledge requires personal communications through discussion and demonstrations. Explicit knowledge refers to manuals, formulas, and specifications that are described in formal language. Explicit knowledge can be managed by placing it in a knowledge database, or it can be managed by a knowledge management system. For example, Fluor Corporation has a web-based knowledge system that gives employees access to all procedures, guidelines, standards, and best practices needed for their specific job function.[50]

**Knowledge management** refers to the process of enhancing company performance by designing and implementing tools, processes, systems, structures, and cultures to improve the creation, sharing, and use of knowledge.[51] Knowledge management can help companies get products to market quicker, better serve customers, develop innovative products and services, and attract new employees and retain current ones by giving people the opportunity to learn and develop.

How might knowledge management occur? There are several ways to help create, share, and use knowledge:[52]

1. Use technology, e-mail, and social networking sites (such as Facebook or MySpace) or portals on the company intranet that allow people to store information and share it with others.
2. Publish directories that list what employees do, how they can be contacted, and the type of knowledge they have.
3. Develop informational maps that identify where specific knowledge is stored in the company.
4. Create chief information officer (CIO) and chief learning officer (CLO) positions for cataloging and facilitating the exchange of information in the company.
5. Require employees to give presentations to other employees about what they have learned from training programs that they have attended.
6. Allow employees to take time off from work to acquire knowledge, study problems, attend training, and use technology.

7. Create an online library of learning resources, such as journals, technical manuals, training opportunities, and video seminars.

8. Design office space to facilitate interaction between employees.

9. Create communities of practice (COPs) using face-to-face meetings, wikis, or blogs for employees who share a common interest in a subject (e. g., product, service, customer, or type of problem), where they can collaborate and share ideas, solutions, and innovations.

10. Use "after-action reviews" at the end of each project to review what happened and what can be learned from it.

Consider the following examples of how companies use different ways to share and create knowledge.

Knowledge sharing can involve reviews or audits of projects after they are completed, followed by sharing insights gained from the review with other employees. For example, the U.S. Army's "After-Action Review" process, adopted by many companies, involves a review of every mission, project, or critical activity.[53] The review involves considering four questions: (1) What did we set out to do? (2) What actually happened? (3) Why did it happen? and (4) What do we do (stop doing, continue to do, consider doing) next? Lessons learned are made available through websites and debriefings up and down the army leadership. Steelcase University Learning Center provides the physical space necessary for sharing knowledge.[54] It provides "information zones" that include whiteboards and tackboards throughout the space. It has flexible furniture arrangements that can accommodate new technologies and can offer individual privacy or can promote group work or collaborative learning.

At MWH Global, an engineering and environmental consulting company, a software program was used to analyze data from employees about which colleagues they most frequently interacted with and whom they turned to for expertise.[55] The program plotted a web of interconnecting nodes and lines representing people and relationships. The web provides a corporate map of how work gets done and who the well-connected technical experts are, and it helps identify informal connections among people that are missing on a traditional organizational chart. Solvay, a Belgian pharmaceutical and chemical company, uses maps to facilitate innovation. After inviting university researchers to the company, Solvay mapped its scientists' internal and external networks before and after the event to see where research overlapped and where the potential existed for collaboration.

As we mentioned in Chapter One, "Introduction to Employee Training and Development," many companies are interested in knowledge management because they are experiencing the loss of explicit and tacit knowledge resulting from older employees retiring. The electric power industry is facing the loss of many talented skilled workers, including engineers and managers.[56] (One estimate is that 30 to 40 percent of employees in the electric power industry will be eligible to retire by 2013.) They also are facing a shortage of high school graduates who have the science, technology, and math skills needed to immediately fill or even train for the jobs. This means that utility companies need to find ways to capture and share knowledge between experienced and less experienced employees. PacificCorp in Portland, Oregon, has a document that it asks employees to use to record the procedures they use. Puget Sound Energy, in Washington State, hired technical writers to interview employees and write reports. DTE Energy Corporation, in Ann Arbor, Michigan, encourages experienced engineers to mentor less experienced engineers. For example, the lead instrumentation and controls engineer at the Fermi II nuclear power plant, with forty-two years of experience, is mentoring a new engineer hired in 2007. They are working together on replacing instruments with new digital equipment, which is helping the less experienced engineer learn about the equipment and control room, as well as pick up the interpersonal skills needed for dealing with maintenance workers.

Chicago-based Grant Thornton LLP, an accounting company, developed and deployed a knowledge management system known as "K-Source."[57] K-Source was designed to help meet key business goals of growing sales, improving customer service, supporting company values, and increasing efficiency of internal services. K-Source includes an online COP for every line of service offered by the company, industry group, and geographic area. Employees are encouraged to contribute to K-Source by a knowledge manager who solicits their participation, as well as by including it as part of their performance evaluation goals. Using K-Source, employees can create personal profiles; set up personalized news feeds from financial websites, access courses, e-books, and webcasts; and participate in online discussions. Datatel, a provider of technology solutions and business services to higher education institutions in North America, provides virtual knowledge cafes for its 500 employees.[58] One cafe includes discussion forums, frequently asked questions, and learning plans for different employee positions. Datatel wants its employees to be able to access knowledge and to have conversations in any area that interests them. Another cafe is part of a productivity improvement initiative. This site includes "ask the experts" discussion boards, job aids, and document sharing.

### Keys for Effective Knowledge Management

There are several key considerations for effective knowledge management. They include collaborating between training and the information technology department, creating leadership positions in charge of knowledge management, providing easy-to-use technology, and ensuring employee trust and willingness to share knowledge.[59]

***Training and Information Technology Collaboration*** For knowledge management to be effective, the training department and information technology department must collaborate.[60] Training can help develop the culture, as well as the content and learning strategies. Information technology develops the systems for accessing, sharing, and storing knowledge and delivering training. For example, the intranet at the Royal Bank of Canada serves as the central depository for information about initiatives completed, planned, or under way in the company. It also contains templates and other tools for training project managers. A separate website features summaries posted by employees who have attended conferences and courses. Technologists developed the infrastructure, and trainers recommended what features should be included.[61] After every U.S. Army mission, project, or critical activity, the lessons learned are identified, codified, and made accessible through websites.[62] The lessons learned include an evaluation of the four simple but critical questions described previously (What did we set out to do? What happened? Why did it happen? and What will we do again the next time and what will we try to improve?). The Center for Army Lessons Learned (CALL) has created a network that has disseminated more than 265,000 products, briefed more than 54,000 soldiers and leaders, and transferred more than 24,000 lessons from military and civilian analysts to forces both in combat and stationed in the United States.

*Create Knowledge Management Leadership Positions*  Some companies, such as IBM, General Mills, and Randstad of North America, have created leadership positions to foster continuous learning and knowledge management. **Chief learning officers (CLOs),** also known as **knowledge officers,** are the leaders of a company's knowledge management efforts. The CLO's job is to develop, implement, and link a knowledge/learning culture with the company's technology infrastructure, including databases and intranets. CLOs locate knowledge and find ways to create, capture, and distribute it. The CLO has to ensure that trainers, information technologists, and business units support and contribute to the development of knowledge management practices. The CLO also is responsible for actively supporting strategic business objectives by providing management direction and support for learning and development activities and by ensuring that knowledge management translates into visible benefits for the business.[63] For example, the CLO at Computer Sciences Corporation (CSC) sponsors a Learning Officer Council, which includes learning officers from the business units who help her understand the training and development needs of the company.[64] Her Department of Global Learning and Development recently created a development program designed to meet the learning needs of 1,800 senior executives and managers with high potential. The program is sponsored by the company's board of directors, chief operating officer, and chief executive officer. At Whirlpool, an appliance company, knowledge management has led to the development of "innovation mentors" around the world who encourage employees to try new ideas.[65]

*Easy-to-Use Technology*  Knowledge management systems fail for two reasons: the technology is too complicated or companies don't give enough consideration to how to motivate employees to share knowledge.[66] Knowledge management systems can make it harder, not easier, for employees to perform their jobs. If the system asks employees to use multiple search engines, collaboration tools, and document management software all on different computer systems, the knowledge management system won't be used. It is important to build the correct technology infrastructure and make it easy for employees to access and share information within the context of their jobs. A new approach to knowledge management imbeds knowledge into the workflow of the job. For example, to help physicians keep up with the many new articles on diseases, medication, and research that are added to the medical literature each year, Partners HealthCare imbeds knowledge though an online patient order management system.[67] The system links the most current clinical knowledge and the patient's history to the management system. The system may question physicians' actions, and they have to respond with a reason. Of course, the physicians still have the ability to override the system.

The sales support staff at Exact Target Inc., a software company, was having difficulty answering all the questions about products and clients from its 75 sales representatives.[68] Some of the technical questions took many hours to answer, and many of the same questions were asked by different sales representatives. To answer the questions, Exact Target started getting sales representatives to answer each other's questions using a website where all posted questions and answers are stored. The website is accessible from a computer, handheld device, or mobile phone. Sales representatives can subscribe to e-mail alerts every time a new question is posted. The sales representatives currently using the system are accessing it an average of three times a week. Twelve sales reps who have found the system to be effective in their work are encouraging and showing others how to use it. Sales representatives can rank each other's questions and answers using a five-star scale to identify the most useful posts or to identify inaccurate or incorrect postings. The search function on the site shows the postings with the highest rankings. Besides posting questions and answers, the sales reps can post useful information or documents they find in their work. Exact Target is combining the informal information exchange between sales representatives with formal training. The company has posted twenty-five training videos and case studies and plans to post more sales training information, client case studies, and videos with online quizzes that the sales reps will be required to pass in order to become certified as competent to sell certain software products or services.

***Employee Trust and Willingness to Share Information*** Trust and a willingness to share information are key personal factors that relate to knowledge sharing. Employees may not know or trust other employees, may hoard knowledge to have power over others, may fear that their ideas will be ridiculed or challenged, or may see knowledge sharing as involving too much work and additional responsibility.[69] To encourage knowledge sharing, companies must recognize and promote employees who learn, teach, and share. For example, the incentive for Xerox field technicians around the world to contribute to the company's maintenance tips database is that they become known as a thought leader or expert.[70] When the system was first available, technicians did not find it natural to submit what they knew. To overcome the engineers' anxiety, managers submitted suggestions from the mat company headquarters and offered rewards such as cash and T-shirts for submitting tips. Managers also featured the names of people who did contribute, resulting in contributors receiving notes from individuals who found their submissions to be helpful. Today, the system holds 70,000 suggestions and saves the company millions of dollars a year in repair costs. Other ways to encourage knowledge sharing are to show that ideas that are shared are used by the company and to show successes. AT&T used knowledge sharing to help global sales force teams share competitive information, which was useful in closing sales.

Because knowledge management has the potential to improve a company's competitive position, companies that are managing knowledge use several measures to evaluate the effectiveness of their knowledge management practices. (Evaluation is discussed in detail in Chapter Six.) These measures are related to company and customer benefits. They include the ability to attract and retain key employees; employee commitment to the company, the encouragement and facilitation of effective teamwork, the use of best practices and the review and updating of these practices, new product introductions, customer satisfaction, and repeat relationships with customers.[71]

## Summary

Learning is an important aspect of any training program. But equally important is encouraging trainees to use learned capabilities on the job (transfer of training). This chapter discussed important program design issues that relate to the three phases of the instructional process: pretraining, during the learning event, and post-training. The chapter discussed effective program design, including selecting and preparing the training site, identifying and choosing the best trainers, communicating with trainees, and deciding how trainers can arrange the training site and create an instructional environment that is conducive to learning. Trainees' age and generation and personality differences should be considered in training design. The chapter introduced and discussed the importance of curriculum, curriculum maps, courses, and lessons, and showed how to use design documents and lesson plans in program design. Because many companies do not have the staff, resources, or expertise needed to design training programs, the chapter also discussed how to identify and choose a vendor or consultant for training services. The chapter concluded by discussing important post-training issues related to transfer of training, including how to create a supportive work environment, provide trainees with self-management skills, and gain manager and peer support. The important role that knowledge management in facilitating learning and transfer of training was discussed. For employees to use a knowledge management system, it needs to be easy to find and use knowledge, and they need to trust and a willingness to share knowledge.

## Key Terms

| | | |
|---|---|---|
| program design, 193 | detailed lesson plan, 209 | opportunity to perform, 220 |
| training site, 195 | lesson plan overview, 211 | electronic performance |
| application assignments, 202 | request for proposal | support system (EPSS), 220 |
| curriculum, 205 | (RFP), 212 | knowledge management, 221 |
| course, 205 | manager support, 215 | chief learning officers |
| program, 205 | action plan, 216 | (CLOs), 224 |
| curriculum road map, 206 | support network, 219 | knowledge officers, 224 |

## Discussion Questions

1. What is a design document? What is included in a design document? How is it useful for training?

2. How might course design differ for baby boomers compared to GenXers?

3. How does a concept map help learners?

4. Explain the three phases of the instructional process, which phase do you think is most important? Why?

5. What could be done to increase the likelihood of transfer of training if the work environment conditions are unfavorable and cannot be changed?

6. Customer service training involves far transfer. What design features would you include in a customer service training program to ensure that transfer of training occurred? What is a curriculum road map? Why is it important?

7. What is an application assignment? Why should it be considered in designing a training program or course?

8. How might you motivate managers to play a more active role in ensuring transfer of training?

9. If you were asked to implement a knowledge management system, what would you recommend to ensure that employees shared and accessed knowledge? Explain your recommendations.

10. What type of seating arrangements would you choose for a training course that involved small-group case discussions? For a lecture including Powerpoint and use of YouTube videos? Explain your choices.

## Application Assignments

1. Develop a questionnaire to measure the degree to which the work environment supports transfer of training. Include the questions and the rating scales that you would use. Use the checklist in Table 5.10 as an example. Provide a rationale for your choice of rating scales and questions, i. e., why did you include them on your questionnaire?

2. Listed here are questions designed to measure trainees' motivation to transfer training. Ask several working friends, colleagues, or fellow employees these questions. Also, ask them to discuss why they responded the way they did.

    For each of the following statements, indicate whether you strongly agree, somewhat agree, somewhat disagree, or strongly disagree.

    a. The skills and knowledge that I have obtained by attending training programs have been helpful in solving work-related problems.

    b. Before I attend training programs, I usually consider how I will use the content of the program.

    c. I believe my job performance will likely improve if I use the knowledge and skills acquired in training programs.

    d. It is unrealistic to believe that mastering the content of training programs can improve my work productivity.

    e. I am usually able to use skills or knowledge acquired in training programs in my work.

    f. There are usually more problems than the trainers realize in applying training program content in my daily work activities.

    g. Before I attend training programs, I usually identify particular problems or projects that I would like the training to help me with.

    Prepare a written summary of what you learned about motivation to transfer training.

3. Design an action planning sheet that a manager and employee could use to facilitate transfer of training. Justify each category included in the action plan.

4. Draw a curriculum map for your major. How does this help you as the learner? How do you think this helps the faculty? Your academic adviser?

5. This assignment relates to Application Assignment 2 in Chapter Four. You now receive the following e-mail from the vice president of operations. Prepare an answer.

    Thanks for your recommendations regarding how to make the "Improving Service Quality Program" a success. To improve hotel staff ability to respond effectively to customer complaints (that is, "recovery"), we have incorporated many of your ideas into the program, including the following:

    a. Having trainees bring an example of a customer problem to class.

    b. Giving trainees the opportunity to practice dealing with irate customers.

    c. Providing trainees with feedback during role plays.

    d. Having trainers identify and communicate objectives of the program to trainees.

    e. Having trainers communicate to the trainees specific key behaviors related to customer service.

I am now concerned about how to make sure that our training investments pay off. That is, I am really interested in seeing that employees effectively and continuously apply in their jobs the skills and knowledge they have gained in training. What recommendations do you have?

6. Go to http://sans.org, the website for the SANS Institute, which provides information security training. Under "Find Training," move down to "Training Curricula" and click on one of the topics listed. What information is provided? How is it useful for learners? For instructors?

7. Go to www.boozallen.com, the website for Booz Allen Hamilton, a consulting firm. Click on Careers. Review the links in this section of the website. Find out information about the company's training programs. Does the company have a work environment that supports training? Explain.

8. One way to diagnose transfer of training problems or to ensure that transfer of training occurs is to complete the matrix shown below. This matrix considers the responsibilities of the manager, the trainer, and the trainee for transfer of training before, during, and after training. Complete each cell of the matrix showing manager, trainer, and trainee responsibilities.

|  | Before Training | During Training | After Training |
| --- | --- | --- | --- |
| **Manager** |  |  |  |
| **Trainer** |  |  |  |
| **Trainee** |  |  |  |

## Case:

# The CEO Institute

The goal of the CEO Institute at the Campbell Soup Company is to create a meaningful leadership experience for its participants. Campbell is trying to help participants learn by formulating ideas and experiences and take time to reflect on what they have learned and apply it to all aspects of their lives. Each class has between twenty and twenty-four participants that represent a cross-section of the company's locations, business units, and functions. Each participant is required to send a letter to the CEO discussing their personal commitment to the program and what they hope to achieve. The program is divided into five modules, each including midday meetings followed by time to reflect and study. Some of the modules include assessment of the participant's leadership style and presentations by members of the executive leadership team in which they share how they developed their leadership style and what they have learned about effective leadership. The five modules focus on leadership fundamentals, understanding leaders across different industries, developing a personal leadership philosophy and model, and what they have learned and will do differently as a leader. In between modules, which are offered several months apart, participants have homework assignments that include readings and peer-coaching meetings with another program participant. The idea is to expose participants to a variety of leadership styles and give them the time and tools to develop their own leadership model.

*Identify the design elements which help ensure that participants learn about leadership and put it into practice. Explain how these design elements encourage learning and transfer.*

Source: Based on N. Reardon, "Making leadership personal," *T+D* (March 2011): 44–49.

# Endnotes

1. B. Smith and B. Delahaye, *How to Be an Effective Trainer* (New York: Wiley, 1987); M. Van Wart, N. Cayer, and S. Cook, *Handbook of Training and Development for the Public Sector.* (San Francisco: Jossey-Bass, 1993).

2. M. Weinstein, "Training spaces," *training* (September/October 2010): 34–37.

3. J. Meister and K. Willyerd, *The 2020 Workplace* (New York, HarperCollins, 2010).

4. L. Nadler and Z. Nadler, *Designing Training Programs,* 2d ed. (Houston: Gulf Publishing Company, 1994); T. W. Goad, "Building Presentations: A Top-Down Approach," in *Effective Training Delivery* (Minneapolis: Lakewood Publishing. 1989): 21–24; F. H. Margolis and C. R. Bell, *Managing the Learning Process* (Minneapolis: Lakewood, 1984).

5. M. Welber, "Save by growing your own trainers," *Workforce* (September 2002): 44–48; T. Adams, A. Kennedy, and M. Marquart, "The reluctant trainer," *T+D* (March 2008): 24–27.

6. P. Hinds, M. Patterson, and J. Pfeffer, "Bothered by abstraction: The effects of expertise on knowledge transfer and subsequent novice performance," *Journal of Applied Psychology,* 86 (2001): 1232–1243; S. Merrill, "Training the Trainer 101," *T+D* (June 2008): 28–31.

7. M. Weinstein, "Training is in SCC's genes," *training* (January/February 2011): 44–46.

8. H. Dolezalek, "Certify me," *Training* (June 2008): 54–59.

9. D. Booher, "Make the room work for you," *Training and Development,* S5–S7; D. Abernathy, "Presentation tips from the pros," *Training and Development* (October 1999): 19–25.

10. Steelcase, "Workplace Issues: One in a Series. Learning Environments for the Information Age," available from the Steelcase website, *www.steelcase.com* (accessed March 1, 2006).

11. G. Dutton, "Are you tuned in to your trainees?" *training* (January/February 2011): 104–105.

12. K. Tyler, "Generation gaps," *HR Magazine* (January 2008): 69–72.

13. P. Ketter, "What can training do for Brown?" *T+D* (May 2008): 30–36.

14. J. Callahan, D. Kiker, and T. Cross, "Does method matter? A meta-analysis of the effects of training method on older learner training performance," *Journal of Management,* 29 (2003): 663–680.

15. R. Daisley, "Considering personality type in adult learning: Using the Myers-Briggs Type Indicator in instructor preparation at PricewaterhouseCoopers," *Performance Improvement* (February 2011): 15–23.

16. E. Albu, "Presenting course outlines in a flow chart format," *T+D* (February 2010): 76–77.

17. K. Albrecht, "Take time for effective learning," *training,* (July 2004): 38–42; K. Kapp, "Matching the right design strategy to the right content," *T+D* (July 2011): 48–52.

18. A. Towler and R. Dipboye, "Effects of trainer expressiveness, organizations, and trainee goal orientation on training outcomes," *Journal of Applied Psychology,* 86 (2001): 664–673.

19. A. Towler and R. Dipboye, "Effects of Trainer Expressiveness, Organization, and Trainee Goal Orientation on Training Outcomes"; T. Sitzmann et al., "A review and meta-analysis of the nomological network of trainee reactions," *Journal of Applied Psychology,* 93 (2008): 280–295.

20. D. Eden and A. Shani, "Pygmalion goes to boot camp: Expectancy, leadership, and trainee performance," *Journal of Applied Psychology,* 67 (1982): 194–199.

21. J. Shapiro, E. King, and M. Quinones, "Expectation of obese trainees: How stigmatized trainee characteristics influence training effectiveness," *Journal of Applied Psychology,* 92 (2007): 239–249.

22. M. Hequet. "Training No One Wants," *training* (January 2004): 22–28.

23. P. Kirschner, C. Carr, and P. Sloep, "How expert designers design," *Performance Improvement Quarterly,* 15 (2002): 86–104.

24. J. Phillips, "Seven issues to consider when designing training curricula," *Performance Improvement* (August 2010): 9–15.

25. Ibid.

26. M. Driscoll and S. Carliner, *Advanced Web-based Training Strategies: Unlocking Instructionally Sound Online Learning* (Hoboken, NJ: Wiley, 2005).

27. G. Piskurich, *Rapid Instructional Design* (San Francisco: Pfeiffer, 2006).

28. Van Wart, Cayer, and Cook, *Handbook of Training and Development for the Public Sector.*

29. G. P. Latham and K. N. Wexley, *Increasing Productivity Through Performance Appraisal,* 2d ed. (Reading, MA: Addison-Wesley, 1994).

30. Ibid.

31. P. Kiger, "Health Partners delivers training that works," *Workforce* (November 2002): 60–64.

32. B. Gerber, "How to buy training programs," *Training* (June 1989): 59–68.

33. D. Blackmen, "Consultants' advice on diversity was anything but diverse," *The Wall Street Journal* (March 11, 1997): A1, A16.

34. R. Zemke and J. Armstrong, "How long does it take? (The sequel)," *Training* (May 1997): 11–15.

35. S. L. Yelon, and J. K. Ford, "Pursuing a multidimensional view of transfer," *Performance Improvement Quarterly,* 12 (1999), 58–78; K. Kapp, "Matching the right design strategy to the right content," *T+D* (July 2011): 48–52; M. Merrill, "First principles of instruction," *Educational Technology Research and Development,* 50 (2002): 43–59.

36. M. Machin, "Planning, Managing, and Optimizing Transfer of Training," in *Creating Implementing, and Managing Effective Training and Development,* ed. K. Kraiger (San Francisco: Jossey-Bass, 2002): 263–301; J. Kim and C. Lee, "Implications of near and far transfer of training on structured on-the-job training," *Advances in Developing Human Resources* (November 2001): 442–451; S. Yelon and J. Ford, "Pursuing a multidimensional view of transfer," *Performance Improvement Quarterly,* 12 (1999): 58–78.

37. S. Yelon and J. Ford, "Pursuing a multidimensional view of transfer," *Performance Improvement Quarterly* 12 (1999): 55–78.

38. H. Martin, "Lessons learned," *The Wall Street Journal* (December 15, 2008): R11.

39. J. M. Cusimano, "Managers as facilitators," *Training and Development,* 50 (1996): 31–33: R. Bates, "Managers as Transfer Agents," in *Improving Learning Transfer in Organizations,* ed. E. Holton and T. Baldwin (San Francisco: Jossey-Bass, 2003): 243–270.

40. S. B. Parry. "Ten ways to get management buy-in," *Training and Development* (September 1997): 21–22; M. L. Broad and J. W. Newstrom, *Transfer of Training* (Reading, MA: Addison-Wesley, 1992)

41. S. Boehle. "Dollars and Sense," *training* (June 2007): 42–25.

42. J. Gordon. "Getting serious about supervisory training," *Training* (February 2006): 27–29.

43. K. Ellis, "Developing for dollars," *Training* (May 2003): 34–39; G. Johnson, "KLA-Tencor," *Training* (Match 2003): 48–49.

44. C. M. Petrini, "Bringing it back to work," *Training and Development Journal* (December 1990): 15–21.

45. H. Martin, "Lessons learned," *The Wall Street Journal* (December 15, 2008): R11.

46. J. Ford, M. Quinones, D. Sego, and J. Sorra. "Factors Affecting the Opportunity to Perform Trained Tasks on the Job," *Personnel Psychology* 45 (1992): 511–527.

47. M. Quinones, J. Ford, D. Sego, and E. Smith, "The effects of individual and transfer environment characteristics on the opportunity to perform trained tasks," *Training Research Journal,* 1 (1995/96): 29–48.

48. G. Stevens and E. Stevens, "The truth about EPSS," *Training and Development,* 50 (1996): 59–61.

49. "In your face, EPSS," *Training* (April 1996): 101–102.

50. T. Davenport, L. Prusak, and B. Strong, "Putting ideas to work," *The Wall Street Journal* (March 10, 2008): R11.

51. D. DeLong and L. Fahey, "Diagnosing cultural barriers to knowledge management," *Academy of Management Executive,* 14 (2000): 113–127; A. Rossett, "Knowledge management meets analysis," *Training and Development* (May 1999): 63–68; M. Van Buren, "A yardstick for knowledge management," *Training and Development* (May 1999): 71–78.

52. Gephart, Marsick, Van Buren, and Spiro, "Learning Organizations Come Alive; Davenport, Prusak, and Strong, "Putting Ideas to Work."

53. "Center for Army Lessons Learned Named in Info World 100 for 2008 Top IT Solutions," at http://usacac .army.mil/cacz/call/index. asp, website for the Center for Army Lessons Learned (accessed March 30, 2009).

54. "A recipe for sharing knowledge," *OD/Leadership Network News* (December 2005). Available at www .steelcase.com/na/ (February 28, 2006).

55. J. MacGregor, "The office chart that really counts," *Business Week* (February 27, 2006): 48–49.

56. B. Roberts, "Can they keep the lights on?" *HR Magazine* (June 2010): 62–68.

57. "Grant Thornton LLP (USA)," *T+D*, October 2010, 74.

58. J. Salopek, "Re-discovering knowledge," *T+D*, October 2010, 36–38.

59. J. Collins, "It's all in here! How do we get it out?" *T+D* (January 2011): 59–61.

60. J. Gordon, "Intellectual capital and you," *Training* (September 1999): 30–38; D. Zielinski, "Have you shared a bright idea today?" *Training* (July 2000): 65–68.

61. K. Ellis, "Share best practices globally," *Training* (July 2001): 32–38.

62. D. Garvin, A. Edmondson, and F. Gino, "Is yours a learning organization?" *Harvard Business Review* (March 2008): 109–116. "Center for Army Lessons Learned Named in Info World 100 for 2008 Top IT Solutions."

63. T. O'Driscoll, B. Sugrue, and M. Vona, "The C-level and the value of learning," *T+D* (October 2005): 70–77.

64. J. Salopek. "Computer Sciences Corporation," *T+D* (October 2005): 58.

65. D. Pringle, "Learning gurus adapt to escape corporate axes," *The Wall Street Journal* (January 7, 2003): B1, B4.

66. P. Babcock, "Shedding light on knowledge management," *HR Magazine* (May 2004): 46–50; R. Davenport, "Does knowledge management still matter?" *T+D* (February 2005): 19–25.

67. Babcock, "Shedding Light on Knowledge Management."

68. K. Spors, "Getting Workers to Share Their Know-how with Their Peers," *The Wall Street Journal* (April 3, 2008): B6.

69. T. Aeppel, "On factory floor, top workers hide secrets to success," *The Wall Street Journal* (July 1, 2002): A1, A10; D. Lepak and S. Snell, "Managing Human Resource Architecture for Knowledge-Based Competition," in *Managing Knowledge for Sustained Competitive Advantage,* ed. S. Jackson, M. Hitt, and A. DeNisi (San Francisco: Jossey-Bass, 2003): 127–154.

70. S. Thurm, "Companies Struggle to Pass on Knowledge That Workers Acquire," *The Wall Street Journal,* (January 23, 2006): B1.

71. M. Van Buren, "A yardstick for knowledge management," *Training and Development* (May 1999): 71–78; L. Bassi and D. McMumer, "Developing measurement systems for managing in the knowledge era," *Organizational Dynamics,* 34 (2005): 185–96.

# Chapter **Six**

# Training Evaluation

## Objectives

After reading this chapter, you should be able to

1. Explain why evaluation is important.
2. Identify and choose outcomes to evaluate a training program.
3. Discuss the process used to plan and implement a good training evaluation.
4. Discuss the strengths and weaknesses of different evaluation designs.
5. Choose the appropriate evaluation design based on the characteristics of the company and the importance and purpose of the training.
6. Conduct a cost-benefit analysis for a training program.
7. Explain the role of workforce analytics and dashboards in determining the value of training practices.

## Evaluation Puts Training Front and Center at Kelly Services

Kelly Services provides a range of services to its clients, including outsourcing, consulting and traditional staffing, HR management, vendor management, and outplacement. Founded in 1946, Kelly's traditional expertise began with providing office services (the "Kelly Girl" brand), call center, light industrial, and electronic assembly staffing. Kelly has evolved from a U.S.-focused company concentrating primarily on traditional office services into a global workforce solutions leader. Kelly Services has approximately 6,700 employees, many of whom work to provide clients with more than 530,000 employees each year. It can provide clients with professional and technical employees in engineering, finance and accounting, information technology, law, science, and health care. Kelly is the world's largest scientific staffing provider. Kelly's business goals include increasing market share outside the United States, improving operational efficiency, and identifying, developing, engaging, and leading top talent. Kelly is challenged to create innovate solutions and generate new business, both for itself and its clients.

Kelly's Global Learning department plays an important strategic role in the company because training is seen as critical to the company's overall success. One example of this was that during the early stages of the economic recession, classroom training continued to receive funding while other departments' budgets were cut. To help reduce training costs, the Global Learning department converted classroom training into virtual instructor-led courses. The Global Learning Group continues to be charged with developing business-related learning solutions and has been able to demonstrate its effectiveness through evaluation. Their measurement strategy includes using anectodal and numerical data to prove causal relationships between learning and outcomes, showing relationships between learning and outcomes, and tracking course completions, enrollments, compliance, cost-per-participant, and employees' evaluations of training courses that they have completed.

For example, when Kelly's senior managers asked Global Learning to help address lagging productivity among new employees and a high turnover rate, Global Learning responded by creating a new program for new employees (known as "the Kelly Experience"). A comparison of turnover rates for employees who participated in the program versus the overall turnover rate demonstrated a 13 percent decrease in turnover related to program participation. Productivity was 27 percent higher for those new employees who participated in the program, compared to those who did not. Also, Global Learning developed Global Solutions Training to grow the profitability of sales employees. Senior leaders and global salespeople helped develop thirteen courses, which emphasized that salespeople have to ask questions about customer needs and know how to recognize cross-selling opportunities. Results showed that the average sales of employees who completed at least one of the thirteen courses were 84 percent higher than for those who did not complete the program. A training initiative designed to train sales employees how to aggressively and effectively sell one of the company's most complex workforce solutions (including outsourcing and consulting) included thirty hours of case studies, role-play exercises, and a case study exam. Participants received a pass/fail grade that determined the scope of their sales responsibility. Evaluation results showed that program participants increased sales opportunities by 63 percent and increased the number of solutions sold per client contact from 22 percent to 26 percent.

**Source:** Based on P. Harris, "Learning, at your service," *T+D* (October 2010): 57–58; www.kellyservices .com, the website for Kelly Services.

# INTRODUCTION

As the opening vignette illustrates, Kelly Services wanted to show that the time, money, and effort devoted to training actually made a difference. That is, the training function was interested in assessing the effectiveness of training programs. **Training effectiveness** refers to the benefits that the company and the trainees receive from training. Benefits for trainees may include learning new skills or behaviors. Benefits for the company may include increased sales and more satisfied customers. A training evaluation measures specific outcomes or criteria to determine the benefits of the program. **Training outcomes** or **criteria** refer to measures that the trainer and the company use to evaluate training programs. To determine the effectiveness of the program, the hospital had to conduct an evaluation. **Training evaluation** refers to the process of collecting the outcomes needed to determine whether training is effective. For Kelly Services, some of the outcomes included employee evaluations of training courses, turnover rate, and sales. Kelly Services also had to be confident that its information-gathering process was providing accurate data that it could use to draw valid conclusions about the effectiveness of its training programs. The **evaluation design** refers to the collection of information—including what, when, how, and from whom—that will be used to determine the effectiveness of the training program. Kelly Services used a post-test comparison group evaluation design to determine the effectiveness of the "Kelly Experience." That is, turnover and productivity data was collected after employees participated in the "Kelly Experience," as well as from employees who did not participate. Kelly Services compared the turnover and productivity data from the two groups of employees and found that turnover was lower and productivity higher for those who participated in the "Kelly Experience." Any organization that evaluates training has to be confident that training—rather than same other factor—is responsible for changes in the outcomes of interest (e.g., turnover, productivity). The degree of confidence that any changes in the outcomes of interest is due to training depends on the type of evaluation design that is used.

Recall the Instructional Systems Design model shown in Chapter One Figure 1.1 and the topics covered in Chapters Two through Five. The information from the needs assessment, the characteristics of the learning environment, and the steps taken to ensure transfer of training should all be used to develop an evaluation plan. In order to identify appropriate training outcomes, a company needs to look at its business strategy, its organizational analysis (Why are we conducting training? How is it related to the business?), its person analysis (Who needs training?), its task analysis (What is the training content?), the learning objectives of the training, and its plan for training transfer.

This chapter will help you understand why and how to evaluate training programs. The chapter begins by discussing the types of outcomes used in training program evaluation. The next section of the chapter discusses the practical factors to consider when choosing an evaluation design. An overview of the types of designs is presented. The chapter reviews the process involved in conducting a program evaluation. The chapter concludes with a discussion of metrics that can be used to evaluate the strategic value of the training function.

# REASONS FOR EVALUATING TRAINING

Companies are investing millions of dollars in training programs to help gain a competitive advantage. Companies invest in training because learning creates knowledge; often, it is this knowledge that distinguishes successful companies and employees from those who are not. Research summarizing the results of studies that have examined the linkage between training and human resource outcomes (such as attitudes and motivation, behaviors, and human capital), organizational performance outcomes (performance and productivity), or financial outcomes (profits and financial indicators) has found that companies that conduct training are likely to have more positive human resource outcomes and greater performance outcomes.[1] The influence of training is largest for organizational performance outcomes and human resource outcomes and weakest for financial outcomes. This result is not surprising, given that training can least affect an organization's financial performance and may do so through its influence on human resource practices. As emphasized in Chapter Two, "Strategic Training," training is more strongly related to organizational outcomes when it is matched with the organization's business strategy and capital intensity. Because companies have made large dollar investments in training and education and view training as a strategy to be successful, they expect the outcomes or benefits related to training to be measurable.

At TELUS, a Canadian telecommunications company, training evaluation involves more than just counting the number of programs that employees attend each year.[2] Employees are asked to complete quarterly surveys that ask about how their use of formal and informal learning has improved their performance and careers. Jim Skinner, the CEO of McDonalds, has three top priorities for the company: long-term sustainable growth for the company, talent management and leadership development, and promoting balanced active lifestyles.[3] McDonalds is well known for the amount of training it provides to all its employees, including crew members, managers, and executives (recall the discussion of McDonald's Hamburger University in Chapter Two). McDonalds evaluates training in a number of different ways. Mystery shoppers and the customer hotline provide evaluations of the service and product quality at its restaurants. Another way is looking at the speed of new product launches. Training has helped reduce new product launches from eighteen months to six months. McDonalds also checks employee turnover at ninety-day and one-year intervals as a measure of training effectiveness. Training is designed to help make employees productive and satisfied, therefore influencing them to stay in their jobs and perhaps commit to a career with the company. In fact, 70 percent of McDonalds managers started as crew members. McDonalds believes if training is not conducted properly, all aspects of the product will suffer, including merchandising and order accuracy, ingredients, portioning, and even temperature. Sales and guest count data show that the regions in which restaurants are located who have more people trained have higher sales and guest counts.

Training evaluation provides a way to understand the investments that training produces and provides information needed to improve training.[4] If the company receives an inadequate return on its investment in training, the company will likely reduce its investment in training or look for training providers outside the company who can provide training experiences that improve performance, productivity, customer satisfaction, or whatever other outcomes the company is interested in achieving. Training evaluation provides the data needed to demonstrate that training does offer benefits to the company. Training evaluation involves both formative and summative evaluation.[5]

## Formative Evaluation

**Formative evaluation** refers to the evaluation of training that takes place during program design and development. That is, formative evaluation helps to ensure that (1) the training program is well organized and runs smoothly, and (2) trainees learn and are satisfied with the program. Formative evaluation provides information about how to make the program better; it usually involves collecting qualitative data about the program. Qualitative data include opinions, beliefs, and feelings about the program. Formative evaluations ask customers, employees, managers, and subject-matter experts (SMEs) their opinions on the description of the training content and objectives and the program design. These people are also asked to evaluate the clarity and ease of use of a part of the training program that is demonstrated to them in the way that it will be delivered (e.g., online, face-to-face, or video).[6] The formative evaluation is conducted either individually or in groups before the program is made available to the rest of the company. Trainers may also be involved to measure the time requirements of the program. As a result of the formative evaluation, training content may be changed to be more accurate, easier to understand, or more appealing. The training method can be adjusted to improve learning (e.g., provide trainees with more opportunities to practice or give feedback). Also, introducing the training program as early as possible to managers and customers helps in getting them to buy into the program, which is critical for their role in helping employees learn and transfer skills. It also allows their concerns to be addressed before the program is implemented.

**Pilot testing** refers to the process of previewing the training program with potential trainees and managers or with other customers (persons who are paying for the development of the program). Pilot testing can be used as a "dress rehearsal" to show the program to managers, trainees, and customers. It should also be used for formative evaluation. For example, a group of potential trainees and their managers may be asked to preview or pilot test a web-based training program. As they complete the program, trainees and managers may be asked to provide their opinions about whether graphics, videos, or music used in the program contributed to (or interfered with) learning. They may also be asked how easy it was to move through the program and complete the exercises, and they may be asked to evaluate the quality of feedback the training program provided after they completed the exercises. The information gained from this preview would be used by program developers to improve the program before it is made available to all employees. St. George Bank developed a new web-based training system for bank tellers.[7] Before the program was provided to all bank tellers, it was reviewed by a small group of them who were considered to be typical users of the program. The tellers provided suggestions for improvement, and the instructional designers incorporated their suggestions into the final version of the program.

## Summative Evaluation

**Summative evaluation** refers to an evaluation conducted to determine the extent to which trainees have changed as a result of participating in the training program. That is, have trainees acquired knowledge, skills, attitudes, behavior, or other outcomes identified in the training objectives? Summative evaluation may also include measuring the monetary benefits (also known as *return on investment* or *ROI*) that the company receives from the program. Summative evaluation usually involves collecting quantitative (numerical) data through tests, ratings of behavior, or objective measures of performance such as volume of sales, accidents, or patents.

From the discussion of summative and formative evaluation, it is probably apparent to you why a training program should be evaluated:

1. To identify the program's strengths and weaknesses. This includes determining if the program is meeting the learning objectives, if the quality of the learning environment is satisfactory, and if transfer of training to the job is occurring.
2. To assess whether the content, organization, and administration of the program— including the schedule, accommodations, trainers, and materials—contribute to learning and the use of training content on the job.
3. To identify which trainees benefit most or least from the program.

4. To assist in marketing programs through the collection of information from participants about whether they would recommend the program to others, why they attended the program, and their level of satisfaction with the program.

5. To determine the financial benefits and costs of the program.

6. To compare the costs and benefits of training versus nontraining investments (such as work redesign or a better employee selection system).

7. To compare the costs and benefits of different training programs to choose the best program.

# OVERVIEW OF THE EVALUATION PROCESS

Before the chapter explains each aspect of training evaluation in detail, you need to understand the evaluation process, which is summarized in Figure 6.1. The previous discussion of formative and summative evaluation suggests that training evaluation involves scrutinizing the program both before and after the program is completed. Figure 6.1 emphasizes that training evaluation must be considered by managers and trainers before training has actually occurred. As was suggested earlier in this chapter, information gained from the training design process shown in Figure 6.1 is valuable for training evaluation.

The evaluation process should begin with determining training needs (as discussed in Chapter Three, "Needs Assessment"). Needs assessment helps identify what knowledge, skills, behavior, or other learned capabilities are needed. Needs assessment also helps identify where the training is expected to have an impact. Needs assessment helps focus the evaluation by identifying the purpose of the program, the resources needed (human, financial, and company), and the outcomes that will provide evidence that the program has been effective.[8] The next step in the process is to identify specific, measurable training objectives to guide the program. The characteristics of good objectives are discussed in Chapter Four,

**FIGURE 6.1**
**The Evaluation Process**

Sources: Based on
D. A. Grove and
C. Ostroff, "Program
Evaluation," in
*Developing Human
Resources*, ed.
K. N. Wexley
(Washington, D. C.:
Bureau of National
Affairs, 1991): 5–185
to 5–220; K. Kraiger,
D. McLinden, and
W. Casper,
"Collaborative
Planning for Training
Impact," *Human
Resource Management*
(Winter 2004):
337–51.

"Learning and Transfer of Training." The more specific and measurable these objectives are, the easier it is to identify relevant outcomes for the evaluation. Besides considering the learning and program objectives in developing learning outcomes, it is also important to consider the expectations of those individuals who support the program and have an interest in it (stakeholders such as trainees, managers, and trainers).[9] If the needs assessment was done well, the stakeholders' interests likely overlap considerably with the learning and program objectives. Analysis of the work environment to determine transfer of training (discussed in Chapter Five, "Program Design") can be useful for determining how training content will be used on the job. Based on the learning objectives and analysis of transfer of training, outcome measures are designed to assess the extent to which learning and transfer have occurred.

Once the outcomes have been identified, the next step is to determine an evaluation strategy. Factors such as expertise, how quickly the information is needed, change potential, and the organizational culture should be considered in choosing a design. Planning and executing the evaluation involves previewing the program (formative evaluation), as well as collecting training outcomes according to the evaluation design. The results of the evaluation are used to modify, market, or gain additional support for the program. The results of the evaluation should also be used to encourage all stakeholders in the training process—including managers, employees, and trainers—to design or choose training that helps the company meet its business strategy and helps managers and employees meet their goals.[10]

# OUTCOMES USED IN THE EVALUATION OF TRAINING PROGRAMS

To evaluate its training program, a company must decide *how* it will determine the program's effectiveness; that is, it must identify what training outcomes or criteria it will measure.

Table 6.1 shows the six categories of training outcomes: reaction outcomes, learning or cognitive outcomes, behavior and skill-based outcomes, affective outcomes, results, and return on investment.[11]

Table 6.1 shows training outcomes, Kirkpatrick's five-level framework for categorizing training outcomes, and a description of each of the outcomes and how they are measured. Both level 1 and level 2 outcomes (reactions and learning) are collected at the completion of training, before trainees return to the job. Level 3 outcomes (behavior/skills) can also be collected at the completion of training to determine trainees' behavior or skill level at that point. To determine whether trainees are using training content back on the job (i.e., whether transfer of training has occurred), level 3, level 4, and/or level 5 outcomes can be collected. Level 3 criteria can be collected to determine whether behavior/skills are being used on the job. Level 4 and level 5 criteria (results and return on investment) can also be used to determine whether training has resulted in an improvement in business results, such as productivity or customer satisfaction. These criteria also help to determine whether the benefits of training exceed their costs. Keep in mind that the levels do not indicate the importance of the outcomes or that lower-level outcomes cause higher-level outcomes.[12] That is, reactions cause learning, which in turn influences skills and results. The outcomes that are collected in evaluation are based on training needs, program objectives, and the strategic reasons for training. We discuss this in the section "Evaluation Practices," later in the chapter.

**TABLE 6.1** Evaluation Outcomes

| Outcome or Criterion | Level | What Is Measured | Examples | Measurement Methods |
|---|---|---|---|---|
| Reactions | 1 | Learners' satisfaction | Comfortable training room<br>Useful materials and program content | Surveys<br>Interviews |
| Learning or cognitive | 2 | Principles, facts, techniques, procedures, or processes that the learners have acquired | Electrical principles<br>Safety rules<br>Steps in interviewing | Tests<br>Work samples |
| Behavior and skill-based | 2 or 3 | Interpersonal<br>Technical or motor skills or behaviors acquired by learners | Preparing a dessert<br>Sawing wood<br>Landing an airplane<br>Listening | Tests<br>Observations<br>Self, peer, customer, and/or managers' ratings<br>Work samples |
| Affective | 2 or 3 | Learners' attitudes and motivation | Tolerance for diversity<br>Safety attitudes<br>Customer service orientation | Attitude surveys<br>Interviews<br>Focus groups |
| Results | 4 | Payoffs for the company | Productivity<br>Quality<br>Costs<br>Repeat customers<br>Customer satisfaction<br>Accidents | Observation<br>Performance data from records or company databases |
| Return on investment | 5 | Identification and comparison of learning benefits with costs | Dollar value of productivity divided by training costs | Economic value |

Sources: Based on K. Kraiger, J. K. Ford, and E. Salas, "Application of cognitive, skill-based, and affective theories of learning outcomes to new methods of training evaluation," *Journal of Applied Psychology,* 78 (2) (1993): 311–328; K. Kraiger, "Decision-Based Evaluation," in K. Kraiger (ed.), *Creating, Implementing, and Managing Effective Training and Development* (San Francisco: Jossey-Bass, 2002): 331–375; D. Kirkpatrick, "Evaluation," in *The ASTD Training and Development Handbook,* 2nd ed., ed. R. L. Craig (New York: McGraw-Hill, 1996): 294–312.

## Reaction Outcomes

**Reaction outcomes** refer to trainees' perceptions of the program, including the facilities, trainers, and content. (Reaction outcomes are often referred to as a measure of "creature comfort.") They are often called *class* or *instructor evaluations.* This information is typically collected at the program's conclusion. You probably have been asked to complete class or instructor evaluations either at the end of a college course or a training program at work. Reactions are useful for identifying what trainees thought was successful or what inhibited learning. Reaction outcomes are level 1 (reaction) criteria in Kirkpatrick's framework.

Reaction outcomes are typically collected via a questionnaire completed by trainees. A reaction measure should include questions related to the trainee's satisfaction with the instructor, training materials, and training administration (e.g., ease of registration and accuracy of course description), as well as the clarity of course objectives and usefulness of the training content.[13] Table 6.2 shows a reaction measure that contains questions about these areas.

An accurate evaluation needs to include all the factors related to a successful learning environment.[14] Most instructor or class evaluations include items related to the trainer's preparation, delivery, ability to lead a discussion, organization of the training materials and content, use of visual aids, presentation style, ability and willingness to answer questions, and ability to stimulate trainees' interest in the course. These items come from trainer's manuals, trainer certification programs, and observation of successful trainers. Conventional wisdom suggests that trainees who like a training program (who have positive reactions) learn more and are more likely to change behaviors and improve their performance (transfer of training). Is this really the case? Recent studies suggest that reactions have the largest relationship to changes in affective learning outcomes.[15] Also, research has found that reactions are significantly related to changes in declarative and procedural knowledge, which challenges previous research suggesting that reactions are unrelated to learning. For courses such as diversity training or ethics training, trainee reactions are especially important because they affect learners' receptivity to attitude change. Reactions have been found to have the strongest relationship with post-training motivation, trainee self-efficacy, and declarative knowledge when technology is used for instructional delivery. This suggests that for online or e-learning training methods, it is important to ensure that it is easy for trainees to access them and the training content is meaningful (i.e., linked to their current job experiences, tasks, or work issues).

**TABLE 6.2**  **Sample Reaction Measure**

Read each statement below. Indicate the extent to which you agree or disagree with each statement using the scale below.

| Strongly Disagree | Disagree | Neither | Agree | Strongly Agree |
|:---:|:---:|:---:|:---:|:---:|
| 1 | 2 | 3 | 4 | 5 |

1. I had the knowledge and skills needed to learn in this course.
2. The facilities and equipment made it easy to learn.
3. The course met all of the stated objectives.
4. I clearly understood the course objectives.
5. The way the course was delivered was an effective way to learn.
6. The materials I received during the course were useful.
7. The course content was logically organized.
8. There was enough time to learn the course content.
9. I felt that the instructor wanted us to learn.
10. I was comfortable asking the instructor questions.
11. The instructor was prepared.
12. The instructor was knowledgeable about the course content.
13. I learned a lot from this course.
14. What I learned in this course is useful for my job.
15. The information I received about the course was accurate.
16. Overall, I was satisfied with the instructor.
17. Overall, I was satisfied with the course.

## Learning or Cognitive Outcomes

**Cognitive outcomes** are used to determine the degree to which trainees are familiar with the principles, facts, techniques, procedures, and processes emphasized in the training program. Cognitive outcomes measure what knowledge trainees learned in the program. Cognitive outcomes are level 2 (learning) criteria in Kirkpatrick's framework. Typically, pencil-and-paper tests are used to assess cognitive outcomes. Table 6.3 provides an example of items from a pencil-and-paper test used to measure trainees' knowledge of decision-making skills. These items help to measure whether a trainee knows how to make a decision (the process that he or she would use). They do not help to determine if the trainee will actually use decision-making skills on the job.

Consider how Grant Thornton, the public accounting and consulting firm, used tests to evaluate one of its training programs. The company introduced a new tax services methodology and tools to approximately 1,400 tax professionals in more than fifty offices.[16] The training solution, known as Tax Symphony, involved blended learning, which included a three-day national- and local-office classroom programs, web-based performance support, and webcasts. The new methodology was introduced during a tax conference. After the conference, the content was taught at local offices using avatars presenting prerecorded audio clips combined with group application activities. Evaluation results showed that 86 percent of the program participants completing the post-test passed it with an average passing score of 85 percent. Average post-test scores improved by 11 percentage points over national classroom post-test scores. Using avatars instead of real instructors in local offices saved $72,000 in costs.

## Behavior and Skill-Based Outcomes

**Skill-based outcomes** are used to assess the level of technical or motor skills and behaviors. Skill-based outcomes include acquisition or learning of skills (skill learning) and use of skills on the job (skill transfer). Skill-based outcomes relate to Kirkpatrick's level 2 (learning) and level 3 (behavior). The extent to which trainees have learned skills can be evaluated by observing their performance in work samples such as simulators. Skill transfer is usually determined by observation. For example, a resident medical student may perform surgery while the surgeon carefully observes, giving advice and assistance as needed. Trainees may be asked to provide ratings of their own behavior or skills (self-ratings).

---

**TABLE 6.3**
**Sample Test Items Used to Measure Learning**

Source: Based on A. P. Carnevale, L. J. Gainer, and A. S. Meltzer, *Workplace Basics Training Manual* (San Francisco: Jossey-Bass, 1990): 8.12.

**For each question, check all that apply.**

1. If my boss returned a piece of work to me and asked me to make changes on it, I would:
   __ Prove to my boss that the work didn't need to be changed.
   __ Do what the boss said, but ask where the boss thought changes were needed
   __ Make the changes without talking to my boss.
   __ Request a transfer from the department.
2. If I were setting up a new process in my office, I would:
   __ Do it on my own, without asking for help.
   __ Ask my boss for suggestions.
   __ Ask the people who work for me for suggestions.
   __ Discuss it with friends outside the company.

Peers, managers, and subordinates may also be asked to rate trainees' behavior or skills based on their observations. Because research suggests that the use of only self-ratings likely results in an inaccurately positive assessment of skill or behavior transfer of training, it is recommended that skill or behavior ratings be collected from multiple perspectives (e.g., managers and subordinates or peers).[17] Table 6.4 shows a sample rating form. This form was used as part of an evaluation of a training program developed to improve school principals' management skills.

## Affective Outcomes

**Affective outcomes** include attitudes and motivation. Affective outcomes that might be collected in an evaluation include tolerance for diversity, motivation to learn, safety attitudes, and customer service orientation. Affective outcomes can be measured using surveys. Table 6.5 shows an example of questions on a survey used to measure career goals, plans, and interests. The specific attitude of interest depends on the program objectives. Affective outcomes relate to Kirkpatrick's level 2 (learning) or level 3 (behavior), depending on how they are evaluated. If trainees were asked about their attitudes on a survey, that would be considered a learning measure. For example, attitudes toward career goals and

**TABLE 6.4   Sample Rating Form Used to Measure Behavior**

*Rating task:* Consider your opportunities over the past three months to observe and interact with the principal/assistant principal you are rating. Read the definition and behaviors associated with the skill. Then complete your ratings using the following scale:

| Always | Usually | Sometimes | Seldom | Never |
|--------|---------|-----------|--------|-------|
| 1 | 2 | 3 | 4 | 5 |

I. *Sensitivity:* Ability to perceive the needs, concerns, and personal problems of others; tact in dealing with persons from different backgrounds; skill in resolving conflict; ability to deal effectively with people concerning emotional needs; knowing what information to communicate to whom.
To what extent in the past three months has the principal or assistant principal:
___ 1. Elicited the perceptions, feelings, and concerns of others?
___ 2. Expressed verbal and nonverbal recognition of the feelings, needs, and concerns of others?
___ 3. Taken actions that anticipated the emotional effects of specific behaviors?
___ 4. Accurately reflected the point of view of others by restating it, applying it, or encouraging feedback?
___ 5. Communicated all information to others that they needed to perform their job?
___ 6. Diverted unnecessary conflict with others in problem situations?

II. *Decisiveness:* Ability to recognize when a decision is required and act quickly. (Disregard the quality of the decision.)
To what extent in the past three months has this individual:
___ 7. Recognized when a decision was required by determining the results if the decision was made or not made?
___ 8. Determined whether a short- or long-term solution was most appropriate to various situations encountered in the school?
___ 9. Considered decision alternatives?
___10. Made a timely decision based on available data?
___11. Stuck to decisions once they were made, resisting pressures from others?

**TABLE 6.5**
**Example of Affective Outcomes: Career Goals, Plans, and Interests**

1. At this time, I have a definite career goal in mind.
2. I have a strategy for achieving my career goals.
3. My manager is aware of my career goals.
4. I have sought information regarding my specific areas of career interest from friends, colleagues, or company career sources.
5. I have initiated conversations concerning my career plans with my manager.

interests might be an appropriate outcome to use to evaluate training focusing on employees self-managing their careers.

## Results

**Results** are used to determine the training program's payoff for the company. Examples of results outcomes include increased production and reduced costs related to employee turnover rates of top talent (managers or other employees), accidents, and equipment downtime, as well as improvements in product quality or customer service.[18] Results outcomes are level 4 (results) criteria in Kirkpatrick's framework. For example, employees of the government of Chesterfield County, Virginia, demonstrate the application of learning through measurements of avoided costs, annual hours saved, and customer service.[19] IKON Office Solutions, Inc., wanted to ensure that the sales force had acceptable proficiency in demonstrating copying equipment.[20] Sales activity was measured before and after the program. Prior to the training, sales activity was below company goals. Four months after training, product placements increased 200 percent.

LQ Management LLC, the parent company of La Quinta Inns and Suites, is responsible for training for the hotels.[21] The company recently implemented a new sales strategy designed to generate the best available rate for each hotel location based on customer demand and occupancy rates. A training program involving an experiential game ("Buddy's View") was used to engage staff in understanding how the new sales strategy would affect the business, as well as to improve customer service. To evaluate the effectiveness of the program, the company collects business results (Kirkpatrick's level 4 criteria)—specifically, percentage changes in service quality and customers' intent to return before and after the program.

## Return on Investment

**Return on investment (ROI)** refers to comparing the training's monetary benefits with the cost of the training. ROI is often referred to as level 5 evaluation (see Table 6.1). Training costs can be direct and indirect.[22] **Direct costs** include salaries and benefits for all employees involved in training, including trainees, instructors, consultants, and employees who design the program; program material and supplies; equipment or classroom rentals or purchases; and travel costs. **Indirect costs** are not related directly to the design, development, or delivery of the training program. They include general office supplies, facilities, equipment, and related expenses; travel and expenses not directly billed to one program; training department management and staff salaries not related to any one program; and administrative and staff support salaries. **Benefits** are the value that the company gains from the training program.

The Northwest Airlines technical operations training department includes 72 instructors who are responsible for training thousands of aircraft technicians and more than 10,000 outside vendors who work on maintaining the Northwest aircraft fleet.[23] Each of the training instructors works with one type of aircraft, such as the Airbus 320. Most of the department's training is instructor-led in a classroom, but other instruction programs use a simulator or take place in an actual airplane.

By tracking department training data, which allowed for training evaluation, the technical operations department was able to demonstrate its worth by showing how its services contribute to the airline's business. For example, the technical operations department reduced the cost of training an individual technician by 16 percent; increased customer satisfaction through training; increased training productivity; made the case for upper management to provide financial resources for training; and improved postcourse evaluations, knowledge, and performance gains.

To achieve these results, the technical operations training department developed the Training Quality Index (TQI). The TQI is a computer application that collects data about training department performance, productivity, budget, and courses, and allows detailed analysis of this data. TQI tracks all department training data into five categories: effectiveness, quantity, perceptions, financial impact, and operational impact. The quality of training is included in the effectiveness category. For example, knowledge gain relates to the difference in trainees' pretraining and post-training knowledge measured by exams. The system can provide performance reports that relate to budgets and the cost of training per student per day and other costs of training. The measures that are collected are also linked to department goals, to department strategy, and ultimately, to the airline's overall strategy. Questions that were often asked before TQI was developed but couldn't easily be answered—such as "How can the cost of training be justified? "What is the operational impact of training?" and "What amount of training have technicians received?"—can now be answered through the TQI system. Training demand can be evaluated against passenger loads and the number of flying routes to determine the right number of trainers in the right locations to support business needs. These adjustments increase customer satisfaction and result in positive views of the training operations.

# DETERMINING WHETHER OUTCOMES ARE APPROPRIATE

An important issue in choosing outcomes is to determine whether they are appropriate. That is, are these outcomes the best ones to measure to determine whether the training program is effective? Appropriate training outcomes need to be relevant, reliable, discriminative and practical.[24]

## Relevance

**Criteria relevance** refers to the extent to which training outcomes are related to the learned capabilities emphasized in the training program. The learned capabilities required to succeed in the training program should be the same as those required to be successful on the job. The outcomes collected in training should be as similar as possible to what trainees learned in the program. That is, the outcomes need to be valid measures of learning. One way to ensure the relevancy of the outcomes is to choose outcomes based on the learning objectives for the program. Recall from Chapter Four that learning objectives show the expected action, the conditions under which the trainee is to perform, and the level or standard of performance.

Figure 6.2 shows two ways that training outcomes may lack relevance. **Criterion contamination** refers to the extent that training outcomes measure inappropriate capabilities

**FIGURE 6.2**
**Criterion deficiency, relevance, and contamination.**

Criteria may also be deficient. **Criterion deficiency** refers to the failure to measure training outcomes that were emphasized in the training objectives.

or are affected by extraneous conditions. For example, if managers' evaluations of job performance are used as a training outcome, trainees may receive higher ratings of job performance simply because the managers know they attended the training program, believe the program is valuable, and therefore give high ratings to ensure that the training looks like it positively affects performance. Criteria may also be contaminated if the conditions under which the outcomes are measured vary from the learning environment. That is, trainees may be asked to perform their learned capabilities using equipment, time constraints, or physical working conditions that are not similar to those in the learning environment.

For example, trainees may be asked to demonstrate spreadsheet skills using a newer version of spreadsheet software than they used in the training program. This demonstration likely will result in no changes in their spreadsheet skills from pretraining levels. In this case, poor-quality training is not the cause for the lack of change in their spreadsheet skills. Trainees may have learned the necessary spreadsheet skills, but the environment for the evaluation differs substantially from the learning environment, so no change in skill level is observed.

Criteria may also be deficient. **Criterion deficiency** refers to the failure to measure training outcomes that were emphasized in the training objectives. For example, the objectives of a spreadsheet skills training program emphasize that trainees both understand the commands available on the spreadsheet (e.g., compute) and use the spreadsheet to calculate statistics using a data set. An evaluation design that uses only learning outcomes such as a test of knowledge of the purpose of keystrokes is deficient because the evaluation does not measure outcomes that were included in the training objectives (e.g., use a spreadsheet to compute the mean and standard deviation of a set of data).

## Reliability

**Reliability** refers to the degree to which outcomes can be measured consistently over time. For example, a trainer gives restaurant employees a written test measuring knowledge of safety standards to evaluate a safety training program that they attended. The test is given before (pretraining) and after (post-training) employees attend the program. A reliable test includes items for which the meaning or interpretation does not change over time. A reliable test allows the trainer to have confidence that any improvements in post-training test scores from pretraining levels are the result of learning that occurred in the training program, not test characteristics (e.g., items are more understandable the second time) or the test environment (e.g., trainees performed better on the post-training test because the classroom was more comfortable and quieter).

## Discrimination

**Discrimination** refers to the degree to which trainees' performance on the outcome actually reflects true differences in performance. For example, a paper-and-pencil test that measures electricians' knowledge of electrical principles must detect true differences in trainees' knowledge of electrical principles. That is, the test should discriminate on the basis of trainees' knowledge of electrical principles. (People who score high on the test have a better understanding of the principles of electricity than do those who score low.)

## Practicality

**Practicality** refers to the ease with which the outcome measures can be collected. One reason companies give for not including learning, performance, and behavior outcomes in their evaluation of training programs is that collecting them is too burdensome. (It takes too much time and energy, which detracts from the business.) For example, in evaluating a sales training program, it may be impractical to ask customers to rate the salesperson's behavior because this would place too much of a time commitment on the customer (and probably damage future sales relationships).

# EVALUATION PRACTICES

Figure 6.3 shows outcomes used in training evaluation practices. Surveys of companies' evaluation practices indicate that reactions (an affective outcome) and cognitive outcomes are the most frequently used outcomes in training evaluation.[25] Despite the less frequent

**FIGURE 6.3**
**Training evaluation practices**

Note: Respondents were 704 high-level business, HR and learning professionals participating in the ASTD/i4cp study, "The Value of Evaluation: Making Training Evaluations More Effective." Source: Based on L. Patel, *2010 State of the Industry Report* (Alexandria, VA: American Society for Training and Development, 2010).

use of cognitive, behavioral, and results outcomes, research suggests that training can have a positive effect on these outcomes.[26] Keep in mind that while most companies are conducting training evaluations, some surveys indicate that 20 percent of all companies are not!

## Which Training Outcomes Should be Collected?

From our discussion of evaluation outcomes and evaluation practices, you may have the mistaken impression that it is necessary to collect all five levels of outcomes to evaluate a training program. While collecting all five levels of outcomes is ideal, the training program objectives determine which ones should be linked to the broader business strategy, as discussed in Chapter Two. To ensure adequate training evaluation, companies should collect outcome measures related to both learning (levels 1 and 2) and transfer of training (levels 3, 4, and 5).

It is important to recognize the limitations of choosing to measure only reaction and cognitive outcomes. Consider the previous discussions of learning and transfer of training in Chapters 4 and 5. Remember that for training to be successful, learning *and* transfer of training must occur. Figure 6.4 shows the multiple objectives of training programs and their implication for choosing evaluation outcomes. Training programs usually have objectives related to both learning and transfer. That is, they want trainees to acquire knowledge and cognitive skills and also to demonstrate the use of the knowledge or strategies they learned in their on-the-job behavior. As a result, to ensure an adequate training evaluation, companies must collect outcome measures related to both learning and transfer.

Ernst & Young's training function uses knowledge testing (level 2) for all of the company's e-learning courses, which account for 50 percent of training.[27] New courses and programs use behavior transfer (level 3) and business results (level 4). Regardless

**FIGURE 6.4**
**Training Program Objectives and Their Implications for Evaluation**

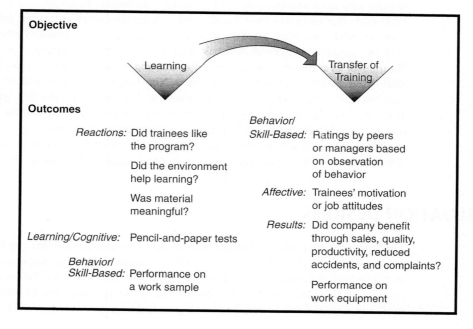

of the program, the company's leaders are interested in whether the trainees believe that training has been a good use of their time and money, and whether they would recommend it to other employees (level 1). The training function automatically tracks these outcomes. Managers use training and development to encourage observable behavior changes in employees that will lead to desirable business results such as client satisfaction and lower turnover.

Note that outcome measures are not perfectly related to each other. That is, it is tempting to assume that satisfied trainees learn more and will apply their knowledge and skills to the job, resulting in behavior change and positive results for the company. However, research indicates that the relationships among reaction, cognitive, behavior, and results outcomes are small.[28]

Which training outcomes measure is best? The answer depends on the training objectives. For example, if the instructional objectives identified business-related outcomes such as increased customer service or product quality, then results outcomes should be included in the evaluation. As Figure 6.4 shows, both reaction and cognitive outcomes may affect learning. Reaction outcomes provide information regarding the extent to which the trainer, facilities, or learning environment may have hindered learning. Learning or cognitive outcomes directly measure the extent to which trainees have mastered training content. However, reaction and cognitive outcomes do not help determine how much trainees actually use the training content in their jobs. As much as possible, evaluation should include behavior or skill-based, affective, or results outcomes to determine the extent to which transfer of training has occurred—that is, whether training has influenced a change in behavior, skill, or attitude or has directly influenced objective measures related to company effectiveness (e.g., sales).

How long after training should outcomes be collected? There is no accepted standard for when the different training outcomes should be collected. In most cases, reactions are usually measured immediately after training.[29] Learning, behavior, and results should be measured after sufficient time has elapsed to determine whether training has had an influence on these outcomes. Positive transfer of training is demonstrated when learning occurs and positive changes in skill-based, affective, or results outcomes are also observed. No transfer of training is demonstrated if learning occurs but no changes are observed in skill-based, affective, or learning outcomes. Negative transfer is evident when learning occurs but skills, affective outcomes, or results are less than at pretraining levels. Results of evaluation studies that find no transfer or negative transfer suggest that the trainer and the manager need to investigate whether a good learning environment (e.g., opportunities for feedback and practice) was provided in the training program, trainees were motivated and able to learn, and the needs assessment correctly identified training needs.

# EVALUATION DESIGNS

The design of the training evaluation determines the confidence that can be placed in the results; that is, how sure a company can be that training is either responsible for changes in evaluation outcomes or has failed to influence the outcomes. No evaluation design can ensure that the results of the evaluation are completely due to training. What the evaluator strives for is to use the most rigorous design possible (given the circumstances under which the evaluation occurs) to rule out alternative explanations for the results of the evaluation.

This discussion of evaluation designs begins by identifying these "alternative explanations" that the evaluator should attempt to control for. Next, various evaluation designs are compared. Finally, this section discusses practical circumstances that the trainer needs to consider in selecting an evaluation design.

## Threats to Validity: Alternative Explanations for Evaluation Results

Table 6.6 presents threats to validity of an evaluation. **Threats to validity** refer to factors that will lead an evaluator to question either (1) the believability of the study results or (2) the extent to which the evaluation results are generalizable to other groups of trainees and situations.[30] The believability of study results refers to **internal validity.** The internal threats to validity relate to characteristics of the company (history), the outcome measures (instrumentation, testing), and the persons in the evaluation study (maturation, regression toward the mean, mortality, initial group differences). These characteristics can cause the evaluator to reach the wrong conclusions about training effectiveness. An evaluation study

**TABLE 6.6** **Threats to Validity**

| Threats to Internal Validity | Description |
| --- | --- |
| **Company** | |
| History | Event occurs, producing changes in training outcomes. |
| **Persons** | |
| Maturation | Changes in training outcomes result from trainees' physical growth or emotional state. |
| Mortality | Study participants drop out of study (e.g., leave company). |
| Initial group differences | Training group differs from comparison group on individual differences that influence outcomes (knowledge, skills, ability, and behavior). |
| **Outcome Measures** | |
| Testing | Trainees are sensitized to perform well on post-test measures. |
| Instrumentation | Trainee interpretation of outcomes changes over course of evaluation. |
| Regression toward the mean | High-and low-scoring trainees move toward the middle or average on post-training measure. |
| **Threats to External Validity** | **Description** |
| Reaction to pretest | Use of a test before training causes trainees to pay attention to material on the test. |
| Reaction to evaluation | Being evaluated causes trainees to try harder in training program. |
| Interaction of selection and training | Characteristics of trainees influence program effectiveness. |
| Interaction of methods | Results of trainees who received different methods can be generalized only to trainees who receive same training in the same order. |

Source: Based on T. D. Cook, D. T. Campbell, and L. Peracchio, "Quasi-Experimentation," in *Handbook of Industrial and Organizational Psychology*, 2d ed., Vol. 1, eds. M. D. Dunnette and L. M. Hough (Palo Alto, CA: Consulting Psychologists Press, 1990): 491–576.

needs internal validity to provide confidence that the results of the evaluation (particularly if they are positive) are due to the training program and not to another factor. For example, consider a group of managers who have attended a communication skills training program. At the same time that they attend the program, it is announced that the company will be restructured. After the program, the managers may become better communicators simply because they are scared that if they don't they will lose their jobs. Perhaps no learning actually occurred in the training program at all.

Trainers are also interested in the generalizability of the study results to other groups and situations (i.e., they are interested in the **external validity** of the study). As shown in Table 6.6, threats to external validity relate to how study participants react to being included in the study and the effects of multiple types of training. Because evaluation usually does not involve all employees who have completed a program (or who may take training in the future), trainers want to be able to say that the training program will be effective in the future with similar groups.

### Methods to Control for Threats to Validity

Because trainers often want to use evaluation study results as a basis for changing training programs or demonstrating that training does work (as a means to gain additional funding for training from those who control the training budget), it is important to minimize the threats to validity. There are three ways to minimize threats to validity: the use of pretests and post-tests in evaluation designs, comparison groups, and random assignment.

*Pretests and Post-tests*   One way to improve the internal validity of the study results is to first establish a baseline or **pretraining measure** of the outcome. Another measure of the outcomes can be taken after training. This is referred to as a **post-training measure.** A comparison of the post-training and pretraining measures can indicate the degree to which trainees have changed as a result of training.

*Use of Comparison Groups*   Internal validity can be improved by using a control or comparison group. A **comparison group** refers to a group of employees who participate in the evaluation study but do not attend the training program. The comparison employees have personal characteristics (e.g., gender, education, age, tenure, and skill level) as similar to the trainees as possible. Use of a comparison group in training evaluation helps to rule out the possibility that changes found in the outcome measures are due to factors other than training. The **Hawthorne effect** refers to employees in an evaluation study performing at a high level simply because of the attention they are receiving. Use of a comparison group helps to show that any effects observed are due specifically to the training rather than the attention the trainees are receiving. Use of a comparison group helps to control for the effects of history, testing, instrumentation, and maturation because both the comparison group and the training group are treated similarly, receive the same measures, and have the same amount of time to develop.

For example, consider an evaluation of a safety training program. Safe behaviors are measured before and after safety training for both trainees and a comparison group. If the level of safe behavior improves for the training group from pretraining levels but remains relatively the same for the comparison group at both pretraining and post-training, the reasonable conclusion is that the observed differences in safe behaviors are due to the training and not some other factor, such as the attention given to both the trainees and the comparison group by asking them to participate in the study.

Keep in mind that a comparison group can be naturally available for training evaluation because all employees may not receive training at the same time or training may be attended by employees at one or several company locations but not at all locations. Employees who do not initially receive training can serve as a comparison group. These employees can be scheduled to receive training at a later time after the evaluation is completed.

***Random Assignment*** **Random assignment** refers to assigning employees to the training or comparison group on the basis of chance alone. That is, employees are assigned to the training program without consideration of individual differences (ability or motivation) or prior experiences. Random assignment helps to ensure that trainees are similar in individual characteristics such as age, gender, ability, and motivation. Because it is often impossible to identify and measure all the individual characteristics that might influence the outcome measures, random assignment ensures that these characteristics are equally distributed in the comparison group and the training group. Random assignment helps to reduce the effects of employees dropping out of the study (mortality) and differences between the training group and comparison group in ability, knowledge, skill, or other personal characteristics.

Keep in mind that random assignment is often impractical. Companies want to train employees who need training. Also, companies may be unwilling to provide a comparison group. One solution to this problem is to identify the factors in which the training and comparison groups differ and control for these factors in the analysis of the data (a statistical procedure known as *analysis of covariance*). Another method is to determine trainees' characteristics after they are assigned and ensure that the comparison group includes employees with similar characteristics.

## Types of Evaluation Designs

A number of different designs can be used to evaluate training programs.[31] Table 6.8 compares each design on the basis of who is involved (trainees or comparison group), when measures are collected (pretraining, post-training), the costs, the time it takes to conduct the evaluation, and the strength of the design for ruling out alternative explanations for the results. As shown in Table 6.7, research designs vary based on whether they include pretraining and post-training measurement of outcomes and a comparison group. In general, designs that use pretraining and post-training measures of outcomes and include a comparison group reduce the risk that alternative factors (other than the training itself) are responsible for the results of the evaluation. This increases the trainer's confidence in using the results to make decisions. Of course, the trade-off is that evaluations using these designs are more costly and take more time to conduct than do evaluations not using pretraining and post-training measures or comparison groups.

### Post-test Only

The **post-test-only** design refers to an evaluation design in which only post-training outcomes are collected. This design can be strengthened by adding a comparison group (which helps to rule out alternative explanations for changes). The post-test-only design is appropriate when trainees (and the comparison group, if one is used) can be expected to have similar levels of knowledge, behavior, or results outcomes (e.g., same number of sales or equal awareness of how to close a sale) prior to training.

**TABLE 6.7**   **Comparison of Evaluation Designs**

| Design | Groups | Measures | | | | |
|---|---|---|---|---|---|---|
| | | **Pretraining** | **Post-training** | **Cost** | **Time** | **Strength** |
| Post-test only | Trainees | No | Yes | Low | Low | Low |
| Pretest/post-test | Trainees | Yes | Yes | Low | Low | Med. |
| Post-test only with comparison group | Trainees and comparison | No | Yes | Med. | Med. | Med. |
| Pretest/post-test with comparison group | Trainees and comparison | Yes | Yes | Med. | Med. | High |
| Time series | Trainees | Yes | Yes, several | Med. | Med. | Med. |
| Time series with comparison group and reversal | Trainees and comparison | Yes | Yes, several | High | Med. | High |
| Solomon Four-Group | Trainees A | Yes | Yes | High | High | High |
| | Trainees B | No | Yes | | | |
| | Comparison A | Yes | Yes | | | |
| | Comparison B | No | Yes | | | |

Consider the evaluation design that the Mayo Clinic used to compare two methods for delivering new manager training.[32] The Mayo Clinic is one of the world's leading centers of medical education and research. Recently, Mayo has undergone considerable growth because a new hospital and clinic have been added in the Phoenix area (the Mayo Clinic is also located in Rochester, Minnesota). In the process, employees who were not fully prepared were moved into management positions, which resulted in increased employee dissatisfaction and employee turnover rates. After a needs assessment indicated that employees were leaving because of dissatisfaction with management, Mayo decided to initiate a new training program designed to help the new managers improve their skills. There was some debate whether the training would be best administered in a classroom or one-on-one with a coach. Because using coaching would be more expensive than classroom training, Mayo decided to conduct an evaluation using a post-test comparison group design. Before training all managers, Mayo held three training sessions with no more than 75 managers included in each. Within each session, managers were divided into three groups: a group that received four days of classroom training, a group that received one-on-one training from a coach, and a group that received no training (a comparison group). Mayo collected reaction (did the trainees like the program?), learning, transfer, and results outcomes. The evaluation found no statistically significant differences in the effects of coaching compared to classroom training and no training. As a result, Mayo decided to rely on classroom courses for new managers and to consider coaching only for managers with critical and immediate job issues.

### Pretest/Post-test

The **pretest/post-test** refers to an evaluation design in which both pretraining and post-training outcome measures are collected. There is no comparison group. The lack of a comparison group makes it difficult to rule out the effects of business conditions or other factors as explanations for changes. This design is often used by companies that want to evaluate a training program but are uncomfortable with excluding certain employees or that intend to train only a small group of employees.

### Pretest/Post-test with Comparison Group

The **pretest/post-test with comparison group** refers to an evaluation design that includes trainees and a comparison group. Pretraining and post-training outcome measures are collected from both groups. If improvement is greater for the training group than the comparison group, this finding provides evidence that training is responsible for the change. This type of design controls for most threats to validity.

Table 6.8 presents an example of a pretest/post-test comparison group design. This evaluation involved determining the relationship between three conditions or treatments and learning, satisfaction, and use of computer skills.[33] The three conditions or treatments (types of computer training) were behavior modeling, self-paced study, and lecture. A comparison group was also included in the study. Behavior modeling involved watching a video showing a model performing key behaviors necessary to complete a task. In this case the task was procedures on the computer. (Behavior modeling is discussed in detail in Chapter Seven, "Traditional Training Methods.")

Forty trainees were included in each condition. Measures of learning included a test consisting of eleven items designed to measure information that trainees needed to know to operate the computer system (e.g., "Does formatting destroy all data on the disk?"). Also, trainees' comprehension of computer procedures (procedural comprehension) was measured by presenting trainees with scenarios on the computer screens and asking them what would appear next on the screen. Use of computer skills (skill-based learning outcome) was measured by asking trainees to complete six computer tasks (e.g., changing directories). Satisfaction with the program (reaction) was measured by six items (e.g., "I would recommend this program to others").

As shown in Table 6.8, measures of learning and skills were collected from the trainees prior to attending the program (pretraining). Measures of learning and skills were also collected immediately after training (post-training time 1) and four weeks after training (post-training time 2). The satisfaction measure was collected immediately following training.

The post-training time 2 measures collected in this study help to determine the occurrence of training transfer and retention of the information and skills. That is, immediately following training, trainees may have appeared to learn and acquire skills related to computer training. Collection of the post-training measures four weeks after training provides information about trainees' level of retention of the skills and knowledge.

**TABLE 6.8**   **Example of a Pretest/Post-test Comparison Group Design**

|  | Pretraining | Training | Post-training Time 1 | Post-training Time 2 |
|---|---|---|---|---|
| Lecture | Yes | Yes | Yes | Yes |
| Self-paced study | Yes | Yes | Yes | Yes |
| Behavior modeling | Yes | Yes | Yes | Yes |
| No training (Comparison) | Yes | No | Yes | Yes |

Source: Based on S. J. Simon and J. M. Werner, "Computer training through behavior modeling, self-paced, and instructional approaches: A field experiment," *Journal of Applied Psychology,* 81 (1996): 648–659.

Statistical procedures known as analysis of variance and analysis of covariance were used to test for differences between pretraining measures and post-training measures for each condition. Also, differences between each of the training conditions and the comparison group were analyzed. These procedures determine whether differences between the groups are large enough to conclude with a high degree of confidence that the differences were caused by training rather than by chance fluctuations in trainees' scores on the measures.

## Time Series

**Time series** refers to an evaluation design in which training outcomes are collected at periodic intervals both before and after training. (In the other evaluation designs discussed here, training outcomes are collected only once after and maybe once before training.) The strength of this design can be improved by using **reversal,** which refers to a time period in which participants no longer receive the training intervention. A comparison group can also be used with a time series design. One advantage of the time series design is that it allows an analysis of the stability of training outcomes over time. Another advantage is that using both the reversal and comparison group helps to rule out alternative explanations for the evaluation results. The time series design is frequently used to evaluate training programs that focus on improving readily observable outcomes (such as accident rates, productivity, and absenteeism) that vary over time. CHG Healthcare Services evaluates the effects of new hire training by first establishing a performance baseline that includes measures of total billing, applications received, and interviews.[34] As new training courses are introduced, CHG can track their influence on new hires performance on these measures.

Figure 6.5 shows a time series design that was used to evaluate how much a training program improved the number of safe work behaviors in a food manufacturing plant.[35]

**FIGURE 6.5**

**Example of a Time Series Design**

Source: J. Komaki, K. D. Badwick, and L. R. Scott, "A behavioral approach to occupational safety: Pinpointing safe performance in a food manufacturing plant," *Journal of Applied Psychology,* 63 (1978). Copyright 1978 by the American Psychological Association. Adapted by permission.

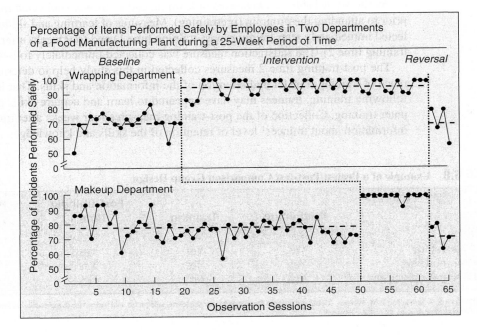

This plant was experiencing an accident rate similar to that of the mining industry, the most dangerous area of work. Employees were engaging in unsafe behaviors, such as putting their hands into conveyors to unjam them (resulting in crushed limbs).

To improve safety, the company developed a training program that taught employees safe behaviors, provided them with incentives for safe behaviors, and encouraged them to monitor their own behavior. To evaluate the program, the design included a comparison group (the Makeup department) and a trained group (the Wrapping department). The Makeup department is responsible for measuring and mixing ingredients, preparing the dough, placing the dough in the oven and removing it when it is cooked, and packaging the finished product. The Wrapping department is responsible for bagging, sealing, and labeling the packages and stacking them on skids for shipping. Outcomes included observations of safe work behaviors. These observations were taken over a twenty-five-week period.

The baseline shows the percentage of safe acts prior to introduction of the safety training program. Training directed at increasing the number of safe behaviors was introduced after approximately five weeks (twenty observation sessions) in the Wrapping department and ten weeks (fifty observation sessions) in the Makeup department. Training was withdrawn from the Wrapping and Makeup departments after approximately sixty-two observation sessions. The withdrawal of training resulted in a reduction of the work incidents performed safely (to pretraining levels). As shown, the number of safe acts observed varied across the observation period for both groups. However, the number of safe behaviors increased after the training program was conducted for the trained group (Wrapping department). The level of safe acts remained stable across the observation period. (See the intervention period.) When the Makeup department received training (at ten weeks, or after fifty observations), a similar increase in the percentage of safe behaviors was observed.

### Solomon Four-Group

The **Solomon four-group** design combines the pretest/post-test comparison group and the post-test-only control group design. In the Solomon four-group design, a training group and a comparison group are measured on the outcomes both before and after training. Another training group and control group are measured only after training. This design controls for most threats to internal and external validity.

An application of the Solomon four-group design is shown in Table 6.9. This design was used to compare the effects of training based on integrative learning (IL) with traditional (lecture-based) training of manufacturing resource planning. Manufacturing resource planning is a method for effectively planning, coordinating, and integrating the use of all resources of a manufacturing company.[36] The IL-based training differed from traditional training in several ways. IL-based training sessions began with a series of activities intended to create a relaxed, positive environment for learning. The students were asked

**TABLE 6.9**
**Example of a Solomon Four-Group Design**

Source: Based on R. D. Bretz and R. E. Thompsett, "Comparing traditional and integrative learning methods in organizational training programs," *Journal of Applied Psychology*, 77 (1992): 941–951.

|  | Pretest | Training | Post-test |
|---|---|---|---|
| Group 1 | Yes | IL-based | Yes |
| Group 2 | Yes | Traditional | Yes |
| Group 3 | No | IL-based | Yes |
| Group 4 | No | Traditional | Yes |

what manufacturing resource planning meant to them, and attempts were made to reaffirm their beliefs and unite the trainees around a common understanding of manufacturing resource planning. Students presented training material and participated in group discussions, games, stories, and poetry related to the manufacturing processes.

Because the company was interested in the effects of IL compared to traditional training, groups that received traditional training were used as the comparison groups (rather than groups who received no training). A test of manufacturing resource planning (knowledge test) and a reaction measure were used as outcomes. The study found that participants in the IL-based learning groups learned slightly less than participants in the traditional training groups. However, IL-group participants had much more positive reactions than did those in the traditional training groups.

## Considerations in Choosing an Evaluation Design

There is no one appropriate evaluation design. An evaluation design should be chosen based on an evaluation of the factors shown in Table 6.10. There are several reasons why no evaluation or a less rigorous evaluation design may be more appropriate than a more rigorous design that includes a comparison group, random assignment, or pretraining and post-training measures. First, managers and trainers may be unwilling to devote the time and effort necessary to collect training outcomes. Second, managers or trainers may lack the expertise to conduct an evaluation study. Third, a company may view training as an investment from which it expects to receive little or no return. A more rigorous evaluation design (pretest/post-test with comparison group) should be considered if any of the following conditions is true:[37]

1. The evaluation results can be used to change the program.
2. The training program is ongoing and has the potential to have an important influence on employees or customers.
3. The training program involves multiple classes and a large number of trainees.
4. Cost justification for training is based on numerical indicators. (Here, the company has a strong orientation toward evaluation.)
5. Trainers or others in the company have the expertise (or the budget to purchase expertise from outside the company) to design and evaluate the data collected from an evaluation study.

**TABLE 6.10**
**Factors That Influence the Type of Evaluation Design**

Source: Based on S. I. Tannenbaum and S. B. Woods, "Determining a strategy for evaluating training: Operating within organizational constraints," *Human Resource Planning,* 15 (1992): 63–81.

| Factor | How the Factor Influences the Type of Evaluation Design |
|---|---|
| Change potential | Can the program be modified? |
| Importance | Does ineffective training affect customer service, safety, product development, or relationships among employees? |
| Scale | How many trainees are involved? |
| Purpose of training | Is training conducted for learning, results, or both? |
| Organization culture | Is demonstrating results part of company norms and expectations? |
| Expertise | Can a complex study be analyzed? |
| Cost | Is evaluation too expensive? |
| Time frame | When is the information needed? |

6. The cost of the training creates a need to show that it works.

7. There is sufficient time for conducting an evaluation. Here, information regarding training effectiveness is not needed immediately.

8. There is interest in measuring change (in knowledge, behavior, skill, etc.) from pretraining levels or in comparing two or more different programs.

For example, if the company is interested in determining how much employees' communications skills have changed as a result of a training program, a pretest/post-test comparison group design is necessary. Trainees should be randomly assigned to training and no-training conditions. These evaluation design features offer a high degree of confidence that any communication skill change is the result of participation in the training program.[38] This type of evaluation design is also necessary if the company wants to compare the effectiveness of two training programs.

Evaluation designs without pretest or comparison groups are most appropriate in situations in which the company is interested in identifying whether a specific level of performance has been achieved. (For example, are employees who participated in training able to communicate their ideas adequately?) In these situations, companies are not interested in determining how much change has occurred, but rather whether the trainees have achieved a certain proficiency level.

One company's evaluation strategy for a training course delivered to the company's tax professionals shows how company norms regarding evaluation and the purpose of training influence the type of evaluation design chosen.[39] This accounting firm views training as an effective method for developing human resources. Training is expected to provide a good return on investment. The company used a combination of affective, cognitive, behavior, and results criteria to evaluate a five-week course designed to prepare tax professionals to understand state and local tax law. The course involved two weeks of self-study and three weeks of classroom work. A pretest/post-test comparison design was used. Before they took the course, trainees were tested to determine their knowledge of state and local tax laws, and they completed a survey designed to assess their self-confidence in preparing accurate tax returns. The evaluators also identified the trainees' (accountants') billable hours related to calculating state and local tax returns and the revenue generated by the activity. After the course, evaluators again identified billable hours and surveyed trainees' self-confidence. The results of the evaluation indicated that the accountants were spending more time doing state and local tax work than before training. Also, the trained accountants produced more revenue doing state and local tax work than did accountants who had not yet received the training (comparison group). There was also a significant improvement in the accountants' confidence following training, and they were more willing to promote their expertise in state and local tax preparation. Finally, after fifteen months, the revenue gained by the company more than offset the cost of training. On average, the increase in revenue for the trained tax accountants was more than 10 percent.

# DETERMINING RETURN ON INVESTMENT

Return on investment (ROI) is an important training outcome. This section discusses how to calculate ROI through a cost-benefit analysis. **Cost-benefit analysis** in this situation is the process of determining the economic benefits of a training program using accounting methods that look at training costs and benefits. Training cost information is important for several reasons:[40]

1. To understand total expenditures for training, including direct and indirect costs
2. To compare the costs of alternative training programs
3. To evaluate the proportion of money spent on training development, administration, and evaluation, as well as to compare monies spent on training for different groups of employees (exempt versus nonexempt, for example)
4. To control costs

There is an increased interest in measuring the ROI of training and development programs because of the need to show the results of these programs to justify funding and to increase the status of the training and development function.[41] Most trainers and managers believe that there is a value provided by training and development activities, such as productivity or customer service improvements, cost reductions, time savings, and decreased employee turnover. ROI provides evidence of the economic value provided by training and development programs. However, it is important to keep in mind that ROI is not a substitute for other program outcomes that provide data regarding the success of a program based on trainees' reactions and whether learning and transfer of training have occurred.

Typically, ROI is used to show a training program's cost effectiveness after it has been delivered. However, ROI is also useful for forecasting the potential value of a new training program, choosing the most cost-effective training method by estimating and comparing the costs and benefits of each approach, and making decisions about whether to fund and offer training programs in the future.[42]

Consider the use of ROI at LensCrafters. LensCrafters brings the eye doctor, a wide selection of frames and lenses, and the lens-making laboratory together in one location.[43] LensCrafters has convenient locations and hours of operations, and it has the ability to make eyewear on-site. Emphasizing customer service, the company offers a one-stop location and promises to make eyewear in one hour. Dave Palm, a training professional at LensCrafters, received a call from a concerned regional manager. He told Palm that although company executives knew that LensCrafters employees had to be well trained to design eyewear and that employees were satisfied with the training, the executives wanted to know whether the money that they were investing in training was providing any return. Palm decided to partner with the operations people to identify how to link training to measurable outcomes such as profitability, quality, and sales. After conversations with the operations employees, he decided to link training to waste from mistakes in quality and remakes, store performance and sales, and customer satisfaction. He chose two geographic regions for the evaluation study and compared the results from these two regions with results from one that had not yet received the training. Palm found that all stores in the two regions that received training reduced waste, increased sales, and improved customer satisfaction. As a result, LensCrafters allotted its training department more financial resources—$10 million a year for training program development and administration—than any other optical retail competitor. Because the training department demonstrated that it does contribute to business operations, it also received money to develop a multimedia-based training system.

The process of determining ROI begins with an understanding of the objectives of the training program.[44] Plans are developed for collecting data related to measuring these objectives. The next step is to isolate, if possible, the effects of training from other factors that might influence the data. Last, the data are converted to a monetary value and ROI is calculated. Choosing evaluation outcomes and designing an evaluation that helps isolate the effects of training were explained earlier in this chapter. The following sections discuss how to determine costs and benefits and provide examples of cost-benefit analysis and ROI calculations.

Because ROI analysis can be costly, it should be limited only to certain training programs. ROI analysis is best for training programs that are focused on an operational issue (measurable identifiable outcomes are available), are linked to a companywide strategy (e.g., better customer service), are expensive, are highly visible, have management interest, are attended by many employees, and are permanent.[45] At Deloitte, the tax and auditing firm, managers don't require analysis of ROI for many training programs.[46] Because knowledge is the product at Deloitte, investment in training is seen as an important part of the business. Deloitte makes money through the billable hours that its consultants provide to clients. Training helps prepare the consultants to serve clients' needs. ROI is primarily calculated for courses or programs that are new or expensive. For example, ROI analysis was conducted for a simulation designed to help new employees learn more quickly how to service clients. At Deloitte, use of the simulation has resulted in new hires being 30 to 40 percent faster in serving clients—resulting in an ROI of over $66 billion after subtracting program costs.

## Determining Costs

One method for comparing costs of alternative training programs is the resource requirements model.[47] The resource requirements model compares equipment, facilities, personnel, and materials costs across different stages of the training process (needs assessment, development, training design, implementation, and evaluation). Use of the resource requirements model can help determine overall differences in costs among training programs. Also, costs incurred at different stages of the training process can be compared across programs.

Accounting can also be used to calculate costs.[48] Seven categories of cost sources are costs related to program development or purchase, instructional materials for trainers and trainees, equipment and hardware, facilities, travel and lodging, salary of trainer and support staff, and the cost of lost productivity while trainees attend the program (or the cost of temporary employees who replace the trainees while they are away from their jobs). This method also identifies when the costs are incurred. One-time costs include those related to needs assessment and program development. Costs per offering relate to training site rental fees, trainer salaries, and other costs that are realized every time the program is offered. Costs per trainee include meals, materials, and lost productivity or expenses incurred to replace the trainees while they attend training.

## Determining Benefits

To identify the potential benefits of training, the company must review the original reasons that the training was conducted. For example, training may have been conducted to reduce production costs or overtime costs or to increase the amount of repeat business. A number of methods may be helpful in identifying the benefits of training:

1. Technical, academic, and practitioner literature summarizes the benefits that have been shown to relate to a specific training program.
2. Pilot training programs assess the benefits from a small group of trainees before a company commits more resources.

3. Observance of successful job performers helps a company determine what successful job performers do differently than unsuccessful job performers.[49]

4. Trainees and their managers provide estimates of training benefits.

For example, a training and development consultant at Apple Computer was concerned with the quality and consistency of the training program used in assembly operations.[50] She wanted to show that training was not only effective but also resulted in financial benefits. To do this, the consultant chose an evaluation design that involved two separately trained groups—each consisting of twenty-seven employees—and two untrained groups (comparison groups). The consultant collected a pretraining history of what was happening on the production line in each outcome that she was measuring (i.e., productivity, quality, and labor efficiency). She determined the effectiveness of training by comparing performance between the comparison and training groups for two months after training. The consultant was able to show that the untrained comparison group had 2,000 more minutes of downtime than the trained group did. This finding meant that the trained employees built and shipped more products to customers—showing definitively that training was contributing to Apple's business objectives.

To conduct a cost-benefit analysis, the consultant had each employee in the training group estimate the effect of a behavior change on a specific business measure (e.g., breaking down tasks will improve productivity or efficiency). The trainees assigned a confidence percentage to the estimates. To get a cost-benefit estimate for each group of trainees, the consultant multiplied the monthly cost-benefit by the confidence level and divided by the number of trainees. For example, one group of 20 trainees estimated a total overall monthly cost benefit of $336,000 related to business improvements and showed an average 70 percent confidence level with that estimate. The calculation is as follows: 70 percent multiplied by $336,000 gave a cost-benefit of $235,200. This number was divided by 20 ($235,200/20 trainees) to give an average estimated cost benefit for each of the trainees ($11,760). To calculate ROI, follow these steps:[51]

1. Identify outcomes (e.g., quality, accidents).

2. Place a value on the outcomes.

3. Determine the change in performance after eliminating other potential influences on training results.

4. Obtain an annual amount of benefits (operational results) from training by comparing results after training to results before training (in dollars).

5. Determine the training costs (direct costs + indirect costs + development costs + overhead costs + compensation for trainees).

6. Calculate the total benefits by subtracting the training costs from benefits (operational results).

7. Calculate the ROI by dividing operational results by costs. The ROI gives an estimate of the dollar return expected from each dollar invested in training.

## Example of a Cost-Benefit Analysis

A cost-benefit analysis is best explained by an example.[52] A wood plant produced panels that contractors used as building materials. The plant employed 300 workers, 48 supervisors, 7 shift superintendents, and a plant manager. The business had three problems. First,

2 percent of the wood panels produced each day were rejected because of poor quality. Second, the production area was experiencing poor housekeeping, such as improperly stacked finished panels that would fall on employees. Third, the number of preventable accidents was higher than the industry average. To correct these problems, the supervisors, shift superintendents, and plant manager attended training in (1) performance management and interpersonal skills related to quality problems and poor work habits of employees, and (2) rewarding employees for performance improvement. Training was conducted in a hotel close to the plant. The training program was a purchased videotape, and the instructor for the program was a consultant. Table 6.11 shows each type of cost and how it was determined.

The benefits of the training were identified by considering the objectives of the training program and the type of outcomes the program was to influence. These outcomes included

**TABLE 6.11**  **Determining Costs for a Cost-Benefit Analysis**

| | |
|---|---:|
| **Direct Costs** | |
| Instructor | $  0 |
| In-house instructor (12 days @ $125 per day) | 1,500 |
| Fringe benefits (25% of salary) | 375 |
| Travel expenses | 0 |
| Materials ($60 × 56 trainees) | 3,360 |
| Classroom space and audiovisual equipment (12 days @ $50 per day) | 600 |
| Refreshments ($4 per day × 3 days × 56 trainees) | 672 |
| **Total direct costs** | **$ 6,507** |
| **Indirect Costs** | |
| Training management | $  0 |
| Clerical and administrative salaries | 750 |
| Fringe benefits (25% of salary) | 187 |
| Postage, shipping, and telephone | 0 |
| Pre- and post-training learning materials ($4 × 56 trainees) | 224 |
| **Total indirect costs** | **$ 1,161** |
| **Development Costs** | |
| Fee for program purchase | $ 3,600 |
| Instructor training | |
|  Registration fee | 1,400 |
|  Travel and lodging | 975 |
|  Salary | 625 |
|  Benefits (25% of salary) | 156 |
| **Total development costs** | **$ 6,756** |
| **Overhead Costs** | |
| General organizational support, top management time (10% of direct, indirect, and development costs) | $ 1,443 |
| **Total overhead costs** | **$ 1,443** |
| **Compensation for Trainees** | |
| Trainees' salaries and benefits (based on time away from job) | $16,969 |
| Total training costs | $32,836 |
| **Cost per trainee** | **$   587** |

the quality of panels, housekeeping in the production area, and the accident rate. Table 6.12 shows how the benefits of the program were calculated.

Once the costs and benefits of the program are determined, ROI is calculated by dividing return or benefits by costs. In this example, ROI was 5.72. That is, every dollar invested in the program returned almost $6 in benefits. How can the company determine if the ROI is acceptable? One way is for managers and trainers to agree on what level of ROI is acceptable. Another method is to use the ROI that other companies obtain from similar types of training. Table 6.13 provides examples of ROIs obtained from several types of training programs.

Recall the discussion of the new manager training program at the Mayo Clinic.[53] To determine Mayo's ROI, the human resource department calculated that one-third of the eighty-four employees retained (twenty-nine employees) would have left Mayo as a result of dissatisfaction. The department believed that this retention was due to the impact of the training. Mayo's cost of a single employee turnover was calculated to be

**TABLE 6.12**   **Determining Benefits for a Cost-Benefit Analysis**

| Operational Results Area | How Measured | Results Before Training | Results After Training | Differences (+ or −) | Costs |
|---|---|---|---|---|---|
| Quality of panels | Percentage rejected | 2 percent rejected— 1,440 panels per day | 1.5 percent rejected— 1,080 panels per day | .5 percent— 360 panels | $720 per day; $172,800 per year |
| Housekeeping | Visual inspection using twenty-item checklist | Ten defects (average) | Two defects (average) | Eight defects | Not measurable in dollars |
| Preventable accidents | Number of accidents | Twenty-four per year | Sixteen per year | Eight per year | $48,000 per year |
| | Direct cost of accidents | $144,000 per year | $96,000 per year | $48,000 per year | |

$$ROI = \frac{Return}{Investment} = \frac{Benefits - Costs}{Costs} = \frac{220,800 - 32,836}{32,836} = 5.72$$

Total benefits = $187,964

Source: Adapted from D. G. Robinson and J. Robinson, "Training for impact," *Training and Development Journal* (August 1989): 30–42.

**TABLE 6.13 Examples of ROIs**

Source: Based on J. J. Philips, "ROI: The search for best practices," *Training and Development* (February 1996): 45.

| Industry | Training Program | ROI |
|---|---|---|
| Bottling company | Workshops on managers' roles | 15:1 |
| Large commercial bank | Sales training | 21:1 |
| Electric and gas utility | Behavior modification | 5:1 |
| Oil company | Customer service | 4.8:1 |
| Health maintenance organization | Team training | 13.7:1 |

75 percent of average total compensation, or $42,000 per employee. Multiplying $42,000 by the twenty-nine employees retained equals a savings of $609,000. However, the cost of the training program needs to be considered. If the annual cost of the training program ($125,000) is subtracted from the savings, the new savings amount is $484,000. These numbers are based on estimates, but even if the net savings figure were cut in half, the ROI is still over 100 percent. By being able to quantify the benefits delivered by the program, Mayo's human resource department achieved greater credibility within the company.

## Other Methods for Cost-Benefit Analysis

Other more sophisticated methods are available for determining the dollar value of training. For example, **utility analysis** is a cost-benefit analysis method that involves assessing the dollar value of training based on estimates of the difference in job performance between trained and untrained employees, the number of individuals trained, the length of time a training program is expected to influence performance, and the variability in job performance in the untrained group of employees.[54] Utility analysis requires the use of a pretest/post-test design with a comparison group to obtain an estimate of the difference in job performance for trained versus untrained employees. Other types of economic analyses evaluate training as it benefits the firm or the government using direct and indirect training costs, government incentives paid for training, wage increases received by trainees as a result of completion of training, tax rates, and discount rates.[55]

## Practical Considerations in Determining ROI

As mentioned earlier in the chapter, ROI analysis may not be appropriate for all training programs. Training programs best suited for ROI analysis have clearly identified outcomes, are not one-time events, are highly visible in the company, are strategically focused, and have effects that can be isolated. In the examples of ROI analysis in this chapter, the outcomes were very measurable. That is, in the wood plant example, it was easy to see changes in quality, to count accident rates, and to observe housekeeping behavior. For training programs that focus on soft outcomes (e.g., attitudes or interpersonal skills), it may be more difficult to estimate the value.

Showing the link between training and market share gain or other higher-level strategic business outcomes can be very problematic. These outcomes can be influenced by too many other factors not directly related to training (or even under the control of the business), such as competitors' performance and economic upswings and downturns. Business units may not be collecting the data needed to identify the ROI of training programs on individual performance. Also, the measurement of training can often be very expensive. Verizon Communications employs 240,000 people.[56] The company estimates that it spends approximately $5,000 for an ROI study. Given the large number of training programs that the company offers, it is too expensive to conduct an ROI for each program.

Companies are finding that, despite these difficulties, the demand for measuring ROI is still high. As a result, companies are using creative ways to measure the costs and benefits of training.[57] For example, to calculate ROI for a training program designed to cut absenteeism, trainees and their supervisors were asked to estimate the cost of an absence. The values were averaged to obtain an estimate. Cisco Systems tracks how often its partners return to its website for additional instruction. A. T. Kearney, a management consulting firm, tracks the success of its training by how much business is generated from past clients.

## Success Cases and Return on Expectations

One way to establish the value of training and overcome the difficulty of evaluating training using a design that can rule out and isolate its effects on results is to rely on return on expectations or success cases. **Return on expectations (ROE)** refers to the process through which evaluation demonstrates to key business stakeholders, such as top-level managers, that their expectations about training have been satisfied.[58] ROE depends on establishing a business partnership with business stakeholders from the start of a training program through its evaluation.

Rather than relying on ROI, Verizon Communications uses training ROE. Prior to training, the senior managers who are financially accountable for the training program are asked to identify their expectations regarding what the training program should accomplish, as well as a cost estimate of the current issue or problem. After training, the senior managers are asked whether their expectations have been met, and they are encouraged to attach a monetary value to those met expectations. The ROE is used as an estimate in an ROI analysis. Verizon Communications continues to conduct ROI analysis for training programs and courses in which objective numbers are available (e.g., sales training) and in which the influence of training can be better isolated (evaluation designs that have comparison groups and that collect pretraining and post-training outcomes).

**Success cases** refer to concrete examples of the impact of training that show how learning has led to results that the company finds worthwhile and the managers find credible.[59] Success cases do not attempt to isolate the influence of training, but rather to provide evidence that it was useful. For example, Federated Department Stores wanted to show the effectiveness of its Leadership Choice program, which was designed to increase sales and profit performance in Federated stores by helping leaders enhance personal effectiveness, develop a customer-focused plan to improve business performance, and recognize the impact of decisions on business results.[60] At the conclusion of the program, participants were asked to set a business and leadership goal to work on in the next three months. Because the managers in the program had a wide range of responsibilities in Federated's various divisions, it was necessary to show that the program produced results for different managers with different responsibilities. As a result, concrete examples were used to illustrate the value of the program to management. Recall from Table 6.10 that a company may want to consider its organizational culture when choosing an evaluation design. Because storytelling is an important part of Federated's culture, using success cases was an acceptable way to show senior managers the impact of the leadership program.

Participants who reported good progress toward their goals were interviewed, and case studies were written to highlight the program's impact in management's priority areas, which were categories such as "in-store shopping experience" and "differentiated assortment of goods." Because the case studies told a retailing story, they communicated the kind of results that the program was designed to achieve. For example, one manager set a goal of increasing sales by designing new neckware assortments so that the selling floor would be visually exciting. He directed a new associate buyer to take more ownership of the neckware business, he reviewed future buying strategies, and he visited competitors' stores. As a result, this manager exceeded his goal of increasing sales 5 percent.

# MEASURING HUMAN CAPITAL AND TRAINING ACTIVITY

So far, this chapter has focused on how to evaluate training programs. It is important to remember that evaluation can also involve determining the extent to which learning and training activities and the training function contribute to the company strategy and help to achieve business goals. Chapter One emphasized that there is increased recognition that training, development, and learning can and should contribute to employee performance and business goals(see Figure 1.1). We discussed the role of metrics in the strategic training and development process in Chapter Two. Metrics are used to determine the value that learning activities or the training function provide to the company.

One way to understand the value that learning activities or the training function provides is through comparisons to other companies. Each year, the American Society of Training and Development (ASTD) prepares a report that summarizes company-provided training in the United States. This report provides information about training hours and delivery methods that companies can use to benchmark, or compare themselves to other companies in similar industries or size.

Table 6.14 provides examples of different measurements, or metrics. These metrics are valuable for benchmarking purposes, for understanding the current amount of training activity in a company, and for tracking historical trends in training activity. However, collecting these metrics does not address such issues as whether training is effective, or whether the company is using the data to make strategic training decisions.[61]

The value of learning activities is best determined through the use of workforce analytics. **Workforce analytics** refers to the practice of using quantitative methods and scientific methods to analyze data from human resource databases, corporate financial statements, employee surveys, and other datasources to make evidence-based decisions and show that human resource practices (including training, development, and learning) influence important company metrics.[62]

Each company needs to use data and metrics that are related to its business strategy or goals. For example, consider how Superior Energy Services in New Orleans relied on workforce analytics to identify and reduce turnover.[63] The oil industry has an annual turnover rate of approximately 35 percent. Superior Energy Services, Inc., was able to quantify the lost revenue for each job type. This was important because the company's business

**TABLE 6.14 Training Metrics**

Sources: M. Green and E. McGill, *State of the Industry, 2011* (Alexandria, VA: American Society for Training and Development, 2011); L. Weatherly, *The Value of People: The Challenges and Opportunities of Human Capital Measurement and Reporting* (Alexandria, VA: Society for Human Resource Management, 2003).

Expenditure per employee
Learning hours received per employee
Expenditure as a percentage of payroll
Expenditure as a percentage of revenue
Cost per learning hour received
Percentage of expenditures for external services
Learning hours received per training and development staff member
Average percentage of learning activities outsourced
Average percentage of learning content by content area (e.g., basic skills, customer service, executive development, etc.)
Average percentage of learning hours provided via different delivery methods (instructor-led, technology-based, etc.)

model operates on billable hours—so turnover means lost revenue. The company identified that about half the employees who quit were skilled operators or supervisors. Using a statistical model for predicting the probability of turnover, the company was able to identify that supervisors who were trained in coaching skills had lower employee turnover rates. As a result, supervisors who had not previously been trained received training in coaching skills. The results showed that after training turnover dropped 8 percent, which translated into less lost revenue. Consider how A. G. Edwards and Accenture measure and determine the value of human capital.[64] A. G. Edwards, a securities and financial services firm based in Saint Louis, Missouri, provided 813,000 hours of training to the company's 15,413 employees located throughout the United States and Europe. Although all human capital investment initiatives are evaluated carefully by A. G. Edwards, they are not part of an annual budgeting process. The chairman of A. G. Edwards wants to make the company stronger in the future by doing whatever it takes to get the best-trained financial planners in the business. One of the metrics that the firm uses to measure progress toward this goal is to count the number of employees who have earned industrywide professional credentials, such as becoming a certified financial planner. Accenture, a global management consulting and technology services company, invested about $400 million in employee development in 2004. The company found that there was a 17 percent to 20 percent increase in demand for consultants who took the most training, and retention rates for these employees were 14 percent greater than for employees who had not taken the highest levels of training available.

Some companies are using dashboards to help measure the effectiveness, financial benefits, and relationship of learning activities to business strategy and goals. A **dashboard** refers to a computer interface designed to receive and analyze the data from departments within the company to provide information to managers and other decision-makers.[65] Dashboards can draw their data from different sources, such as the company's human resource information system orlearning management or course enrollment system. Dashboards are useful because they can provide a visual display using charts of the relationship between learning activities and business performance data, including measures related to intangible assets such as human capital (recall the discussion of human capital in Chapter One). The dashboard allows the user to access and use the data in different ways, including isolating problem areas and creating categories based on precalculated formulas (such as cost per learning hour received).

Key Bank, headquartered in Cleveland, Ohio, is one of the largest bank-based financial services companies in the United States.[66] Its business strategy is to build client relationships through client-focused solutions and extraordinary service. Key Bank provides a wide variety of training and development programs to help employees grow personally and professionally. To help ensure the efficiency and effectiveness of its training and development activity, Key Bank uses a dashboard that allows access to real-time data providing access to information about the strategic alignment, effectiveness, and investment in training programs across the company. The training activity dashboard provides historical information on learning and training (a "rear-view" perspective). The user identifies the time period that he or she is interested in and then can select companywide or business-specific information. The dashboard offers information on total training activities, the distribution of training activities across the company or business, identifies which training areas are receiving the most funding, and can identify employee progress in completing training and acquiring skills. The dashboard also can be used to provide a perspective of future learning (a "windshield" perspective). Users can look at completion rates for training courses and programs and identify the progress rates at Key Bank locations across the United States. This information is useful for training managers to understand whether local training goals are met, in progress, or behind completion dates, helping them better plan future training and adjust training goals with local managers.

**Summary**

Evaluation provides information used to determine training effectiveness. Evaluation involves identifying the appropriate outcomes to measure. The chapter notes that a good evaluation requires thinking about evaluation before conducting training. Information from the needs assessment and specific and measurable learning objectives help identify outcomes that should be included in the evaluation design. The outcomes used in evaluating training programs include trainees' satisfaction with the training program, learning of knowledge or skills, use of knowledge and skills on the job, and results such as sales, productivity, or accident prevention. Evaluation may also involve comparing the costs of training to the benefits received (ROI). Outcomes used in training evaluation help to determine the degree to which the program has resulted in both learning and transfer of training. Evaluation also involves choosing the appropriate design to maximize the confidence that can be placed in the results. The design is based on a careful analysis of how to minimize threats to internal and external validity, as well as the purpose, expertise, and other company and training characteristics. The types of designs used for evaluation vary on the basis of whether they include pretraining and post-training measures of outcomes and use of a training group and a comparison group. The chapter concludes with a discussion of how to measure and display the contribution of training to a company's human capital assets.

## Key Terms

training effectiveness, *233*
training outcomes, *233*
criteria, *233*
training evaluation, 233
evaluation design, *234*
formative evaluation, *235*
pilot testing, *236*
summative evaluation, *236*
reaction outcomes, *239*
cognitive outcomes, *241*
skill-based outcomes, *241*
affective outcomes, *242*
results, *243*
return on investment (ROI), 243
direct costs, *243*

indirect costs, *243*
benefits, *243*
criteria relevance, *244*
criterion contamination, 244
criterion deficiency, *245*
reliability, *245*
discrimination, 245
practicality, *246*
threats to validity, *249*
internal validity, *249*
external validity, *250*
pretraining measure, *250*
post-training measure, *250*
comparison group, *250*
Hawthorne effect, *250*
random assignment, *251*

post-test-only, *251*
pretest/post-test, *252*
pretest/post-test with comparison group, *253*
time series, *254*
reversal, *254*
Solomon four-group, *255*
cost-benefit analysis, *257*
utility analysis, *263*
return on expectations (ROE), *243*
success cases, *264*
workforce analytics, *265*
dashboard, *266*

## Discussion Questions

1. What can be done to motivate companies to evaluate training programs?
2. What do threats to validity have to do with training evaluation? Identify internal and external threats to validity. Are internal and external threats similar? Explain.
3. What are the strengths and weaknesses of each of the following designs: post-test-only, pretest/post-test with comparison group, and pretest/post-test only?
4. What are results outcomes? Why do you think most organizations don't use results outcomes to evaluate their training programs?
5. This chapter discussed several factors that influence the choice of evaluation design. Which of these factors would have the greatest influence on your choice of an evaluation design? Which would have the least influence? Explain your choices.
6. How might you estimate the benefits of a training program designed to teach employees how to use the Internet to monitor stock prices?
7. A group of managers ($N = 25$) participated in the problem-solving module of a leadership development program two weeks ago. The module consisted of two days in which the group focused on the correct process to use in problem solving. Each manager supervises fifteen to twenty employees. The company is willing to change the program, and there is an increasing emphasis in the company to show that training expenses are justifiable. You are asked to evaluate this program. Your boss would like the results of the evaluation no later than six weeks from now. Discuss the outcomes you would collect and the design you would use. How might your answer change if the managers had not yet attended the program?
8. What practical considerations need to be taken into account when calculating a training program's ROI?
9. What metrics might be useful for evaluating the effectiveness of a company's training function? Discuss and rate their importance.
10. What is return on expectations (ROE)? How can it be used to show the costs and benefits of training without collecting statistics and conducting analyses? Explain its strengths and weaknesses compared to a cost-benefit analysis.

## Application Assignments

1. Consider this course as a training program. In teams of up to five students, identify (a) the types of outcomes you would recommend to use in evaluating this course and (b) the evaluation design you would use. Justify your choice of a design based on minimizing threats to validity and practical considerations.
2. Domino's Pizza was interested in determining whether a new employee could learn how to make a pizza using a computer-based training method (CD-ROM). The CD-ROM application addresses the proper procedure for "massaging" a dough ball and stretching it to fit a 12-inch pizza pan. Domino's quality standards emphasize the roundness of the pizza, an even border, and uniform thickness of the dough. Traditionally, on-the-job training is used to teach new employees how to stretch pizza dough to fit the pizza pan.

a. What outcomes or criteria should Domino's Pizza measure to determine if CD-ROM training is an effective method for teaching new employees how to stretch pizza dough to fit a 12-inch pan? Who would be involved in the evaluation?

b. Describe the evaluation design that you would recommend using to determine if CD-ROM training is more effective than on-the-job training.

3. Ask your instructor for a copy of the evaluation form, survey, or rating sheet that is used by your college, university, or business to evaluate the course or program in which you are using this text. As you look over the evaluation, answer the following questions:

a. What are the strengths and weaknesses of the evaluation form?

b. What changes would you suggest to improve the evaluation form (e.g., different questions, additional questions, etc.)?

c. How should the evaluation be used to actually improve the instruction that you receive?

4. Sears designed a training program to improve tool and hardware sales. The two-hour program involved distance learning and was broadcast from the Sears training facility to fifty salespersons at ten store locations in the United States. The salespersons are paid $15 per hour. The program involved training salespeople in how to set up merchandise displays so they attract buyers' attention. Sales of tools and merchandise at the ten stores included in the program averaged $5,000 per week before the program and $6,500 per week after the program. Program costs included:

| | |
|---|---|
| Instructor | $10,000 |
| Distance learning (satellite space rental) | 5,000 |
| Materials ($100 per trainee @ 50 trainees) | 5,000 |
| Trainees' salaries and benefits (50 trainees with wages of $15 per hour in a 2-hour training program) | 1,500 |

What is the ROI from this program?

5. Cablevision developed an e-learning course that taught salespersons how to increase the number of cable television subscribers, thereby increasing revenue. The company wants to know if salespersons will increase upselling of cable television services (e.g., premium channels) and will try to sell other products (e.g., e-mail and web access). The company also wants to know the ROI of this training program.

a. What training outcomes should the company collect? From whom should the outcomes be collected?

b. What evaluation design would you recommend? Defend your recommendation.

c. Show how Cablevision can conduct an ROI analysis. Describe the information that the company should collect and how it should be collected.

6. The 100-employee information technology department of a financial services company had a high turnover rate. A survey of employees revealed that the reason that most of

them left was dissatisfaction with the level of training. The average turnover rate was 23 percent per year. The cost to recruit and train one new employee was $56,625. To address the turnover problem, the company developed a skills training program that averaged 80 hours per year per employee. The average employee wage was $35 per hour. Instructor, classroom, and other costs were $170,000.

   a. What is the total cost of training? The total cost of turnover?

   b. If the turnover rate dropped 8 percent (from 23 percent to 15 percent), what was the financial benefit of the training program?

   c. What was the ROI of the training program?

   d. How much would the turnover rate have to be reduced (from 23 percent) for the training program to show a benefit?

7. Go to www.roiinstitute.net, the website for ROI Institute, Inc., the leading resource on research, training, and networking for practitioners of the Phillips ROI Methodology™. Click on "Tools." Review the "Nations Hotels—Measuring the ROI in Business Coaching." What are the strengths of this approach for determining ROI? What are the weaknesses?

## Case: *A Healthy Investment at Sisters of Charity Providence Hospital*

At Sisters of Charity Providence Hospital, a 304-bed hospital in Columbia, South Carolina, a training function that addresses performance gaps and supports quality service is a top priority. Training and development programs are linked to the hospital's strategic goals: to become an employer of choice and to provide service and operational excellence. It is not only important to develop programs supporting the strategy, but also to provide evidence as to how they contribute. One priority has been to develop leaders from its current managers. The hospital's first program, Leading Edge, included a curriculum that focused on financial and performance management, identifying and recruiting top talent, and change management. The focus of the training was based on the middle managers' performance needs and weaknesses. The training used a variety of methods, but each program included a set of team building activities and a performance review of the organization. Formal processes were implemented to hold leaders accountable for the performance of their area. The principle objectives included (1) increased earnings before interest, depreciation, and amortization; and (2) improvement of employee and patient satisfaction.

*What outcomes should the hospital collect to determine the effectiveness of the Leading Edge Program? What evaluation design should it use? Explain your choice of outcomes and design.*

**Source:** Based on "The healthy glow of learning," *T + D* (October 2008): 63–64.

# Endnotes

1. P. Tharenou, A. Saks, and C. Moore, "A review and critique of research on training and organizational-level outcomes," *Human Resource Management Review,* 17 (2007): 251–273.

2. P. Galagan, "Measure for measure," *T+D* (May 2011): 28–30.

3. T. Bingham and P. Galagan, "M training: They're lovin' it," *T+D* (November 2006): 29–32; *www.mcdoalds.com*, website for McDonalds, accessed September 15, 2011.

4. A. Purcell, "20/20 ROI," *Training and Development* (July 2000): 28–33.

5. M. Van Wart, N. J. Cayer, and S. Cook, *Handbook of Training and Development for the Public Sector* (San Francisco: Jossey-Bass, 1993).

6. K. Brown and M. Gerhardt, "Formative evaluation: An integrative practice model and case study," *Personnel Psychology,* 55 (2002): 951–983.

7. J. Salopek, "BEST 2005: St. George Bank," *T + D* (October 2005): 68.

8. D. Russ-Eft and H. Preskill, "In search of the Holy Grail: Return on investment evaluation in human resource development," *Advances in Developing Human Resources,* 7 (February 2005): 71–85.

9. K. Kraiger, D. McLinden, and W. Casper, "Collaborative planning for training impact," *Human Resource Management,* 43 (4) (2004): 337–351; F. Nickols, "Why a stakeholder approach to evaluating training," *Advances in Developing Human Resources,* 7 (February 2005): 121–134.

10. K. Kraiger, D. McLinden, and W. Casper, "Collaborative planning for training impact," *Human Resource Management* (Winter 2004): 337–51; R. Brinkerhoff, "The success case method: A strategic evaluation approach to increasing the value and effect of training," *Advances in Developing Human Resources,* 7 (February 2005): 86–101.

11. K. Kraiger, J. K. Ford, and E. Salas, "Application of cognitive, skill-based, and affective theories"; J. J. Phillips, "ROI: The search for best practices"; D. L. Kirkpatrick, "Evaluation of Training," in *Training and Development Handbook,* 2d ed., ed. R. L. Craig (New York: McGraw-Hill, 1976): 18-1 to 18-27.

12. K. Kraiger, J. K. Ford, and E. Salas, "Application of cognitive, skill-based, and affective theories of learning outcomes to new methods of training evaluation," *Journal of Applied Psychology,* 78 (1993): 311–328; J. J. Phillips, "ROI: The search for best practices," *Training and Development* (February 1996): 42–47; G. M. Alliger et al., "A meta-analysis of the relations among training criteria," *Personnel Psychology,* 50 (1997): 341–355; K. Kraiger, "Decision-Based Evaluation," in *Creating, Implementing, and Managing Effective Training and Development,* ed. K. Kraiger (San Francisco: Jossey-Bass, 2002): 331–375; G. Alliger and E. Janek, "Kirkpatrick's levels of training criteria: Thirty years later," *Personnel Psychology,* 42 (1989): 331–342.

13. R. Morgan and W. Casper, "Examining the factor structure of participant reactions to training: A multidimensional approach," *Human Resource Development Quarterly,* 11 (2000): 301–317; K. Brown, "An examination of the structure and nomological network of trainee reactions: A closer look at 'smile sheets,'" *Journal of Applied Psychology,* 90 (2005): 991–1001; G. Vellios, "On the level," *T+D* (December 2008): 26–29.

14. G. Hopkins, "How to design an instructor evaluation," *Training and Development* (March 2000): 51–53.

15. T. Sitzmann et al., "A review and meta-analysis of the nomological network of trainee reactions," *Journal of Applied Psychology,* 93 (2008): 280–295.

16. "Grant Thornton," *T+D* (October 2010): 75.

17. P. Taylor, D. Russ-Eft, and H. Taylor, "Transfer of management training from alternative perspectives," *Journal of Applied Psychology,* 94 (2009): 104–121.

18. J. J. Phillips, "Was it the training?" *Training and Development* (March 1996): 28–32.

19. Chesterfield County, Virginia, "2011 Training Top 125," *Training* (January/February 2011): 87.

20. Ikon Office Solutions, "2011 Training Top 125," *Training* (January/February 2011): 87.

21. "LQ Management LLC," *T+D* (October 2008): 76–77.

22. J. J. Phillips, "ROI: The search for best practices," *Training and Development* (February 1996): 42–47.

23. J. Schettler, "Homegrown solutions," *Training* (November 2002): 76–79.

24. D. A. Grove and C. Ostroff, "Program Evaluation." In *Developing Human Resources,* ed. K. N. Wexley (Washington, D. C.: Bureau of National Affairs, 1991): 5-185 to 5-220.

25. H. J. Frazis, D. E. Herz, and M. W. Horrigan, "Employer-provided training: Results from a new survey," *Monthly Labor Review,* 118 (1995): 3–17.

26. W. Arthur, Jr. et al., "Effectiveness of training in organizations: A meta-analysis of design and evaluation features," *Journal of Applied Psychology,* 88 (2003): 234–245.

27. J. Gordon, "Eye on ROI," *Training* (May 2007): 43–45.

28. G. Alliger and E. Janek, "Kirkpatrick's levels of training criteria: Thirty years later," *Personnel Psychology,* 42 (1989): 331–342.

29. W. Arthur, Jr., W. Bennett, P. Edens, and S. Bell, "Effectiveness of training in organizations: A meta-analysis of design and evaluation features," *Journal of Applied Psychology,* 88 (2003): 234–245.

30. T. D. Cook, D. T. Campbell, and L. Peracchio, "Quasi-experimentation." In *Handbook of Industrial and Organizational Psychology,* 2d ed., Vol. 1, eds. M. D. Dunnette and L. M. Hough (Palo Alto, CA: Consulting Psychologists Press, 1990): 491–576.

31. Ibid.; J. J. Phillips, *Handbook of Training Evaluation and Measurement Methods,* 2d ed. (Houston, TX: Gulf Publishing, 1991).

32. D. Sussman, "Strong medicine required," *T+D* (November 2005): 34–38.

33. S. J. Simon and J. M. Werner, "Computer training through behavior modeling, self-paced, and instructional approaches: A field experiment," *Journal of Applied Psychology,* 81 (1996): 648–659.

34. CHG Healthcare Services, "2011 Training Top 125," *Training* (January/February 2011): 87.

35. J. Komaki, K. D. Bardwick, and L. R. Scott, "A behavioral approach to occupational safety: Pinpointing and reinforcing safe performance in a food manufacturing plant," *Journal of Applied Psychology,* 63 (1978): 434–445.

36. R. D. Bretz and R. E. Thompsett, "Comparing traditional and integrative learning methods in organizational training programs," *Journal of Applied Psychology,* 77 (1992): 941–51.

37. S. I. Tannenbaum and S. B. Woods, "Determining a strategy for evaluating training: Operating within organizational constraints," *Human Resource Planning,* 15 (1992): 63–81; R. D. Arvey, S. E. Maxwell, and E. Salas, "The relative power of training evaluation designs under different cost configurations," *Journal of Applied Psychology,* 77 (1992): 155–160.

38. P. R. Sackett and E. J. Mullen, "Beyond formal experimental design: Toward an expanded view of the training evaluation process," *Personnel Psychology,* 46 (1993): 613–627.

39. B. Gerber, "Does your training make a difference? Prove it!" *Training* (March 1995): 27–34.

40. A. P. Carnevale and E. R. Schulz, "Return on investment: Accounting for training," *Training and Development Journal* (July 1990): S1–S32.

41. J. Phillips and P. Phillips, "Distinguishing ROI myths from reality," *Performance Improvement* (July 2008): 12–17.

42. J. Mattox, "ROI: The report of my death is an exaggeration," *T+D* (August 2011): 30–33.

43. A. Purcell, "20/20 ROI," *Training and Development* (July 2000): 28–33.

44. J. Phillips and P. Phillips, "Using action plans to measure ROI," *Performance Improvement,* 42 (2003): 22–31.

45. K. Ellis, "What's the ROI of ROI?" *Training* (January 2005): 16–21; B. Worthen, "Measuring the ROI of training," *CIO* (February 15, 2001): 128–136; D. Russ-Eft and H. Preskill, "In search of the Holy Grail: Return on investment evaluation in human resource development," *Advances in Developing Human Resources* (February 2005): 71–85.

46. J. Gordon, "Eye on ROI," *Training* (May 2007): 43–45.

47. A. P. Carnevale and E. R. Schulz, "Return on investment: Accounting for training," *Training and Development Journal* (July 1990): S1–S32; G. Kearsley, *Costs, Benefits, and Productivity in Training Systems* (Boston: Addison-Wesley, 1982).

48. S. D. Parry, "Measuring training's ROI," *Training and Development* (May 1996): 72–77.

49. D. G. Robinson and J. Robinson, "Training for impact," *Training and Development Journal* (August 1989): 30–42; J. J. Phillips, "How much is the training worth?" *Training and Development* (April 1996): 20–24.

50. A. Purcell, "20/20 ROI," *Training and Development* (July 2000): 28–33.

51. J. J. Phillips, *Handbook of Training Evaluation and Measurement Methods,* 2d ed. (Houston, TX: Gulf Publishing, 1991); J. J. Phillips, "ROI: The search for best practices," *Training and Development* (February 1996): 42–47; J. Phillips and P. Phillips, "Moving from evidence to proof," *T+D* (August 2011): 34–39.

52. D. G. Robinson and J. Robinson, "Training for impact," *Training and Development Journal* (August 1989): 30–42.

53. D. Sussman, "Strong medicine required," *T+D* (November 2005): 34–38.

54. J. E. Matheiu and R. L. Leonard, "Applying utility analysis to a training program in supervisory skills: A time-based approach," *Academy of Management Journal,* 30 (1987): 316–335; F. L. Schmidt, J. E. Hunter, and K. Pearlman, "Assessing the economic impact of personnel programs on workforce productivity," *Personnel Psychology,* 35 (1982): 333–347; J. W. Boudreau, "Economic considerations in estimating the utility of human resource productivity programs," *Personnel Psychology,* 36 (1983): 551–576.

55. U. E. Gattiker, "Firm and taxpayer returns from training of semiskilled employees," *Academy of Management Journal,* 38 (1995): 1151–1173.

56. B. Worthen, "Measuring the ROI of training," *CIO* (February 15, 2001): 128–136.

57. D. Abernathy, "Thinking outside the evaluation box," *Training and Development* (February 1999): 19–23; E. Krell, "Calculating success," *Training* (December 2002): 47–52; D. Goldwater, "Beyond ROI," *Training* (January 2001): 82–90.

58. J. Kirpatrick and W. Kirkpatrick, "Creating ROE: The end is the beginning," *T+D* (November 2011): 60–64. J. Kirkpatrick and W. Kirkpatrick, "ROE's rising star: Why return on expectations is getting so much attention," *T+D* (August 2010): 34–38.

59. R. Brinkerhoff, "The success case method: A strategic evaluation approach to increasing the value and effect of training," *Advances in Developing Human Resources,* 7 (February 2005): 86–101; J. Kirkpatrick and W. Kirkpatrick, "ROE's rising star: Why return on expectations is getting so much attention," *T+D* (August 2010): 34–38.

60. C. Wick and R. Pollock, "Making results visible," *T+D* (June 2004): 46–51.

61. E. Holton and S. Naquin, "New metrics for employee development," *Performance Improvement Quarterly,* 17 (2004): 56–80.

62. E. Frauenheim, "Numbers game," *Workforce Management,* March 2011:20–21; P. Gallagher, "Rethinking HR," *Human Resource Executive,* September 2, 2009: 1, 18–23; B. Roberts, "How to put analytics 'on your side,'" *HR Magazine,* October 2009: 43–46; A. Rossett, "Metrics matter," *T+D* (March 2010): 64–69.

63. B. Roberts, "Analyze this!," *HR Magazine,* October 2009: 35–41.

64. R. Stolz, "The capital idea," *Human Resource Executive* (February 2005): 1, 24–29.

65. D. Galloway, "Achieving accurate metrics using balanced scorecards and dashboards," *Performance Improvement* (August 2010): 38–45.

66. D. Mallon, "At a glance," *T+D* (December 2009): 66-68; www.key.com, webpage for Key Bank, accessed September 15, 2011.

## Case 2                                               Learning in Practice

### Business Goals Drive Learning at Verizon

Verizon's three business goals for 2011 were to build a business and a workforce that were as good as its networks, to lead in shareholder value creation, and to be recognized as an iconic technology company. The company's strategic business units align their priorities with the overall company business goals. The Learning and Development section of Verizon establishes training priorities and initiatives that support the business unit and overall company goals. To help create shareholder value, a customized executive education development program sponsored by the company president and CEO was developed to help senior managers understand how to drive long-term value creation. The program provides them with tools, processes, and metrics to help them understand how to positively influence shareholder value. As part of the program, senior managers work in cross-functional teams and are given an assignment to identify barriers to creating more shareholder value. At the end of the session, each team presents its recommendations to top executives. Many of these recommendations have been implemented, resulting in such changes as new budgeting processes and new process improvement programs. Also, as part of the program, each manager chooses one or two actions that they will commit to for positively influencing shareholder value. These actions are part of the senior manager's performance review. Because innovation and new technology drives Verizon's success, the company is using social media for training and on-demand learning. Videos distributed through the company's YouTube site are one of the employees' favorite ways to learn. For example, videos are used to demonstrating

system processes for sales teams. Many videos go "viral," with employees recommending to their peers a video they may have just watched. Verizon also expanded its internal social network for peer-to-peer collaboration. Also, Yammer.com was recently launched. It has more than 8,000 members and over 400 groups using it. Sales teams use the site to post questions and share best practices. Verizon is exploring the use of tablet computers to allow retail employees access to information they need while working with a customer. Verizon envisions that by 2022, its learning organization will have a greater emphasis on facilitating and moderating user-generated content rather than generating or providing content itself. The company expects that its workforce will use mobile online performance support on an as-needed basis into the future.

### Questions

1. Do you think it is easier for a company like Verizon, which emphasizes technology and innovation, to adopt and use new technologies such as social media for training? Why?

2. What metrics should Verizon use to show the effectiveness of its internal YouTube video site?

3. Should all training that Verizon offers be available to employees on an "as-needed" basis? Explain your answer. Is performance support the same as learning?

**Sources:** Based on L. Freifeld, "Verizon's new # is 1," *training* (January/February 2012): 28–30; M. Weinstein, "Verizon Connects to Success," *training* (January/February 2011): 40–42.

# Training and Development Methods

Part Three of this book covers the different types of training and development methods. Chapter Seven, "Traditional Training Methods," introduces you to presentational, hands-on, and group training methods, which include on-the-job training (OJT), simulations and games, lectures, and various group building methods such as action learning and team training. Chapter Eight, "Technology-Based Training Methods," covers topics such as Twitter and Facebook and focuses on some of the newest technology-based methods that are being used for training and development. E-learning, online learning, distance learning, virtual reality, virtual worlds such as Second Life, collaboration tools such as blogs and wikis, and mobile learning using social media smart phones and tablet computers such as i-Pads are examples of some of the methods discussed. Blended learning is also covered. Chapters Seven and Eight both show how each method is used and help you understand the potential strengths and weaknesses of each method, as well as important research results. Many companies are moving toward a blended learning approach to take advantage of the strengths of both face-to-face and technology-aided instruction.

Chapter Nine, "Employee Development and Career Management," details development planning and different types of development activities, including assessment, formal courses and programs, experiences, and interpersonal relationships involving mentoring and coaching. Chapter Nine also provides you with examples of companies' development systems.

The Part Three case, "Development Is Served 24/7 in InterContinental Hotel Group's Leaders Lounge," illustrates how companies can use technology to develop leadership talent.

---

7. Traditional Training Methods
8. Technology-based Training Methods
9. Employee Development and Career Management

# Traditional Training Methods

## Objectives

After reading this chapter, you should be able to

1. Discuss the strengths and weaknesses of presentational, hands-on, and group building training methods.
2. Provide recommendations for effective on-the-job training (OJT).
3. Develop a case study.
4. Develop a self-directed learning module.
5. Discuss the key components of behavior modeling training.
6. Explain the conditions necessary for adventure learning to be effective.
7. Discuss what team training should focus on to improve team performance.

## Training at La Quinta Hotels Helps Delight Guests

La Quinta operates more than eight hundred hotels in forty-six U.S. states, Canada, and Mexico, under the La Quinta Inns and La Quinta Inns and Suites brands. La Quinta wants its 9,000 employees to provide the best rooms, atmosphere, and courteous service at every hotel. La Quinta's culture emphasizes continuous improvement and its operating philosophy stresses taking care of employees, guests, and keeping the hotels spotlessly cleaned and well maintained. This means that training plays an important role in the success of every employee.

All employees have a personal training plan that is specifically tailored to their jobs. This helps them focus their attention on what they need to know to be successful in their job. La Quinta uses different training methods to help employees learn, including web-based training, small group training involving games where they are challenged with real-world scenarios that have occurred at hotel properties, and DVDs. The goal of the small group training is to make learning fun and, at the same time, promote learning through conversation and idea sharing.

One type of training method used is a game similar to Monopoly that guides employees through front-desk operations and helps them learn how to deliver superior service. The training program involves small groups working with a facilitator to review different service scenarios and situations that occur. The groups are asked to consider how employees can deliver the best service in each scenario. Front-desk employees are better "experts" at customer service than any trainer. For housekeeping and maintenance employees, La Quinta uses DVDs for training. Employees are provided with small portable DVD players when they need to learn tasks that they frequently perform on the job. For example, DVDs for cleaning the bathroom review the entire cleaning cycle. Employees take the DVD into the bathroom and watch the process of cleaning a bathroom before they try it themselves. They can fast-forward and review the DVD as needed to learn at their own pace. DVDs are available in both English and Spanish to accommodate the employee's language. La Quinta also uses games that include employees from different functions and levels, including maintenance workers, front-desk employees, housekeepers, and supervisors. The purpose of the game is to help employees work together and understand the need to communicate with each other to solve guest problems. Based on a photograph of a room, employees are asked to determine which small detail might lead to a larger problem. For example, if the TV remote requires batteries and it hasn't been checked to see if it works correctly, the next guest in the room will not be able to watch TV and will be inconvenienced by having to wait for new batteries to be delivered to the room.

Training is also provided for new hotel managers. New hotel managers complete an eighteen-day on-the-job training (OJT) program delivered by an instructor who is an experienced manager at his or her own hotel. Following the OJT program, new managers travel to the corporate offices in Dallas, Texas, for a four-day class delivered by corporate trainers and company executives. As part of the class, the new managers develop an action plan specific to their hotel property.

**Sources:** Based on "Who is La Quinta?" "Culture," and "Training/Development," from www.lq.com, website for La Quinta Inns and Suites, accessed January 23, 2012. "La Quinta Hotels: Hands-On Training," *Training* (March/April 2008): 38–39.

# INTRODUCTION

La Quinta uses a combination of training methods to ensure that its housekeepers, maintenance employees, and front-desk employees deliver excellent customer service. For most companies, including La Quinta, training methods have to be developed or purchased within a budget, there usually is a sense of urgency for the training, and training must be made available to those employees who need it.

Before we discuss specific training methods, it is important for you to consider more broadly the training methods that companies are using to help employees learn and how the emphasis placed on these different methods is changing. Figure 7.1 shows a learning system with four quadrants. This learning system shows that how and what employees learn varies and influences the type of training methods used.[1] Guided competency development means that the company has defined a broad set of competencies or skills for positions or for the entire company. Training and development methods such as lectures or online training are directed at the most common needs in the company. Context-based learning, learning that occurs on the job and during the everyday performance of work, tends to be more unique to the employee's needs and includes training methods such as OJT, simulations,

**FIGURE 7.1**

**A Learning System**

Source: From
J. Meister and
K. Willyerd, *The 2020 workplace. How innovative companies attract, develop, and keep tomorrow's employees today* (New York: Harper Business 2010).

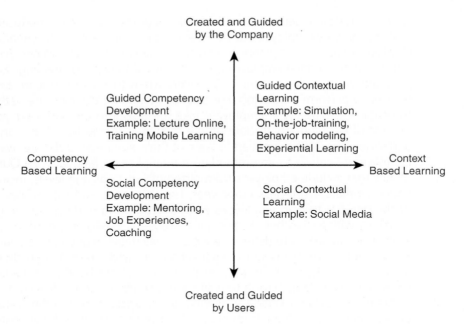

Created and Guided
by the Company

Guided Competency
Development
Example: Lecture Online,
Training Mobile Learning

Guided Contextual
Learning
Example: Simulation,
On-the-job-training,
Behavior modeling,
Experiential Learning

Competency
Based Learning

Context
Based Learning

Social Competency
Development
Example: Mentoring,
Job Experiences,
Coaching

Social Contextual
Learning
Example: Social Media

Created and Guided
by Users

and mobile learning. Both guided competence development and guided contextual learning are usually formal training activities designed and developed by the company to achieve specific learning goals. Employees are expected to participate in these learning activities. The bottom quadrants include social learning; i.e., learning activities that involve employees collaborating with each other either one-to-one or in groups or teams. Social competency development enhances specific job-related competencies through interaction with others such as a mentor or coach, or through encountering challenging job experiences. The competencies that are developed are typically not necessary for successful performance of one's job but help prepare employees for future roles or positions. As a result, mentoring, coaching, and job experiences are considered development activities. We discuss development activities in Chapter Nine, "Employee Development and Career Management." Social contextual learning is informal and peer-to-peer, and it occurs spontaneously on an as-needed basis. It usually involves employees sharing knowledge on issues, problems, and topics related to their current job. Employees have always learned from face-to-face meetings and phone conversations with peers. What is new is that the increased availability and access to phones and tablet computers provide a multimedia, low-cost, easy-to-use, and familiar way to interact with others on using social media such as blogs, wikis, social networks (such as Facebook), and microblogs (such as Twitter). This provides many possibilities for technology-aided social contextual learning. We will discuss blogs, wikis, social networks, and microblogs in Chapter 8, "Technology-Based Training Methods." Keep in mind that training methods can cut across the quadrant shown in Figure 7.1 if they include multiple types of learning, such as a virtual classroom that includes simulations and use of social networks.

Today, most companies' training methods would be found in Quadrants 1, 2, and 3, but some are beginning to explore how to facilitate learning from peers either face to face or through the use of social media. This is because traditionally training and development activities have been largely "instructor focused." This means that the instructor or trainer, along with the company, has the primary responsibility for ensuring that employees learn.[2] The learner plays a passive role as the receiver of information, and learning occurs to the extent that the appropriate conditions are provided by the learning "experts" or are inherent in the learning method. For example, the instructor bears the responsibility for identifying what should be learned, determining the most appropriate methods, and evaluating the extent to which knowledge and skill acquisition resulted from the learning activity. Recently, training and development have emphasized a more active role for the learner because of the increased recognition that the learner is at least as important as the instructor and the learning conditions in determining whether learning occurs.[3] Also, there is increased recognition of the importance of informal learning and the greater availability and use of online and mobile technology (e.g., iPods) to deliver instruction and social collaboration.[4] Using technology to deliver instruction or social collaboration gives the employee the opportunity to choose when, how, from whom, and even what content to learn. Figure 7.1 provides an overview of how much companies are using different training methods. Instructor-led classroom training remains the most frequently used method, but the use of online learning, virtual classroom, or a combination of methods continues to grow.

Regardless of whether the training method is traditional or technology-based, for training to be effective, it needs to be based on the training design model shown in Figure 1.2 in Chapter One, "Introduction to Employee Training and Development." Needs assessment, a positive learning environment, and transfer of training are critical for training program effectiveness. Recall the discussions of needs assessment, learning, and transfer of training in Chapters Three, Four, and Five.

This chapter and Chapter Eight present various training methods. This chapter focuses on **traditional training methods,** which require an instructor or facilitator and involve face-to-face interaction between trainees. However, most methods discussed here can be adapted for online, virtual reality, mobile learning, or other new training technologies used for training delivery or instruction. For example, a classroom lecture can occur face-to-face with trainees (traditional training) or can be delivered through a virtual classroom, in which the instructor is not in the same room as the trainees. Also, instruction can be real-time (synchronous) or time-delayed (asynchronous). Through technology, a lecture can be attended live (although the trainees are not in the same classroom as the trainer), or the lecture can be videotaped or burned onto a DVD. The lecture can be viewed by the trainees at their convenience on a personal computer that gives them access to the appropriate medium for viewing the lecture (e.g., DVD player or Internet connection).

Chapter Eight, "Technology-Based Training Methods," discusses web-based training, e-learning, virtual reality, and social media. The increased use of technology-based training for delivery of instruction is occurring because of the potential increases in learning effectiveness, as well as the reductions in training costs.

Keep in mind that many companies' training programs use a combination of methods to capitalize on each method's strengths for learning and transfer. For example, the training program at Colorado Springs Utilities begins with a brainstorming session to engage trainees and help them enjoy the training and retain more of what they learn.[5] In a safety training class, students experience a simulated emergency and have to respond using their new skills, along with their knowledge of an evacuation plan. The trainees perform different roles and activities in response to a power shutdown. Afterward, the trainer critiques their performance and trainees discuss what they have learned (or still need to learn). Trainees complete a written exam and review to ensure knowledge retention. Whataburger, a family-owned business that includes 700 restaurants in 10 states, hosts its annual WhataGames training activity to boost employees' loyalty, pride in their work, and productivity.[6] The WhataGames training includes a quiz show that tests employees' knowledge of menu items, procedures, and company history (e.g., "At what temperature does chicken have to reach to be properly cooked? Answer: 165 degrees"). To prepare for the competition, employees review company history as well as operations manuals. During the What's Cooking competition, employee teams are tested in a simulated lunch rush. Inspectors examine every order prepared for accuracy and presentation. Besides benefiting the company, winning teams split more than $140,000 in prize money.

The traditional training methods discussed in this chapter are organized into three broad categories: presentation methods, hands-on methods, and group building methods.[7] The following sections provide a description of each method, a discussion of its advantages and disadvantages, and tips for the trainer who is designing or choosing the method. The chapter concludes by comparing methods based on several characteristics, including the learning outcomes influenced, the extent to which the method facilitates learning transfer, cost, and effectiveness.

# PRESENTATION METHODS

**Presentation methods** are methods in which trainees are passive recipients of information. This information may include facts, processes, and problem-solving methods. Lectures and audiovisual techniques are presentation methods. It is important to note that instructor-led classroom presentation methods may include lectures, video, workbooks and manuals, DVDs, and games. That is, a mix of methods can actively engage trainees in learning and can help transfer of training to occur.

## Lecture

In a **lecture,** trainers communicate through spoken words what they want the trainees to learn. The communication of learned capabilities is primarily one-way—from the trainer to the audience. As Figure 7.2 shows, instructor-led classroom presentation remains a popular training method despite new technologies such as interactive video and computer-assisted instruction.

A lecture is one of the least expensive, least time-consuming ways to present a large amount of information efficiently in an organized manner.[8] The lecture format is also useful because it is easily employed with large groups of trainees. Besides being the primary means to communicate large amounts of information, lectures are also used to support other training methods such as behavior modeling and technology-based techniques. For example, a lecture may be used to communicate information regarding the purpose of the training program, conceptual models, or key behaviors to trainees prior to their receiving training that is more interactive and customized to their specific needs.

Table 7.1 describes several variations of the standard lecture method. All have advantages and disadvantages.[9] Team teaching brings more expertise and alternative perspectives to the training session. Team teaching does require more time on the part of trainers to

**FIGURE 7.2**
**Use of training methods**

Source: Based on
"2011 training
industry report,"
*Training* (November/
December 2011): 30.

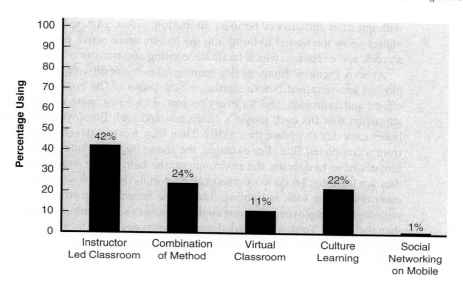

**TABLE 7.1**
**Variations of the Lecture Method**

| Method | Description |
| --- | --- |
| Standard lecture | Trainer talks and may use visual aids provided on the blackboard, whiteboard, or Microsoft PowerPoint slides, while trainees listen and absorb information. |
| Team teaching | Two or more trainers present different topics or alternative views of the same topic. |
| Guest speakers | A speaker or speakers visit the session for a predetermined time period. Primary instruction is conducted by the instructor. |
| Panels | Two or more speakers present information and ask questions. |
| Student presentations | Groups of trainees present topics to the class. |

not only prepare their particular session but also coordinate with other trainers, especially when there is a great deal of integration between topics. Panels are good for showing trainees different viewpoints in a debate. A potential disadvantage of a panel, however, is that trainees who are relatively naive about a topic may have difficulty understanding the important points. Guest speakers can motivate learning by bringing to the trainees relevant examples and applications. For guest speakers to be effective, trainers need to set expectations with speakers regarding how their presentation should relate to the course content. Student presentations may increase the material's meaningfulness and trainees' attentiveness, but it can inhibit learning if the trainees do not have presentation skills.

The lecture method has several disadvantages. Lectures tend to lack participant involvement, feedback, and meaningful connection to the work environment—all of which inhibit learning and transfer of training. Lectures appeal to few of the trainees' senses because trainees focus primarily on hearing information or seeing facts, principles, or processes. Lectures also make it difficult for the trainer to judge quickly and efficiently the learners' level of understanding. To overcome these problems, the lecture is often supplemented with question-and-answer periods, discussion, video, games, or case studies. These techniques allow the trainer to build into the lecture more active participation, job-related examples, and exercises, which facilitate learning and transfer of training.

At Sony Pictures' Imageworks, training takes many different forms.[10] For example, employees are retrained before starting a new project. The company creates digital visual effects and animation, and for every project, it uses new methods and technology to create animation that fits each movie's characters and feel. Employees take classes for several hours each day to update their skills. Then they work at developing a frame of animation from a completed film. For example, the frame might include the characters, but the employees have to develop the environment, the hair, or the animation, depending on what they are learning. Imageworks has online tutorials that employees can access to learn about other disciplines such as lighting. The online tutorials help employees learn the basic terminology so employees can communicate and work with employees from disciplines other than their own. To showcase good work, employees or teams whose work has received exemplary peer review are asked to give lunchtime lectures to teach techniques to others. At Constellation Energy, new-hire training involves thirty hours of pretraining work, plus two weeks of classroom instruction that focuses on developing sales skills relevant to an energy company.[11] Trainees learn about the issues that their potential customers face and learn models to help customers manage costs and risks over time. They also prepare tools and materials for their target markets and participate in role playing. Finally, trainees meet with their managers at the end of training to develop a plan to implement what they have learned.

## Audiovisual Techniques

**Audiovisual instruction** includes overheads, slides, and video. Video is a popular instructional method.[12] It has been used for improving communications skills, interviewing skills, and customer-service skills and for illustrating how procedures (e.g., welding) should be followed. Video is, however, rarely used alone. It is usually used in conjunction with lectures to show trainees real-life experiences and examples. Here is how one company is using video in its training program.

At 5:30 A.M., the Morse Bros., an Oregon company that supplies aggregate products, such as concrete, gravel, and quarry rock, drivers prepare to deliver the first of many loads. In the concrete business, a perishable product needs to be delivered on a timely basis to construction sites. Morse Bros. has been able to reduce costs and raise customer satisfaction by providing drivers with product training and by instructing drivers to avoid rollovers and excessive idling at construction sites.

What method does Morse Bros. use to train its drivers? The company produces training videos that are presented by mentor-drivers. The mentor-driver's job is to select the weekly video, schedule viewing sessions, keep attendance records, and guide a wrap-up discussion following each video. The mentor-drivers are trained to call attention to key learning points covered in the video and relate the topic to issues that the drivers deal with on the job. Because training sessions are scheduled early in the morning at the beginning of the drivers' shift, time is limited. Videos seldom run more than 10 minutes. For example, one called *Another Pair of Eyes* trains drivers to observe test procedures used by testing agencies at job sites. Samples are tested several times a month. A sample that fails can leave the company liable for demolition and removal of the concrete structure. Morse Bros. provides training on test procedures because samples often fail a test due to contamination (e.g., dirt) that gets into the test cylinder. Another video emphasizes cold-weather precautions: Drain all tanks and hoses at the end of the day, park the drum in neutral. At each training session, drivers are asked to answer several questions related to the content of the program. At the end of a session, drivers and the mentor-driver discuss anything that might be interfering with the quality of the product or timeliness of delivery. Mentor-drivers then share this information with company managers.[13]

Video is also a major component of behavior modeling and, naturally, interactive video instruction. The use of video in training has a number of advantages.[14] First, trainers can review, slow down, or speed up the lesson, which gives them flexibility in customizing the session depending on trainees' expertise. Second, trainees can watch the video multiple times if they have access to it during and after the training session. This gives them control over their learning. Third, trainees can be exposed to equipment, problems, and events that cannot be easily demonstrated, such as equipment malfunctions, angry customers, or emergencies. Fourth, trainees are provided with consistent instruction. Program content is not affected by the interests and goals of a particular trainer. Fifth, videotaping trainees allows them to see and hear their own performance without the interpretation of the trainer. That is, video provides immediate objective feedback. As a result, trainees cannot attribute poor performance to the bias of external evaluators such as the trainer or peers. Sixth, video requires minimal knowledge of technology and equipment. Most trainers and trainees can easily use a VCR or DVD player.

Most problems in video result from the creative approach used.[15] These problems include too much content for the trainee to learn, poor dialogue between the actors (which hinders the credibility and clarity of the message), overuse of humor or music, and drama that makes it confusing for the trainee to understand the important learning points emphasized in the video.

# HANDS-ON METHODS

**Hands-on methods** are training methods that require the trainee to be actively involved in learning. These methods include OJT, simulations, case studies, business games, role playing, and behavior modeling. These methods are ideal for developing specific skills, understanding how skills and behaviors can be transferred to the job, experiencing all aspects of completing a task, or dealing with interpersonal issues that arise on the job.

## On-the-job training (OJT)

**On-the-job training (OJT)** refers to new or inexperienced employees learning in the work setting and during work by observing peers or managers performing the job and then trying to imitate their behavior. OJT is one of the oldest and most used types of informal training.[16] It is considered informal because it does not necessarily occur as part of a training program, and because managers, peers, or mentors serve as trainers. If OJT is too informal, learning is less likely to occur. OJT can be useful for training newly hired employees, upgrading experienced employees' skills when new technology is introduced, cross-training employees within a department or work unit, and orienting transferred or promoted employees to their new jobs.

OJT takes various forms, including apprenticeships and self-directed learning programs. (Both of these are discussed later in this section.) OJT has several advantages over other training methods.[17] It can be customized to the experiences and abilities of trainees. Training is immediately applicable to the job because OJT occurs on the job using actual tools and equipment. As a result, trainees are highly motivated to learn. Both trainees and trainers are at the job site and continue to work while training occurs. This means that companies save the costs related to bringing trainees to a central location, hiring trainers, and renting training facilities. OJT can be offered at any time, and trainers will be available because they are peers or managers. Finally, OJT uses actual job tasks and occurs at work. As a result, skills learned in OJT more easily transfer to the job.

Reliance Industries, one of India's largest businesses, uses OJT in its Nagothane Manu-facturing Division (a refinery that makes polymers and chemicals).[18] Because of rapid company growth and the demand for experienced employees, the company needed to de-crease the length of time required for new engineers to contribute. In response to this need, the training staff identified mentors who would help accelerate learning for the new engineers. The mentors and new hires are carefully matched based on an assessment of the mentor's training style and the new employee's learning style. Mentors are paired with up to three new employees, each for nine months. The mentors and new employees work to-gether on four learning modules, each of which takes two months to complete. Each mod-ule includes predetermined lesson plans, and progress is tracked using an online portal. As a result, the length of time that it takes new engineers to contribute at work has decreased from twelve to six months.

At Sweets Candy, a candy maker based in Salt Lake City, Utah, new employees receive training in basic safety and emergency evacuation procedures in an orientation session and then are assigned a mentor.[19] The mentor works with the new employee for two weeks, providing hands-on, one-on-one training. Teams hold weekly meetings, and managers pro-vide training on safety issues throughout the year. Employees also receive a weekly safety contact card on which they note safety hazards that they have encountered on their job and how they have fixed the problem. The safety contact cards are turned in, and each month the company has a safety celebration where the cards are put into a drawing. Employees win prizes such as a day off or a $10 gift card. All of the safety contact cards are reviewed to identify safety issues and hazards, which are then communicated to the employees.

OJT is an attractive training method because compared to other methods, it needs less investment in time or money for materials, the trainer's salary, or instructional design. Managers or peers who are job knowledge experts are used as instructors. As a result, it may be tempting to let them conduct the training as they believe it should be done.

There are several disadvantages to this unstructured approach to OJT. Managers and peers may not use the same process to complete a task. They may pass on bad habits as well as useful skills. Also, they may not understand that demonstration, practice, and feedback are important conditions for effective OJT. Unstructured OJT can result in poorly trained employees, employees who use ineffective or dangerous methods to produce a product or provide a service, and products or services that vary in quality.

OJT must be structured to be effective. Table 7.2 shows the principles of structured OJT. Because OJT involves learning by observing others, successful OJT is based on the principles emphasized by social learning theory. These include the use of a credible trainer, a manager or peer who models the behavior or skill, communication of specific key behav-iors, practice, feedback, and reinforcement. For example, at Rochester Gas and Electric in Rochester, New York, radiation and chemistry instructors teach experienced employees

**TABLE 7.2   Principles of OJT**

**Preparing for Instruction**

1. Break down the job into important steps.
2. Prepare the necessary equipment, materials, and supplies.
3. Decide how much time you will devote to OJT and when you expect the employees to be competent in skill areas.

**Actual Instruction**

1. Tell the trainees the objective of the task and ask them to watch you demonstrate it.
2. Show the trainees how to do the task without saying anything.
3. Explain the key points or behaviors. (Write out the key points for the trainees, if possible.)
4. Show the trainees how to do it again.
5. Have the trainees do one or more single parts of the task and praise them for correct reproduction (optional).
6. Have the trainees do the entire task and praise them for correct reproduction.
7. If mistakes are made, have the trainees practice until accurate reproduction is achieved.
8. Praise the trainees for their success in learning the task.

**Transfer of Training**

Provide support materials and job aids such as flowcharts, checklists, or procedures.
Arrange for manager or trainer support and observation on the job, especially for difficult or complex tasks.

**Evaluation**

Prepare and allow time for final tests and exercises and surveys of trainee reactions.

Sources: Based on R. Buckley and J. Caple, "Developing one-to-one training programs," *T+D* (April 2010): 108–109; W. J. Rothwell and H. C. Kazanas, "Planned OJT Is Productive OJT," *Training and Development Journal* (October 1990): 53–55; P. J. Decker and B. R. Nathan, *Behavior Modeling Training* (New York: Praeger Scientific, 1985).

how to conduct OJT.[20] While teaching these employees how to demonstrate software to new employees, the trainer may ask the employees to watch other OJT instructors as they train new recruits so that they can learn new teaching techniques. Regardless of the specific type, effective OJT programs include:

1. A policy statement that describes the purpose of OJT and emphasizes the company's support for it.
2. A clear specification of who is accountable for conducting OJT. If managers conduct OJT, this is mentioned in their job descriptions and is part of their performance evaluations.
3. A thorough review of OJT practices (program content, types of jobs, length of program, cost savings) at other companies in similar industries.
4. Training of managers and peers in the principles of structured OJT (see Table 7.2).
5. Availability of lesson plans, checklists, procedure manuals, training manuals, learning contracts, and progress reports for use by employees who conduct OJT.
6. Evaluation of employees' levels of basic skills (reading, computation, and writing) before OJT.[21]

For example, the OJT program utilized by Borden's North American Pasta Division has many of these characteristics.[22] Not all managers and peers are used as trainers. Borden's invests in trainer selection, training, and rewards to ensure OJT's effectiveness. Employees and managers interested in being instructors are required to apply for the position. Those chosen as instructors are required to complete a demanding train-the-trainer course that involves classroom training, as well as time on the manufacturing floor to learn how to operate machinery such as pasta machines and to correctly teach other employees to use the equipment. Borden's also builds accountability into the OJT program. Trainees are responsible for completing a checklist that requires them to verify that the trainer helped them learn the skills needed to operate the equipment and used effective instructional techniques.

## Self-Directed Learning

**Self-directed learning** has employees take responsibility for all aspects of learning, including when it is conducted and who will be involved.[23] Trainees master predetermined training content at their own pace without an instructor. Trainers may serve as facilitators. That is, trainers are available to evaluate learning or answer questions for the trainee. The trainer does not control or disseminate instruction. The learning process is controlled by the trainee. Self-directed learning for salespersons could involve reading newspapers or trade publications, talking to experts, or surfing the Internet to find new ideas related to the salesperson industry.[24] Also, self-directed learning could involve the company providing employees with information such as databases, training courses, and seminars while still holding them responsible for taking the initiative to learn. Because the effectiveness of self-directed learning is based on an employee's motivation to learn, companies may want to provide seminars on the self-directed learning process, self-management, and how to adapt to the environment, customers, and technology.

Self-directed learning has several advantages.[25] It allows trainees to learn at their own pace and receive feedback about the learning performance. For the company, self-directed learning requires fewer trainers, reduces costs associated with travel and meeting rooms, and makes multiple-site training more realistic. Self-directed learning provides consistent training content that captures the knowledge of experts. Self-directed learning also makes it easier for shift employees to gain access to training materials. For example, Four Seasons Hotels faced the challenge of opening a new hotel in Bali, Indonesia.[26] It needed to teach English skills to 580 employees, none of whom spoke English or understood Western cuisine or customs. Four Seasons created a self-directed learning center that enables employees to teach themselves English. The center emphasizes communications as a whole, not simply learning to speak English. As a result of this emphasis, the center features video recorders, training modules, books, and magazines. Monetary incentives are provided for employees to move from the lowest to the highest level of English skills. Besides English, the center also teaches Japanese (the language of 20 percent of the Bali hotel's visitors) and provides training for foreign managers in Bahasa Indonesian, the native language of Indonesia.

A major disadvantage of self-directed learning, however, is that trainees must be willing to learn on their own and feel comfortable doing so. That is, trainees must be motivated to learn. From the company perspective, self-directed learning results in higher development costs, and development time is longer than with other types of training programs.

Several steps are necessary to develop effective self-directed learning:[27]

1. Conduct a job analysis to identify the tasks that must be covered.
2. Write trainee-centered learning objectives directly related to the tasks. Because the objectives take the place of the instructor, they must indicate what information is important, what actions the trainee should take, and what the trainee should master.

3. Develop the content for the learning package. This involves developing scripts (for video) or text screens (for computer-based training). The content should be based on the trainee-centered learning objectives. Another consideration in developing the content is the medium (e.g., paper, video, computer, or website) that will be used to communicate the content.

4. Break the content into smaller pieces ("chunks"). The chunks should always begin with the objectives that will be covered and include a method for trainees to evaluate their learning. Practice exercises should also appear in each chunk.

5. Develop an evaluation package that includes evaluation of the trainee and evaluation of the self-directed learning package. Trainee evaluation should be based on the objectives (a process known as *criterion referencing*). That is, questions should be developed that are written directly from the objectives and can be answered directly from the materials. Evaluation of the self-directed learning package should involve determining ease of use, how up-to-date the material is, whether the package is being used as intended, and whether trainees are mastering the objectives.

Self-directed learning is likely to become more common in the future, as companies seek to train staff flexibly, take advantage of technology, and encourage employees to be proactive in their learning rather than driven by the employer.

## Apprenticeship

**Apprenticeship** is a work-study training method with both on-the-job and classroom training.[28] To qualify as a registered apprentice under state or federal guidelines, apprentices in most cases must complete at least 144 hours of classroom instruction and must obtain 2,000 hours, or one year, of on-the-job experience.[29] Once their training is complete, apprentices are called *journey workers,* and they earn certification from the U.S. Department of Labor or a state apprenticeship agency. Table 7.3 shows the top occupations for apprentices. Apprenticeships can be sponsored by individual companies or by groups of companies cooperating with a union. As Table 7.3 shows, most apprenticeship programs are in the skilled trades such as plumbing, carpentry, electrical work, and pipe fitting. Table 7.4 is an example of an apprenticeship program for a machinist.

In an apprenticeship program, the hours and weeks that must be devoted to completing specific skill units are clearly defined. The OJT involves assisting a certified tradesperson (a journey worker) at the work site. The OJT portion of the apprenticeship follows the guidelines for effective OJT by including modeling, practice, feedback, and evaluation.[30] First, the employer verifies that the trainee has the required knowledge of the operation or process. Next, the trainer (who is usually a more experienced, licensed employee) demonstrates each step of the process, emphasizing safety issues and key steps. The senior employee provides the apprentice with the opportunity to perform the process until all are satisfied that the apprentice can perform it properly and safely.

A major advantage of apprenticeship programs is that learners can earn pay while they learn. This is important because programs can last several years. Learners' wages usually increase automatically as their skills improve. Also, apprenticeships are usually effective learning experiences because they involve learning why and how a task is performed through classroom instruction provided by local trade schools, high schools, or community colleges. Apprenticeships also usually result in full-time employment for trainees at the company

**TABLE 7.3**
Top 25
Occupations
for Active
Apprentices

Source: Based on
"Top 25 Apprentice-
ship Occupations
Ranked by Total as of
September 30, 2007,"
from U.S. Department
of Labor, Employment
and Training Admin-
istration. Available at
www.doleta.gov/OA/
top-25-occupations.cfm.

| Rank | Occupation | Total Active Enrolled | Number of Active Programs |
|------|------------|----------------------:|--------------------------:|
| 1 | Electrician | 45,609 | 3,209 |
| 2 | Heavy truck driver | 37,805 | 39 |
| 3 | Carpenter | 33,027 | 446 |
| 4 | Plumber | 18,578 | 2,644 |
| 5 | Construction craft laborers | 9,836 | 94 |
| 6 | Pipe fitter (construction) | 9,542 | 722 |
| 7 | Sheet metal worker | 8,754 | 518 |
| 8 | Structural-steel worker | 8,659 | 131 |
| 9 | Roofer | 5,943 | 139 |
| 10 | Elevator constructor | 5,746 | 62 |
| 11 | Drywall installers | 5,541 | 44 |
| 12 | Sprinkler fitter | 5,433 | 124 |
| 13 | Operating engineer | 4,837 | 131 |
| 14 | Painter (construction) | 4,795 | 248 |
| 15 | Boilermaker | 4,089 | 32 |
| 16 | Bricklayer (construction) | 3,729 | 194 |
| 17 | Millwright | 3,185 | 381 |
| 18 | Heating/air-conditioner-installer | 3,099 | 601 |
| 19 | Powerline maintainer | 3,087 | 297 |
| 20 | Powerline installer and repairer | 2,886 | 92 |
| 21 | Insulation worker | 2,328 | 101 |
| 22 | Correction officer | 2,290 | 58 |
| 23 | Child care development specialist | 2,282 | 971 |
| 24 | Cook (hospitality and cruise ship) | 2,259 | 1 |
| 25 | Cement mason | 2,240 | 127 |
| | **All Occupations** | **292,163** | **25,290** |

that the employee is training at when the program is completed. From the company's perspective, apprenticeship programs meet specific business training needs and help attract talented employees. At its manufacturing facility in Toledo, Ohio, Libbey Glass has apprenticeship programs in mold making, machine repair, millwrighting, and maintenance repair.[31] These programs are viewed as the best jobs within the company because the wage rates are high and because most apprentices are scheduled to work day shifts instead of afternoon or midnight shifts. The apprenticeship program has been costly for the company but has paid dividends. Each apprentice requires the support of a journey worker for each work assignment. This means that work is being performed by two employees when only one worker is normally required. The program also requires apprentices to be evaluated every 1,000 hours to meet U.S. Department of Labor standards. The reviews are conducted by a committee that includes management and department journey workers. The committee also develops tests and other evaluation materials. The committee members cannot perform their normal duties during the time they are reviewing apprentices, so their workload has to be distributed among other employees or rescheduled for some other time. The program offers many benefits to Libbey: The company is developing employees who are more receptive to changes in the work environment; work can be performed at Libbey, so the company does not have to outsource jobs to contract labor; and Libbey is given an edge

**TABLE 7.4**
**Example of a Machinist Apprenticeship**

Source: A. H. Howard III, "Apprenticeship." In *The ASTD Training and Development Handbook*, 4th ed., ed. R. L. Craig (New York: McGraw-Hill, 1996): 808.

| Hours | Weeks | Unit |
|---|---|---|
| 240 | 6.0 | Bench Work |
| 360 | 9.0 | Drill Press |
| 240 | 6.0 | Heat Treat |
| 200 | 5.0 | Elementary Layout |
| 680 | 17.0 | Turret Lathe (Conventional and Numerical Control) |
| 800 | 20.0 | Engine Lathe |
| 320 | 8.0 | Tool Grind |
| 640 | 16.0 | Advanced Layout |
| 960 | 24.0 | Milling Machine |
| 280 | 7.0 | Profile Milling |
| 160 | 4.0 | Surface Grinding |
| 240 | 6.0 | External Grinding |
| 280 | 7.0 | Internal Grinding |
| 200 | 5.0 | Thread Grinding |
| 520 | 13.0 | Horizontal Boring Mills |
| 240 | 6.0 | Jig Bore/Jig Grinder |
| 160 | 4.0 | Vertical Boring |
| 600 | 15.0 | Numerical Control Milling |
| 240 | 6.0 | Computer Numerical Control |
| 640 | 16.0 | Related Training |
| 8,000 | 200.0 | TOTAL |

*Probationary:* **The following hours are included in the totals above, but must be completed in the first 1,000 hours of apprenticeship:**

| | | |
|---|---|---|
| 80 | 2.0 | Drill Press (probation) |
| 280 | 7.0 | Lathe Work (probation) |
| 360 | 9.0 | Milling Machine (probation) |
| 40 | 1.0 | Elementary Layout (probation) |
| 80 | 2.0 | Related Training (probation) |
| **840** | **21.0** | **TOTAL** |

in attracting talented employees who like the idea that after completing an apprenticeship, they are eligible for promotions to other positions in the company, including management positions. Also, the apprenticeship program helps Libbey tailor training and work experiences to meet specific needs in maintenance repair, which is necessary to create and repair production mold equipment used in making glass products.

Apprentice-like programs are also used to prepare new managers. The president and chief executive officer of Goldcorp, a company in the mining industry, offers the chance for MBAs to apply for a nine-month apprenticeship.[32] The apprentice shadows Goldcorp's CEO and observes board meetings, negotiations, mine acquisitions, and other important aspects of the mine industry. Goldcorp hopes the apprenticeships will attract more MBAs to the mining industry, which is viewed by many graduates as an unsafe and dirty business. Hyatt Hotels offers several programs in which management trainees complete training in the areas of facilities, culinary arts, sales, hotel operations, accounting, and catering.[33] Trainees rotate through all parts of the hotel and perform all aspects of each job, ranging from washing dishes to catering, and then spend the rest of the training time in their specialty area. Employees who complete the training are placed in entry-level management positions.

Besides the development costs and time commitment that management and journey workers have to make to apprenticeship programs, another disadvantage of many of these programs is that despite efforts to be inclusive, there still may be limited access for minorities and women.[34] Also, there is no guarantee that jobs will be available when the program is completed. Finally, apprenticeship programs prepare trainees who are well trained in one craft or occupation. Due to the changing nature of jobs (thanks to new technology and use of cross-functional teams), many employers may be reluctant to employ workers from apprenticeship programs. Employers may believe that because apprentices are narrowly trained in one occupation or with one company, program graduates may have only company-specific skills and may be unable to acquire new skills or adapt their skills to changes in the workplace.

## Simulations

A **simulation** is a training method that represents a real-life situation, with trainees' decisions resulting in outcomes that mirror what would happen if they were on the job. A common example of the use of simulators for training is flight simulators for pilots. Simulations, which allow trainees to see the impact of their decisions in an artificial, risk-free environment, are used to teach production and process skills as well as management and interpersonal skills. As you will see in Chapter Eight, new technology has helped in the development of virtual reality, a type of simulation that even more closely mimics the work environment.

Simulators replicate the physical equipment that employees use on the job. For example, Time Warner Cable installers learn how to correctly install cable and high-speed Internet connections by crawling into two-story houses that have been built inside the company's training center.[35] Trainees drill through the walls and crawl around inside these houses, learning how to work with different types of homes. New call center employees at American Express learn in a simulated environment that replicates a real call center.[36] Trainees go to a lab that contains cubicles identical to those in the call center. All materials (binders, reference materials, supplies, etc.) are exactly the same as they would be in the call center. The simulator uses a replica of the call center database and includes a role play that uses speech recognition software to simulate live calls. After the call center trainees learn transactions, they answer simulated calls that require them to practice them. The simulator gives them feedback about errors that they made during the calls and shows them the correct action. The simulator also tracks the trainees' performance and alerts the instructors if a trainee is falling behind. The simulator prepares call center employees in thirty-two days, an improvement over the previous twelve-week program of classroom and OJT. Turnover among call center employees is 50 percent lower since employees began training in the simulated environment. American Express believes that the reduction in turnover is because the training environment better prepares new employees to deal with the noise and pace of a real call center.

Thirty high-potential global managers at Automatic Data Processing, Inc., in teams of six, participate in a computer-based business simulation that replicates the company's business model.[37] The team acts as the company's executive board, must operate a financially sound and profitable business through five rounds by creating growth opportunities in a competitive global market.

A key aspect of simulators is the degree to which they are similar to the equipment and situations that the trainee will encounter on the job. Recall the discussion of near transfer in Chapter Five, "Program Design." Simulators need to have elements identical to those found in the work environment. The simulator needs to respond exactly like the equipment would under the conditions and response given by the trainee. For example, flight simulators include distractions that pilots have to deal with, such as hearing chimes in the cockpit from traffic alerts generated by an onboard computer warning system while listening to directions from an air traffic controller.[38] For this reason, simulators are expensive to develop and need constant updating as new information about the work environment is obtained.

## Case Studies

A **case study** is a description about how employees or an organization dealt with a difficult situation. Trainees are required to analyze and critique the actions taken, indicating the appropriate actions and suggesting what might have been done differently.[39] A major assumption of the case study approach is that employees are most likely to recall and use knowledge and skills if they learn through a process of discovery.[40] Cases may be especially appropriate for developing higher-order intellectual skills such as analysis, synthesis, and evaluation. These skills are often required by managers, physicians, and other professional employees. Cases also help trainees develop the willingness to take risks given uncertain outcomes, based on their analysis of the situation. To use cases effectively, the learning environment must give trainees the opportunity to prepare and discuss their case analyses. Also, face-to-face or electronic communication among trainees must be arranged. Because trainee involvement is critical for the effectiveness of the case method, learners must be willing and able to analyze the case and then communicate and defend their positions.

Table 7.5 presents the process used for case development. The first step in the process is to identify a problem or situation. It is important to consider if the story is related to the instructional objectives, will provoke a discussion, forces decision making, can be told in a reasonable time period, and is applicable to the situations that trainees may face. Information on the problem or situation must also be readily accessible. The next step is to research documents, interview participants, and obtain data that provide the details of the case. The third step is to outline the story and link the details and exhibits to relevant points in the story. Fourth, the media used to present the case should be determined. Also, at this point in case development, the trainer should consider how the case exercise will be conducted. This may involve determining if trainees will work individually or in teams, and how the students will report results of their analyses. Finally, the actual case materials need to be prepared. This includes assembling exhibits (figures, tables, articles, job descriptions, etc.), writing the story, preparing questions to guide trainees' analysis, and writing an interesting, attention-getting case opening that will attract trainees' attention and provide a quick orientation to the case.

**TABLE 7.5**
**Process for Case Development**

Source: Based on J. Alden and J. K. Kirkhorn, "Case Studies," in *The ASTD Training and Development Handbook,* 4th ed., ed. R. L. Craig (New York: McGraw-Hill, 1996): 497–516.

1. Identify a story.
2. Gather information.
3. Prepare a story outline.
4. Decide on administrative issues.
5. Prepare case materials.

There are a number of available sources of preexisting cases. A major advantage of preexisting cases is that they are already developed, but a disadvantage is that the case may not actually relate to the work situation or problem that the trainee will encounter. It is especially important to review preexisting cases to determine how meaningful they will be to the trainee. Preexisting cases on a wide variety of problems in business management (e.g., in human resource management, operations, marketing, advertising, etc.) are available from Harvard Business School, the Darden Business School at the University of Virginia, Ivey Business School at the University of Western Ontario, and various other sources.

One organization that has effectively used case studies is the Central Intelligence Agency (CIA).[41] The cases are historically accurate and use actual data. For example, "The Libyan Attack" is used in management courses to teach leadership qualities. "The Stamp Case" is used to teach new employees about the agency's ethics structure. The CIA uses approximately 100 cases. One-third are focused on management; the rest focus on operations training, counterintelligence, and analysis. The cases are used in the training curriculum, where the objectives include teaching students to analyze and resolve complex, ambiguous situations. The CIA found that for the cases used in training programs to be credible and meaningful to trainees, the material had to be as authentic as possible and had to stimulate students to make decisions similar to those that they must make in their work environment. As a result, to ensure case accuracy, the CIA uses retired officers to research and write cases. The CIA has even developed a case writing workshop to prepare instructors to use the case method.

## Business Games

**Business games** require trainees to gather information, analyze it, and make decisions. Business games are primarily used for management skill development. Games stimulate learning because participants are actively involved and because games mimic the competitive nature of business. The types of decisions that participants make in games include all aspects of management practice: labor relations (agreement in contract negotiations), ethics, marketing (the price to charge for a new product), and finance (financing the purchase of new technology).

Typical games have the following characteristics.[42] The game involves a contest among trainees or teams of trainees or against an established criterion such as time or quantity. The game is designed to demonstrate an understanding of or application of a knowledge, skill, or behavior. Several alternative courses of action are available to trainees, and trainees can estimate the consequences of each alternative, but only with some uncertainty. Trainees do not know for certain what the consequences of their actions will be because the consequences are partially based on the decisions of other game participants. Finally, rules limit participant behavior.

To ensure learning and transfer of training, games used in training should be simple enough that trainees can play them in a short period of time. The best games generate excitement among the participants and interest in the game. Meaningfulness of the game is enhanced if it is realistic. Trainees need to feel that they are participating in a business and acquiring knowledge, skills, and behaviors that are useful on the job.[43] Debriefing from a trainer can help trainees understand the game experience and facilitate learning and transfer. Debriefing can include feedback, discussions of the concepts presented during the game, and instructions in how to use at work the knowledge, skills, or behavior emphasized in the game. Table 7.6 contains some questions that can be used for debriefing.

**TABLE 7.6**
**Questions to Use When Debriefing a Game**

Source: Based on S. Sugar, "Using Games to Energize Dry Material." In *The ASTD Handbook of Training Design and Delivery,* ed. G. Piskurich, P. Beckschi, and B. Hall (New York: McGraw-Hill, 2000): 107–120.

How did the score of the game affect your behavior and the behavior of the team?
What did you learn from the game?
What aspects of the game remind you of situations at work?
How does the game relate to your work?
What did you learn from the game that you plan to use at work?

At ConAgra Foods, new vice-presidents participate in a game on the last of eight days of leadership training.[44] Teams run a simulated business based on ConAgra, rotating through roles including sales and marketing, research and development, and finance. The teams compete for business and market share while developing their teamwork and other interpersonal skills. At the end of the game, ConAgra executives determine the winning teams based on financial measures, as well as team work skills. Sun Microsystems uses games to teach new employees the company structure, strategy, and history and to portray the company as innovative, with strong values. The game is set on a planet known as "Solaris," which has a society based on Sun's core values. The game includes groups of lost colonists who settle on the planet after wandering through space. The colonists make it their goal to create an information network (Sun is the company that founded the network). Enemies threaten the planet, and the players' task is to save it.

A review of research on computer games shows that trainees learn more when they are actively involved in learning the content (rather than reading text or listening), they have unlimited access to the game, and the game is used as a supplement to other training methods such as lecturing.[45] Games may give team members a quick start at developing a framework for information and may help develop cohesive groups. For some groups (such as senior executives), games may be more meaningful training activities (because the game is realistic) than are presentation techniques such as classroom instruction.

## Role Plays

**Role plays** refer to experiences in which trainees take on a role such as a manager, client, or disgruntled employee, and explore what is involved in the role.[46] Role plays are usually included in training programs involving interpersonal skills such as communications, sales, providing performance feedback, coaching, leadership, and team building. Role plays can be completed in small groups of two to three persons in which all trainees complete the role play. Or several trainees can volunteer to role play while the remaining trainees observe them. In a role play, outcomes depend on the emotional (and subjective) reactions of the other trainees.

At Wequassett Resort and Golf Club in Chatham, Massachusetts, the training schedule considers both the need to make guests happy and the need to help both new and returning employees learn to do that.[47] From April to October, the resort is closed, but 340 employees start work in the spring before the resort opens. Half of the employees are receiving training for the first time, while the returning employees need refresher training. Wequassett Academy offers seventy courses in four schools (customer intimacy, technical training, information and technology, and management). The goal of training is to provide the kind of service that will encourage guests to come back again, as well as recommend the resort to their friends. The resort's training is in step with its business, which requires a

**TABLE 7.7
Activities for
Effective Role
Plays**

Sources: Based on
S. Karve, "Setting the
stage for effective role
plays," *T+D*
(November 2011):
76–77; S. Thiagarajan,
"Instructional Games,
Simulations, and Role
Plays." In *The ASTD
Training and Devel-
opment Handbook*:
517–533.

Provide background information on the purpose of and context for the role play.
Make sure that a script is provided with enough detail for trainees to understand
their role.
The room is arranged so trainees can see and hear the role players.
Observations sheets and checklists that emphasize the issues in the role play are developed
and used.
Debriefing occurs on the experience of the role players and observers, the relationship of
the role play to the company context, and important learning points.

personal touch. Training involves classroom instruction with role plays, as well as the use
of DVDs. Employees have to successfully complete competency checklists before they are
able to work. For example, food servers may have to take courses in menu knowledge, food
service, and wine knowledge.

For role plays to be effective, trainers need to engage in several activities before, during,
and after the role play. Table 7.7 shows the activities that comprise effective role plays.

## Behavior Modeling

**Behavior modeling** presents trainees with a model who demonstrates key behaviors to
replicate and provides trainees with the opportunity to practice the key behaviors. Behavior
modeling is based on the principles of social learning theory (discussed in Chapter Four,
"Learning and Transfer of Training"), which emphasize that learning occurs by (1) observation of behaviors demonstrated by a model and (2) vicarious reinforcement. **Vicarious
reinforcement** occurs when a trainee sees a model receiving reinforcement for using
certain behaviors.

Behavior modeling is more appropriate for teaching skills and behaviors than for teaching factual information or knowledge. Research suggests that behavior modeling is one of
the most effective techniques for teaching interpersonal and computer skills.[48]

Table 7.8 presents the activities in a behavior modeling training session. These activities include an introduction, skill preparation and development, and application planning.[49]
Each training session, which typically lasts four hours, focuses on one interpersonal skill

**TABLE 7.8
Activities in
a Behavior
Modeling
Training
Program**

**Introduction (45 mins.)**
- Watch video that presents key behaviors.
- Listen to rationale for skill module.
- Discuss experiences in using skill.

**Skill Preparation and Development (2 hrs., 30 mins.)**
- View model.
- Participate in role plays and practice.
- Receive oral and video feedback on performance of key behaviors.

**Application Planning (1 hr.)**
- Set improvement goals.
- Identify situations in which to use key behaviors.
- Identify on-the-job applications of the key behaviors.

such as coaching or communicating ideas. Each session includes a presentation of the rationale behind the key behaviors, a video of a model performing the key behaviors, practice opportunities using role playing, evaluation of a model's performance in the videotape, and a planning session devoted to understanding how the key behaviors can be used on the job. In the practice sessions, trainees are provided with feedback regarding how closely their behavior matches the key behaviors demonstrated by the model. The role playing and modeled performance are based on actual incidents in the employment setting in which the trainee needs to demonstrate success.

Well-prepared behavior modeling training programs identify the key behaviors, create the modeling display, provide opportunities for practice, and facilitate transfer of training.[50] The first step in developing behavior modeling training programs is to determine (1) the tasks that are not being adequately performed due to lack of skill or behavior and (2) the key behaviors that are required to perform the task. A **key behavior** is one of a set of behaviors that are necessary to complete a task. In behavior modeling, key behaviors are typically performed in a specific order for the task to be completed. Key behaviors are identified through a study of the skills and behaviors necessary to complete the task and the skills or behaviors used by employees who are effective in completing the task.

Table 7.9 presents key behaviors for a behavior modeling training program on problem analysis. The table specifies behaviors that the trainee needs to engage in to be effective in problem analysis skills. Note that the key behaviors do not specify the exact behaviors needed at every step of solving a problem. Rather, the key behaviors in this skill module specify more general behaviors that are appropriate across a wide range of situations. If a task involves a clearly defined series of specific steps that must be accomplished in a specific order, then the key behaviors that are provided are usually more specific and explained in greater detail. For example, tennis players learning how to serve must follow a detailed sequence of activities (e.g., align feet with the baseline, take the racquet back over the head, toss the ball, bring the racquet forward over the head again, pronate the wrist, and strike the ball). People learning interpersonal skills must develop more general key behaviors because there is always more than one way to complete the task. The development of general key behaviors promotes far transfer (discussed in Chapter Five). That is, trainees are prepared to use the key behaviors in a variety of situations.

Another important consideration in developing behavior modeling programs is the modeling display. The **modeling display** provides the key behaviors that the trainees will practice to develop the same set of behaviors. Videotape is the predominant method used to present modeling displays, although computerized modeling displays are also being used.

**TABLE 7.9**

**Example of Key Behaviors in Problem Analysis**

Get all relevant information by:
- Rephrasing the question or problem to see if new issues emerge
- Listing the key problem issues
- Considering other possible sources of information

Identify possible causes.

If necessary, obtain additional information.

Evaluate the information to ensure that all essential criteria are met.

Restate the problem considering new information.

Determine what criteria indicate that the problem or issue has been resolved.

(The use of new technology in training is discussed in Chapter Eight.) Effective modeling displays have six characteristics:[51]

1. The display clearly presents the key behaviors. The music and the characteristics of the situation shown in the display do not interfere with the trainee seeing and understanding the key behaviors.
2. The model is credible to the trainees.
3. An overview of the key behaviors is presented.
4. Each key behavior is repeated. The trainee is shown the relationship between the behavior of the model and each key behavior.
5. A review of the key behaviors is included.
6. The display presents models engaging in both positive use of key behaviors and negative use (i.e., ineffective models not using the key behaviors).

Providing opportunities for practice involves (1) having trainees cognitively rehearse and think about the key behaviors and (2) placing trainees in situations (such as role plays) in which they have to use the key behaviors. Trainees may interact with one other person in the role play or in groups of three or more in which each trainee can practice the key behaviors. The most effective practice session allows trainees to practice the behaviors multiple times, in a small group of trainees where anxiety or evaluation apprehension is reduced, with other trainees who understand the company and the job.

Practice sessions should include a method for providing trainees with feedback that should provide reinforcement to the trainee for behaviors performed correctly, as well as information needed to improve behaviors. For example, if role plays are used, trainees can receive feedback from the other participants who serve as observers when not playing the role. Practice sessions may also be videotaped and played back to the trainees. The use of video objectively captures the trainees' behavior and provides useful, detailed feedback. Having the trainees view the video shows them specifically how they need to improve their behaviors and identifies behaviors that they are successfully replicating.

Behavior modeling helps ensure that transfer of training occurs by using application planning. **Application planning** prepares trainees to use the key behaviors on the job (i.e., enhances transfer of training). Application planning involves having all participants prepare a written document identifying specific situations in which they should use the key behaviors. Some training programs actually have trainees complete a "contract" outlining the key behaviors that they agree to use on the job. The trainer may follow up with the trainees to see if they are performing according to the contract. Application planning may also involve preparing trainees to deal with situational factors that may inhibit their use of the key behaviors (similar to relapse prevention, discussed in Chapter Four). As part of the application planning process, a trainee may be paired with another participant, with the stated expectation that the two should periodically communicate with each other to discuss successes and failures in the use of key behaviors.

# GROUP BUILDING METHODS

**Group building methods** are training methods designed to improve team or group effectiveness. A **team** refers to two or more people with specific roles or functions who work together with shared responsibility to achieve a common goal or mission or complete tasks in a company.[52] In group building methods, trainees share ideas and experiences, build group identity, understand the dynamics of interpersonal relationships, and get to know their own strengths and weaknesses and those of their coworkers. Group techniques focus on helping teams increase their skills for effective teamwork. A number of training techniques are available to improve work group or team performance, to establish a new team, or to improve interactions among different teams. All involve examination of feelings, perceptions, and beliefs about the functioning of the team; discussion; and development of plans to apply what was learned in training to the team's performance in the work setting. Group building methods include adventure learning, team training, and action learning.

Group building methods often involve experiential learning. **Experiential learning** training programs have four stages: (1) gain conceptual knowledge and theory; (2) take part in a behavioral simulation; (3) analyze the activity; and (4) connect the theory and activity with on-the-job or real-life situations.[53]

For experiential training programs to be successful, several guidelines should be followed. The program needs to tie in to a specific business problem. The trainees need to be moved outside their personal comfort zones, but within limits so as not to reduce trainee motivation or ability to understand the purpose of the program. Multiple learning modes should be used, including audio, visual, and kinesthetic. When preparing activities for an experiential training program, trainers should ask trainees for input on the program goals. Clear expectations about the purpose, expected outcomes, and trainees' role in the program are important. Finally, the training program needs to be evaluated. Training programs that include experiential learning should be linked to changes in employee attitudes, behaviors, and other business results. If training programs that involve experiential learning do not follow these guidelines, they may be questioned. For example, the U.S. Postal Inspector resigned after criticisms surfaced about postal team training activities. Current and former postal employees complained to several U.S. senators about training activities that included having employees wrap each other in toilet paper, dress as cats, and hold signs that spelled "teamwork."[54]

## Adventure Learning

**Adventure learning** is an experiential learning method that focuses on the development of teamwork and leadership skills through structured activities.[55] Adventure learning includes wilderness training, outdoor training, improvisational activities, drum circles, and even cooking classes. Adventure learning appears to be best suited for developing skills related to group effectiveness, such as self-awareness, problem solving, conflict management, and risk taking. Adventure learning may involve strenuous, challenging physical activities such as dogsledding or mountain climbing. Adventure learning can also use structured individual and group activities, such as wall climbing, rope courses, trust falls, ladder climbing, and traveling from one tower to another using a device attached to a wire that connects the two towers.

For example, "The Beam" requires team members to cross a six-foot-high beam placed between two trees, using only help from the team. Trainees can help by shouting advice and encouragement.[56] Rope-based activities may be held three to four feet or twenty-five to thirty feet above the ground. The high-ropes course is an individual-based exercise whose purpose is to help the trainee overcome fear. The low-ropes course requires the entire team of trainees to complete the course successfully. The purpose is to develop team identity, cohesiveness, and communication skills.

To improve their leadership skills and teamwork, lawyers at Weil, Gotshal, & Manges in New York worked with New York City firefighters to learn how to hook up a fire hose, set the water pressure, and extinguish fires.[57] At the fire academy, four-person teams rushed into burning buildings and rescued passengers in simulated subway accidents or other emergency drills. The Fire Department of New York (FDNY) program, Firefighter for a Day Team Challenge, was created to help teams develop decision-making and problem-solving skills. These skills are especially necessary for work teams made up of employees from different specialties or areas of expertise who work on large projects or deal with complex problems requiring coordination, delegation. Companies pay up to $2,500 for each four-person team.

Adventure learning can also include demanding activities that require coordination but place less of a physical strain on team members. In drum circles, each team member is given a drum, and facilitators work with the team to create a drumming orchestra. Toyota spent $20,000 for drums to accommodate forty people at its training center in Torrance, California.[58] Drum circles are held twice a week. Toyota believes that the drum circles are metaphors for how high-performance teams should operate: cooperatively and smoothly. Cookin' Up Change is one of many team-building courses offered around the United States by chefs, caterers, hotels, and cooking schools.[59] These courses have been used by companies such as Honda and Microsoft. The idea is that cooking classes help strengthen communications and networking skills by requiring team members to work together to create a full-course meal. Each team has to decide who does what kitchen tasks (e.g., cooking, cutting, cleaning, etc.) and who prepares the main course, salads, and dessert. Often, team members are required to switch assignments in mid-preparation to see how the team reacts to change.

For adventure learning programs to be successful, exercises should relate to the types of skills that participants are expected to develop. Also, after the exercises, a skilled facilitator should lead a discussion about what happened in the exercise, what was learned, how events in the exercise relate to the job situation, and how to set goals and apply what was learned on the job.[60] California-based Quantum Corporation developed a project to overhaul the company's online infrastructure across global operations.[61] The project included a diverse group of team members from the information technology, engineering, marketing, and graphic design departments. The team consisted of very talented employees who were not used to working with each other. Many of the team members were geographically dispersed, which increased the difficulties of working together. Quantum hired a group of actors to lead the team through a series of improvisational activities designed to get the team members to share personal stories. Using music, props, lighting, and costumes, the actors interpreted the stories told by team members. The actors portrayed team members who, for example, expressed isolation and frustration. Other times, team members would play the parts. The sessions allowed each team member to ask questions of the actors or each other. The team came away from the activity with more empathy and understanding for each other. Development of the personal relationships created positive interpersonal bonds that helped the team meet deadlines and complete projects.

This approach does have disadvantages, however. The physical demands of some types of adventure learning and the requirement that trainees often touch each other in the exercises may increase a company's risk for negligence claims due to personal injury, intentional infliction of emotional distress, and invasion of privacy. Also, the Americans with Disabilities Act (ADA) raises questions about requiring disabled employees to participate in physically demanding training experiences.[62]

Given the physically demanding nature of adventure learning, it is important to consider when to use it instead of another training method. Adventure learning allows trainees to interact interpersonally in a situation not governed by formal business rules. This type of environment may be important for employees to mold themselves into a cohesive work team. Also, adventure learning exercises allow trainees to share a strong emotional experience. Significant emotional experiences can help trainees break difficult behavior patterns and open trainees to change their behaviors. One of the most important characteristics of adventure learning is that the exercises can serve as metaphors for organizational behavior. That is, trainees will behave in the same way in the exercises that they would when working as a team (e.g., developing a product launch plan). As a result, by analyzing behaviors that occur during the exercise, trainees gain insight into ineffective behaviors.

Does adventure learning work? Rigorous evaluations of its impact on productivity or performance have not been conducted. However, former participants often report that they gained a greater understanding of themselves and how they interact with coworkers.[63] One key to an adventure learning program's success may be the insistence that whole work groups participate together so that group dynamics that inhibit effectiveness can emerge and be discussed.

## Team Training

**Team training** refers to training that is designed to improve team effectiveness. There are many different types of teams in companies, including production teams, service teams, committees, project teams, and management teams. Teamwork tends to be episodic.[64] That is, teams engage in a cycle of identifying their goals, engage in interpersonal interactions, and take actions to achieve their goals. They repeat this cycle as goals are reached and tasks are completed and they move on to new tasks or goals. Regardless of the type of team, successful team performance depends on the knowledge, attitudes, and behaviors of its members. Figure 7.3 shows the three components of team performance: knowledge, attitudes, and behavior.[65] The behavioral requirement means that team members must perform actions that allow them to communicate, coordinate, adapt, and complete complex tasks to accomplish their objective. The knowledge component requires team members to have mental models or memory structures that allow them to function effectively in unanticipated or new situations. Team members' beliefs about the task and feelings toward each other relate to the attitude component. Team morale, cohesion, and identity are related to team performance. For example, in the military, as well as many areas of the private sector (e.g., nuclear power plants and commercial airlines), much work is performed by crews, groups, or teams. Successful performance depends on coordination of individual activities to make decisions, on team performance, and on readiness to deal with potentially

**FIGURE 7.3**
**Components of team performance**

Source: Based on E. Salas and J. A. Cannon-Bowers, "Strategies for Team Training." In *Training for 21st-Century Technology: Applications of Psychological Research,* eds. M. A. Quinones and A. Dutta (Washington, D.C.: American Psychological Association, 1997): 249–281.

**FIGURE 7.4**

**Main Elements of the Structure of Team Training**

Sources: Based on E. Salas and J. A. Cannon-Bowers, "Strategies for Team Training," in *Training for 21st-Century Technology: Applications of Psychological Research*, eds. M. A. Quinones and A. Dutta (Washington, D.C.: American Psychological Association, 1997): 249–281; J. Cannon-Bowers and C. Bowers, "Team Development and Functioning." In S. Zedeck (eds.). *APA Handbook of Industrial and Organizational Psychology* (Washington, D.C.: American Psychological Association, 2011): 597–650.

dangerous situations (e.g., an overheating nuclear reactor). Research suggests that teams that are effectively trained develop procedures to identify and resolve errors, coordinate information gathering, and reinforce each other.[66]

Figure 7.4 illustrates the four main elements of the structure of team training (tools, methods, strategies, and team training objectives). Several tools help to define and organize the delivery of team training.[67] These tools also provide the environment (e.g., feedback) needed for learning to occur. These tools work in combination with different training methods to help create instructional strategies. These strategies are a combination of the methods, tools, and content required to perform effectively.

The strategies include cross training, coordination training, and team leader training. **Cross training** has team members understand and practice each other's skills so that members are prepared to step in and take the place of a member who may temporarily or permanently leave the team. Research suggests that most work teams would benefit from providing members with at least enough understanding of teammates' roles to discuss trade-offs of various strategies and behaviors that affect team performance.[68] **Coordination training** instructs the team in how to share information and decision-making responsibilities to maximize team performance. Coordination training is especially important for commercial aviation or surgical teams who are in charge of monitoring different aspects of equipment and the environment but who must share information to make the most effective decisions regarding patient care or aircraft safety and performance. **Team leader training** refers to training that the team manager or facilitator receives. This may involve training the manager on how to resolve conflict within the team or helping the team coordinate activities or other team skills. **Scenario-based training** refers to training that places team members in a realistic context while learning. This type of team training helps trainees experience the consequences of their actions, make adjustments, accomplish their tasks, and build team self-efficacy (feeling that the team can successfully perform tasks). **Guided team self-correction** refers to training that emphasizes continuous learning and knowledge sharing in teams. In this type of training, team members observe each other's behavior and give and receive performance feedback.

Employees obviously need technical skills that can help the team accomplish its task. But team members also need skills in communication, adaptability, conflict resolution, and other teamwork issues.[69] Team training usually involves multiple methods. For example, a lecture or video may be used to disseminate knowledge regarding communication skills to trainees. Role plays or simulations may be used to give trainees the opportunity to put into practice the communication skills emphasized in the lecture. Regardless of the method chosen, opportunities for practice and feedback need to be included.

For example, Aquarius is an undersea laboratory used during the NASA Extreme Environment Mission Operations (NEEMO). The base, located several miles off the coast of Key Largo, Florida, is owned by the National Oceanic and Atmospheric Administration (NOAA) and managed by the University of North Carolina.[70] The NEEMO experience places astronauts in an environment with challenges that parallels the hostile physical and stressful psychological environment experienced in long-duration missions. These challenges can include allowing the crew to experience the effects of gravity in space, on the moon, and Mars, providing a compressed timeline for completing tasks, practicing procedures such as spacewalks to repair or replace equipment and emergency procedures used to rescue crew members, and performing tasks with delayed and limited communications with the mission control crew. The NEEMO experience helps crew members develop important team processes, such as communication, coordination, performance monitoring and back up behaviors, to successfully meet the challenges and perform the task they encounter, both in Aquarius and on their space missions.

United Airlines sent its supervisor, or lead, ramp employees to Pit Instruction and Training (Pit Crew U), which focuses on the preparation, practices, and teamwork of NASCAR pit crews. United is using the training to develop standardized methods to safely and more efficiently unload, load, and send off its airplanes.[71] Pit Instruction and Training, located outside Charlotte, North Carolina, has a quarter-mile race track and a pit road with pit stops for six cars. The school offers programs to train new racing pit crews, but most of its business comes from companies interested in teaching their teams to work as safely, efficiently, and effectively as NASCAR pit crews do. NASCAR pit crews work safely, quickly, and efficiently because each crew member knows what tasks to do (change tires, use an air gun, add gasoline, or clean up spills), and after the crew members have finished servicing the race car, they move new equipment into position in anticipation of the next pit stop. At Pit Crew U, trainees actually work as pit crews. They learn how to handle jacks, change tires, and fill fuel tanks on race cars. They are videotaped and timed just like real pit crews, and they receive feedback from trainers and from professional pit crew members who work on NASCAR teams. Also, the program requires trainees to deal with unforeseen circumstances similar to what they may encounter on the job. For example, at one pit stop, lug nuts had been sprinkled intentionally in the area where the race car stops, and the United employees were observed to see whether they noticed the lug nuts and cleaned them up. On their jobs, ramp employees are responsible for removing debris from the tarmac so that it is not sucked into jet engines or does not harm equipment. At another pit stop, United teams had to work with fewer members, which sometimes occurs when ramp crews are understaffed due to absences.

United's training is part of a multimillion-dollar investment that includes updating equipment and providing bag scanners. The purpose of the training is to standardize the tasks of ramp team members, to reinforce the need for ramp teams to be orderly and communicative, and to increase morale. Training has been optional for ramp employees, and they have survived layoffs and have been asked to make wage concessions to help pull the company out of bankruptcy. United has already started scheduling shorter ground times at some airports in anticipation of the positive results of the program. With shorter ground times, United can offer more daily flights without having to buy more airplanes. United hopes to make the airline more competitive by cutting the average airplane ground time by eight minutes.

## Action Learning

**Action learning** gives teams or work groups an actual problem, has them work on solving it and committing to an action plan, and then holds them accountable for carrying out the plan.[72] Companies use action learning to solve important problems, develop leaders, quickly build high-performance teams, and transform the organizational culture. Table 7.10 shows the steps involved in action learning. Several types of problems are addressed in action learning, including how to change the business, better use technology, remove barriers between the customer and company, and develop global leaders. Typically, action learning involves between six and thirty employees. It may also include customers and vendors. There are several variations in the composition of the group. One variation is that the group includes a single customer for the problem being dealt with. Sometimes

**Table 7.10 Steps in Action Learning**

Sources: Based on M. Marquardt, "Harnessing the power of action learning," *T+D* (June 2004): 26–32; D. Dotlich and J. Noel, *Action Learning* (San Francisco: Jossey-Bass, 1998).

- Identification of the sponsors of action learning, including CEOs and top managers
- Identification of the problem or issue
- Identification and selection of the group who can address the problem
- Identification of coaches who can help the group reframe the problem and improve its problem solving by listening, giving feedback, offering assumptions, and so on
- Presentation of the problem to the group
- Group discussion that includes reframing the problem and agreement on what the problem is, what the group should do to solve the problem, and how the group should proceed
- Data gathering and analysis relevant to solving the problem, done by the group as a whole as well as by individual members
- Group presentation on how to solve the problem, with the goal of securing a commitment from the sponsors to act on the group's recommendations
- Self-reflection and debriefing (e.g., What have the group and group members learned? What might they have done differently?)

the groups include cross-functional representatives who all have a stake in the problem. For example, Novartis, a company that has business in pharmaceuticals (such as Sandoz) and in consumer and animal health care, uses action learning to work on issues (such as marketing) that are important to all of the company's core businesses.[73] Or the group may involve employees from multiple functions who all focus on their own functional problems, each contributing to solving the problems identified. Employees are asked to develop novel ideas and solutions in a short period of time. The teams usually need to gather data for problem solving by visiting customers, employees, academics, and/or industry leaders. Once the teams have gathered data and developed their recommendations they are required to present them to top-level executives.

ATC, a public transportation services management company in Illinois, used action learning to help boost profitability by reducing operating costs.[74] Employees were divided into Action Workout Teams to identify ways of reducing costs and to brainstorm effective solutions. The process assumed that employees closest to where the work gets done have the best ideas about how to solve problems. Teams of five to seven employees met once a week for a couple of hours for forty-five to sixty days. For example, a team working on parts inventory might have had a parts clerk, a couple of people from maintenance, a supervisor, and an operations employee. These teams studied problems and issues such as overtime, preventive maintenance, absenteeism, parts inventory, and inefficient safety inspection procedures. The teams brainstormed ideas, prioritized them according to their highest potential, developed action plans, installed them, tested them, and measured the outcomes. The solutions that the teams generated resulted in more than $1.8 million in savings for the company.

### Six Sigma, Black Belt Training, and Kaizen

Six Sigma and Kaizen, black belt training programs, involve principles of action learning. Six Sigma and Kaizen provide employees with measurement and statistical tools to help reduce defects and to cut costs.[75] Six Sigma is a quality standard with a goal of no more than 3.4 defects per million processes. There are several levels of Six Sigma training, resulting in employees becoming certified as green belts, champions, or black belts.[76] To become black belts, trainees must participate in workshops and written assignments coached by expert instructors. The training involves four four-day sessions over about sixteen weeks. Between training sessions, candidates apply what they learn to assigned projects and then use them in the next training session. Trainees are also required to complete not only oral and written exams but also two or more projects that have a significant impact on the company's bottom line. After completing black belt training, employees are able to develop, coach, and lead Six Sigma teams; mentor and give advice to management on useful Six Sigma projects; and provide Six Sigma tools and statistical methods to team members. After black belts lead several project teams, they can take additional training and be certified as master black belts. Master black belts can teach other black belts and help senior managers integrate Six Sigma into the company's business goals.

McKesson Corporation trained fifteen to twenty black belts and reassigned them to their original business units as their team's Six Sigma representatives.[77] When the two-year commitment ends, the black belts return to the business at higher positions, helping to spread the approach throughout the organization and ensuring that key leaders are committed to the Six Sigma philosophy. In most divisions of the company, Six Sigma training is mandated for senior vice presidents, who attend training that introduces Six Sigma and details how to identify a potential Six Sigma project. Across the company, every manager and director is expected to attend basic training. The Six Sigma effort has shown benefits every year since the program started in 1999.

Just Born, the company that makes Mike and Ike and Peeps candies, uses the Wow . . . Now Improvement Process, a customized Kaizen process to improve business processes and results.[78] The Wow . . . Now Improvement Process includes training employees how to identify improvement opportunities, collect data, make improvements, measure results, and refine practices based on the results. *Kaizen,* the Japanese word for improvement, is one of the underlying principles of lean manufacturing and total quality management (we discussed lean thinking in Chapter One). **Kaizen** refers to practices participated in by employees from all levels of the company that focus on continuous improvement of business processes.[79] As the Wow . . . Now Improvement Process illustrates, Kaizen involves considering a continuous cycle of activities, including planning, doing, checking, and acting (PDCA). Statistical process control techniques are used by employees to identify causes of problems and potential solutions. They include process flow analysis, cause-and-effect diagrams, control charts, histograms, and scattergrams.

Although action learning has not been formally evaluated, the process appears to maximize learning and transfer of training because it involves real-time problems that employees are facing. Also, action learning can be useful for identifying dysfunctional team dynamics that can get in the way of effective problem solving. Action learning at General Electric has required employees to use and apply skills to team building, problem solving, change management, conflict resolution, communications, coaching, and facilitation. General Electric believes that action learning has resulted in such benefits as greater speed in decision making and implementation, employees who work more easily across borders and business units, management that is willing to take more risks, and an increase in open dialogue and trust among employees.[80]

# CHOOSING A TRAINING METHOD

As a trainer or manager, you will likely be asked to choose a training method. Given the large number of training methods available to you, this task may seem difficult. One way to choose a training method is to compare methods. Table 7.11 evaluates each training method discussed in this chapter according to a number of characteristics. The types of learning outcomes related to each method are identified. Also, for each method, a high, medium, or low rating is provided for each characteristic of the learning environment, for transfer of training, for cost, and for effectiveness.

How might you use this table to choose a training method? The first step in choosing a method is to identify the type of learning outcome that you want training to influence. As discussed in Chapter Four, these outcomes include verbal information, intellectual skills, cognitive strategies, attitudes, and motor skills. Training methods may influence one or several learning outcomes. Research on specific learning methods has shown that for learning to be effective, the instructional method needs to match the desired learning outcome. For example, research on behavior modeling and role playing shows that these methods lead to positive results, but their effectiveness varies according to the evaluation criteria used.[81] This emphasizes that the particular learning *method* used to deliver learning is not

**TABLE 7.11** Comparison of Training Methods

| | Presentation | | | Hands-On | | | | | | | Group Building | | |
| | Lecture | Video | OJT | Self-Directed Learning | Apprenticeship | Simulation | Case Study | Business Games | Role Playing | Behavior Modeling | Adventure Learning | Team Training | Action Learning |
|---|---|---|---|---|---|---|---|---|---|---|---|---|---|
| **Learning Outcome** | | | | | | | | | | | | | |
| Verbal information | Yes | Yes | Yes | Yes | Yes | No | Yes | Yes | No | No | No | No | No |
| Intellectual skills | Yes | No | No | Yes | Yes | Yes | Yes | Yes | No | No | No | Yes | No |
| Cognitive strategies | Yes | No | Yes | Yes | No | Yes | Yes | Yes | Yes | Yes | Yes | Yes | Yes |
| Attitudes | Yes | Yes | No | No | No | No | No | No | Yes | No | Yes | Yes | Yes |
| Motor skills | No | Yes | Yes | No | Yes | Yes | No | No | No | Yes | No | No | No |
| **Learning Environment** | | | | | | | | | | | | | |
| Clear objective | Medium | Low | High | High | High | High | Medium | High | Medium | High | Medium | High | High |
| Practice | Low | Low | High | High | High | High | Medium | Medium | Medium | High | Medium | High | Medium |
| Meaningfulness | Medium | Medium | High | Medium | High | High | Medium | Medium | Medium | Medium | Low | High | High |
| Feedback | Low | Low | High | Medium | High | High | Medium | High | Medium | High | Medium | Medium | High |
| Observation and interaction with others | Low | Medium | High | Medium | High | High | High | High | High | High | High | High | High |
| **Transfer of Training** | Low | Low | High | Medium | High | High | Medium | Medium | Medium | High | Low | High | High |
| **Cost** | | | | | | | | | | | | | |
| Development | Medium | Medium | Medium | High | High | High | Medium | High | Medium | Medium | Medium | Medium | Low |
| Administrative | Low | Low | Low | Medium | High | Low | Low | Medium | Medium | Medium | Medium | Medium | Medium |
| **Effectiveness** | High for verbal information | Medium | High for structured OJT | Medium | High | High | Medium | Medium | Medium | High | Low | Medium | High |

what is most important. Rather, the choice of the learning method should be based on the desired learning outcomes and the features that facilitate learning and transfer of training. Once you have identified a learning method, the next step is to consider the extent to which the method facilitates learning and transfer of training, the costs related to the development and use of the method, and its effectiveness.

As was discussed in Chapter Four, for learning to occur, trainees must understand the objectives of the training program, training content should be meaningful, and trainees should have the opportunity to practice and receive feedback. Also, a powerful way to learn is through observing and interacting with others. As you may recall from Chapter Five, transfer of training refers to the extent to which training will be used on the job. In general, the more the training content and environment prepare trainees for use of learning outcomes on the job, the greater the likelihood that transfer will occur. As discussed in Chapter Six, "Training Evaluation," two types of costs are important: development costs and administrative costs. Development costs relate to design of the training program, including costs to buy or create the program. Administrative costs are incurred each time that the training method is used. These include costs related to consultants, instructors, materials, and trainers. The effectiveness rating is based on both academic research and practitioner recommendations.

Several trends in Table 7.11 are worth noting. First, there is considerable overlap between learning outcomes across the training methods. Group building methods are unique because they focus on individual as well as team learning (e.g., improving group processes). If you are interested in improving the effectiveness of groups or teams, you should choose one of the group building methods (e.g., adventure learning, team training, or action learning). Second, comparing the presentation methods to the hands-on methods illustrates that most hands-on methods provide a better learning environment and transfer of training than do the presentation methods. The presentation methods are also less effective than the hands-on methods. If you are not limited by the amount of money that can be used for development or administration, choose a hands-on method over a presentation method. The training budget for developing training methods can influence the method chosen. If you have a limited budget for developing new training methods, use structured OJT—a relatively inexpensive yet effective hands-on method. If you have a larger budget, you might want to consider hands-on methods that facilitate transfer of training, such as simulators. Keep in mind that many of the methods discussed in this chapter can be adapted for use in online learning, e-learning, and distance learning. These training methods are discussed in Chapter Eight.

If possible, you may want to use several different methods within a single training program to capitalize on the different strengths of each method for facilitating learning and transfer. For example, the Home Depot uses self-paced materials, a video-based course, and instructor-led training to train appliance salespeople.[82] Self-paced training is used to instruct employees about an appliance category (e.g., dishwashers) and to help them understand the products available at the store. The video-based program teaches salespersons to emphasize each product's features and benefits to customers. Salespeople participate in role playing and are evaluated on their ability to follow the company's selling strategies. All salespeople must also complete an eight-hour instructor-led course that helps them evaluate customers' needs, answer questions, and make the sale. The instructor-led course includes role plays so salespeople can practice selling to customers.

**Summary**

Companies are using a variety of training methods to guide competency development and contextual learning. Although new technology such as social networks are being used by some companies for training delivery and instruction, most training is still conducted face to face with an instructor. This chapter discussed traditional face-to-face training methods, including presentation, hands-on, and group building training methods. Presentation methods (such as lecturing) are effective for efficiently communicating information (knowledge) to a large number of trainees. Presentation methods need to be supplemented with opportunities for trainees to practice, discuss, and receive feedback to facilitate learning. Hands-on methods get trainees directly involved in learning. Hands-on methods are ideal for developing skills and behaviors. Hands-on methods include OJT, simulations, self-directed learning, business games, case studies, role playing, and behavior modeling. These methods can be expensive to develop but incorporate the conditions needed for learning and transfer of training to occur. Group building methods such as team training, action learning, and adventure learning focus on helping teams increase the skills needed for effective teamwork (e.g., self-awareness, conflict resolution, and coordination) and help build team cohesion and identity. Group building techniques may include the use of presentation methods, as well as exercises during which team members interact and communicate with each other. Team training has a long history of success in preparing flight crews and surgical teams, but its effectiveness for developing management teams has not been clearly established.

## Key Terms

traditional training methods, *279*
presentation methods, *280*
lecture, *280*
audiovisual instruction, *282*
hands-on methods, *283*
on-the-job training (OJT), *283*
self-directed learning, *286*
apprenticeship, *287*
simulation, *290*

case study, *290*
business games, *292*
role plays, *293*
behavior modeling, *294*
vicarious reinforcement, *294*
key behavior, *295*
modeling display, *295*
application planning, *296*
group building methods, *296*
team, *296*

experiential learning, *297*
adventure learning, *297*
team training, *299*
cross training, *300*
coordination training, *300*
team leader training, *301*
scenario-based training, *301*
guided team self-correction, *301*
action learning, *302*
kaizen, *304*

## Discussion Questions

1. What are the differences between social contextual learning and guided competency development? Are both types of learning (and associated training methods) necessary? Explain.
2. What are the strengths and weaknesses of the lecture, the case study, and behavior modeling?
3. If you had to choose between adventure learning and action learning for developing an effective team, which would you choose? Defend your choice.
4. Discuss the process of behavior modeling training.

5. How can the characteristics of the trainee affect self-directed learning?

6. What are the components of effective team performance? How might training strengthen these components?

7. Table 7.11 compares training methods on a number of characteristics. Explain why simulation and behavior modeling receive high ratings for transfer of training.

8. What are some reasons why on-the-job training (OJT) can prove ineffective? What can be done to ensure its effectiveness?

9. Why are apprenticeship programs attractive to employees? Why are they attractive to companies?

10. Discuss the steps of an action learning program. Which aspect of action learning do you think is most beneficial for learning? Which aspect is most beneficial for transfer of training? Explain why. Defend your choices.

## Application Assignments

1. Choose a job with which you are familiar. Develop a self-directed learning module for a skill that is important for that job.

2. Go to www.sabrehq.com, the website for Sabre Corporate Development. Click on Team Building Events. Choose one of the activities and events found on this page, and review it. Discuss what you would do to ensure that the team building event you selected is successful.

3. Divide into teams of two students. One student should be designated as a "trainer," the other as a "trainee." The trainee should briefly leave the room while the trainer reads the instructions for folding a paper cup. After the trainers have read the instructions, the trainees should return to the room. The trainers should then train the trainees in how to fold a paper cup (which should take about 15 minutes). When the instructor calls time, the trainers should note the steps they followed to conduct the training. The trainees should record their evaluations of the strengths and weaknesses of the training session (5–10 minutes). If time allows, switch roles.

## SUPPLEMENT TO APPLICATION ASSIGNMENT 3
*Steps and Key Points in Folding a Paper Cup:*

| Steps in the Operation | Key Points |
| --- | --- |
| Step: A logical segment of the operation in which something is done to advance the task. | Key point: Any directions or bits of information that help to perform the step correctly, safely, and easily. |
| Place 8 1/2″ × 11″ sheet of paper in front of you on a flat surface. | 1. Be sure that the surface is flat—free of interfering objects. |
| Fold the lower-left corner up. | 2a. Line up the right edges.<br>  b. Make a sharp crease. |

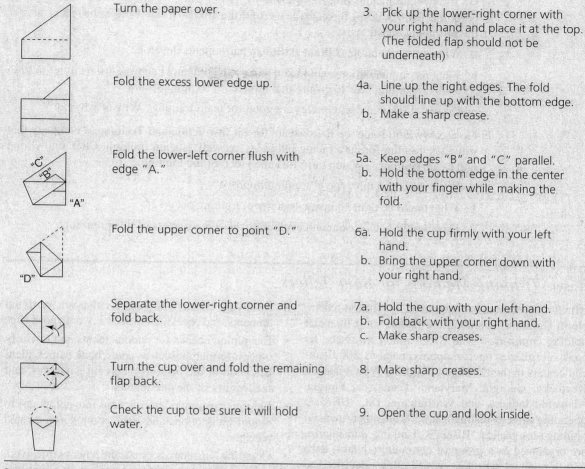

| | |
|---|---|
| Turn the paper over. | 3. Pick up the lower-right corner with your right hand and place it at the top. (The folded flap should not be underneath) |
| Fold the excess lower edge up. | 4a. Line up the right edges. The fold should line up with the bottom edge.<br>b. Make a sharp crease. |
| Fold the lower-left corner flush with edge "A." | 5a. Keep edges "B" and "C" parallel.<br>b. Hold the bottom edge in the center with your finger while making the fold. |
| Fold the upper corner to point "D." | 6a. Hold the cup firmly with your left hand.<br>b. Bring the upper corner down with your right hand. |
| Separate the lower-right corner and fold back. | 7a. Hold the cup with your left hand.<br>b. Fold back with your right hand.<br>c. Make sharp creases. |
| Turn the cup over and fold the remaining flap back. | 8. Make sharp creases. |
| Check the cup to be sure it will hold water. | 9. Open the cup and look inside. |

Source: From P. Decker and B. Nathan, *Behavior Modeling Training* (New York: Praeger Scientific, 1985).

Be prepared to discuss the training process and your reactions as a trainer or trainee. Also, be prepared to discuss the extent to which the training followed the steps for effective OJT.

4. Review one of the following websites, which feature simulations: www.income-outcome.com or www.celemi.com.

   Describe the situation that the simulation is designed to represent. What elements in the simulation replicate the work environment? How could the simulation be improved to ensure that learning and transfer of training occur?

5. Watch the Wendy's training video on YouTube at www.youtube.com/watch?v=eOuHZDGK-kY.

   How is this video effective for helping staff learn how to serve Wendy's food to customers? What would you add to the video to increase its effectiveness?

6. Go to www.drumcafe.com, the website for Drum Cafe, a company that specializes in corporate team building through the use of drum circles. Review the website and answer the following questions:

   a. What are drum circles? What skills can participants develop?

   b. What recommendations would you make to a company that uses drum circles to train teams regarding how to ensure that transfer of training occurs?

   c. Do you think that drum circles are good for team training? Why or why not?

7. Go to www.5off5on.com, the website for Pit Instruction and Training, a company that provides training for auto racing pit crews, as well as team training. Click on "Group and Lean Training." Watch the YouTube video of the training.

   a. What skills can this type of training improve?

   b. What could be done to insure transfer of training occurs?

   c. How would you recommend evaluating the effectiveness of this program?

---

# Case: *Training Methods for Bank Tellers*

BB&T Corporation, headquartered in Winston-Salem, North Carolina, is among the nation's top financial holding companies, with $152 billion in assets. Its bank subsidiaries operate approximately 1,500 financial centers in the Carolinas, Virginia, West Virginia, Kentucky, Georgia, Maryland, Tennessee, Florida, Alabama, Indiana, and Washington, D.C. BB&T's operating strategy distinguishes it from other financial holding companies. BB&T's banking subsidiaries are organized as a group of community banks, each with a regional president, which allows decisions to be made locally, close to the client. This also makes BB&T's client service more responsive, reliable, and empathetic. BB&T was experiencing a 30 percent annual turnover rate for bank tellers and decided that its on-the-job training (OJT) was ineffective. The bank tellers' tasks include:

- Balancing currency, coin, and checks in cash drawers at the end of each shift, and calculating daily transactions using computers, calculators, or adding machines
- Cashing checks and paying out money after verifying that signatures are correct, that written and numerical amounts agree, and that accounts have sufficient funds

- Receiving checks and cash for deposit, verifying amounts, and checking the accuracy of deposit slips
- Examining checks for endorsements and to verify other information such as dates, bank names, identification of the persons receiving payments, and the legality of the documents
- Entering customers' transactions into computers to record transactions and issue computer-generated receipts
- Counting currency, coins, and checks received, either by hand or using a currency-counting machine, to prepare them for deposit or shipment to branch banks or the Federal Reserve Bank
- Preparing and verifying cashier's checks
- Sorting and filing deposit slips and checks
- Ordering a supply of cash to meet daily needs
- Receiving and counting daily inventories of cash drafts and travelers' checks

On a daily basis, tellers use a variety of skills to complete their tasks. These include:

- *Communicating with supervisors, peers, or subordinates*—Providing information to supervisors, coworkers, and subordinates either by telephone, in written form, via e-mail, or in person

- *Monitoring process, materials, or surroundings*— Monitoring and reviewing information from materials, events, or the environment, to detect or assess problems
- *Identifying objects actions, and events*—Identifying information by categorizing, estimating recognizing differences or similarities, and detecting changes in circumstances or events
- *Establishing and maintaining interpersonal relationships*—Developing constructive and cooperative working relationships with others, and maintaining them over time
- *Performing for or working directly with the public*— This includes providing services for bank customers
- *Interacting with computers*—Using computers and computer systems (including hardware and software) to program, write software, set up functions, enter data, or process information
- *Evaluating information to determine compliance with standards*—Using relevant information and individual judgment to determine whether events or processes comply with laws, regulations, or standards
- *Getting information*—Observing, receiving, and otherwise obtaining information from all relevant sources
- *Making decisions and solving problems*—Analyzing information and evaluating results to choose the best solution and solve problems
- *Processing information*—Compiling, coding, categorizing, calculating, tabulating, auditing, or verifying information or data

*Describe the training method or combination of training methods that you would recommend to train BB&T's bank tellers. Justify your choice of methods.*

**Sources:** Based on "BB&T Winston-Salem, North Carolina, Channeling Aristotle," *T+D* (October 2008): 50–52; www.bbt.com, website for BB&T. Tasks and work responsibilities are taken from http://onlinecenter.onet.org, O*Net online summary report for bank tellers (Job Code 43-0071.00). (Accessed January 23, 2012.)

# Endnotes

1. J. Meister and K. Willyerd, *The 2020 Workplace* (New York: HarperCollins, 2010).
2. K. Kraiger, "Transforming our models of learning and development: Web-based instruction as enabler of third-generation instruction," *Industrial and Organizational Psychology: Perspectives on Science and Practice*, 1 (2008): 454–457.
3. B, Bell, and S. Kozlowski,"Goal orientation and ability: Interactive effects on self-efficacy, performance, and knowledge,"*Journal of Applied Psychology*, 87 (2002): 495–505; J. Colquitt, J. LePine, and R. Noe, "Toward an integrative theory of training motivation: A meta-analytic path analysis of 20 years of research," *Journal of Applied Psychology*, 85 (2000): 678–707.
4. M. Green, and E. McGill, E. *State of the Industry, 2011* (Alexandria, VA: American Society for Training and Development, 2011).
5. J. Salopek, "Colorado Springs Utility: 2005 BEST Award Winner," *T+D* (October 2005): 38–40.
6. J. Breal, "Secret Sauce," *Fast Company* (May 2007): 61–63.
7. M. Green, and E. McGill, *State of the Industry, 2011* (Alexandria, VA: American Society for Training and Development, 2011); "2011 Training Industry Report," *Training* (November/December 2011): 22–35.
8. M. Van Wart, N. J. Cayer, and S. Cook, *Handbook of Training and Development for the Public Sector* (San Francisco: Jossey-Bass, 1993); R. S. House, "Classroom Instruction."In *The ASTD Training and Development Handbook,* 4th ed., ed. R. L. Craig (New York: McGraw-Hill, 1996): 437–452.
9. M. Van Wart, N. J. Cayer, and S. Cook, *Handbook of Training and Development for the Public Sector* (San Francisco: Jossey-Bass, 1993).
10. K. Tyler, "15 Ways to Train on the Job," *HR Magazine* (September 2008): 105–108.
11. "Constellation Energy," *T+D* (October 2008): 35–36.
12. H. Dolezalek, "Industry Training Report," *Training* (October 2004): 33–34.

13. T. Skylar, "When Training Collides with a 35-Ton Truck," *Training* (March 1996): 32–38.

14. L. Ford, "Caught on Tape," *T+D* (December 2005): 63–64.

15. R. B. Cohn, "How to Choose a Video Producer," *Training* (July 1996): 58–61.

16. R. DeRouin, T. Parrish, and E. Salas, "On-the-job training: Tips for ensuring success," *Ergonomics in Design* 13 (Spring 2005): 23–26; D. Gallup and K. Beauchemin, "On-the-job training." In *The ASTD Handbook of Training Design and Delivery,* ed. G. Piskurich, P. Beckschi, and B. Hall (New York: McGraw-Hill, 2000): 121–132.

17. R. DeRouin, T. Parrish, and E. Salas, "On-the-job training: Tips for ensuring success," *Ergonomics in Design* 13 (Spring 2005): 23–26; C. Aik, "The synergies of the learning organization, visual factory management, and on-the-job training," *Performance Improvement* 44 (2005): 15–20.

18. "Reliance Industries Limited, Nagothane Manufacturing Division," *T+D* (October) 2008: 78.

19. N. Woodward, "Making safety job no. 1," *HR Magazine* (January 2007): 60–65.

20. B. Filipczak, "Who owns your OJT?" *Training* (December 1996). 44–49; R. DeRouin, T. Parrish, and E. Salas, "On-the-job training: Tips for ensuring success," *Ergonomics in Design* 13 (Spring 2005): 23–26; D. Gallup and K. Beauchemin, "On-the-job training," in *The ASTD Handbook of Training Design and Delivery,* ed. G. Piskurich, P. Beckschi, and B. Hall (New York: McGraw-Hill, 2000): 121–132

21. W. J. Rothwell and H. C. Kazanas, "Planned OJT is productive OJT," *Training and Development Journal* (October 1996): 53–56; R. Buckley and J. Caple, "Developing one-to-one training programs," *T+D* (April 2010): 108–109.

22. B. Filipczak, "Who owns your OJT?" *Training* (December 1996): 44–49.

23. G. M. Piskurich, *Self-Directed Learning* (San Francisco: Jossey-Bass, 1993).

24. S. Boyer and B. Lambert, "Take the handcuffs off sales team development with self-directed learning," *T+D* (November 2008): 62–66.

25. G. M. Piskurich, "Self-Directed Learning," in *The ASTD Training and Development Handbook,* 4th ed., ed. R. L. Craig (New York: McGraw-Hill, 1996), 453–72; G. M. Piskurich, "Developing Self-Directed Learning," *Training and Development* (March 1994): 31–36.

26. C. M. Solomon, "When training doesn't translate," *Workforce* (March 1997): 40–44.

27. P. Warr and D. Bunce, "Trainee characteristics and the outcomes of open learning," *Personnel Psychology* 48 (1995): 347–375; T. G. Hatcher, "The ins and outs of self-directed learning," *Training and Development* (February 1997): 35–39.

28. R. W. Glover, *Apprenticeship Lessons from Abroad* (Columbus, OH: National Center for Research in Vocational Education, 1986).

29. Commerce Clearing House, *Orientation-Training* (Chicago: Personnel Practices Communications, Commerce Clearing House, 1981): 501–505.

30. A. H. Howard III, "Apprenticeships." In *The ASTD Training and Development Handbook:* 803–813.

31. M. Rowh, "The rise of the apprentice," *Human Resource Executive* (February 2006): 38–43.

32. A. Ciaccio, "'You're hired': Goldcorp stint touts opportunities in mining," *The Wall Street Journal,* September 25, 2005: B6.

33. M. Rowh, "The rise of the apprentice," *Human Resource Executive* (February 2006): 38–43.

34. *Eldredge v. Carpenters JATC* (1981), 27 Fair Employment Practices (Bureau of National Affairs): 479.

35. M. Pramik, "Installers learn on practice dwellings," *Columbus Dispatch,* February 7, 2003: F1.

36. H. Dolezalek, "Pretending to learn," *Training* (July/August 2003): 20–26.

37. "Best practices and outstanding initiatives: Automatic Data Processing, Inc.: Leaders in action," *Training* (January/February 2011): 94–95.

38. S. McCartney, "Addressing small errors in the cockpit," *The Wall Street Journal* (September 13, 2005): D5.

39. J. Alden and J. Kirkhorn, "Case Studies." In *The ASTD Training and Development Handbook:* 497–516.

40. H. Kelly, "Case method training: What it is and how it works," in *Effective Training Delivery,* ed. D. Zielinski (Minneapolis: Lakewood Books, 1989): 95–96.

41. T. W. Shreeve, "On the case at the CIA," *Training and Development* (March 1997): 53–54.

42. S. Wiebenga, "Guidelines for selecting, using, and evaluating games in corporate training," *Performance Improvement Quarterly* 18 (2004): 19–36; S. Sugar, "Using games to energize dry material," in *The ASTD Handbook of Training Design and Delivery:* 107–120.

43. D. Schwartz, J. Bransford, and D. Sears, "Efficiency and Innovation in Transfer" In *Transfer of Learning: Research and Perspectives,* ed. J. Mestre (Greenwich, CT: Information Age Publishing, 2004).

44. D. Zielinski, "Training games," *HR Magazine* (March 2010): 64–66.

45. T. Sitzmann, "A meta-analytic examination of the instructional effectiveness of computer-based simulation games," *Personnel Psychology,* 64 (2011): 489–528.

46. S. Thiagarajan, "Instructional Games, Simulations, and Role Plays," in *The ASTD Training and Development Handbook:* 517–533; S. Karre, "Setting the stage for effective role plays," *T+D* (November 2011): 76–77.

47. "Wequassett Resort and Golf Club: Heroic customer service," *Training* (March/April 2008): 36–37.

48. S. J. Simon and J. M. Werner, "Computer training through behavior modeling, self-paced, and instructional approaches: A field experiment," *Journal of Applied Psychology* 81 (1996): 648–659; P. Taylor, D. Russ-Eft, and D. Chan, "A meta-analytic review of behavior modeling training," *Journal of Applied Psychology* 90 (2005): 692–709.

49. W. C. Byham and A. Pescuric, "Behavior modeling at the teachable moment," *Training* (December 1996): 51–56.

50. P. Decker and B. Nathan, *Behavior Modeling Training* (New York: Praeger Scientific, 1985).

51. Ibid.; T. T. Baldwin, "Effects of alternative modeling strategies on outcomes of interpersonal/skills training," *Journal of Applied Psychology,* 77 (1992): 147–154.

52. J. Cannon-Bowers and C. Bowers, "Team development and functioning." in S. Zedeck (ed.) *APA Handbook of Industrial and Organizational Psychology* (Washington, D.C.: American Psychological Association, 2010): 597–650; J. Mathieu et al., "Team effectiveness 1997–2007: A review of recent advancements and a glimpse into the future," *Journal of Management* 34 (2008): 410–476; S. Kozlowski and D. Ilgen, "Enhancing the effectiveness of work groups and teams," *Psychological Science in the Public Interest* 7 (2006): 77–124.

53. D. Brown and D. Harvey, *An Experiential Approach to Organizational Development* (Englewood Cliffs, NJ: Prentice Hall, 2000); J. Schettler, "Learning by doing," *Training* (April 2002): 38–43; P. Mirvis, "Executive development through consciousness-raising experiences," *Academy of Management Learning and Education* (June 2008): 173–188.

54. S. Lueck, "Postal Service's top inspector should be fired, senators say," *The Wall Street Journal,* (May 2, 2003): A2.

55. R. J. Wagner, T. T. Baldwin, and C. C. Rowland, "Outdoor training: Revolution or fad?" *Training and Development Journal* (March 1991): 51–57; C. J. Cantoni, "Learning the ropes of teamwork," *The Wall Street Journal,* (October 2, 1995): A14.

56. C. Steinfeld, "Challenge courses can build strong teams," *Training and Development* (April 1997): 12–13.

57. G. Kranz, "From fire drills to funny skills," *Workforce Management* (May 2011): 28–32.

58. M. Regan, "Execs scale new heights in the name of teamwork," *Columbus Dispatch* (February 15, 2004): F2.

59. D. Mishev, "Cooking for the company," *Cooking Light* (August 2004): 142–147.

60. G. M. Tarullo, "Making outdoor experiential training work," *Training* (August 1992): 47–52.

61. J. Schettler, "Learning by doing," *Training* (April 2002): 38–43

62. C. Clements, R. J. Wagner, and C. C. Roland, "The ins and outs of experiential training," *Training and Development* (February 1995): 52–56.

63. G. M. McEvoy, "Organizational change and outdoor management education," *Human Resource Management* 36 (1997): 235–250.

64. M. Marks, J. Mathieu, and S. Zaccaro, "A temporally based framework and taxonomy of team processes," *Academy of Management Review* 26 (2001): 356–376.

65. E. Salas and J. A. Cannon-Bowers, "Strategies for Team Training." In *Training for 21st-Century Technology: Applications for Psychological Research,* ed. M. A. Quinones and A. Dutta (Washington, D.C.: American Psychological Association, 1997): 249–281.

66. R. L. Oser et al., *Toward a Definition of Teamwork: An Analysis of Critical Team Behaviors,* Technical Report 89-004 (Orlando, FL: Naval Training Research Center, 1989).

67. E. Salas and J. A. Cannon-Bowers, "Strategies for Team Training." In *Training for 21st-Century Technology: Applications of Psychological Research,* eds. M. A. Quinones and A. Dutta (Washington, D.C.: American Psychological Association, 1997): 249–281.

68. M. Markset al., "The impact of cross-training on team effectiveness," *Journal of Applied Psychology,* 87 (2002): 3–13.

69. E. Salas, C. Burke, and J. Cannon-Bowers, "What We Know about Designing and Delivering Team Training: Tips and Guidelines." In *Creating, Implementing, and Managing Effective Training and Development,* ed. K. Kraiger (San Francisco: Jossey-Bass, 2002): 234–262.

70. R. Noe, A. Dachner, B. Saxton, and K. Keeton, *Team Training for Long-Duration Missions in Isolated and Confined Environments: A Literature Review, Operational Assessment, and Recommendations for Practice and Research.* National Aeronautics and Space Administration (NASA) Technical Report NASM/TM-2011-216162, available from http://ston.jsc.nasa.giv/collections/TRS.

71. S. Carey, "Racing to improve," *The Wall Street Journal* (March 24, 2006): B1, B6.

72. D. Dotlich and J. Noel, *Active Learning: How the World's Top Companies Are Recreating Their Leaders and Themselves* (San Francisco: Jossey-Bass, 1998).

73. M. Marquardt, "Harnessing the power of action learning," *T+D* (June 2004): 26–32; "Learning at Novartis,"from the Novartis website, www.novartis.com/careers/learning-at-novartis/index.shtml (accessed June 21, 2012, ).

74. "A Team Effort," *Training* (September 2002): 18.

75. H. Lancaster, "This kind of black belt can help you score some points at work," *The Wall Street Journal,* (September 14, 1999): B1; S. Gale, "Building frameworks for six sigma success," *Workforce* (May 2003): 64–66.

76. J. DeFeo, "An ROI story," *Training and Development* (July 2000): 25–27.

77. S. Gale, "Six Sigma is a way of life," *Workforce* (May 2003): 67–68.

78. M. Sallie-Dosunmu, "Born to grow," *TD* (May 2006): 33–37.

79. A. Brunet and S. New, "Kaizen in Japan: an empirical study," *International Journal of Production and Operations Management* 23 (2003): 1426–1446.

80. M. Marquardt, "Harnessing the power of action learning," *T+D* (June 2004): 26–32

81. M. Burke and R. Day, "A cumulative study of the effectiveness of managerial training," *Journal of Applied Psychology* 71 (1986): 232–245.

82. "Outstanding Training Initiatives. The Home Depot: Appliance Within," *training* (March 2006): 64–66.

# Chapter **Eight**

# Technology-Based Training Methods

## Objectives

After reading this chapter, you should be able to:

1. Explain how new technologies are influencing training.
2. Evaluate a web-based training site.
3. Explain how learning and transfer of training are enhanced by new training technologies.
4. Explain the strengths and limitations of e-learning, mobile learning training methods (such as iPads), and simulations.
5. Explain the different types of social media and the conditions conducive to their use for training.
6. Describe to a manager the different types of distance learning.
7. Recommend what should be included in an electronic performance support system.
8. Compare and contrast the strengths and weaknesses of traditional training methods versus those of technology-based training methods.
9. Identify and explain the benefits of learning management systems.

## Learning Methods Evolve at Farmers Insurance Group

Farmers Insurance Group is the third-largest insurer of auto and homeowners insurance in the United States and also provides other insurance and financial products. Farmers has 60,000 employees and exclusive and independent agents in every one of the fifty states. It processes millions of insurance quotes, new policies, renewals, and bills each year. In the insurance industry, legal requirements and the introduction of new products, processes, and services make training and development critical for business success. At Farmers Insurance, learning professionals are rewarded based on the degree to which training programs change the behavior of employees and help the business meet its objectives. Learning is delivered based on the desired result.

Farmers uses a blended learning approach to deliver effective training to its multigenerational employees and agents who are located across the United States. Farmers believes that rather than allowing learners to chose the type of training method that they believe best fits their style, a blended learning approach is more effective. As a result, its training programs integrate face-to-face instruction, print, online, video, audio, virtual simulations, and coaching. Technology is used for delivering knowledge, and instructor-led training is used for skill development. In the past five years, the amount of learning delivered through instructor-led classroom based training has dropped from 90 to 50 percent. The other 50 percent is online or informal learning. For example, Farmers is using various training methods to help its employees cope with the changes made in claims processing, ratings, billing, and product systems in support of the Farmers business strategy (Farmers Future 2020), which emphasizes customer experience, distribution, and product management excellence. For example, field managers were required to complete online training and webinars (web-based seminars) designed to provide the new knowledge that they needed. Then the managers received instructor-led training, videos, and coaching guides. Farmers also revised its training program for new agents as a result of an increased failure rate of new agencies. The revised program includes more coaching, performance support aids, and multimedia methods. It also ensures that new agents learn knowledge and skills when they are relevant to their jobs, rather than forcing them to learn everything at once and having them frustrated with being unable to recall the information when they need it later. As a result of the program revision, converting new agents to full-time status improved by 12 percent, sales results exceeded sales goals by 11 percent, and agency success rates increased 10 percent.

Recognizing that new technologies are potentially useful for training delivery and instruction, Farmers has started to use virtual classrooms, mobile learning, social networks, iPads, and learning simulations. For example, Farmers developed iFarmers apps for customers, sales agents, and employees. The iFarmers customer app helps customers learn about different insurance products. An iClaims app gives customers access to input and manage their insurance claims. The iAgent app provides business-focused learning for sales agents. Farmers has also been experimenting with social networking for employees to collaborate, create and share knowledge, and provide performance support. Some training programs are using the social network for collaborative exercises. Farmer's "Agency Insider" program allows learners to specify whether they want to use Twitter, Facebook, e-mail, or a Really Simple Syndication (RSS) feed.

**Sources:** Based on www.farmers.com, the website for Farmers Insurance; L. Freifeld, "Farmers' Premier Position," *training* (January/February 2011): 26–31; J. Salopek, "Thriving through change, cultivating growth," *T+D* (October 2010): 53–54.

# INTRODUCTION

As the opening vignette illustrates, technology is having a major impact on the delivery of training programs. Farmers Insurance is using a combination of traditional and new technology training methods (a blended learning approach). Online learning provides trainees with access to training at any time and place. The use of technology such as online learning requires collaboration among the areas of training, information technology, and top management. In addition, needs assessment, design, transfer, and evaluation (training design) are critical components of the effective use of training technology. Although technologies such as social media, tablet computers, and virtual reality provide exciting capabilities and possibilities, it is critical that companies use training technologies that support both business and learner needs.

Farmers Insurance is not alone in its use of new training technologies. Technology is changing learning and training in corporate settings, as well as in grade schools, high schools, colleges, and universities. At Ohio State University, students taking its Women, Culture, and Society course find themselves immersed in Second Life, a computer-based, three-dimensional virtual classroom.[1] Students explore the realities of how race, class, sexual orientation, economic equality, physical ability, violence, and the environment are experienced in a virtual society in which they can choose and change their identity, gender, and race. For example, one student studying disabilities was able to meet a Second Life resident who has cerebral palsy in real life. The Second Life resident gave her a wheelchair, allowing her to tour the virtual world in it, learning about people's attitudes regarding disability. The Second Life simulation includes a replica of an actual university building, display space, ocean top and hillside gathering places for discussion groups, and a virtual women's studies library. At the College of Medicine, students use the iPod Touch in classrooms and clinics.[2] The iPod Touch provides students with an opportunity to access a wide variety of online materials, including lecture recordings, readings, materials, and videos from the university's learning management system, as well as download high-quality images.

As we discussed in Chapter Seven, "Traditional Training Methods," instructor-led classroom training is still the most popular training method. However, the use of technology for training delivery and instruction is increasing and anticipated to grow in the future. Table 8.1 provides a snapshot of the use of new technology in training. The use of training technologies is expected to increase dramatically in the next decade as technology improves, the cost of technology decreases, companies recognize the potential cost savings of training via tablets, mobile phones, and social media, and the need for customized training increases.[3] As you will see later in this chapter, new training technologies are unlikely to totally replace face-to-face instruction. Rather, face-to-face instruction will be combined with new training technologies (a combination known as *blended learning*) to maximize learning.

The development, availability, and use of social media such as Twitter and Facebook have the potential to have a significant influence on training and learning. These tools are used by many people in their daily lives, especially the millennial generation. Many companies are beginning to use these tools for recruiting new employees and marketing and developing products and services. These tools are also being used for learning. Figure 8.1 shows the use of social media tools for work-related learning. Social media tools are reshaping learning by giving employees access to and control of their own learning through

**TABLE 8.1**

**Use of New Technology in Training**

Sources: M. Green and E. McGill, *State of the Industry, 2011* (Alexandria, VA: American Society for Training and Development, 2011); "2011 training industry report," *Training* (November/December 2011): 22–35.

- 11 percent of training hours are delivered in a virtual classroom and 22 percent is delivered online.
- 33 percent of learning hours involve technology-based training methods.
- 69 percent of companies use learning management systems. Broken down by size, 85 percent of large (10,000 or more employees), 54 percent of midsize (1,000–9,999 employees), and 52 percent of small companies (100–999 employees) use learning management systems.
- 28 percent of large companies (10,000 or more employees) deliver training online, compared to 20 percent of midsize (1,000–9,999 employees) and 21 percent of small (100 or less employees) companies.

**FIGURE 8.1**

**Use of Social Media Tools for Work-Related Learning**

Source: Based on L. Patel, "The rise of social media," *T+D* (July 2010): 60–61.

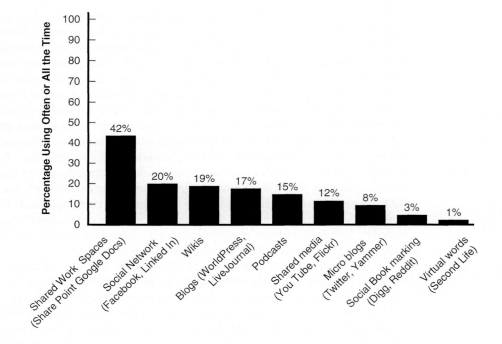

relationships and collaborations with others. Social media tools, including shared workspaces, social networks, wikis, blogs, podcasts, and microblogs, are being used for learning. As shown in Figure 8.1, shared workspaces, social networks, and wikis are the most commonly used social media for learning.[4] There appear to be generational differences in using and realizing the potential benefits of social media tools. Millennials believe that social media tools are helpful for learning and getting work done, and do so to a greater extent than baby boomers or Generation Xers. This may be because millennials are more likely to use social media tools in their personal lives, resulting in their being more comfortable using them at work.

The development of tablet computers such as the iPad also have the potential to influence training and learning. One estimate is that nearly 40 percent of executives plan to incorporate tablets such as the iPad into their new training and development initiatives.[5] These devices are expected to be used for learning and performance support, but also for coaching and mentoring employees, mobile gaming, and microblogging (e.g., Twitter).

This chapter begins by discussing the influence of new technology on training delivery, support, and administration. How technology has changed the learning environment also is addressed. Next, the chapter explores computer-based training, online-learning, and e-learning. E-learning emphasizes learning through interaction with training content, sharing with other trainees, and using Internet resources. Technologies that are familiar to us in our non-work life, such as social media, tablets such as iPads, and mobile smartphones, which are just beginning to be used for training purposes, are introduced. Next, the use of expert systems and intelligent tutoring systems as an instructional method and for on-the-job performance support is discussed. The chapter also shows how learning management systems aid in the delivery and administration of training programs. The last section of the chapter compares the various training methods that are based on new technology. A blended learning approach combining traditional face-to-face and technology-based training methods may be the best way to capitalize on the strengths of available training methods.

# TECHNOLOGY'S INFLUENCE ON TRAINING AND LEARNING

Chapters One and Two discussed the role that training and development should play in helping companies to execute their business strategy and deal with forces influencing the workplace. For training to help a company gain a competitive advantage, it needs to support business goals and be delivered as needed to geographically dispersed employees who may be working at home or in another country. Training costs (such as travel costs) should be minimized and maximum benefits gained, including learning and transfer of training. For learning and transfer to occur (i.e., for the benefits of training to be realized), the training environment must include learning principles such as practice, feedback, meaningful material, and the ability to learn by interacting with others.

New technologies have made it possible to reduce the costs associated with delivering training to employees, to increase the effectiveness of the learning environment, and to help training contribute to business goals. Table 8.2 lists, describes, and provides examples of some of the new technology training methods that we will discuss in this chapter. New technologies have influenced the delivery of training, training administration, and training support. Technology has made several benefits possible:[6]

- Employees can gain control over when and where they receive training.
- Employees can access knowledge and expert systems on an as-needed basis.
- Through the use of avatars, virtual reality, and simulations, the learning environment can look, feel, and sound just like the work environment.
- Employees can choose the type of media (print, sound, video, etc.) that they want to use in a training program.
- Course enrollment, testing, and training records can be handled electronically, reducing the paperwork and time needed for administrative activities.
- Employees' accomplishments during training can be monitored.
- Traditional training methods, such as classroom instruction and behavior modeling, can be delivered to trainees rather than requiring them to come to a central training location.

Consider how technology has influenced training at IBM and UPS.[7] At IBM, the learning strategy is for employees to learn every day in a dynamic way based on their current job and what they need to do in the future. To better prepare the company's next generation of leaders and to best use its global workforce, IBM is using new technology—such as collaborative online learning platforms that allow employees to learn from their peers—and virtual tools that give them instant access to experts. Peer learning can occur spontaneously online just as it would if all of IBM's employees were located in the same building. IBM employees participating in the company's virtual, three-dimensional online environment create avatars (computer depictions of humans) to interact with each other and discuss and share ideas. At UPS, technology has made the driver's job more complex. Drivers have to

**TABLE 8.2**

**New Technologies Used for Training**

Sources: Based on R. Johnson and H. Gueutal, *Transforming HR Through Technology* (Alexandria, VA: SHRM Foundation, 2010); American Society for Training and Development, *Transforming Learning with Web 2.0 Technologies*, 2010 survey report; T. Bingham and M. Conner, *The New Social Learning* (Alexandria, VA: American Society for Training and Development Press, 2010); A. Kaplan and M. Haenlein, "Users of the world unite! The challenges and opportunities of social media," *Business Horizons*, 53 (2010): 59–68.

**E-learning, Online Learning, Computer-Based Training (CBT), Web-Based Training**
Training delivered using a computer or the web. Can include CDs or DVDs of text and/or video.

**Webcasts/Webinars**
Live web-based delivery of instruction to trainees in dispersed locations.

**Podcasts**
Web-based delivery of audio and video files.

**Mobile Learning**
Delivery of training through handheld mobile devices such as smartphones or tablet computers.

**Blended Learning**
Training is delivered using a combined technology and face-to-face instructional delivery approach, such as classroom and WBT.

**Wikis**
Websites that allow many users to create, edit, and update content and share knowledge

**Distance Learning**
Training delivered to trainees in other locations online, or through webcasts or virtual classroom often supported with communications tools such as chat, e-mail, and online discussions.

**Social Media**
Online and mobile technology used to create interactive communications allowing the creation and exchange of user-generated content. They include wikis, blogs, networks such as Facebook, MySpace, and LinkedIn, microsharing sites such as Twitter, and shared media such as YouTube.

**Shared Workspaces (Example: Google Docs)**
A space hosted on a web server where people can share information and documents.

**RSS Feeds**
Updated content sent to subscribers automatically instead of by e-mail.

**Blogs (Example: WorldPress)**
A webpage where an author posts entries and readers can comment.

**Chat Rooms and Discussion Boards**
An electronic room or message board on which learners communicate. Communications between learners can occur at the same or different times. A facilitator or instructor can moderate the conversations, which may be grouped by topic.

**Microblogs or Microsharing (Example: Twitter)**
Software tools that enable communications in short bursts of text, links, and multimedia, either through stand-alone applications or through online communities or social networks.

handle the truck safely, be proficient on the DIAD (handheld computer), and understand how to stay safe during a package delivery. As a result, UPS developed the Integrad training center in Maryland. Integrad includes a simulator designed to teach new hires how to load and unload packages from shelves, the floor, and the rear door while also meeting company time standards for such activities and minimizing the stress and strain that cause injuries. On average, drivers have to step off and on the truck at least 120 times on their routes, which can strain ankles if done incorrectly. At Integrad, trainees deliver packages while trainers and trainees serve as customers in a simulated town with stores, streets, and even a loading dock.

## Technology and Collaboration

Technology allows digital collaboration to occur. **Digital collaboration** is the use of technology to enhance and extend employees' abilities to work together regardless of their geographic proximity.[8] Digital collaboration includes electronic messaging systems, electronic meeting systems, online communities of learning organized by subject where employees can access interactive discussion areas and share training content and web links, social networks, and document-handling systems with collaboration technologies that allow interpersonal interaction. Digital collaboration requires a computer, tablet, or phone with a web browser or app, but collaborative. Digital collaboration can be synchronous or asynchronous.[9] In **synchronous communication,** trainers, experts, and learners interact with each other live and in real time, the same way they would in face-to-face classroom instruction. Technologies such as video teleconferencing and live online courses (virtual classrooms) make synchronous communication possible. **Asynchronous communication** refers to non-real-time interactions. That is, persons are not online and cannot communicate with each other without a time delay, but learners can still access information resources when they desire them. E-mail, self-paced courses on the web or on CD-ROM, discussion groups, and virtual libraries allow asynchronous communication.

The Shoney's and Captain D's restaurant chains have more than 350 restaurants in more than twenty states.[10] Over 8,000 employees each year must be trained on the basics of the operational parts of the business, including how to make French fries, hush puppies, and coleslaw. Also, each year, 600 new managers must be trained in business issues and back-office operations of the restaurants. The biggest challenge that Shoney's faced was how to consistently train geographically dispersed employees. Shoney's solution was to implement OneTouch, a live integrated video and two-way voice and data application that combines synchronous video, voice, data, and live webpages so that team members can interact with trainers. OneTouch can be delivered to desktop PCs, as well as to warehouses and repair bays. Desktop systems can be positioned in any appropriate location in the restaurant, and individuals or a group of employees can gather around the PC for training. The training modules include topics such as Orientation, Kitchen, and Dining Room. Each module is interactive. Topics are introduced and are followed up by quizzes to ensure that learning occurs. For example, the coleslaw program shows trainees what the coleslaw ingredients are and where they can be found in the restaurant. The coleslaw program includes a video that trainees can watch and refer to as they practice. After they practice, they have to complete a quiz, and their manager has to verify that they completed the topic before they move on to the next program. The training is consistent and easy to update. In addition, the program allows kitchen and counter staff to learn each other's skills, which gives Shoney's flexibility in its staffing (e.g., counter employees who also know how to cook).

## Technology and Learning Environment

As discussed in Chapter Seven, learning used to be a very linear process. That is, instructors presented information to the learners, and practice and applications occurred after instruction was completed (see the classroom learning environment shown in Figure 8.1). Traditionally, the learning environment included only the instructor or trainer and the learners. The trainer was responsible for delivering content, answering questions, and testing learning. Trainees played a passive role in learning. Communication on course content was one-way: from the instructor to the learner. Experts and resource materials were separate from the learning environment. Contact with resource materials and experts beyond the instructor and course materials assigned for the course required learners to go outside the formal learning environment. Also, learners had to wait to access resource materials and experts until instruction was completed. Interaction among learners occurred primarily outside the training room and tended to be limited to those who worked in the same geographic area.

Technology has allowed learning to become a more dynamic process. As shown on the right side of Figure 8.2, the learning environment can be expanded to include greater interaction between learners and the training content, as well as between learners and the

**FIGURE 8.2  Types of Learning Environments**

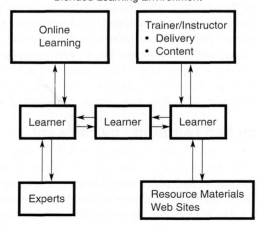

instructor. The trainer may help design the instruction, but the instruction is delivered to the learners primarily through technology such as online learning, simulations, iPods, or iPads. The instructor becomes more of a coach and resource person to answer students' questions and is less involved in the delivery of content. Learning occurs primarily through exchanges with other learners, using blogs, wikis, or other types of social media training, working on virtual team projects, participating in games, listening, exchanging ideas, interacting with experts (engineers, managers, etc.), and discovering ideas and applications using hyperlinks that take the learner to other websites. Experts and resource materials may be part of the learning environment. While learners interact with the training content through exercises, applications, and simulations, they can discuss what they are learning with other learners or access experts or resource materials available on the Internet. Training delivery and administration (e.g., tracking learner progress) is all done through a learning management system (discussed later in the chapter). In the blended learning environment, shown at the bottom of Figure 8.2, trainees have access to a blended training curriculum that consists of both online and classroom instruction. Collaboration can occur between learners, between learners and training content (e.g., simulation or game), between learners and instructors, and between learners and experts. It is important that new technologies create a dynamic learning environment, including collaboration, active learner involvement, and access to other resources. A dynamic learning environment likely includes the use of **Web 2.0** technologies, including social networking, so-called blogs, wikis, and Twitter.[11] Qualcomm's initiative, Learning 2.0, involves the use of Web 2.0 technologies such as social bookmarking/tagging, blogs, and tools similar to those found on Facebook and YouTube to build relationships between trainees and training content.

Recent technology, including smartphones, tablets, and personal computers, has enabled training to be delivered to different geographical locations, to accompany trainees whether they are at work or at home. The training content can be delivered in a consistent manner to multiple trainees of different locations and times. Many of the training methods discussed in this chapter have these features. For example, online learning, or e-learning, includes instruction and delivery of training using the Internet or web. Distance learning typically involves videoconferencing and/or computers for delivery of instruction from a trainer to trainees who are not in the same location as the trainer. Mobile technologies allow training to be delivered through iPods, iPhones, personal data assistants (PDAs), iPads, and handheld computers that allow trainees to tune in to training programs at any time or place. New training technologies allow for the use of multiple media including text, graphics, video, and audio. This allows for learning content to be presented in multiple ways, appealing to trainee preferences and learning styles. The next section of the chapter describes new training technologies, how they are used, and their potential learning advantages and disadvantages.

# COMPUTER-BASED TRAINING, ONLINE LEARNING, WEB-BASED TRAINING, E-LEARNING

**Computer-based training (CBT), online learning, e-learning,** and **web-based training** refer to instruction and delivery of training by computer through the Internet or the web.[12] All of these training methods can include and integrate into instruction text, interaction using simulations and games, and video, and collaboration using blogs, wikis, and social networks, and hyperlinks to additional resources. In some types of CBT training, content is provided stand-alone using software or DVDs with no connection to the Internet. Trainees can still interact with the training content, answer questions, and choose responses regarding how they would behave in certain situations, but they cannot collaborate with other learners. For example, Wipro Technologies developed a tool they call a Unified Learning Kit (ULK), a portable laptop programmable computer that enables new employees to experiment in engineering subjects.[13] One ULK can teach more than ten different technical subjects related to hardware and software engineering.

Online learning, e-learning, and web-based training all include delivery of instruction using the Internet or web. The training program can be accessed using a password through the public Internet or the company's private intranet. There are many potential features that can be included in online learning to help trainees learn and transfer training to their jobs. For example, online programs that use video may make it an interactive experience for trainees. That is, trainees watch the video and have the opportunity to use the keyboard or touch the screen to answer questions, provide responses to how they would act in certain situations, or identify the steps they would take to solve a problem. Interactive video is especially valuable for helping trainees learn technical or interpersonal skills. We discuss more of the potential features and advantages of online learning below.

For example, during training needs assessment, Bayer Pharmaceuticals discovered that its technical experts needed new skills to manage large projects.[14] These skills related to keeping project managers focused on the task, managing competing priorities, managing large cross-functional teams, and supervising employees who did not report to them. These skills are important to reduce the time needed to bring research discoveries to the marketplace. To train in these skills, Bayer used a computer-based simulation that requires teams of trainees to manage a large-scale project. The management decisions they make affect their odds of being successful. A computer calculates each team's probability of succeeding. The simulation includes obstacles that can affect a project negatively, such as unmotivated employees, absenteeism, and projects being completed late. The simulation also includes online work that trainees complete prior to training. The prework provides trainees with an overview of the steps involved in project management. All trainees complete a self-assessment of their team-related behavior (e.g., conflict resolution). The assessments are used for discussing leader/team-member relationships. After completing the simulation, trainees can access a program website that includes a newsletter and tips for project management. Employees who have completed the simulation are demonstrating increased confidence in their ability to manage a project and to handle changing priorities, and they are addressing team issues more quickly.

Chiquita, the fresh fruit company, needed to help employees understand how they could contribute to the company's business goals through a new performance management system, Perform to Grow.[15] Although e-learning modules were developed to help employees learn how to practice the tools and steps within the Perform to Grow system, offices in Central America, Africa, Asia, and Eastern Europe did not have the technology that was available in the North American and Western European offices. As a result, Chiquita burned the e-learning modules and tool kit onto CD-ROMs for distribution to employees in those locations.

Federal Express's twenty-five-disk interactive video curriculum includes courses related to customer etiquette, defensive driving, and delivery procedures.[16] As Federal Express discovered, interactive video has many advantages. First, training is individualized. Employees control what aspects of the training program they view. They can skip ahead when they feel competent, or they can review topics. Second, employees receive immediate feedback concerning their performance. Third, training is accessible on a twenty-four-hour basis regardless of employees' work schedules. From the employer's standpoint, the high cost of developing interactive video programs and purchasing the equipment was offset by the reduction in instructor costs and travel costs related to a central training location. At Federal Express, interactive video has made it possible to train 35,000 customer-contact employees in 650 locations nationwide, saving the company millions of dollars. Without interactive video, Federal Express could not deliver consistent high-quality training.

## *Potential Features of Online Learning*

In online learning, it is possible to enable learners to interact with the training content and other learners and to decide how they want to learn.[17] Figure 8.3 shows the possible features that can be built into online learning. These features include content, collaboration and sharing, links to resources, learner control, delivery, and administration. It is important to note that not all these features are incorporated into online learning methods. One reason is that certain methods make it difficult to incorporate some of these features. For example, as you will see later in the chapter, distance learning that involves teleconferencing may limit the amount of collaboration between trainees and the instructor. Also, in distance learning, trainees do not have control over the content, practice, and speed of learning. Another reason why a feature may not be incorporated is that the designers may have chosen not to include it. Although e-learning *can* include all the features to facilitate learning that are shown in Figure 8.3, it may fall short of its potential because, for example, program developers do not include opportunities for trainees to collaborate. As Figure 8.3 shows, not only can online learning provide the trainee with content, but it also can give learners the ability to control what they learn, the speed at which they progress through the program, how much they practice, and even when they learn. In addition, online learning can allow learners to collaborate or interact with other trainees and experts and can provide links to other learning resources such as reference materials, company websites, and other training programs. Text, video, graphics, and sound can be used to present course content. Online learning may also include various aspects of training administration such as course enrollment, testing and evaluating trainees, and monitoring of trainees' learning progress.

## *Advantages of Online Learning*

The possible features that can be built into online learning give it potential advantages over other training methods. The advantages of e-learning are shown in Table 8.3. E-learning initiatives are designed to contribute to a company's strategic business objectives.[18] E-learning supports company initiatives such as expanding the number of customers, initiating new ways to carry out business such as e-business (providing products and services through the internet), and speeding the development of new products or services. E-learning may involve a larger audience than traditional training programs that focus on employees. E-learning may involve partners, suppliers, vendors, and potential customers. For example, Lucent Technologies, which designs and delivers communications network technologies,

**FIGURE 8.3    Potential Features of E-learning**

**TABLE 8.3**
**Advantages of E-learning**

Sources: Based on D. Hartley, "All aboard the e-learning train," *Training and Development* (July 2000): 37–42; V. Beer, *The Web Learning Field Book: Using the World Wide Web to Build Workplace Learning Environments* (San Francisco: Jossey-Bass, 2000).

It supports the company's business strategy and objectives.
It is accessible at any time and any place.
The audience can include employees and managers, as well as vendors, customers, and clients.
Training can be delivered to geographically dispersed employees.
Training can be delivered faster and to more employees in a shorter period of time.
Updating is easy.
Practice, feedback, objectives, assessment, and other positive features of a learning environment can be built into the program. Learning is enhanced through the use of multiple media (sound, text, video, graphics, etc.) and trainee interaction.
Paperwork related to training management (enrollment, assessment, etc.) can be eliminated.
It can link learners to other content, experts, and peers.

has devoted significant resources to ensure that customers and business partners have access to e-learning.[19] Training affects customer satisfaction with Lucent's products and solutions. It also influences employees' ability to sell to and service customers. Product training courses that deal with installing, repairing, and operating Lucent equipment are available to customers on the company's website. Users can take the courses, register and pay for the classes, and track their progress. Lucent also provides training to its business partners, who are required to be certified in Lucent's products before they can receive special discounts. As Lucent increases its electronically delivered courses, the company is also trying to increase the percentage of learners who take courses online. Today, about half the users attend classroom-based training.

E-learning allows training to be delivered faster and to more employees in a shorter period of time. Ritz Camera Centers uses an e-learning program to help keep its employees up to date on product information and enhance their selling skills.[20] E-learning was selected because the company needed a systematic way to reach all associates quickly with materials that could be easily managed and updated. Ritz Camera employees can access short training courses online on a wide variety of technologies and brands. Each module provides insight into product features, competitive differences, and benefits. Training modules are created monthly and can stay live for up to a year based on product cycles. The modules feature training assessments in the form of a quiz that employees must complete successfully. In addition, Ritz can track employees' participation through a web portal.

E-learning offers training to geographically dispersed employees at their own locations, reducing travel costs associated with bringing trainees to a central location. This is one reason why online learning is the second most popular approach to training (after print-based materials) for small businesses.[21] For small businesses, online learning helps reduce travel costs related to bringing employees to a central location for training and gives employees flexibility as they try to fit training into their work schedules. Golden Harvest Seeds, Inc., found that its sales training program for 250 employees and 2,000 independent crop-seed dealers was not well attended and the training sessions took too much valuable work time. To overcome the attendance problem and increase training effectiveness, Golden Harvest hired a company to produce and post online videos for teaching salespersons how to sell Golden Harvest seeds. Golden Harvest found that employees were watching the videos, sales and the demand for more courses increased, and training costs per person were reduced from over $175 to less than $100.

In another example, Nike was challenged to design a training program for retailers with stores throughout the country and high levels of staff turnover.[22] Nike wanted a program to deliver information in short time periods to make it easier for salespeople to learn but not keep them off the sales floor. Nike developed the Sports Knowledge Underground, which looks like a subway map in which different stations represent different product training. For example, the Apparel Union Station branches off to the apparel technologies line, the running products line, and the Nike Pro products line. Each segment lasts no more than five minutes and gives the salesperson the needed product knowledge. Salespersons are tested at the end of the training and are asked for feedback about the program, which is sent to the e-learning program developers. The program is currently used by more than 20,000 sales associates, and more are expected to complete the training as it becomes available in more stores. The program appears to be having a positive impact on the business—stores that have the program have seen a 4 percent increase in sales.

Some companies have training requirements that all employees have to complete for the company to meet quality or legal requirements. Online learning allows more employees to gain access to these types of programs in a quicker time period than if face-to-face instruction is used. For example, financial services companies are often challenged to keep their global employees up to date on constant changes in products, policies, and government regulations. Face-to-face training is not timely or cost-efficient. For example, Sanofi U.S. was behind its competition in product knowledge within the diabetes sales force.[23] The company needed a training solution that the sales force could complete in the field or while traveling. As a result, the company developed a self-paced, e-learning solution—a virtual campus called Diabetes University. Learners can be guided through the campus by a "professor" and participate in different types of learning activities, including games, videos, and narrated text. E-learning allows retailers to track every employee's course performance and match it with his or her sales performance.[24] Product lines are tied to specific certificate tracks. To sell those products, employees must first complete the learning for that track and pass the certification exam. A grocery store chain had to train its pharmacy staff about the privacy rules that were part of the Health Insurance Portability and Accountability Act (HIPAA). To quickly train the staff, a training course was posted online, making it easier for employees to access it through a laptop computer, cash register, smartphone, or iPad.[25] Online training allows retailers such as Luxottica, the eyeware and optical company, the ability to track who enrolls and complete online courses that are required for certification to some positions (such as licensed opticians).

E-learning is also easy to update, thanks to user-friendly authoring languages such as HTML. Changes can be made on the server that stores the e-learning program. Employees worldwide can access the updated program. The administrative features of e-learning make training management a more efficient, paperless process. For example, CCH developed Shared Learning, an online administration module that allows companies to monitor employees' completion of e-learning. It tracks how many times employees complete the same class and how much time employees spend per class, and it bookmarks the point at which trainees leave an online class so they can enter the program at the place they left it when they again begin training.[26]

### Effectiveness of Online Learning

Is e-learning effective for all types of learning outcomes and trainees? Both research and company experiences suggest that e-learning is effective for a wide range of outcomes, including knowledge, skills, and behaviors.[27] Table 8.4 shows some of the research results regarding the effectiveness of online learning compared to other training methods. Online learning may be most effective for training that emphasizes cognitive outcomes, such as declarative and procedural knowledge (recall the discussion of learning outcomes in Chapters Four and Six). Online learning may facilitate greater social interaction between trainees than face-to-face learning methods because other trainees are equally accessible or more accessible than the instructor and there are more methods available that allow learners to interact, such as e-mail, blogs, wikis, and chat rooms.[28] Also, trainees may be more motivated to participate because they avoid feelings of inadequacy and low self-confidence, which can hinder participation in face-to-face learning. Delaware North Companies (DNC), a hospitality and food services company based in Buffalo, New York, provides hospitality and food services to national parks, stadiums, and airports. DNC delivers self-paced interactive training via the web, followed by virtual classes.[29] At DNC, soft skills, such as

**TABLE 8.4**   **Research Results Regarding the Effectiveness of Online Learning**

- Online instruction is more effective than face-to-face classroom instruction for teaching declarative knowledge (cognitive knowledge assessed using written tests designed to measure whether trainees remember concepts presented in training).
- Web-based instruction and classroom instruction are equally effective in teaching procedural knowledge (the ability of learners to perform the skills taught in training).
- Learners are equally satisfied with web-based and classroom instruction.
- Web-based instruction appears to be more effective than classroom instruction (1) when learners are provided with control over content, sequence, and pace; (2) in long courses; and (3) when learners are able to practice the content and receive feedback.
- Web-based instruction and classroom instruction are equally effective when similar instructional methods are used (for example, both approaches use video, practice assignments, and learning tests).
- The employees who get the most from online learning are those who complete more of the available practice opportunities and take more time to complete the training.
- E-learning is not effective for all learners, especially those with low computer self-efficacy.

Sources: Based on K. Kraiger, "Transforming our models of learning and development: Web-based instruction as enabler of third-generation instruction," *Industrial Organizational Psychology* 1 (2008): 454–467; T. Sitzmann et al., "The comparative effectiveness of web-based and classroom instruction: A meta-analysis," *Personnel Psychology* 59 (2006): 623–634; E. Welsh et al., "E-learning: Emerging uses, empirical results and future directions," *International Journal of Training and Development* 7 (2003): 245–258.

managing a team, effective communication techniques, delegation, empowerment, and conflict resolution, have been identified as best for online training. Functional and technical skills have been found to be best suited for OJT

Despite the increasing popularity of online learning, many companies such as Home Depot, Inc., Recreational Equipment, Inc., and Qwest Communications International still prefer face-to-face training methods for teaching skills for complex jobs involving selling and repairing equipment.[30] Online learning is used to train employees when their job requires them to use a standard set of facts or procedures. For example, Recreational Equipment, Inc., uses role playing between new employees and trainers who simulate a wide range of customer behaviors, helping them understand the difference between customers who want a specific product and customers who want to discuss different product choices. Qwest Communications estimates that 80 percent of training in its network department is completed face to face, compared to 20 percent online. To learn how to fix and install equipment, the company believes that employees must have hands-on experience that is similar to what they will encounter working in homes and commercial locations. Online learning may be valuable, but it is insufficient for teaching complex analytical, conceptual, and interpersonal skills.[31] This may be because online learning lacks communication richness, some online learners may be reluctant to interact with other learners, and, although online learning increases accessibility to training, employees with busy work schedules have a greater opportunity to more easily delay, fail to complete, or poorly perform learning activities. Later in the chapter, we discuss how online learning can be combined with face-to-face instruction, known as blended learning, to take advantage of the strengths of both methods. Learning can be enhanced by combining face-to-face instruction and e-learning because learners are more engaged; the use of video, graphics, sound, and text is combined with active learning experiences such as cases, role playing, and simulations. Also, blended learning provides opportunities for learners to practice, ask questions, and interact with other learners and peers both face to face and online.

# DEVELOPING EFFECTIVE ONLINE LEARNING

Table 8.5 provides tips for developing effective online learning.[32] The training design or ADDIE model discussed in Chapter One, "Introduction to Employee Training and Development," should still be used in designing e-learning. However, the emphasis at each stage should be slightly different.[33] Needs assessment, creating a positive online learning experience, learner control, and providing time and space for online learning are three central issues that need to be addressed for effective online learning, including web-based training.

**TABLE 8.5**   **Tips for Developing Effective Online Learning**

| Needs assessment | Identify the connection between online learning and the needs of the business. Get management to buy in. Make sure that employees have access to technology and technology support. Consult with information technology experts about system requirements. Identify specific training needs (knowledge, skills, competencies, behaviors). If needed, train learners on computer and Internet basics. |
|---|---|
| Creating a positive learning experience | Incorporate learning principles (practice, feedback, meaningful material, an appeal to active learner involvement, and an appeal to multiple senses). Design the course for the available bandwidth (or increase the available bandwidth to suit the course needs). Use games and simulations, which are attractive to learners. Structure materials properly. Allow trainees the opportunity to communicate and collaborate with each other and with the trainer, experts, or facilitators. Make the program user-friendly: Learning modules should be kept short, the content should not overload trainees, and webpages should not be confusing. Provide incentives for completing training. Keep each instructional segment self-contained. "Chunk" training modules. Create smooth transitions between instructional segments. Any audio, video, or animation should be useful to the learner; otherwise, it is a waste of time and bandwidth. Provide the developer/producer with clear specifications regarding required file formats, maximum file sizes, window and image dimensions, navigation, screen fonts, and available bandwidth. Provide writers and instructional designers with clear guidelines for the maximum number of words per screen, how many interactive exercises to include, and which exercises are best suited to the content. Conduct a formative evaluation (pilot test) before large scale use of online learning. |
| Provide time and space under learner control | Provide learners with control, including the opportunity to skip sections or modules and the ability to pause, bookmark, review, and return to where they left off. Give learners dedicated training time to participate in online learning. |

Sources: Based on K. Dobbs, "What the online world needs now: Quality," *Training* (September 2000): 84–94; P. Galagan, "Getting started with e-learning." *Training and Development* (May 2000): 62–64; D. Zielinski, "Can you keep learners online?" *Training* (March 2000): 65–75; V. Beer, *The Web Learning Field Book: Using the World Wide Web to Build Workplace Learning Environments* (San Francisco Jossey-Bass, 2000); E. Zimmerman, "Better training is just a click away," *Workforce* (January 2001): 36–42; R. Clark and R. Mayer, *E-Learning and the Science of Instruction* (San Francisco: John Wiley, 2003); E. Salas, R. DeRouin, and L. Littrell, "Research-Based Guidelines for Designing Distance Learning: What We Know So Far," in *The Brave New World of eHR*, ed. H. Gueutal and D. Stone (San Francisco: Jossey-Bass, 2005): 104–137; S. Boehle, "Putting the learning back into e-learning," *Training* (January 2006): 29–35; A Rossett and L. Schafer, "What to do about e-dropouts," *T+D* (June 2003): 40–46; M. Morrison, "Leaner e-learning," *Training* (January 2008): 16–18.

# Needs Assessment

Needs assessment includes getting management to support online learning. Also, the information technology department needs to be involved in the design of any web-based program to ensure that the technology capabilities of the company network are understood, to guarantee that trainees can get access to the browsers and connections that they need to participate in e-learning and use all of the tools (e.g., e-mail, chat rooms, hyperlinks) that may accompany it, and to get technical support when needed. Online tutorials may be needed to acquaint trainees with the capabilities of the e-learning system and how to navigate the web. Recall from Chapter Three, "Needs Assessment," that a needs assessment determines the company's resources for training and the tasks to be trained for, and it analyzes the employees who may need training. The needs assessment process for web-based training or any other type of online learning should include a technology assessment (as part of the organizational analysis) and an assessment of the skills that users need for online training (person analysis). This should include a technical analysis focused on identifying minimum computing requirements (bandwidth, memory, hard drive space, software, processing speed).

**Bandwidth** refers to the number of bytes and bits (information) that can travel between computers per second. Graphics, photos, animation, and video in courses can be slow to download and can "crash" the system. Online learning courses should be designed for the available bandwidth on the company's system. Bandwidth can be increased by upgrading access speed on the users' computers, buying and installing faster servers and switches (computer hardware) on the company's network, or encouraging trainees to access the web when demand is not high.[34] Soon bandwidth may not be an issue because computer servers will be able to transfer more data faster, personal computers will have greater processing speed, and cables and wireless communications systems that carry data will have greater capacity. Online learning should also try to build in interactivity without requiring the use of plug-ins. A **plug-in** refers to additional software that needs to be loaded on the computer to listen to sound, watch video, or perform other functions. Plug-ins can be expensive because they may require the company to pay licensing fees. Plug-ins also can affect how the computer processes tasks. If trainees experience repeated technology problems (such as slow download times, network downtimes, or plug-in difficulties), they are likely to lose patience and be reluctant to participate in online learning.

Grant Thornton LLP, a global accounting, tax, and business advisory firm, created Grant Thornton University (GTU), one place for all of its employees' training needs.[35] Through GTU, employees can register for any course, whether it is classroom-based or online, and have access to more than 1,000 hours of self-paced, live webcasts and virtual classroom courses. To ensure that GTU was successful, the company investigated its business learning needs and the best delivery method for each topic (a needs assessment). Learning paths are broken down by competencies and skill requirements and are related to job performance. For example, if employees receive performance feedback suggesting that they need to improve their teamwork skills, managers can identify an appropriate course by position and required competencies. A combination of self-paced lessons and live virtual classroom is the optimal instructional method. The self-paced lessons deliver content, and the live training is used for question-and-answer sessions and case studies. Live training also provides trainees with the opportunity to interact with peers and course experts. To obtain support for GTU, the company's chief learning officer invited managers to participate in a virtual kickoff from their desktop personal computers. The kickoff covered the strategic goals of the initiative, showed managers how the technology worked, and let them sample various content.

## Creating a Positive Online Learning Experience

In the design and development phase, the characteristics of a positive learning environment discussed in Chapter Four (e.g., objectives, practice, interaction) should be included to help aid retention of learning content and create a meaningful experience that motivates learners. Flowcharts or storyboards should be created that include all of the course components such as a main menu, modules, webpages for each lesson, assessments, discussion forums, images, color specifications, and help menus. Rapid prototyping should be used for designing the program.[36] **Rapid prototyping** refers to an iterative process in which initial design ideas are proposed and provided in rough form in an online working prototype that is reviewed and refined by design team members. Also, multiple types of media should be chosen in order to appeal to different learning styles to the greatest possible extent. This includes text, animation, pictures, video, audio, games, simulations, or even e-books. E-learning should be designed to minimize content or work that is unrelated to the learning objectives. Extraneous content may take up trainees' limited cognitive processing resources, resulting in less learning. Table 8.6 provides several design principles that should be considered to create a positive online learning experience.

Remember that just putting text online isn't necessarily an effective way to learn. **Repurposing** refers to directly translating an instructor-led, face-to-face training program to an online format. Online learning that merely repurposes an ineffective training program will still result in ineffective training. Unfortunately, in their haste to develop online learning, many companies are repurposing bad training. The best e-learning uses the advantages of the Internet in combination with the principles of a good learning environment. Effective online learning takes advantage of the web's dynamic nature and ability to use many positive learning features, including linking to other training sites and content through the use of hyperlinks, providing learner control, and allowing the trainee to collaborate with other learners. Effective online learning uses video, sound, text, and graphics to hold learners' attention. Effective online learning provides trainees with meaningful content related

**TABLE 8.6**
**Principles for Creating a Positive Learning Experience**

Sources: Based on R. Clark and R. Mayer, "Learning by doing: Evidence-based guidelines for principled learning environments," *Performance Improvement* 47 (2008): 5–13; R. Mayer, "Applying the science of learning: Evidence-based principles for the design of multimedia instruction," *American Psychologist* (November 2008): 760–769; R. Clark and R. Mayer, *E-Learning and the Science of Instruction*, 2d ed. (San Francisco: Jossey-Bass/Pfeiffer, 2008); T. Sitz Mann and K. Ely. "Sometimes you need a reminder: The effects of prompting self-regulation on regulatory processes, learning, and attrition." *Personnel Psychology* 95 (2010): 132–144.

Instruction includes relevant visuals and words.
Text is aligned close to visuals.
Complex visuals are explained by audio or text, rather than by both text and audio that narrates the text.
Extraneous visuals, words, and sounds are omitted.
Learners are socially engaged through conversational language agents.
Key concepts are explained prior to the full process or task associated with the concepts.
Prompts are provided that encourage self-regulation.
Content is presented in short sequences over which learners have control.
Activities and exercises that mimic the context of the job are provided.
Explanations are provided for learner responses to quizzes and exercises.
Exercises are distributed within and among the module(s) rather than in a single place.

to realistic on-the-job activities, relevant examples, and the ability to apply content to work problems and issues. Also, trainees have opportunities to practice and receive feedback through the use of problems, exercises, assignments, and tests.

To ensure that materials are not confusing or overwhelming to the learner, online learning content needs to be properly arranged.[37] An orientation to the new program should be provided to learners to explain how to learn online, how to get help, and how to interact with peers, trainers, and facilitators.[38] Participants should be provided with an overview of the course or program and success factors for completion. After an e-learning program is implemented, the focus should shift to on how to best distribute, maintain, update, and improve it. Evaluation still involves collecting some combination of reaction, learning, behavior, and results outcomes, including an emphasis on questions related to the number and quality of the interactive exercises and multimedia and the ease of use of the navigation tools. Materials in online learning need to be organized in small, meaningful modules of information. Each module should relate to one idea or concept. The modules should be connected in a way that encourages the learner to be actively involved in learning. Active involvement may include asking trainees to find resources on the Internet, try quizzes or games, choose between alternative actions, or compare what they know to the knowledge of an expert or model. Objectives, videos, practice exercises, links to material that elaborates on the module content, and tests should be accessible within each module. The modules should be linked in an arrangement that makes sense, such as by importance or by the order in which content has to be learned (prerequisites). Trainees can choose to skip over material that they are familiar with or that they are competent in, based on a test of the content, or they can return to modules they need more practice in.

## Learner Control

One of the web's major potential advantages is that it gives learners control. **Learner control** refers to giving trainees the option to learn actively though self-pacing, exercises, exploring links to other material, and conversations with other trainees and experts. It includes the ability to select how content is presented (e.g., text, picture, video, etc.), to pause, skip, or review content, and to link to additional resources. That is, online learning allows activities typically led by the instructor (presentation, visuals, slides) or trainees (discussion, questions), as well as group interaction (discussion of application of training content), to be incorporated into training without trainees or the instructor having to be physically present in a training room. Simply providing learner control does not ensure that trainees will use all the features provided by online learning (e.g., practice exercises).[39] Trainees should have access to instructions on how to use learner control tools, or else difficulty using them will take away from time and attention that they can devote to learning. Companies must communicate the importance and meaningfulness of the training content for employees' jobs and must hold employees accountable for completing the training.

Research provides several recommendations for maximizing the benefits of learner control.[40] Training programs should not allow trainees to control the amount of feedback they receive because they may rely too much on the feedback, reducing their long-term retention of the training material. The program should offer practice on each topic repeatedly throughout the program so that trainees will not forget topics they have already completed. The program should provide practice to trainees using different examples to help the transfer of training content (skills or knowledge), not only to the full range of situations that trainees may encounter on the job, but also to unexpected situations. Trainees should be allowed to control the sequence in which they receive instruction but not be able to skip practice. Prompting self-regulation improves performance in online training. As was discussed in Chapter Four, **self-regulation** refers to the learner's involvement with the training material and assessing their progress toward learning. Online prompts asking trainees to recall key points or to set goals to help them use and remember the content after the course will help trainees to remember the key principles/objectives presented in training and how to apply their knowledge and skills.

## Provide Time and Space for Online Learning

Using formative evaluation of prototypes of web training can be helpful in identifying the appropriate length and time of modules (formative evaluations were discussed in Chapter Six, "Training Evaluation"). End users (managers, potential trainees) should be involved in a formative evaluation to ensure that music, graphics, icons, animation, video, and other features facilitate rather than interfere with learning. Also, end users need to test the content, the navigator, and the site map to guarantee that they can easily move through the learning module and access resources and links to other websites as needed. Online learning blurs the distinction between training and work. Expectations that trainees will be motivated and able to complete web-based training during breaks in their normal workday or on their personal time are unrealistic.[41] Companies need to ensure that employees are given time and space for e-learning to occur.[42] That is, employees need dedicated time, protected from work tasks, for learning to occur. As with other training programs, employees need to understand why they should attend e-learning and the benefits they will receive so as to enhance their motivation to learn. Accurate communications about the content and types of learning activities in e-learning courses need to be provided to employees.[43] Managers need to give employees time in their schedules, and employees need to schedule "training time" to complete training and avoid interruptions that can interfere with learning. Some companies are moving away from their initial expectation that online learning can be completed at the employee's desktop without time away from the job; instead, they are setting up learning labs for online learning to occur without the distractions of the workplace. "Chunking," or using one- to two-hour training modules, helps trainees learn and retain more than they might in a standard full-day or half-day training class. Training can also be more easily integrated into the typical workday. Trainees can devote one to two hours to a learning session from their office and then return to their work responsibilities.

Given the work demands that employees face, trainees need incentives to complete online learning. Some companies present cash awards and merchandise to employees who pass online competency tests that show they have completed and learned online course content. Other companies use certification programs to ensure that online courses are completed. For example, at Symbol Technologies, a manufacturer of handheld bar-code scanners and computers, sales trainees must complete online courses to be certified as salespersons.[44] If they don't complete the training, they can't continue into other training programs needed to be a successful salesperson. Aventis Pharma AG, a pharmaceutical company, has simply eliminated other training options such as classroom learning. If employees want training, their only option is online learning.

## Technology for Collaboration and Linking

Chapter Four emphasized that learning often occurs as a result of interaction or sharing between employees. Employees learn by informal, unstructured contact with experts and peers. Collaboration can involve an exchange among two or more trainees or among the trainer or other experts.

**Hyperlinks** are links that allow a trainee to access other websites that include printed materials, as well as communications links to experts, trainers, and other learners. Owens Corning's learning resource home page has hyperlinks to all available forms of training information, including CD-ROM, web-based, and trainer-led programs. The site supports online course registration and allows tests to be sent to trainees, scored, and used to register trainees in appropriate courses.[45]

Research suggests that the reason some employees fail to complete online learning and prefer instructor-led face-to-face instruction over online learning is that they want to be able to learn and network with their peers.[46] Effective online learning connects trainees and facilitates interaction and sharing through the use of collaborative learning tools such as chat rooms, discussion boards, or social media. Other methods for learner interaction and sharing include having trainees participate in collaborative online projects and receive tutoring, coaching, and mentoring by experts. Online learning also should provide a link between the trainees and the "instructor," who can answer questions, provide additional learning resources, and stimulate discussion between trainees on topics such as potential applications of the training content and common learning problems.

# SOCIAL MEDIA: WIKIS, BLOGS, MICROBLOGS, AND SOCIAL NETWORKS

**Social media** are online and mobile technology used to create interactive communications allowing the creation and exchange of user-generated content.[46a] They include blogs, wikis, networks such as Facebook, MySpace, and LinkedIn, microsharing sites such as Twitter, and shared media such as YouTube. Social media can be useful for:

- Providing links to resources such as webinars, videos, and articles related to new learning content
- Helping determine future training needs and issues by using tagging capabilities
- Reinforcing and sustaining learning
- Being used as a coaching and mentoring tool
- Linking learners before, during, and after a formal training event
- Engaging Generation X and millennial employees
- Providing content before a face-to-face learning event

A **blog** refers to a webpage where an author posts entries and readers often can comment. There are many different types of blogs, including personal blogs written by one person, company blogs used for marketing and branding purposes, topic blogs focusing on a specific topic area, and blogs based on media (video blogs) and devices (mobile device blog). There are several consideration for effectively using blogs in training.[47] For a blog to be useful for training, it should be related to the learning objectives; otherwise, trainees will find it to be "busy work" and fail to see its benefits. Blogs can be especially useful for trainees to analyze and synthesize information, for learners to reflect on the lesson or course content, and to share ideas and applications of learning content. Instructors need to provide timely and relevant feedback on blog entries. Also, instructors must provide guidelines regarding how blog entries will be evaluated or what types of blog entries are desired (e.g., new ideas, application-related, "what did I learn?"). Blogs can also be useful for training courses involving group work such as projects and cases. Blogs provide a way for team members to share comments, insights, and even get involved in brainstorming.

A **wiki** refers to a website that allows many users to create, edit, and update content and share knowledge. A **microblog or microsharing** refers to software tools such as Twitter that enable communications in short bursts of text, links, and multimedia either through stand-alone applications or through online communities or social networks. **Shared media** refers to audio or video such as YouTube that can be accessed and shared with others.

How are social media being used for learning, training, and development? Many companies are using social networking tools to help employees learn informally and share knowledge both on an as-needed basis and as part of formal training courses.

Consider the following companies and nonprofit organizations' use of social networking tools.[48] U.S. intelligence, diplomatic, and military organizations use Intellipedia to capture, share, and cross-reference reports of situations across the world. The site has been valuable in giving these communities real-time information. For example, during the Iraq war, when insurgents conducted attacks with improvised explosive devices using chlorine, someone asked what officers in the field should do to collect evidence of chlorine use. More than twenty experts located around the world helped to create a set of instructions in two days, without ever meeting face to face. Intellipedia is reviewed by volunteers who answer questions and keep track of wiki pages in their areas of expertise. The identity of the experts who contribute is provided to users.

Advantage Sales and Marketing (ASM), a sales and marketing agency based in Irvine, California, added social networking to its sales training program (Accelerated Career Excellence in Sales—ACES), which teaches individuals to become business development managers. The five-month learning program involves participants meeting face to face for a two-day training session and then returning to their home sales markets. The reaming time in the program is spent working in the field with mentors and completing online training modules. During the program, employees have access to the ACES workplace community online for interaction with senior sales leaders, peers, mentors, and other sales persons in the program. Adding the social networking platform to the training program has encouraged employees to share knowledge. For example, one learner in the program contacted all of the ACES mentors to identify best practices on a specific topic. He compiled this information into a document that he shared with the entire learner community. Verizon uses social networking tools to train employees to support new products and devices. Device Blog, Device Forum, and Learning Communities help ensure that employees are ready to support customers when new products and devices are introduced to the market, engages Verizon's multigenerational workforce, and facilitates peer-to-peer learning. Device Blog makes available information and updates on wireless devices (such as the Droid), frequently asked questions (FAQs), how-to videos, and troubleshooting tips. Device Forums enable retail employees to learn from peers and product manufacturers. Employees can ask each other questions, share issues, post tips, make suggestions, and access product experts.

Learning communities are accessed through the Device Blog. They include video blogs, message boards, links to online training modules, and product demonstrations. In addition to these tools, employees have access to My Network for collaborating with their peers, knowledge and document sharing, and creating working groups. Some instructors also use it for posting supplemental content for learners' use.

IBM uses social media to connect its employees around the world. IBM's site, known as w3, contributes to the global integration of the company. The w3 On Demand Workplace is a powerful productivity and collaboration tool for 400,000 IBM employees in seventy-five countries. The w3 can be used by employees to find resources and knowledge from peers around the world to help clients innovate and succeed. Employees can create personal profiles, bookmark websites and stories that they are interested in, comment on company blogs, contribute to wikis, share files, and read and review position papers, videos, and podcasts.

Special People in Northeast, Inc. (SPIN), a nonprofit organization that provides services to individuals with disabilities, makes webcasts as well as videos, how-to manuals, and process flowcharts electronically available to employees to ensure that knowledge of key employees is documented and current practices and procedures are available and shared. Intel encourages informal learning two ways: through knowledge sharing and providing employees with "performer support." Both knowledge sharing and performer support are part of Planet Blue, a social media platform for Intel employees. Employees also have access to Intelpedia, an internal wiki that employees can edit. Intelpedia has millions of pages, and thousands of employees have contributed to it. Intelpedia helped create a culture for using technology-based information-sharing solutions at Intel.

How would you determine if social media would be an effective learning tool in a company? Table 8.7 shows the questions to ask to address this issue. The more "yes" answers to these questions, the more likely that social media will be an effective learning solution. The most important consideration is whether social media is already being used in the company, which would make it easier to determine how it fits into the company's learning strategy and how easily it could be adapted to training.

It is important to consider if the ideas, content, and recommendations provided in social media are high quality and match company priorities. IBM conducts expertise assessment to ensure the quality of the recommendations.[49] All employees conduct an annual self-evaluation that defines their skill level and ability to serve clients. The skills level choices

**TABLE 8.7**
**Factors to Consider in Deciding to Use Social Media for Training and Learning**

Sources: Based on T. Bingham and M. Conner, *The New Social Learning* (Alexandria, VA: American Society for Training and Development, 2010); M. Derven, "Social networking: A force for development?" *T+D* (July 2009): 59–63.

Are social networks already being used in the company?
Does social networking fit into the company's learning strategy?
Are employees geographically dispersed?
Does the learning strategy support on-the-job learning?
Is there is a need to foster collaboration?
Are a significant number of employees from the millennial generation or Generation X?
Are employees comfortable using social networks?
Does the business require substantial teamwork?
Does knowledge need to be shared quickly?
Does the company value innovation?
Does the culture support decentralized decision making?

include entry, foundational, experienced, expert, and thought leader. These rankings help employees find those who have the knowledge and experience that they need for a particular skill or solution. Self-evaluations of "thought leader" and "expert" are verified by a second line manager and subject matter experts (SMEs). Also, it may also be necessary to have an editor monitor online postings to ensure that they reflect how the company wants to be perceived. The tradeoff of quality evaluations and monitoring are that they may inhibit collaboration and networking.

# BLENDED LEARNING

Because of the limitations of online learning related to technology (e.g., insufficient bandwidth and lack of high-speed web connections), trainee preference for face-to-face contact with instructors and other learners, and employees' inability to find unscheduled time during their workday to devote to learning from their desktops, many companies are moving to a hybrid, or blended, learning approach. **Blended learning** combines online learning, face-to-face instruction, and other methods for distributing learning content and instruction. Blended learning courses provide learners with the positive features of both face-to-face instruction and technology-based delivery and instructional methods (such as online learning, distance learning, or mobile technologies like tablet computers or iPhones), while minimizing the negative features of each.[50] In comparison to classroom delivery, blended learning provides increased learner control, allows for self-directedness, and requires learners to take more responsibility for their learning—all factors consistent with the recommendations of adult learning theory discussed in Chapter Four.[51] In comparison to pure online learning, blended learning provides more face-to-face social interaction and ensures that at least some of the instruction is presented in a dedicated learning environment. Blended learning uses the classroom to allow learners to learn together and to discuss and share insights, which helps bring learning to life and make it meaningful. Live feedback from peers is preferable to feedback received online.[52] Blended learning has been found to be more effective than face-to-face instruction for motivating trainees to learn and for teaching declarative knowledge or information about ideas or topics.[53] It appears that blended learning capitalizes on the positive learning features inherent in both face-to-face and web-based instruction. Interestingly, learners react more favorably toward classroom instruction than blended learning. This may be because blended learning courses are more demanding, requiring a greater time commitment because of the use of two learning approaches. Research suggests that the most significant issues or problems with blended learning are fast-changing technology, insufficient management support and commitment to blended learning, and a lack of understanding of what blended learning really is and how to implement it.[54]

Cisco Systems offers "Management 101," a foundational program for management development.[55] Cisco used to offer seven separate courses to its managers. The current program integrates the management development curriculum. In phase 1, for the first nine weeks, a different topic that managers need to know is covered online each week. The online learning includes testing to ensure that the managers have gained knowledge, multimedia exercises, case studies, and weekly facilitated online discussions. In phase 2, managers attend a four-day program in which they come together in a classroom to discuss and build on what they have learned online. Phase 3 involves each manager learning alongside his or her own manager. At the conclusion of the program, each manager receives a 360-degree feedback evaluation. This evaluation is used to tailor each manager's development plan. Gilbane Building Company offers a change management course that includes an eight-hour face-to-face class combined with a two-hour online prerequisite module presenting change management principles. The face-to-face class allows trainees to apply the change management principles to possible project scenarios. Gilbane also includes a performance support system that trainees can refer to when they return to their jobs.

Training at Dunkin' Donuts is based on a blended learning approach that involves online, classroom, and on-site work with follow-up and reinforcement.[56] Franchisees attend an introductory course that focuses on the business as well as their roles and responsibilities and those of the franchisor. This helps the franchisees learn from and build relationships with important individuals and teams at the corporation. Franchisees then complete 60 hours of online training on their own time in how doughnuts are made, equipment maintenance, food safety, and shift management. A five-and-one-half-week instructor-led course and certification program runs at the same time as the online training. The online and the instructor-led courses are both designed to simulate restaurant experiences, with the goal of facilitating on-the-job practice that occurs in the restaurant. Practice sessions are supported with skills checklists so that trainees can monitor their progress and review training materials.

# SIMULATIONS AND GAMES

Simulations and games were introduced as a traditional training method in Chapter Seven. This chapter discusses how development in software and computer technology has improved the learning and transfer that can result from simulators and games. Simulation and games that can be delivered via a personal computer (or gaming technology such as an Xbox immerse trainees in decision-making exercises in an artificial yet realistic environment that allow them to learn the consequences of their decisions. Simulation games are widely popular—one estimate is that 40 percent of adults play video games![57] The key is how to use the fun and motivational aspects of games to help employees acquire knowledge and skills. Table 8.8 shows four different types of simulations and games. UrbanSim is a branching story U.S. Army game that teaches counterinsurgency techniques to battalion commanders.[58] UrbanSim resembles a militarized version of SimCity that many of us

**TABLE 8.8**
**Types of Simulations**

Sources: Based on C. Cornell, "Better than the real thing?" *Human Resource Executive* (August 2005): 34–37; S. Boehle, "Simulations: The next generation of e-learning," *Training* (January 2005): 22–31.

| Type of Simulation | Description |
|---|---|
| Branching story | Trainees are presented with a situation and asked to make a choice or decision. Trainees progress through the simulation on the basis of their decisions. |
| Interactive spreadsheet | Trainees are given a set of business rules (usually finance-based) and asked to make decisions that will affect the business. The decisions are entered into a spreadsheet that shows how the decisions affect the business. |
| Game-based | Trainees play a video game on a computer. |
| Virtual lab | Trainees interact with a computer representation of the job for which they are being trained. |

enjoy at home. However, UrbanSim is a sophisticated simulation that incorporates factors such as economic conditions and social networking ties and analyzes how these factors sway the population to back the government or the insurgents. Traditionally, Army simulations have involved battlefield tactics and deciding how much, when, and which firepower to use to overtake the enemy. However, in today's counterinsurgency missions in which the enemy does not wear a uniform and lives among the peaceful civilian population, and there is not necessarily an identifiable battlefield, winning the hearts and minds of locals depends more on psychology, sociology, and political skills than firepower. These games require military leaders to make the types of decisions that they have to make in their operations and to see the consequences. For example, they can kick down doors, bribe local leaders, smash insurgent cells, and fix sewer lines. They help the leaders understand how to best use the resources they have available and to understand the immediate consequences of each decision, as well as how each decision can contribute to or deter from the effectiveness of other actions. For example, repairing the local sewer system shifts the population's mood, which in turn changes support for the insurgents, which affects the number of attacks from improvised explosive devices and could eventually help the army overcome the counterinsurgency.

At NetApp Inc., twenty-five managers participated in a game in which they played the role of top executives in an imaginary company modeled after their employer.[59] The managers worked in five-person teams and competed to produce the strongest sales and operating profit. They were faced with challenges such as balancing long-term investments against short-term results. Managers received information including market analyses based on actual NetApp data and a menu of strategic initiatives such as improving college recruiting. The teams had to choose strategies and allocate employees and money. They were given scenarios such as an important customer seeking to add last-minute product features; in responding, they had to decide whether to add the features (which included determining their related costs) or refuse and risk angering an important client. The teams saw the consequences of their decisions. For example, one team declined to add the product features, which resulted in a decline in customer satisfaction and market share. At the end of the simulation, the sales and total profits of each team, as well as the effects of their strategies, were discussed.

Miller Brewing Company uses a mini-game, "Tips on Tap," to help teach bartenders how to serve the perfect beer, card customers, and provide good service to increase their tips.[60] "Tips on Tap" includes simulations such as Score Your Pour, which teaches how to pour beer using the proper angle and height. Trainees move the glass using a computer mouse and measure the distance and angle of the glass to the beer tap to create the proper "head" (the foam on top of a glass of beer). Points are subtracted if the tap is hit while pouring or if the beer is spilled. Feedback is provided to trainees after each session. Mini-games are becoming increasingly popular for a number of reasons. At Miller, the online game does a better job of replicating how to pour a beer correctly than traditional classroom instruction; it is more convenient and accessible for trainee practice; and the real product is not used, thus eliminating waste and reducing costs. Also, mini-games are easy to access, engage the learner with music and graphics, require less than twenty minutes of student participation, and have low development costs. Mini-games may be most appropriate for learning skills that can be taught and learned through repetition, such as pouring beer or conducting emergency procedures.

Before launching its new product, Rapid Release Gelcaps, Tylenol used a game called "The Need for Speed Trivia," to help salespersons learn about the product.[61] The game was burned onto a CD-ROM for salespersons to play either by themselves or online against their peers. The game used a timer and scoring system. Salespersons who played against each other raced to see who could answer the most questions in the shortest time. A high-score system was posted so that anyone who played the game could see who had the leading score. Questions about the product were designed to reinforce the information sales reps had received about the new gelcaps at a national sales meeting. The results suggest the game was an effective training tool. Each salesperson played an average of forty-seven games and interacted with the program for seventy-one minutes. Feedback from the sales reps indicates that they learned about the product and enjoyed playing the game.

An **avatar** refers to a computer depictions of humans that are used as imaginary coaches, coworkers, and customers in simulations.[62] Typically, trainees can see the avatar, who appears throughout the training course. For example, a sales training course at CDW Corporation, a technology products and service company, guides trainees through mock interviews with customers. The avatar introduces the customer situation, and trainees hear the customer speaking to them in a simulated phone conversation. Trainees have to "read" the customer's voice, with help from the avatar, to determine what is happening in the sales process. The Loews hotel chain uses Virtual Leader, a program that helps participants learn how to be effective in meetings (e.g., how to build alliances or how to get a meeting agenda approved). As trainees attend the simulated meetings, what they say (or do not say) results in scores that relate to their influence in the meeting.

As you can see from these examples, simulations can be effective for several reasons.[63] First, trainees can use them on their desktop computer, eliminating the need to travel to a central training location. Second, simulations are meaningful, they get trainees involved in learning, and they are emotionally engaging (they can even be fun!). This increases employees' willingness to practice, encourages retention, and improves their skills. Third, simulators provide a consistent message of what needs to be learned; trainees can work at their own pace; and, compared to face-to-face instruction, simulators can incorporate more situations or problems that a trainee might encounter. Fourth, simulations can safely put employees in situations that would be dangerous in the real world. Fifth, simulations have been found to result in such positive outcomes as shorter training times and increased return on investment.

Simulations do have some disadvantages. The use of simulations has been limited by their development costs. Games and simulations are useful for practicing skills, but trainees must first acquire knowledge and then apply it while playing the game.[64] Debriefing learners after a game is useful for helping trainees understand how their simulation experience relates to their work. A customized simulation can cost between $200,000 and $300,000, while a simulation purchased from a supplier without any customization typically costs $100 to $200 per trainee.[65] However, although they continue to be an expensive training method, development costs for simulations continue to decrease, making them a more popular training method. Also, the use of simulations as a training method is likely to increase as technology development allows more realism to be built into simulations. Finally, trainees may not be comfortable in learning situations that lack human contact.

## Virtual Reality

**Virtual reality** is a computer-based technology that provides trainees with a three-dimensional learning experience. Virtual reality allows simulations to become even more realistic. Using specialized equipment or viewing the virtual model on the computer screen, trainees move through the simulated environment and interact with its components.[66] Technology is used to stimulate multiple senses of the trainee.[67] Devices relay information from the environment to the senses. For example, audio interfaces, gloves that provide a sense of touch, treadmills, or motion platforms are used to create a realistic, artificial environment. Devices also communicate information about the trainee's movements to a computer. These devices allow the trainee to experience **presence** (the perception of actually being in a particular environment). Presence is influenced by the amount of sensory information available to the trainee, control over sensors in the environment, and the trainees' ability to modify the environment.

For example, Motorola uses virtual reality in its advanced manufacturing courses for employees learning to run the Pager Robotic Assembly facility. Employees are fitted with a head-mount display that allows them to view the virtual world, which includes the actual lab space, robots, tools, and assembly operation. Trainees hear and see the actual sounds and sights as if they were using the real equipment. Also, the equipment responds to the employees' actions (e.g., turning on a switch or moving a dial).

One advantage of virtual reality is that it allows trainees to practice dangerous tasks without putting themselves or others in danger. Research suggests that virtual reality training is likely to have the greatest impact on complex tasks or tasks that involve extensive use of visual cues.[68] The key to the success of the virtual reality environment is to use visual, spatial, and audio cues to design engaging experiences that are as close as possible to the actual work environment.[69] Learning in virtual reality occurs when a teachable moment occurs. That is, the learners' lack of knowledge or skill clashes with their need to acquire knowledge or skills to overcome a challenge. The experience of the learner in the environment cause learning to occur and helps in its retention and application. Virtual worlds need to allow learners to act and interact toward a common goal, to make errors and try again, and to eventually achieve the learning outcomes. Learners need to be provided with minimal guidelines, allowing them to learn from their peers, the environment, and their experience. Two of the advantages of virtual worlds, collaboration and knowledge and skill transfer, can be facilitated by creating an environment where learners participate in the same space at the same time and providing time for instructor (avatar) review of the application of the knowledge or skills taught or for peer review of actions, behaviors, or results. Another potential advantage relates to the cognitive processing required by the learner. The use of such a realistic environment in training may make more memory available for learning. Memory that was previously used to convert one- or two-dimensional training scenarios into three-dimensional space can now be used for processing information.

Obstacles to developing effective virtual reality training include poor equipment that results in a reduced sense of presence (e.g., poor tactile feedback and inappropriate time lags between sensing and responding to trainees' actions). Poor presence may result in the trainee experiencing vomiting, dizziness, and headaches (simulator sickness) because senses are distorted.

# Virtual Worlds

**Virtual worlds** refer to computer-based, simulated online three-dimensional representations of the real world where learning programs or experiences can be hosted. In Second Life, one popular virtual world, trainees use an avatar to interact with each other in classrooms, webinars, simulations, or role-play exercises. The virtual world of Second Life allows for learning to be real without being dangerous or risky for patients, employees, or customers. Second Life allows employees to learn alone, with their peers, or in teams. Second Life can be used to create virtual classrooms, but its strength is its ability to create virtual reality simulations that actively involve the learner, such as putting the trainee's avatar in a realistic role play in which it has to deal with an upset customer. Stapoil, a Norwegian oil company, has an oil platform in Second Life that allows trainees to walk around it. Stapoil uses the oil platform for safety training. It catches fire and employees have to find lifeboats to safely exit the platform.[70]

Employees at Silicon Image learn about making silicon chips by exploring a virtual world that represents a corporate campus and interacting with avatars.[71] Employees can visit the company's departments while watching videos and slide shows explaining what type of work is done within each unit. British Petroleum (BP) uses Second Life to train new gas station employees in the safety features of gasoline storage tanks and piping systems.[72] BP's virtual world includes three-dimensional replicas of the tank and pipe systems at a gas station. Trainees are able to see the underground storage tanks and piping systems and observe how safety devices control gasoline flow—something they could never do in real life. A pharmaceutical company developed a virtual world to train physicians how to expand their practices by offering vaccinations.[73] Physicians can tour a virtual practice and visit different rooms to learn how to order and store vaccines, administer doses to patients and bill for their services.

Besides Second Life, ProtoSphere, Forterra, and Virtual Heroes are other providers of virtual worlds.[74] Paidera, a technology company that provides English-as-second-language training, uses Forterra to teach English. Trainees create avatars and then enter the virtual world to practice language skills in real situations. Trainees are placed in a virtual situation, such as talking to a cab driver or ordering food at a restaurant, that requires use of their language skills. The cost to rent space from a virtual-world program's campus within a public space is $200–$300 per day; it costs $1,000 to $2,000 for a customized simulation within the space.[75] Leased space in a virtual world is expensive. It can can range from $5,000 to $100,000 annually, depending on the size and type of the space leased ($10,000–$20,000 is required for a private space on a public server or a private, customized island).

## Advantages of Virtual Worlds

There are several advantages of using a virtual world for training.[76] Although few studies have been conducted so far, research suggests that learners are more satisfied with virtual world experiences and learn more and faster than in traditional courses.[77] The virtual environment can imitate an actual workplace such as a lab, processing plant, or hospital emergency room, allowing trainees to both practice their skills without harming products or patients and, at the same time, see the real-life consequences of their actions and decisions. It also provides a place to meet with trainers, managers, or other employees who can serve as teachers. Virtual worlds are useful for skill building for non-routine job tasks and difficult to define procedures based on judgment and problem solving. Virtual worlds also can be useful for teaching interpersonal skills such as time management, communications, leadership, and working under pressure. Teamwork exercises and group problem solving are possible because avatars can be created to simulate other trainees or other trainees can simultaneously be involved in the simulation. Second Life and other virtual worlds motivate learners by making learning fun and interactive. Second Life also can enhance transfer of training because the virtual world used for training can replicate the real-life work environment identically. Second Life can be used for e-learning, collaboration, and meetings. As with other technology-based training methods, it is an especially effective way for employees who are not in the same location or country to have access to training.

### *Disadvantages of Virtual Worlds*

Despite the seemingly unlimited potential for training and development in virtual worlds such as Second Life, this method also has significant disadvantages. Research suggests that disadvantages include lack of ease of use for first-time users; the potential risk of a difficult keyboard and mouse interface, which can demotivate learners; the high investment of time and money required for programming content; and the lack of evidence supporting its effectiveness for learning.[78] The novelty of the experience of a three-dimensional virtual world such as Second Life and the appearance of the avatars may help trainees recall the experience, but they may also interfere with retention and transfer of the training content to the job. Learning in a virtual world may be better for those who already have some job experiences because for learners totally new to the work world, a virtual environment may confuse and overwhelm them.

# MOBILE TECHNOLOGY AND LEARNING

Mobile technology allows learning to occur anywhere, at any time. Mobile technology consists of[79]

- Wireless transmission systems such as Wi-Fi and Bluetooth that allow transmission of data without the need for physical connections between devices or between a device and an Internet connection.
- Mobile devices such as PDAs, smartphones, tablet computers, iPods, iPads, global positioning system (GPS) devices, and radio frequency identification chips (RFIDs).
- Software applications related to processing audio files, word processing, spreadsheets, Internet, e-mail, and instant messaging.

GPS and RFID devices are used for tracking customers, employees, and property. For example, many cars and trucks are equipped with GPS devices to allow operators to locate drivers. Trucking companies use GPS devices to track loads and to determine expected arrival times. RFID chips are embedded in products to track their movement and to help in inventory control. Hotels are providing mobile devices such as PDAs to allow customers to access information about guest services, dining, entertainment, and accommodations anywhere on the hotel property.

**Mobile learning** refers to training delivered using a mobile device such as a smartphone, netbook, notebook computer, or iPad. Mobile learning can involve both formal and informal learning. Formal learning might include e-learning courses, podcasts, or videos on the mobile device. Informal learning includes engaging in communication and messaging with other employees or experts via Twitter, blogs, or Facebook. The advantages of mobile learning include that it is an easy way to get up-to-date information to employees; it can be useful for enhancing transfer of training through providing follow-up; it brings training to employees who constantly traveling, out of the office visiting customers or clients, or don't have the time to attend a face-to-face course or program (such as salespeople or executives); and learners can complete training on their own time and pace. Mobile devices can also provide RSS feeds, shared media (such as YouTube), and podcasts. **Podcasts** are audio or video program content distributed in episodes using software such as RSS. The best use of podcasts is for narrative-based content that inspires the user's imagination using music and sound effects.[80] Podcasts are great for sharing expertise of SMEs using interviews, stories, and role plays. It is cheap and easy to produce using a microphone, computer with audio software, portable digital recorder, Skype phone recorder, headphones, or speakers. An advantage of podcasts is that learners can listen at any time or place time using many different mobile devices such as iPhones, iPads, or notebook computers. Through mobile technologies, training and learning can occur naturally throughout the workday or at home, employees can be connected to communities of learning, and employees are given the ability to learn at their own pace by reviewing material or skipping over content that they already know.[81]

Some companies are using PDAs as their primary method for delivering training or as a follow-up to training programs delivered face-to-face or online. At Tyco International Ltd., a safety products producer, service technicians use PDAs to manage service orders, conduct inspections, and generate quotes for customers.[82] Tyco is using the PDAs to deliver a short course that teaches sales technicians how to program and set a burglar alarm. The course includes a simulation of an alarm panel. The ability to use their PDAs for learning is perfect for Tyco's sales technicians; because they are constantly traveling, responding to service requests, they have little time for traditional training or online learning. The PDAs are also used for electronic performance support, providing technicians with access to job aids and procedure guides for tasks such as how to remove and replace a failed alarm or how to troubleshoot a specific piece of equipment. This is important because with the more than 200 categories of equipment serviced by Tyco, it is difficult for the technicians to recall all of the necessary procedures and programming, even when they have been reviewed in earlier training courses.

Many companies are considering using tablets such as the iPad for training because of their ease of use, colorful, easy-to-read display, ability to connect to the web, and availability of powerful apps. **Apps** refer to applications designed specifically for smartphones and tablet computers. Apps are primarily being used to supplement training, manage the path or sequence of training, and to help employees maintain training records.[83] An app for the U.S. military combat medical teams provides details on specific medical procedures such as controlling bleeding. The American Ophthalmological Society (AOS) is using apps in its continuous medical education courses to supplement training. Courses are provided online, but learning tips and techniques are provided as mobile apps.

Some companies are beginning to use apps as primary training. To ensure that learning and transfer of training occurs using these apps, they are designed to catch the learner's attention by incorporating attention-getting videos, stories, and interactions. For example,

Coca-Cola uses multiplayer gaming on electronic devices to train executives in team problem solving. Hilton Worldwide is distributing 1,000 iPads to senior executives. These executives spend almost 8 percent of their time traveling, which makes classroom learning difficult.[84] The iPads are loaded with customized apps and videos. SAP, a technology company, gave its employees 1,500 iPads and is expected to distribute an additional 17,000 in 2011. SAP is using the iPad because it can help facilitate personalized learning for salespeople around the world. A new salesperson in China will need a different set of skills and apps than a saleperson who is experienced at selling SAP solutions in Canada. Watson Pharmaceuticals has developed an app for its corporate university, allowing pharmaceutical representatives to access videos and product knowledge from their iPhones. Unisys Corporation offers employees both an e-learning and mobile version of a compliance training program.[85] The mobile version includes four twenty-minute segments compared to the one-and-one-half-hour e-learning program. The mobile version also has less content on each screen and limited use of video. Unisys is also providing samples of e-learning or face-to-face programs on mobile devices to entice learners to get involved in other training courses. Northrop Grumman, a defense contractor, is developing games for tablets and iPads that train users on information technology security using an interface that looks like a motherboard. Learners move around the game board in their "truck" and are presented with questions about information technology security. Correctly answering all of the questions earns them the opportunity to play an action game in which they shoot down logic bombs, malicious code, and Trojan horses.

For mobile learning to be effective, it needs to be short, easy to use, and meaningful.[86] One estimate is that the course length should not exceed ten minutes because users likely do not have long periods of time for learning, and attention spans are limited when looking at the small screens on many mobile devices. The screen layout should work with or without graphics. Images should be used only where relevant to the content because download time may be slow due to bandwidth limitations. Images used should be sized so that the user can see them without scrolling horizontally or vertically. Technical requirements due to screen size, web browsers, and mobile operating systems need to be considered, as well as the availability and ability to use plug-ins such as flash, Java, and Portable Document Format (PDF). Also, simply repurposing lectures by digitizing them and distributing them to employees will not facilitate learning. For example, Capital One creates simulated radio shows with phone-in questions and answers given by announcers to create an audio learning environment that is enjoyable and interesting. As with e-learning, training that uses mobile technology may be most effective if it is part of a blended learning approach that involves face-to-face interaction among trainees as well as audio learning.

# INTELLIGENT TUTORING SYSTEMS

An **Intelligent tutoring system (ITS)** is an instructional system that uses artificial intelligence.[87] There are three types of ITS environments: tutoring, coaching, and empowering. Tutoring is a structured attempt to increase trainee understanding of a content domain. Coaching provides trainees with the flexibility to practice skills in artificial environments. Empowering refers to the student's ability to explore the content of the training program freely. The five components of ITS are shown in Figure 8.4. The ITS has information about the content domain, as well as expectations about the trainee's level of knowledge.

**FIGURE 8.4**
**Components of ITS**

Source: Based on D. Steele-Johnson and B. G. Hyde, "Advanced Technologies in Training: Intelligent Tutoring Systems and Virtual Reality." In *Training for a Rapidly Changing Workplace*, ed. M. A. Quinones and A. Ehrenstein (Washington, D.C.: American Psychological Association, 1997): 225–248.

**Domain Expert**
- Provides information about how to perform the task

**Trainee Model**
- Provides information about student's knowledge

**User Interface**
- Enables trainee to interact with the system

**Training Session Manager**
- Interprets trainees' actions and reports the results or provides coaching

**Trainee Scenario Generator**
- Determines difficulty and order in which problems are presented to trainee

ITS can be distinguished from other new training technologies in several ways:[88]

- ITS has the ability to match instruction to individual student needs.
- ITS can communicate and respond to the student.
- ITS can model the trainee's learning process.
- ITS can decide, on the basis of a trainee's previous performance, what information to provide.
- ITS can make decisions about the trainee's level of understanding.
- ITS can complete a self-assessment resulting in a modification of its teaching process.

ITS has been used by the National Aeronautics and Space Administration (NASA) in astronaut training.[89] For example, the Remote Maneuvering System ITS was used to teach astronauts how to use the robotic arm on the space shuttle. Astronauts had to learn to complete tasks and procedures related to grappling a payload. The ITS generated processes that were matched to individual astronauts. Feedback was matched to each astronaut's pattern of success and failure in learning the tasks. The system recorded performance data for each astronaut, made decisions regarding the student's level of understanding, and used those decisions to provide appropriate feedback.

# DISTANCE LEARNING

**Distance learning** is used by geographically dispersed companies to provide information about new products, policies, or procedures, as well as deliver skills training and expert lectures to field locations.[90] Distance learning can include virtual classrooms, which have the following capabilities: projection of still, animated, and video images; instructor-participant audio discussion; sharing of computer software applications; interactions using instant polling technology; and whiteboard marking tools.[91] Distance learning features two-way communications between people, and it currently involves two types of technology.[92] The first technology is teleconferencing. **Teleconferencing** refers to synchronous exchange of audio, video, and/or text between two or more individuals or groups at two or more locations. Trainees attend training programs in training facilities in which they can communicate with trainers (who are at another location) and other trainees using the telephone or personal computer. The second type of distance learning also includes individualized, personal computer–based training.[93] Employees participate in training anywhere they have access to a personal computer. This type of distance learning may involve multimedia training methods, such as web-based training. Course material and assignments can be distributed using the company's intranet, video, or CD-ROM. Trainers and trainees interact using e-mail, bulletin boards, and conferencing systems.

Teleconferencing usually includes a telephone link so that trainees viewing the presentation can call in questions and comments to the trainer. Also, satellite networks allow companies to link up with industry-specific and educational courses for which employees receive college credit and job certification. IBM, Hewlett-Packard, and Milliken.Corporation are among the many firms that subscribe to the National Technological University (now part of Walden University), which broadcasts courses throughout the United States that technical employees need to obtain advanced degrees in engineering.[94]

A **virtual classroom** refers to using a computer and the Internet to distribute instructor-led training to geographically dispersed employees. The potential advantages of the virtual classroom include its cost savings and convenience: geographically dispersed employees can be brought together for training for several hours each week, and content experts can be brought into the classroom as needed. However, the training delivered using a virtual classroom is not the same as the training delivered face to face by an instructor. There are a number of guidelines for developing effective training in the virtual classroom:[95]

- Design short modules and follow up with an assignment that applies the learning to the job.
- Make learning interactive and interesting, such as modeling the program after a phone-in radio show.
- Include media such as video and audio.
- Limit classroom size to no more than twenty-five learners.
- Offer learners multiple ways of interacting with each other and the instructor, including webinars, e-mail, discussion rooms, message boards, and blogs.

**Interactive distance learning (IDL)** refers to the latest generation of distance learning, which uses satellite technology to broadcast programs to different locations and allows trainees to respond to questions posed during the training program using a keypad.[96] IDL is being used by companies that have employees in many different locations and who lack computers or online access. IDL allows employees in different locations to see behaviors and how to get things done rather than just read or hear about them. For example, JCPenney Company, which produces more than 200 different IDL programs each year, uses distance learning to reach every associate. Each store has a training room where up to twelve employees can sign in to the program and watch on a large television screen. Each employee has his or her own keypad to interact with the program. Employees are able to watch the satellite broadcast live or view a tape of the program later. Regardless of whether watching the program live or via tape, employees can answer questions such as, "How many square feet does your store have for lingerie?" At the end of the program, managers and trainers can access a report on how every store answered. Evaluations of the interactive distance learning program have been positive. IDL has allowed JCPenney to deliver training to every employee in the company, and 86 percent of its employees report that they have the training needed to perform their jobs effectively.

An advantage of distance learning is that the company can save on travel costs. It also allows employees in geographically dispersed sites to receive training from experts who would not otherwise be available to visit each location. Intuit finds that a traditional classroom environment is good for introducing software and providing trainees with the opportunity to network. Virtual classroom training is used for courses on special software features, for demonstrations, and for troubleshooting using application-sharing features. General Mills uses virtual classrooms at smaller plants where offering a class on site is not cost effective.[97] Employees have access to courses in product-specific knowledge (e.g., cereal production), general technical skills (e.g., food chemistry), and functional-specific knowledge (e.g., maintenance). FileNeT Corporation was concerned with how its sales force was going to keep up with new software and software updates.[98] FileNeT tried self-paced online learning but discovered that salespeople did not like to read a lot of material about new products on the web. Enrollment in online courses dwindled, and salespeople flooded the company's training department with requests for one-on-one assistance. To solve the training problem, the company decided to use webcasting. **Webcasting,** or **web conferencing,** involves instruction that is provided online through live broadcasts. Webcasting helped spread the sales force training throughout the year rather than cramming it into twice-a-year sales meetings. Webcasting also helped ensure that the salespeople all received the same information. The salespeople liked the webcasts because of the timely information that helped them have conversations with customers. The live sessions were also popular because participants could ask questions. Webcasting has not replaced face-to-face training at FileNeT; classroom training is still about 80 percent of training, but that percentage has decreased from 90 percent. Webcasting has also resulted in savings of $500,000 annually (because one of the twice-yearly sales meetings was canceled).

The major disadvantages of distance learning are the lack of interaction between the trainer and the audience, technology failures, and unprepared trainers. A high degree of interaction among trainees or between the trainees and the trainer is a positive learning feature that is missing from distance learning programs that use the technology only to broadcast a lecture to geographically dispersed employees. All this does is repurpose a traditional lecture (with its limitations for learning and transfer of training) for a new training technology. To engage trainees in a distance learning environment, it is useful to limit online sessions to sixty to ninety minutes in length, maintain a good instructional pace, avoid presenting unnecessary text, use relevant and engaging visuals (e.g., graphs and animation), and allow trainees to participate using polling devices and small-group breakout rooms for discussion and projects.[99] A group spokesperson can be assigned to summarize and communicate the group's ideas. Weather conditions and satellite glitches can occur at any time, disconnecting the instructor from the audience or making it difficult to show video or other multimedia presentations. Instructors need backup plans for dealing with technical issues. Because many instructors have difficulty speaking to trainees in another location without a live group of trainees in front of them, it is important to prepare instructors for distance delivery. For example, a producer who is familiar with the technology can work with the instructor and help facilitate the training session.

# TECHNOLOGIES FOR TRAINING SUPPORT

Technologies such as expert systems, groupware, and electronic support systems are being used to support training efforts. Training support means that these technologies are helping to capture training content so that it is available to employees who may not have attended training. Training support also means that these technologies provide information and decision rules to employees on an as-needed basis (i.e., they are job aids). Employees can access these technologies in the work environment.

Table 8.9 shows when training support technologies are most needed. Many conditions shown in the table relate to characteristics of the task or the environment that can inhibit transfer of training. For example, employees may work some distance away from their manager, the manager may be difficult to contact, or employees may need special expertise that the manager lacks. These situations make it difficult for employees to find answers to problems that arise on the job. Training support technologies can assist in transfer of training by helping employees generalize training content to the work environment and by providing employees with new information (not covered in training).

## Expert Systems

**Expert systems** refer to technology (usually software) that organizes and applies the knowledge of human experts to specific problems.[100] Expert systems have three elements:

1. A knowledge base that contains facts, figures, and rules about a specific subject
2. A decision-making capability that, imitating an expert's reasoning ability, draws conclusions from those facts and figures to solve problems and answer questions
3. A user interface that gathers and gives information to the person using the system

Expert systems are used as a support tool that employees refer to when they have problems or decisions that they feel exceed their current knowledge and skills. For example, a large international food processor uses an expert system called Performer, which is designed to provide training and support to its plant operators. One problem that the company was facing was determining why potato chips were being scorched in the fryer operation. An operator solved the problem using Performer. He selected the Troubleshooting menu,

**TABLE 8.9**
**Conditions When Training Support Technologies Are Most Needed**

Source: Based on A. Rossett, "Job Aids and Electronic Performance Support Systems." In *The ASTD Training and Development Handbook,* 4th ed., ed. R. L. Craig (New York: McGraw-Hill, 1996): 554–577.

- Performance of task is infrequent.
- The task is lengthy, difficult, and information intensive.
- The consequences of error are damaging.
- Performance relies on knowledge, procedures, or approaches that frequently change.
- There is high employee turnover.
- Little time is available for training, or there are few resources for training.
- Employees are expected to take full responsibility for learning and performing tasks.

then Product Texture/Flavor, then Off Oil Flavor. The program listed probable causes, beginning with high oxidation during frying. The operator chose that cause, and the system recommended adjusting the cooking line's oil flush, providing detailed steps for that procedure. Following those steps resolved the problem.[101]

Although expert systems are discussed as a technology that supports training, expert systems can also be used as a delivery mechanism. Expert systems can be used to train employees in the decision rules of the experts. For example, a financial company dramatically increased the portfolio of products that it offered to customers.[102] The sales force needed to be prepared to introduce these products to clients and to make sales. The company developed an expert system to capture the sales processes used by top sales performers. This web-based expert system allowed salespersons to access information on each financial product, alerted salespersons to information they needed from the customer, and used expert logic to identify opportunities to introduce new products to customers based on data entered by the salesperson (the expert system matches general client characteristics with specific customer characteristics).

Expert systems can deliver both high quality and lower costs. By using the decision processes of experts, the system enables many people to arrive at decisions that reflect experts' knowledge. An expert system helps avoid the errors that can result from fatigue and decision biases. The efficiencies of an expert system can be realized if it can be operated by fewer or less skilled (and likely less costly) employees than the company would otherwise require.

## Electronic Performance Support Systems (EPSSs)

An **electronic performance support system (EPSS)** is an electronic infrastructure that captures, stores, and distributes individual and corporate knowledge assets throughout an organization to enable individuals to achieve required levels of performance in the fastest possible time and with a minimum of support from other people.[103] An EPSS includes all the software needed to support the work of individuals (not just one or two specific software applications). It integrates knowledge assets into the interface of the software tools rather than separating them as add-on components. For example, company policy information may be presented in a dialog box rather than in a separate online document. The typical EPSS includes:

- An "assistant" to automate tasks and lighten the workload
- A "librarian" to provide task-specific information
- A "teacher" to guide the user through the process step by step
- An "advisor" to provide expert advice

Chapter Five, "Program Design," discussed EPSS as a means to help training transfer. EPSS can also be used as a substitute for training. Microsoft's Office software has "wizards," a help function that recognizes the task that the user is starting to perform (e.g., writing a letter) and offers information related to that task. Also, retailers such as Sephora and JCPenney are supplying employee with iPads that they can use as a product-reference guide (a performance support tool). At Reuters, the news and financial information company, employees who deal with orders for financial systems information and data needed a way to get their questions answered on an as-needed basis because they did not have time to attend training sessions.[104] Typical questions included how to register financial traders to access Reuters's information and systems and how to coordinate installation of Reuters's technology on the trading floor. Reuters purchased an EPSS that provides employees with Help tabs on their computer screens as they perform tasks. The Help tabs provide answers to questions about the steps required to complete different processes, such as user registration.

To use EPSS as a substitute for training, trainers must determine whether problems and tasks require employees to actually acquire knowledge, skill, or ability (learned capability) and whether periodic assistance through an EPSS is sufficient.

# LEARNING MANAGEMENT SYSTEMS: SYSTEMS FOR TRAINING DELIVERY, SUPPORT, AND ADMINISTRATION

A **learning management system (LMS)** refers to a technology platform that can be used to automate the administration, development, and delivery of all of a company's training programs. LMSs can provide employees, managers, and trainers with the ability to manage, deliver, and track learning activities. Some of the features of LMSs are shown in Table 8.10. New developments in LMSs include providing the ability for users to search the database and their company's intranet simultaneously for information on training courses, contact experts who are identified by the company as topic experts, enroll in all courses related to a certification or particular training topic at one time, and use simulations to determine whether employees are complying with ethical standards and skills that they have been trained in using by the LMS.[105]

There are a number of reasons LMSs are becoming more popular. An LMS can help a company reduce travel and other costs related to training, reduce time for program completion, increase employees' accessibility to training across the business, and provide administrative capabilities to track program completion and course enrollments. LMSs allow companies to track all learning activity in the business. For example, FedEx Office has

**TABLE 8.10**
**Features of LMSs**

Source: Based on "Learning management systems: An executive summary," *Training* (March 2002): 4.

| | |
|---|---|
| Trainee management and reporting | Track and report on trainee progress and activity. |
| Training event and resource management | Organize courses and learning events in catalogs; manage and track course resources such as classrooms and instructors; support communications among administrators and students. |
| Online course delivery infrastructure | Deliver online courses; register and track trainees. |
| Authoring tools | Create new courses; promote consistency in courses. |
| Skill assessment | Create, edit, distribute, and deliver assessment tests; review trainee achievements. |
| Professional development management | Track and compare trainee learning against goals, based on the trainee's job or function. |
| Knowledge bases | Integrate links to learning references that supplement online learning. |
| Personalization | Engage employees in learning through the use of target courses, references, and e-mails. |

document and shipping centers around the world and employs more than 20,000 people. The LMS at FedEx includes a software package that creates individualized training for each employee, schedules classrooms, tracks employee progress, manages all aspects of the training curriculum, and delivers e-learning courses.[106] Employees have access via their personal computer to their personal learning plan, which is based on their job, what their manager requires, and their own personal interests.

Smaller companies can also gain the advantages of an LMS by hiring a vendor to own and operate the system, maintain the hardware, and handle security and upgrades.[107] This allows smaller companies to offer training and development opportunities that they could not otherwise offer due to the small number of training staff. Using an LMS, GECU, a Texas-based credit union, has improved its training staff's ability to manage, deliver, and evaluate learning. Before the LMS, there were few courses and programs at the company for professional development. The LMS has allowed GECU to offer courses for career development for all employees.

## Why Develop an LMS?

Tracking the learning activity in a business is important for human capital management. **Human capital management** integrates training with all aspects of the human resource function (e.g., performance evaluation, human resource planning, etc.) to determine how training dollars are spent and how training expenses translate into business dollars for the company. The major reasons that companies adopt an LMS are to centralize management of learning activities, track regulatory compliance, measure training usage, and measure employee performance.[108] A total of 38 percent of companies report integrating an LMS with human resource information systems.[109]

LMSs are also important for companies to be able to track the number of employees who have completed courses that are required to meet state, federal, or professional regulations (compliance training).[110] These courses cover a wide range of topics, including financial integrity, health and safety, environmental protection, and employee rights. For example, various regulations mandate that companies be able to prove that employees have completed courses in sexual harassment or defensive driving. Employees from a variety of for-profit businesses, including financial services, oil refining, and pharmaceuticals, as well as employees in nonprofit organizations such as government agencies and hospitals, have to complete certain required courses. The Gunderson Lutheran Health System includes hospitals, community clinics, nursing homes, home care, pharmacies, ambulances, mental health services, and vision centers.[111] Employees are required to take courses to comply with national standards on protecting patient privacy, as well as courses related to providing a safe and healthy work environment. Gunderson developed an LMS that includes all mandatory compliance courses, as well as other courses. Employees can access courses on the LMS through computers located at their desks, in computer labs, or at health sciences libraries. Gunderson has realized many benefits from the LMS. The LMS has been useful in reducing the time employees spend on compliance courses (for example, safety courses now take twenty minutes compared to the two hours required for classroom training). The online courses provide employees with flexibility to fit learning into their schedules. For example, nurses can leave their online course to visit patients and then return to continue learning right where they left off. The online courses offer more interactivity through the use of exercises, assessments, and role plays than did the classroom training, and such interactivity holds employees' interest. Finally, since the LMS was developed, the demand for learning has increased: Departments want more classroom courses to be converted to online courses.

An LMS can help companies understand the strengths and weaknesses of their employees, including where talent gaps exist.[112] Also, an LMS can be linked to other human resource systems, such as performance management or employee development systems, to identify learning opportunities for employees to strengthen their performance weaknesses. Turner Construction has a competency model that divides jobs into nine job families and divides the families into job levels (senior management, administrative/clerical, and management). Employees receive an online performance evaluation of their skills based on their job family and level. The performance management system links to the company's LMS. The LMS analyzes the employees' skill weaknesses and provides recommendations of courses that can improve those skills. The LMS system allows Turner Construction to identify skill gaps for entire levels, job families, or business units. The results can be used to identify where to spend monies allocated for training to develop new courses.

## Developing an LMS

How does a company go about developing an LMS? First, senior management needs to be convinced that an LMS will benefit employees, improve business functions, and contribute to overall business strategies and goals.

Second, a company that wants to develop an LMS must have an e-learning culture that supports online learning and encourages employee participation. Third, the online learning environment needs to be under the control of the learner. Learners require not just choices in what and when to learn, but also involvement in learning (practice, feedback, appeals to multiple senses, etc.).[113]

To maximize its effectiveness, an LMS should be integrated with talent management systems. The interfaces between the systems will provide basic employee information such as business unit, geographic location, and job title. Information about which courses employees have completed and are eligible to complete should also be stored in the LMS. Consider how VCA Animal Hospitals, Vanguard, and Gales Residential LMS contributes to the business, encourage employee participation in training, and integrate talent management practices and systems.[114] VCA Animal Hospitals has a geographically dispersed workforce with 13,000 workers in over 500 animal hospitals across forty states. It used to rely on training based on Microsoft PowerPoint presentations with audio narration but recognized that it had to improve the quality of its courses. VCA Animal Hospitals purchased a new LMS that now allows more engaging training methods, including video clips of veterinarians discussing medical practices, simulations, online collaboration between learners and learners and between learners and the instructors, and safety inspection checklists. The LMS is used for online courses, registering veterinarians for classroom-based courses, and tracking who has completed training and how well they scored on post-training tests. Vanguard, the financial services firm, uses an LMS that allows its employees, known as crew members, to get learning recommendations from Vanguard's University based on their career interests, development goals, and relevant content for their current jobs. It also makes it easier for crew members to find and access videos, audio clips, interactive flash demonstrations, and articles, as well as enrolling in classes. The LMS categorizes informal learning sources, such as podcasts, articles, and video clips, with formal learning solutions, including online and classroom-based courses. Informal and formal learning solutions as well as outside courses offered by vendors can also be found using a key work search. Gables Residential develops, builds, and manages multifamily communities and mixed-use developments in urban markets such as Houston, Texas, and Washington, D.C. Gables Residential associates, primarily consisting of millennials and Generation Xers, wanted a system that was exciting and easily customizable. Associates can use the LMS to take assessments and courses that are linked to their development plans. The LMS also gives associates access to e-learning courses and a WebEx Training Center through which instructors can lead live virtual classes. The LMS has helped the company reduce travel and hotel costs by 21 percent.

# CHOOSING NEW TECHNOLOGY TRAINING METHODS

Table 8.11 compares technology-based training methods based on the same characteristics used to compare traditional training programs in Chapter Seven. Several trends are apparent in this table. First, these methods require considerable investment in development.

**TABLE 8.11**  **Comparison of Technology-Based Training Methods**

| | Online E-learning Web Based Computer-Based | Computer-Based (No Internet) | Distance Learning | Intelligent Tutoring | Simulations Games Virtual Reality | Mobile Learning | Social Media |
|---|---|---|---|---|---|---|---|
| **Learning Outcome** | | | | | | | |
| Verbal information | Yes | Yes | Yes | Yes | Yes | Yes | Yes |
| Intellectual skills | Yes | Yes | Yes | Yes | Yes | Yes | No |
| Cognitive strategies | Yes | Yes | Yes | Yes | Yes | No | Yes |
| Attitudes | Maybe | No | No | No | Yes | No | No |
| Motor skills | No | No | No | Yes | Yes | No | No |
| **Learning Environment** | | | | | | | |
| Objective | High | High | High | High | High | High | Medium |
| Practice | High | High | Low | High | High | Low | Medium |
| Meaningfulness | High | High | Medium | High | High | Medium | Medium |
| Feedback | High | High | Low | High | High | Low | High |
| Interaction | | | | | | | |
|   Learner content | High | High | Medium | High | High | Medium | High |
|   Learner-Instructor | Medium | Low | Medium | High | Medium | Low | Medium |
|   Learner-Learner | Medium | Low | Medium | Low | High | Low | High |
| **Transfer of Training** | High | Medium | Medium | High | High | Medium | Medium |
| **Cost** | | | | | | | |
| Development | High | High | Medium | High | High | Medium | Medium |
| Administrative | Low | Low | Low | Low | Low | Low | Medium |
| **Effectiveness** | High | Medium | Medium | ? | High | ? | ? |

Development costs are related to purchasing hardware and software, as well as developing programs and transferring programs to new media (e.g., mobile phones using apps). However, although development costs are high, costs for administering the program are low. Advantages of these methods include (1) cost savings due to training being accessible to employees at their home or office, (2) reduced number of trainers needed, and (3) reduced costs associated with employees traveling to a central training location (e.g., airfare, food, and lodging). Moreover, with the exception of distance learning and mobile learning, most of the important characteristics needed for learning to occur (practice, feedback, etc.) can be built into these methods. Note that only a limited number of studies of the effectiveness of several methods (e.g., mobile learning, social networks, and intelligent tutoring) are available because companies are just starting to use these technologies for training.

Recall the discussion in Chapter Six of how to determine the costs and benefits of training programs. Caterpillar has found that it spends approximately one-third as much for e-learning as for classroom instruction because of the reduced number of instructors, the lower costs associated with course materials, and the reduced travel expenses.[115] For a one-hour course with a class size of 100 trainees, e-learning is 40 percent less expensive than classroom training ($9,500 versus $17,062, or $76 per trainee). As the number of trainees increases to, for example, 40,000 trainees (Caterpillar has more than 70,000 employees worldwide), the company's cost savings are 78 percent ($1.1 million versus $5 million, or $99 per trainee).[116]

You might assume that e-learning is superior to other methods, but this is not necessarily the case. Its major advantage is that web-based programs can offer collaboration and sharing (connecting trainees to other trainees, experts, and chat rooms) and links to resources available on the web. Web-based training also allows the learner to be given assignments requiring open-ended responses (e.g., write a report on a customer's needs) rather than only yes/no or multiple-choice responses. In web-based training, the instructor can read the assignment and provide detailed feedback. However no training method is inherently superior to other methods. Rather, for any method to be effective it has to create a positive learning environment and aid in training transfer. Face-to-face classroom instruction can be ineffective for the same reasons as online learning, or distance learning. For example, the material is not meaningful, there are limited opportunities for practice, and managers don't support use of training content on the job.

How do new technology training methods relate to traditional training methods discussed in Chapter Seven? Virtual reality and intelligent tutoring systems are best suited for teaching complex processes related to operating machinery, tools, and equipment. These methods are an extension of simulations. Online training is best suited for teaching facts, figures, cognitive strategies (e.g., how to hold an effective meeting), and interpersonal skills (e.g., closing a sale). These methods are technological extensions of traditional training methods such as behavior modeling, on-the-job training, and apprenticeship. Mobile learning is probably best suited for teaching facts given the limited personal interaction, and interaction with the content using many mobile devices. Currently, mobile learning and social media are best used as supplements to face-to-face instruction to facilitate learning and transfer of training. Social media are also good tools for knowledge management because they facilitate collaboration on documents, reports (wikis), and personal interaction (blogs, Twitter, and Facebook). Although traditional training methods can be effective, managers and trainers should consider using new technology training methods under certain conditions:[117]

1. Sufficient budget and resources will be provided to develop and support the purchase and use of new technology.
2. Trainees are geographically dispersed, and travel costs related to training are high.
3. Trainees are comfortable using technology, including the Internet, web, iPads, and smartphones.
4. The increased use of new technology is part of the company's business strategy. New technology is being used or implemented in manufacturing of products or service processes.
5. Employees have limited or no time for training.
6. Current training methods allow limited time for practice, feedback, and assessment.
7. Use of new technology fits into the organizational culture or business strategy.

The best uses for classroom instruction may be when trainees need interaction, instructor support, or visual cues. It is important to note that many companies recognize the strengths and weaknesses of both traditional training methods and technology-based training methods and are using both in a blended learning approach. Technology-based training methods can be used to provide consistent delivery of training content involving transfer of information (knowledge and skills) to geographically dispersed employees who work at their own pace, practice, and collaborate with the trainer and other trainees online. Then trainees can be brought to a central location for face-to-face training using traditional methods (classroom, action learning, games, and role plays) that emphasizes through the use of cases and problems the application of the knowledge and skills. Face-to-face instruction is also more useful for facilitating interaction among trainees as well as collaboration, networking, and discussion. For example, at Pitney Bowes, a mailing equipment provider, e-learning is used for content that many geographically dispersed employees must know, such as legal compliance requirements or new product training.[118] Learning that requires interaction with others—such as leadership management training, problem solving, or decision making—requires face-to-face classroom instruction or a blended learning approach.

## Summary

This chapter provided an overview of the use of new technologies in training delivery, support, and administration. Many new technologies have features that help to ensure learning and transfer of training (e.g., e-learning). If designed correctly these technologies can create a positive learning environment by appealing "to multiple senses and allow" employees to pace themselves, receive feedback and reinforcement, and find information from experts on an as-needed basis. Mobile learning methods (such as iPads) allow employees to participate in training from home or work on a twenty-four-hour basis. Employees control not only the presentation of training content but also when and where they participate in training. Simulations and virtual reality also can create a more realistic training environment, which can make the material more meaningful and increase the probability that training will transfer to the job. Expert systems and electronic support systems are tools that employees can access on an as-needed basis to obtain knowledge and information. Social media help to capture the knowledge that employees gain from training and facilitate their sharing of information. Learning management systems make it easier to store and record training information such as course enrollments and employee training records. This makes it easier for employees to participate in training and to retrieve training-related information for managerial decision making.

Most new technology training methods are superior to traditional methods in one way because they allow trainees to participate in courses at any time or place. However, similar to traditional training methods, technology-based training methods will be ineffective if they do not include interaction, feedback, practice, and other features of a positive learning environment. Considerations in choosing a training method include monies for development, geographic dispersion of employees, employees' difficulty in attending training, and whether new technologies are part of the company's business strategy. Rather than choosing between face-to-face and technology-based training methods, companies are often choosing to use both in a blended learning approach.

# Key Terms

| | | |
|---|---|---|
| digital collaboration, *321* | social media, *335* | distance learning, *347* |
| synchronous communication, *321* | blog, *335* | virtual classroom, *348* |
| | hyperlinks, *335* | teleconferencing, 348 |
| asynchronous communication, *321* | microsharing, *336* | interactive distance learning (IDL), *348* |
| Web 2.0, *323* | wiki, *336* | webcasting or web conferencing, *349* |
| computer-based training (CBT), *323* | shared media, *336* | |
| | blended learning, *338* | expert systems, *350* |
| online learning, *323* | avatar, *341* | electronic performance |
| e-learning, *323* | virtual reality, *342* | support system |
| web-based training, *323* | presence, *342* | (EPSS), *351* |
| bandwidth, *331* | virtual worlds, *343* | learning management |
| plug-in, *331* | microblog or | system (LMS), *352* |
| rapid prototyping, *332* | mobile learning, *344* | human capital |
| repurposing, *332* | apps, *345* | management, *353* |
| learner control, *333* | intelligent tutoring system | |
| self-regulation, *334* | (ITS), *346* | |

# Discussion Questions

1. Explain how technology has changed the learning environment.
2. What types of learning outcomes are best suited for mobile learning? Explain.
3. What are the differences between expert systems and electronic performance tools?
4. Are training support technologies always needed? Justify your answer.
5. Discuss how new technologies make it easier to learn. How do they facilitate transfer of training?
6. Is all Internet training the same? Explain.
7. What are some potential problems with using virtual reality technology for training?
8. What is social media? Explain how it can be used for training.

9. Explain learner control, sharing, and linking. How do they contribute to the effectiveness of e-learning?

10. What is repurposing? How does it affect the use of new technologies in training?

11. Distance learning can be used to deliver a lecture to geographically dispersed trainees. How might distance learning be designed and used to avoid some of the learning and transfer of training problems of the traditional lecture method?

12. Why would a company use a combination of face-to-face instruction and web-based training?

13. What conditions are best for the use of social media tools as part of a learning solution?

14. What should a manager do to help ensure that online learning is effective?

## Application Assignments

1. Using only the web, further investigate any new technology discussed in this chapter. With any search engine on the web (e.g., Google, Yahoo, etc.), conduct a search for information about the technology that you have chosen. Find information describing the technology, hints for developing or purchasing the technology, and examples of companies marketing and/or using the technology. Include web addresses in your summary.

2. Go to www.allencomm.com, website for Allen Communications, creator of DesignJot, an app to help design effective training. Watch the video and review the website. What features does this app have that help design training programs? Why are they useful?

3. Go to www.skillsoft.com, the website for Skillsoft, a company that specializes in providing e-learning solutions. Move the cursor over Info Center, then over Demos. Click on Business Skills Demos. View one of the demos for the e-learning courses. Does the program create a positive learning environment? How? What suggestions do you have for improving the program?

4. Go to www.mzinga.com. Mzinga provides software solutions for learning. Click on Products. Then click on Omni Social Suite. What learning solutions are provided by the Omni Social Suite? Do you believe that these solutions are effective? Why?

5. Go to www.isense.com, the website for Intersense, a company that develops and markets motion tracking projects used for commercial applications. Click on either Military or Industrial markets. Click on Learn More and then review the simulation. What are the advantages of the simulation you reviewed? What are the potential weaknesses?

6. Go to www.capellauniversity.edu, the website for Capella University—a university that offers online courses. Click on Online Learning on the left side of the page. Click on the "See how it works" short course demo and watch the video *Night in the Life of a Capella Learner*. Based on the information provided, what are the strengths and weaknesses of online courses? What will be most effective for helping students learn?

7. Go to www.youtube.com. Search for "Training in Second Life" or "Training Simulations in Second Life." Choose and review a video of one of the many different types of training offered in Second Life (e.g., medicine, nursing, or management). Provide a brief description of the training and the Universal Resource Locator (URL) for the video. Discuss the strengths and weaknesses of the training. Based on the video you reviewed, do you think that companies, interest in Second Life for training will increase or decrease in the future? Why?

8. Go to www.kahnacademy.org, the website for The Kahn Academy. The Kahn Academy is a non-profit organization dedicated to providing a free world-class education to anyone anywhere. Click on About. Watch the videos (Under How it works for students) and read about the learning tools used by the Academy. How is the Academy using technology to facilitate learning? What are the strengths and weaknesses of these technologies?

---

# Case: *Cisco Systems Account Managers Are Too Busy for Training*

Cisco Systems of San Jose, California, helps people make connections in business, education, philanthropy, or creativity. Cisco hardware, software, and service offerings are used to create the Internet solutions that make networks possible—providing easy access to information anywhere, at any time. Cisco's account managers are the company's front-line sales force. A needs assessment found that account managers were concerned because learning content was not being delivered to them in a way that fit their work patterns or learning styles. Because account managers spend a lot of time traveling, they wanted to get on the Internet, find what they needed, and get out again. They preferred not to sit in front of a personal computer for a long e-learning course.

As a result, Cisco is creating the Account Manager Learning Environment (AMLE). The AMLE is intended to be a development tool and performance support system based on four business objectives: increase sales, increase revenue, increase speed at which account managers become competent in a topic, and reduce travel and costs. Cisco's goal in developing the AMLE is to create a learning environment that will motivate account managers to use it.

*What new technology training methods would you recommend including in Cisco's AMLE? Why? Discuss the knowledge, skills, behavior, or competencies that your training method(s) would focus on.*

**Sources:** Based on M. Delahoussaye and R. Zemke, "Ten things we know for sure about learning on-line," *Training* (September 2001): 48–59; P. Galayan, "Delta force," *T+D* (July 2002): 21–28.

## Endnotes

1. L. Hurtubise, "iPod adds a touch of education innovation," *Insight* (December 2008): 1.
2. J. McCallister, "The popular online world inspires new ways to teach and learn," *onCampus* (January 24, 2008): 1–14; D. Naraghi, "Brave new (virtual) world," *Ohio State University Alumni Magazine* (May/June 2008): 24–29.
3. P. Ketter "2010: Six trends that will change workplace learning forever," *T+D* (December 2010): 34–40; T. Bingham and M. Conner, *The New Social Learning* (Alexandria, VA: American Society for Training and Development, 2010).
4. L. Patel, "The rise of social media," *T+D* (July 2010): 60–61.
5. B. Mirza, "Social media tools redefine learning," *HR Magazine,* December 2010, 74; L. Patel, "The rise of social media," *T+D*, July 2010, 60–61; J. Meister, E. Kaganer, and R. Von Feldt, "2011: The year of the media tablet as a learning tool," *T+D*, April 2011, 28–31.
6. P. Shank, "When to use instructional technology," *T+D* (September 2004): 30–37; S. E. O'Connell, "New technologies bring new tools, new rules," *HR Magazine* (December 1995): 43–48; S. E. O'Connell, "The virtual workplace moves at warp speed," *HR Magazine* (March 1996): 51–57.
7. M. Weinstein, "Virtually integrated," *Training* (April 2007): 10; A. Hira, "The making of a UPS driver," *Fortune* (November 12, 2007): 118–129; P. Ketter, "What can training do for Brown?" *T+D* (May 2008): 30–36.
8. J. Salopek, "Digital collaboration," *Training and Development* (June 2000): 39–43.
9. V. Beer, *The Web Learning Fieldbook* (New York: John Wiley, 2000); A. Chute, P. Sayers, and R. Gardner, "Network learning environments," *New Directions for Teaching and Learning* 71 (1997): 75–83.
10. E. Hollis, "Shoney's: Workforce development on the side," *Chief Learning Officer* (March 2003): 32–34.

11. "Qualcomm, Inc: Learning 2.0," *Training* (February 2009): 100.

12. M. Rosenberg, *E-Learning: Strategies for Delivering Knowledge in the Digital Age* (New York: McGraw-Hill, 2001); "What Is Web-Based Training?" (from www.clark.net/pub/nractive/fl.html); R. Johnson and H. Gueutal, *Transforming HR through Technology* (Alexandria, VA: SHRM Foundation, 2010).

13. P. Harris, "Where innovative learning is the norm," *T+D* (October 2011): 61–62.

14. "Project leadership," *Human Resource Executive* (2000): A16.

15. M. Weinstein, "Satellite success," *Training* (January 2007): 36–38.

16. F. Filipowski, "How Federal Express makes your package its most important," *Personnel Journal* (February 1992): 40–46.

17. M. Moore, "Three types of interaction," *American Journal of Distance Education* 3(2) (1989): 1–6.

18. P. Galagan, "The e-learning revolution," *Training and Development* (December 2000): 24–30; D. Khirallah, "A new way to learn," *Information Week Online,* May 22, 2000; G. Wang, R. Von Der Linn, D. Foucar-Szocki, O. Griffin, and E. Sceiford, "Measuring the business impact of e-learning—An empirical study," *Performance Improvement Quarterly* 16 (2003): 17–30.

19. M. Gold, "E-learning, the Lucent way," *T+D* (July 2003): 46–50.

20. S. Murphy, "Ritz Camera focuses on web-based teaching tools," *Chain Store Age* (December 23, 2008).

21. R. Flandez, "Firms go online to train employees," *The Wall Street Journal* (August 14, 2007): B4.

22. J. Marquez, "Faced with high turnover, retailers boot up e-learning programs for quick training," *Workforce Management* (August 2005): 74–75.

23. "Sanofi-aventis U.S.," *T+D*, October 2009, 83.

24. S. Gale, "Making e-learning more than 'pixie dust,'" *Workforce* (March 2003): 58–62.

25. G. Wright, "Retailers buy into e-learning," *HR Magazine* (December 2010): 87–90.

26. Shared learning demo, January 24, 2001 (from the CCH website, *hr.cch.com*).

27. K. Brown, "Using computers to deliver training: Which employees learn and why?" *Personnel Psychology* 54 (2001): 271–96; E. T. Welsh et al., "E-learning: Emerging uses, empirical results, and future directions," *International Journal of Training and Development* 7(4) (2003): 245–258; T. Sitzmann et al., "The comparative effectiveness of web-based and classroom instruction: A meta-analysis," *Personnel Psychology* 59 (2006): 623–624.

28. K. Kraiger, "Transforming our models of learning and development: Web-based instruction as enabler of third-generation instruction," *Industrial Organizational Psychology,* 1(4) (December 2008): 454–467.

29. B. Roberts, "Hard facts about soft-skills e-learning," *HR Magazine* (January 2008): 76–78.

30. G. Anders, "Companies find on-line training has its limits," *The Wall Street Journal* (March 26, 2007): B3.

31. E. T. Welsh et al., "E-learning: Emerging uses, empirical results, and future directions," *International Journal of Training and Development* 7(4) (2003): 245–258

32. K. Kiser, "10 things we know so far about online training," *Training* (November 1999): 66–70; R. Wells, "Back to the (Internet) classroom," *Training* (March 1999): 50–54; L. Martins and F. Kellermans, "A model of business school students' acceptance of a Web-based course management system," *Academy of Management Learning and Education* 3 (2004): 7–26; H. Klein, R. Noe, and C. Wang, "Motivation to learn and course outcomes: The impact of delivery mode, learning goal orientation, and perceived barriers and enablers," *Personnel Psychology* 59 (2006): 665–702.

33. B. Neal, "e-Addie!" *T+D* (March 2011): 76–77.

34. D. Schaaf, "Bandwidth basics," *Training* (September 1999): OL23–OL37; J. Adams, "Rapid talent development," *T+D* (March 2008): 68–73.

35. S. Gale, "Making e-learning more than 'pixie dust,'" *Workforce* (March 2003): 58–62.

36. B. Neal, "e-Addie!" *T+D* (March 2011): 76–77; N. Miner and J. Hofman, "It's not the technology, stupid," *T+D* (February 2009): 30–32; E. Edwards, "Quick draw," *T+D* (August 2009): 92–93.

37. K. Brown and J. Ford, "Using Computer Technology in Training: Building an Infrastructure for Active Learning." In *Creating, Implementing, and Managing Effective Training and Development,* ed. K. Kraiger (San Francisco: Jossey-Bass, 2002): 192–233.

38. B. Neal, "e-Addie!" *T+D* (March 2011): 76–77; N. Miner and J. Hofman, "It's not the technology, stupid," *T+D* (February 2009): 30–32; E. Edwards, "Quick draw," *T+D* (August 2009): 92–93.

39. S. Boehle, "Putting the learning back in e-learning," *Training* (January 2006): 29–35; Brown, "Using computers to deliver training: Which employees learn and why?"

40. R. DeRouin, B. Fritzsche, and E. Salas, "Learner control and workplace learning: Design, person, and organizational issues," in *Research in Personnel and Human Resource Management,* vol. 24, ed. J. Martocchio (New York: Elsevier, 2005): 181–214; T. Sitzmann, B. Bell, K. Kraiger, and A. Kanar, "A multilevel analysis of the effect of prompting self-regulation in technology-delivered instruction. *Personnel Psychology* 62 (2009): 697–734; T. Sitzmann and K. Ely, "Sometimes you need a reminder: The effects of prompting self-regulation on regulatory processes, learning, and attrition," *Journal of Applied Psychology* 95 (2010): 132–144.

41. D. Zielinski, "The lie of online learning," *Training* (February 2000): 38–40; D. Zielinski, "Can you keep learners on-line?" *Training* (March 2000): 65–75.

42. K. Brown, "A field study of employee e-learning activity and outcomes," *Human Resource Development Quarterly* (Winter 2005): 465–80.

43. S. Chyung and M. Vachon, "An investigation of the profiles of satisfying and dissatisfying factors in e-learning," *Performance Improvement Quarterly* 18 (2005): 97–113.

44. D. Zielinski, "Can you keep learners on-line?" *Training* (March 2000): 65–75.

45. C. Pollack and R. Masters, "Using Internet technologies to enhance training," *Performance Improvement* (February 1997): 28–31.

46. D. Zielinski, "Can you keep learners on-line?" *Training* (March 2000): 65–75; K. Brown and J. Ford, "Using Computer Technology in Training: Building an Infrastructure for Active Learning." In *Creating, Implementing, and Managing Effective Training and Development,* ed. K. Kraiger (San Francisco: Jossey-Bass, 2002): 192–233.

46a. M. Derven, "Social networking a force for development," *T+D* (July 2009): 58–63; A. Kaplan and M. Haenlein, "Users of the world unite! The challenges and opportunities of social media," *Business Horizons* 53 (2010): 59–68.

47. B. Livingston "Harnessing blogs for learning," *T+D* (May 2011): 76–77.

48. T. Bingham, M. Connor, and M. Weinstein, "Netting know-how," *Training,* September/October 2010, 26–29; J. Roy, "Transforming informal learning into a competitive advantage," *T+D,* October 2010, 23–25; P. Galagan, "Unformal, the new normal?," *T+D,* September 2010, 29–31; M. Weinstein, "Verizon connects to success," *training,* January/February 2011, 40–42.

49. M. Derven, "Social networking: A force for development?" *T+D* (July 2009): 59–63.

50. S. J. Hysong and L. M. Mannix, "Learning Outcomes in Distance Education versus Traditional and Mixed Environments" (paper presented at the annual conference of the Society for Industrial and Organizational Psychology, Orlando, FL, 2003).

51. M. Knowles, *The Adult Learner,* 4th ed. (Houston, TX: Gulf Publishing, 1990).

52. M. Weinstein, "Got class," *Training* (December 2005): 29–32.

53. T. Sitzmann et al., "The comparative effectiveness of web-based and classroom instruction: A meta-analysis," *Personnel Psychology* 59 (2006): 623–624; H. Klein, R. Noe, and C. Wang, "Motivation to learn and course outcomes: The impact of delivery mode, learning goal orientation, and perceived barriers and enablers," *Personnel Psychology* 59 (2006): 665–702.

54. K. Kim, C. Bonk, and E. Oh, "The present and future of blended learning in workplace settings in the United States," *Performance Improvement* (September 2008): 5–14.

55. M. Weinstein, "A better blend," *Training* (September 2008): 30–39.

56. W. Webb, "Training = franchise success," *Training* (October 2008): 54–55 and the Dunkin' Donuts website at www.dunkindonuts.com.

57. M. Slagle, "Poll: 4 in 10 Americans play video games," May 8, 2006, Accessed from www.washigtonpost .com, the website for the *Washington Post.*

58. M. Peck, "Confessions of an X-Box general," *Foreign Policy* (September 28, 2011). From www .foreignpolicy.com, the website for *Foreign Policy,* accessed September 31, 2011.

59. P. Dvorak, "Theory and practice: Simulation shows what it is like to be the boss; middle managers at NetApp receive useful taste of reality," *The Wall Street Journal* (March 31, 2008): B7.

60. C. Aldrich, "Engaging minigames find niche in training," *T+D* (July 2007): 22–24.

61. M. Weinstein, "Winning games," *Training* (April 2007): 16–18.

62. J. Borzo, "Almost human," *The Wall Street Journal,* May 24, 2004: R1, R10; J. Hoff, "My virtual life," *BusinessWeek,* May 1, 2006: 72–78.

63. C. Cornell, "Better than the real thing?" *Human Resource Executive* (August 2005): 34–37; E. Frauenheim, "Can video games win points as teaching tools?" *Workforce Management* (April 10, 2006): 12–14; S. Boehle, "Simulations: The next generation of e-learning," *Training* (January 2005): 22–31; J. Borzo, "Almost human," *The Wall Street Journal,* May 24, 2004: R1, R10.

64. T. Sitzmann, "A meta-analytic examination of the instructional effectiveness of computer-based simulation games," *Personnel Psychology* 64: 489–528.

65. L. Freifeld, "Solid Sims," *Training* (October 2007): 48.

66. N. Adams, "Lessons from the Virtual World," *Training* (June 1995): 45–48.

67. D. Steele-Johnson and B. G. Hyde, "Advanced Technologies in Training: Intelligence Tutoring Systems and Virtual Reality." In *Training for a Rapidly Changing Workplace,* ed. M. A. Quinones and A. Ehrenstein (Washington, D.C.: American Psychological Association, 1997): 225–248.

68. Ibid.

69. K. Kapp and T. O'Driscoll, "Designing virtual immersive environments," *T+D* (April 2010): 30–32.

70. H. Dolezalek, "Virtual vision," *Training* (October 2007): 40–46.

71. R. Flandez, "Small business link: Chip maker trains in the virtual world," *The Wall Street Journal* (April 3, 2008): B6.

72. P. Galagan, "Second that," *T+D* (February 2008): 34–37.

73. P. Harris, "Immersive learning seeks a foothold," *T+D* (January 2009): 40–45.

74. H. Dolezalek, "Virtual vision," *Training* (October 2007): 40–46.

75. "What does it cost to use a virtual world learning environment?" *T+D* (November 2008): 88.

76. A. Nancheria, "Robots in the room," *T+D* (November 2008): 18; R. Clark, "Accelerating expertise with scenario-based learning," *T+D* (January 2009): 84–85.

77. For example, see S. Kumta et al., "Fostering critical thinking skills through a web-based tutorial programme for first year medical students—A randomized controlled study," *Journal of Educational Multimedia and Hypermedia* 12 (2003): 267–273.

78. K. Taylor and S. Chyung, "Would you adopt Second Life as a training and development tool?" *Performance Improvement* (September 2008): 17–25.

79. D. Gayeski, "Goin' mobile," *T+D* (November 2004): 46–51; D. Gayeski and M. Petrillose, "No strings attached," *Performance Improvement* (February 2005): 25–31; D. Hartley, "Pick up your PDA," *T+D* (February 2004): 22–24.

80. J. Halls, "Give learning a listen: Audio podcasting and learning," *T+D* (October 2010): 92–93.

81. E. Wagner and P. Wilson, "Disconnected," *T+D* (December 2005): 40–43; J. Bronstein and A. Newman, "IM learning," *T+D* (February 2006): 47–50.

82. M. Weinstein, "Mobility movement," *Training* (September 6, 2007): 15–16.

83. G. Dutton, "There's an app for that!" *Training* (September/October 2011): 36–37.

84. J. Meister, E. Kaganer, and R. Von Feldt, "2011: The year of the media tablet as a learning tool," *T+D,* April 2011, 28–31.

85. L. Stevens, "Up close and insightful," *Human Resource Executive* (September 16, 2011): 24–29.

86. E. Wagner and P. Wilson, "Disconnected," *T+D* (December 2005): 40–43; J. Brink, "M-learning: The future of training technology," *T+D* (February 2011): 27–29; G. Woodwill, "Getting started with mobile learning," *T+D* (December 2010): 76–77; A. Ahmad and P. Norton, "Smartphones make IBM smarter, but not as expected," *T+D* (January 2010): 46–50.

87. D. Steele-Johnson and B. G. Hyde, "Advanced Technologies in Training: Intelligence Tutoring Systems and Virtual Reality." In *Training for a Rapidly Changing Workplace,* ed. M. A. Quinones and A. Ehrenstein (Washington, D.C.: American Psychological Association, 1997): 225–248.

88. R. J. Seidel, O. C. Park, and R. S. Perez, "Expertise of ICAI: Developmental requirements," *Computers in Human Behavior,* 4 (1988): 235–256.

89. D. Steele-Johnson and B. G. Hyde, "Advanced Technologies in Training: Intelligence Tutoring Systems and Virtual Reality." In *Training for a Rapidly Changing Workplace*, ed. M. A. Quinones and A. Ehrenstein (Washington, D.C.: American Psychological Association, 1997): 225–248.

90. "Putting the distance into distance learning," *Training* (October 1995): 111–118.

91. R. Clark, "Harnessing the virtual classroom," *T+D* (November 2005): 40–45.

92. D. Picard, "The future is distance training," *Training* (November 1996): s3–s10.

93. A. F. Maydas, "On-line networks build the savings into employee education," *HR Magazine* (October 1997): 31–35.

94. J. M. Rosow and R. Zager, *Training: The Competitive Edge* (San Francisco: Jossey-Bass, 1988).

95. M. Lewis, "Moving into the live virtual classroom," *T+D* (July 2011): 76–77; R. Ubell, "How to run a virtual classroom," *T+D* (October 2011): 92–93.

96. M. Weinstein, "Satellite success," *Training* (January 2007): 36–38.

97. "Training Top 100 Best Practices 2006: General Mills," *Training* (March 2006): 61.

98. S. Alexander, "Reducing the learning burden," *Training* (September 2002): 32–34.

99. R. Clark, "Harnessing the virtual classroom," *T+D* (November 2005): 40–45; R. Clark and R. Mayer, *E-Learning and the Science of Instruction* (San Francisco: John Wiley, 2003; 2d ed. published in 2008 by Jossey-Bass/Pfeiffer).

100. W. Hannum, *The Application of Emerging Training Technologies* (Alexandria, VA: The American Society for Training and Development, 1990).

101. P. A. Galagan, "Think performance: A conversation with Gloria Gery," *Training and Development* (March 1994): 47–51.

102. "Module Example: Financial Products Sales Applications," from PortBlue website, www.portblue.com/pub/solutions-sales-marketing (April 24, 2006).

103. S. Caudron, "Your learning technology primer," *Personnel Journal* (June 1996): 120–136; A. Marquardt and G. Kearsley, *Technology-Based Learning* (Boca Raton, FL: St. Lucie Press, 1999).

104. M. Weinstein, "Wake-up call," *Training* (June 2007): 48–50.

105. S. Boehle, "LMS leaders," *Training* (October 2008): 30–34.

106. D. Sussman, "The LMS value," *T+D* (July 2005): 43–45.

107. B. Roberts, "Educate yourself," *HR Magazine* (September 2010): 109–112.

108. "LMS Survey Results," from www.learningcircuits.org/2005/jun2005/LMS_survey.htm (July 7, 2006).

109. E. Cohen, "At the ready," *Human Resource Executive* (August 2003): 40–42.

110. K. Oakes, "Mission critical," *T+D* (September 2005): 25–28; D. Sussman, "The LMS value," *T+D* (July 2005): 43–45; H. Johnson, "Prescription for success," *Training* (October 2003): 52.

111. Johnson, "Prescription for Success."

112. J. Barbian, "Great Expectations," *Training* (September 2002): 10–12; D. Sussman, "The LMS value," *T+D* (July 2005): 43–45.

113. K. Dobbs, "Take the gamble out of an LMS," *Workforce* (November 2002): 52–58.

114. "LMS goes to the dogs," *training*, (September/October 2010): 8; L. Freifeld, "LMS lessons," *training* (September/October 2010): 20–24; "A new lease on learning," *Training* (October 2009): 44–46.

115. I. Speizer, "Value-minded," *Workforce Management* (July 2005): 55–58.

116. M. Weinstein, "Got class," *Training* (December 2005): 29–32.

117. P. Shank; "When to use instructional technology," *T+D* (September 2004): 30–37; H. Dolezalek, "Dose of reality," *Training* (April 2004): 28–34; E. Salas, R. DeRouin, and L. Littrell, "Research-Based Guidelines for Designing Distance Learning," in *The Brave New World of eHR*, ed. H. Gueutal and D. Stone (San Francisco: Jossey-Bass, 2005): 104–137; G. Piskurich, "E-learning: Fast, cheap, good," *Performance Improvement* (January 2006): 18–24.

118. M. Weinstein, "Got class," *Training* (December 2005): 29–32.

# Chapter Nine

# Employee Development and Career Management

## Objectives

After reading this chapter, you should be able to:

1. Discuss the steps in the development planning process.
2. Explain the employees' and company's responsibilities in planning development.
3. Discuss current trends in using formal education for development.
4. Relate how assessment of personality type, work behavior, and job performance can be used for employee development.
5. Explain how job experiences can be used for development and suggest a job experience to match an employee's development goal or need.
6. Identify the characteristics of an effective mentoring program.
7. Describe the succession planning process and how the nine-box grid is used.
8. Design an effective on-boarding process.

## Developing Managers at Tyson Foods

Tyson Foods, Inc., headquartered in Springdale, Arkansas, is one of the world's largest processors and marketers of chicken, beef, and pork. The company produces a wide variety of protein-based and prepared food products and is the recognized market leader in the retail and food-service markets. Tyson provides products and services to customers throughout the United States and more than 90 other countries. The company has approximately 117,000 employees (known as Team Members) in more than four hundred facilities and offices in the United States and around the world.

Tyson Foods recognizes that its success depends on the development of its managers. Specifically, Tyson needs to identify employees with high leadership potential and quickly develop them into leaders and managers capable of leading process improvements and cost efficiencies to drive and sustain business profits. To accomplish this, Tyson, with the help of consulting firm SVI, created a two-year development program known as Leaders Into Champions (LINC). The objectives of LINC were to create a group of managers who were ready to take executive management positions, ensure that they had the correct skills and attitudes to drive innovation and create competitive advantage in the business, expand their involvement and influence within the industry and within Tyson Foods, and provide development opportunities.

To identify participants in the LINC program, leaders from every business unit are asked to nominate high-potential leaders who received performance evaluations in the top 5 percent. A selection process then occurs that includes a review of operational results, peer and manager recommendations, and an evaluation of future growth potential. Nominees are also asked to present to an executive panel the most personal challenges that helped shape them. Asking nominees to share these challenges communicates to them that the LINC program will require courage, honesty, and sharing with others. Following the presentations, twenty managers are chosen for the LINC program.

The program begins by having participants read the book *The Organization Champion*, written by SVI, which emphasizes that leaders need to adjust their mindset to adapt to changing business needs. Also, participants complete an assessment that measures participants' skills in being an organization champion. The assessment is used by LINC participants to identify their strengths and areas for improvement and is used to create individual development plans. Next, participants complete a two-day event that helps them consider their life perspectives. Through the event, participants focus on what they are good at doing, what makes them come alive, and how they uniquely contribute to the company. LINC participants have opportunities to interact directly with Tyson's executives in monthly meetings, either in person at company headquarters or using video conferencing. A business unit executive hosts each meeting and shares information on the business, his or her own personal challenges in their jobs, and present a leadership-competency–based topic. The meetings are useful for development for both participants and executives. LINC participants gain exposure and networking opportunities with executives and executives have the opportunity to "size up" high-potential leaders who may someday work in their business unit. The monthly meetings also involve peer coaching that takes place among LINC participants. LINC participants share ideas and provide feedback to each other.

The second year of the program includes an experiential event designed to measure the development progress of the participants. It requires participants to rely on what they have learned. After the experiential event, participants are given an assignment based on their interests, which is called a "stretch assignment." This task forces them to experience new challenges and exposes them to different parts of the business. The stretch assignments involve important roles that require LINC participants to face actual business challenges and opportunities. Participants need to develop new skills to successfully complete the stretch assignments. These assignments might include participation in an action learning team, research project, or executive internship. Stretch assignments have resulted in new products and competitive advantages for Tyson Foods.

Overall, the LINC program has been successful. LINC is considered the best development program within Tyson Foods, and most LINC participants are promoted into executive positions.

**Source:** Based on M. Thompson, "What makes Tyson's high-potential leadership program critical to company success?" *T+D,* April 2011, 98–100; www.tysonfoods.com, website for Tyson Foods.

# INTRODUCTION

As the Tyson Food example illustrates, employee development is a key contributor to a company's competitive advantage by helping high-potential managers understand their strengths, weaknesses, and interests and by showing them how new jobs and expanded job responsibilities are available to them to meet their personal growth needs. This helps retain valuable managers who might otherwise leave to join clients or competitors. It is also important to emphasize that development is important for all employees, not just managers. Employee development is a necessary component of a company's talent management efforts. Employee development is key to ensuring that employees have the competencies necessary to serve customers and create new products and customer solutions. Regardless of the business strategy, development is also important for retaining talented employees. As we noted in Chapter One, "Introduction to Employee Training and Development," employee engagement is directly related to how employees are treated by their managers. Employee development can help increase employee engagement by (1) showing employees that the company is interested in their skill development, and (2) by developing managers who can create a positive work environment that makes employee's want to come work and contribute to company goals.

This chapter begins by discussing the relationship between development, training, and careers. Choosing an approach is one part of development planning. Second, before employees choose development activities, the employee and the company must have an idea of the employee's development needs and the purpose of development. Identifying the needs and purpose of development are part of its planning. The second section of the chapter describes the steps of the development planning process. Employee and company responsibilities at each step of the process are emphasized. Third, we look at development approaches, including formal education, assessment, job experiences, and interpersonal relationships. The chapter emphasizes the types of skills, knowledge, and behaviors that are strengthened by each development method. The chapter concludes with a discussion of special issues in employee development, including succession planning, developing dysfunctional managers, and on-boarding.

# THE RELATIONSHIP AMONG DEVELOPMENT, TRAINING, AND CAREERS

## Development and Training

**Development** refers to formal education, job experiences, relationships, and assessment of personality and skills that help employees prepare for the future. The Tyson Foods example illustrates that although development can occur through participation in planned programs, it often results from performing different types of work. Because it is future-oriented, it involves learning that is not necessarily related to the employee's current job.[1] Table 9.1 shows the differences between training and development. Traditionally, training focuses on helping employees' performance in their current jobs. Development prepares them for other positions in the company and increases their ability to move into jobs that may not yet exist.[2] Development also helps employees prepare for changes in their current jobs that may result from new technology, work designs, new customers, or new product markets.

**TABLE 9.1**
Comparison
Between
Training and
Development

| | Training | Development |
|---|---|---|
| **Focus** | Current | Future |
| **Use of work experiences** | Low | High |
| **Goal** | Preparation for current job | Preparation for changes |
| **Participation** | Required | Voluntary |

Development is especially critical for talent management, particularly for senior managers and employee's with leadership potential (recall our discussion of attracting and retaining talent in Chapter One). Companies report that the most important talent management challenges they face include developing existing talent and attracting and retaining existing leadership talent.[3] Chapter Two, "Strategic Training," emphasized the strategic role of training. As training continues to become more strategic (that is, related to business goals), the distinction between training and development will blur. Both training and development will be required and will focus on current and future personal and company needs.

## Development and Careers

Traditionally, careers have been described in various ways.[4] Careers have been described as a sequence of positions held within an occupation. For example, a university faculty member can hold assistant, associate, and full professor positions. A career has also been described in the context of mobility within an organization. For example, an engineer may begin her career as a staff engineer. As her expertise, experience, and performance increase, she may move through advisory engineering, senior engineering, and senior technical positions. Finally, a career has been described as a characteristic of the employee. Each employee's career consists of different jobs, positions, and experiences.

Today's careers are known as protean careers.[5] A **protean career** is based on self-direction, with the goal of psychological success in one's work. Employees take major responsibility for managing their careers. For example, an engineer may decide to take a sabbatical from her position to work in management at the United Way Agency for a year. The purpose of this assignment could be to develop her managerial skills, as well as help her evaluate if she likes managerial work more than engineering.

The protean career has several implications for employee development. The goal of the new career is **psychological success**: the feeling of pride and accomplishment that comes from achieving life goals that are not limited to achievements at work (such as raising a family and having good physical health). Psychological success is more under the employee's control than the traditional career goals, which were not only influenced by employee effort but were controlled by the availability of positions in the company. Psychological success is self-determined rather than solely determined through signals the employee receives from the company (like salary increase and promotion). For example, a 55-year-old management consultant used to work in Manhattan.[6] After more than ten years in the business, she decided to become a stay-at-home mom. As she focused on raising her two children, she also worked for several different nonprofits creating a preschool program for economically disadvantaged children. After she moved with her husband and family to Japan for four years due to his job transfer, she became interested in food. When the family returned to the United States, she realized that she had a passion for farming. She studied online and visited local farms to learn about how to make goat cheese. Today, she owns and operates a working farm in New York, about a one-hour drive from New York City. The farm produces goat cheese, grows vegetables, and hosts classes for children and adults. The farm demands mean that she sometimes has to put in as much as fourteen hours each day. She plans to work as long as she is physically able to and hopes to make the business self-sustainable. She also doesn't believe the farm is her last career move. She hopes someday that she will apply what she has learned to projects in Africa and India.

Employees need to develop new skills rather than rely on a static knowledge base. This has resulted from companies' need to be more responsive to customers' service and product demands. As we emphasized in Chapter One, learning is continuous, often informal, and involves creating and sharing knowledge. The emphasis on continuous learning has altered the direction and frequency of movement within careers (career pattern).[7] Traditional career patterns consisted of a series of steps arranged in a linear hierarchy, with higher steps related to increased authority, responsibility, and compensation. Expert career patterns involve a lifelong commitment to a field or specialization (such as law, medicine, or management). These types of career patterns will not disappear. Rather, career patterns involving movement across specializations or disciplines (a spiral career pattern) will become more prevalent. These new career patterns mean that developing employees (as well as employees taking control of their own careers) must be provided with the opportunity to (a) determine their interests, skill strengths, and weaknesses; and (b) based on this information, seek appropriate development experiences that will likely involve job experiences and relationships as well as formal courses.

The most appropriate view of today's careers are that they are "boundaryless and often change."[8] It includes movement across several employers (also known as job hopping) or even different occupations. Job hopping is discussed in Chapter Ten, "Social Responsibility: Legal Issues, Managing Diversity, and Career Challenges," but keep in mind that statistics indicate that the average employment tenure at any given company for all American workers is only five years.[9] One study found that 60 percent of employees of all ages rate time and flexibility as very important reasons for staying with a company.[10]

"Boundaryless" means that careers may involve identifying more with a job or profession than with the present employer. A career can also be considered boundaryless in the sense that career plans or goals are influenced by personal or family demands and values. One way that employees cope with changes in their personal lives, as well as in employment relationships, is to rearrange and shift their roles and responsibilities. Employees can change their careers throughout their life based on awareness of strengths and weaknesses, perceived need to balance work and life, and the need to find stimulating and exciting work.[11] Career success may not be tied to promotions but to achieving goals that are personally meaningful to the employee rather than those set by parents, peers, or the company. As we discuss later in the chapter, careers are best managed through partnerships between employees and their company that create a positive relationship through which employees are committed to the organization but can take personal control for managing their own careers to benefit themselves and the company.

As this discussion shows, to retain and motivate employees, companies need to provide a system to identify and meet employees' development needs. This is especially important to retain good performers and employees who have potential for managerial positions. **Development planning or career management system** refers to a system to retain and motivate employees by identifying and helping to meet their development needs. We discuss these systems below.

## DEVELOPMENT PLANNING SYSTEMS

Companies' development planning systems (also known as development planning processes) vary in the level of sophistication and the emphasis they place on different components of the process. Steps and responsibilities in the development planning system are shown in Figure 9.1.

**Self-assessment** refers to the use of information by employees to determine their career interests, values, aptitudes, and behavioral tendencies. It often involves psychological tests such as the Myers-Briggs Type Indicator (MBTI, a type of personality assessment described later in the chapter), the Strong-Campbell Interest Inventory, and the Self-Directed Search. The Strong-Campbell helps employees identify their occupational and job interests; the Self-Directed Search identifies employees' preferences for working in different types of environments (like sales, counseling, landscaping, and so on). Tests may also help employees identify the relative values they place on work and leisure activities.

Through the assessment, a development need can be identified. This need can result from gaps between current skills and/or interests and the type of work or position the employee wants. For example, Verizon Wireless provides an online tool that allows employees to assess their current skills and abilities in order to benchmark themselves against job openings throughout the company. The assessment allows employees to

**FIGURE 9.1** **Steps and responsibilities in the Development Planning Process**

| | Self-assessment | Reality check | Goal setting | Action planning |
|---|---|---|---|---|
| **Employee responsibility** | Identify opportunities and needs to improve. | Identify what needs are realistic to develop. | Identify goal and method to determine goal progress. | Identify steps and timetable to reach goal. |
| **Company responsibility** | Provide assessment information to identify strengths, weaknesses, interests, and values. | Communicate performance evaluation, where employee fits in long-range plans of the company, changes in industry, profession, and workplace. | Ensure that goal is SMART (specific, measurable, attainable, relevant, and timely); commit to help employee reach the goal. | Identify resources employee needs to reach goal, including additional assessment, courses, work experiences, and relationships. |

identify capabilities they are lacking and provides them with specific information about what they can do to develop skills through training, job experience, or enrolling in an academic program.[12]

## Reality Check

**Reality check** refers to the information employees receive about how the company evaluates their skills and knowledge and where they fit into the company's plans (potential promotion opportunities, lateral moves). Usually, this information is provided by the employee's manager as part of the performance appraisal. Some companies also use the 360-degree feedback assessment, which involves employees completing a self-evaluation of their behaviors or competencies and their managers, peers, direct reports, and even customers also providing evaluations of them. The concept of 360-degree feedback is discussed later in the chapter.

It is not uncommon for managers to hold separate performance appraisals and development discussions. This is done because performance appraisal and development discussions have different objectives. Discussing performance and development in the same meeting is difficult because they have different objectives. Performance appraisal discussions are focused on an employee's job performance during a defined period of time (such as six months or a year) and usually involve a discussion of what financial incentives or pay increases the employee can expect to receive as a result of performance. Development discussions do not involve pay or rewards. They focus on the employee's skill set or competencies, how to develop them, and the manager and the employee identifying and agreeing on realistic short- and long-term development goals (responsibilities or positions that the employee can achieve).

For example, as part of Caterpillar's performance management process, career development is discussed between the employee and his or her manager.[13] To facilitate this discussion, employees complete a data sheet that serves as an internal resume. The data sheet includes information about the employee's skills, education, academic degrees, languages spoken, and previous positions. Managers are expected to indicate an employee's readiness for a new job, whether the job will be a promotion or lateral move, and what education or training the employee needs to be ready for the move. Managers discuss with employees where they want to go next and what they have to do to prepare themselves for the next position. Managers also identify where they think the employee has the best opportunities in different functional areas and provide an overall rating of potential and promotability.

## Goal Setting

**Goal setting** refers to the process of employees developing short- and long-term development objectives. These goals usually relate to desired positions (such as becoming sales manager within three years), level of skill application (use one's budgeting skills to improve the unit's cash flow problems), work setting (move to corporate marketing within two years), or skill acquisition (learn how to use the company's human resource information system). These goals are usually discussed with the manager and written into a development plan. A development plan for a product manager is shown in Figure 9.2. Development plans usually include descriptions of strengths and weaknesses, career goals, and

**FIGURE 9.2**   **Development Plan**

---

**Name:** _____   **Title:** Project Manager   **Immediate Manager:** _____

**Competencies**
*Please identify your three greatest strengths and areas for improvement.*
**Strengths**
• Strategic thinking and execution (confidence, command skills, action orientation)
• Results orientation (competence, motivating others, perseverance)
• Spirit for winning (building team spirit, customer focus, respect colleagues)

**Areas for Improvement**
• Patience (tolerance of people or processes and sensitivity to pacing)
• Written communications (ability to write clearly and succinctly)
• Overly ambitious (too much focus on successful completion of projects rather than developing
  relationships with individuals involved in the projects)

**Development Goals**
*Please describe your overall career goals.*
• **Long-term:** Accept positions of increased responsibility to a level of general manager (or beyond).
  The areas of specific interest include but are not limited to product and brand management,
  technology and development, strategic planning, and marketing.
• **Short-term:** Continue to improve my skills in marketing and brand management while utilizing my skills
  in product management, strategic planning, and global relations.

**Next Assignments**
*Identify potential next assignments (including timing) that would help you develop toward your
goals.*
• Manager or director level in planning, development, product, or brand management. Timing estimated
  to be Spring 2014.

**Training and Development Needs**
*List both training and development activities that will either help you develop in your current assignment
or provide overall development.*
• Master's degree classes will allow me to practice and improve my written communications skills. The
  dynamics of my current position, teamwork, and reliance on other individuals allow me to practice
  patience and to focus on individual team members' needs along with the success of the projects.

---

**Employee** _____   **Date** _____
**Immediate Manager** _____   **Date** _____
**Mentor** _____   **Date** _____

---

development activities for reaching the career goal. An effective development plan focuses
on development needs that are most relevant to the organization's strategic objectives.

Consider Just Born's Career Development Process (CDP), which is used by employees
to identify their career path within the company and ready themselves for their next position.[14] The development plan involves identifying both short- and long-term career goals.

Employees commit to two goals to help them progress in their career. Just Born provides a competency dictionary on the company's intranet that can be used for identifying development needs. The CDP gives both employees and their managers the opportunity to discuss future career plans and becomes a reality check by raising expectations and increasing performance standards. Employees initiate the CDP by first defining future job interests, identifying work experiences that help prepare for the future job, and establishing the long-term career goal. The CDP is discussed with the employee's manager. The manager can support the CDP or suggest changes. If employees' future job interests are outside their current department, the interests are communicated to the manager of that department.

## Action Planning

During this phase, employees complete an action plan. An **action plan** is a written strategy that employees use to determine how they will achieve their short- and long-term career goals. Action plans may involve any one or combination of development approaches discussed later in the chapter (such as enrolling in courses and seminars, getting additional assessment, obtaining new job experiences, or finding a mentor or coach).[15] The development approach used depends on the needs and developmental goal.

## Examples of Career Management and Development Systems

Effective career development systems include several important features (see Table 9.2). Also, companies are using technology to provide employees with greater access and give them more responsibility for managing their own careers. Sprint's individual development plan is based on five core competencies: act with integrity, focus on the customer, deliver results, build relationships, and develop leadership.[16] These competencies are used by each business unit to establish its strategy as well as by each manager and employee in creating development plans. The competencies are the foundations for development

**TABLE 9.2**
**Design Factors of Effective Development Systems**

Sources: Based B. Conaty and R. Charan, *The Talent Masters* (New York: Crown Business, 2010); D. Hall, *Careers in and out of Organizations* (Thousand Oaks, CA: Sage, 2002).

1. The system is positioned as a response to a business need or to support the business strategy.
2. Employees and managers participate in developing the system.
3. Employees are encouraged to take an active role in career management and development.
4. Evaluation is ongoing and used to improve the system.
5. Business units can customize the system for their own purposes (with some constraints).
6. Employees have access to development and career information sources (including advisors and positions available).
7. Senior management and the company culture support the development system.
8. The development system uses competencies, skills, and behavior that are common to the company's other human resource practices, including performance management, training, and recruiting.
9. The development system is linked to other human resource practices, such as performance management, training, and recruiting systems.
10. A large, diverse talent pool is created.
11. Development plans and talent evaluation information are available and accessible to all managers.

conversations between managers and employees. Among the resources available to support the development plan is a development activities guide, which includes audiotapes, books, and specific courses designed to improve each of the competencies, as well as a website where employees can learn about the process. At Automatic Data Processing, managers are trained to promote development, and they are held accountable in part of their performance evaluation for the number of employees they have coached and prepared for promotion.[17] Managers receive training on how to hold effective development discussions. Employees can attend information sessions where they can learn about career options within ADP from other employees holding many different positions. ADP also provides a web-based tool for its sales associates, which they can use to access sales and sales leadership career descriptions and opportunities across the company's markets, products, and international locations. General Mills's development plan is similar to the one shown in Figure 9.2. Each employee completes a development plan that asks employees to consider four areas:

- *Professional goals and motivation:* What professional goals do I have? What excites me to grow professionally?
- *Talents or strengths:* What are my talents and strengths?
- *Development opportunities:* What development needs are important to improve?
- *Development objectives and action steps:* What will be my objective for this plan? What steps can I take to meet the objective?

Every year, managers and employees are expected to have a development discussion and create an individual development plan. Speakers, online tools, and workshops to help employees complete the development plan and prepare for a development discussion with their manager increase the visibility and emphasize the importance of the development planning process. Evaluation data showed that more than 80 percent of employees report having an effective and motivating development plan. Also, annual survey results show that General Mills ranks 20 percent to 30 percent higher on continued improvement and impact of learning and growth compared to companies it is benchmarked against.

Walgreens, the neighborhood drugstore and retailer, has an online career development site called Blueprints, which allows employees to manage their own careers. Career management products available on Blueprints include e-learning modules, competencies and performance standards for different jobs, and descriptions of roles, career paths, and job rotations related to specific career goals. White Lodging Services, a hospitality service company, provides each leader with a career steward, who provides mentoring and coaching needed for the person's success. Each leader has a "2 Sheet," which is an online dashboard that provides a snapshot of the leader's performance over time based on the company's balanced scorecard, presents their short- and long-term goals and actions to reach the goals, and identifies the training they have completed and what types of training they will need to achieve their goals.

IBM's Blue Opportunities reinforces to employees that growing their careers is important to obtain challenging and interesting work and that they need to take responsibility, working with their managers, for identifying training and development activities that interest them. Blue Opportunities highlights the company's training and development opportunities such as short- and long-term job rotation, on-site job shadowing, and cross-functional projects on an employee-only intranet site that is accessible to employees in the United States and other global locations. The goals of Blue Opportunities are developing employees' skills and knowledge and offering them potential job or career changes. Blue Opportunities provides a way for employees to develop skills across business units and explore career options that they would not have previously considered.

The Role of the Manager @ IBM is an expert system that provides a customized learning portfolio for each manager based on their background, training, and management style. The expert system guides managers through prework that has to be completed prior to attending learning labs. Learning is reinforced through the use of a knowledge management system that allows managers to post suggestions and store ideas. Managers who have completed the Role of the Manager @ IBM program have created action plans that have generated revenues of $184 million.

# APPROACHES TO EMPLOYEE DEVELOPMENT

Four approaches are used to develop employees: formal education, assessment, job experiences, and interpersonal relationships.[18] Many companies use a combination of these approaches. Figure 9.3 shows the frequency of use of different employee development practices. Larger companies are more likely to use leadership training and development planning more frequently than smaller companies. Children's Healthcare of Atlanta, a medical system specializing in pediatric care, has a Center for Leadership that includes assessment, workshops, action learning, and personal coaches.[19] High-performing employees with potential to become managers complete a full day of assessment that includes participating in a business simulation that requires them to pretend they are managing a division of a major company. They also complete a personality inventory. Employees are given feedback about their behavior in the simulation and the results of the personality inventory.

**FIGURE 9.3**
**Frequency of Use of Employee Development Practices**

Source: Based on E. Esen and J. Collison, *Employee Development* (Alexandria, VA: SHRM Research, 2005).

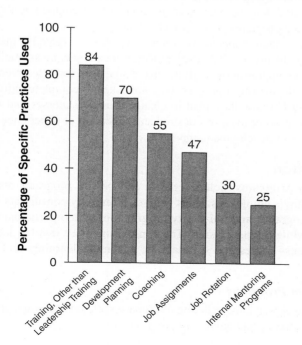

Employees attend five workshops each year that focus on helping employees work with the feedback they received during the assessment. The workshops cover topics such as leading change, developing a business strategy, and creating a personal vision. Action learning requires participants to work in teams on a topic that is of strategic importance to the medical system. Coaches work with the employees to identify long-term improvement goals.

Regardless of the approach used to ensure that development programs are effective, the programs should be developed through the same process used for training design: assessing needs, creating a positive development environment, ensuring employees' readiness for development, identifying the objectives for development, choosing a combination of development activities that will help achieve the objectives, ensuring that the work environment supports development activities and the use of skills and experiences acquired, and evaluating the program. To determine the development needs of an individual, department, or company, an analysis of strengths and weaknesses needs to be completed so that appropriate development activities can be chosen. Many companies have identified key competencies for successful managers. Recall from the discussion in Chapter Three, "Needs Assessment," that competencies are areas of personal capability that enable employees to successfully perform their jobs. Competencies can include knowledge, skills, abilities, or personal characteristics.

For example, Schwan Food Company, a Minnesota-based frozen food delivery service, determined the need for development and then used assessment to determine appropriate development activities and create its own corporate university.[20] As part of the process, the company had to determine what kind of managers it wanted and how they were supposed to perform. Schwan identified fifteen important competencies, including "managing vision and purpose," and "developing direct reports." After the competencies were identified, the company used 360-degree feedback to measure managers' competency strengths and weaknesses and created development activities related to strengthening the competencies (e.g., coaches, training programs, job experiences, etc.).

Keep in mind that although much development activity is targeted at managers, all levels of employees may be involved in development. For example, most employees typically receive a performance appraisal (an activity that can be used for assessment) at least once per year. As part of the appraisal process, they are asked to complete individual development plans outlining (1) how they plan to change their weaknesses and (2) their future plans (including positions or locations desired and education or experience needed). Next, we explore each type of development approach.

## Formal Education

**Formal education programs** include off-site and on-site programs designed specifically for the company's employees, short courses offered by consultants or universities, executive MBA programs, and university programs in which participants actually live at the university while taking classes. These programs may involve lectures by business experts, business games and simulations, adventure learning, and meetings with customers.

### *Formal Education Programs*

Employee development programs, including short courses offered by consultants or universities, executive MBA programs, and university programs.

Many companies rely primarily on in-house development programs offered by training and development centers or corporate universities, rather than sending employees to programs offered by universities.[21] Companies rely on in-house programs because they can be tied directly to business needs, can be easily evaluated using company metrics, and can get senior-level management involved.

Most formal education programs actively involve the employees in learning. Separate programs are usually offered for supervisors, middle managers, and executives. Special programs for particular jobs (such as engineer) are also available. At Whirlpool, the largest manufacturer of large home appliances in the world, the company's leadership development program focuses on twelve critical attributes: (1) character and enduring values, (2) communications, (3) customer champion, (4) confidence, (5) developing talent, (6) diversity with inclusion, (7) driver of change/transformation, (8) extraordinary results, (9) management skills, (10) strategy, (11) thought leadership, and (12) vision.[22] The leadership development program is organized into three tiers. The first tier (Leadership Development Programs) includes programs to train new graduates for higher-level positions in functional areas such as marketing, engineering, finance, or human resources. Each program runs three to four years and includes formal training, mentoring, and rotations through job assignments. A total of 100 new employees attend the program each year, with over 300 involved in the rotations at any one time. The second tier of programs (Leading the Whirlpool Enterprise), required for the top 700 company leaders, involves two one-week classes. One class includes a 360-degree assessment evaluating each executive's attributes and providing feedback. The second week focuses on asking the executives to consider the company's strategic objectives, identify the most important business issue, and develop a plan to solve the issue. The third tier (Leaders Developing Leaders) includes the twenty top company executives from around the world. These executives are given an intensive assessment of their skills and personality and they are matched with a coach who works with them to help improve their weaknesses and capitalize on their strengths. To ensure that the company's investment in the Leadership Development Program is well spent, managers and company leaders are held accountable for developing future leaders by serving as teachers in the courses. Also, managers' and company leaders' performance evaluations include objectives related to leadership development, as well as financial results.

General Electric (GE) has one of the oldest and most widely known management development centers in the world. GE invests approximately $1 billion each year for training and education programs for its employees.[23] GE develops managers at the John F. Welch Leadership Center at Crotonville, New York.[24] The facility has residence buildings where participants stay while attending programs, as well as classrooms for courses, programs, and seminars. Each year, GE employees chosen by their managers based on their performance and potential attend management development programs. The programs include professional skills development and specialized courses in areas such as risk analysis and loan structuring. All of the programs emphasize theory and practical application. Course time is spent discussing business issues facing GE. The programs are taught by in-house instructors, university faculty members, and even CEO Jeff Immelt. Examples of management development programs available at GE are shown in Table 9.3. As you can see, GE uses a combination of coursework and job experiences to develop entry-level and top levels of management. Other programs such as the Business Manager Course and the

**TABLE 9.3**   **Examples of Leadership Development Programs at General Electric**

| Program | Summary | Qualifications to Attend |
|---|---|---|
| Entry-level Commercial Leadership Program | Formal courses to develop commercial skills and techniques. Challenging assignments in key sales and marketing roles within a business. | Bachelor's degree; minimum 3.0 GPA; prior internship or co-op experience, willingness to relocate; demonstrated interest in sales career and results-oriented. |
| Experienced Commercial Leadership Program (ECLP) Sales and Marketing | Receive at least six weeks of training to develop marketing and sales capabilities, strengthen leadership skills, foster ECLP culture. Three eight-month business rotations within a GE business; the rotations are marketing focused and sales focused. Every four months, review self-assessment and manager evaluations to identify accomplishments, development needs, and career interests. Training includes classroom and online training and in-residence symposiums at the John F. Welch Learning Center. | MBA; five to eight years marketing or sales experience; demonstrated achievement and leadership in sales or marketing communications, and analytical skills; willingness to relocate; expertise aligned with a GE business |

Source: Based on "Program Details," www.ge.com/careers/students/eclp/program_details.html (Accessed February 1, 2012).

Executive Development Course involve action learning. As discussed in Chapter Seven, "Traditional Training Methods," action learning involves assigning a real problem that GE is facing to program participants who must present their recommendations to CEO Jeff Immelt. Besides programs and courses for management development, GE also holds seminars to better understand customer expectations and leadership conferences designed specifically for African-American, female, and Hispanic managers to discuss leading and learning.

## Executive Education

A number of institutions in the United States and abroad provide executive education, including Harvard, Stanford, Columbia, INSEAD, and Ohio State University. Executive education includes executive MBA programs, as well as specialized curriculum on topics such as leadership, entrepreneurship, change, innovation, and global business.[25] Executive education programs typically involve a blended learning approach (blended learning was discussed in Chapter Eight, "Technology-Based Training Methods"). This means that managers visit campus for face-to-face instruction and, between sessions, work online on assignments such as team projects, cases, or reading assignments. For example, Xerox Corporation's Emerging Leaders Program (ELP) is a five-month program that includes a two-hour program kickoff using web-based conferencing, e-modules that employees complete at their own pace, face-to-face meetings, online assessment, coaching, and mentoring.[26] Employees from North America and Europe have participated in ELP. Each session in the European ELP includes high-potential managers from 14 countries who work in different functions and speak different languages. The most challenging part of ELP involves working as a cross-functional, cross-cultural, geographically dispersed team to identify, plan, and begin a business project based on the strategic initiatives. Each team presents their results to vice presidents and executives at the conclusion of the program.

In addition to blended learning, business schools or other educational institutions have begun offering companies in-house, customized programs to help managers gain real-world skills and study problems in real-world environments—without requiring the managers to disrupt their work by requiring them to travel to campus. These programs supplement formal courses from consultants or university faculty with other types of development activities. For example, Duke Corporate Education conducts custom programs for Arcelor-Mittal, which was formed by the merger of two steel companies.[27] One of the challenges the company faces is how to get its managers to understand the global challenges facing the steel industry. As a result, the program involves middle managers visiting steel plants in both mature and emerging markets to gain an understanding of the technology and management processes of a more established steel plant compared to a growing steel plant. The managers are asked to develop proposals for improving the growing plant, such as how to identify environmental problems and expanding health and safety features. The Haas School of Business at the University of California, Berkeley, worked with StatoilHydro, a Norwegian oil and gas company that focuses on preparing employees to work in different cultures. The program includes challenges such as working with contractors who may not have the employees or equipment to complete a project on time or learning to deal with local government officials.

Managers who attend the Center for Creative Leadership development program take psychological tests; receive feedback from managers, peers, and direct reports; participate in group-building activities (like adventure learning, discussed in Chapter Seven); receive counseling; and set improvement goals and write development plans.[28]

## Tuition Reimbursement

Enrollment in executive education programs or MBA programs may be limited to managers or employees identified to have management potential. As a result, many companies also provide tuition reimbursement as a benefit for all employees to encourage them to develop on their own. **Tuition reimbursement** refers to the practice of reimbursing employees' costs for college and university courses and degree programs. Companies spend about $10 billion on tuition reimbursement for courses offered by nonprofit colleges and universities, as well as for-profit universities like Capella University.[29] These courses include face-to-face classroom instruction, online learning, and blended learning. Companies that have evaluated tuition reimbursement programs have found that the programs increase employee retention rates and readiness for promotion, and improve job performance.[30] Verizon Wireless invests $26 million annually in tuition assistance program participated in by 18 percent of its employees.[31] Employees can receive tuition assistance for attending a university or college or for the costs of the company's on-site program conducted at call centers and corporate offices. The on-site program classes, taught by university faculty, help employees earn degrees by attending classes where they work and when they have free time in their work schedules. They are eligible for tuition reimbursement from the day they are hired and have to make no commitment to stay employed with the company. Their expenses are limited to $8,000 per year for full-time employees and $4,000 for part-time employees. This exceeds the $5,250 annual reimbursement limit that most companies use based on the tax-free maximum established by the Internal Revenue Service (IRS). To be eligible for reimbursement, coursework has to relate to an employee's current job or career path within Verizon Wireless. Evaluation of the program has shown that it has resulted in increased morale and helped to attract new and retain current employees.

## Assessment

**Assessment** involves collecting information and providing feedback to employees about their behavior, communication style, or skills.[32] The employees, their peers, managers, and customers may provide information. Assessments are used for several reasons. First, assessment is most frequently used to identify employees with managerial potential and to measure current managers' strengths and weaknesses. Assessment is also used to identify managers with the potential to move into higher-level executive positions, and it can be used with work teams to identify the strengths and weaknesses of individual team members and the decision processes or communication styles that inhibit the team's productivity. Assessments can help employees understand their tendencies, needs, the type of work environment they prefer, and the type of work they might prefer to do.[33] This information, along with the performance evaluations they receive from the company, can help employees decide what type of development goals might be most appropriate for them (e.g., leadership position, increase scope of their current position, etc.). Popular assessment tools include personality test and inventories, assessment centers, performance appraisal, and 360-degree feedback systems.

### Personality Tests and Inventories

Tests are used to determine if employees have the personality characteristics necessary to be successful in specific managerial jobs or jobs involving international assignments. They are used to help employees gain self-awareness of how they respond to conflict, what motivates them, how they solve problems, and how they react to stress. Some personality tests such as the NEO Personality Inventory (or the NEO-PRI) measure openness to new experiences, conscientiousness or dependability, emotional stability, assertiveness, and the ability to get along with other people. For example, Carmeuse North America uses personality tests in its leadership development program. The personality tests for employees who have been identified as having high potential for top management positions will be used to guide employees into development activities including coaching and formal courses.[34] Starwood Vacation Ownership, a subsidiary of Starwood Hotels and Resorts, uses several assessment tools to determine if its top managers value the commercial success of the business, as well as tolerance for ambiguity, the ability to create and communicate a business strategy, the ability to build business partnerships, and the ability to develop staff. The assessment identifies managers who are ready for international assignments, may not fit their current position, or need coaching to better understand the company culture.[35] CareSource, a Medicaid-managed care provider in Dayton, Ohio, has a defined process for identifying and developing employees who have the potential to be strong leaders and effective managers.[36] Assessment of fit with the organizational values and culture which emphasize serving the underserved, begins with the recruiting process. The company uses multiple assessment tools to evaluate managers' competencies (recall our discussion of competencies in Chapter Three). These assessments include the Myers-Briggs Type Indicator (MBTI; discussed below), the Gallup's Strength Finder to identify managers' strengths and develop plans for using their strengths with their employee team, and the Leadership Practices Inventory, which provides managers with an idea of their leadership skills as evaluated by peers, their boss, and their own self-assessment, and is used to build a personal leadership development plan. Also twice a year, using the performance management system, they are evaluated on competencies and behavior that CareSource believes are characteristics of an effective leader and manager: service orientation, organizational awareness, teamwork, communications, and organizational leadership. Based on the assessment results, managers with high leadership potential are encouraged to participate in a variety of development activities.

Two popularly used assessment tools are DiSC and the MBTI. Both of these tools can be used to help employees better understand how to adapt and change their behavior to be a more effective leader or team member. These tools can be used to place employees in job experiences they will be most successful in, give them experiences requiring them to adapt their behavior or personality, or assign a mentor or coach who can help them learn how to adapt to different situations. The DiSC measures personality and behavioral style, including dominance (direct, strong-willed, forceful), influence (sociable, talkative), steadiness (gentle, accommodating) and conscientiousness (private, analytical).[37] See www.discprofile .com for more information on DiSC. The **Myers-Briggs Type Inventory (MBTI)** refers to an assessment that is based on Carl Jung's personality type theory. This theory emphasizes that we have a fundamental personality type that shapes and influences how we understand the world, process information, and socialize. The assessment determines which one of sixteen personality types fits best. The sixteen unique personality types are based on preferences for introversion (I) or extraversion (E), sensing (S) or intuition (N), thinking (T) or feeling (F), and judging (J) or perceiving (P). The assessment tool identifies an individual's preferences for energy (introversion versus extroversion), information gathering (sensing versus intuition), decision making (thinking versus feeling), and lifestyle (judging versus perceiving).[38] Each personality type has implications for work habits and interpersonal relationships. For example, individuals who are introverted, sensing, thinking, and judging (known as ISTJs) tend to be serious, quiet, practical, orderly, and logical. These persons can organize tasks, be decisive, and follow through on plans and goals. ISTJs have several weaknesses, however, because they do not tend to use the opposite preferences: extroversion, intuition, feeling, and perceiving. These weaknesses include problems dealing with unexpected opportunities, appearing too task-oriented or impersonal to colleagues, and making overly quick decisions. Visit the website www.cpp.com for more information on the personality types.

Hallmark Cards has helped people express their feelings and celebrate important events and occasions for over 100 years.[39] Hallmark executives want to change the company's culture from that of a manufacturing company focused on developing products to a consumer-based company focusing on engaging its key customers. It recognizes the importance of developing leaders that can view situations from different perspectives, provide support to each other and work together, inspire employees, and efficiently implement new ideas. To help make this cultural shift, Hallmark Cards is using the MBTI to help managers increase their self-insight into how their actions and communications are perceived by other employees and managers, as well as how they tend to interact in teams, and their work and leadership styles.

Hallmark Cards has realized several positive results from using the MBTI. The speed of managers' decision making and clarity of communications to employees have improved. There has been a noticeable improvement in employees feeling comfortable expressing their thoughts and managers communicating in ways that appeal to all employee types.

## Assessment Center

At an **assessment center,** multiple raters or evaluators (assessors) evaluate employees' performance on a number of exercises.[40] An assessment center is usually an off-site location such as a conference center. From six to twelve employees usually participate at one time. Assessment centers are primarily used to identify if employees have the personality characteristics, administrative skills, and interpersonal skills needed for managerial jobs. They are also increasingly being used to determine if employees have the necessary skills to work in teams.

The types of exercises used in assessment centers include leaderless group discussions, interviews, in-baskets, and role plays.[41] In a **leaderless group discussion,** a team of five to seven employees is assigned a problem and must work together to solve it within a certain time period. The problem may involve buying and selling supplies, nominating a subordinate for an award, or assembling a product. In the **interview,** employees answer questions about their work and personal experiences, skill strengths and weaknesses, and career plans. An **in-basket** is a simulation of the administrative tasks of the manager's job. The exercise includes a variety of documents that may appear in the in-basket, e-mail, or on a manager's desk. The participants read the materials and decide how to respond to them. Responses might include delegating tasks, scheduling meetings, writing replies, or completely ignoring the memo! Role plays refer to the participant taking the part or role of a manager or other employee. For example, an assessment center participant may be asked to take the role of a manager who has to give a negative performance review to a subordinate. The participant is told about the subordinate's performance and is asked to prepare for and actually hold a forty-five-minute meeting with the subordinate to discuss the performance problems. The role of the subordinate is played by a manager or other member of the assessment center design team or company. The assessment center might also include interest and aptitude tests to evaluate an employee's vocabulary, general mental ability, and reasoning skills. Personality tests may be used to determine if employees can get along with others, their tolerance for ambiguity, and other traits related to success as a manager.

Assessment center exercises are designed to measure employees' administrative and interpersonal skills. Skills typically measured include leadership, oral and written communication, judgment, organizational ability, and stress tolerance. Table 9.4 shows an example of the skills measured by the assessment center. As we see, each exercise gives participating employees the opportunity to demonstrate several different skills. For example, the exercise requiring scheduling to meet production demands evaluates employees' administrative and problem-solving ability. The leaderless group discussion measures interpersonal skills such as sensitivity toward others, stress tolerance, and oral communication skills.

Managers are usually used as assessors. The managers are trained to look for employee behaviors that are related to the skills that will be assessed. Typically, each

**TABLE 9.4**  **Examples of Skills Measured by Assessment Center Exercises**

| | Exercises | | | | |
|---|---|---|---|---|---|
| Skills | In-Basket | Scheduling Exercise | Leaderless Group Discussion | Personality Test | Role-Play |
| Leadership (dominance, coaching, influence, resourcefulness) | X | | X | X | X |
| Problem solving (judgment) | X | X | X | | X |
| Interpersonal (sensitivity, conflict resolution, cooperation, oral communication) | | | X | X | X |
| Administrative (organizing, planning, written communications) | X | X | X | | |
| Personal (stress tolerance, confidence) | | | X | X | X |

X indicates a skill measured by the exercise.

assessor observes and records one or two employee's behaviors in each exercise. The assessors review their notes and rate each employee's level of skills (for example, 5 = high level of leadership skills, 1 = low level of leadership skills). After all employees have completed the exercises, the assessors discuss their observations of each employee. They compare their ratings and try to agree on each employee's rating for each of the skills.

Research suggests that assessment center ratings are related to performance, salary level, and career advancement.[42] Assessment centers may also be useful for development because employees who participate in the process receive feedback regarding their attitudes, skill strengths, and weaknesses.[43] For example, Steelcase, the office furniture manufacturer based in Grand Rapids, Michigan, uses assessment centers for first-level managers.[44] The assessment center exercises include in-basket, interview simulation, and a timed scheduling exercise requiring participants to fill positions created by absences. Managers are also required to confront an employee on a performance issue, getting the employee to commit to improve. Because the exercises relate closely to what managers are required to do at work, feedback given to managers based on their performance in the assessment center can target specific skills or competencies that they need to be successful managers.

### Performance Appraisals and 360-Degree Feedback Systems

**Performance appraisal** is the process of measuring employees' performance. Performance appraisal information can be useful for employee development under certain conditions.[45] The appraisal system must tell employees specifically about their performance problems and how they can improve their performance. This includes providing a clear understanding of the differences between current performance and expected performance, identifying causes of the performance discrepancy, and developing action plans to improve performance. Managers must be trained in frequent performance feedback. Managers also need to monitor employees' progress in carrying out action plans.

Consider how Just Born, the company that makes Mike and Ike, Hot Tamales, and Peeps, uses performance appraisals for evaluation and development.[46] The appraisal starts with a planning meeting between employee and manager. The strategic initiatives of the department are discussed along with the employee's role. The employee and manager agree on four personal objectives that will help the department reach its goals, as well as key performance outcomes related to the employee's job description. Competencies that the employee needs to reach the personal objectives are identified. The manager and employee jointly develop a plan for improving or learning the competencies. During the year, the manager and employee monitor the progress toward reaching the performance and personal objectives and achievement of the learning plan. Pay decisions made at the end of each year are based on the achievement of both performance and learning objectives.

Upward feedback and 360-degree feedback are popular tools for development, particularly for managers. **Upward feedback** refers to appraisal that involves collecting subordinates' evaluations of managers' behaviors or skills. The 360-degree feedback process is a special case of upward feedback. In **360-degree feedback systems,** employees' behaviors or skills are evaluated not only by subordinates but by peers, customers, their bosses, and themselves. The raters complete a questionnaire asking them to rate the person on a number of different dimensions. Table 9.5 provides an example of the types of skills related to management success that are rated in a 360-degree feedback questionnaire. Typically, raters are asked to assess the manager's strength in a particular item or whether development is needed. Raters may also be asked to identify how frequently they observe a competency or skill (e.g., always, sometimes, seldom, never).

The results of a 360-degree feedback system show how the manager was rated on each item. The results also show how self-evaluations differ from evaluations from the other raters. Table 9.6 shows the type of activities involved in using 360-degree feedback for development.[47] Typically, managers review their results, seek clarification from the raters, and set specific development goals based on the strengths and weaknesses identified.[48]

The benefits of 360-degree feedback include collecting multiple perspectives of managers' performance, allowing employees to compare their own personal evaluations with the views of others, and formalizing communications about behaviors and skill ratings between employees and their internal and external customers. Several studies have shown that performance improves and behavior changes as a result of participating in upward feedback and 360-degree feedback systems.[49] The most change occurs in individuals who receive lower ratings from others than they gave themselves (overraters).

Potential limitations of 360-degree feedback include the time demands placed on the raters to complete the evaluations, managers seeking to identify and punish raters who provided negative information, the need to have a facilitator help interpret results, and companies' failure to provide ways that managers can act on the feedback they receive (development planning, meeting with raters, taking courses, etc.).

Effective 360-degree feedback systems include several factors. The system must provide reliable or consistent ratings and competencies, raters' confidentiality is maintained,

**TABLE 9.5**  **Skills Related to Managerial Success**

| Resourcefulness | Can think strategically, engage in flexible problem solving, and work effectively with higher management |
|---|---|
| Doing whatever it takes | Has perseverance and focus in the face of obstacles |
| Being a quick study | Quickly masters new technical and business knowledge |
| Building and mending relationships | Knows how to build and maintain working relationships with coworkers and external parties |
| Leading subordinates | Delegates to subordinates effectively, broadens their opportunities, and acts with fairness toward them |
| Compassion and sensitivity | Shows genuine interest in others and sensitivity to subordinates' needs |
| Straightforwardness and composure | Is honorable and steadfast |
| Setting a developmental climate | Provides a challenging climate to encourage subordinates' development |
| Confronting problem subordinates | Acts decisively and fairly when dealing with problem subordinates |
| Team orientation | Accomplishes tasks through managing others |
| Balance between personal life and work | Balances work priorities with personal life so that neither is neglected |
| Decisiveness | Prefers quick and approximate actions to slow and precise ones in many management situations. |
| Self-awareness | Has an accurate picture of strengths and weaknesses and is willing to improve. |
| Hiring talented staff | Hires talented people for the team |
| Putting people at ease | Displays warmth and a good sense of humor |
| Acting with flexibility | Can behave in ways that are often seen as opposites |

Source: Adapted with permission from C. D. McCauley, M. M. Lombardo, and C. J. Usher, "Diagnosing management development needs: An instrument based on how managers develop," *Journal of Management* 15 (1989): 389–403.

**TABLE 9.6**

**Activities in Using 360-Degree Feedback for Development**

1. **Understand strengths and weaknesses.**
   Review ratings for strengths and weaknesses.
   Identify skills or behaviors where self-ratings and others' (manager, peer, customer) ratings agree and disagree.

2. **Identify a development goal.**
   Choose a skill or behavior to develop.
   Set a clear, specific goal with a specified outcome.

3. **Identify a process for recognizing goal accomplishment.**
   Identify a timeframe for achieving the development goal.
   Identify development goal outcomes that can be measured and tracked.

4. **Identify strategies for reaching the development goal.**
   Establish strategies such as reading, job experiences, courses, and relationships.
   Establish strategies for receiving feedback on progress.
   Establish strategies for reinforcing the new skill or behavior.

the behaviors or skills assessed are job-related (valid), the system is easy to use, and managers receive and act on the feedback.[50]

Technology allows 360-degree questionnaires to be delivered to the raters via their personal computers. This increases the number of completed questionnaires returned, makes it easier to process the information, and speeds feedback reports to managers.

Regardless of the assessment method used, the information must be shared with the employee for development to occur. Along with assessment information, the employee needs suggestions for correcting skill weaknesses and using skills already learned. These suggestions might be to participate in training courses or develop skills through new job experiences. Based on the assessment information and available development opportunities, employees should develop action plans to guide their self-improvement efforts.

At AlliedBarton Security Systems, its 360-degree feedback report maps onto the company's core values and what it calls its Leadership Non-Negotiables.[51] The process is linked to an online talent tool kit, which gives managers leadership tips based on their 360-degree feedback. Capital One has developed an effective 360-degree feedback system.[52] Capital One, a consumer credit company, has included a number of features in its 360-degree feedback system to minimize the chance that the ratings will be used to get back at an employee or turned into popularity contests. The 360-degree assessments are based on the company's competency model, so raters are asked for specific feedback on a competency area. Rather than a lengthy form that places a large burden on raters to assess many different competencies, Capital One's assessment asks the raters to concentrate on three or four strengths or development opportunities. It also seeks comments, rather than limiting raters to merely circling numbers corresponding to how much of each competency the employee has demonstrated. These comments often provide specific information about what aspect of a competency needs to be developed or identifies work situations in which a competency needs to be improved. This comment system helps tailor development activities to fit competency development. To increase the chances that the assessment will result in change, the feedback from the 360-degree assessment is linked to development plans, and the company offers coaching and training to help employees strengthen their competencies. Employees are encouraged to share feedback with their coworkers. This creates a work environment based on honest and open feedback that helps employees personally grow.

## Job Experiences

Most employee development occurs through **job experiences:**[53] relationships, problems, demands, tasks, or other features that employees face in their jobs. A major assumption of using job experiences for employee development is that development is most likely to occur when there is a mismatch between the employee's skills and past experiences and the skills required for the job. To succeed in their jobs, employees must stretch their skills—that is, they are forced to learn new skills, apply their skills and knowledge in a new way, and master new experiences.[54] New job assignments help take advantage of employees' existing skills, experiences, and contacts, while helping them develop new ones.[55] General Electric uses experienced managers to integrate newly acquired companies. The Rainforest Alliance, an international nonprofit organization with 265 employees that helps product makers employ sustainable land practices, is challenged by quick growth (it has doubled in size since 2003) and the need it created to identify and develop managerial staff.[56] The Rainforest Alliance gives many junior employees the chance to lead research and other initiatives and, if they are successful, promotes them to manage the initiatives. For example, one employee who, started with the company as an administrative assistant was asked to take on more responsibilities, including researching climate change, and she is now the coordinator of a new climate initiative. Junior employees also can take part in internship programs in foreign offices to learn more about the organization and work on the "front lines" in implementing sustainable land practices.

Most of what we know about development through job experiences comes from a series of studies conducted by the Center for Creative Leadership.[57] Executives were asked to identify key career events that made a difference in their managerial styles and the lessons they learned from these experiences. The key events included those involving the job assignment (such as fixing a failing operation), those involving interpersonal relationships (getting along with supervisors), and the specific type of transition required (situations in which the executive did not have the necessary background). The job demands and what employees can learn from them are shown in Table 9.7.

One concern in the use of demanding job experiences for employee development is whether they are viewed as positive or negative stressors. Job experiences that are seen as positive stressors challenge employees to stimulate learning. Job challenges viewed

**TABLE 9.7   Job Demands and the Lessons Employees Learn from Them**

| | |
|---|---|
| Making transitions | *Unfamiliar responsibilities:* The manager must handle responsibilities that are new, very different, or much broader than previous ones. |
| | *Proving yourself:* The manager has added pressure to show others that they can handle the job. |
| Creating change | *Developing new directions:* The manager is responsible for starting something new in the organization, making strategic changes in the business, carrying out a reorganization, or responding to rapid changes in the business environment. |
| | *Inherited problems:* The manager has to fix problems created by a former incumbent or take over handling problem employees. |
| | *Reduction decisions:* Decisions about shutting down operations or staff reductions have to be made. |
| | *Problems with employees:* Employees lack adequate experience, are incompetent, or are resistant. |
| Having a high level of responsibility | *High stakes:* Clear deadlines, pressure from senior managers, high visibility, and responsibility for key decisions make success or failure in this job clearly evident. |
| | *Managing business diversity:* The scope of the job is large with responsibilities for multiple functions, groups, products, customers, or markets. |
| | *Job overload:* The sheer size of the job requires a large investment of time and energy. |
| | *Handling external pressure:* External factors that affect the business (e.g., negotiating with unions or government agencies, working in a foreign culture, coping with serious community problems, etc.) must be dealt with. |
| Being involved in nonauthority relationships | *Influencing without authority:* Getting the job done requires influencing peers, higher management, external parties, or other key people over whom the manager has no direct authority. |
| Facing obstacles | *Adverse business conditions:* The business unit or product line faces financial problems or difficult economic conditions. |
| | *Lack of top management support:* Senior management is reluctant to provide direction, support, or resources for current work or new projects. |
| | *Lack of personal support:* The manager is excluded from key networks and gets little support and encouragement from others. |
| | *Difficult boss:* The manager's opinions or management style differs from those of the boss, or the boss has major shortcomings. |

Source: C. D. McCauley, L. J. Eastman, and J. Ohlott, "Linking management selection and development through stretch assignments," *Human Resource Management* 84 (1995): 93–115. Copyright © 1995 Wiley Periodicals, Inc., a Wiley Company.

**FIGURE 9.4**

**How Job Experiences Are Used for Employee Development**

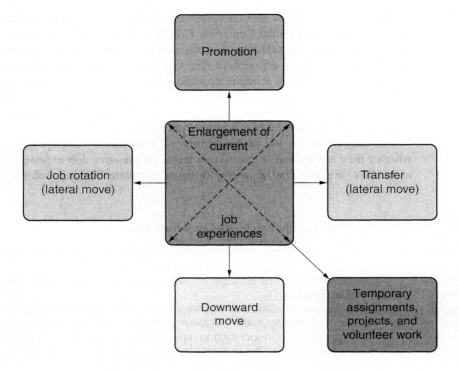

as negative stressors create high levels of harmful stress for employees exposed to them. Recent research findings suggest that all of the job demands, with the exception of obstacles, are related to learning.[58] Managers reported that obstacles and job demands related to creating change were more likely to lead to negative stress than the other job demands. This suggests that companies should carefully weigh the potential negative consequences before placing employees in development assignments involving obstacles or creating change.

Although the research on development through job experiences has focused on executives and managers, line employees can also learn from job experiences. As we noted earlier, for a work team to be successful, its members now need the kinds of skills that only managers were once thought to need (such as dealing directly with customers, analyzing data to determine product quality, and resolving conflict among team members). Besides the development that occurs when a team is formed, employees can further develop their skills by switching work roles within the team.

Figure 9.4 shows the various ways that job experiences can be used for employee development. These include enlarging the current job, job rotation, transfers, promotions, downward moves, and temporary assignments. For companies with global operations (multinationals), it is not uncommon for employee development to involve international assignments that require frequent travel or relocation.

### *Enlarging the Current Job*

**Job enlargement** refers to adding challenges or new responsibilities to employees' current jobs. This could include special project assignments, switching roles within a work team, or researching new ways to serve clients and customers. For example, an engineering employee may join a task force developing new career paths for technical employees. Through this project work, the engineer may lead certain aspects of career path development (such as reviewing the company's career development process). As a result, the engineer not only learns about the company's career development system, but uses leadership and organizational skills to help the task force reach its goals. Some companies are enlarging jobs by giving two managers the same responsibilities and job title and allowing them to divide the work (two-in-a-box).[59] This helps managers learn from a more experienced employee, helps companies fill jobs that require multiple skills, and, for positions requiring extensive travel, ensures that one employee is always on site to deal with work-related issues. For example, at Cisco Systems, the head of the Cisco routing group, who was trained as an engineer but now works in business development, shared a job with an engineer. Each employee was exposed to the other's skills, which has helped both perform their jobs better.

## *Job Rotation*

**Job rotation** gives employees a series of job assignments in various functional areas of the company or movement among jobs in a single functional area or department. Cianbro Corporation, a construction company, uses a rotational program for new hires that exposes them to estimating, engineering, and field experience.[60] The Financial Department provides a program that includes rotations through field assignments, business unit assignments, and a corporate rotation. At the senior level, top talent are rotated to provide them with the exposure and experiences they need to succeed in senior management positions in the company. The job rotation program at India-based Tata Consultancy Services sends native employees to operations in China, Hungary, and South America.[61] The program helps the company have skilled employees who are prepared to work in any of the company's offices in forty-two countries. Employees also gain an understanding of the culture of the country they work in. It also helps improve customer service because the company can draw on the strength of its entire workforce, rather than just relying on employees who are located close to the customer. The assignments typically last eighteen to twenty-four months, involving learning from both the customers and the local employees based at the location. After the assignment is completed, the employee usually works on the same kinds of projects they worked on in the overseas assignment, which helps transfer the knowledge gained to their home operations.

Job rotation helps employees gain an overall appreciation of the company's goals, increases their understanding of different company functions, develops a network of contacts, and improves problem-solving and decision-making skills.[62] For example, Sanofi-Aventis Pharmaceuticals encourages high-performing sales professionals to take on a temporary project or assignment with the Commercial Training Department to determine if they are interested in a training specialist role.[63] The length of the project assignments vary from a few days to several weeks, depending on the needs of the employee and training unit. Sales professionals who accept full-time training positions rotate to another role in the corporate office in two to three years (such as in marketing), go back to the field in a different sales unit, or accept a promotion to the district sales manager position. Job rotation has also been shown to be related to skill acquisition, salary growth, and promotion rates. But there are several potential problems with job rotation for both the employee and the work unit. The rotation may create a short-term perspective on problems and solutions in

**TABLE 9.8**

**Characteristics of Effective Job Rotation Systems**

1. Job rotation is used to develop skills, as well as give employees experience they will need for managerial positions.
2. Employees understand specific skills that will be developed by rotation.
3. Job rotation is used for all levels and types of employees.
4. Job rotation is linked with the career management process so that employees know the development needs addressed by each job assignment.
5. Benefits of rotation are maximized and costs are minimized through timing the rotations to reduce work load costs and help employees understand the job rotation's role in their development plans.
6. All employees have equal opportunities for job rotation assignments, regardless of their demographic group.

Sources: Based on L. Cheraskin and M. Campion, "Study clarifies job rotation benefits," *Personnel Journal* (November 1996): 31–38; M. Fiester, A. Collis, and N. Cossack, "Job rotation, total rewards, measuring value," *HR Magazine* (August 2008): 33–34.

rotating employees and their peers. Employees' satisfaction and motivation may be adversely affected because they find it difficult to develop functional specialties and they don't spend enough time in one position to receive a challenging assignment. Productivity losses and workload increases may be experienced by both the department gaining a rotating employee and the department losing the employee due to training demands and loss of a resource.

Table 9.8 shows characteristics of effective job rotation systems. Effective job rotation systems are linked to the company's training, development, and career management systems. Also, job rotation is used for all types of employees, not just those with managerial potential.

### Transfers, Promotions, and Downward Moves

Upward, lateral, and downward mobility is available for development purposes in most companies.[64] In a **transfer,** an employee is assigned a job in a different area of the company. Transfers do not necessarily increase job responsibilities or compensation. They are likely lateral moves (a move to a job with similar responsibilities). **Promotions** are advancements into positions with greater challenges, more responsibility, and more authority than in the previous job. Promotions usually include pay increases.

Transfers may involve relocation within the United States or to another country. This can be stressful not only because the employee's work role changes, but if the employee is in a two-career family, the spouse must find new employment. Also, the family has to join a new community. Transfers disrupt employees' daily lives, interpersonal relationships, and work habits.[65] People have to find new housing, shopping, health care, and leisure facilities, and they may be many miles from the emotional support of friends and family. They also have to learn a new set of work norms and procedures; they must develop interpersonal relationships with their new managers and peers; and they are expected to be as productive in their new jobs as they were in their old jobs, even though they may know little about the products, services, processes, or employees for whom they are responsible.

Because transfers can provoke anxiety, many companies have difficulty getting employees to accept them. Research has identified the employee characteristics associated with a willingness to accept transfers:[66] high level of career ambition, a belief that one's future with the company is promising, and a belief that accepting a transfer is necessary for success in the company. Employees who are not married and not active in the community are generally most willing to accept transfers. Among married employees, the spouse's willingness to move is the most important influence on whether an employee will accept a transfer.

A **downward move** occurs when an employee is given less responsibility and authority.[67] This may involve a move to another position at the same level (lateral demotion), a temporary cross-functional move, or a demotion because of poor performance. Temporary cross-functional moves to lower-level positions, which give employees experience working in different functional areas, are most frequently used for employee development. For example, engineers who want to move into management often take lower-level positions (like shift supervisor) to develop their management skills.

Because of the psychological and tangible rewards of promotions (such as increased feelings of self-worth, salary, and status in the company), employees are more willing to accept promotions than lateral or downward moves. Promotions are more readily available when a company is profitable and growing. When a company is restructuring or experiencing stable or declining profits—especially if numerous employees are interested in promotions and the company tends to rely on the external labor market to staff higher-level positions—promotion opportunities may be limited.[68]

Unfortunately, many employees have difficulty associating transfers and downward moves with development. They see them as punishment rather than as opportunities to develop skills that will help them achieve long-term success with the company. Many employees decide to leave a company rather than accept a transfer. Companies need to successfully manage transfers not only because of the costs of replacing employees but because of the relocation costs such as home sales and purchases directly associated with them. One challenge that companies face is learning how to use transfers and downward moves as development opportunities—convincing employees that accepting these opportunities will result in long-term benefits for them.

To ensure that employees accept transfers, promotions, and downward moves as development opportunities, companies can provide

- Information about the content, challenges, and potential benefits of the new job and location
- Involvement in the transfer decision by sending the employees to preview the new location and giving them information about the community
- Clear performance objectives and early feedback about their job performance
- A host at the new location to help them adjust to the new community and workplace
- Information about how the job opportunity will affect their income, taxes, mortgage payments, and other expenses
- Reimbursement and assistance in selling and purchasing or renting a place to live
- An orientation program for the new location and job
- Information on how the new job experiences will support employees' career plans
- Assistance for dependent family members, including identifying schools and child care and elder care options
- Help for the spouse in identifying and marketing skills and finding employment[69]

**Externship** refers to a company allowing employees to take a full-time operational role at another company. Mercer Management, a consulting firm, uses externship to develop employees interested in gaining experience in a specific industry.[70] Mercer Management promises to employ the externs after their assignments end. For example, one employee who had been a Mercer consultant became a vice president of Internet services for Binney & Smith, the maker of Crayola crayons. He had served as a consultant on an Internet project for Binney & Smith. But he wanted to actually implement his recommendations rather than just give them to the client and move on to another project—so he started working at Binney & Smith. He remains on Mercer Management's payroll, though his salary comes from Binney & Smith. Mercer believes that employees who participate in the externship program will remain committed to the company because they have had the opportunity to learn and grow professionally and have not had to disrupt their personal and professional lives with a job search. Although externships give employees other employment options and some employees will leave as a result, Mercer believes that it not only is a good development strategy, but also helps in recruitment. The externship program signals to potential employees that Mercer is creative and flexible with its employees.

### Temporary Assignments, Projects, Volunteer Work, and Sabbaticals

**Temporary assignments** refer to job tryouts such as employees taking on a position to help them determine if they are interested in working in a new role, employee exchanges, sabbaticals, and voluntary assignments. All temporary assignments have a predetermined ending date after which the employee returns to their permanent position. For example, Sanofi-Aventis Pharmaceuticals encourages high-performing sales professionals to take on a temporary project or assignment with the Commercial Training department to determine if they are interested in a training specialist role.[71] The length of the project assignments vary from a few days to several weeks, depending on the needs of the employee and training unit. Sales professionals who accept a full-time training position rotate to another role in the corporate office in two to three years (such as in marketing), go back to the field in a different sales unit, or accept promotion to a district sales manager position.

Employee exchange is another type of temporary assignment. Procter & Gamble (P&G) and Google have started to swap employees.[72] Employees from the two companies participate in each other's training programs and attend meetings where business plans are discussed. Both companies hope to benefit from the employee swap. P&G is trying to increase its understanding of how to market laundry detergent, toilet paper, and skin cream products to a new generation of consumers, who spend more time online than watching television. Google wants to gain more ad revenue by persuading companies to shift from showcasing their brands on television to video-sharing sites such as YouTube. The idea of the employee swap occurred when P&G recognized that a switch to a smaller Tide laundry soap bottle with a more concentrated formula did not include an online campaign, where buyers could find answers as to why the bottle decreased in size. Employees of both companies have benefited from the swap. Google employees have learned that Tide's bright orange packaging is a critical part of the brand and have adopted P&G's marketing language; and P&G employees have recognized that online ad campaigns can increase brand awareness, even for products such as diapers that are not purchased online. P&G has invited mommy-bloggers to visit their baby division to better understand how their diapers can meet their needs.

Temporary assignments can include a **sabbatical** (a leave of absence from the company to renew or develop skills). Employees on sabbatical often receive full pay and benefits. Sabbaticals improve employee well-being through reducing stress and burnout and helping them acquire new skills and perspectives.[73] Sabbaticals also allow employees more time for personal pursuits such as writing a book or spending more time with young children. Sabbaticals are common in a variety of industries ranging from consulting firms to the fast-food industry.[74] Fallon Worldwide, an advertising agency, offers a program called Dreamcatchers to staff members who want to work on a project or travel.[75] Dreamcatchers was developed to help the agency avoid having employees burn out and lose their creative edge. Employees have taken time off to write novels, kayak, and motorcycle through the Alps. Fallon Worldwide matches employee contributions of up to $1,000 annually for two years and offers up to two extra weeks of paid vacation. The agency partners believe that the program has helped in the retention of key employees and the recruiting of new ones. The partners also believe that the program helps recharge employees' creativity, which is key for employees to do their best work for customers.

Volunteer assignments can also be used for development. Volunteer assignments may give employees opportunities to manage change, teach, have a high level of responsibility, and be exposed to other job demands shown earlier in Table 9.7. For General Mills, volunteer assignments and involvement with community projects is one of the ways the company lives its corporate values.[76] Employees work in a wide variety of charities, with duties ranging from serving meals to the homeless, painting child care center rooms, or serving as corporate board members. Besides providing valuable services to community organizations, General Mills believes volunteer assignments help employees improve team relationships and develop leadership and strategic thinking skills.

## How to Match Job Experiences to Employees' Development Needs and Goals

Job experiences are used for development in companies of all sizes, but their type and availability vary.[77] Large companies, such as HCA, Inc., with 195,000 employees in the health care business, have the ability to provide high-potential employees with many different kinds of developmental experiences. For example, an administrator can begin working in a position in a smaller heath-care facility, and then move to a larger facility, including a hospital or health-care business. Smaller companies might not have the same type or number of development experiences at work, but can encourage employees to get relevant experiences outside of work. For example, Murray Martin, the CEO at Pitney Bowes, learned a lot about conflict management through his role as vice president of his homeowners' association. Regardless of the size of the company, for job experiences to be an effective development activity, they should be tailored to employees' development needs and goals. Table 9.9 shows which job experiences are most appropriate for different types of employee development needs or goals.

## Interpersonal Relationships

Employees can also develop skills and increase their knowledge about the company and its customers by interacting with a more experienced organization member. Mentoring and coaching are two types of interpersonal relationships that are used to develop employees.

**TABLE 9.9**
**Matching Job Experiences to Employees Development Needs**

Source: Based on B. Kaye, "Up is not the only way . . . really!" *T+D* (September 2011): 41–45.

| Job Experience | Employee Development Need or Goal |
|---|---|
| Job enlargement | Interested in developing new skills, would like to continue in their current position, and their position has opportunities for skill development |
| Job rotation or transfer | Desire a job with similar responsibilities to their current position but assignments requiring new skills, interest in learning about another function, division, or product of the organization |
| Promotion | Want and are ready to assume more responsibility, accountability for other employees and projects, and desire to influence business decisions |
| Downward move | Considering changing or trying out a new profession or career and needs to acquire new skill, wants to reduce job stress or achieve better work and non-work balance, prefers a previous job |
| Temporary assignments, project work, volunteer work, sabbatical | Want a new understanding or perspective of customers, products, community issues, obtain job experiences and develop skills in jobs not available in the company, use and develop current skills in a new context, avoid burnout and alleviate stress. |

## *Mentoring*

A **mentor** is an experienced, productive senior employee who helps develop a less experienced employee (the protégé). Because of the lack of potential mentors and recognizing that employees can benefit from relationships with peers and colleagues, some companies have initiated and supported group and peer mentoring. In **group mentoring programs,** a successful senior employee is paired with a group of four to six less experienced protégés. One potential advantage of peer mentoring is that protégés are encouraged to learn from each other, as well as from a more experienced senior employee. Also, group mentoring acknowledges the reality that it is difficult for one mentor to provide an employee with all the guidance and support he or she needs. Group mentoring provides a development network for employees: a small group that an employee can use for mentoring support and also can rely on to take an interest in his or her learning and development. The leader helps protégés understand the organization, guides them in analyzing their experiences, and helps them clarify career directions. Each member of the group may complete specific assignments, or the group may work together on a problem or issue.[78]

Most mentoring relationships develop informally as a result of interests or values shared by the mentor and protégé. Research suggests that employees with certain personality characteristics (like emotional stability, the ability to adapt their behavior based on the situation, and high needs for power and achievement) are most likely to seek a mentor and be an attractive protégé for a mentor.[79] Mentoring relationships can also develop as part of a formal mentoring program (that is, a planned company effort to bring together successful senior employees with less experienced employees). Table 9.10 shows examples of how companies are using formal mentoring programs. Mentoring programs have many important purposes including socializing new employees, developing managers, and providing opportunities for women and minorities to share experiences, and gain the exposure and skills needed to move into management positions.

**TABLE 9.10**
**Examples of Mentoring Programs**

Sources: Based on www.sodexousa.com, the website for Sodexo, Inc.; "Best practices and outstanding initiatives," *training*, January/February 2011, 94–98; "Training Top 125," *training*, January/February 2011, 54–93; R. Emelo, "Conversations with mentoring leaders," *T+D*, June 2011, 32–37.

**SCC Soft Computer**—Every new hire is assigned a mentor. The mentor creates a personalized learning passport, including the new employee's photo, and identifies the competency areas that the new hire needs to develop. After identifying the competency the mentor is responsible for, the mentor follows up with the employee regularly. When the employee's personal learning passport is complete, he or she is eligible for advancement.

**Microsoft**—The mentoring program includes career development mentoring and peer mentoring. Career development mentoring focuses on career and professional development through structured, yearlong, cross-group mentoring. Peer mentoring is less structured and focuses on transfer of work-related knowledge among members of the same work team.

**Sacramento Municipal Utility District (SMUD)**—Includes a one-year mentoring program in its Building Leadership Talent program. The program matches protégés with mentors who are outside their business unit. SMUD provides an orientation and half-day session for the mentors that includes skill building, role-playing, a process model for effective mentoring, templates for documenting goals and progress toward meeting the goals, skill practice, and web-based training.

**Sodexo**—Peer-to-peer mentoring is a program managed directly by Sodexo's Network Groups. Networks are organized around a common dimension of diversity and are created by employees who want to raise awareness in Sodexo of their identity groups. They include network groups based on national orientation, race, sexual preference, military service, and employees from mixed generations. The Spirit of Mentoring Bridge Programs are informal divisional pairings in which newly hired employees and front-line managers come together to expand professional development opportunities and increase the depth and diversity of Sodexo's management.

**Agilent Technologies**—The Next Generation Leadership Program accelerates development for top talent by matching senior executives with high potential.

**McDonalds**—Offers a virtual online mentoring program that employees can use to build their skill sets and develop relationships.

*Developing Successful Mentoring Programs*   One major advantage of formalized mentoring programs is that they ensure access to mentors for all employees, regardless of gender or race. An additional advantage is that participants in the mentoring relationship know what is expected of them.[80] One limitation of formal mentoring programs is that mentors may not be able to provide counseling and coaching in a relationship that has been artificially created.[81] To overcome this limitation, it is important that mentors and protégés spend time discussing work styles, their personalities, and their backgrounds, which helps build the trust needed for both parties to be comfortable with their relationship.[82] Toshiba America Medical Systems doesn't have a formal mentoring program. However, Toshiba encourages informal mentoring from the first day employees are hired. Both managers and HR business partners take the time to help new employees meet their colleagues and show them around the workplace.[83]

Table 9.11 presents the characteristics of a successful formal mentoring program. Mentors should be chosen based on interpersonal and technical skills. They also need to be trained.[84] For mentors, protégés, and the company to get the most out of mentoring, tools and support are needed.[85] For example, at the University of New Mexico Hospitals

**TABLE 9.11**
**Characteristics of Successful Formal Mentoring Programs**

1. Mentor and protégé participation is voluntary. The relationship can be ended at any time without fear of punishment.
2. The mentor–protégé matching process does not limit the ability of informal relationships to develop. For example, a mentor pool can be established to allow protégés to choose from a variety of qualified mentors.
3. Mentors are chosen on the basis of their past record in developing employees, willingness to serve as a mentor, and evidence of positive coaching, communication, and listening skills.
4. Mentor–protégé matching is based on how the mentor's skills can help meet the protégé's needs.
5. The purpose of the program is clearly understood. Projects and activities that the mentor and protégé are expected to complete are specified.
6. The length of the program is specified. The mentor and protégé are encouraged to pursue the relationship beyond the formal period.
7. A minimum level of contact between the mentor and protégé is specified. Mentors and protégés need to determine when they will meet, how often, and how they will communicate outside the meetings.
8. Mentors and protégés need to determine the mechanics of the relationship: when they will meet, how often, and how they will communicate outside of the meetings.
9. Protégés are encouraged to contact one another to discuss problems and share successes.
10. The mentor program is evaluated. Interviews with mentors and protégés give immediate feedback regarding specific areas of dissatisfaction. Surveys gather more detailed information regarding benefits received from participating in the program.
11. Employee development is rewarded, which signals to managers that mentoring and other development activities are worth their time and effort.

(UNMH), a "Mentorship Program Partnering Guide" provides information on the mentor and protégé roles, monthly meeting structure, and ideas for development activities and how to build relationships. Yum! Brands provides goal sheets, discussion guides, websites, books, and self-guided e-learning modules.

A key to successful mentoring programs is that the mentor and protégé are well-matched and can interact with each other face-to-face or virtually using video-conferencing. American Fidelity Assurance Company created a specialized mentoring program for developing leaders.[86] Current leaders serve as mentors but also can serve as protégés. In the program, participants are paired based on assessment results and mentee goals and objectives. Paying attention to mentor–protégé pairings has paid off: 88 percent of protégés indicated that their mentors played a key role in reaching their goals, and 88 percent plan to continue the mentoring relationship. At UNMH, quarterly "Speed Networking" sessions are an important part of the mentoring program. These sessions provide the opportunity for up to fifteen mentors to meet and interact with fifteen protégés. These sessions provide the protégé with exposure to the guidance and tips of multiple leaders and the opportunity to network. Microsoft provides an online portal that provides assistance in matching mentors and protégés and a social networking function that helps employees connect with each other.

Web-based matching systems are also available to help match mentors and protégés. Mentors enroll themselves into a database of experts. Similar to the results of a Google search, the program provides a list of mentors with a percentage indicator that helps identify mentors whose skills and expertise best match the protégés development needs. Protégés can then choose the mentor who they believe can best further their development. Software is also available to track mentor's and protégé's work, help build development plans, and schedule mentor and protégé meetings.[87] For example, at SAIC, a company specializing in technology solutions, a web-based tool is used to provide online forms, make calendar appointments, set goals for mentoring relationships, and outline an action plan to ensure that protégé needs are discussed.

***Benefits of Mentoring Relationships***   Both mentors and protégés can benefit from a mentoring relationship. Research suggests that mentors provide career and psychosocial support to their protégés. **Career support** includes coaching, protection, sponsorship, and providing challenging assignments, exposure, and visibility. **Psychosocial support** includes serving as a friend and a role model, providing positive regard and acceptance, and creating an outlet for the protégé to talk about anxieties and fears. Additional benefits for the protégé include higher rates of promotion, higher salaries, and greater organizational influence.[88]

Mentoring relationships provide opportunities for mentors to develop their interpersonal skills and increase their feelings of self-esteem and worth to the organization. For individuals in technical fields such as engineering or health services, the protégé may help them gain knowledge about important new scientific developments in their field (and therefore prevent them from becoming technically obsolete). Protégés can also help mentors learn about how to use social media such as Twitter and Facebook and to understand the needs and motivations of younger employees.[89] This is especially the case in reverse mentoring programs, where more senior employees are paired with a younger employee. Tamara Trummer summarizes some of the benefits she gained from mentoring relationships: "I found mentors in two of my earlier companies, both male and female managers who 'taught me the ropes' in an informal sense by giving me inside information about the company, certain executives—and even such practical things as how to conduct business travel and handle an expense account."[90] One mentor arranged for her to travel from the remote manufacturing plant where she worked to the corporate office and set up meetings to meet key employees she would have to work with. Her mentors have also included co-workers, peers, and even subordinates who have taught her computer software skills. As a result of her positive experiences as a protégé Trummer now mentors others employees.

Mentoring can also occur between mentors and protégés from different organizations and can allow small business owners access to experienced mentors they might not otherwise meet.[91] Websites such as MicroMentor are available to help small business owners find online mentors. For example, Sturdy McKee wanted to expand his physical therapy practice but needed help understanding financial statements so that he could plan the growth of his business and seek outside funding. Using MicroMentor, he completed a personal profile, listed his goals, and then searched potential mentor profiles. Sturdy and his mentor had weekly phone conversations discussing the basics of balance sheets and financial vocabulary. As a result of his positive experience, Sturdy has mentored other entrepreneurs seeking help starting a physical therapy practice.

Mentoring programs can also help encourage women and minorities who tend to be under represented in leadership positions to develop management skills and move into management positions.[92] The Economical Insurance Group (TEIG), one of the largest property and casualty insurance groups in Canada, is focused on women's leadership development.

TEIG's women's leadership development program includes an instructor-led workshop focusing on the fundamentals of achievement, leadership, and legacy specific to women in the company. Following the workshop female leaders were invited to participate in the TEIG Women's Leadership Network, held quarterly. The network meetings use the company's virtual classroom to discuss business ideas and challenges unique to women and to share leadership experiences.

## Coaching

A **coach** is a peer or manager who works with employees to motivate them, help them develop skills, and provide reinforcement and feedback. There are three roles that a coach can play.[93] The main reasons that coaches are used include developing high-potential managers, acting as a sounding board for managers, or specifically trying to change behaviors that are making managers ineffective.[94] Part of coaching may be one-on-one with an employee (such as giving feedback). Another role is to help employees learn for themselves. This involves helping them find experts who can assist them with their concerns and teaching them how to obtain feedback from others. Third, coaching may involve providing resources such as mentors, courses, or job experiences that employees may not be able to gain access to without the coach's help. BD, a medical technology company, uses peer coaching as part of its leadership development programs.[95] The topics discussed include job challenges as a development method, ambiguity as a change agent, and how to influence others. Evaluation of the peer coaching has found that coaches gain confidence in their abilities and participants learn about the topics discussed. Wachovia Corporation, a financial services company, has an executive coaching program that uses both internal and external coaches.[96] Participants in the executive leadership development program receive 360-degree assessments that they take to their internal coaches, who are from a different division in the company. Together, the manager and coach review the assessment results and agree on an action plan. The coaches are trained how to coach and understand the positive and negative aspects of 360-degree feedback. Research suggests that coaching improves managers' use of 360-degree feedback by helping them set specific improvement goals and solicit ideas for improvement, which results in improved performance.[97]

PG&E, an energy company, hired a coach to work with a skilled manager whose brash personality was hurting her relationships with her associates and her career.[98] The coach videotaped her as she role-played an actual clash that she had had with another manager over a new information system. During the confrontation (and the role play), she was aloof, abrasive, cold, and condescending. The coach helped her see the limitations of her approach. She apologized to colleagues and listened to their ideas. Coaching helped this manager learn how to maintain her composure and focus on what is being said rather than on the person saying it, or the way it made her feel.

The best coaches should be empathetic, supportive, practical, and self-confident, but not appear as someone who knows all the answers or wants to tell others what to do.[99] Employees who are going to be coached need to be open-minded and interested, not defensive, closed-minded, or concerned with their reputation. Both the coach and the employee to be coached take risks in the relationship. Coaches use their expertise and experiences to help an employee. Employees are vulnerable by honestly communicating about their weaknesses.

To develop coaching skills, training programs need to focus on four issues related to managers' reluctance to provide coaching.[100] First, managers may be reluctant to discuss performance issues even with a competent employee because they want to avoid confrontation. This is especially an issue when the manager is less of an expert than the employee. Second, managers may be better able to identify performance problems than to help employees solve them. Third, managers may also feel that the employee interprets coaching as criticism. Fourth, as companies downsize and operate with fewer employees, managers may feel that there is not enough time for coaching.

## Special Topics in Employee Development: Succession Planning, Developing Dysfunctional Managers, Onboarding

### Succession Planning

**Succession planning** refers to the process of identifying, evaluating, developing, and tracking high potential employees who are capable of moving into higher-level managerial positions. Succession planning helps organizations on several different ways. It identifies and prepares future company leaders, help ensure that the company runs smoothly when key employees and managers leave, and creates opportunities for development and promotion. It provides a set of development experiences that managers must complete to be considered for top management positions: This avoids the premature promotion of managers who are not ready to move into leadership positions. Succession planning also helps attract and retain managerial employees by providing them with development opportunities that they can complete if upper management is a career goal for them. However, one estimate is that less than 45 percent of companies have a succession planning process.[101] **High-potential employees** are those people that the company believes are capable of being successful in higher-level managerial positions, such as general manager of a strategic business unit, functional director (such as director of marketing), or CEO.[102] High-potential employees typically complete an individual development program that involves education, executive mentoring and coaching, and rotation through job assignments. Job assignments are based on the successful career paths of the managers whom the high-potential employees are being prepared to replace. High-potential employees may also receive special assignments, such as making presentations and serving on committees and task forces.

### Process of Developing a Succession Plan

Table 9.12 shows the process used to develop a succession plan. The first step is to identify what positions are included in the succession plan, such as all management positions or only certain levels of management. The second step is to identify which employees are part of the succession planning system. For example, in some companies, only high-potential employees are included in the succession plan. Third, the company needs to identify how positions will be evaluated. For example, will the emphasis be on competencies needed for each position or on the experiences an individual needs to have before moving into the position? Fourth, the company should identify how employee potential will be measured. That is, will employees' performance in their current jobs as well as ratings of potential be used? Will employees' position interests and career goals be considered? Fifth, the succession planning review process needs to be developed. Typically, succession planning reviews first involve employees' managers and human resources. A talent review could also include an overall assessment of leadership talent in the company, an identification

**TABLE 9.12**

**The Process of Developing a Succession Plan**

Sources: Based on W. Rothwell, "The Future of Succession Planning," *T+D*, September 2010. 51–54; B. Dowell, "Succession Planning," in *Implementing Organizational Interventions*, ed. J. Hedge and E. Pulaskos (San Francisco: Jossey-Bass, 2002), 78–109; R. Barnett and S. Davis, "Creating greater success in succession planning," *Advances in Developing Human Resources* 10 (2008): 721–739.

1. Identify what positions are included in the plan.
2. Identify the employees who are included in the plan.
3. Develop standards to evaluate positions (e.g., competencies, desired experiences, desired knowledge, developmental value, etc.).
4. Determine how employee potential will be measured (e.g., current performance and potential performance).
5. Develop the succession planning review.
6. Link the succession planning system with other human resource systems, including training and development, compensation, performance management, and staffing systems.
7. Determine what feedback is provided to employees.
8. Measure the effectiveness of the succession plan.

of high-potential employees, and a discussion of plans to keep key managers from leaving the company. Sixth, succession planning depends on other HR systems, including compensation, training and development, and staffing. Incentives and bonuses may be linked to completion of development opportunities. Activities such as training courses, job experiences, mentors, and 360-degree feedback can be used to meet development needs. Companies need to make decisions (such as will they fill an open management position internally with a less experienced employee who will improve in the role over time, or will they hire a manager from outside the company who can immediately deliver results?). Seventh, employees need to be provided with feedback on future moves, expected career paths, and development goals and experiences. Finally, the succession planning process needs to be evaluated. This includes identifying and measuring appropriate results outcomes (such as reduced time to fill manager positions, increased use of internal promotions, etc.) as well as collecting measures of satisfaction with the process (reaction outcomes) from employees and managers. Also, modifications that will be made to the succession planning process need to be identified, discussed, and implemented.

### Assessing and Making Development Plans Using the Nine-Box Grid

Many companies use the nine-box grid for conducting the succession planning review. The **nine-box grid** is a three-by-three matrix used by groups of managers and executives to compare employees within one department, function, division, or the entire company.[103] The nine-box grid is used for analysis and discussion of talent, to help formulate effective development plans and activities, and to identify talented employees who can be groomed for top-level management positions in the company. As shown in Figure 9.5, one axis of the matrix is based on an assessment of job performance. The other axes are typically labeled "potential" or "promotability." The manager's assessment of performance and potential influences employees' development plans. For example, as shown in Figure 9.5, high-potential employees who are high performers are found in the top-right corner of the matrix. These are employees who should be developed for leadership positions in the company. Contrast the development plans of high-potential, high-performance employees with employees in the other areas of the grid. The development plans for employees with low potential and low performance emphasize performance improvement in their current position, rather than finding them challenging new job experiences. If they do not improve in

**FIGURE 9.5**

**Example of a Nine-Box Grid**

Sources: Based on K. Tyler, "On the grid," *HR Magazine* (August 2011): 67–69; D. Day, *Developing Leadership Talent* (Alexandria, VA: SHRM Foundation, 2007).

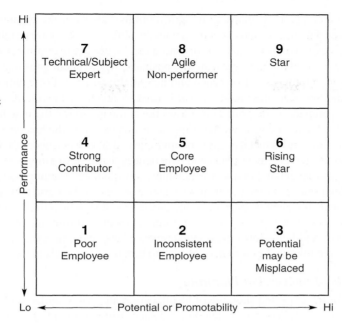

their current position, they are likely to be fired. Employees in the top-left corner of the grid are outstanding performers but have low potential. These employees are likely experts in their field of expertise. Their development plans likely emphasize keeping their knowledge, skills, and competencies current and finding them experiences that will continue to motivate them and facilitate creativity and innovation. Employees who are low performers with high potential (located in the bottom-right corner of the grid) may have just taken a new position and haven't had the time to demonstrate high performance or these employees' knowledge, skills, or competencies might not match their job requirements. Development plans for these employees might emphasize moving them to a position that best matches their skill set, or if they have just moved to the job, ensuring that they get the training and development opportunities and resources necessary to help them attain high performance levels. Employees in the middle of the grid, core employees, are solid but not outstanding performers who have moderate potential. Development plans for these employees will include a mix of training and development designed to help ensure that their solid performance continues. Also, core employees' development plans likely include some development experiences that can help grow their skills and determine their interest and ability to perform in positions requiring different skills and/or more responsibility.

How can companies use the nine-box grid? The process begins by clearly defining each box (e.g., what does a star performer look like?) and provide examples of desirable behavior to managers. Next, managers categorize their direct reports on the grid and then meet with other managers to compare, discuss, and defend their categorizations (a process often referred to as a *calibration meeting*). Managers use the nine-box grid to determine the development plans for their direct reports and to decide who to recommend for high-potential leadership positions or development programs. Typically, each manager's grid is consolidated into an overall grid that can represent a department, division, geographic area, and even the entire company. Collapsing the grid to higher levels of the organization provides HR and top-level managers and executives with the ability to see the mix of the potential and performance of the workforce. This information can be used to determine if the talent exists to meet strategic needs such as growing the business, where talent gaps and excesses exist, and changes in employees performance and potential over time. For example, at Discover Card Financial Services, the nine-box grid is used in seven business units and is then collapsed into a company-wide grid. This allows the company to see the match (or mismatch) between the leadership talents and the company needs based on the business strategy.

The value of the grid is that it is based on multiple and shared perspectives of talent, it helps managers provide development plans and experiences that best fit employees based on their performance and potential (such as mentorships, job rotations, training opportunities, etc.), and it provides a snapshot of the company's talent. For the nine-box grid to be effectively used for development and talent management, the process must include a frank and honest discussion of employees by their managers, the information gathered from the process is discussed with employees and helps form their development plans, and employees are identified and placed in key job roles and experiences needed to best use their skills in the company.

### An Example of Succession Planning

To prepare for the expected shortage of health care managers, Gunderson Lutheran Health System in La Crosse, Wisconsin, developed a succession planning process to identify and develop high-potential candidates in one of four leadership levels: physician executives, physician administrative leadership, administrative executives, and administrative leaders at the director level.[104] Selection of candidates was based on demonstrating a high level of competency in nine areas, including operations, finance, strategic thinking, building partnerships and teams, staff development, change management, performance management, and leadership development. Candidates also needed to demonstrate an interest and willingness for promotion, to participate in a leadership assessment process to determine skill gaps and development needs, to receive development feedback and coaching to get a realistic view of current performance and develop skills and competencies for future positions, to accept assignments that provided development opportunities, and to invest the time and effort required to learn new skills and review their progress with their vice president or manager and a review group headed by the vice president of Operations and Human Resources. Behavioral interviews, 360-degree assessment, the MBTI, and assessments of values and leadership skills are used to identify individuals' strengths and development needs or gaps. Based on the assessment, individual development plans are discussed and agreed upon with the review group. Development plans are based on both the candidate's and the organization's needs. The development plans include activities such as coaching, continuing education, mentoring, project assignments, committee appointments, job enlargement, job rotation, or cross-functional assignments. For example, projects have included work in developing an electronic medical record and assignments. New job experiences include moving an administrative director from the rehabilitation area into the HR operation role for three years before moving into a larger role overseeing all hospital operations. These activities allow candidates to learn while the leadership team can evaluate how they perform when given increased responsibility and stretch assignments.

Gunderson measures the impact of development activities and the success of the succession planning process through performance and feedback from peers and colleagues. The review group studies annual progress. Sixty high-potential employees in all levels of leadership have been identified, and their career paths are discussed. Four high-potential directors have been promoted into chief roles and six high-potential managers into director roles. Nine high-potential managers and directors now have expanded roles.

## Issues in Succession Planning

One of the important issues in succession planning is deciding whether to tell employees if they are on or off the list of potential candidates for higher-level manager positions.[105] There are several advantages and disadvantages that companies need to consider. One advantage to making a succession planning list public or telling employees who are on the list is that they are more likely to stay with the company because they understand they likely will have new career opportunities. Another is that high-potential employees who are not interested in other positions can communicate their intentions. This helps the company avoid investing costly development resources in them and allows the company to have a more accurate idea of its high-potential managerial talent. The disadvantages of identifying high-potential employees are that those not on the list may become discouraged and leave the company, or changes in business strategy or employees' performance could take them off the list. Also, employees might not believe they have had a fair chance to compete for leadership positions if they already know that a list of potential candidates has been established. One way to avoid these problems is to let employees know they are on the list but not discuss a specific position that they will likely reach. Another is to review the list of candidates frequently and clearly communicate plans and expectations. Managers at Midmark Corporation, a medical equipment manufacturer based in Versailles, Ohio, identify successors every six months as part of the company's performance review process and produce a potential list of candidates. Some employees are labeled as "high professionals." "High professionals" are employees who are strong performers, happy in their current position, and unlikely or not interested in more demanding leadership positions. Other employees are identified as having high potential for leadership positions. Employees with high potential for leadership positions are considered for challenging development assignments involving overseas relocation. Using interviews, the company determines if employees on the succession list are interested and qualified for leadership positions.

## Developing Managers with Dysfunctional Behaviors

A number of studies have identified managerial behaviors that can cause an otherwise competent manager to be a "toxic" or ineffective manager. These behaviors include insensitivity to others, inability to be a team player, arrogance, poor conflict-management skills, inability to meet business objectives, and inability to change or adapt during a transition.[106] For example, a skilled manager who is interpersonally abrasive, aggressive, and autocratic may find it difficult to motivate subordinates, may alienate internal and external customers, and may have trouble getting their ideas accepted by superiors. These managers are in jeopardy of losing their jobs and have little chance of future advancement because of their dysfunctional behavior. Typically, a combination of assessment, training, and counseling is used to help managers change dysfunctional behavior. For example, a chief technical officer at TaylorMade-adidas Golf (TMaG), a golf equipment company and U.S.-based subsidiary of the Adidas Group, had decades of experience, and his education and technical abilities were sufficient to effectively manage the more than 100 engineers and other staff who reported to him.[107] However, his people skills needed improvement. In meetings, he made cynical comments and quickly reviewed technical information with his staff, not taking time to answer their questions. His lack of people skills caused a high turnover rate in his department. To improve his people skills, the manager began working with a coach to help him identify his strengths and weaknesses. Now he meets his coach twice a month to develop his people skills based on a set of clearly defined improvement objectives which they developed together. As a result of the coaching, employees now come to him first with their issues and problems because he is a good listener.

One example of a program designed specifically to help managers with dysfunctional behavior is the Individual Coaching for Effectiveness (ICE) program.[108] Research suggests that managers' participation in these programs results in skill improvement and reduced likelihood of termination.[109] The ICE program includes diagnosis, coaching, and support activities. The program is tailored to the manager's needs. Clinical, counseling, or industrial/organizational psychologists are involved in all phases of the ICE program. They conduct the diagnosis, coach and counsel the manager, and develop action plans for implementing new skills on the job.

The first step in the ICE program, diagnosis, involves collecting information about the manager's personality, skills, and interests. Interviews with the manager and the manager's supervisor and colleagues plus psychological tests are used to determine whether the manager can actually change the dysfunctional behavior. For example, personality traits such as extreme defensiveness may make it difficult for the manager to change the problem behavior. If it is determined that the manager can benefit from the program, then typically the manager and the manager's supervisor set specific developmental objectives tailored to the manager's needs.

In the coaching phase of the program, the manager is first presented with information about the targeted skills or behavior. This information may be about principles of effective communication or teamwork, tolerance of individual differences in the workplace, or methods for conducting effective meetings. The second step is for the manager to participate in behavior-modeling training, which was discussed in Chapter Seven. The manager also receives psychological counseling to overcome beliefs that may inhibit learning the desired behavior.

### Onboarding

**Onboarding** or socialization refers to the process of helping new hires adjust to social and performance aspects of their new jobs.[110] This is important to help employees adjust to their jobs by establishing relationships to increase satisfaction, clarifying goals and expectations to improve performance, and providing feedback, coaching, and follow-up activities to reduce turnover. There is wide variation in the types of onboarding programs across companies. However, effective onboarding involves the four steps shown in Figure 9.6. Effective onboarding includes understanding mundane tasks, such as completing tax forms and knowing how to complete time sheets or travel reimbursement forms. But it goes beyond compliance to include enhancing new hires' self-confidence, feeling socially comfortable and accepted by their peers and manager, understanding their role and job expectations, responsibilities, and performance requirements, and helping them "fit" into and understand the company culture. Effective onboarding is related to many important outcomes for the employee and the company including higher job satisfaction, organizational commitment, lower turnover, higher performance, reduced stress and career effectiveness.[111]

**FIGURE 9.6**
**The Four Steps in Onboarding**

Sources: Based on T. Bauer, *Onboarding New Employees: Maximizing Success* (Alexandria, VA: SHRM Foundation, 2010); G. Chao et al., "Organizational socialization: Its content and consequences," *Journal of Applied Psychology*, 79 (1994): 730–743.

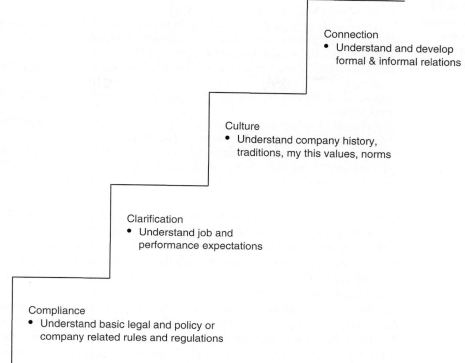

Connection
• Understand and develop formal & informal relations

Culture
• Understand company history, traditions, my this values, norms

Clarification
• Understand job and performance expectations

Compliance
• Understand basic legal and policy or company related rules and regulations

Table 9.13 shows the characteristics of effective orientation programs. Effective onboarding programs actively involve the new employee. Several companies offer onboarding programs that include the characteristics shown in this table. New hires at Sierra Nevada Corporation, a company in the defense and aerospace industry, are contacted by the company's talent acquisition and training teams before orientation.[112] The program includes a review of the company's history, culture, vision, and values. On their first day on the job, new hires have a meet-and-greet lunch date with their manager. Employees continue onboarding for ninety days, which includes e-learning, mentoring, on-the-job training, and a performance review. Booz Allen, a strategy and technology consulting company, revised their onboarding program to reduce the time that it took for new employees to become productive, support their decision to join the company, and develop knowledge regarding the company culture and core values.[113] The onboarding programs involve face-to-face and online activities to enhance the effectiveness of their process. The new program, which spans twelve months, includes learning activities and events organized into three phases. The first phase, known as "Engage," is designed to motivate and prepare new hires for their first year. Engage spans two to three weeks. It includes learning activities that actively involve the new hires in working in cross-functional teams with members from different offices and levels. New hires can use their laptops to explore online resources for career planning and development. Teams of three new hires each begin to compete in a simulated yearlong client project. They have access to an experienced employee who can provide

**TABLE 9.13**
**Characteristics of Effective Onboarding Programs**

| |
|---|
| Employees are encouraged to ask questions. |
| The program includes information on both technical and social aspects of the job. |
| The employee's manager has some onboarding responsibility. |
| Debasing or embarrassing new employees is avoided. |
| Employees learn about the company culture, history, language, products, services, and customers. |
| Follow-up of employee progress occurs at different points up to one year after joining the company. |
| The program involves participation, active involvement, and formal and informal interaction between new hires and current employees. |
| Relocation assistance is provided (such as house hunting or information sessions on the community for employees and their significant others). |

insights and examples of how they have worked with clients during their career. Also, senior company leaders deliver welcome messages and lead discussions of how to succeed at the company. The second phase of the onboarding program, "Equip," begins in the new hire's second week and continues through their first six months. "Equip" provides employees with the skills, behaviors, and tools that they need for success at the company. It includes thirty-, sixty-, and ninety-day meetings with their manager, a series of e-newsletters, and detailed onboarding tool kit designed to reinforce and build on what they learned in the first phase of the program. The third and final phase, "Excel," emphasizes professional development, relationship building, and acceptance of the company's values. "Excel" involves the seven month period through the end of the new hires first year of employment. The employees first annual performance review occurs at the end of "Excel." In addition to the three phases, new hires have access to and are encouraged to use the company's social media and knowledge management tool, known as the Onboarding Community, to discover and share information via blogs and take part in online activities and resources that support the onboarding program.

The results of the program have been positive. More than 8,000 new employees have completed the program. Over 95 percent report that the program had a positive impact on their decision to join and stay at the company and improved their job readiness. Turnover for new employees who have been with the company six months or less has been reduced by 4 percent. New employees' time to productivity has been reduced, saving the company millions of dollars in lost revenue.

IBM redesigned their new employee onboarding program to include both face-to-face interactions and technology-based features that help employees prepare for their current job, as well as plan for their future careers.[114] The new onboarding program takes into account that many new employees don't spend much of their time in the office—they work at home and on the road, and members of their work group are likely to be located around the world. But new employees still need to quickly learn to perform their jobs, feel comfortable, and develop a network of friends. The program, known as Succeeding @IBM, helps employees learn how their job relates to other IBM business units and locations and is customized to address the needs of employees in different types of jobs such as consultants, college graduates, and managers. Following a classroom experience on the first day, new employees work toward online to complete four different phases of onboarding. Discovery IBM covers IBM's values, history, and businesses. Share and Connect encourage new employees to collaborate with each other and experienced employees for support, career guidance, and technical expertise. Grow My Career provides a roadmap for employees to use to identify different learning and career paths within IBM. Find Support connects new employees with mentors, career coaches, websites, and other resources. New employees can also use IBM's instant messaging and have access to an online employee directory that includes job descriptions, resume, skills, languages spoken, and photos.

## Summary

This chapter emphasized the various development methods that companies use: formal education, assessment, job experiences, and interpersonal relationships. Most companies use one or more of these approaches to develop employees. Formal education involves enrolling employees in courses or seminars offered by the company or educational institutions. Assessment involves measuring the employee's performance, behavior, skills, or personality characteristics. Job experiences include job enlargement, rotating to a new job, promotions, or transfers. More experienced, senior employees (mentors) can help employees better understand the company and gain exposure and visibility to key persons in the organization. Part of a manager's job responsibility may be to coach employees. Regardless of the development approaches used, employees should have a development plan to identify (1) the type of development needed, (2) development goals, (3) the best approach for development, and (4) whether development goals have been reached. For development plans to be effective, both the employee and the company have responsibilities that need to be completed. The chapter concluded by discussing important issues in employee development including succession planning, dealing with dysfunctional manger, and onboarding.

## Key Terms

development, *367*
protean career, *368*
psychological success, *368*
development planning or career management system, *370*
self-assessment, *371*
reality check, *371*
goal setting , *371*
action plan, *373*
formal education programs, *376*
tuition reimbursement, *379*
assessment, *380*
Myers-Briggs Type Inventory (MBTI), *381*

assessment center, *382*
leaderless group discussion, *382*
interview, *382*
in-basket, *382*
performance appraisal, *383*
upward feedback, *384*
360-degree feedback systems, *384*
job experiences, *386*
job enlargement, *388*
job rotation, *389*
transfer, *390*
promotions, *390*
downward move, *391*

externship, *391*
temporary assignments, *392*
sabbatical, *392*
mentor, *394*
group mentoring programs, *394*
career support, *397*
psychosocial support, *397*
coach, *398*
succession planning, *399*
high-potential employees, *399*
nine-box grid, *400*
on-boarding, *404*

## Discussion Questions

1. How could assessment be used to create a productive work team?

2. List and explain the characteristics of effective 360-degree feedback systems.

3. Why do companies develop formal mentoring programs? What are the potential benefits for the mentor? For the protégé?

4. Your boss is interested in hiring a consultant to help identify potential managers among current employees of a fast-food restaurant. The manager's job is to help wait on customers and prepare food during busy times, oversee all aspects of restaurant operations (including scheduling, maintenance, on-the-job training, and food purchase), and help motivate employees to provide high-quality service. The manager is also responsible for resolving disputes that might occur between employees. The position involves working under stress and coordinating several activities at one time. She asks you to outline the type of assessment program that you believe would do the best job of identifying employees who will be successful managers. What will you tell her?

5. Many employees are unwilling to relocate because they like their current community, and their spouses and children prefer not to move. Yet employees need to develop new skills, strengthen skill weaknesses, and be exposed to new aspects of the business to prepare for management positions. How could an employee's current job be changed to develop management skills without having to relocate them?

6. What is coaching? Is there one type of coaching? Explain.

7. Why are many managers reluctant to coach their employees?

8. Why should companies be interested in helping employees plan their development? What benefits can companies gain? What are the risks?

9. What are the manager's roles in a development system? Which role do you think is most difficult for the typical manager? Which is the easiest role? List the reasons why managers might resist involvement in career management.

10. What should be included in a development plan? What do you think is the most important part of the plan for ensuring that employees develop? Explain your choice.

11. Should a company identify and formally acknowledge its high-potential managers or should it be kept secret? Should managers know they are considered high-potential managers? Explain your positions.

12. Nationwide Financial, a 5,000-employee life insurance company based in Columbus, Ohio, uses the nine-box grid for its succession review. What type of development plans and activities would you recommend for solid but not outstanding performers with moderate leadership potential? How would these plans differ from employees with high potential and high performance (stars)? Explain.

13. Explain the four steps in on-boarding. What should new hires learn at each step? How might social media or the Internet aid the on-boarding process?

## Application Assignments

1. Your manager wants you to create a one-page form for development planning. Create the form, and provide a rationale for each category you include on it.

2. Go to www.shrm.org/foundation, click on "Foundation Products," under "SHRM Foundation DVD Series." Watch the video *Seeing Forward: Succession Planning at 3M*.

Answer the following questions:

a. Why is development important at 3M?

b. How does 3M develop employees?

c. In addition to development activities, what else is necessary for effective employee development?

3. Go to GE's website, www.gecareers.com. Review the entry-level leadership and experienced leadership programs. Overall, what type of development activities are included in these programs? Choose one program and describe it (development activities, length, participants, etc.). Compare the development activities used in the entry-level and experienced leadership programs. How are they similar? How are they different? Why might they differ? Click on the KTS-II under the "About the KTS-II" tab.

4. Go to www.checkster.com. Checkster provides tools that individuals and companies can use to grow talent. Click on "Tools for Individuals" at the top of the page. Click on "Start Now" and register (free). After you register, you can complete a self-assessment and ask your friends or work colleagues to also evaluate your talents. This is an example of a 360-degree feedback process. You will receive a report summarizing your results. Is this a useful tool for getting feedback and identifying development needs and interest? Why or why not? If you wanted to improve your weaknesses, what next steps would you take?

5. Go to www.keirsey.com., the website for Keirsey.com, an organization offering publications, assessments, and professional services for employee and leadership development. Complete the Keirsey Temperament Sorter or the Keirsey Character Sorter. (You will have to register first.) These are examples of assessment instruments that can be used for development. What did you learn about yourself? How could the instrument that you completed be useful for management development? What might be some disadvantages of using this instrument?

6. Go to www.dukece.com, a provider of custom corporate education programs. Under "Clients," click on "Client Stories" and read one of the client success stories. Prepare a brief summary of the business issue, approach, learning experience, execution, and outcome. Why do you think the program was successful?

## Case: *Trustmark's Leadership Development Program*

Trustmark provides more than 2 million people with flexible medical, life, and disability benefits and fitness and wellness services. The company, headquartered in Lake Forest, Illinois, has more than 6,200 full- and part-time employees working in twenty-five locations across the United States. Trustmark experienced steady growth until mid-1990, when it experienced financial pressures that forced it to re-evaluate its operations. Trustmark concentrated on core competencies, sold off businesses, and focused on generating capital. Once the company was financially sound, Trustmark executives moved to create a culture that would be open to innovation and opportunity. The challenge was to create a culture where all employees felt they could challenge the status quo and seek new opportunities. The key to creating this culture was developing effective leaders who supported it.

Trustmark used workshops and 360-degree feedback to help the "Trustmark Renaissance," a radical change in the organizational culture and mind-set, succeed. The leadership program includes sessions, attended by senior leaders, directors, and managers, during which participants learn about leadership practices, such as how to inspire a shared vision, challenge the process, enable others to act, and encourage with the heart. During these sessions, participants also receive feedback from their 360-degree assessments. Participants also get one-on-one coaching where they can discuss their leadership challenges and their feedback. Participants are asked to identify development areas to focus on during the next step in the process, a two-day workshop. At the workshop, participants learn more about the leadership practices and how to improve the areas identified in their feedback. Participants leave the workshop with an improvement plan for improving their leadership effectiveness. Participants are paired with partners who are expected to provide post-workshop support, exchange action plans, and commit to follow-up to ensure success in using what they learned.

## Questions

1. What development activities are used in this program? Why are they important?

2. What data or outcomes should be collected to monitor the effectiveness of the leadership development program? Explain the business reason for your choice of outcomes or data.

**Source:** Based on T. Welch, "Setting the Stage for a Renaissance at Trustmark," *T+D*, December 2010, 70–72.

## Endnotes

1. D. Day, *Developing Leadership Talent* (Alexandria, VA: SHRM Foundation, 2007); M. London, *Managing the Training Enterprise* (San Francisco: Jossey-Bass, 1989); C. McCauley and S. Heslett, "Individual Development in the Workplace," in *Handbook of Industrial, Work, and Organizational Psychology,* Vol. 1, ed. N. Anderson et al. (London: Sage Publications, 2001), 313–335.

2. R. W. Pace, P. C. Smith, and G. E. Mills, *Human Resource Development* (Englewood Cliffs, NJ: Prentice Hall, 1991); W. Fitzgerald, "Training versus development," *Training and Development Journal,* May 1992, 81–84; R. A. Noe et al., "Employee Development: Issues in Construct Definition and Investigation of Antecedents," in *Improving Training Effectiveness in Work Organizations,* ed. J. K. Ford (Mahwah, NJ: Lawrence Erlbaum, 1997), 153–189.

3. Towers-Perrin HR Services, *Talent Management: The State of the Art* (Chicago, IL: Towers Perrin, 2005). Available at www.towersperrin.com.

4. J. H. Greenhaus and G. A. Callanan, *Career Management,* 2nd ed. (Fort Worth, TX: Dryden Press, 1994); D. C. Feldman, *Managing Careers in Organizations* (Glenview, IL: Scott Foresman, 1988); D. Hall, *Careers In and Out of Organizations* (Thousand Oaks, CA: Sage, 2002).

5. D. T. Hall, "Protean careers of the 21st century," *Academy of Management Executive* 11 (1996), 8–16; Hall, *Careers In and Out of Organizations*; S. Sullivan and Y. Baruch, "Advances in career theory and research: A critical review and agenda for future exploration," *Journal of Management,* 35 (2009): 1542–1571.

6. K. Essick, "The good life-second acts," *The Wall Street Journal,* May 6, 2011, R7.

7. K. R. Brousseau et al., "Career pandemonium: Realigning organizations and individuals," *Academy of Management Executive* 11 (1996), 52–66.

8. M. B. Arthur, "The boundaryless career: A new perspective of organizational inquiry," *Journal of Organization Behavior* 15 (1994): 295–309; P. H. Mirvis and D. T. Hall, "Psychological success and the boundaryless career," *Journal of Organization Behavior* 15 (1994): 365–380; M. Lazarova and S. Taylor, "Boundaryless careers, social capital, and knowledge management: Implications for organizational performance," *Journal of Organizational Behavior* 30 (2009): 119–139; D. Feldman and T. Ng, "Careers: Mobility, embeddedness, and success," *Journal of Management* 33 (2007): 350–377; S. Tams and M. Arthur, "New directions for boundaryless careers: Agency and interdependence in a changing world," *Journal of Organizational Behavior,* 31 (2010), 629–646.

9. B. P. Grossman and R. S. Blitzer, "Choreographing careers," *Training and Development,* January 1992, 67–69.

10. Harris Interactive, *Emerging Workforce Study* (Ft. Lauderdale, FL: Spherion, 2005); available at www .spherion.com/pressroom; L. Chao, "What GenXers need to be happy at work," *The Wall Street Journal,* November 29, 2005, B6; E. Kaplan-Leiserson, "The changing workforce," *T+D,* February 2005, 10–11.

11. L. Mainiero and S. Sullivan, "Kaleidoscope careers: An alternative explanation for the "opt-out" revolution," *Academy of Management Executive* 19 (2005), 106–23; S. Sullivan and L. Mainiero, "Benchmarking ideas for fostering family-friendly workplaces," *Organizational Dynamics* 36 (2007), 45–62.

12. B. Yovovich, "Golden opportunities," *Human Resource Executive,* August 2008, 30–34.

13. S. Needleman, "New career, same employer," *The Wall Street Journal,* April 21, 2008, B9.

14. M. Sallie-Dosunmu, "Born to grow," *T+D,* May 2006, 34–37.

15. D. T. Jaffe and C. D. Scott, "Career Development for Empowerment in a Changing Work World," in *New Directions in Career Planning and the Workplace,* ed. J. M. Kummerow (Palo Alto, CA: Consulting Psychologists Press, 1991), 33–60; L. Summers, "A logical approach to development planning," *Training and Development* 48 (1994), 22–31; D. B. Peterson and M. D. Hicks, *Development First* (Minneapolis, MN: Personnel Decisions, 1995).

16. K. Ellis, "Individual development plans: The building blocks of development," *training,* December 2004, 20–25; "Training Top 10 Hall of Fame," *training,* February 2010, 60, 62.

17. "Training Top 125 2010," *training,* February 2010, 64–101.

18. T. Shawel, "Homegrown career development," *HR Magazine,* April 2011, 36–38; "Training Top 125," *Training,* January/February 2011, 54–93; T. Barron, "IBM's new fangled, old-fashioned pep," *T+D,* April 2004, 64–65; D. Robb, "Succeeding with succession," *HR Magazine,* January 2006, 89–92; N. Lewis and P. Orton, "The five attributes of innovative e-learning," *Training and Development,* June 2000, 47–51; N. Davis, "One-on-one training crosses continents," *HR Magazine,* November 2007, 54–56.

19. M. Weinstein, "Teaching the top," *training,* February 2005, 30–33.

20. C. Cornell, "Fail safe," *Human Resource Executive* (June 2, 2003): 33–36.

21. C. Waxer, "Course review," *Human Resource Executive,* December 2005, 46–48.

22. F. Hansen, "Building better leaders . . . faster," *Workforce Management* (June 9, 2008): 25–28.

23. GE website: www.ge.com/company/culture/leaderhip_learning.html (accessed February 2, 2012).

24. R. Knight, "GE's corporate boot camp cum talent spotting venue," *Financial Times Business Education,* March 20, 2006, 2; J. Durett, "GE hones its leaders at Crotonville," *training,* May 2006, 25–27.

25. J. Bolt, *Executive Development* (New York: Harper Business, 1989); M. A. Hitt et al., "Understanding strategic intent in the global marketplace," *Academy of Management Executive* 9 (1995), 12–19.

26. Center for Creative Leadership, "Xerox Corporation" (2007), from the CCL website, www.ccl.org.

27. "Client Stories," www.dukece.com, the website of Duke Corporate Education.

28. L. Bongiorno, "How'm I doing?" *BusinessWeek,* October 23, 1995, 72, 74. www.ccl.org, website for Center for Creative Leadership, accessed February 2, 2012.

29. C. Waxer, "Course review," *Human Resource Executive,* December 2005, 46–48.

30. R. Johnson, "The learning curve: The value of tuition reimbursement," *training* (November 2005): 30–33; G. Benson, D. Finegold, and S. Mohrman, "You paid for the skills, now keep them: Tuition reimbursement and voluntary turnover," *Academy of Management Journal* 47 (2004): 315–331.

31. P. Babcock, "Always more to learn," *HR Magazine* (September 2009): 51–56.

32. D. Day, *Developing Leadership Talent* (Alexandria, VA: SHRM Foundation, 2007).

33. M. Weinstein, "Personalities and Performance," *training,* July/August 2008, 36–40.

34. E. Krell, "Personality counts," *HR Magazine,* November 2005, 47–52.

35. C. Cornell, "The Value of values," *Human Resource Executive,* November 2004, 68–72.

36. M. Weinstein, "The X factor," *training,* May/June 2011, 65–67.

37. From www.discprofile.com, the website for DiSc, accessed February 1, 2012.

38. S. K. Hirsch, *MBTI Team Member's Guide* (Palo Alto, CA: Consulting Psychologists Press, 1992); A. L. Hammer, *Introduction to Type and Careers* (Palo Alto, CA: Consulting Psychologists Press, 1993); J. Llorens, "Taking inventory of Myers-Briggs," *T+D,* April 2010, 18–19.

39. J. Overbo, "Using Myers-Briggs personality type to create a culture adapted to the new century," *T+D*, February 2010, 70–72.

40. G. C. Thornton II and W. C. Byham, *Assessment Centers and Managerial Performance* (New York: Academic Press, 1982); L. F. Schoenfeldt and J. A. Steger, "Identification and Development of Management Talent," in *Research in Personnel and Human Resource Management,* ed. K. N. Rowland and G. Ferris (Greenwich, CT: JAI Press, 1989), Vol. 7, 151–181.

41. Thornton and Byham, *Assessment Centers and Managerial Performance.*

42. B. B. Gaugler, D. B. Rosenthal, G. C. Thornton III, and C. Bentson, "Metaanalysis of assessment center validity," *Journal of Applied Psychology* 72 (1987), 493–511; D. W. Bray, R. J. Campbell, and D. L. Grant, *Formative Years in Business: A Long-Term AT&T Study of Managerial Lives* (New York: Wiley, 1974).

43. R. G. Jones and M. D. Whitmore, "Evaluating developmental assessment centers as interventions," *Personnel Psychology* 48 (1995), 377–88.

44. J. Schettler, "Building bench strength," *training,* June 2002, 55–58.

45. S. B. Silverman, "Individual development through performance appraisal," in *Developing Human Resources,* 5–120 to 5–151.

46. M. Sallie-Dosunmu, "Born to grow," *T+D,* May 2006, 34–37.

47. Center for Creative Leadership, *Skillscope for Managers: Development Planning Guide* (Greensboro, NC: Center for Creative Leadership, 1992); G. Yukl and R. Lepsinger, "360-degree feedback," *Training,* December 1995, 45–50.

48. J. S. Lublin, "Turning the tables: Underlings evaluate bosses," *The Wall Street Journal,* October 4, 1994, B1, B14; D. O'Reilly, "360-degree feedback can change your life," *Fortune,* October 17, 1994, 93–100; J. F. Milliman et al., "Companies evaluate employees from all perspectives," *Personnel Journal,* November 1994, 99–103.

49. L. Atwater, P. Roush, and A. Fischthal, "The influence of upward feedback on self- and follower ratings of leadership," *Personnel Psychology* 48 (1995), 35–59; J. F. Hazucha, S. A. Hezlett, and R. J. Schneider, "The impact of 360-degree feedback on management skill development," *Human Resource Management* 32 (1993), 325–351; J. W. Smither et al., "An examination of the effects of an upward feedback program over time," *Personnel Psychology* 48 (1995), 1–34; J. Smither and A. Walker, "Are the characteristics of narrative comments related to improvements in multirater feedback ratings over time?" *Journal of Applied Psychology* 89 (2004), 575–581; J. Smither, M. London, and R. Reilly, "Does performance improve following multisource feedback? A theoretical model, meta-analysis, and review of empirical findings," *Personnel Psychology* 58 (2005), 33–66.

50. D. Bracken, "Straight talk about multirater feedback," *Training and Development,* September 1994, 44–51; K. Nowack, J. Hartley, and W. Bradley, "How to evaluate your 360-feedback efforts," *Training and Development,* April 1999, 48–52; M. Levine, "Taking the burn out of the 360-degree hot seat," *T+D,* August 2010, 40–45.

51. "Training Top 125," *training,* January/February 2011, 54–93.

52. A. Freedman, "The evolution of 360s," *Human Resource Executive,* December 2002, 47–51.

53. M. W. McCall Jr., M. M. Lombardo, and A. M. Morrison, *Lessons of Experience* (Lexington, MA: Lexington Books, 1988); L. Dragoni et al., (2009). "Understanding managerial development: integrating developmental assignments, learning orientation, and access to developmental opportunities in predicting managerial competencies," *Academy of Management Journal* 52 (2009), 731–43.

54. R. S. Snell, "Congenial ways of learning: So near yet so far," *Journal of Management Development* 9 (1990), 17–23.

55. R. Morrison, T. Erickson, and K. Dychtwald, "Managing middlescence," *Harvard Business Review,* March 2006, 78–86.

56. K. Spors, "Top small workplaces 2008: Rainforest Alliance," *The Wall Street Journal,* October 13, 2008, R9.

57. M. McCall, M. Lombardo, and A. Morrison, *Lessons of Experience;* M. W. McCall, "Developing executives through work experiences," *Human Resource Planning* 11 (1988), 1–11; M. N. Ruderman, P. J. Ohlott, and C. D. McCauley, "Assessing Opportunities for Leadership Development," in *Measures of Leadership,*

547–62; C. D. McCauley, L. J. Estman, and P. J. Ohlott, "Linking management selection and development through stretch assignments," *Human Resource Management* 34 (1995), 93–115.

58. C. D. McCauley et al., "Assessing the developmental components of managerial jobs," *Journal of Applied Psychology* 79 (1994), 544–60; J. LePine, M. LePine, and C. Jackson, "Challenge and hindrance stress: Relationships with exhaustion, motivation to learn, and learning performance," *Journal of Applied Psychology* 89 (2004): 883–91.

59. S. Thurm, "Power-sharing prepares managers," *The Wall Street Journal,* December 5, 2005, B4.

60. "Training Top 125," *training,* January/February 2011, 54–93.

61. M. Weinstein, "Foreign but familiar," *training,* January 2009, 20–23.

62. M. London, *Developing Managers* (San Francisco: Jossey-Bass, 1985); M. A. Campion, L. Cheraskin, and M. J. Stevens, "Career-related antecedents and outcomes of job rotation," *Academy of Management Journal* 37 (1994), 1518–1542; M. London, *Managing the Training Enterprise* (San Francisco: Jossey-Bass, 1989).

63. "Training Top 125," *training,* January/February 2011, 54–93.

64. D. C. Feldman, *Managing Careers in Organizations* (Glenview, IL: Scott Foresman, 1988); D. Hall, *Careers In and Out of Organizations* (Thousand Oaks, CA: Sage, 2002).

65. J. M. Brett, L. K. Stroh, and A. H. Reilly, "Job Transfer," in *International Review of Industrial and Organizational Psychology: 1992,* ed. C. L. Cooper and I. T. Robinson (Chichester, U.K.: John Wiley and Sons, 1992); D. C. Feldman and J. M. Brett, "Coping with new jobs: A comparative study of new hires and job changers," *Academy of Management Journal* 26 (1983), 258–72.

66. R. A. Noe, B. D. Steffy, and A. E. Barber, "An investigation of the factors influencing employees' willingness to accept mobility opportunities," *Personnel Psychology* 41 (1988), 559–80; S. Gould and L. E. Penley, "A study of the correlates of willingness to relocate," *Academy of Management Journal* 28 (1984), 472–478; J. Landau and T. H. Hammer, "Clerical employees' perceptions of intraorganizational career opportunities," *Academy of Management Journal* 29 (1986), 385–405; R. P. Duncan and C. C. Perruci, "Dual-occupation families and migration," *American Sociological Review* 41 (1976), 252–261; J. M. Brett and A. H. Reilly, "On the road again: Predicting the job transfer decision," *Journal of Applied Psychology* 73 (1988), 614–620.

67. D. T. Hall and L. A. Isabella, "Downward moves and career development," *Organizational Dynamics* 14 (1985), 5–23.

68. H. D. Dewirst, "Career Patterns: Mobility, Specialization, and Related Career Issues," in *Contemporary Career Development Issues,* ed. R. F. Morrison and J. Adams (Hillsdale, NJ: Lawrence Erlbaum, 1991), 73–108.

69. J. M. Brett, "Job transfer and well-being," *Journal of Applied Psychology* 67 (1992), 450–63; F. J. Minor, L. A. Slade, and R. A. Myers, "Career Transitions in Changing Times," in *Contemporary Career Development Issues,* 109–20; C. C. Pinder and K. G. Schroeder, "Time to proficiency following job transfers," *Academy of Management Journal* 30 (1987), 336–353; G. Flynn, "Heck no—We won't go!" *Personnel Journal,* March 1996, 37–43.

70. R. E. Silverman, "Mercer tries to keep employees through its 'externship' program," *The Wall Street Journal,* November 7, 2000, B18.

71. "training Top 125," *training* (January/February 2011), 54–93.

72. E. Byron, "A new odd couple: Google, P&G swap workers to spur innovation," The *Wall Street Journal,* November 19, 2008, A1, A18.

73. O. Davidson et al., "Sabbatical leaves: Who gains and how much?" *Journal of Applied Psychology* 95 (2010): 953–964.

74. C. J. Bachler, "Workers take leave of job stress," *Personnel Journal,* January 1995, 38–48.

75. F. Jossi, "Taking time off from advertising," *Workforce,* April 2002, 15.

76. M. Weinstein, "Charity begins @ work," *training,* May 2008, 56–58; K. Ellis, "Pass it on," *Training,* June 2005, 14–19.

77. R. Grossman, "The care and feeding of high-potential employees," *HR Magazine* (August 2011): 34–39.

78. B. Kaye and B. Jackson, "Mentoring: A group guide," *Training and Development,* April 1995, 23–27.

79. D. B. Turban and T. W. Dougherty, "Role of protégé personality in receipt of mentoring and career success," *Academy of Management Journal* 37 (1994), 688–702; E. A. Fagenson, "Mentoring: Who needs it? A comparison of protégés' and nonprotégés' needs for power, achievement, affiliation, and autonomy," *Journal of Vocational Behavior* 41 (1992), 48–60.

80. A. H. Geiger, "Measures for mentors," *Training and Development Journal,* February 1992, 65–67.

81. K. E. Kram, *Mentoring at Work: Developmental Relationships in Organizational Life* (Glenview, IL: Scott Foresman, 1985); K. Kram, "Phases of the mentoring relationship," *Academy of Management Journal* 26 (1983), 608–625; G. T. Chao, P. M. Walz, and P. D. Gardner, "Formal and informal mentorships: A comparison of mentoring functions and contrasts with nonmentored counterparts," *Personnel Psychology* 45 (1992), 619–636; C. Wanberg, E. Welsh, and S. Hezlett, "Mentoring Research: A Review and Dynamic Process Model," in *Research in Personnel and Human Resources Management,* ed. J. Martocchio and G. Ferris (New York: Elsevier Science, 2003), 39–124.

82. E. White, "Making mentorships work," *The Wall Street Journal,* October 23, 2007, B11; E. Holmes, "Career mentors today seem short on advice but give a mean tour," *The Wall Street Journal,* August 28, 2007, B1; J. Sandberg, "With bad mentors it's better to break up than to make up," *The Wall Street Journal,* March 18, 2008, B1.

83. M. Weinstein, "Please don't go," *training,* May/June 2011, 28–34.

84. L. Eby, M. Butts, A. Lockwood, and A. Simon, "Protégés' negative mentoring experiences: Construct development and nomological validation," *Personnel Psychology* 57 (2004), 411–47; M. Boyle, "Most mentoring programs stink—but yours doesn't have to," *training,* August 2005, 12–15.

85. R. Emelo, "Conversations with mentoring leaders," *T+D,* June 2011, 32–37.

86. M. Weinstein, "Please don't go," *training,* May/June 2011, 28–34; "Training Top 125," *Training,* January/February 2011, 54–93.

87. M. Weinstein, "Tech connects," *training,* September 2008, 58–59; L. Francis, "Mentoring makeover," *T+D* (July 2007): 53–57.

88. G. F. Dreher and R. A. Ash, "A comparative study of mentoring among men and women in managerial, professional, and technical positions," *Journal of Applied Psychology* 75 (1990), 539–46; T. D. Allen et al., "Career benefits associated with mentoring for protégés: A meta-analysis," *Journal of Applied Psychology* 89 (2004), 127–36; R. A. Noe, D. B. Greenberger, and S. Wang, "Mentoring: What We Know and Where We Might Go," in *Research in Personnel and Human Resources Management,* ed. G. Ferris and J. Martucchio (New York: Elsevier Science, 2002), 129–74; R. A. Noe, "An investigation of the determinants of successful assigned mentoring relationships," *Personnel Psychology* 41 (1988), 457–79; B. J. Tepper, "Upward maintenance tactics in supervisory mentoring and nonmentoring relationships," *Academy of Management Journal* 38 (1995), 1191–205; B. R. Ragins and T. A. Scandura, "Gender differences in expected outcomes of mentoring relationships," *Academy of Management Journal* 37 (1994), 957–71.

89. L. Kwoh, "Reverse mentoring cracks workplace," *The Wall Street Journal* (November 28, 2011): B7.

90. S. Wells, "Tending talent," *HR Magazine,* May 2009, 53–60.

91. K. Spors, "Websites offer access to mentors," *The Wall Street Journal,* June 3, 2008, B7.

92. "TEIG locks in on leadership," *training,* January/February 2011, 34–39.

93. D. B. Peterson and M. D. Hicks, *Leader as Coach* (Minneapolis, MN: Personnel Decisions, 1996).

94. D. Coutu and C. Kauffman, "What coaches can do for you," *Harvard Business Review,* January 2009, 91–97.

95. J. Toto, "Untapped world of peer coaching," *T+D,* April 2006, 69–71; R. Barner, "The 5 hidden roles of the managerial coach," *T+D,* June 2011, 38–45.

96. H. Johnson, "The ins and outs of executive coaching," *training,* May 2004, 36–41.

97. J. Smither et al., "Can working with an executive coach improve multisource ratings over time? A quasi-experimental field study," *Personnel Psychology* 56 (2003), 23–44.

98. J. Lublin, "Did I just say that?! How you can recover from foot-in-mouth," *The Wall Street Journal,* June 18, 2002, B1.

99. J. Toto, "Untapped world of peer coaching," *T+D,* April 2006, 69–71.

100. R. Zemke, "The corporate coach," *training,* December 1996, 24–28.

101. W. J. Rothwell, *Effective Succession Planning,* 4th ed. (New York: AMACOM, 2010); A. Paradise, "Many barriers inhibit success of succession planning," *T+D* (June 2010): 60–61.

102. C. B. Derr, C. Jones, and E. L. Toomey, "Managing high-potential employees: Current practices in thirty-three U.S. corporations," *Human Resource Management* 27 (1988), 273–90.

103. K. Tyler, "On the grid," *HR Magazine* (August 2011): 67–69; D. Day, *Developing Leadership Talent* (Alexandria, VA: SHRM Foundation, 2007).

104. N. Noelke, "Leveraging the present to build the future," *HR Magazine,* March 2009, 34–36.

105. M. Steen, "Where to draw the line on revealing who's next in line," *Workforce Management,* June 2011, 16–18.

106. M. W. McCall, Jr., and M. M. Lombardo, *Off the Track: Why and How Successful Executives Get Derailed,* Technical Report No. 21 (Greensboro, NC: Center for Creative Leadership, 1983); E. V. Veslor and J. B. Leslie, "Why executives derail. Perspectives across time and cultures," *Academy of Management Executive* 9 (1995): 62–72.

107. S. Boehle, "Crafting a coaching culture," *training* (May 18, 2007): 22–24.

108. L. W. Hellervik, J. F. Hazucha, and R. J. Schneider, "Behavior Change: Models, Methods, and a Review of Evidence," in *Handbook of Industrial and Organizational Psychology,* 2d ed., ed. M. D. Dunnette and L. M. Hough (Palo Alto, CA: Consulting Psychologists Press, 1992), 3: 823–99.

109. D. B. Peterson, "Measuring and Evaluating Change in Executive and Managerial Development." Paper presented at the annual conference of the Society for Industrial and Organizational Psychology, (Miami, FL, 1990).

110. T. Bauer, *"Onboarding New Employees: Maximizing Success,"* (Alexandria, VA: SHRM Foundation, 2010).

111. H. Klein and N. Weaver, "The effectiveness of organizational-level orientation program in the socialization of new hires," *Personnel Psychology,* 23 (2000): 47–66; C. Wanberg, J. Kammeyer-Mueller, "Predictors and outcomes of proactivity in the socialization process," *Journal of Applied Psychology,* 85 (2000): 373–385; T. Bauer et al., "Newcomer adjustment during organizational socialization: A meta-analytic review of antecedents, outcomes, and methods," *Journal of Applied Psychology* 92 (2007): 707–721; D. Allen, "Do organizational socialization tactics influence newcomer embeddedness and turnover? *Journal of Management,* 32 (2006): 237–256.

112. "training Top 125," *training,* January/February 2011, 91.

113. D. Milliken, "Poised for discovery," *T+D* (August 2011): 70–71.

114. T. Starner, "Big Blue welcomes you," *Human Resource Executive* (September 16, 2010): 30–33.

| Case 3 | Learning in Practice |
|---|---|

# Development Is Served 24/7 in InterContinental Hotel Group's Leaders Lounge

Intercontinental Hotel Group (IHG), an Atlanta-based company, operates by a simple strategy: "Great hotels guest's love." IHG operates brands such as InterContinental, Crowne Plaza, Hotel Indigo, Holiday Inn, Holiday Inn Express, Staybridge Suites, and Candlewood Suites. These brands include 4,400 hotels, with 652,000 rooms, in more 100 countries around the world. The company believes that how its employees feel about its brands and how they deliver the guest experience is what distinguishes it from the competition. "Winning Ways," IHG's core values, help guide and motivate employees to improve their personal and professional lives, take ownership, work together, and engage in responsible behavior. IHG makes four promises to employees:

- Room to Have a Great Start
- Room to Be Involved
- Room to Grow
- Room for You

The "Room to Grow" promise means that employees are given support for development opportunities and encouraged to pursue a rewarding career. "Room to Grow" ensures that employees know what success means for their job, they receive regular, high-quality feedback, they have opportunities to develop in their current and future roles, and they are aware of career opportunities within IHG around the world.

In keeping with its "Room to Grow" promise, IHG wanted to create a way to respond to the needs of many of its global corporate and hotel-level managers, who had indicated in surveys that they did not feel connected to each other and senior management. To develop managers' leadership skills, IHG created a virtual leadership development community called the Leaders Lounge, for the general managers in its hotels, as well as for employees holding corporate director or higher-level positions. The Leaders Lounge features short and concise information on leadership, which is provided in articles, tips, videos, downloadable tools, and best practices within IHG. Employees who access the site can use social networks to post tips and react to the leadership content. There are several dedicated areas within the Leaders Lounge, including the "Leadership Gym," which features assessment tools designed to help employees identify their leadership strengths and weaknesses; and "Problem Solver," which asks employees for input on leadership issues. Also included is a section known as "The Academy," for users to access e-learning opportunities on business topics including finance, customer service, and coaching skills. Use of "The Academy" also allowed IHG to move several modules of its Senior Leadership Program online, generating cost savings resulting from reducing travel costs related to global managers having to travel to the training site.

There is compelling evidence that the Leaders Lounge has been effective for developing managers. The Lounge costs 5 percent of the costs for a typical three-day on-site leadership workshop. More than 70 percent of Lounge members use it in any one month, averaging six times per year. More than 3,000 leadership tools have been downloaded and shared with leadership teams around the world. Lounge members across the globe have taken content from the Lounge and used it to build local learning workshops and training sessions. Surveys for hotel general managers (who make up 75 percent of the Leaders Lounge membership) show that their engagement scores increased approximately 3 percent.

**Sources:** Based on www.ihgplc.com, the website for InterContinental Hotels Group; P. Harris, "Where people power makes the difference," *T+D* (October 2010): 32–34; "Best practices and outstanding initiatives: InterContinental Hotels Group Leaders Lounge," *training* (January/February 2011): 96–97.

## Questions

1. What are the advantages and disadvantages of IHG's virtual leadership development program for the company? For employees?
2. Many companies are using a blended approach for employee development. That is, they are using both face-to-face and technology-aided training and development activities for leadership development. What more traditional development activities would you recommend the IHG include in the development program to make it more effective? Explain how these development activities will enhance the program's effectiveness.
3. Do you think that IHG's evaluation of the program makes a strong business case for it? Why or why not? What other metrics or outcomes would you suggest that IHG include to improve its overall evaluation of the effectiveness of the virtual leadership program for employees and the business? What other outcomes or metrics should IHG use to determine whether the program contributes to the "Winning Ways" core values?

# Social Responsibility and the Future

Chapter Ten, "Social Responsibility: Legal Issues, Managing Diversity, and Career Challenges," focuses on how training contributes to a company's social responsibility through partnerships with unions, community colleges, and other educational institutions. Also, socially responsible companies take steps to manage diversity and help employees work effectively in different cultures, as well as preparing employees to cope with career challenges like balancing work-life, coping with career breaks, recycling their careers, dealing with job loss, and preparing for retirement.

Chapter Eleven, "The Future of Training and Development," discusses how training and development will evolve in the future. Many factors will influence the future of training and development, including the development of new technology, which can affect how training is delivered and the quality and realism of instruction; the increased emphasis on just-in-time learning; and the increased value placed on intellectual capital, which can be developed through social relationships and networks.

Part Four concludes with a case that explores how companies are changing their vacation policy to encourage employees to use their vacation time.

# Chapter **Ten**

## Social Responsibility: Legal Issues, Managing Diversity, and Career Challenges

### Objectives

After reading this chapter, you should be able to

1. Discuss the role of training partnerships in developing skills and contributing to local communities.
2. Discuss the potential legal issues that relate to training.
3. Develop a program for effectively managing diversity.
4. Design a program for preparing employees for cross-cultural assignments.

5. Discuss the importance of career paths and dual career paths for employees and companies.
6. Develop policies to help employees achieve work-life balance.
7. Describe how companies are helping veterans develop skills and get employment.
8. Explain the value of phase retirement programs for older employees.

## Eliminating the Skills Gap and Reducing Unemployment Through Job Training Programs

Both workers and companies are suffering from a skills gap. Over 14 million American are searching for work, but companies are struggling to find employees who have the skills necessary for the job openings they have. For example, despite the estimated loss of thousands of jobs as the manufacturing sector shrinks in the next ten years, it will still experience a shortage of skilled labor as manufacturing workers retire and few are available to replace them. Companies, job seekers, and federal and local government are hoping that training programs can help the unemployed get jobs, the underemployed get jobs that better match their skills, and prepare the workforce with the skills necessary for the jobs that will be added when the economy recovers.

Consider one example of many job training programs funded by the Workforce Investment Act of 1998, which is responsible for providing the majority of federal funding, approximately $3 billion, for job training (renewed funding of the act is currently being debated in Congress). The Machinist Training Institute (MTI) is a program run by a Detroit, Michigan–based nonprofit organization called Focus: HOPE. Focus: HOPE is an organization dedicated to solving the problems of hunger, economic disparity, inadequate education, and racial divisiveness. Focus: HOPE also offers six months to one-and-one-half-year training programs leading to technology certifications in personal computer support and network and server maintenance and technology degrees in information systems. Since the 1980s, Focus: HOPE has trained 11,000 people, and MTI has trained 2,400 people and helped diversify the machinist trades. Many graduates were the first African Americans or female machinists hired by companies.

In 2011, Focus: HOPE received almost $6 million in Workforce Investment Act funds for its training programs, along with donations from professional organizations such as the Society of Manufacturing Engineers. The MTI program is a twenty-week program in which students are in "class" five days each week. The current MTI class includes both older and younger students who come from a variety of backgrounds. Some students have been laid off from their high-paying jobs, have dropped out of community college, or have been unable to get employment due to criminal backgrounds. MTI includes classroom instruction but also requires students to practice and gain experience working in its labs and shops, both with conventional equipment used in skilled trades such as metalworking lathes and newer, computer-controlled versions that are used in many of today's manufacturing operations. These require students to have high levels of literacy and numerical and computer skills needed to program the equipment. Focus: HOPE takes many steps to help the students succeed. They find scholarships for students to cover tuition costs, offer subsidized child care, give them free bus tickets so they can get to class, and have a credit union that is open to all students, regardless of their credit rating.

There is currently ongoing political debate fueled by contradictory research results about whether the investment of public money in job training programs is paying off. That is, although in theory, training helps people help themselves, turning them from an unemployment cost to a revenue-producing citizen, it is uncertain whether job training programs make it easier for the unemployed to find a job or lead to better pay for the underemployed. Yet Focus: HOPE has found jobs for sixty-four of its ninety-two students who have graduated since 2008. Tranor Industries, a small manufacturer of car parts, hired three MTI graduates. One of the graduates didn't stay long with the company, but the company has been impressed with the skills of the remaining two MTI graduates and plans to hire more.

**Sources:** Based on D. Bennett, "Do the unemployed get a second act?" *Bloomberg Business Week,* September 19–September 25, 2011, 64–70; www.focushope.edu, the website for Focus: HOPE.

# INTRODUCTION

Training and development should help companies achieve their business goals, resulting in profits and positive returns to stockholders. But stockholders represent only one of the parties (or stakeholders) that have an interest in a company's success. Other important stakeholders include the local community and employees who can also benefit from training and development. Companies have a social responsibility to help improve the communities where they are located by protecting the environment, supporting cultural activities, and helping to reduce poverty and unemployment. For example, companies can develop partnerships with schools, community colleges, and universities to design programs that can increase the skills of the workforce. These partnerships benefit the company because they provide a source of skilled employees. They also contribute to the local community because they improve the skill level of the local labor market. This helps keep employers from moving to other locations in the United States and abroad to find the skills they need and can help attract new employers. This chapter's opening vignette highlights a federally funded program that helps the unemployed find jobs and provides companies with a source for skilled workers. Focus: Hope is one example of a nontraditional source that companies are using as they struggle to find workers with skill sets needed for many jobs (recall the discussion in Chapter One, "Introduction to Employee Training and Development," of the mismatch between the skills available in the workforce and skills that companies need). The first section of this chapter discusses the different types of training partnerships that companies are participating in with schools, unions, and nonprofit organizations to provide them with skilled workers.

Social responsibility also means that companies need to comply with laws and regulations, but perhaps more importantly, take actions and create conditions to help all employees grow, develop, and contribute to company goals, regardless of their background and career issues they are facing. The second section of the chapter discusses how laws and regulations influence training and development and how to ensure the talents and skills of a diverse workforce are best used. This includes managing diversity and inclusion, melting the glass ceiling that women face in trying to achieve higher-level management positions, and preparing employees to work in cross-cultural assignments,. The final section of the chapter discusses specific career challenges that employees face and what employees can do to help them manage and cope with them. These challenges include balancing work and life, career breaks, coping with job loss, job hopping and recycling careers, and retirement.

## Training Partnerships

Government agencies, trade groups, foundations, and companies are working with schools to develop employee skills and provide jobs. **Sector partnerships** refer to government agencies, industry trade groups that help identify the skills that local employers require and work with community colleges, universities, and other educational institutions to provide qualified employees. Sector partnerships can focus on jobs that require more than a high school diploma but less than a four-year college degree, and some provide skills that are needed for professional employees such as engineers. Through such partnerships, workforce skill needs can be met faster than if individual employers worked alone. For example, the federal government gave Maine $14 million to establish a partnership designed to provide the workforce skills needed for boat building.[1] The Michigan Energy, Labor, and Economic Growth Department created the Michigan Academy for Green Mobility Alliance to start developing the workforce skills needed in the electric vehicle industry. The alliance of university researchers, auto manufacturers, and suppliers develops training programs that the auto industry needs for hybrid and electric vehicle production. The training focuses on electric batteries and automobile electronic systems. Both employed and jobless workers can participate, and the state of Michigan pays a portion of the tuition costs. Participation in the programs can lead to certificates, as well as bachelor's or master's degrees related to "green" fields of study. The Finger Lakes Advanced Manufacturing Partnership, in upstate New York, is trying to help the area prepare for the anticipated retirements of skilled equipment and machinery operators by visiting high school teachers, parents, and students about career opportunities in fields such as photonics (the study of photons), which lead to jobs in developing precision optics and optical components. Job Corps is a career and technical training program funded by Congress and administered by the U.S. Department of Labor.[2] Job Corps trains young people between the ages of 16 and 24 in academic, information technology, and vocational skills needed in jobs such as masonry, carpentry, and nursing. Education, training, and support services are provided to students at 125 Job Corps center campuses located throughout the United States and Puerto Rico and through private contractors. Troy Carter dreamed of becoming a music industry success and received his GED from a Job Corps center in Maryland. He is now the CEO of Coalition Media Group, a Beverly Hills, California, artist management and digital marketing company that has worked with Sean "Diddy" Combs, Nelly, and Will Smith and includes Lady Gaga among his current clients.

Some programs are specifically directed at helping the hard-to-employ, such as low-income or homeless people or individuals with a criminal record, escape the poverty cycle through learning marketable skills and helping them get a job. For example, The Center for Energy Workforce Development (CEWD) received a grant of more than $1 million from the Bill and Melinda Gates Foundation to work with low-income young adults to help them find careers in the energy industry.[3] Youths will be placed in jobs in natural gas and electrical utilities, construction, and manufacturing. CEWD was formed to help utilities work together to develop solutions to the coming workforce shortage in the utility industry due to retirement or employees leaving the industry. One estimate is that over 40 percent of the U.S. workforce in energy will be eligible for retirement in the next five years. It is the first partnership between utilities, their associations, contractors, and unions to focus on the need to build a skilled workforce pipeline that will meet future industry needs.

Project Vacant Streets, a Miami-based program founded by Frank Kelley, a Johnson & Johnson executive, tries to get jobs for persons who are "crisis homeless"; that is, everyday people who end up homeless due to losing their jobs because of the recession.[4] One estimate is that 80 percent of the homeless are crisis homeless, with the remaining 20 percent including individuals who have chronic physical or mental health problems. Many of the crisis homeless are qualified for jobs but have lost their homes and now live in homeless shelters. Project Vacant Streets helps the crisis homeless develop skill sets that can get them back into the workforce. It focuses on emotional, professional, and physical issues needed for success. Kelley works with the program participants to identify their passions, develop their interviewing skills, physical presence, and develop strategies to leave a lasting impression built around his Attitude, Communication, External Image (ACE) approach. Exercises, simulations, and workshops are delivered to participants to improve their attitude toward the job search and communicate their positive attitude to prospective employers. Also, the program involves companies such as Starbucks presenting to the homeless the same types of courses that their employees would receive (e.g., a customer service class). Because of the comprehensive nature of the program, Kelley works with a small number of participants at one time. But despite the small numbers, he has helped program participants get jobs in local Miami hotels, including the Eden Roc, Hilton, and Doubletree.

Mark Goldsmith, a former Revlon executive, started his own nonprofit organization called Getting Out and Staying Out (GOSO).[4a] GOSO is currently working with more than 200 inmates serving prison sentences in New York. GOSO works with young prisoners who are attending school and have been in prison for only a short time. It provides individual job and education counseling and interview preparation, maintains a job bank of openings from employers willing to hire former inmates, provides educational scholarships, and holds seminars. One seminar taught by a retired construction company executive focused on the skills required to become a successful tradesperson. GOSO has been successful. Fewer than 10 percent of the 400 released inmates GOSO has worked with have been arrested again, compared with two-thirds of prisoners nationwide who are rearrested following their release. A total of 75 percent of former prisoners in GOSO are employed or attending school. Former inmates stop by to share good news about a job, discuss problems they are having at home or at work, or return for counseling if they lose or don't get a job, want to change jobs, or decide to go back to school.

Federal legislation encourages partnerships between educational institutions, employers, and labor unions. The **School-to-Work Opportunities Act** is designed to assist the states in building school-to-work systems that prepare students for high-skill, high-wage jobs or future education. The act encourages partnerships between educational institutions, employers, and labor unions. The act requires that every school-to-work system include work-based learning, school-based learning, and connecting activities that match students with employers and bring classrooms and workplaces together. For example, a high school in Wisconsin has a program that combines engineering classes at school with paid, on-the-job engineering experience.[5] Wisconsin has one of the most fully developed school-to-work programs. Apprenticeships are offered in thirteen fields ranging from tourism to engineering. Committees of employers and educators developed the skill sets to be covered and identified appropriate classroom and work experiences.

Federal Tool & Engineering, a customized metal stamping company based in Wisconsin, received a $1.5 million order because the company had taken the time and invested the money to get several employees certified in advanced manufacturing skills.[6] Because of grants made by the state of Wisconsin to technical college and workforce development boards, four employees were able to obtain certification by attending a standardized training program that focuses on quality practices and measurement, safety, process and production, and maintenance awareness. The program also helps employees develop math, science, communications, computing, problem-solving, and teamwork skills.

The **Workforce Investment Act of 1998** created a comprehensive workforce investment system. The reformed system is intended to be customer-focused, help Americans manage their careers through information and high-quality services, and help U.S. companies find skilled workers. The cornerstone of the system is One-Stop service delivery, which unifies numerous training, education, and employment programs into a single, customer-friendly system in each community. The underlying notion of One-Stop is the coordination of programs, services, and governance structures so that customers have access to a seamless system of workforce investment services. It is envisioned that a variety of programs could use One-Stop's common intake, case management, and job development services in order to take full advantage of One-Stop's potential for efficiency and effectiveness.

A wide range of services, including training and employment programs, are available to meet the needs of employers and job seekers. The challenge in helping One-Stop live up to its potential is to make sure that the state and local boards can effectively coordinate and collaborate with the network of other service agencies, including Temporary Assistance for Needy Families (TANF) agencies, transportation agencies and providers, metropolitan planning organizations, child care agencies, nonprofit and community partners, and the broad range of partners who work with youth.

O*NET, the Occupational Information Network, is a unique, comprehensive database and directory of occupational titles, worker competencies, and job requirements and resources.[7] O*NET, which supports One-Stop service delivery, is the primary source of occupational information in the United States. The O*NET database includes information on skills, abilities, knowledge, work activities, and interests associated with occupations. O*NET information can be used to facilitate career exploration, vocational counseling, and a variety of human resource (HR) functions, such as developing job orders, creating position descriptions, and aligning training with current workplace needs. Job seekers can use O*NET to find out which jobs fit with their interests, skills, and experience and to identify the skills, knowledge, and abilities needed for their dream job.

## Lifelong Learning

A **Lifelong Learning Account (LiLA)** refers to an account for adult education into which both the employee and the company contribute and the employee keeps—even if he or she leaves the company. The money in the LiLA can be used to pay for a range of educational expenses, including tuition, books, fees, supplies, and non-job-specific certification courses. The money in the account can be rolled over from year to year. The federal Lifelong Learning Account Act of 2010 (proposed but not yet voted on) supports these LiLAs, which can be used to save for a wide range of educational opportunities, including part-time education, job training, and apprenticeships.[8] The bill provides several financial incentives to workers and employers to participate. Like a 401(k) retirement plan, employers can choose to match workers' contributions, and contributions to the accounts will grow tax-free. A total of $2,500 can be contributed to the account during a year, and workers can receive up to a $750 tax credit for making these contributions. Employers will receive a 25 percent tax credit on their contributions. The accounts will also be portable and employee-owned, meaning that they will stay with the individual even if they lose their job, switch jobs, or stop working.

Some companies have taken the initiative to introduce their own type of LiLA to make continuing education a priority.[9] IBM's Matching Accounts for Learning Initiative program allows employees to contribute up to $1,000 per year into a portable, interest-bearing account with a 50 percent company match. Employees can use the money to gain skills not directly related to their current jobs, such as learning a new language. The University of California at San Francisco (UCSF) Medical Center set up a small pilot LiFA program that was so successful that it is now being expanded. During the pilot phase of the program, employees took training in health care–related skills, as well as real estate, finance, and word processing. Managers at the UCSF Medical Center believe that, although employees are using the LiLA accounts to learn skills unrelated to their jobs, they are unlikely to leave for other job opportunities because of the investment that UCSF has made in their careers.

## Joint Union-Management Programs

The initial goal of these programs was to help displaced employees find new jobs by providing skill training and outplacement assistance. Currently, **joint union-management training programs** provide a wide range of services designed to help employees learn skills that are directly related to their jobs and also develop skills that are "portable"—that is, valuable to employers in other companies or industries.[10] Both employers and unions contribute money to run the programs, and both oversee their operation. The National Coalition for Telecommunications Education and Learning (NACTEL) is a partnership between telecommunications companies, including AT&T, Century Link, Frontier, and Verizon, and labor unions, such as Communication Workers of America (CWA) and International Brotherhood of Electrical Workers (IBEW), that has developed online education programs.[11] NACTEL includes courses that allow employees to work toward associate degrees (e.g., in telecommunications) and certificate programs (e.g., Introduction to Telecommunications). The NACTEL programs are offered by Pace University's School of Computer Science and Information Systems.

Chrysler recently implemented the World Class Manufacturing (WCM) process, designed to improve quality, reduce costs, and empower employees. The process saved Fiat from going out of business by improving the quality of its cars and making production more efficient.[12] Chrysler worked with the United Auto Workers (UAW) to renovate its training center in Warren, Michigan, and introduce technology-based training methods to teach problem-solving skills that employees use in their plant jobs. Chrysler wants to have more than 1,200 hourly and salaried employees attend the WCM Academy each year to create a culture of continuous improvement and learning. The UAW was initially resistant to supporting WCM but is now supportive because of the high level of employee involvement. The UAW labor agreement provides a $500 annual bonus, which can increase to $1,000 for each employee if a plant reaches WCM goals. Also, UAW members understand that WCM and the Academy are important for driving changes needed in the plants to maintain Chrysler's competitiveness and keep manufacturing jobs.

Unlike previous training, only 30 percent will involve classroom instruction. A total of 70 percent of the training at the Academy involves hand-on training activities, including high-tech simulations and games designed to focus on the specific needs of manufacturing facilities. For example, at a simulated work station, employees put on a special suit containing motion detectors. While employees work at the station, the system identifies stressful actions and provides diagnostic feedback designed to help them use more safe and efficient motions. Three-dimensional goggles allow employees to become immersed in a plant full of unsafe behaviors and working conditions. Employees watch videos emphasizing unsafe conditions and identify potential risks and solutions within the three-dimensional plant environment. Workers train on a simulated door line which helps them learn how to create kits that reduce inventory and materials handling. After spending two days at the Academy, workers return to their plants to work with a trainer on applying what they have learned. Workers return to the Academy at a later time to share best practices and how they have applied what they have learned to project assignments. This enables workers to share their knowledge and expertise and provides ideas for trainers about how to improve the Academy experience.

# LEGAL ISSUES AND MANAGING A DIVERSE WORKFORCE AT HOME AND ABROAD

## Legal Issues

Table 10.1 shows potential training activities and situations that can make an employer vulnerable to legal actions and harm the company's reputation. The following sections describe each situation and potential implications for training.[13]

### *Failing to Provide Training or Providing Inadequate Training*

To comply with a wide range of laws and regulations, companies are required to show that employees not only have completed training programs, but also are applying their new knowledge on the job. Most companies provide training to reduce the potential for a hostile work environment for employees protected by Title VII of the Civil Rights Act (covering race, color, gender, religion, nationality, and national origin), the Age Discrimination in Employment Act (ADEA; covering age), or the Americans with Disabilities Act (ADA; covering disability).[14] For example, the U.S. Supreme Court considers sexual harassment training to be an important factor for companies that wish to avoid punitive damages in sexual harassment cases. Employers must also train employees to comply with practices designed to prevent harassment of any class protected by Title VII.

Federal laws may require a certain number of training hours and types of training for employees in certain industries. For example, initial training for flight attendants must include how to handle passengers, use galley equipment, evacuate the airplane, and use the public address system. The safe landing of U.S. Airways Flight 1549 on the Hudson River in 2009 was one of the rare moments when a U.S. passenger plane completed a forced landing without loss of life of passengers or crew. As a result, the Federal Aviation Administration (FAA) has implemented new training regulations and rules for airlines, calling for hands-on drills on the use of emergency equipment and procedures for all flight attendants.[15]

The FAA has also introduced training standards requiring scenario-based simulations to help pilots operate today's new aircraft, which have integrated systems, greater speed, range, and altitude, and new multifunctional flight displays.[16]

Companies in health care are required to comply with the Health Insurance Portability and Accountability Act (HIPPA); companies in finance are required to comply with the

**TABLE 10.1**
**Situations That May Result in Legal Action**

- Failing to provide required training or providing inadequate training
- Incurring employee injury during a training activity
- Incurring injuries to employees or others outside the training session
- Breach of confidentiality or defamation
- Reproducing and using copyrighted material in training classes without permission
- Excluding women, minorities, and older Americans from training programs
- Failing to ensure equal treatment while in training
- Requiring employees to attend training programs that they may find offensive
- Revealing discriminatory information during a training session
- Not accommodating trainees with disabilities
- Incorrectly reporting training as an expense, or failing to report training reimbursement as income

Bank Secrecy Act; and companies in the gaming industry (such as casinos) are required to train employees on how to handle money and report suspicious activity.[17] In several states, candidates interested in being hired as full-time police officers must complete approved police training. Legislation can also require training that is related to providing a drug-free workplace (e.g., training about drug abuse and making counseling available) and a safe workplace (e.g., training about the handling of hazardous materials and the use of safety equipment as dictated by the Occupational Safety and Health Act/OSHA).

### Incurring Employee Injury During a Training Activity

OJT and simulations often involve the use of work tools and equipment (e.g., welding machinery, printing press, etc.) that could cause injury if incorrectly used. Workers' compensation laws in many states make employers responsible for paying employees their salary and/or providing them with a financial settlement for injuries received during any employment-related activity such as training. Managers should ensure that (1) employees are warned of potential dangers from incorrectly using equipment and (2) safety equipment is used.

### Incurring Injuries to Employees or Others Outside a Training Session

Managers should ensure that trainees have the necessary level of competence in knowledge, skills, and behaviors before they are allowed to operate equipment or interact with customers. Even if a company pays for training to be conducted by a vendor, it is still liable for injuries or damages resulting from the actions of poorly, incorrectly, or incompletely trained employees. A company that contracts out training to a vendor or consultant should ensure that the vendor has liability insurance, be sure that the trainers are competent, and determine if there has been previous litigation against the trainer or the vendor providing the training. Also, trainers should be sure to keep copies of notes, activities, and training manuals that show that training procedures were correct and followed the steps provided by licensing or certification agencies (if appropriate).

### Incurring Breach of Confidentiality or Defamation

Managers should ensure that information placed in employees' files regarding performance in training activities is accurate. Also, before discussing an employee's performance in training with other employees or using training performance information for promotion or salary decisions, managers should tell employees that training performance will be used in that manner.

### Reproducing and Using Copyrighted Material in Training Classes Without Permission

**Copyrights** protect the expression of an idea (e.g., a training manual for a software program) but not the ideas that the material contains (e.g., the use of help windows in the software program).[18] Copyrights also prohibit others from creating a product based on the original work and from copying, broadcasting, or publishing the product without permission.

   The use of videotapes, learning aids, manuals, and other copyrighted materials in training classes without obtaining permission from the owner of the material is illegal. Managers should ensure that all training materials are purchased from the vendor or consultant who developed them, or that permission to reproduce materials has been obtained. Material on Internet sites is not necessarily free from copyright law.[19] Many websites and published material are governed by the fair use doctrine, which means that you can use small amounts of copyrighted material without asking permission or paying a fee so long as the use meets four standards. The standards relate to (1) the purpose for which the copyrighted materials are being used, (2) what the copyrighted work is, (3) the proportion of the copyrighted material you are using, and (4) how much money the copyright owner can lose as a result of the use. Republishing or repackaging under your own name material that you took from the Internet can be a violation of copyright law. For example, Crisp Learning, a small training company, frequently finds itself in court defending copyright issues. Crisp Learning develops and sells video and training courses that deal with skills such as business report writing and time management. The series of courses, known as the Fifty-Minute series, is popular because it is easily applied and can be completed in a short period of time. Crisp Learning has found that copyright violators have actually retyped its books and sold them as their own work.

Violating copyright can be expensive. Copyright violators can end up paying expensive legal fees and paying damages that are more expensive than what it would have cost to legally purchase the training materials. To obtain copyright permission, you need to directly contact the owners of the material and explain how the material will be used and how ownership will be cited. Another way to get copyright permission is to seek permission from organizations such as the Copyright Clearance Center (www.copyright.com) or iCopyright.com.

### *Excluding Women, Minorities, and Older Employees from Training Programs*

Two pieces of legislation make it illegal for employers to exclude women, minorities, or older persons from training programs. **Title VII of the Civil Rights Act** (amended in 1991) makes it illegal to deny access to employment or deprive a person employment because of the person's race, color, religion, gender, or national origin. The **Age Discrimination in Employment Act (ADEA)** prohibits discrimination against persons who are age 40 or older. The Equal Employment Opportunity Commission (EEOC) is responsible for enforcing both the Civil Rights Act and the ADEA.

Although these two pieces of legislation have existed for several years, a study by the U.S. Department of Labor found that training experiences necessary for promotion are not as available or accessible to women and minorities as they are to white males.[20] Women, minorities, and older employees sometimes are illegally excluded from training programs, either by not being made aware of opportunities for training or by purposeful exclusion from enrollment in training programs. Denial of training opportunities and better treatment of younger employees can be used to support claims of age discrimination.[21] Older employees may bring lawsuits against companies based on a denied promotion or discharge. As evidence for age discrimination, the courts will investigate whether older workers were denied training opportunities that were provided to younger workers. To avoid age discrimination in training, managers and trainers need to ensure that the organization's culture and policies are age-neutral. Decisions about training and development opportunities should not be made on the basis of stereotypes about older workers and should take into account job-relevant factors such as performance. Managers should be held accountable for fair training and development practices and for ensuring that all employees have development plans. Finally, all employees should receive training on the ADEA and on how age stereotypes can affect treatment of older employees. Stereotypes such as "Older workers are resistant to change" may result in exclusion of older workers from training and development programs.

The University of Phoenix had to pay over $1 million in 2008 for demonstrating a religious bias against non-Mormon employees who worked as enrollment counselors in the university's Online Division.[22] The religious bias occurred when tuition waivers for non-Mormon employees were denied for failing to meet student registration goals, yet waivers were provided to Mormon employees who failed to meet the same goals.

In another example, New Prime, Inc, a large trucking company violated federal law by discriminating against female truck driver job applicants when it required that they be trained only be female trainers.[23] Training was provided for male job applicants with no delay, but female job applicants were put on a waiting list, resulting in delaying or denying them jobs.

### *Not Ensuring Equal Treatment of All Employees While in Training*

Equal treatment of all trainees means that conditions of the learning environment, such as opportunities for practice, feedback, and role playing, are available for all trainees regardless of their background. Also, trainers should avoid jokes, stories, and props that might create a hostile learning environment. For example, because of claims that female employees were being harassed at air traffic control centers, the FAA required employees to attend diversity training where male employees were made to experience what it felt like to be taunted and jeered at as you walked down the aisle in an air traffic control facility (known as "walking the gauntlet"). One of the male employees found the experience to be distasteful and psychologically stressful, sued the FAA, and won.

### *Requiring Employees to Attend Programs That Might Be Offensive*

Allstate Insurance has been the focus of several religious discrimination lawsuits brought by insurance agents. Some agents charged that the principles emphasized in training programs were based on Scientology were offensive and counter to their religious beliefs. For example, the training program taught concepts such as the "tone scale" which catalogs emotions and Scientologists believe can influence behavior.[24]

### *Revealing Discriminatory Information During a Training Session*

At Lucky Store Foods, a California supermarket chain, notes taken during a diversity training program were used as evidence of discrimination.[25] In the training session, supervisors were asked to verbalize their stereotypes. Some comments ("Women cry more," "Black women are aggressive") were derogatory toward women and minorities. The plaintiff in the case used the notes as evidence that the company conducted the training session to avoid an investigation by the EEOC. The case was settled out of court.

### *Not Accommodating Trainees with Disabilities*

The **Americans with Disabilities Act (ADA)** of 1990 prohibits individuals with disabilities from being discriminated against in the workplace. The ADA prohibits discrimination based on disability in employment practices, including hiring, firing, compensation, and training. The ADA defines a disability as a physical or mental impairment that substantially limits one or more major life activities, a record of having an impairment, or being regarded as having such an impairment. This includes serious disabilities such as epilepsy, blindness, or paralysis, as well as persons who have a history of heart disease, mental illness, or cancer that is currently in remission.

The ADA requires companies to make "reasonable accommodation" to the physical or mental condition of a person with a disability who is otherwise qualified, unless doing so would impose an "undue hardship" on the organization's operations. Determination of undue hardship is made by analyzing the type and cost of the accommodation in relation to the company's financial resources. Even if the undue hardship can be justified, the ADA requires that the person with the disability be provided the option of paying the part of the cost that causes the undue hardship.

In the context of training, **reasonable accommodation** refers to making training facilities readily accessible to and usable by individuals with disabilities. Reasonable accommodation may also include modifying instructional media, adjusting training policies, and providing trainees with readers or interpreters. Employers are not required to make reasonable accommodation if the person does not request them. Employers are also not required to make reasonable accommodation if persons are not qualified to participate in training programs (e.g., they lack the prerequisite certification or educational requirements).

One example of how the ADA might influence training activities involves adventure learning. Some adventure learning experiences demand a high level of physical fitness. Employees who have a disability cannot be required to attend adventure learning training programs.[26] If it does not cause an undue hardship, employees should be offered an alternative program for developing the learned capabilities emphasized in the adventure learning program.

It is impossible to give specific guidelines regarding the type of accommodations that trainers and managers should make to avoid violating the ADA. It is important to identify if the training is related to "essential" job functions. That is, are the tasks or knowledge, skills, and abilities that are the focus of training fundamental to the position? Task analysis information (discussed in Chapter Three, "Needs Assessment") can be used to identify essential job functions. For example, tasks that are frequently performed and critical for successful job performance would be considered essential job functions. If training relates to a function that may be performed in the job but does not have to be performed by all persons (a marginal job function), then a disability in relation to that function cannot be used to exclude that person from training. To the extent that the disability makes it difficult for the person to receive the training necessary to complete essential job functions, the trainer must explore whether it is possible to make reasonable accommodations.

### Incorrectly Reporting Training as an Expense or Failing to Report Training Reimbursement as Income

The cost of training is covered by the Internal Revenue Code. Companies can often deduct the cost of training provided to employees as a business expense. The Employer Assistance Program, part of the IRS Code, allows an employer to pay an employee up to $5,250 per year for certain educational expenses. This amount can be deducted by the employer as a business expense without adding the payment to the employee's yearly gross income. In other programs (e.g., the Educational Reimbursement Program), the employer can decide which training is paid for and how it is funded. Reimbursement for training expenses that an employee incurs may be considered part of the employee's taxable income. Employees may be able to deduct work-related educational expenses as itemized deductions on their income taxes. To be deductible, the expenses must be for training that maintains or improves skills required in the job or that serves a business purpose of the company and is required by the company, or by law or regulations, in order for employees to keep their present salary, status, or job. See www.irs.gov for more information about business and individual reporting of educational expenses.

### Managing Workforce Diversity and Inclusion

Diversity can be considered any dimension that differentiates a person from another.[27] For example, at Verizon, diversity means embracing differences and variety, including age, ethnicity, education, sexual orientation, work style, race, gender, and more. **Inclusion** refers to creating an environment in which employees share a sense of belonging, mutual respect, and commitment from others so they can perform their best work.[28]

**Diversity training** refers to learning efforts that are designed to change employee attitudes about diversity and/or develop skills needed to work with a diverse workforce. The goals of diversity training are (1) to eliminate values, stereotypes, and managerial practices that inhibit employees' personal development; and therefore (2) to allow employees to contribute to organizational goals regardless of their race, sexual orientation, gender, family status, religious orientation, or cultural background.[29] Equal Employment Opportunity (EEO) laws help ensure that women and minorities are adequately represented in a company's labor force. That is, companies have focused on ensuring equal access to jobs. However, diversity training and a focus on EEO laws are insufficient for a company to truly capitalize on the value of a diverse workforce. They are one part of a larger emphasis on managing diversity and inclusion.

More generally, a survey of diversity training efforts found that[30]

- The most common area addressed through diversity efforts is the pervasiveness of stereotypes, assumptions, and biases.
- Fewer than one-third of companies do any kind of long-term evaluation or follow-up. The most common indicators of success were reduced grievances and lawsuits, increased diversity in promotions and hiring, increased self-awareness of biases, and increased consultation of human resource management specialists on diversity-related issues.
- Most programs lasted only one day or less.
- Three-fourths of the survey respondents indicated they believed that the typical employee leaves diversity training with positive attitudes toward diversity. However, more than 50 percent reported that the programs have no effect over the long term.
- A total of 29 percent of survey respondents reported that no tools were provided to reinforce diversity training, and 22 percent reported that no development or advancement issues were addressed.

**Managing diversity and inclusion** involves creating an environment that allows all employees to contribute to organizational goals and experience personal growth. This environment includes access to jobs, as well as fair and positive treatment of all employees. The company must develop employees who are comfortable working with people from a wide variety of ethnic, racial, and religious backgrounds. Managing diversity may require changing the company culture. It includes the company's standards and norms about how employees are treated, competitiveness, results orientation, innovation, and risk taking. The value placed on diversity is grounded in the company culture.

Managing diversity and inclusion can provide companies with a competative advantage in several different ways. It helps a company develop a reputation as a favorable employer, which attracts talent, women and minority employees. Women and minority employees will feel valued and free to contribute their insights, which can help develop new products and improve marketing efforts focused on specific consumer segments such as Hispanics.

Diversity may enhance performance when organizations have an environment that promotes learning from diversity.[31] There is no evidence to support the direct relationship between diversity and business.[32] Rather, a company will see the success of its diversity efforts only if it makes a long-term commitment to managing diversity and has a zero tolerance policy toward discrimination. Successful diversity requires that it be viewed as an opportunity for all employees to (1) learn from each other how to better accomplish their work, (2) be provided with a supportive and cooperative organizational culture, and (3) be taught leadership and process skills that can facilitate effective team functioning. Diversity is a reality in labor and customer markets and is a social expectation and value. Managers should focus on building an organizational environment, on HR practices, and on managerial and team skills that all capitalize on diversity. As you will see in the discussion that follows, managing diversity requires difficult cultural change, not just slogans on the wall.

Table 10.2 shows the characteristics associated with the long-term success of diversity programs. It is critical that a diversity program be tied to business objectives. For example, cultural differences affect the type of skin cream consumers believe they need or the fragrance they may be attracted to. Understanding cultural differences is part of understanding the consumer (which is critical to the success of companies such as Avon). Top management support can be demonstrated by creating a structure to support the initiative.

**TABLE 10.2**    **Characteristics Associated with Diversity Programs' Long-Term Success**

- Top management provides resources, personally intervenes, and publicly advocates diversity.
- The program is structured.
- Capitalizing on a diverse workforce is defined as a business objective.
- Capitalizing on a diverse workforce is seen as necessary to generate revenue and profits.
- The program is evaluated using metrics such as sales, retention, and promotion rates.
- Manager involvement is mandatory.
- The program is seen as a culture change, not a one-shot program.
- Managers and demographic groups are not blamed for problems.
- Behaviors and skills needed to successfully interact with others are taught.
- Managers are rewarded on progress toward meeting diversity goals.
- Management collects employee feedback and responds to it.
- Create a safe and open culture that all employees want to belong to, in which employees can discover and appreciate differences and where the benefits of diversity are recognized by all employees.

Sources: K. Bezrvkova, K. Jehn, & C. Spell, "Reviewing diversity training: Where we have been and where we should go", Academy of Management Learning and Education 11 (2012): 207–227; S. Rynes and B. Rosen, "A field survey of factors affecting the adoption and perceived success of diversity training," *Personnel Psychology* 48 (1995), 247–270; J. Gordon, "Different from what? Diversity as a performance issue," *Training,* May 1995, 25–33; Corporate Leadership Council, *The Evolution of Corporate Diversity* (Washington, D.C.: Corporate Executive Board, 2002); R. Anand and M. Winters, "A retrospective view of corporate diversity training from 1964 to the present," *Academy of Management Learning and Education* 7 (2008), 356–372; C. Chavez and J. Weisinger, "Beyond diversity training: A social infusion for cultural inclusion," *Human Resource Management* 47 (2008), 331–350.

Consider Sodexo's diversity effort.[33] Sodexo is the leading food and facilities management company in the United States, Canada, and Mexico, daily serving 10 million customers. With employees in 80 countries representing 128 nationalities connecting with customers on a daily basis, a policy of inclusion is not an option or a choice—it is a business necessity. Sodexo is focused on gender representation, generational opportunities in the workplace, people with disabilities, and ethnic minority representation. As a result, diversity and inclusion are core elements of the business strategy. Sodexo believes that diversity and inclusion is a fundamental business objective focused on employees (e.g., work culture, recruitment, talent development, work-life effectiveness, etc.), customers, clients, and shareholders (e.g., supplier diversity, cross-market diversity council, diversity consulting, etc.), and communities (e.g., Sodexo Foundation and Community Partners). For example, some of the objectives include understanding and living the business case for diversity and inclusion; increasing awareness of how diversity relates to business challenges; creating and fostering a diverse work environment by developing management practices that drive hiring, promotion, and retention of talent; engaging in relationship management and customer service to attract and retain diverse clients and customers; and partnering with women and minority businesses to deliver food and facility management services. Diversity and inclusion are core competencies at Sodexo. Diversity and inclusion are part of employees' training and managers' annual performance review; new employee orientation emphasizes Sodexo's values and expectations regarding diversity and inclusion.

Sodexo separates Equal Employment Opportunity (EEO) and legal compliance training from diversity training. At Sodexo, diversity training is part of the managing diversity strategy. Every three years, employees are required to take EEO and affirmative action refresher courses. Top management is also involved in and committed to managing diversity. The senior executives program includes ongoing classroom training that is reinforced with community involvement, sponsoring employee groups, and mentoring diverse employees. Executives are engaged in learning the business case for diversity and are personally held accountable for the company's diversity agenda. Every manager takes an eight-hour introductory class (called Spirit of Diversity). Sodexo's diversity training involves learning labs focused on skill building and diversity awareness. Examples of these learning labs include Generations in the Workplace, Disability Awareness Training, Cross-Cultural Communications, and Improving Team Effectiveness Through Inclusion. The company's learning and development team develops customized learning solutions for different functions and work teams. For example, a course related to selling to a diverse client base was developed and offered to the sales force, and a cross-cultural communications program was provided for recruiters.

In addition to diversity training activities, Sodexo has six employee network groups— such as the African American Leadership Forum, People Respecting Individuality, Diversity, and Equality, Honoring Our Nation's finest with Opportunity and Respect (HONOR), and the Intergenerational Network Group. These network groups provide forums for employees' professional development and sharing input and ideas to support companys' diversity efforts. Sodexo's "Champions of Diversity" program rewards and recognizes employees who advance diversity and inclusion.

To emphasize the importance of diversity for the company, at Sodexo, each manager has a diversity scorecard that evaluates his or her success in recruitment, retention, promotion, and development of all employees. The scorecard includes both quantitative goals and evaluation of behaviors such as participating in training, mentoring, and doing community outreach. A proportion of their pay bonuses is determined by success in these areas.

Sodexo has found that its diversity training and efforts to manage diversity are having a positive impact on business results. Its mentoring program has led to increased productivity, engagement, and retention of women and people of color. There was an estimated ROI of $19 for every dollar spent on the program. Sodexo also has been awarded several new business contracts and retained clients because of its involvement in managing diversity. Sodexo has also been recognized for its diversity and inclusion efforts, which helps attract talented employees by signaling that the company cares about the well-being of all of its employees. Sodexo was ranked number 2 on the 2011 Diversity Inc Top 50 Companies for Diversity list. This marks the sixth consecutive year that the company has been recognized by Diversity Inc for the success of its diversity efforts. Sodexo is also recognized as a top company for executive women and ranked among the top ten companies for Latinos, blacks, global diversity, and people with disabilities. Most effective programs to manage diversity, such as Sodexo's diversity program, include the key components shown in Table 10.3.

As should be apparent from this discussion, successful diversity programs involve more than just an effective training program. They require an ongoing process of culture change that includes top management support, as well as diversity policies and practices in the areas of recruitment and hiring, training and development, and administrative structures, such as conducting diversity surveys and evaluating managers' progress on diversity goals.[34] They also focus on enhancing diversity and inclusion with suppliers, vendors, and in the communities where the company conducts business. One way that top management is supporting the management of diversity and reinforcing its importance for the business is by creating Chief Diversity Officer executive positions. For example, Ingersoll Rand, a heating and ventilating equipment manufacturer, created a Chief Diversity Officer position to help identify and develop more women and minority leaders in the company who could provide ideas to help improve sales growth in foreign markets.[34a] The Chief Diversity Officer has created employee networking groups for women, African Americans, and veterans in North America. In Europe, she is developing a one-year leadership training program for twelve carefully selected female employees.

## Melting the Glass Ceiling

A major development issue facing companies today is how to get women and minorities into upper-level management positions—how to break the glass ceiling. The **glass ceiling** refers to a barrier to advancement to higher-level jobs in the company that adversely affects women and minorities. The barrier may be due to lack of access to training programs, development experiences, or relationships (e.g., mentoring). Surveys show that in Fortune 500 companies, women represent less than 3 percent of CEOs and approximately 14 percent of executive officers.[35] Two-thirds of these companies lack specific programs targeted at the needs of women leaders, and 23 percent offer some activities or programs targeted to the needs of women. These activities include flexible scheduling, diversity recruiting, and coaching and mentoring. One of the dilemmas is that companies may be reluctant to treat women any differently than men from a leadership development perspective despite acknowledging that women lack executive sponsors or mentors, have insufficient experience, and need better work-life balance. The glass ceiling is a barrier to advancement to higher levels of the organization. This barrier may be due to stereotypes or company systems that adversely affect the development of women or minorities.[36] The glass ceiling is likely caused by lack of access to training programs, appropriate developmental job experiences, and developmental relationships (such as mentoring).[37] Women and minorities often have trouble finding mentors because of their lack of access to the "old-boy network,"

**TABLE 10.3  Key Components of Effective Managing Diversity Programs**

**Top Management Support**
- Make the business case for diversity.
- Include diversity as part of the business strategy and corporate goals.
- Participate in diversity programs, and encourage all managers to attend.
- Ensure that the composition of the executive management team mirrors the diversity of the workforce.

**Recruitment and Hiring**
- Ask search firms to identify wider arrays of candidates.
- Enhance the interviewing, selection, and hiring skills of managers.
- Expand college recruitment at historically minority colleges.

**Identifying and Developing Talent**
- Form a partnership with internship programs that target minority students for management careers.
- Establish a mentoring process.
- Refine the company's global succession planning system to improve identification of talent.
- Improve the selection and development of managers and leaders to help ensure that they are capable of maximizing team performance.
- Ensure that all employees, especially women and minorities, have access to management development and leadership programs.

**Employee Support**
- Form resource groups or employee network groups, including employees with common interests, and use them to help the company develop business goals and understand the issues they are concerned with (e.g., Asian Pacific employees, women, gays, lesbians, transgenders, Native Americans, veterans, Hispanics).
- Celebrate cultural traditions, festivities, and holidays.
- Make work-life balance initiatives (such as flextime, telecommuting, elder care, etc.) available to all employees.

**Ensuring Fair Treatment**
- Conduct extensive diversity training.
- Implement an alternative dispute resolution process.
- Include women and minorities on all human resources committees throughout the company.

**Holding Managers Accountable**
- Link managers' compensation to their success in meeting diversity goals and creating openness and inclusion in the workplace.
- Use employee attitude or engagement surveys to track employees' attitudes about such things as inclusion, fairness, opportunities for development, work-life balance, and perceptions of the company culture.
- Implement 360-degree feedback for all managers and supervisors.

**Improving Relationships with External Stakeholders**
- Increase marketing to diverse communities.
- Provide customer service in different languages.
- Broaden the company's base of suppliers and vendors to include businesses owned by minorities and women.
- Provide scholarships and educational and neighborhood grants to diverse communities and their members.

Sources: Based on R. Anand and M. Winters, "A retrospective view of corporate diversity training from 1964 to the present," *Academy of Management Learning and Education* 7 (2008), 356–372; C. Chavez and J. Weisinger, "Beyond diversity training: A social infusion for cultural inclusion," *Human Resource Management* 47 (2008), 331–350; V. Smith, "Texaco outlines comprehensive initiatives," *Human Resource Executive*, February 1997, 13; Verizon's diversity program available at the company website, www.verizon.com.

managers' preference to interact with other managers of similar status rather than with line employees, and intentional exclusion by managers who have negative stereotypes about women's and minorities' abilities, motivation, and job preferences.[38] Research has found no gender differences in access to job experiences involving transitions or creating change.[39] However, male managers receive significantly more assignments involving high levels of responsibility (high stakes, managing business diversity, handling external pressure, etc.) than female managers of similar ability and managerial level. Also, female managers report experiencing more challenges due to lack of personal support (which makes it more difficult to cope with stress) than male managers. Career encouragement from peers and senior managers does help women advance to higher management levels.[40] Managers making developmental assignments need to carefully consider whether gender biases or stereotypes are influencing the types of assignments given to women versus men.

Best Buy Company developed the Talent Readiness Program to help middle-managers who were participating in its Women's Leadership Forum (known as WOLF) advance into senior management.[41] The Talent Readiness Program is designed to prepare female managers to take on new leadership roles, bringing greater diversity to those positions. The Talent Readiness Program is unique in its approach to development because it emphasizes skills related to business and leadership, experience, and social and emotional intelligence. In the Talent Readiness Program, women work on public speaking skills, take classes on meeting effectiveness and career planning, and learn how to present themselves with confidence. In the first phase of the program, lasting one year, participants are involved in training and leadership sessions including ongoing self-work. During phase two lasting one year, participants work on "boards" creating strategies and working cross-functionally to influence business outcomes and provide solutions to company initiatives. The program also uses technology to connect participants so that they can learn and share experiences. As of January 2011, 146 participants have completed the first phase of the program, and 12 of them have moved into new roles with increased responsibility, while dozens more have reported interviewing for new leadership roles in both traditional and nontraditional spaces. Nearly 60 percent of program participants believe that they are ready to take on a new role and are aligned with their managers in this belief, while 18 percent admitted that, based on their participation in the program, they are looking at roles outside their original plan for the next role they may wish to take. The Economical Insurance Group (TEIG), one of the largest property and casualty insurance groups in Canada, women's leadership development program includes an instructor-led workshop focusing on the fundamentals of achievement, leadership, and legacy specific to women in the company.[42] Following the workshop, female leaders are invited to participate in the TEIG Women's Leadership Network, held quarterly. The network meetings use the company's virtual classroom to discuss business ideas and challenges unique to women and to share leadership experiences. Table 10.4 provides recommendations for melting the glass ceiling and helping retain talented women.

# CROSS-CULTURAL PREPARATION

As we mentioned in Chapter One, companies today are challenged to expand globally. Because of the increase in global operations, employees often work outside their country of origin or work with employees from other countries. An **expatriate** works in a country

**TABLE 10.4**
**Recommenda-
tions for
Melting the
Glass Ceiling**

Source: Based on
D. McCracken, "Win-
ning the talent war
for women," *Harvard
Business Review*,
November–December
2000, 159–167.

| |
|---|
| Make sure senior management supports and is involved in the program. |
| Make a business case for change. |
| Make the change public. |
| Gather data on problems that cause the glass ceiling using task forces, focus groups, and questionnaires. |
| Create awareness of how gender attitudes affect the work environment. |
| Force accountability through reviews of promotion rates and assignment decisions. |
| Promote development for all employees. |

other than his or her country of origin. The most frequently selected locations for expatriate assignments include the United States, China, the United Kingdom, Singapore, Germany, and Japan.[43] Many U.S. companies are using international rotational assignments as a training tool. Guardian Industries, a glass manufacturer in Michigan, has expats in eighteen different countries.[44] Guardian's expat retention rate is close to 90 percent, which is likely due to how it treats the expats during and after their assignments. Guardian values expat experience by looking at these employees first when considering who to fill open positions. While on their assignments, Guardian stays in contact with the expats. Expat assignments can be of varying lengths depending on business needs. One former expat spent thirteen years in Saudi Arabia and Thailand, moving from department head to plant manager. The expat and his family asked to return to the United States, but the company had no plant manager openings. The expat was willing to take a lower-level position to learn things he didn't yet know about the business. When a plant manager position became available, it was offered to him.

**Cross-cultural preparation** educates employees (expatriates) and their families who are to be sent to a foreign country. To successfully conduct business in the global market-place, employees must understand the business practices and the cultural norms of different countries.

## Steps in Cross-Cultural Preparation

To prepare employees for cross-cultural assignments, companies need to provide cross-cultural preparation. Most U.S. companies send employees overseas without any prepa-ration. As a result, the number of employees who return home before completing their assignments is higher for U.S. companies than for European and Japanese companies.[45] One estimate is that U.S. companies lose more than $2 billion a year as a result of failed overseas assignments.

To succeed overseas, expatriates (employees on foreign assignments) need to be

1. Competent in their areas of expertise
2. Able to communicate verbally and nonverbally in the host country
3. Flexible, tolerant of ambiguity, and sensitive to cultural differences
4. Motivated to succeed, able to enjoy the challenge of working in other countries, and willing to learn about the host country's culture, language, and customs
5. Supported by their families[46]

One reason for U.S. expatriates' high failure rate is that companies place more em-phasis on developing employees' technical skills than on preparing them to work within other cultures. Research suggests that the comfort of an expatriate's spouse and family is the most important determinant of whether the employee will complete the assignment.[47] Studies have also found that personality characteristics are related to expatriates' desire to terminate the assignment and performance in the assignment.[48] Expatriates who were extroverted (outgoing), agreeable (cooperative and tolerant), and conscientious (dependable, achievement-oriented) were more likely to want to stay with the assignment and perform well. This suggests that cross-cultural preparation may be effective only when expatriates' personalities predispose them to be successful in assignments in other cultures.

The key to a successful foreign assignment is a combination of training and career management for the employee and family. Cross-cultural preparation involves three phases: predeparture, on-site, and repatriation (preparing to return home).

### *Predeparture Phase*

Before departure, employees need to receive language training and training focused on the new country's culture and customs. English is the common language at many multinational companies. But failing to speak the native language can cause employees to risk being misinterpreted or fail to understand informal conversations. Speaking and understanding the local language can help employees avoid misunderstandings and gain greater respect from business partners, subordinates, and customers. For example, at Intel, employees with a business need can take classes in Mandarin, Japanese, and Spanish at various offices throughout the United States, free of charge.[49] Also, it is critical that the family be included in orientation programs.[50] Expatriates and their families need information about housing, schools, recreation, shopping, and health care facilities in the areas where they will live. Expatriates also must discuss with their managers how the foreign assignment fits into their career plans and what types of positions they can expect upon their return.

Cross-cultural training methods include presentational techniques, such as lectures that expatriates and their families attend on the customs and culture of the host country, e-learning, immersion experiences, or actual experiences in the home country in culturally diverse communities.[51] Experiential exercises, such as miniculture experiences, allow expatriates to spend time with a family in the United States from the ethnic group of the host country. For example, an Indian trainer took twenty managers from Advanced Micro Devices on a two-week immersion trip during which the group traveled to New Delhi, Bangalore, and Mumbai, meeting with business persons and government officials.[52] The program required six months of planning, including providing the executives with information on foods to eat, potential security issues, and how to interact in business meetings. For example, Indians prefer a relatively indirect way into business discussions, so the managers were advised to discuss current events and other subjects before talking business.

VF Asia Limited is a Hong Kong–based unit of VF Corporation. VF Corporation is the world's largest apparel company and the owner of many brands, including Nautica, Wrangler, Jansport, and North Face.[53] VF Asia's Self-Enhancement Learning Fundamentals (SELF) program is an online customer training program that includes instruction on topics that help employees understand and communicate with individuals from the diverse cultures throughout Asia with whom they do business. Course topics include business etiquette, holding successful meetings, and negotiations. VF Asia's training team maintains a partnership with the VF Corporation development team. Both teams work together to develop and implement global initiatives to ensure that they are customized to local needs and requirements.

Research suggests that the degree of difference between the United States and the host country (cultural novelty), the amount of interaction with host country citizens and host nationals (interaction), and the familiarity with new job tasks and work environment (job novelty) all influence the "rigor" of the cross-cultural training method used.[54] Hands-on and group-building methods are most effective (and most needed) in assignments with a high level of cultural and job novelty that require a good deal of interpersonal interaction with host nationals.

### On-Site Phase

On-site training involves continued orientation to the host country and its customs and cultures through formal programs or through a mentoring relationship. Expatriates and their families may be paired with an employee from the host country, who helps them understand the new, unfamiliar work environment and community.[55] Companies are also using websites and social media to help employees on expatriate assignments get answers to questions.[57] Expatriates can use a website to get answers to questions such as, "How do I conduct a meeting here?" or "What religious or business philosophy might have influenced today's negotiation behavior?" Companies also are using websites and social media to help employees who are not expatriates but interact with clients around the world or who work on cross-cultural teams requiring limited travel. IBM uses social networking tools to connect its employees around the world. IBM's site, known as w3, contributes to the global integration of the company. The w3 On Demand Workplace is a powerful productivity and collaboration tool for 400,000 IBM employees in seventy-five countries. The w3 can be used by employees to find resources and knowledge from peers around the world to help clients innovate and succeed. Employees can create personal profiles, bookmark websites and stories they are interested in, comment on company blogs, contribute to wikis, share files, and read and review position papers, videos, and podcasts.

A major reason that employees refuse expatriate assignments is that they can't afford to lose their spouse's income or are concerned that their spouse's career could be derailed by being out of the workforce for a few years.[58] Some "trailing" spouses decide to use the time to pursue educational activities that could contribute to their long-term career goals. But it is difficult to find these opportunities in an unfamiliar place. GlaxoSmithKline's International Service Center, which handles all of its relocations from or to the United States, offers a buddy system for spouses to connect with others who have lived in the area for the past several years.[59] General Motors (GM) offers career continuation services that reimburse spouses $2,500 each year during the expatriate assignment for maintaining professional licenses or certifications. The World Bank manages an Internet site dedicated to expatriates, where spouses can post resumes and ask for job leads.

### Repatriation Phase

**Repatriation** prepares expatriates for return to the parent company and home country from the foreign assignment. Expatriates and their families are likely to experience high levels of stress and anxiety when they return because of changes that have occurred since their departure. Employees should be encouraged to self-manage the repatriation process.[60] Before they go on the assignment, they need to consider what skills they want to develop and the types of jobs that might be available in the company for an employee with those skills. Because the company changes and colleagues, peers, and managers may leave while the expatriate is on assignment, they need to maintain contact with key company and industry contacts. Otherwise, on return, the employees' reentry shock will be heightened when they have to deal with new colleagues, a new job, and a company culture that may have changed. This includes providing expatriates with company newsletters and community newspapers and ensuring that they receive personal and work-related mail from the United States while they are on foreign assignment. It is also not uncommon for employees and their families to have to readjust to a lower standard of living in the United States than they had in the foreign country, where they may have enjoyed maid service, a limousine, private schools, and clubs. Salary and other compensation arrangements should be worked out well before employees return from overseas assignments.

Aside from reentry shock, many expatriates decide to leave the company because the assignments they are given upon returning to the United States have less responsibility, challenge, and status than their foreign assignments.[61] As noted earlier, career planning discussions need to be held before the employees leave the United States to ensure that they understand the positions they will be eligible for upon repatriation.

Royal Dutch Shell, a joint Dutch and British oil and gas company, has one of the world's largest expatriate workforces. To avoid expatriates who feel undervalued and leave the company, Royal Dutch Shell gets involved with expatriates and their careers. Resource planners track workers abroad, helping to identify their next assignment. Most expatriates know their next assignment three to six months before the move, and all begin the next assignment with a clear job description. Expatriates who have the potential to reach top-level management positions are placed in the home office every third assignment to increase their visibility to company executives. Expatriates are also assigned technical mentors who evaluate their skills and help them improve their skills through training at Royal Dutch Shell's training center.

Because of family issues, poor economic times, and security issues, many companies are using virtual expatriates, relying more on short-time assignments, frequent business travel, and international commutes in which an employee lives in one country and works in another.[62] **Virtual expatriates** refer to employes who have an assignment to manage an operation abroad without being located permanently in that country. The employees periodically travel to the overseas location, return, and later use video conferencing and communications technology to manage the operation.[63] Virtual expatriates eliminate exposing the family to the culture shock of an overseas move. This setup also allows the employee to manage globally while keeping in close touch with the home office. Virtual expatriates are less expensive than traditional expatriates, who can cost companies over three times as much as a host national employee. One major disadvantage of virtual expatriates is that visiting a foreign operation on a sporadic basis may lengthen the time needed to build a local management team, so it will take longer to solve problems because of the lack of a strong personal relationship with local employees. One of the potential difficulties of short-term international assignments is that employees may be perceived as foreigners rather than colleagues because they haven't had the time to build relationships and develop trust among coworkers in their short-term location. Another is that traveling can take a physical and emotional toll on employees as they try to juggle business responsibilities with maintaining contact with family and friends. Procter & Gamble (P&G) helps employees on short-term assignments by providing a trip fund that is based on the length of time that an employee is on an extended business trip. For example, a U.S.-based employee working in Western Europe for six months would get a fund containing the cost of five business-class round trips. The employee can use money from the fund to take trips home or to cover family visits to the employee's location.

# CAREER CHALLENGES FACING A MULTIGENERATIONAL WORKFORCE

Employees' careers involve four stages: exploration, establishment, maintenance, and decline.[64] In the exploration stage, employees attempt to identify the type of work that interests them. They consider their interests, values, and work preferences and begin pursuing the type of education and training they need. Establishment involves finding employment, making an independent contribution, achieving more responsibility and financial success, and establishing a suitable lifestyle. In the maintenance stage, individuals are concerned with keeping their skills up to date and being perceived as someone who is still contributing to the company. They have many years of experience, much job knowledge, and an in-depth understanding of how business is conducted. The last stage, disengagement, involves individuals preparing to phase out of work and retire. Although individuals can go through these stages in a linear fashion and at certain ages (for example, exploration typically occurs before age 30), most individuals do not because today's careers are boundaryless and often change.[65] This means that careers may involve identifying more with the profession than the present employer, resulting in job changes. Also, at different times in their lives, individuals reconsider their interests, values, and how to best use their skills, resulting in one or more career changes.

It is important to recognize that there are likely generational differences in what employees want in their career. Generation Xers (Gen Xers), more than previous generations, appear to place higher importance on work-life balance, opportunities for growth, and good work relationships.[66] Millennials and Gen Xers are more used to change and job insecurity than baby boomers, and as a result, they are more likely to leave jobs to develop their skills. Baby boomers tend to be loyal to one company and therefore willing to relocate for a promotion or new assignment than Gen Xers, who want to stay in an area where they have formed social and work relationships. Although there are generational differences, similarities also exist. All generations share similar values related to family, respect, and trust.[67] Regardless of potential generational differences affecting employees' career needs, the reality is that most companies' workforce includes four or five generations of employees. As a result, to attract, motivate, and retain a talented multigenerational workforce companies need to understand and manage career challenges and help employees deal with career issues. These career challenges and issues include balancing work-life needs, providing career ladders, career recycling, understanding job hopping, helping employees return to work after career breaks, helping employees deal with job loss, and meeting the needs of older employees, including retirement. These career challenges and issues are discussed next.

## Work-Life Balance

Maintaining a healthy work-life balance is a concern for all employees, regardless of whether they have families, significant others, or dependents. It is difficult for employees to maintain work-life balance due to long work hours, night shift work, travel, and technologies such as pagers, smartphones, and notebook computers that bombard employees on a 24/7 basis with work demands and family member requests. One study found that due to work demands, 75 percent of employees report having not enough time for their children, and 61 percent reporting not having enough time for their spouse. However, only half of employees in the United States strongly agree that they have the flexibility they need to successfully manage their work and personal or family life.[68] **Work-life balance** refers to helping employees deal with the stresses, strains, and conflicts related to trying to balance work and non-work demands. Work-life conflict has been found to be related to increased health risks, decreased productivity, tardiness, turnover, and poor mental health.[69] Work-life conflict occurs due to competing time demands, the stress of work and life roles, and when employees behavior in their work roles is not appropriate for their behavior in non-work roles (such as when a manager has to be logical and impartial at work, but they are expected to be warm, emotional, and friendly with family members and friends).

Social legislation has been approved to help employees balance work and family. The **Family and Medical Leave Act (FLMA)** is a federal law that provides up to twelve weeks of unpaid leave in a one-year period for parents with new infants or newly adopted children.[70] The FMLA also covers employees who must take a leave of absence from work to care for a family member who is ill or to deal with their own personal illness. Employees can also take twenty-six workweeks of leave during a single twelve-month period to care for a service member with a serious injury or illness if the eligible employee is the service member's spouse, son, daughter, parent, or next of kin (military caregiver leave). Companies are required to provide employees with health care benefits during their leave of absence.

Many companies have gone beyond relying on the FMLA to help employees balance work and family life. Work-family programs include paid/unpaid elder care leave, flexible spending accounts for dependent care, elder care resources and referrals, flexible spending accounts for elder care and on-site child care. Research has found that employees working at companies that offer these programs believe that the organization supports their family and this leads to more positive job attitudes and better job performance.[71] Also, employees who use work-family programs have less work-family conflict than employees who do not. Additionally, companies are recognizing the benefits that can be gained by providing all employees, regardless if they have a spouse, children, or elders, with work-life balance through flexible work schedules, protecting their free time, and more productively using work time.[72] The benefits include the ability to have an advantage in attracting and retaining talented employees and reduced stress, resulting in healthier employees and a rested workforce that can maximize the use of their skills. As a result, typically companies provide programs and practices that assist employees in coping with both family and broader non-work-life demands. Table 10.5 shows examples of work-life balance practices.

Consider the following examples of work-family and work-life balance practices and programs.[73] Amerisure Mutual Insurance in Farmington Hills, Michigan, built a work environment and provides flexible programs designed to increase employee retention and engagement. A new computer system makes it easier for employees to work at home by giving them access to work files using their home computers. **Telecommuting** refers to a work arrangement that gives employees flexibility in both work location and hours. Employees meet with their managers to discuss the feasibility of working off site and how their performance will be evaluated. Amerisure also allows employees to take days off each year for volunteer work, and provides five paid days each year for family commitments related to medical care, such as caring for ill grandparents and immediate family members. The company's turnover rate has dropped from 18 percent to 10 percent, and

**TABLE 10.5**
**Examples of**
**Work-Life**
**Balance**
**Practices**

Flexible work schedules
Job sharing
Childcare
Eldercare
Personal leave
Telecommuting
Reduced meeting times
Reduced work hours
Adoption support
Paid vacation time
Personal services (supply meals, purchase gifts, arrange home and auto services)

employee engagement survey scores have increased. Hourly employees at health care provider Kaiser Permanente can get paid time off for several hours during the workday so they can manage doctor or school appointments without having to miss an entire day's work. They are also providing employees with more flexibility on when they want to start and end work. This helps employees more easily accommodate dropping off kids at school or running errands for elderly parents. At Marriott International, 87 percent of its employees are hourly workers. To help keep hourly workers at their best at work, the company offers many different flexibility options, including compressed workweeks, shift swapping, and work-at-home positions. A **compressed workweek** refers to a work schedule that allows employees to work fewer days but with longer hours, for example, four days, ten hours each day. Also, Marriott offers a cross-training program that allows employees such as housecleaners to get trained in a different unit (such as catering), which will give them more opportunities to choose to work when they are available. Employee survey results suggest that over 75 percent of employees with access to flexible scheduling options report that it is a major reason that they intend to remain employed at Marriott.

Fenwick & West LLP, a law firm in San Francisco, California, with 245 employees, has created special positions known as "workflow coordinators" and "balanced hour advisors," who regularly review attorneys' hours to ensure that employees on reduced assignments are not overworked or overlooked for key assignments. KPMG uses Wellness Scorecards to determine if consultants are working too much overtime or skipping vacations. RSM McGladrey, a consulting firm in Rochester, Minnesota, gives employees several flextime options, including FlexYear, which provides a schedule similar to a teacher (work nine months with pay distributed over the entire year), and FlexCareer, which enables employees to take up to five years off for personal reasons and provides resources such as training to keep employees connected with the firm and the industry so they can more easily transition back to work at the end of their sabbaticals. **Flextime** refers to giving employees the option of choosing when to work during the workday, workweek, or work year. Flexible work arrangements focused on the workweek usually give employees the choice as to how they want to arrange their start and ending time, so long as they work a total of eight hours each day. They also require employees to work during certain core hours (such as 9 A.M. to 3 P.M.). At Bon Secours Health System employees can work compressed workweeks, with options including four ten-hour shifts or three twelve-hour shifts per week. They can also choose other options, such as working weekends only, four- and eight-hour shifts, and seven consecutive workdays followed by seven days off. At U.S. Bank, tellers can choose to job-share. **Job sharing** refers to having two employees divide the hours, the responsibilities, and the benefits of a full-time job. Companies may also use two job-sharing employees to fill one full-time position.

There are several challenges with the use of work-life balance policies. The first challenge is using them to help employees achieve work-life balance without hurting business needs such as customer service and productivity. Second, managers need to understand and accept the idea that employees should not be punished for use of work-life balance policies. Employees' performance and development should be based on what they accomplish and how they do it, not whether they are seen around the office or put in "face time" with their manager. Third, it is important to ensure that work-life balance practices are accessible to everyone and meet the needs of all employees, not just those with families. Consider how Windstream and Wequasset Resort and Golf Club address these challenges.[74] At Windstream, managers are able to design and implement flexible work programs that they believe are best for their individual work groups. The guidelines that managers are given to follow in implementing flexible work programs emphasize that administration of the programs should be consistent across employees, and the programs need to maintain overall service levels and not hinder the achievement of business objectives. Flexible work programs are available to all full-time hourly non-exempt and salaried employees but exclude some managers and employees in jobs where their daily contribution and availability are necessary for the company's business success. For example, employees in direct customer support jobs must be available to meet customer needs. Wequassett Resort and Golf Club takes a similar approach. Department managers are allowed to give employees the flexibility they need, so long as the company goals are met. Its flextime policy is based on the company's operating philosophy, which emphasizes "going above and beyond" to please the customer. To assist employees in making the necessary commitment to please the customer, Wequassett recognizes the need to help employees balance work and life. Wequassett believes that employees do their best work if they have balance in their work and life because they are rested and not anxious. During weekly meetings, Wequasset's leadership committee considers flextime requests and provides immediate decisions. The company rarely denies request for time off or for unique work schedules, and they allow employees to leave and return to work when they have appointments or need to run errands. To ensure that the flexible schedules are not abused by employees, its flextime policy clearly states what is expected from both the employee and the company. Measurable goals including timetables and quotas are used to ensure that productivity goals are met. If issues do occur, the company uses individual performance plans and peer reviews to provide feedback and correct performance problems.

## CAREER PATHS AND DUAL CAREER PATHS

A **career path** is a sequence of job positions involving similar types of work and skills that employees move through in the company.[75] Career paths help companies offer career options to their employees that help them make job choices that best fit their life situations. Also, career paths help companies build employees' skills through a series of jobs or roles. This maximizes their value to the company. Figure 10.1 shows the career paths in Whole Foods Market stores and communicates the company's perspective of career management.

Developing career paths involves analyzing work and information flows, important development experiences, qualifications and the types of tasks performed across jobs,

**FIGURE 10.1**

**Career Paths
in Whole Foods
Market Stores**

Source: From
http://www
.wholefoodsmarket
.com/career/paths.php
(accessed February 14,
2012).

**Career Paths**

Whole Foods Market seeks individuals who believe in our mission of
Whole Foods, Whole People, Whole Planet — people who are
enthusiastic about food and our products, and who want to join a culture
of shared fate.

We mentor our team members through education and on-the-job
experience. We encourage participation and involvement at all levels of
our business. Team expertise is developed by fostering creativity, self-
responsibility and self-directed teamwork, and by rewarding productivity
and performance.

**Opportunities That Grow With You**

We encourage all qualified team members to apply for any available
opportunity in their store or facility, their region or the company as they
expand their product knowledge, develop their skills and enhance their
value to their teams. To support advancement from within, all openings
for positions at team leader level and higher are listed on our internal job
site. Many other openings are posted as well, from all around the
company.

**Opportunities in our Stores**

Departments
- Bakery
- Customer Service
- Grocery
- Facilities
- Floral
- Meat
- Prepared Foods
- Produce
- Seafood
- Specialty
- Whole Body

Store Team Leaders
Associate Store Team Leaders
Specialized Store Support*
Department Team Leaders
Associate Team Leaders
Specialized Team Members**
Team Members

Department Descriptions    * HR, Accounting, IT/Store Systems, Marketing
                           ** Buyers, Specialists, Receivers, Supervisors, Chefs/Cooks, Estheticians, etc.

similarities and differences in working environments, and the historical movement patterns of employees into and out of jobs (i.e., where in the company employees come from
and what positions they take after leaving a job).[76]

## Dual Career Path

For companies with professional employees such as engineers and scientists, an important
issue is how to ensure that they feel valued. Many companies' career paths are structured so
that the only way engineers and scientists (individual contributors) can advance and receive
certain financial rewards (such as stock options) is by moving into managerial positions.
Figure 10.2 shows examples of traditional career paths for scientists and managers. Advancement opportunities within a technical career path are limited. Individual contributors
who move directly into management may lack the experience and/or competencies needed
to be successful. Managerial career paths may be more highly compensated than technical
career paths. A career path system such as the one in Figure 10.2 can have negative consequences for the company. Scientists may elect to leave the company because they have

**FIGURE 10.2**
**Traditional Career Paths for Scientists and Managers**

Individual Contributor Career Path

Management Career Path

lower status, less salary, and fewer advancement opportunities than managers enjoy. Also, if scientists want to gain status and additional salary, they must choose to become managers. Scientists who cannot meet the challenges of a managerial position may leave the company.

Many companies are using multiple- or dual-career-path systems to give additional career opportunities to scientists and other individual contributors such as salespersons. A **dual-career-path system** enables employees to remain in a technical or sales career path or move into a management career path.[77] Figure 10.3 shows a dual-career-path system. Research scientists have the opportunity to move into three different career paths: a scientific path and two management paths. It is assumed that because employees can earn comparable salaries and have similar advancement opportunities in all three paths, they will choose the path that best matches their interests and skills. For example, Toshiba Medical Systems is reconsidering its retention strategies as baby boomers retire and Gen Xers move into leadership positions in the company.[78] Recognizing that baby boomers may tend to judge the success of their careers based on promotions, but younger employees place less value on level, title, and money, Toshiba has developed both technical and managerial career ladders. The technical career ladders allow employees to continue to perform hands-on work in areas they enjoy, but still allow them to move up in the company.

Effective dual-career paths have several characteristics:[79]

- Salary, status, and incentives for technical employees compare favorably with those of managers.

- Individual contributors' base salaries may be lower than that of managers, but they are given opportunities to increase their total compensation through bonuses (e.g., for patents and developing new products).

**FIGURE 10.3**
**Example of a Dual-career Path System**

Source: Z. B. Leibowitz, B. L. Kaye, and C. Farren, "Multiple career paths," *Training and Development Journal* (October 1992): 31–35.

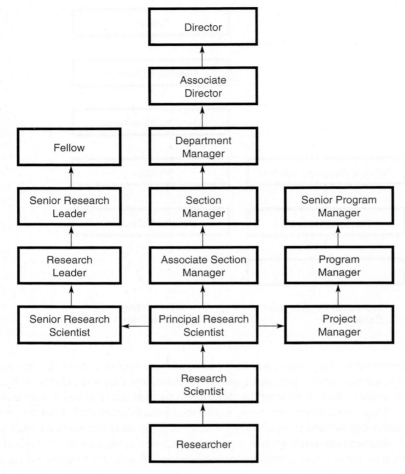

- The individual contributor career path is not used to satisfy poor performers who have no managerial potential. The career path is for employees with outstanding technical skills.
- Individual contributors are given the opportunity to choose their career path. The company provides assessment resources (such as psychological tests and developmental feedback, as discussed in Chapters Nine and Eleven). Assessment information enables employees to see how similar their interests, work values, and skill strengths are to those of employees in technical and managerial positions.

# CAREER RECYCLING

**Recycling** involves changing one's major work activity after having been established in a specific field. Recycling is accompanied by a re-exploration of values, skills, interests, and potential employment opportunities. For example, the global entertainment company Cirque du Soleil has a career transition program that helps artistic staff plan for their post-performing years.[80] The program relies on Cirque's expertise of what skills are needed to work backstage in the entertainment business. Cirque can help artists obtain the training they need for careers as fitness coaches, naturopaths, or makeup artists. A corporate manager at General Electric in his mid-50s started a new career and a lifelong dream of becoming a fashion designer as a result of taking early retirement.[81] One woman gave up a five-year career teaching fifth-graders to work with the importer of Zyr Vodka.[82] While on vacation, this woman agreed to help a friend market a new Russian vodka during a business trip to Las Vegas. The work was very different from what she had been doing, but she found the work interesting and exciting. After the trip, her friend asked her to join the company as vice president. The job did not offer the woman the same security as the teaching job, and she would be taking a pay cut as well. Despite those negative aspects of the job, however, she accepted the position and has been working hard to build the brand by meeting with restaurant owners, liquor distributors, and club owners. She finds that working for a small distributor gives her a sense of ownership in the success (or failure) of the business. Also, she enjoys being accountable for all her decisions.

Recycling is not just limited to older employees who are nearing retirement. Many companies that face a serious shortage of qualified employees are developing retraining programs in hopes of filling labor shortages with employees from other fields.[83] Companies are using these training programs to help recycle employees into new jobs and careers. For example, in the IT field, companies face a shortage of qualified staff for internal help desks and customer service. Also, many persons with computer skills who seek these positions lack the interpersonal skills needed to give counsel and advice to users of software, databases, and company intranets. The computer consulting industry is training former stockbrokers, flight attendants, and bank tellers to work at help desks. These training programs are referred to as "boot camps" because the training emphasizes total immersion in the job, one-on-one supervision, and cramming into a short training program what knowledge and skills the employee needs to have.

It is also not uncommon for employees who are considering recycling to conduct **informational interviews** with managers or other employees who hold jobs in functional areas that they believe may be congruent with their interests and abilities, to gather information about the skills, job demands, and benefits of their jobs. For example, a 30-year-old manager at Intel Corporation was unhappy with her job as a consumer marketing manager.[84] To find new job opportunities, she conducted informational interviews with managers and had discussions with colleagues at work. She also researched different departments, such as corporate communications, and searched Intel's intranet for job information. Because she was interested in education, she also looked outside Intel for opportunities at universities, educational software firms, and toy companies. She found a job as a program marketing manager with Intel's worldwide education group.

## Job Hopping

**Job hopping** refers to employees changing jobs, usually between companies, every two to three years. Job hopping is prevalent today, especially among Gen Xers and millennials, as more employees view themselves as "free agents" who must actively manage their own careers. It is estimated that employees in all age groups are staying at jobs for a shorter period of time compared to the 1980s. They recognize that they have a protean career, which means they to take responsibility for their own careers because companies may lay them off if business declines or changes in the business strategy make them expendable. Loyalty does not guarantee job security. Employees recognize that their employability and economic well-being depends on their personal growth and pay, and as a result, they will leave for another job offer if the company offers more learning opportunities or better compensation.[85] Although job hopping was once considered damaging to an employee's career, today, companies are more used to the practice. This is especially true in high-technology industries, where talented employees are in demand and new start-ups offer stock options that can result in substantial financial gains if the company grows.

Is job hopping good for companies and employees? There are advantages and disadvantages to it, for both employees and companies.[86] For companies, job hopping results in a loss of talent and productivity that results from turnover, retraining, and recruitment costs. Also, job hopping makes it difficult to create and sustain a culture that supports relationships between employees or continuity in employee-customer relationships. Job hopping does provide companies with the opportunity to hire employees who have a variety of experiences in different companies, which can allow the company to understand and implement best practices. Hiring employees who job hop may increase company's flexibility and adaptability because these employees are capable of quickly learning different jobs. Also, employees who job hop likely do not need or have high expectations for job security, making it easier for the company to downsize if necessary. For employees, in addition to better pay and growth opportunities, job hopping can provide opportunities to work in a variety of industries, in different-sized companies, and to gain new skills, experiences, and personal contacts. The downside of job hopping for employees is that they may not be staying in any one job long enough to complete important projects, develop personal networks, or gain relevant experiences. This may hurt their opportunity to obtain attractive job and career opportunities in the future.

Companies are unlikely to eliminate job hopping. However, companies can reduce job hopping and attract and retain talented employees by creating conditions for employee engagement, providing employees with growth opportunities, and offering incentives and rewards for good performance.

# COPING WITH CAREER BREAKS

Both men and women face major problems in trying to return to work after taking several months or years off for family-related or other reasons.[87] This is especially the case for returning troops from Iraq and Afghanistan, who often have difficulty returning to their jobs and finding employment. The unemployment rate for veterans tends to be higher than the rate for the overall labor force, with the unemployment rate for those ages 22 to 24 more than three times as high as for non-veterans of the same age.[88] Returning troops face many obstacles to finding employment or returning to their jobs, including lack of experience in the workplace, incomplete skill sets and education credentials, difficulty to work in less structured situations without clear-cut guidelines and expectations, and psychological and physical challenges. But veterans are known to have many characteristics and skills that are valuable for employers including attention to detail, self-discipline, problem solving, decision-making in stressful situations, and teamwork.

Both the federal government and companies are involved in helping veterans return to work or find new jobs.[89] The **Uniformed Services Employment and Reemployment Act** covers deployed employees' rights, such as guaranteeing jobs when they return except under certain circumstances. However, the job a service member returns to may be different from the one he or she left, and it could require new skills or be in a different location. Also, veterans who return to work have to prove themselves all over again, and some may have received disabling physical or psychological injuries from their military service. At Booz Allen Hamilton, about 28 percent of its employees have a military background. The company recruits veterans, makes accommodations based on their physical needs, works with organizations that help them transition between military and civilian life, and offers them onboarding programs and mentoring. Aon, an insurance and consulting company, offers a peer mentoring program that matches veterans with managers who can help them address their job skills and knowledge needs. Aon has worked with other companies and the Wounded Warrior Project to identify disabled veterans who need help. They have provided training for job interviews and networking and resume development. American Electric Power, one of the largest electric utilities in the United States, is one of four U.S. electric companies participating in the Troops to Energy Jobs program. The Troops to Energy Jobs Program, developed under CEWD, provides training in community and technical colleges and four-year universities to help veterans complete and finish their education in order to complement their current skill sets. The program helps veterans get placed in internships and permanent jobs, including engineering, security, line workers, and technicians. The United Association of Plumbers, Pipefitters, and Sprinkler Fitters partnered with the U.S. military to create a program that provides veterans with two weeks of transitional training to help them adjust to civilian life, followed by sixteen weeks of accelerated technical training in topics such as welding, piping, and heating and ventilation, and then a four-year apprenticeship. Veterans are paid during the training and apprenticeship and are guaranteed employment when they complete the program.

In general, women are more likely than men to leave jobs for family reasons. Women trying to return to work often find that their skills and knowledge are out of date and that they have lost their professional network. Because of the need to retain skilled employees in the areas of accounting, finance, and consulting, many companies are helping women cope during their family leave by offering special work arrangements, such as small project work, training, and mentoring.[90] Booz Allen Hamilton provides small work contracts that can be done at home. The contracts include proposal writing, idea development, and client contact.

## COPING WITH JOB LOSS

Coping with job loss is a major career issue because of the increased use of downsizing to deal with excess staff resulting from corporate restructurings, mergers, acquisitions, and takeovers. Research suggests that layoffs do not result in improved profits, they have mixed effects on productivity, and they have adverse effects on the morale, workload, and commitment of employees who remain with the company.[91] Job loss also causes stress and disrupts the personal lives of laid-off employees.[92] Because of the potential damaging effects of downsizing, companies should first seek alternative ways to reduce head count (the number of employees) and lower labor costs. These alternatives may include asking employees to work fewer hours, offering early retirement plans, delaying wage increases, and deciding not to fill position openings created by turnover and retirements. However, job loss may be inevitable in the case of mergers or acquisitions (which may create redundant positions and an excess of employees with similar skills) or downturns in business that force the company to reduce labor costs by eliminating employees in order to survive.

Job loss is especially traumatic for older workers. They may find it difficult to find a job because of their age. For example, a sixty-two year old middle manager who had been making $65,000 a year was laid off from his job at Boston Mutual Life Insurance Company.[93] He and his wife are down to their last $2,500 after using up all his unemployment benefits. He now finds himself standing on a street corner with a sign that says "I need a job . . . 36 yrs exper; Insur/mngmnt" and includes his phone number. He has no pension, and he cannot live on the $1,200 per month that Social Security would pay.

Pillowtex Corporation, a North Carolina–based textile company, recently laid off 5,500 employees.[94] One of them was Ruth Jones, an 83-year-old employee with over 50 years of service at Pillowtex, and she doesn't know how she will meet her expenses. She gets unemployment benefits and Social Security benefits, but because the company is bankrupt, she is unlikely to get severance pay from Pillowtex. She does get two small pensions from two companies that preceded Pillowtex (Cannon Mills and Fieldcrest Cannon), and her home is paid off. She plans to seek other jobs at the local grocery store or the gas station.

From a career management standpoint, companies and managers have two major responsibilities. First, they are responsible for helping employees who will lose their jobs. Second, steps must be taken to ensure that the "survivors" of the layoff (the remaining employees) remain productive and committed to the organization.

To prepare employees for layoffs and reduce their potential negative effects, companies need to provide outplacement services. Outplacement services should include:[95]

- Advance warning and an explanation for the layoff
- Psychological, financial, and career counseling
- Assessment of skills and interests
- Job seeking services, such as résumé-writing assistance and interview training
- Job banks where job leads are posted and where out-of-town newspapers, phones, and books regarding different occupations and geographic areas are available
- Electronic delivery of job openings, self-directed career management guides, and values and interest inventories

Some companies provide training and education to assist outplaced employees. Ford Motor Company closed several of its North American factories and cut more than 34,000 jobs.[96] Ford offered its Educational Opportunity Program to laid-off workers at these factories. Under the program, Ford paid as much as $15,000 per year in tuition for UAW members who go to school full time to earn a degree, certificate, or license. Employees received half their usual hourly salary plus medical benefits. Boeing, the aircraft manufacturer in Washington, worked with Washington State and local business and government officials to offer a small business training program to outplaced employees.[97] Selection for the program—which involved classes, reviews of business plans, and consultation—was rigorous. Applicants had to have a viable business idea, identify competitors and customers, and indicate how they would support themselves until the business made a profit. Laid-off workers started such businesses as restaurants, bookstores, and accounting offices. Besides helping former employees, the program allowed Boeing to hold down its unemployment insurance contributions and improve its image in the community.

Many laid-off workers, frustrated by long job searches and craving independence, have started their own businesses despite high odds against success.[98] For example, when Michele Free, a technical writer, was laid off and unable to find a job, she started an online literary agency. Her agency helps writers find publishers. She has nine clients on contract and has sold a fantasy trilogy and a Civil War history book. Free is much happier, although to make ends meet, she has had to sell food grown on her property and cash in stock that she received from her last job.

Typically, companies devote more resources to outplacing employees who have lost their jobs than to employees who remain. Employees in upper-level managerial and professional positions typically receive more personalized outplacement services (e.g., office space, a private secretary, etc.) than do lower-level employees.[99] Although losing a job causes grief and denial in employees, once employees have worked through their emotions, they are capable of carrying on a campaign to find a new job. Laid-off employees are certain of their future, in that they know that they need to seek alternative employment. However, for the **survivors** (employees who remain with the company following a downsizing), uncertainty about their future remains. Survivors feel some sense of gratification because they have kept their jobs. However, they do not know how safe their current job is, nor do they know in what direction the company is heading. Also, in many cases, survivors are expected to perform the work of the laid-off employees as well as their own. As a result, survivors experience considerable anxiety, anger toward top-level managers, cynicism toward reorganization and new business plans, resentment, and resignation.[100]

Survivors are more likely to view layoffs as fair if employees are asked to cut costs to avoid layoffs, if the factors used to decide whom to lay off (e.g., performance, seniority, etc.) are applied equally to individual contributors and management employees, if advance notice is provided, and if clear and adequate explanations are given for the layoffs.[101] Survivors need to be trained to deal with increased workloads and job responsibilities due to the consolidation and loss of jobs. The company also needs to provide survivors with realistic information about their future with the company.

## MEETING THE NEEDS OF OLDER WORKERS

A survey of 150 Fortune 500 companies found that one-third expect some of their executives to leave within the next five years, and the companies lack confidence that they will be able to find talented people to replace them.[102] As was discussed in Chapter One, this shortage of talented employees goes beyond the managerial ranks. Because of the shortage of skilled and experienced employees in many industries, companies are likely to try to keep talented older employees working. Also, many potential retirees plan to cut back on work but not completely quit working. The AARP/Roper Report has found that 80 percent of baby boomers plan to work at least part time during their retirement.[103] This is due to both personal preferences and economic reasons. Because of the stock market plunge and the decrease in home values, many recent retirees are finding themselves low on money and looking to reenter the workforce. For example, a 71-year-old retiree who gave up a long career in the defense industry and retired in Tucson, Arizona, is looking for work at local hardware stores and considering filing for bankruptcy.[104] To meet the needs of older workers and to avoid skill shortages, companies are offering alternative work schedules and arrangements, including part-time work, rehiring of retirees, and phased retirement programs in which employees gradually reduce their work hours.

When are employees considered "older" employees? As discussed earlier in the chapter, the ADEA begins protecting employees at age 40. This includes denying access for training programs and forcing employees to retire (without a legitimate reason) who are covered by the act. Mandatory retirement ages vary according to occupation; for air traffic controllers, it is 56, for pilots, it is 65, and for federal law enforcement officers, it is 57. Professional football players and other professional athletes are considered "old" at age 30. Older employees do not have higher absenteeism rates and are not more likely to put less effort into work as they approach retirement. However, they do require more help in learning new technology and prefer hands-on practice during training.[105] Older employees are as productive and customer-savvy as younger employees, and they have valuable experience.

Companies can take several actions to meet the needs of older employees. First, flexibility in scheduling allows older employees to take care of sick spouses, go back to school, travel, or work fewer hours. CVS Caremark learned that many customers prefer to discuss their health issues with an older, more experienced pharmacist. As a result, to retain older pharmacists, Caremark has a program that allows them to work in the northern U.S. states in the summer and in the warmer, southern states in the winter.[106] Southern Company, an electric utility, found that many of its employees were planning to retire in the next five to ten years but were also interested in coming back to work on a part-time basis. The company created a "retired reservists pool" consisting of retired employees who can be called back during hurricanes and other emergencies to train new employees and to staff short-term projects.[107] Second, research suggests that the probability of receiving company-sponsored training peaks at age 40 and declines as an employee's age increases.[108] Companies need to ensure that older employees receive the training that they need to avoid obsolescence and to be prepared to use new technology. Third, older employees need resources and referral help that address long-term health care and elder care. Fourth, assessment and counseling are necessary to help older employees recycle to new jobs or careers, or transition to less secure positions whose responsibilities are not as clearly defined. Fifth, it is important to recognize that as older employees' physical and mental abilities decline, they can rely on experience and motivation to avoid poor performance. Companies should consider moving valuable older employees who are suffering skill deterioration to other jobs. Bon SecoursHealth System in Richmond, Virginia, credits the company's success to its older employees. Because 30 percent of Bon Secours's employees are over 50, the company tries to accommodate them. For example, a licensed practical nurse at Bon Secours found the physical aspects of her job (walking, lifting, and helping patients to stand up) too demanding. In response, the company moved her to the employee wellness program, where she gives innoculations and performs less strenuous duties.[109] Finally, companies need to ensure that employees do not hold inappropriate stereotypes about older employees (e.g., that they fear new technology or cannot learn new skills).

## Preretirement Socialization

**Preretirement socialization** is the process of helping employees prepare to exit from work. It encourages employees to learn about retirement life; plan for adequate financial, housing, and health care resources; and form accurate expectations about retirement. Employees' satisfaction with life after retirement is influenced by their health, their feelings about their jobs, and their level of optimism. Employees who attend preretirement socialization programs have fewer financial and psychological problems and experience greater satisfaction with retirement compared to employees who do not attend these programs. These programs typically address the following topics:[110]

- Psychological aspects of retirement, such as developing personal interests and activities
- Housing, including a consideration of transportation, living costs, and proximity to medical care
- Health during retirement, including nutrition and exercise
- Financial planning, insurance, and investments
- Health care plans
- Estate planning
- The collection of benefits from company pension plans and Social Security

Preretirement socialization or retirement planning can help employees avoid being forced to return to work because of poor financial planning. For example, a 58-year-old retiree took an early retirement package from GTE, the telecommunications company.[111] He accepted a buyout from GTE after its merger talks with Bell Atlantic. Stock market losses and his decision to withdraw $2,000 from his retirement account each month have made it necessary for him to seek employment again. He now works for $10.50 an hour at a car dealership chain, loading and delivering car parts. After paying his bills, he is able to save $100 per week in a savings account. He is considering retirement again at age 60, when he will begin collecting his military pension. But the turbulence in the stock market and rising health insurance expenses (which have increased between $150 and $450 per quarter) may make it difficult for him to retire until he reaches age 62, when he can collect Medicare and Social Security benefits.

Many companies are also using phased retirement and alternative work arrangements such as rehiring retired employees to help employees make the transition into retirement while at the same time continuing to use their talents. **Phased retirement** involves employees transitioning from full-time employment to full-time retirement by working part time. Phased retirement can benefit both companies and their employees. It can help companies cope with the shortages of skilled employees in the labor market. It provides a source of income for employees who have seen the value of their retirement funds decrease during the economic recession. There are several different passed retirement plans. An employee can retire and return as an independent contractor, consultant, or part-time worker. The use of phased retirement plans is complicated by regulations regarding taxation of retirement benefits and concerns about continued health care coverage (e.g., there is no legal definition of phased retirement, and the tax code has few regulations for how to offer phased retirement within a defined retirement benefits plan). Consider the programs that several companies are offering to capitalize on older employees' skills and accommodate their needs.[112] At Stanley Consultants, an engineering, environmental, and construction services consulting firm, retirees are often hired for project work that matches their backgrounds and the company's skill needs. Another method is to allow employees to phase into retirement by reducing their work hours. SC Johnson offers retirees temporary work assignments, consulting and contract work, telecommuting, and part-time work. Centegra Health System's phased retirement program offers flexible scheduling, including part-time work, compressed workweeks, job sharing, summers off, and long-distance contract work. L.L. Bean allows employees to trade, take on, or give away work shifts, and volunteer to stay late or leave early.

Formal preretirement socialization programs are primarily for employees who are considering retirement, but financial planning, estate planning, and purchasing insurance need to be done much earlier in their careers to ensure that employees will have the financial resources necessary to live comfortably during retirement.

## Retirement

**Retirement** involves leaving a job and a work role and making a transition into life without work. For some employees, retirement involves making a transition out of their current job and company, seeking full- or part-time employment elsewhere, or recycling into another career.

By 2018, almost one out of four employees of the U.S. labor force will be over 55 years old. Recent changes in the Social Security system have led to no mandatory retirement age for most jobs, and financial needs suggest that employees may elect to work longer for whatever reason.[113] The oldest members of the baby boom generation should be retiring soon because they are reaching age 62, the earliest age for collecting Social Security benefits.[114] However, many employees are postponing retirement because of economic reasons, including the shrinking value of investment portfolios, falling housing prices, and the reduction or loss of health care benefits upon retirement. For example, a 63-year-old project manager was laid off from a company that makes medical devices and has been looking for part-time work as a grant writer in a nonprofit organization. He recently shifted his job search to full-time employment after realizing that his 401(k) retirement account had lost 16 percent of its value, translating into a loss of four years of retirement income.[115] A couple who recently retired from SAP AG, the German software company, thought they had done a good job of planning for their financial needs during retirement. However, the husband of the couple is now interviewing for a new full-time job because declines in the stock market have resulted in substantial declines in the available assets that they expected to live on during retirement. Although delayed retirement is disappointing for employees, it is potentially good news for many companies, particularly those in knowledge-based industries, which are predicted to suffer from retirements due to the loss of experienced, expert employees.

Despite the need for employees to work longer because of economic reasons, historically over half of all employees retire before age 63, and 80 percent leave by the time they are 70. This may be because employees accept companies' offers of early retirement packages, which usually include generous financial benefits. Also, employees may find work less satisfying and be interested in pursuing primarily non-work activities as a source of satisfaction.

The aging workforce and the use of early retirement programs (discussed next) to shrink companies' workforces have three implications. First, companies must meet the needs of older employees. Second, companies must take steps to prepare employees for retirement. Third, companies must be careful that early retirement programs do not unfairly discriminate against older employees.

## Early Retirement Programs

**Early retirement programs** offer employees financial benefits to leave the company. These programs are usually part of the company's strategy to reduce labor costs without having to lay off employees. Financial benefits usually include a lump sum of money and a percentage of salary based on years of service. These benefits can be quite attractive to employees, particularly those with long tenure with the company. Eligibility for early retirement is usually based on age and years of service. Ford offered its workers several different early retirement programs, including a special retirement incentive in which employees with thirty years of service or more receive $35,000 to retire with full retiree benefits. Workers 55 years or older with at least ten years on the job can leave and receive lifetime retiree benefits, and in another plan, workers with twenty-eight years of service can leave and receive 85 percent of their pay until they reach the thirty-year anniversary of their hiring.[116]

Early retirement programs have two major problems. First, employees who may be difficult to replace may elect to leave the company. Second, older employees may believe that early retirement programs are discriminatory because they feel they are being forced to retire. To avoid costly litigation, companies need to make sure that their early retirement programs contain the following features:[117]

- The program is part of the employee benefit plan.
- The company can justify age-related distinctions for eligibility for early retirement.
- Employees are allowed to choose early retirement voluntarily.

Eligibility requirements should not be based on stereotypes about ability and skill decrements that occur with age. Research suggests that age-related declines in specific abilities and skills have little effect on job performance.[118] Employees' decisions are considered voluntary if they can refuse to participate, if they are given complete information about the plan, and if they receive a reasonable amount of time to make their decisions.

Training plays an important role in early retirement programs. Companies teach employees to understand the financial implications of early retirement. Training programs are also used to help employees understand when and in what forms health benefits and retirement savings can be received. For example, retirement savings can often be distributed to retirees either as a one-time lump sum of money or as a payout of a specific amount of money each month, quarter, or year.

---

## Summary

Public and privately-held companies are in business to create financial returns. But they also have a social responsibility to improve the communities where they are located by helping to reduce poverty and unemployment, comply with laws and regulations, and help all employees contribute to company goals by helping them grow, develop, and address their career challenges. This directly benefits the local community and the workforce, but it also enhances the company's reputation, which helps attract, motivate, and retain talented employees. Through partnerships with government agencies, trade groups, labor unions, and foundations, a company's training and development function can develop the skills of the labor force to improve their employability and attract jobs to the local community. Also, being socially responsible means that training and development practices are accessible to all employees, they are treated appropriately during training activities, and copyright laws are followed (i.e., credit is given and payment is provided for materials used in courses). Today's workforce is not only diverse in race, gender, and national origin, but it is also multigenerational. To fully capitalize on the competitive advantage of diversity and meet social responsibility goals, companies need to proactively manage diversity and inclusion. This means going beyond diversity training to ensure that top management support diversity, managers are held accountable for diversity goals, employees are supported, and recruitment, hiring, and development are focused on identifying and nurturing the talent of all employees. Finally, company's need to help employees manage career challenges to increase their engagement, productivity, and reduce stress. The chapter discusses these challenges and the types of policies and programs that can help employees cope with them. The career challenges include balancing work and life, career breaks, coping with job loss, job hopping, recycling careers, and retirement.

## Key Terms

sector partnerships, *422*
School-to-Work Opportunities Act, *424*
Workforce Investment Act of 1998, *424*
Lifelong Learning Account (LiLa), *425*
joint union-management training programs, *426*
copyrights, *428*
Title VII, *429*
Age Discrimination in Employment Act (ADEA), *429*
Americans with Disabilities Act (ADA), *430*
reasonable accommodation, *431*
inclusion, *432*

diversity training, *432*
managing diversity and inclusion, *432*
glass ceiling, *435*
expatriates, *437*
preparation, *438*
repatriation, *440*
cross-cultural virtual expatriate, *441*
work-life balance, *443*
telecommuting, *443*
Family and Medical Leave Act (FMLA), *443*
compressed workweek, *444*
flextime, *444*
job sharing, *445*
career path, *445*

dual-career-path system, *447*
recycling, *448*
informational interviews, *449*
job hopping, *449*
Uniformed Services Employment and Reemployment Rights Act, *450*
survivors, *453*
preretirement socialization, *454*
phased retirement, *455*
retirement, *456*
early retirement programs, *457*

## Discussion Questions

1. What is a sector partnership? Why is it important? Provide an example of a sector partnership.
2. What are some of the potential legal issues that a trainer should consider while planning an adventure learning program?
3. Explain the relationship between "managing diversity and inclusion" and "diversity training." Which is most effective? Why?
4. How would you prepare a team of three managers to go to Warsaw, Poland, to oversee the operations of a recently acquired financial services firm? They will be leaving in one month, and the assignment lasts two years.

5. What should companies do to develop talented women to take top management positions? Provide support for your recommendations.

6. How are career paths useful for employees? How can they contribute to company effectiveness?

7. What is job hopping? Which career challenges might a company focus on to reduce job hopping?

8. What advantages and disadvantages might a company gain by using phased retirement?

9. What are work-life programs? How are they related to work-family programs? What are some of the challenges in developing and using work-life programs?

10. How could you help the survivors of a downsizing remain motivated and productive? Which of your recommendations is most important? Explain why.

## Application Assignments

1. Go to www.wholefoods.com, the website for Whole Foods. At the bottom of the page, click on "Careers FAQ" under "Careers." Review the discussion under "Career Paths" and "Training and Development." What is a career path? How do you think career paths help Whole Foods? Whole Foods employees? Should there be a relationship between training and development activities and career paths? Why?

2. Go to www.sodexousa.com, the website for Sodexo. Click on "Careers," then click on "Annual Diversity Report." Review the Annual Diversity Report. Why is managing diversity important to Sodexo? What are the strengths and weaknesses of Sodexo's approach for managing diversity? What role does learning, training, and development play in managing diversity at Sodexo?

3. Go to www.workingmother.com, the website for *Working Mother* magazine. Review any five of the "2011 Working Mother Best Companies." What practices do they use to help employees balance work-life and work-family? What types of outcomes or metrics would you collect to see if these practices were effective?

4. Go to http://fairuse.stanford.edu, a website called Copyright and Fair Use created by Stanford Universities library system How does work fall in the public domain? That is, how can you use someone else's work without having to obtain permission to use it?

5. Go to www.hp.com, the website for Hewlett-Packard (HP). Click on "About Us," then "Corporate Objectives." Next, in the drop-down menu for "More," click on "Diversity and Inclusion." Find the diversity value chain. Explain the evolution of thinking about how to manage a diverse workforce shown in the diversity value chain.

6. Go to www.wolfatbestbuy.com, the website for Best Buy's Women's Leadership Forum. Review "About Wolf" and "Talent Readiness Program." What are WOLF and the Talent Readiness Program? How does it contribute to Best Buy's efforts to manage diversity and inclusion and melting the glass ceiling?

7. Go to www.aep.com, the website for American Electric Power. Click on "Careers," then click on "A Military-Friendly Employer." Download and read the brochure for "Troops to Energy" jobs. What are the steps that an interested veteran would take to get started in the program? Explain why each of the steps is important from a career or developmental perspective.

8. Go to www.youtube.com, and search for "World Manufacturing Academy." Watch the video *Chrysler World Class Manufacturing Academy Feature.* What is the purpose of the Academy? What type of training is used? What are the learning advantages of the training shown in the video compared to classroom instruction?

---

# Case: *Successful Management Requires International Experience*

As companies become more global, economic patterns and business practices in one area of the world can determine the success of a company on the other side of the world. At P&G, being a successful global leader requires an international background. A majority of P&G's 140,000 employees work outside the United States. P&G uses international assignments for employees to learn how business is conducted in another country so that lessons learned there can be applied at home or in another region. Only a quarter of relocations originate in the United States; the majority are from place to place across the world. An important goal of employees who receive international assignments is to develop local talent to replace themselves.

For example, a manager who is being prepared to take over a top finance position in Russia might go to Britain to gain experience working in a more structured and complex market. P&G managers in Europe must learn to keep the company's products on big-box-store shelves such as Carrefour, the European supermarket and discount chain and one of the largest retailers in the world. P&G might send junior U.S. managers to work with European managers who are responsible for products at Carrefour, expecting that they will transfer skills learned in these assignments to dealing with product placement in big-box retailers such as Walmart and Costco. As the economies of Poland, Hungry, and the Czech Republic continue to develop their economies may become similar to those of Britain and Germany. Providing managers experiences in Western Europe would be useful for transferring the knowledge to jobs in Eastern Europe.

*What steps should P&G take to prepare employees for international assignments to help them succeed? Should P&G also include spouses and family members in preparation for international assignments? Why or why not?*

**Source:** Based on M. Schoeff, "P&G places a premium on international experience," *Workforce Management* (April 10, 2006): 28.

## Endnotes

1. J. Kogel, "O captain! My captain! I know not how to build an app for that," *Workforce Management* (July 2011): 3–4.

2. "Workforce readiness programs prepare future workforce," *T+D* (December 2010): 23; www.cewd.org, the website for Center for Energy Workforce Development; www.jobcorps.gov, the website for Job Corps.

3. Ibid.

4. M. Weinstein, "Homeless but hopeful," *training*, March/April 2010, 22–26; www.unleashyourace.com, the website for Frank Kelley; L. Germinsky, "Back to Life, One Man at A Time" from http://blog.tonic.com/project-vacant-streets, August 20, 2009.

4a. C. Hymowitz, "Executives teach inmates how to be employees," *The Wall Street Journal* (March 17, 2008): B1, B3.

5. D. Stamps, "Will school-to-work transition work?" *training* (June 1996): 72–81.

6. J. Dresang, "Factory workers' new skills help lure business," *Columbus Dispatch* (August 24, 2008): D3.

7. See http//online.onetcenter.org/. the website for the Occupational Information Network (O*NET), U.S. Department of Labor, accessed June 27, 2012.

8. "Larson introduces Lifelong Learning Accounts Act" (July 14, 2010), from http//BigNews.biz, a press release and news distribution service, accessed February 13, 2012.

9. S. Ladika, "When learning lasts a lifetime," *HR Magazine* (May 2008): 56–60.

10. M. Hequet, "The union push for lifelong learning," *Training* (March 1994): 26–31; S. J. Schurman, M. K. Hugentoble, and H. Stack, "Lessons from the UAW-GM Paid Education Leave Program," in *Joint Training Programs,* ed. L. A. Ferman et al. (Ithaca, NY: ILR Press, 1991): 71–94. See also www.nactel.org, the website for the National Coalition for Telecommunications Education and Learning (accessed February 12, 2012).

11. See www.nactel.org, the website for the National Coalition for Telecommunications Education and Learning (accessed February 12, 2012).

12. "Chrysler Group LLC opens state-of-the-art world class manufacturing academy in Warren, Michigan," PR Newswire, accessed February 1, 2012; B. Snavely, "High-tech retraining," *Columbus Dispatch* (February 4, 2012): A1 and A9.

13. J. Sample, *Avoiding Legal Liability for Adult Educators, Human Resource Developers, and Instructional Designers* (Malabar, FL: Krieger Publishing, 2007); A. Cardy, "The legal framework of human resource development: Overview mandates, structures, and financial implications," *Human Resource Development Review* 2 (2003): 26–53; A. Cardy, "The legal framework of human resource development, Part II: Fair employment, negligence, and implications for scholars and practitioners," *Human Resource Development Review* 2 (2003): 130–154; A. Cardy, "Reputation, goodwill, and loss: Entering the employee training audit question,"*Human Resource Development Review* (September 2005): 279–304.

14. W. Turner and C. Thrutchley, "Employment Law and Practices Training: No Longer the Exception—It's the Rule," in *Legal Report* (Alexandria, VA: Society for Human Resources Management, July–August 2003): 1–4.

15. A. Pasztor and S. Carey, "Rescue renews focus on training," *The Wall Street Journal* (January 17–18, 2009): A3.

16. From www.faa.gov, "FAA Industry Training Standards" (accessed February 12, 2012).

17. D. Zielinski, "A closer look," *Training* (November 2005): 16–22.

18. G. Kimmerling, "A licensing primer for trainers," *Training and Development* (January 1997): 30–35; M. Partridge, "Copyrights and wrongs," *HR Magazine* (November 2008): 101–104.

19. R. Ganzel, "Copyright or copywrong?" *Training* (2002): 36–44.

20. U.S. Department of Labor, *A Report on the Glass Ceiling Initiative* (Washington, D.C.: U.S. Government Printing Office, 1991); C. Petrini, "Raising the ceiling for women," *Training and Development* (November 1995): 12.

21. T. Maurer and N. Rafuse, "Learning, not litigating: Managing employee development and avoiding claims of age discrimination," *Academy of Management Executive* 15 (2001): 110–121.

22. "University of Phoenix to Pay $1,875,000 for Religious Bias Against Non-Mormons," November 10, 2008, press release from www.eeoc.gov, the website for the Equal Employment Opportunity Commission (EEOC).

23. "EEOC Brings Class Lawsuit Against New Prime Trucking for Sex Discrimination," September 22, 2011, press release from www.eeoc.gov, accessed February 12, 2012.

24. R. Sharpe, "In whose hands? Allstate and Scientology," *The Wall Street Journal* (March 22, 1995): A1, A4.

25. Bureau of National Affairs, "Female grocery store employees prevail in sex-bias suit against Lucky Stores," *BNAs Employee Relations Weekly* 10 (1992): 927–938; *Stender v. Lucky Store Inc.,* DCN California, No. C-88-1467, 8/18/92.

26. J. Sample and R. Hylton, "Falling off a log—and landing in court," *Training* (May 1996): 67–69.

27. H. Dolezalek, "The path to inclusion," *Training,* May 2008, 52–54.

28. E. McKeown, "Quantifiable inclusion strategies," *T+D,* October 2010, 16.

29. S. E. Jackson et al., *Diversity in the Workplace: Human Resource Initiatives* (New York: Guilford Press, 1992).

30. S. Rynes and B. Rosen, "A field study of factors affecting the adoption and perceived success of diversity training," *Personnel Psychology* 48 (1995): 247–270; N. Aparna, "Why diversity training doesn't work . . . right now," *T+D,* November 2008, 52–57.

31. For example, see P. McKay, D. Avery, and M. Morris, "A tale of two climates: Diversity climate from subordinates' and managers' perspectives and their role in store unit sales performance," *Personnel Psychology,* 62 (2009): 767–791; M. Triana, M. Garcia, and A. Colella, "Managing diversity: How organizational efforts to support diversity moderate the effects of perceived racial discrimination on affective commitment," *Personnel Psychology* 63 (2010): 817–844.

32. T. Kochan et al., "The effects of diversity on business performance: Report of the Diversity Research Network," *Human Resource Management* 42 (2003): 8–21; F. Hansen, "Diversity's business case just doesn't add up," *Workforce*, June 2003, 29–32; M. J. Wesson and C. I. Gogus, "Shaking hands with the computer: An examination of two methods of newcomer socialization," *Journal of Applied Psychology* 90 (2005), 1018–1026; H. J. Klein and N. A. Weaver, "The effectiveness of an organizational-level orientation training program in the socialization of new hires," *Personnel Psychology* 53 (2000): 47–66.

33. R. Anand and M. Winters, "A retrospective view of corporate diversity training from 1964 to the present," *Academy of Management Learning and Education,* 7 (2008), 356–372; H. Dolezalek, "The path to inclusion," *Training,* May 2008, 52–54; "Sodexo 2010 Diversity and Inclusion Annual Report," available at www.sodexousa.com, the website for Sodexo USA, accessed June 20, 2011.

34. K. Bezrvkova, K. Jehn, & C. Spell, "Reviewing diversity training: Where we have been and where we should go", Academy of Management Learning and Education 11 (2012)207–227; C. T. Schreiber, K. F. Price, and A. Morrison, "Workforce diversity and the glass ceiling: Practices, barriers, possibilities," *Human Resource Planning* 16 (1994): 51–69.

34a. L. Kwoh, "Firms hail new chiefs (of diversity)," *The Wall Street Journal* (January 5, 2012): B10.

35. "Most Employers Lacking a Strategy for Developing Women Leaders," press release from October 25, 2010, at www.mercer.com, the website of Mercer, a global provider of consulting, outsourcing, and investment services; R. Pyrillis, "Programs that help women take the lead," *Workforce Management,* January 2011, 3–4.

36. U.S. Department of Labor, *A Report on the Glass Ceiling Initiative* (Washington, D.C.: U.S. Department of Labor, 1991).

37. P. J. Ohlott, M. N. Ruderman, and C. D. McCauley, "Gender differences in managers' developmental job experiences," *Academy of Management Journal* 37 (1994): 46–67; D. Mattioli, "Programs to promote female managers win citations," *The Wall Street Journal,* January 30, 2007, B7.

38. U.S. Department of Labor, *A Report on the Glass Ceiling Initiative* (Washington, D.C.: U.S. Government Printing Office, 1991); R. A. Noe, "Women and mentoring: A review and research agenda," *Academy of Management Review* 13 (1988): 65–78; B. R. Ragins and J. L. Cotton, "Easier said than done: Gender differences in perceived barriers to gaining a mentor," *Academy of Management Journal* 34 (1991): 939–951.

39. L. A. Mainiero, "Getting anointed for advancement: The case of executive women," *Academy of Management Executive* 8 (1994): 53–67; J. S. Lublin, "Women at top still are distant from CEO jobs," *The Wall Street Journal,* February 28, 1995, B1, B5; P. Tharenov, S. Latimer, and D. Conroy, "How do you make it to the top? An examination of influences on women's and men's managerial advancement," *Academy of Management Journal* 37 (1994): 899–931.

40. P. Tharenou, "Going up? Do traits and informal social processes predict advancement in management?" *Academy of Management Journal* 44 (2001): 1005–1017.

41. R. Pyrillis, "Programs help women take the lead," *Workforce Management* (January 2011): 3–4; Talent Readiness Program at www.wolfatbestbuy.com, accessed September 13, 2011.

42. L. Freifeld, "TEIG locks in on leadership," *Training,* January/February 2011, 34–39.

43. I. Speizer, "Rolling through the downturn," *Workforce Management,* August 11, 2008, 31–37.

44. A. Andors, "Happy returns," *HR Magazine* (March 2010): 61–62.

45. R. L. Tung, "Selection and training of personnel for overseas assignments," *Columbia Journal of World Business* 16 (1981): 18–78.

46. W. A. Arthur Jr. and W. Bennett Jr., "The international assignee: The relative importance of factors perceived to contribute to success," *Personnel Psychology* 48 (1995): 99–114; G. M. Spreitzer, M. W. McCall Jr., and Joan D. Mahoney, "Early identification of international executive potential," *Journal of Applied Psychology* 82 (1997): 6–29.

47. J. S. Black and J. K. Stephens, "The influence of the spouse on American expatriate adjustment and intent to stay in Pacific Rim overseas assignments," *Journal of Management* 15 (1989), 529–544; M. Shaffer and D. A. Harrison, "Forgotten partners of international assignments: Development and test of a model of spouse adjustment," *Journal of Applied Psychology* 86 (2001): 238–254.

48. M. Shaffer et al., "You can take it with you: Individual differences and expatriate effectiveness," *Journal of Applied Psychology* 91 (2006): 109–125; P. Caligiuri, "The big five personality characteristics as predictors of expatriatesesire to terminate the assignment and supervisor-rated performance," *Personnel Psychology* 53 (2000): 67–88.

49. G. Weber, "Intel's internal approach," *Workforce Management* 83 (2004): 49.

50. E. Dunbar and A. Katcher, "Preparing Managers for Foreign Assignments," *Training and Development Journal,* September 1990, 45–47.

51. J. S. Black and M. Mendenhall, "A Practical but Theory-Based Framework for Selecting Cross-Cultural Training Methods," in *Readings and Cases in International Human Resource Management,* ed. M. Mendenhall and G. Oddou (Boston: PWS-Kent, 1991), 177–204.

52. P. Tam, "Culture course," *The Wall Street Journal,* May 25, 2004, B1, B12.

53. "Success is in the details," *T+D* (October 2009): 37–38; D. Zielinski, "Training game," *HR Magazine* (March 2010): 64–66.

54. S. Ronen, "Training the International Assignee," in *Training and Development in Organizations,* ed. I. L. Goldstein (San Francisco: Jossey-Bass, 1989), 417–453.

55. P. R. Harris and R. T. Moran, *Managing Cultural Differences* (Houston: Gulf, 1991).

56. S. Ladika, "Socially evolved," *Workforce Management* (September 2010): 18–22.

57. J. Carter, "Globe trotters," *Training,* August 2005, 22–28.

58. C. Solomon, "Unhappy trails," *Workforce,* August 2000, 36–41.

59. C. Patton, "Coming to America," *Human Resource Executive* (January/February 2012): 22, 26–29.

60. H. Lancaster, "Before going overseas, smart managers plan their homecoming," *The Wall Street Journal,* September 28, 1999, B1; A. Halcrow, "Expats: The squandered resource," *Workforce,* April 1999, 42–48.

61. P. R. Harris and R. T. Moran, *Managing Cultural Differences* (Houston: Gulf, 1991).

62. J. Cook, "Rethinking relocation," *Human Resources Executive,* June 2, 2003, 23–26.

63. J. Flynn, "E-mail, cellphones, and frequent-flier miles let 'virtual' expats work abroad but live at home," *The Wall Street Journal,* October 25, 1999, A26; J. Flynn, "Multinationals help career couples deal with strains affecting expatriates," *The Wall Street Journal,* August 8, 2000, A19; C. Solomon, "The world stops shrinking," *Workforce,* January 2000, 48–51.

64. J. H. Greenhaus, G. Callanan, and V. Godshalk, *Career Management,* 4th ed. (Sage Publications, 2010).

65. L. Chao, "What Gen Xers need to be happy at work," *The Wall Street Journal,* (November 29, 2005): B6; E. Kaplan-Leiserson, "The changing workforce," *T+D* (February 2005): 10–11.

66. S. Hewlett, L. Sherbin, and K. Sumberg, "How Gen Y and boomers will reshape your agenda," *Harvard Business Review*(July–August 2009): 71–76; A. Fox, "Mixing it up," *HR Magazine* (May 2011): 22–27; K. Ball and G. Gotsill, *Surviving the Baby Boomer Exodus* (Boston: Cengage, 2011).

67. *Generational Differences: Myths and Realities* 4 (Alexandria, VA: Society for Human Resource Management, 2007).

68. C. Patton, "On the frontier of flexibility," *Human Resource Executive,* May 2, 2009: 48–51.

69. J. H. Greenhaus and N. Beutell, "Sources of conflict between work and family roles," *Academy of Management Review* 10 (1985): 76–88; J. H. Pleck, *Working Wives/Working Husbands* (Newbury Park, CA: Sage, 1985); R. Kelly and P. Voydanoff, "Work/family role strain among employed parents," *Family Relations,* 34 (1985): 367-374 J. Quick, A. Henley, and J. Quick, "At work and at home," *Organizational Dynamics* 33 (2004): 426–438.

70. Family and Medical Leave Act; from U.S. Department of Labor, Wage and Hour Division website, www.dol.gov/whd/fmla/index.htm, accessed February 14, 2012.

71. W. Casper and M. Butts, *Is There a Business Case for Work-Family Programs*? (Alexandria, VA: SHRM Foundation Research Report).

72. A. Fox, "Achieving integration," *HR Magazine,* April 2011: 42–47.

73. R. Silverman, "For manual jobs, white collar perks," *The Wall Street Journal* (October 3, 2011): B8; M. O'Brien, "Balancing work/life by the hour," *Human Resource Executive* (July/August 2011): 40–42; Families and Work Institute, *2009 Guide to Bold Ideas for Making Work Work,* New York: Families and Work Institute, 2009; S. Shellenberger, "Time-zoned: Working round the clock workforce," *The Wall Street Journal,* February 15, 2007, D1; D. Meinert, "The gift of time," *HR Magazine* (November 2011): 37–41.

74. M. Weinstein, "A minute can win it," *training* (July/August 2011): 28–32.

75. G. Carten, K. Cook, and D. Dorsey, *Career Paths* (Chichester, U.K., 2009); J. Greenhaus, G. Callanan and V. Godshalk, *Career Management,* 4th ed. (Thousand Oaks, CA: SAGE Publications, 2010).

76. R. H. Vaughn and M. C. Wilson, "Career management using job trees: Charting a path through the changing organization," *Human Resource Planning* 17 (1995): 43–55.

77. H. D. Dewirst, "Career Patterns: Mobility, Specialization, and Related Career Issues," in *Contemporary Career Development Issues,* ed. R. F. Morrison and J. Adams (Hillsdale, NJ: Lawrence Erlbaum, 1991): 73–107.

78. M. Weinstein, "Please don't go," *training* (May/June 2011): 28–34.

79. Z. B. Leibowitz, B. L. Kaye, and C. Farren, "Multiple career paths," *Training and Development Journal* (October 1992): 31–35.

80. E. Demby, "Do your family-friendly programs make cents?" *HR Magazine* (January 2004): 74–78.

81. M. Hammers, "A 'family friendly' backlash," *Workforce Management* (August 2003): 77–79.

82. J. Spencer, "Shirk ethic: How to fake a hard day at the office," *The Wall Street Journal* (May 15, 2003): D1, D3.

83. S. Shellenbarger, "Some employees begin to find what helps shiftworker families," *The Wall Street Journal* (September 20, 2000): B1.

84. C. Hymowitz and K. Dunham, "How to get unstuck," *The Wall Street Journal* (March 29, 2004): R1, R4.

85. I. DeBare, "Keeping a bag packed at work: Employees today are more apt to job hop than ever before," *San Francisco Chronicle*, accessed from website for Integral Talent Systems, www.itsinc.net/job-hop.htm on October 7, 2011; M. Korn, "The young are happy at work," *The Wall Street Journal* (October 17, 2011): B7.

86. T. Khadder, "Job-hopping: Career killer or savior?" *Excelle* (June 25, 2009), accessed at http://excelle .monster.com on October 7, 2011; A. Balderrama, "Is job hopping the new normal?," February 2, 2011, accessed at www.azcentral.com on October 7, 2011.

87. A. Chaker and H. Stout, "After years off, women struggle to renew their careers," *The Wall Street Journal* (May 4, 2004): A1, A8; S. Shellenbarger, "Rewriting the rule book on when mothers work," *The Wall Street Journal;* E. Simon, "Smoothing war-to-work shift takes care," *Columbus Dispatch* (October 21, 2007): D3.

88. L. Freifeld, "Warriors to workers," *training* (September/October 2010): 14–18; E. Glazer, "Vets join tough job market," *The Wall Street Journal* (November 21, 2011): B7.

89. S. Greengard, "When Johnny or Janey comes marching home," *Workforce Management* (June 2011): 3–4; Troops to Energy Jobs Program at www.cewd.org, the website for Center for Energy Workforce Development; T. Ridout, "AEP to Attract Military Veterans Through Troops to Energy Jobs Pilot Program," AEP Press Releases, accessed from www.aep.com on July 11, 2011; L. Freifeld, "Warriors to workers," *training* (September/October 2010): 14–18.

90. S. Shellenbarger, "Employers step up efforts to lure stay-at-home mothers back to work," *The Wall Street Journal* (February 9, 2006): D1; A. Chaker and H. Stout, "After years off, women struggle to renew their careers," *The Wall Street Journal* (May 4, 2004): A1, A8.

91. W. Cascio, *Responsible Restructuring: Creative and Profitable Alternatives to Layoffs* (San Francisco: Berrett-Koehler, 2002).

92. J. Brockner, "The Effects of Work Layoffs on Survivors: Research, Theory, and Practice," in *Research in Organizational Behavior,* Vol. 10, ed. B. M. Staw and L. L. Cummings (Hillsdale, NJ: Lawrence Erlbaum, 1988): 45–95; L. Greenhalgh, A. T. Lawrence, and R. I. Sutton, "Determinants of workforce reduction strategies in declining organizations," *Academy of Management Review* 13 (1988): 241–254; J. Nocera, "Living with layoffs," *Fortune* (April 1, 1996): 69–71; J. Martin, "Where are they now?" *Fortune* (April 1, 1996): 100–108.

93. J. Pereira, "A worker's quest for a job lands on a street corner," *The Wall Street Journal* (March 5, 2003): A1, A7.

94. D. Morse, "Older workers in the lurch," *The Wall Street Journal* (August 20, 2003): B1, B10.

95. J. C. Latack and J. B. Dozier, "After the ax falls: Job loss as career transition," *Academy of Management Review* 11 (1986): 375–392; J. Brockner, "Managing the effects of layoffs on survivors," *California Management Review* (Winter 1992): 9–28; S. L. Guinn, "Outplacement programs: Separating myth from reality," *Training and Development Journal* 42 (1988): 48–49; D. R. Simon, "Outplacement: Matching needs, matching services," *Training and Development Journal* 42 (1988): 52–57; S. Rosen and C. Paul, "Learn the inner workings of outplacement," *The Wall Street Journal* (July 31, 1995): editorial page; S. Spera,

a

E. D. Buhrfeind, and J. P. Pennebaker, "Expressive writing and coping with job loss," *Academy of Management Journal* 37 (1994): 722–733.

96. J. McCracken and J. White, "Ford Will Shed 28% of workers in North America," *The Wall Street Journal* (January 24, 2006): A1, A16; J. McCracken, "To shed idled workers, Ford offers to foot the bill for college," *The Wall Street Journal* (January 18, 2006): B1, B3.

97. J. Cole, "Boeing teaches employees how to run small business," *The Wall Street Journal* (November 7, 1995): B1–B2.

98. K. Dunham, "Frustrated laid-off workers take risk of entrepreneurship," *The Wall Street Journal* (July 8, 2003): B10.

99. E. B. Picolino, "Outplacement: The view from HR," *Personnel* (March 1988): 24–27.

100. H. M. O'Neill and D. J. Lenn, "Voices of survivors: Words that downsizing CEOs should hear," *Academy of Management Executive* 9 (1995): 23–34.

101. J. Brockner, "Managing the effects of layoffs on survivors," *California Management Review* (Winter 1992): 9–28; J. Brockner et al., "Interactive effects of procedural justice and outcome negativity on victims and survivors of job loss," *Academy of Management Journal* 37 (1994): 397–409.

102. W. Byham, "Grooming next-millennium leaders," *HR Magazine* (February 1999): 46–53.

103. S. Brown, "Staying ahead of the curve 2003: The AARP Working in Retirement Study," American Association for Retired Persons (September 2003). Available in the "Policy and Research" section of the AARP website at www.aarp.org.; H. Dolezalek, "Boomer reality," *Training* (May 10, 2007): 16–21.

104. H. Green, "The unretired," *BusinessWeek* (December 15, 2008): 46–49.

105. R. Grossman, "Mature workers: Myths and realities," *HR Magazine* (May 2008): 40–41; G. Callahan and J. Greenhaus, "The Baby boomer generation and career management: A call to action," *Advances in Developing Human Resources* 10 (2008): 70–85.

106. C. Leahey, "What–me retire?," *Fortune* (January 16, 2012): 56.

107. K. Greene, "Bye-Bye Boomers," *The Wall Street Journal* (September 20, 2005): B1, B6.

108. C. A. Olson, "Who Receives Formal Firm-Sponsored Training in the U.S.?" October 15, 1996, National Center for the Workplace, Institute of Industrial Relations, University of California (Berkeley). Document at http://violet.lib.berkeley.edu/~ iir/.

109. R. Grossman, "Keep Pace with Older Workers," *HR Magazine* (May 2008): 38-46.

110. A. L. Kamouri and J. C. Cavanaugh, "The impact of preretirement education programs on workers' preretirement socialization," *Journal of Occupational Behavior* 7 (1986): 245–256; N. Schmitt and J. T. McCune, "The relationship between job attitudes and the decision to retire," *Academy of Management Review* 24 (1981): 795–802; N. Schmitt et al., "Comparison of early retirees and non-retirees," *Personnel Psychology* 32 (1981): 327–340; T. A. Beehr, "The process of retirement," *Personnel Psychology* 39 (1986): 31–55; S. M. Comrie, "Teach employees to approach retirement as a new career," *Personnel Journal* 64(8) (1985): 106–108; L. Grensing-Pophal, "Departure plans," *HR Magazine* (July 2003): 83–86.

111. K. Greene, "Back on an early shift, but at half the pay," *The Wall Street Journal* (March 5, 2003): B1, B2.

112. AARP website, www.aarp.org, "2009 AARP best employers for workers over 50," accessed May 6, 2011; M. Prost, "Phasing out," *Human Resource Executive* (July/August 2011): 22–24.

113. K. Greene, "Many older workers to delay retirement until after age 70," *The Wall Street Journal* (September 23, 2003): D2; C. Leahey, "What–me retire?," *Fortune* (January 16, 2012): 56.

114. J. Levitz, "Americans delay retirement as housing, stocks, swoon," *The Wall Street Journal* (April 1, 2008): A1, A13. (January 18, 2006): B1, B3.

115. K. Greene, "Baby boomers delay retirement," *The Wall Street Journal* (September 22, 2008): A4.

114. J. McCracken, "To shed idled workers, Ford offers to foot the bill for college," *The Wall Street Journal* (January 18, 2006): B1, B3.

117. M. L. Colusi, P. B. Rosen, and S. J. Herrin, "Is your early retirement package courting disaster?" *Personnel Journal* (August 1988): 60–67.

118. B. Rosen and T. Jerdee, "Managing Older Workers' Careers." In *Research in Personnel and Human Resources Management,* Vol. 6, ed. G. Ferris and K. Rowland (Greenwich, CT: JAI Press, 1998): 37–74.

# Chapter **Eleven**

## The Future of Training and Development

### Objectives

After reading this chapter, you should be able to

1. Identify the future trends that are likely to influence training departments and trainers.
2. Discuss how these future trends may affect training delivery and administration, as well as the strategic role of the training department.
3. Discuss how rapid instructional design differs from traditional training design.
4. Discuss the advantages of embedded learning.
5. Discuss how training can contribute to a company's sustainability initiative.
6. Discuss the implications of cloud computing for learning, training, and development.

## Welcome to the Office of the Future!

What might the office of the future look like? Physically, it will look the same as today's offices. Employees still will have desks, meet in conference rooms, and eat in the cafeteria. There likely will be new technology, such as smaller tablet computers. Teleconferences will provide instantaneous language translations, making it easier for employees who do not speak each other's language to talk to each other. "Tables" will be able to make three-dimensional holograms of real-world objects without requiring special glasses to see them. Offices will have special window glass that can change from a solar panel to a multimedia screen to a frosted privacy shade. Technology like that found in game consoles will allow employees to navigate computer screens just by moving their wrists. Computer programs will be available to tell employees who they should work with on their next project. People will also work with computers that capitalize on the innate strengths of humans—computers are strong on routine processing, repetitive arithmetic, and error-free consistency, while we humans are better at complex communications, pattern matching, intuition, and creativity. For example, consider two examples of how people and computers can capitalize on each other's strengths to help make the workplace more efficient and effective. In 2011, Watson, a specially programmed computer, was able to beat the best human *Jeopardy!* players (including Ken Jennings, who won more consecutive episodes of the game show than anyone in history) by quickly extracting the correct answer from huge datasets of information. Watson was the first step in the development of "Search bots," which will be used to review the web to find information that fits a profile provided by employees. This will include major developments, news feeds and alerts, and searches of relevant professional publications. The search bot will improve with feedback telling it that you like some content but not other content. Store managers at the Zara chain of clothing stores are asked to determine fashion trends in their communities and stores. This supplements computer models that are used to predict future fashion trends and sales demands. Staples uses software to test customer responses to different ideas about packaging its copy paper and find the best match. But humans identify the elements of the packaging, such as colors, logos, and slogans.

Keep in mind that regardless of advances in computer pattern recognition and complex communication, human skills in applied math and statistics, negotiation and group dynamics, writing, solving open-ended problems, persuasion, nurturing, and interaction cannot be replaced and will remain in demand.

Nanotechnology advances will be available to help us enhance our learning and computational skills. Three-atom-wide nanobots injected into the brain could assist in memory and cognition. We may also pop ampakine pills to enhance our attention spans and aid learning and memory without experiencing the side effects of sleeplessness. Learning will likely occur 24/7 using mobile devices such as smart phones, tablets such as the iPad, and netbooks. This learning will be brief and available wherever we need it. Using global positioning system (GPS) sensitivity, we will be able to set our social networking profile to alert us when topic experts are available and tell us their physical proximity from our location. Social learning via shared workspaces, social networks, and wikis (learning from others) will supplement traditional training, encouraging employees to learn from each other, from trainers and instructors, and from other work experts.

**Sources:** Based on "Brave new work: The office of tomorrow," *Fortune* (January 16, 2012): 49–54; J. Meister and K. Willyerd, "Looking ahead at social learning: 10 predictors," *T+D* (July 2010): 34–41; P. Galagan, "How would you train a transhuman?" *T+D* (January 2012): 27–29; P. Ketter, "2010 six trends that will change workplace learning forever," *T+D* (December 2010): 34–40; E. Brynjolfsson and A. McAfee, "Winning the race with ever-smarter machines," *MIT Sloan Management Review* (Winter 2012): 53–60.

# INTRODUCTION

The previous ten chapters discussed training design and delivery, development and career management, and training's role in contributing to social responsibility through managing diversity and inclusion and helping the multigenerational workforce prepare and successfully deal with career challenges. This chapter takes a look at what the future of training and development might look like. The chapter opener highlights how technological advancements will shape where and how we work and learn. Technological advances represent one trend that is likely to influence the future of training and development and your future as a trainer. Table 11.1 shows the future trends discussed in this chapter that will influence training.

**TABLE 11.1**
**Future Trends**
**That Will**
**Affect Training**

- Need to contribute to sustainability
- Use of new technologies for training delivery
- Increased demand for training for virtual work arrangements
- Greater emphasis on speed in design, focus on content
- Increased emphasis on capturing and sharing intellectual capital
- Increased use of true performance support and social learning
- Increased emphasis on performance analysis and learning for business enhancement
- Increased use of training partnerships and outsourcing training

## Training for Sustainability

**Sustainability** refers to a company's ability to make a profit without sacrificing the resources of its employees, the community, or the environment. A growing number of companies have made sustainability an important part of their business strategy. Training and development can contribute to companies sustainability initiatives by providing learning opportunities for employees in organizations in developing countries that lack the resources, providing development experiences for employees in poor and emerging countries that benefit the local community, and teaching employers to protect the environment. Consider how training at Novartis, DHL Express Europe, and Gilbane Building Company is helping these companies reach their sustainability goals.[1]

For example, the pharmaceutical company Novartis supports the Regional Psychosocial Support Initiative (REPSSI), an African-based philanthropic organization that provides emotional and psychological support to children affected by the HIV/AIDS epidemic. The company's trainers provide REPSSI's employees with leadership development training. To help meet the organization's goal of helping children and youth so that they can live with hope and dignity, REPSSI managers need training in communication skills, providing feedback, intercultural skills, and project management. Novartis has transformed its corporate training programs into a form useful for REPSSI. The training content is delivered through instructor-led courses and e-learning. Novartis and training vendor partners, including business schools, send speakers at their own expense to Africa. Instructors are also available for follow-up after each course is completed.

DHL Express Europe has launched GoGreen, a carbon-neutral product line. After GoGreen shipments are delivered, their environmental impact—including truck transport, sorting, long-distance flights, and distribution—is calculated using software that accounts for all of the carbon emissions released during the shipments. Customers are charged a fee to offset the emissions. The fee is then used to fund carbon reduction projects, such as the development of alternative fuel vehicles and solar cells and the planting of trees. DHL Express Europe uses e-learning to help its sales force understand the facts about global warming, why it is a concern for the company, and the company programs in place to reduce its impact on global warming. The company also has an environmental training program for all employees, including the GoGreen Academy, which includes numerous assignments on global business practices.

Gilbane Building Company is a family-owned construction business headquartered in Rhode Island. Concerns about building in an environmentally friendly way have been an important part of the company culture for many years, and recently customers have been showing more interest in "green buildings." Green buildings are buildings that have been designed so that construction wastes fewer materials and uses less electricity. Gilbane's customers enjoy the energy cost savings and the available tax breaks for choosing to build green buildings. As a result of adopting environmentally friendly building practices, Gilbane can be both socially responsible and profitable.

Training plays an important role in helping Gilbane exceed customer expectations and provide the greener buildings that customers desire. Gilbane University includes instructor-led and online courses, as well as distance learning and a virtual classroom. Gilbane offers certification and training for employees in the Leadership in Energy and Environmental Design (LEED) rating system. LEED is a set of standards for constructing buildings in an environmentally responsible way with minimal waste. The standards were developed by the U.S. Building Green Council, which consists of building product managers, owners, utilities, and government agencies in the construction trade. Buildings that are built according to the LEED standards become LEED-certified. One course at Gilbane University helps employees prepare for the LEED exam. The course covers the LEED scorecard, reviews design decisions, and explains the documentation that a builder must keep for the building to be LEED-certified. Course participants can also use Gilbane's green portal, a page on the company's intranet that includes course resources such as study guides and practice exams. Another course offered by Gilbane University, New Construction Success, teaches construction managers how to work with all departments (such as purchasing) to produce a LEED-certified building. For example, if a builder wants to use a high level of recycled material in a building, steel may be the choice. However, it is important to know that steel takes longer to deliver, and the manager needs to be sure that the building schedule takes into account the longer lead time. Besides offering training, Gilbane positions green teams in each of the company's nine operating regions to help the region develop and use sustainable business practices and to keep the region up-to-date on the latest green construction methods and materials.

Dow Corning is among a number of large companies that are sending small teams of employees to developing countries such as India, Ghana, Brazil, and Nigeria to provide free consulting services to nonprofit organizations.[2] These experiences benefit the local communities, as well as the company and employee participants. The programs are good for internal and external public relations, help recruit and retain talented employees, provide training for future leaders, generating new ideas, and helping companies gain name recognition needed to sell their products and services in emerging markets. Dow Corning employees continue to receive their regular salaries during the assignments, which usually last between two and four weeks. Employee demand for the assignments exceed available openings because the assignments help them develop new skills and meet personal needs to donate time and expertise to those in need. For example, a customs and trade coordinator for Dow Corning spent four weeks in rural India helping women examine stitchery and help set process for garments sold in local markets. She found the experience worthwhile despite working nine-hour days and sleeping in a lodge that had limited access to electricity and hot water. Dow Corning is currently evaluating fifteen new business-related ideas related to affordable housing and energy which were generated by the twenty employees sent to India since 2010.

# INCREASED USE OF NEW TECHNOLOGIES FOR TRAINING DELIVERY

The use of social media, mobile learning (iPods), and other new technologies will likely increase in the future for several reasons. First, the cost of these technologies will decrease. Second, companies can use technology to better prepare employees to serve customers and generate new business. Third, use of these new technologies can substantially reduce the training costs related to bringing geographically dispersed employees to one central training location (e.g., travel, food, and housing). Fourth, these technologies allow trainers to build into training many of the desirable features of a learning environment (e.g., practice, feedback, reinforcement, etc.). Fifth, as companies employ more contingent employees (e.g., part-timers and consultants) and offer more alternative work arrangements (e.g., flexible work schedules and working from home), technology will allow training to be delivered to any place and at any time.

New technology also makes it possible to create "smart" products.[3] For example, packages sent by UPS leave an electronic trail that can be used to improve shipping and delivery processes. In the future, training products may also leave an electronic trail that will enable trainers and managers to better understand how these products are being used. New technologies that combine computer science, instructional design, and graphic interfaces have the potential to increase our ability to learn.[4] Employees may soon learn in their sleep. One device detects when a person is dreaming, which is a good time to acquire new skills. Teleimmersion—which is a technology that provides realistic, life-sized holographic projections in which employees can hear and see collaborators as if they were physically present in the office—can be used to create a holographic training room in the office with virtual trainees beamed in from other locations. Virtual retinal display is a technology that projects images directly on the retina of the eye. Virtual retinal display allows real-time, on-site performance support. The technology takes what is shown on a computer monitor and reduces it through special glasses directly onto the retina in full color. The image looks like it is floating in air about two feet away. Digital Avatar is an animated virtual teacher. With this technology, corporate trainers can create animated versions of themselves for online instruction. Training in the future will also include greater use of two- and three-dimensional simulations and virtual worlds (such as Second Life) that feature interactions between employees and between employees and customers (such as pharmaceutical salespersons interacting with physicians, pharmacists, and other health care professionals).[5] The content of the simulations can be changed quickly to make it appropriate for global audiences. Instant messaging, personal digital assistants (PDAs), networking websites, blogs, and social software such as Meetup and MySpace are making collaboration very easy.[6] The knowledge exchanged through these types of collaboration may be tacit knowledge that is difficult to communicate through other training.

# INCREASED DEMAND FOR TRAINING FOR VIRTUAL WORK ARRANGEMENTS

**Virtual work arrangements** include virtual teams as well as **telecommuting,** work that is conducted in a remote location (distant from central offices) where the employee has limited contact with peers but is able to communicate electronically. The critical feature of virtual work arrangements is that location, organization structure, and employment relationships are not limiting factors.[7] For example, employees from two or three organizations may work together on projects designed to meet the strategic and operational needs of their organizations. Similarly, employees within a single organization may work with peers from different units or functions on a project team. Virtual knowledge teams have members that are distributed across multiple time zones, countries, and/or companies. They are more diverse than other knowledge teams, with team members representing different specialties and perhaps different cultures, languages, and organizational allegiances. These teams do not have constant membership. Team members may move onto and off the team at different points in a project. Some members may participate in all team tasks, whereas others may work only on some. Successful virtual knowledge teams need structure (e.g., reporting relationships, membership, etc.), leadership (empowered, shared leadership, integration with other teams, etc.), shared values (such as what do we value as a team, and how will we run meetings, make decisions, and solve problems?), and rewarded goals (what are our key goals, what do customers need from us, and how will we reward goal accomplishment?). If team members are from different cultures, working from a distance can make language and cultural differences even more difficult to deal with. For example, teams responsible for evaluating business opportunities for Shell Technology Ventures, a subsidiary of Royal Dutch/Shell, found that it was challenging to create a team process structured so that team members who prefer structure can move forward without creating so much bureaucracy that it inhibits team members who do best in an unstructured environment. Dutch team members prefer more details about how a process works, who will make a decision, and what the next steps are than do their colleagues from the United States.

There are two training challenges for virtual work arrangements. First, companies have to invest in training delivery methods that facilitate digital collaboration.[8] **Digital collaboration** refers to an interaction between two or more people mediated by a computer. Social media and the web enable employees to access training from their desktops and to collaborate with others on an as-needed basis. Virtual work arrangements rely on digital collaboration. Virtual team members need training in teamwork skills and understanding cultural differences, as well as in the technical skills and competencies needed to perform their jobs. Second, for companies with virtual work arrangements, having knowledge, knowing which employees possess it, and sharing it within and across functions, teams, and individuals are critical for effectiveness. Teams and employees must be provided with the tools that they need for finding knowledge—knowledge that can be used to provide a service, develop or manufacture a product, or refine a process.

# INCREASED EMPHASIS ON SPEED IN DESIGN, FOCUS ON CONTENT, AND USE OF MULTIPLE DELIVERY METHODS

Because of new technology, trainers are being challenged to find new ways to use instructional design.[9] Shifts are taking place in who is leading the learning (from the instructor to the employee), as well as where learning is taking place (from workplace to mobile learning). For example, trainers need to determine the best way to design an effective training course using podcasting. Despite the use of new technology for learning, the fundamental questions remain: Why is training occurring? Who is the audience? What resources are necessary so that employees can learn what they need to know?

As discussed in Chapter One, "Introduction to Employee Training and Development," the traditional training design model has been criticized for several reasons. First, it is a linear approach driven by subject-matter experts (SMEs). Second, the instructional system design model uses a rational, step-by-step approach that assumes that the training content is stable. Third, given the accelerated demand for training to be delivered just in time, traditional training takes too long. **Rapid instructional design (RID)** is a group of techniques that allows training to be built more quickly. RID modifies the training design model, which consists of needs analysis, design, development, implementation, and evaluation (recall the discussion of training design in Chapter One). There are two important principles in RID.[10] One is that instructional content and process can be developed independently of each other. The second is that resources that are devoted to design and delivery of instruction can be reallocated as appropriate. *Design* includes everything that happens before the training experience; *delivery* is what happens during the training experience. For example, if a company has limited resources for training delivery, such as large groups of trainees and a tight schedule, extra time should be allocated to the design process. Table 11.2 lists RID strategies. For example, learning style differences make it difficult to develop a training program that maximizes learning for all employees. As a result, if possible, training content can be offered through books, manuals, audiotapes, videotapes, and online learning. It may also be possible to combine some steps of the design process, such as analyses and evaluation. For example, knowledge tests and other evaluation outcomes may be based on task analysis and other needs analysis results. There is no need to conduct separate analyses of training needs and learning outcomes. If the client is convinced that there is a training need and if the trainer can quickly confirm this need, then there is no reason to conduct a full needs analysis (e.g., new regulations that affect business transactions in financial services, or product changes). Job aids such as checklists, worksheets, and performance support tools can be provided to employees based on the results of a task analysis to identify activities and decisions needed to complete a procedure. Job aids can be chosen to help employees complete the procedure, and training can be provided to teach employees how to use the job aid. The point to keep in mind is that use of a training design process (or instructional design process), as discussed in Chapter One, should not be abandoned. Rather, in the future, trainers will further develop RID techniques to reduce

| | |
|---|---|
| **TABLE 11.2**<br>**Examples of**<br>**RID Strategies**<br><br>Source: Based on<br>S. Thiagarajan, "Rapid<br>Instructional Develop-<br>ment." In *The ASTD<br>Handbook of Training<br>Design and Delivery*,<br>ed. G. Piskurich,<br>P. Beckschi, and<br>B. Hall (New York:<br>McGraw-Hill, 2000):<br>54–75. | Focus on accomplishment and performance.<br>Develop a learning system instead of an instructional system.<br>Use shortcuts (e.g., use existing records for needs assessment; conduct focus groups).<br>Combine different steps of the instructional design process.<br>Implement training and continuously improve it.<br>Skip steps in the instructional design process.<br>Use existing course materials that can be customized with examples, exercises, and assignments.<br>Develop instruction around job aids.<br>Use recording equipment, Internet, and e-mail to collect data and exchange information with SMEs. |

the time and cost and to increase the efficiency of training design in order to better meet business needs.

Managers are demanding training courses that are shorter and that focus only on the necessary content.[11] Training departments will be expected to reduce the number of courses and programs that are offered without directly addressing a business issue or performance problem. SMEs used as trainers will be expected to focus their presentations on information that is directly relevant to trainees. Seminars and classes that take place over several days or half-days will have to be retooled to be more accessible and individualized. At Hartford Life Insurance Company, training managers are receiving more requests for shorter training sessions.[12] To ensure that learning and transfer of training occur in the shorter courses, trainers have asked managers to act as coaches to supplement the training and have created more on-the-job learning opportunities. Other companies are asking trainees to complete more pre-class assignments and are using more post-course job aids. The development of focused content will become easier because of blogs and podcasts that allow training content to be developed without programming languages such as Hypertext Markup Language (HTML). Content-developed authoring tools will likely continue to become more user-friendly.

Given the increased popularity of notebooks and tablets, new types of apps for learning will be developed. These likely will include apps related to locating experts, the training scheduler, retirement planners, and the development activities chooser. For example, the Assessment and Development Group International has developed apps to help increase coaching success and facilitate behavioral change, engage and retain employees, and improve sales and customer relationships.[13] Using a smart phone, the Coach app allows users to identify their interaction style (driver, analytical, expressive, and supportive). A graph of team members' interaction styles is generated, and coaching tactics specific to each style are provided. The app also suggests how to modify behavior and be more responsive to team members and a question-and-answer exercise to help address specific issues that may occur during coaching.

# INCREASED EMPHASIS ON CAPTURING AND SHARING INTELLECTUAL CAPITAL

Companies that recognize the strategic value of becoming a learning organization and are concerned about the loss of valuable knowledge because their baby boomer employees are retiring (see the discussions in Chapters One and Five) will continue to seek ways to turn employees' knowledge (human capital) into a shared company asset. As emphasized in Chapter Two, "Strategic Training," training functions will focus on learning, with an emphasis on employee training and development and the management and coordination of organizational learning. Sharing knowledge and contributing to the company's intellectual capital is going to become more common as collaborative social networking technology and Web 2.0 tools make this simpler to implement. The rise of intelligent tutors and on-demand learning technologies will make connections to information faster, more current and accurate, and more easily customizable to employees' needs and work. More teams and groups of employees will make use of social media and Web 2.0 tools to share links and content with each other, participate in discussions, collaborate, and create learning content.

For example, to improve productivity at MWH, an engineering firm specializing in water projects, employees are asked to indicate which employees they talk to and ask for help.[14] This information is used to create a "map" of connections. The map shows communications gaps, places where information gets stuck, and employees who are not connected to their colleagues. MWH's purpose in developing the map of informal connections between employees, known as **social network analysis,** was to reduce costs and improve communications between its seven technology centers. MWH found that information flowed well within each center, but not between centers. For example, employees in Denver had little contact with employees in California and the least amount of contact with employees in New Zealand. To remove communication barriers, U.S. employees were sent to fill vacation openings in the United Kingdom. Top managers were trained to become less authoritarian and more collaborative, therefore helping to facilitate information flow. After five years, the employees within MWH are now more closely connected to each other. It takes employees an average of 2.4 steps to get the information they need, down from 3.2.

The increasing use of new technologies to deliver training and to store and communicate knowledge means that trainers must be technologically literate. That is, they must understand the strengths and weaknesses of new technologies and implementation issues such as overcoming users' resistance to change (which is discussed later in this chapter). Also, many companies have created positions such as knowledge manager or chief information officer, whose job is to identify reliable knowledge and make sure it is accessible to employees.

# INCREASED USE OF TRUE PERFORMANCE SUPPORT AND SOCIAL LEARNING

Companies are moving away from courseware and classes as a performance improvement method and are instead adopting true performance support that is available during the work process.[15] **Embedded learning** refers to learning that occurs on the job as needed; it involves collaboration and nonlearning technologies such as microblogs, and it is integrated with knowledge management.[16] Embedded learning will include social learning. **Social learning** refers to learning with and from others. We can learn from others in face-to-face interactions occurring in classrooms, conferences, and group meetings, as well as online using social media such as Twitter, blogs, and social networks such as Facebook. Potentially, through sharing ideas, information, and experiences, we can learn more with others than we can alone.[17]

Embedded learning may become increasingly prevalent in the future because companies can no longer have employees attend classroom instruction or spend hours on online learning that is not directly relevant to their current job demands. Formal training programs and courses will not disappear but will focus more on the development of competencies that can benefit the employee and the company over the long term, whereas embedded learning will focus on providing the learning that the employee needs to complete key job tasks. Embedded-learning products include task-specific, real-time content and simulation that are accessible during work, as well as real-time collaboration in virtual workspaces. Recent, rapid adoption of wireless technology is connecting employees directly to business processes. For example, radio frequency identification chips are implanted in products such as clothing, tires, and mechanical parts. These chips contain information that is beamed via radio waves to employees processing handheld wireless devices. The device, the task context, and the performance environment are incompatible with class-room or courseware-based learning but with performance support. Learning is a business process that is integrated with several other business processes. Learning is expected as a result of collaboration with employees and machines in the work process. Employees can be provided with real-time performance support through communications with experts and through automated coaching.

One vision of the future is that employees will be presented with short learning episodes embedded in their work, be alerted when the learning episodes are needed, have direct connections to experts, be continuously connected online wirelessly, and have simulations for guidance.[18] Every employee will have a dynamic display (a personalized "dashboard") that provides a unique view into the company. The display will be customized to each em-ployee's role and background and will give the employee a current picture of specific job responsibilities within the scope of the entire workflow. The dashboard will allow the em-ployee to collaborate with others, request information, or participate in a simulation to deal with a problem. Another vision is that the personal computer will be the hub that allows employees not only to share data but also to access training content and subject matter ex-perts automatically, on an as-needed basis. This will occur through the interface of e-mail, instant messaging, virtual offices supplied through three-dimensional environments, video conferencing, social media, and shared meetings applications.[19]

More learning will become just-in-time, using mobile devices such as notebooks and tab-lets such as the iPad. As a result, instead of having to complete specific training classes, learn-ing functions will focus on setting standards required to achieve accreditation, create systems to allow employees to meet accreditation standards, and track completion of standards.[20] To achieve accreditation may involve having specific job experiences, observing a expert-level employee, contributing content for helping peers and less experienced learn, and passing a test.

There is a new type of learner emerging, the "social cyborg," who integrates social networks into the way they think, learn, and solve problems.[20] As Facebook and other so-cial networking sites and smart phones with communications and internet access continue to spread and evolve, employees will spend more time on computers and online playing games, working, and connecting to friends and work associates using e-mail and text. "So-cial cyborgs" are already prevalent among the millennial generation who expect companies to accommodate their need to access the latest tools and technologies at work including tablets and mobile devices, Really Simple Syndication (RSS) feeds, and social networking sites. This means that training, development, and learning functions will need to adjust their assumptions about how and where we learn. Design and development strategies based on individual learners who learn alone and without technology will continue to become obsolete. Employees will expect training and development to include simulations, games, and virtual reality, which will become more realistic than they are today. For example, researchers are developing wearable devices that allow the use of hand gestures to interact with environment and contact lenses that act as a computer display. Also, learners will expect training and development to use social media, as well as learning that is delivered when it is needed rather than during a scheduled course.

A new set of learning strategies will be need to be adopted including learning environ-ments that include online mentoring and collaborative learning platforms. This means that companies will need to consider how, when, and for which employees to use social media such as Facebook and Twitter, as well as mobile devices for learning. Social networking platforms will be part of learning management systems. This will allow managers to determine which learning content is in most demand and take content developed by social network contributors and use it in formal training courses. Not using or forbidding the use of social media will no longer be an option to attract, motivate, and retain talented employees (and customers!). Instead, companies will need to establish policies regarding the use of social media.

# INCREASED EMPHASIS ON PERFORMANCE ANALYSIS AND LEARNING FOR BUSINESS ENHANCEMENT

Because of an increasing focus on contributing to the company's competitive advantage, training departments will have to ensure that they are seen as helping the business functions (e.g., marketing, finance, production, etc.) meet their needs.[22]

This means that you understand the business enough to ask the right questions to develop an appropriate learning solution (recall the discussion of needs assessment in Chapter Three, "Needs Assessment"). Such questions might include how success will be measured and why the company has not thus far seen desired results. The role of the learning professional is to understand business challenges and consistently work to fill employee performance gaps. To enhance the business means that learning professionals have to be aligned with the business and take responsibility for the relationship and the business outcomes from learning solutions, have an agreed-upon business outcome that is included in the learning function and business performance plan, attend business staff meetings and network with internal customers, and identify as a partner with the business with the joint goal of improving performance.

Consider how companies in three different industries expect training to influence their bottom line.[23] The training offered at TRX, a company that provides transaction processing and data integration services, is expected to have a direct influence on boosting customer satisfaction scores and agents' productivity. Metrics such as hours of training delivered are not as important as showing how training is contributing to customer service, productivity, and profitability. Supply-chain training for Coca-Cola must be tied in some way to the company's three-year business plan or it will not be supported. At Ho-Chunk Casino in Wittenberg, Wisconsin, the director of training spends time educating managers on how the training unit adds value to the business. One of the director's biggest challenges is convincing first-line supervisors to support transfer of training. The training director has found that explaining Kirkpatrick's evaluation model (reaction, learning, behavior, results) to the supervisors helps them understand that training is a process, not a one-time event, and that they play an important role in determining the success or failure of training. (Kirkpatrick's model is discussed in more detail in Chapter Six, "Training Evaluation.") Training departments must shift the focus from training as *the* solution to business problems to a performance analysis approach. A **performance analysis approach** involves identifying performance gaps or deficiencies and examining training as one possible solution for the business units (the customers). Training departments will need to continue instructing managers to consider all potential causes of poor performance before deciding that training is the solution. Poor employee performance may be due to poor management, inefficient technologies, or outdated technology rather than deficiencies in skill or knowledge (recall the discussion of person analysis in Chapter Three). Three ways that training departments will need to be involved are (1) focusing on interventions related to performance improvement, (2) providing support for high-performance work systems, and (3) developing systems for training administration, development, and delivery that reduce costs and increase employees' access to learning.

Training departments' responsibilities will likely include a greater focus on systems that employees can use for information (such as expert systems or electronic performance support systems) on an as-needed basis. This need is driven by the use of contingent employees and the increased flexibility necessary to adapt products and services to meet customers' needs. For example, companies do not want to spend money to train employees who may be with the company only a few weeks. Instead, through temporary employment agencies, companies can select employees with the exact skill set needed. Training departments need to provide mechanisms to support the temporary employees once they are on the job and encounter situations, problems, rules, and policies they are unfamiliar with because they are not yet knowledgeable about the company.

As was discussed in Chapter One, more companies are striving to create high-performance workplaces because of the productivity gains that can be realized through this type of design. High-performance work requires that employees have the interpersonal skills necessary to work in teams. High-performance work systems also require employees to have high levels of technical skills. Employees need to understand statistical process control and the Total Quality Management (TQM) philosophy. Employees also must understand the entire production and service system so that they can better serve both internal and external customers. As more companies move to high-performance work systems, training departments will need to be prepared to provide effective training in interpersonal, quality, and technical skills, as well as to help employees understand all aspects of the customer-service or production system.

Business competitiveness can be realized by quick change, speed in delivery, and reductions in costs and time constraints. Cypress Semiconductors, a supplier of integrated circuits for network equipment that is based in San Jose, California, uses competency models that are linked to success profiles that detail employees' roles, activities, responsibilities, career development initiatives, and training options.[24] The profiles are used for employee performance evaluations, and they are also used in the hiring process. For example, a training plan can be developed for new hires as soon as they are on the job so that they can be successful as quickly as possible.

Just-in-time learning is many companies' answer to quick learning and the quick application of learning to the business.[25] Memorial Sloan-Kettering Cancer Center developed a set of simulation tools that are integrated with the implementation of several clinical support systems (order management, electronic medical records, picture archival and communications, and disease management) available to the entire medical center. IBM Global Services has moved its training from three days in the classroom to just-in-time on the web. E-business consultants can now access a website that provides them with the training they need or with information or case studies from which the training was built. They can also collaborate with other consultants to share knowledge.

Because the direction in training is away from learning as the primary outcome and more toward learning as a way to enhance business performance, companies have started to purchase learning management systems (LMSs) that provide training administration, development tools, and online training. (LMSs are discussed in Chapter Eight, "Technology-Based

Training Methods.") LMS software contains learning analytics, or analysis tools, that can track learning activity and costs and can relate learning results to product revenues or sales goals.[26]

Today, most companies own their own software and hardware and keep them on site in their facilities. However, cloud computing allows companies to lease software and hardware, and employees don't know the location of computers, databases, and applications that they are using (this is known as being in the "cloud"). **Cloud computing** refers to a computing system that provides information technology infrastructure over a network in a self-service, modifiable, and on-demand.[27] Clouds can be delivered on-demand via the Internet (public cloud) or restricted to use by a single company (private cloud). Cloud computing gives companies and their employees access to applications and information from smart phones and tablets rather than relying solely on personal computers. It also allows groups to work together in new ways, can make employees more productive by allowing them to more easily share documents and information, and provide greater access to large company databases. From a learning perspective, this means that tools for conducting workforce analytics using metrics on learning, training and development programs, and social media and collaboration tools such as Twitter, blogs, Google documents, and YouTube videos will be more easily accessible and available for use. Cloud computing also can make it easier for employees to access formal training programs from a variety of vendors and educational institutions.

# INCREASED USE OF TRAINING PARTNERSHIPS AND OUTSOURCING TRAINING

Chapter Two discussed several reasons for companies to outsource their training. Two main reasons were that employees need to learn specialized new knowledge and that companies want to gain access to best practices and cost savings. External suppliers may be consultants, academics, graduate students, or companies in the entertainment and mass communications industries. External suppliers can be partners or be sole providers of training services. The key decision for companies will not be whether to outsource but rather how much training to outsource.

BellSouth developed a new training program on the basics of wireless communications for its own employees. Members of the training team believed that if employees within BellSouth could benefit from knowing more about how wireless communications work, then key suppliers, end-user customers, and companies that sell the wireless products would also benefit. This type of training might give BellSouth an advantage over its competitors. As a result, BellSouth's Intro to Wireless Communications training is being offered both within the company and to companies that sell BellSouth's products, such as Best Buy. Best Buy is making the training available to their customers. BellSouth is also providing training that can help make its networks of suppliers and customers more knowledgeable in other areas, such as basic personal computer skills for managing computer networks. BellSouth offers courses from training suppliers on its company website. The company charges a fee for the training.

Why train suppliers, customers, and vendors? The intent is to build a broad understanding of what wireless technology does, how it works, where it works, why it works, its strengths and weaknesses, and its potential applications. Providing training also enhances the value of BellSouth's services. That customers, vendors, and suppliers are learning more about BellSouth's products and services translates into higher sales. For example, the more that salespeople understand the products and the technology they are selling, the better they can match customer needs and product capabilities. This knowledge increases customer satisfaction and word-of-mouth advertising, and it lowers the number of returns and complaints—thus cutting the costs of doing business.[28]

As discussed in Chapter One, the demographic, global, and technological changes are creating a skills gap that presents challenges for companies in the United States and around the world. Also, the current education-to-employment system is not preparing students and adults for the twenty-first-century economy. Barriers between business and educational institutions make it difficult for many employees to update their skills and knowledge that they need for their current jobs or preparation for jobs in another career. Recall our discussion of business and education partnerships in Chapter Ten, "Social Responsibility: Legal Issues, Managing Diversity, and Career Challenges." To cope with the skills gap, we will likely see a greater incidence of business, education, and community partnerships working on rebuilding education to employment systems.[29] The goal of these partnerships is to help individuals prepare for higher-skill and higher-wage jobs and attract new companies to the area by integrating employee retraining, elementary through high school career education programs, career academies, and higher education programs into a lifelong learning system. A lifelong learning system can provide better opportunities for more people to develop the talent needed to suit multiple jobs and careers that they will likely hold during their lifetimes.

Also, due to an increased urgency to find ways to eliminate unemployment, underemployment, and meet skill gaps, federal, state, and local governments probably will provide more economic incentives for retraining employees, including tax credits and tax breaks for companies to invest in training and the spread of lifelong learning accounts, which employees can use to pay for additional education at vocational schools and colleges and universities.

For example, Sematech, the semiconductor industry association, worked with community colleges in the Phoenix, Arizona, area to develop a curriculum for training entry-level manufacturing technicians.[30] Displaced auto workers in Michigan have been recruited to fill nursing positions.[31] Oakland University recruits auto workers into a one-year nursing program. After completing the program, participants can gain employment with St. John Health, the largest health network in Detroit. In San Francisco, material handlers who have lost jobs in the aviation industry have been retrained to work for Genentech, a biotechnology company. The Integrated Basic Education and Skills Training (IBEST) program offered by Washington State allows participants to receive training for jobs in nursing, hospitality, corrections, and welding. The program is targeted to the underemployed and the unemployed. Completion of the one-year program prepares participants with sufficient skills to obtain an entry-level job in their chosen field with the opportunity to return for additional training.

Trainers and other learning professionals will need to identify outsource providers who can deliver effective training solutions, particularly in technology-based learning solutions in which they lack the internal expertise to develop in house. Baker Hughes Incorporated, an oilfield services provider, was challenged to deliver training to a growing global workforce in sixteen countries, including Nigeria and Russia. Baker Hughes outsourced the design and support of their learning processes to Expertus, a training and learning outsourcing provider. Expertus developed processes and ongoing support through an LMS for training administration, report management, onboarding, and compliance training.[32]

One type of training outsourcing involves the use of an **application service provider (ASP),** a company that rents out access to software for a specific application.[33] Some ASPs have relationships with courseware developers that provide online learning. These relationships allow the ASP to offer structured courses, as well as custom options. The major benefit is that company resources are not used to purchase or maintain an internal network or intranet. Also, companies save the costs associated with building, renting, or maintaining a training facility. Typically, the company pays for a license along with a maintenance contract. Training delivery and administration programs are run on the ASP's computers. The ASP can track how many employees use the software contracted for, which areas are accessed the most, and how employees perform on post-training tests. The ASP also provides technical support, including software upgrades. The company pays the ASP a fee. For example, KPMG Consulting challenged its e-learning department to develop a program that would train 8,500 employees worldwide in e-business.[34] The national director of e-learning recognized that he had to ensure that the program didn't overload KPMG's computer system. The solution was to use an ASP to host the company's computer-based training program, providing access to employees worldwide while using none of KPMG's computer resources. The use of an ASP allowed KPMG to quickly develop and make the training available to its workforce.

## Implications of Future Trends for Trainers' Skills and Competencies

A recent study found that the competencies and expertise included in the ASTD competency model (see Figure 1.4 in Chapter One) are likely to be needed in the future. However, increased emphasis will also be placed on the ability of trainers to more effectively use technology. Also, as companies become more global, they will need to adapt training methods and content to local cultures.[35] Table 11.3 shows the skills that trainers will need to develop in the future.

| | |
|---|---|
| **TABLE 11.3**<br>**Skills for**<br>**Future**<br>**Trainers**<br><br>Source: Based on M. Laff, "Trainers Skills 2020," *T+D* (December 2008): 42; P. Galagan, "New Skills for a New Work Reality," *T+D* (November 2011): 26–29. | • Matching training content and methods to the local culture of the workforce<br>• Designing learning space, as well as content in technology-driven learning environments<br>• Use of multimedia tools, including audio, video, webcasts, and live action<br>• Delivering and packaging training in different formats for beginners and experts<br>• Use of assessments to determine trainees' learning styles<br>• Developing search-and-identify techniques so employees can find information and training when they need it<br>• Facilitating learning and staying in touch with employees, managers, and business units to identify what they need and making suggestions regarding tools, processes, or procedures that could help them work more effectively<br>• Developing and delivering learning that is integrated with the job<br>• Understand how social media can be used for learning, the limitations of social media, and ability to make a business case for it<br>• Identify the root cause of job and business problems |

**Summary**    This chapter discussed future trends that are likely to influence training and development. These trends relate to training delivery and structure of the training function. Training will contribute to a company's sustainability goals. Trainers will be asked to design focused content more quickly and to deliver training using multiple methods. New technology will have a growing impact on training delivery in the future. Also, new technology will allow training departments to store and share human capital throughout the company. There will be an increased emphasis on integrating training with other human resource functions and showing how training helps the business. Training departments are more likely to develop partnerships with vendors and other companies in the future.

## Key Terms

sustainability *468*

virtual work arrangements, *470*

telecommuting, *470*

digital collaboration, *471*

rapid instructional design (RID), *472*

social network analysis, *474*

embedded learning, *474*

social learning, *474*

performance analysis approach, *476*

cloud computing, *478*

application service provider (ASP), *480*

## Discussion Questions

1. Discuss how new technologies are likely to impact training in the future.
2. What new skills will trainers need to be successful in the future?
3. What is rapid instructional design? How does it differ from the traditional training design process discussed in Chapter One? (See Figure 1.1.)
4. How does the use of a learning management system better link training to business strategy and goals?
5. What is cloud computing? How does it enable just-in-time training delivery?
6. How will social learning and social networks influence employee expectations about learning, training, and development?
7. What are the implications of virtual work arrangements for training?
8. How can training contribute to a sustainability initiative?

## Application Assignments

1. Interview a manager. Ask this person to evaluate his or her company's training department in terms of training delivery, service, expertise, and contribution to the business. Ask him or her to explain the rationale for the evaluation. Summarize this information. Based on the information you gathered, make recommendations regarding how the training department can be improved.

2. This chapter discussed several trends that will influence the future of training. Based on future social, economic, political, or technological factors, identify one or two additional trends that you think will influence training. Write a two- to three-page paper summarizing your ideas. Make sure you provide a rationale for your trends. Many organizations are moving from a training perspective to a performance perspective. That is, they are interested in performance improvement, not training just for the sake of training.

3. SumTotal is an ASP. Visit www.sumtotalsystems.com. What services and products does this ASP provide?

4. Go to http://2oms.com/apps/ website for the Assessment and Development Group International. Click on "Mobile Apps". Read about and install on your smart phone Performance Coach. What are the strengths and weaknesses of the Performance Coach app?

5. Go to www.youtube.com website for YouTube. First, watch the video "IBM's Watson Supercomputer Destroys All Humans on Jeopardy." Then watch the video *IBM Watson: Watson After Jeopardy!* How can Watson and the technology that it uses help make us "smarter" and improve performance?

---

## Case: *The Role of Learning Technologies in Empowering Employees and Environmental Sustainability at TELUS*

TELUS an information technology company that employs 38,000 people found in its annual survey that employees understood the business strategy but they didn't feel empowered to address business issues. As a result, TELUS created the TELUS Leadership Philosophy (TLP). The TLP emphasizes that employees should generate ideas and share opinions that help improve company performance. The TLP supports key business goals including Customers First, an initiative designed to create a customer-focused culture and Work Styles, an initiative with the goal of having 30 percent of employees working in offices, 40 percent mobile, and 30 percent working at home by 2014. The Work Styles initiative was started to enhance employee productivity, help employees stay healthy by promoting practices that enhance their work-life balance, and support TELUS commitment to environmental sustainability by reducing its real estate footprint, and therefore carbon emissions from buildings and commuting. Currently, many TELUS employees work in virtual teams that are managed from a distance.

*How might social media and apps help empower employees to delight their customers and help the learning function contribute to enhancing environment sustainability? What are the challenges of delivering learning to employees who work in virtual teams or work at home or travel on the road?*

**Source:** Based on J. Salopek, "Getting social to create transparency," *T+D* (October 2011): 68–70; www.telus.ca, the website for TELUS (accessed February 15, 2012).

## Endnotes

1. M. Weinstein, "Charity Begins @ Work," *training* (May 2008): 56–58; A. Fox, "Get in the business of being green," *HR Magazine* (June 2008): 45; J. Jarventaus, "Training a green workforce," *T+D* (September 2007): 28–34; H. Dolezalek, "Good news: Training can save the world," *training* (May 2006): 28–33; Gilbane Building Company website, www.gilbanebuilding.com.

2. A. Tergesen, "Doing good to do well," *The Wall Street Journal* (January 9, 2012): B7.

3. J. Meister and K. Willyerd, *The 2020 Workplace* (Harper Business: New York, 2010); P. Ketter, "Six trends that will change workplace learning forever," *T+D* (December 2010): 34–40.

4. J. Barbian, "The future training room," *training* (September 2001): 40–45.

5. P. Harris, "Immersive learning seeks a foothold," *T+D* (January 2009): 40–45.

6. M. Green, "Better, smarter, faster," *T+D* (April 2011): 70–72; H. Dolezalek and T. Galvin, "Future scan," *training* (September 2004): 30–38; A. Kamenetz, "The network unbound," *Fast Company* (June 2006): 68–73.

7. J. Meister and K. Willyerd, *The 2020 Workplace* (Harper Business: New York, 2010).

8.  J. Salopek, "Digital collaboration," *Training and Development* (June 2000): 38–43.

9.  H. Dolezalek, "Who has the time to design?" *training* (January 2006): 24–28.

10. S. Thiagarajan, "Rapid Instructional Development." In *The ASTD Handbook of Training Design and Delivery,* ed. G. Piskurich, P. Beckschi, and B. Hall (New York: McGraw-Hill, 2000): 54–75.

11. M. Weinstein, "Six for '06," *training* (January 2006): 18–22.

12. D. Zielinski, "Wanted: Training manager," *training* (January 2006): 36–39.

13. "Manage employees and clients like a hero," *T+D* (February 2012): 17.

14. P. Dvorak, "Engineering firm charts ties," *The Wall Street Journal* (January 26, 2009): B7.

15. S. Adkins, "The brave new world of learning," *T+D* (June 2003): 28–37.

16. M. Littlejohn, "Embedded learning," *T+D* (February 2006): 36–39.

17. T. Bingham and M. Conner, *The New Social Learning* (American Society for Training and Development: Alexandria, VA, 2010).

18. J. Cross and T. O'Driscoll, "Workflow learning gets REAL," *training* (February 2005): 30–35.

19. A. Nancherta, "Tools 2020," *T+D* (December 2008): 34-35; J. Llorens, "Technology 2020," *T+D* (December 2008): 36–37.

20. J. Meister and K. Willyerd, "Looking ahead at social learning: 10 predictors," *T+D* (July 2010): 34–41.

21. J. Campbell and W. Finegan, "Dawn of the social cyborg," *training* (September/October 2011): 20–27; J. Meister and K. Willyerd, *The 2020 Workplace* (Harper Business: New York, 2010); A. Thompson, "Delivering meaningful outcomes for your organization," *T+D* (February 2012): 38–41; J. Meister and K. Willyerd, "Looking ahead at social learning: 10 predictors," *T+D* (July 2010): 34–41.

22. E. Salas, S. Tannenbaum, K. Kraiger, & K. Smith-Jentsch, "The science of training and development in organizations: What matters in practice," *Psychological Science in the Public Interest* 13 (2012): 74–101. A. Thompson, "Delivering meaningful outcomes for your organization," *T+D* (February 2012): 38–41.

23. D. Zielinski, "Wanted: Training manager," *training* (January 2006): 36–39.

24. H. Dolezalek, "Mining for Gold," *training* (September 2003): 36–42.

25. R. Weintraub and J. Martineau, "The just-in-time imperative," *T+D* (June 2002): 50–58.

26. M. Hequet, "The state of the e-learning market," *training* (September 2003): 24–29.

27. A. McAfee, "What every CEO needs to know about the cloud," *Harvard Business Review* (November 2011): 124–132; B. Roberts, "The grand convergence," *HR Magazine* (October 2011): 39-46; M. Paino, "All generations learn in the cloud," *Chief Learning Officer* (September 28, 2011), accessed from http://blog.clomedia.com, October 11, 2011.

28. D. Garrett, "Crossing the channel," *training* (September 1999): OL14–OL20.

29. E. Gordon, "Talent challenge: Renewing the vision," *T+D* (June 2010): 42–47.

30. S. Jackson, "Your local campus: Training Ground Zero," *BusinessWeek* (September 30, 1996): 68.

31. M. Laff, "Switching gears leads to new careers," *T+D* (September 2007): 39–43.

32. "Baker Hughes taps Expertus to Streamline Learning practices" from www.expertus.com website for Expertus, a company that provides human capital management service and training solutions, accessed February 17, 2012.

33. D. Schaaf, "ERP or oops?" *training* (May 2000): S4–S12; J. Ryder, "Future of HR technology," *HR Magazine 50th Anniversary Issue* (2005): 67–68.

34. M. Kaeter, "Training for rent," *training* (May 2000): S14–S22.

35. P. Galagan, "New skills for a new work reality," *T+D* (November 2011): 26–29; J. Salopek, "Keeping it real," *T+D* (August 2008): 42–45.

| Case 4 | Learning in Practice |
|--------|----------------------|

# Please Take Your Vacation!

In some companies your boss gives you as much vacation as you want whenever you want to take it. Open-ended vacation plans have gained in popularity especially among high-tech, professional services, and other white-collar employers. Employers are using these plans to help employees take time off. Some estimates are that less than forty percent of all employees use their vacation time. Intense and long work hours can lead to employee burnout, more errors, and lower quality products and services. Employees have no guaranteed amount or limit of vacation time but they do have to get approval.

At IBM employees inform their managers but take time off when they want it. Best Buy doesn't track the hour's employee's work. Instead it emphasizes a "results only work environment," where workers are measured on their performance and results. Netflix stopped tracking employee vacations to focus on what was accomplished instead of how many days or hours employees worked. Netflix has a strong performance culture. Employees work 24/7 including weekends often from home using their laptop computer or smartphone. Employees are taking about three to five weeks off a year more than in the past under the "no vacation policy." Employees are never questioned about how much vacation time they have taken because it is their personal choice. Also, they have to discuss when and how much time to take in order to balance the workload with their peers. Netflix employees do keep in touch using e-mail or phone when on vacation so their never is really any "down time." Hulu studied Netflix's vacation policy and decided not to copy it because their employees expressed concerns about doing away with taking vacation time. They were worried that

there would be pressure to adopt their managers' work habits. For example, if they had a workaholic boss it would be difficult for them to ask for time off. Ryan LLC, a tax services company, uses open-ended vacations as part of a move to a flexible work policy to lower employee turnover. Motley Fool, the financial services company, found that most people take about four weeks off using its open-ended vacation policy. Motley Fool has a ritual that requires employees to be ready to take a vacation on short notice. At an employee meeting, one name is drawn from a hat. The employee chosen must go on vacation for two back-to-back weeks during the next month. When they return to work they have to tell their peers what they did during the time off.

## Questions

1. What should be done to insure that employees take advantage of open-ended vacation policies, but at the same time it doesn't increase their colleague's workload and hurt the business?

2. Why do you think that employees don't take vacation time?

3. What type of work is best suited for an open-ended vacation policy? For what types of jobs would it not work?

4. How do open-ended vacation policies help the company?

**Sources:** Based on S. Shellenbarger, "Unlimited vacation, but can you take it?, *The Wall Street Journal* (July 20, 2011): D3; S. DuBois, "Flexible vacation policies are here to stay," *CNN Money* (February 1, 2011) accessed at http://money .cnn.com, February 17, 2012.

# Glossary

**360-degree feedback**   A special case of the upward feedback system. Here employees' behaviors or skills are evaluated not only by subordinates but also by peers, customers, bosses, and employees themselves via a questionnaire rating them on a number of dimensions.

**ability**   The physical and mental capacity to perform a task.

**action learning**   A training method that involves giving teams or work groups a problem, having them work on solving it and committing to an action plan, and then holding them accountable for carrying out the plan.

**action plan**   A written document detailing steps that a trainee and the manager will take to ensure that training transfers to the job.

**advance organizers**   Outlines, texts, diagrams, and graphs that help trainees organize information that will be presented and practiced.

**adventure learning**   A training method focusing on developing teamwork and leadership skills using structured outdoor activities.

**affective outcomes**   Outcomes including attitudes and motivation.

**Age Discrimination in Employment Act**   A federal law that prohibits discrimination against individuals 40 years of age or older.

**alternative work arrangements**   Independent contributors, on-call workers, temporary workers, and contract company workers.

**Americans with Disabilities Act (ADA)**   A 1990 act prohibiting workplace discrimination against people with disabilities.

**andragogy**   The theory of adult learning.

**application assignments**   Assignments which require trainees to identify work problems or situations and to apply training content to solve them.

**application planning**   The preparing of trainees to use key behaviors on the job.

**application service provider (ASP)**   A company that rents out access to software for specific applications.

**apprenticeship**   A work-study training method with both on-the-job and classroom training.

**apps**   Applications designed specifically for smartphones and tablet computers that are being used to supplement training, manage the path or sequence of training, and to help employees maintain training records.

**assessment**   The collecting of information and providing of feedback to employees about their behavior, communication style, or skills.

**assessment center**   A process in which multiple raters or evaluators (also known as assessors) evaluate employees' performances on a number of exercises.

**asynchronous communication**   A non–real-time interaction in which people cannot communicate with each other without a time delay.

**attitude**   Combination of beliefs and feelings that predispose a person to behave in a certain way.

**audiovisual instruction**   Media-based training that is both watched and heard.

**automatization**   Making performance of a task, recall of knowledge, or demonstration of a skill so automatic that it requires little thought or attention.

**avatars**   Computer depictions of humans that are used as imaginary coaches, co-workers, and customers in simulations.

**balanced scorecard**   A means of performance measurement that allows managers to view the overall company performance or the performance of departments or functions (such as training) from the perspective of internal and external customers, employees, and shareholders.

**bandwidth**   The number of bytes and bits (information) that can travel between computers per second.

**basic skills**   Skills necessary for employees to perform their jobs and learn the content of training programs.

**behavior modeling**   A training method in which trainees are presented with a model who demonstrates key behaviors to replicate and provides them with the opportunity to practice those key behaviors.

**benchmarking**   The use of information about other companies' training practices to help determine the appropriate type, level, and frequency of training.

**benefits**   The value company gains from a training program.

**blended learning**   Learning that involves a combination of online learning, face-to-face instruction, and other methods.

**blog**   A webpage where an author posts entries and readers can comment.

**brand**   The look and feeling of the training function that is used to create expectations for its customers.

**business-embedded (BE) model**   A training function model that aligns closely with the company's business strategy and that is characterized by five competencies: strategic direction, product design, structural versatility, product delivery, and accountability for results.

**business game**   A training method in which trainees gather information, analyze it, and make decisions.

**business process outsourcing**   The outsourcing of any business process, such as human resource management, production, or training.

**business strategy**   A plan that integrates a company's goals, policies, and actions.

**career path**   A sequence of job positions involving similar types of work and skills that employees move through in a company.

**career support**   Coaching, protection, sponsorship, and provision of challenging assignments, exposure, and visibility to an employee.

**case study**   A description of how employees or an organization dealt with a situation.

**centralized training**   Organizing the training department so that training and development programs, resources, and professionals are primarily housed in one location and decisions about training investment, programs, and delivery are made from that department.

**change**   The adoption of a new idea or behavior by a company.

**chief learning officer (CLO)**   A leader of a company's knowledge management efforts (also called knowledge officer).

**climate for transfer**   Trainees' perceptions about a wide variety of characteristics of the work environment; these perceptions facilitate or inhibit use of trained skills or behavior.

**closed skills**   Training objectives that are linked to learning specific skills that are to be identically produced by the trainee on their job.

**cloud computing**   A computing system that provides information technology infrastructure over a network in a self-service, modifiable, and on-demand.

**coach**   A peer or manager who works with employees to motivate them, help them develop skills, and provide reinforcement and feedback.

**cognitive ability**   Verbal comprehension, quantitative ability, and reasoning ability.

**cognitive outcomes**   Outcomes that are used to measure what knowledge trainees learned in a training program.

**cognitive strategies**   Strategies that regulate the learning processes; they relate to the learner's decision regarding what information to attend to, how to remember, and how to solve problems.

**community of practice (COP)**   A group of employees who work together, learn from each other, and develop a common understanding of how to get work accomplished.

**comparison group**   A group of employees who participate in an evaluation study but do not attend a training program.

**competency**   An area of personal capability that enables employees to perform their job.

**competency model**   A model identifying the competencies necessary for each job as well as the knowledge, skills, behavior, and personal characteristics underlying each competency.

**competitive advantage**   An upper hand over other firms in an industry.

**competitiveness**   A company's ability to maintain and gain market share in an industry.

**compressed work week**   A work schedule that allows employees to work fewer days but with longer hours, for example, four days ten hours each day.

**computer-based training (CBT)**   An interactive training experience in which the computer provides the learning stimulus, the trainee must respond, and the computer analyzes the responses and provides feedback to the trainee.

**concentration strategy**   A business strategy that focuses on increasing market share, reducing costs, or creating a market niche for products and services.

**consequences**   Incentives that employees receive for performing well.

**continuous learning**   A learning system in which employees are required to understand the entire work system including the relationships among their jobs, their work units, and the company. Also, employees are expected to acquire new skills and knowledge, apply them on the job, and share this information with fellow workers.

**control**   A manager's or employee's ability to obtain and distribute valuable resources.

**coordination training**   Training a team in how to share information and decision-making responsibilities to maximize team performance.

**copyright**   Legal protection for the expression of an idea.

**corporate university model**   A training model in which the client group includes not only company employees and managers but also stakeholders outside the company.

**cost-benefit analysis**   The process of determining the economic advantages of a training program using accounting methods.

**course or program**   Includes units or lessons which are smaller sections or modules covering different topics that can involve several hours, half-days, full days or even weeks.

**criteria**   Measures or outcomes that trainer and the company use to evaluate training programs.

**criteria relevance**   The extent to which training outcomes relate to the learned capabilities emphasized in training.

**criterion contamination**   When a training program's outcomes measure inappropriate capabilities or are affected by extraneous conditions.

**criterion deficiency**   The failure to measure training outcomes that were emphasized in training objectives.

**cross-cultural preparation**   The education of employees (expatriates) and their families who are to be sent to a foreign country.

**cross training**   A training method in which team members understand and practice each other's skills so that members are prepared to step in and take another member's place should someone temporarily or permanently leave the team; also, more simply, training employees to learn the skills of one or several additional jobs.

**crowdsourcing**   Asking a large group of employees (the crowd) using social media or the web to help provide information for needs assessment that they are not traditionally asked to do.

**curriculum**   An organized program of study designed to meet a complex learning objective such as preparing a learner to become a salesperson, certified computer network technician or a licensed nurse.

**curriculum road map**   A figure showing all of the courses in a curriculum, the paths learners can take through it, and the sequences in which courses have to be completed.

**customer capital**   The value of relationships with persons or other organizations outside a company for accomplishing the goals of the company (e.g., relationships with suppliers, customers, vendors, government agencies).

**dashboards**   A computer interface designed to receive and analyze the data from departments within the company to provide information to managers and other decision-makers.

**detailed lesson plan**   The translation of the content and sequence of training activities into a guide used by the trainer to help deliver training.

**development**   Formal education, job experiences, relationships, and assessments of personality and abilities that help employees prepare for the future.

**development planning or career management system**   A system to motivate and retain employees by identifying and meeting their career and development needs.

**digital collaboration**   An interaction between two or more people mediated by a computer; the use of technology to enhance and extend employees' ability to work together regardless of their geographic proximity.

**direct costs**   Costs that are actually connected to training, including the salaries and benefits of all employees involved, program supplies, equipment and classroom rental or purchase, and travel costs.

**discrimination**   The degree to which trainees' performances on an outcome actually reflect true differences in performance.

**disinvestment strategy**   A business strategy that emphasize the liquidation and divestiture of businesses.

**distance learning**   Training method in which geographically dispersed companies provide information about new products, policies, or procedures as well as skills training and expert lectures to field locations.

**diversity training**   Training programs designed to change employees' attitudes about diversity and/or to develop skills needed to work with a diverse work force.

**downward move**   The reduction of an employee's responsibility and authority.

**dual-career-path system**   A career path system that enables technical employees to either remain in a technical career path or move into a management career path.

**early retirement program**   A system of offering (usually older) employees financial benefits to leave a company.

**elaboration**   A learning strategy requiring the trainee to relate the training material to other more familiar knowledge, skills, or behavior.

**e-learning**   Instruction and delivery of training by computer online through the Internet or web.

**electronic performance support system (EPSS)**
A computer application that can provide, as requested, skills training, information access, and expert advice.

**embedded learning**   Learning that occurs on the job as needed.

**employee engagement**   The extent to which employees are fully involved in their work and the strength of their commitment to their job and the company.

**error management training**   Training in which trainees are given opportunities to make errors, which can aid in learning and improve trainees' performance on the job.

**evaluation design**   Designation of what information is to be collected, from whom, when, and how to determine the effectiveness of training.

**expatriate**   A person working in a country other than his or her nation of origin.

**expectancy**   The belief about the link between trying to perform a behavior (or effort) and actually performing well; the mental state that the learner brings to the instructional process.

**experiential learning**   A training method in which participants (1) are presented with conceptual knowledge and theory, (2) take part in a behavioral simulation, (3) analyze the activity, and (4) connect the theory and activity with on-the-job or real-life situations.

**expert systems**   Technology (usually software) that organizes and applies human experts' knowledge to specific problems.

**explicit knowledge**   Knowledge that can be formalized, codified, and communicated.

**external analysis**   Examining the company's operating environment to identify opportunities and threats.

**external conditions**   Processes in the learning environment that facilitate learning.

**external growth strategy**   A business strategy emphasizing acquiring vendors and suppliers or buying businesses that allow the company to expand into new markets.

**external validity**   The generalizability of study results to other groups and situations.

**externship**   Situation in which a company allows an employee to take a full-time, temporary operational role at another company.

**Family and Medical Leave Act (FMLA)**   A federal law that provides for up to 12 weeks of unpaid leave for parents with new infants or newly adopted children; also covers employees who must take a leave of absence from work to care for a family member who is ill or to deal with a personal illness.

**far transfer**   Trainees' ability to apply learned capabilities to the work environment even though it is not identical to the training session environment.

**feedback**   Information that employees receive while they are performing about how well they are meeting objectives.

**fidelity**   The extent to which a training environment is similar to a work environment.

**flextime**   Providing employees with the option of choosing when to work during the work day, workweek, or work year.

**focus group**   A face-to-face meeting with subject-matter experts (SMEs) in which specific training needs are addressed.

**formal education program**   An off-site or on-site program designed for a company's employees, a short course offered by a consultant or school, an executive MBA program, or a university program in which students live at the university while taking classes.

**formal training and development**   Training and development programs, courses and events that are developed and organized by the company.

**formative evaluation**   Evaluation conducted to improve the training process; usually conducted during program design and development.

**generalization**   A trainee's ability to apply learned capabilities to on-the-job work problems and situations that are similar but not identical to problems and situations encountered in the learning environment.

**generalizing**   Adapting learning for use in similar but not identical situations.

**glass ceiling**   A barrier to advancement to an organization's higher levels.

**goal**   What a company hopes to achieve in the medium- to long-term future.

**goal orientation**   A trainee's goals in a learning situation.

**goal setting**   An employee's process of developing short- and long-term career objectives.

**goal setting theory**   A theory assuming that behavior results from a person's conscious goals and intentions.

**gratifying**   The feedback that a learner receives from using learning content.

**group building methods**   Training methods designed to improve team or group effectiveness.

**group mentoring program**   A program in which a successful senior employee is paired with a group of four to six less experienced protégés to help them understand the organization, guide them in analyzing their experiences, and help them clarify career directions.

**guided team self-correction**   Training that emphasizes continuous learning and knowledge sharing in teams through team members observing each other's behavior and giving and receiving performance feedback.

**hands-on method**   A training method in which the trainee is actively involved in learning.

**Hawthorne effect**   A situation in which employees in an evaluation study perform at a high level simply because of the attention they are receiving.

**high-potential employee**   An employee who the company believes is capable of succeeding in a higher-level managerial position.

**human capital**   The sum of the attributes, life experiences, knowledge, inventiveness, energy, and enthusiasm that a company's employees invest in their work.

**human capital management**   The integration of training with other human resource functions so as to track how training benefits the company.

**human resource development**   The integrated use of training and development, organizational development, and career development to improve individual, group, and organizational effectiveness.

**human resource management**   The policies, practices, and systems that influence employees' behavior, attitudes, and performance.

**human resource management (HRM) practices**   Management activities relating to investments in staffing, performance management, training, and compensation and benefits.

**human resource planning**   The identification, analysis, forecasting, and planning of changes needed in a company's human resources area.

**hyperlinks**   Links that allow a user to easily move from one web page to another.

**in-basket**   A training exercise involving simulation of the administrative tasks of the manager's job.

**inclusion**   Creating an environment in which employees share a sense of belonging, mutual respect, and commitment with others so they can perform their best work.

**indirect costs**   Costs not related specifically to a training program's design, development, or delivery.

**informal learning**   Learning that is learner initiated, involves action and doing, is motivated by an intent to develop, and does not occur in a formal learning setting.

**informational interview**   An interview an employee conducts with a manager or other employee to gather information about the skills, job demands, and benefits of that person's job.

**input**   Instructions that tell employees what, how, and when to perform; also, the resources that employees are given to help them perform their jobs.

**instruction**   The characteristics of the environment in which learning is to occur.

**Instructional System Design (ISD)**   A process for designing and developing training programs.

**instrumentality**   In expectancy theory, a belief that performing a given behavior is associated with a particular outcome.

**intellectual capital**   The codified knowledge that exists in a company.

**intellectual skills**   The mastery of concepts and rules.

**intelligent tutoring system (ITS)**   An instructional system using artificial intelligence.

**interactive distance learning (IDL)**   The use of satellite technology to broadcast programs to different locations, allowing trainees to respond to questions posed during the training program using a keypad.

**internal analysis**   Identifying the company's strength and weaknesses based on examining the available quantity and quality of financial, physical, and human capital.

**internal conditions**   Processes within the learner that must be present for learning to occur.

**internal growth strategy**   A business strategy focusing on new market and product development, innovation, and joint ventures.

**internal validity**   Establishing that a treatment (training) made a difference.

**interview**   Employees answer questions about their work and personal experiences, skill strengths and weaknesses, and career plans.

**ISO 10015**   A quality management tool designed to ensure that training is linked to a company's needs and performance.

**ISO 9000:2000**   A family of standards developed by the International Organization for Standardization that includes 20 requirements for dealing with such issues as how to establish quality standards and document work processes.

**job**   A specific position requiring completion of certain tasks.

**job analysis**   The process of developing a description of a job (duties, tasks, and responsibilities) and the specifications (knowledge, skills, and abilities) that an employee must have to perform it.

**job enlargement**   The adding of challenges or new responsibilities to an employee's current job.

**job experience**   The relationships, problems, demands, tasks, and other features that an employee faces on the job.

**job hopping**   The practice of employees changing jobs usually between companies every two to three years.

**job incumbent**   An employee currently holding a particular job.

**job rotation**   Assigning employees a series of jobs in various functional areas of a company or movement among jobs in a single functional area or department.

**job sharing**   A work situation in which two employees divide the hours, responsibilities, and benefits of a full-time job.

**joint union-management training program**   A program created, funded, and supported by both union and management to provide a range of services to help employees learn skills that are directly related to their jobs and that are "portable" (valuable to employers in other companies or industries).

**kaizen**   Practices in which employees from all levels of the company focus on continuous improvement of business processes.

**key behaviors**   A set of behaviors that is necessary to complete a task; an important part of behavior modeling training.

**knowledge**   Facts or procedures that individuals or teams of employees know or know how to do (human and social knowledge); also a company's rules, processes, tools, and routines (structured knowledge).

**knowledge management**   The process of enhancing company performance by designing and implementing tools, processes, systems, structures, and cultures to improve the creating, sharing, and use of knowledge.

**knowledge officer**   A leader of a company's knowledge management efforts (also called a chief learning officer).

**knowledge workers**   Employees who own the means of producing a product or service. These employees have a specialized body of knowledge or expertise that they use to perform their jobs and contribute to company effectiveness.

**lapse**   Situation in which a trainee uses previously learned, less effective capabilities instead of trying to apply capabilities emphasized in a training program.

**leaderless group discussion**   A training exercise in which a team of five to seven employees must work together to solve an assigned problem within a certain time period.

**lean thinking**   Doing more with less effort, equipment, space, and time, but providing customers with what they need and want. Part of lean thinking includes training workers in new skills or how to apply old skills in new ways so that they can quickly take over new responsibilities or use new skills to help fill customer orders.

**learner control**   A trainee's ability to learn actively through self-pacing, exercises, exploring links to other material, and conversations with other trainees and experts.

**learner-content interaction**   The learner interacts with the training content such as reading text on the web or in books, listening to multimedia modules and in activities that require the manipulation of tools or objects such as writing and completing case studies.

**learner-instructor interaction**   Discussion between the learner and the expert (trainer).

**learner-learner interaction**   Discussion between learners with or without an instructor.

**learning**   The acquisition of knowledge by individual employees or groups of employees who are willing to apply that knowledge in their jobs in making decisions and accomplishing tasks for the company; a relatively permanent change in human capabilities that does not result from growth processes.

**learning management systems (LMS)**   A system for automating the administration of online training programs.

**learning organization**   A company that has an enhanced capacity to learn, adapt, and change; an organization whose employees continuously attempt to learn new things and then apply what they have learned to improve product or service quality.

**learning orientation**   Learners who try to increase their ability or competence in a task.

**lecture**   A training method in which the trainer communicates through spoken words what trainees are supposed to learn.

**lesson plan overview**   A plan that matches a training program's major activities to specific times or time intervals.

**Lifelong Learning Account (LiLA)**   An account for adult education to which both the employee and the company contribute and the employee keeps—even if he or she leaves the company.

**logical verification** Perceiving a relationship between a new task and a task that has already mastered.

**maintenance** The process of continuing to use newly acquired capabilities over time.

**Malcolm Baldrige National Quality Award** A national award created in 1987 to recognize U.S. companies' quality achievements and to publicize quality strategies.

**managing diversity and inclusion** The creation of an environment that allows all employees (regardless of their demographic group) to contribute to organizational goals and experience personal growth.

**massed practice** A training approach in which trainees practice a task continuously without resting.

**mental requirements** The degree to which a person must use or demonstrate mental skills or cognitive skills or abilities to perform a task.

**mentor** An experienced, productive senior employee who helps develop a less experienced employee (a protégé).

**metacognition** A learning strategy whereby trainees direct their attention to their own learning process.

**metrics** Business-level outcomes chosen to measure the overall value of training or learning initiatives.

**micro blogs or micro sharing** Software tools such as Twitter that enable communications in short bursts of text, links, and multimedia either through standalone applications or through online communities or social networks.

**mission** A company's long-term reason for existing.

**mobile learning** refers to informal or formal learning delivered using a mobile device such as a smartphone, netbook, notebook computer, or i-Pad.

**modeling** Having employees who have mastered the desired learning outcomes demonstrate them for trainees.

**modeling display** A training method in which trainees are shown key behaviors, which they then practice; often done by videotape or computer.

**motivation to learn** A trainee's desire to learn the content of a training program.

**motor skills** Coordination of physical movements.

**Myers-Briggs Type Inventory (MBTI)** A psychological test for employee development consisting of over 100 questions about how the person feels or prefers to behave in different situations.

**near transfer** A trainee's ability to apply learned capabilities exactly to the work situation.

**need** A deficiency that a person is experiencing at any point in time.

**needs assessment** The process used to determine if training is necessary; the first step in the Instructional System Design (ISD) model.

**nine-box grid** A three-by-three matrix used by groups of managers and executives to compare employees within one department, function, division, or the entire company for analysis and discussion of talent, to help formulate effective development plans and activities, and to identify talented employees who can be groomed for top-level management positions in the company.

**norms** Accepted standards of behavior for work-group members.

**objective** The purpose and expected outcome of training activities.

**offshoring** The process of moving jobs from the United States to other locations in the world.

**onboarding** The orientation process for newly hired managers.

**online learning** Instruction and delivery of training by computer online through the Internet or web.

**on-the-job training (OJT)** Training in which new or inexperienced employees learn through first observing peers or managers performing a job and then trying to imitate their behavior.

**open skills** Training objectives linked to general learning principles.

**opportunity to perform** The chance to use learned capabilities.

**organizational analysis** A training analysis that determines the appropriateness of training, considering the context in which training will occur.

**organizing** A learning strategy that requires the learner to find similarities and themes in training materials.

**other** In task analysis, a term referring to the conditions under which tasks are performed; for example, physical condition of the work environment or psychological conditions, such as pressure or stress.

**output** A job's performance standards.

**outsourcing** The acquisition of training and development activities from outside a company.

**overall task complexity** The degree to which a task requires a number of distinct behaviors, the number of choices involved in performing the task, and the degree of uncertainty in performing the task.

**overlearning**  Employees' continuing to practice even if they have been able to perform the objective several times.

**part practice**  A training approach in which each objective or task is practiced individually as soon as it is introduced in a training program.

**past accomplishments**  A system of allowing employees to build a history of successful accomplishments.

**perception**  The ability to organize a message from the environment so that it can be processed and acted upon.

**performance analysis approach**  An approach to solving business problems that identifies performance gaps or deficiencies and examines training as a possible solution.

**performance appraisal**  The process of measuring an employee's performance.

**performance orientation**  A learner's focus on task performance and how the learner compares to others.

**person analysis**  Training analysis that involves (1) determining whether performance deficiencies result from lack of knowledge, skill, or ability or else from a motivational or work-design problem, (2) identifying who needs training, and (3) determining employees' readiness for training.

**person characteristics**  An employee's knowledge, skill, ability, behavior, or attitudes.

**phased retirement**  A phase during which older employees gradually reduce their hours, which helps them transition into retirement.

**physical requirements**  The degree to which a person must use or demonstrate physical skills and abilities to perform and complete a task.

**pilot testing**  The process of previewing a training program with potential trainees and managers or other customers.

**plug-in**  Extra software that needs to be loaded on a computer, for example, to listen to sound or watch video.

**posttest only**  An evaluation design in which only posttraining outcomes are collected.

**posttraining measure**  A measure of outcomes taken after training.

**power**  The ability to influence others.

**practicality**  The ease with which outcome measures can be collected.

**practice**  An employee's demonstration of a learned capability; the physical or mental rehearsal of a task, knowledge, or skill to achieve proficiency in performing the task or skill or demonstrating the knowledge.

**preretirement socialization**  The process of helping employees prepare for exit from work.

**presence**  In training, the perception of actually being in a particular environment.

**presentation methods**  Training methods in which trainees are passive recipients of information.

**pretest/posttest**  An evaluation design in which both pretraining and post-training outcome measures are collected.

**pretest/posttest with comparison group**  An evaluation design that includes trainees and a comparison group. Both pretraining and posttraining outcome measures are collected.

**pretraining measure**  A baseline measure of outcomes.

**program design**  The organization and coordination of a training program.

**promotion**  An advancement into a position with greater challenges, more responsibility, and more authority than the previous job provided; usually includes a pay increase as well.

**protean career**  A career that is frequently changing based on changes in the person's interests, abilities, and values as well as changes in the work environment.

**psychological success**  A feeling of pride and accomplishment that comes from achieving life goals.

**psychosocial support**  Serving as a friend and role model to an employee; also includes providing positive regard, acceptance, and an outlet for the protégé to talk about anxieties and fears.

**random assignment**  The assignment of employees to training or a comparison group on the basis of chance.

**rapid instructional design (RID)**  A group of techniques that allows training to be built more quickly; the two principles of RID are that instructional content and process can be developed independently of each other and that resources devoted to design and delivery of instruction can be reallocated as appropriate.

**rapid needs assessment**  A needs assessment that is done quickly and accurately but without sacrificing the quality of the process or the outcomes.

**rapid prototyping**  An iterative process used in designing e-learning in which initial design ideas are proposed and provided in rough form in an online working prototype that is reviewed and refined by design team members.

**reaction outcomes**  A trainee's perceptions of a training program, including perceptions of the facilities, trainers, and content.

**readability** Written materials' level of difficulty.

**readiness for training** The condition of (1) employees having the personal characteristics necessary to learn program content and apply it on the job, and (2) the work environment facilitating learning and not interfering with performance.

**realistic job preview** Stage in which a prospective employee is provided accurate information about attractive and unattractive aspects of a job, working conditions, company, and location to be sure that the employee develops appropriate expectations.

**reality check** The information employees receive about how the company evaluates their skills and knowledge and where they fit into the company's plans (potential promotion opportunities, lateral moves).

**reasonable accommodation** In terms of the Americans with Disabilities Act (ADA) and training, making training facilities readily accessible to and usable by individuals with disabilities; may also include modifying instructional media, adjusting training policies, and providing trainees with readers or interpreters.

**recycling** Changing one's major work activity after having been established in a particular field.

**rehearsal** A learning strategy focusing on learning through repetition (memorization).

**reinforcement theory** A theory emphasizing that people are motivated to perform or avoid certain behaviors because of past outcomes that have resulted from those behaviors.

**reliability** The degree to which outcomes can be measured consistently over time.

**repatriation** Preparing expatriates for return to the parent company and country from a foreign assignment.

**repurposing** Directly translating a training program that uses a traditional training method onto the web.

**request for proposal (RFP)** A document that outlines for potential vendors and consultants the requirements for winning and fulfilling a contract with a company.

**resistance to change** Managers' and/or employees' unwillingness to change.

**results** Outcomes used to determine a training program's payoff.

**retirement** The leaving of a job and work role to make the transition into life without work.

**retrieval** The identification of learned material in long-term memory and use of it to influence performance.

**return on expectations (ROE)** The process through which evaluation demonstrates to key business stakeholders, such as top level managers, that their expectations about training have been satisfied.

**return on investment (ROI)** A comparison of a training program's monetary benefits and costs.

**reversal** A time period in which training participants no longer receive training intervention.

**role play** A training exercise in which the participant takes the part or role of a manager or some other employee; training method in which trainees are given information about a situation and act out characters assigned to them.

**sabbatical** A leave of absence from the company to renew or develop skills.

**scenario-based training** Training that places team members in a realistic context while learning.

**School-to-Work Opportunities Act** A federal law designed to assist states in building school-to-work systems that prepare students for high-skill, high-wage jobs or future education.

**sector partnerships** Government agencies and industry trade groups that help identify the skills that local employers require and work with community colleges, universities and other educational institutions to provide qualified employees.

**self-assessment** An employee's use of information to determine career interests, values, aptitudes, and behavioral tendencies.

**self-directed learning** Training in which employees take responsibility for all aspects of their learning (e.g., when it occurs, who is involved).

**self-efficacy** Employees' belief that they can perform their job or learn the content of a training program successfully.

**self-management** Person's attempt to control certain aspects of his or her decision making and behavior.

**self-regulation** Learner's involvement with the training material and assessing their progress toward learning.

**semantic encoding** The actual coding process of incoming memory.

**shared media** Audio or video such as YouTube that can be accessed and shared with others.

**simulation** A training method that represents a real-life situation, with trainees' decisions resulting in outcomes that mirror what would happen if they were on the job.

**situational constraints**   Work environment characteristics that include lack of proper equipment, materials, supplies, budgetary support, and time.

**Six Sigma process**   A process of measuring, analyzing, improving, and then controlling processes once they have been brought within the Six Sigma quality tolerances or standards.

**skill**   Competency in performing a task.

**skill-based outcomes**   Outcomes used to assess the level of technical or motor skills or behavior; include skill acquisition or learning and on-the-job use of skills.

**social capital**   The value of relationships among employees within a company.

**social learning**   Learning with and from others.

**social learning theory**   A theory emphasizing that people learn by observing other persons (models) who they believe are credible and knowledgeable.

**social media**   Online and mobile technology used to create interactive communications allowing the creation and exchange of user-generated content

**social network analysis**   A map of employee relationships that can be used to help identify informal employee communications and information- and knowledge-sharing patterns.

**social support**   Feedback and reinforcement from managers and peers.

**Solomon four-group**   An evaluation design combining the pretest/post-test comparison group and the post-test-only control group designs.

**spaced practice**   A training approach in which trainees are given rest intervals within the practice session.

**staffing strategy**   A company's decisions regarding where to find employees, how to select them, and the mix of employee skills and statuses.

**stakeholders**   The parties with an interest in a company's success (include shareholders, employees, customers, and

**strategic choice**   The strategy believed to be the best alternative to achieve the company goals.

**strategic training and development initiatives** Learning-related actions that a company takes to achieve its business strategy.

**strategic value**   Employees potential to improve company effectiveness and efficiency.

**subject-matter expert (SME)**   A person who knows a great deal about (1) training issues, (2) the knowledge, skills, and abilities required for task performance, (3) necessary equipment, and (4) the conditions under which tasks have to be performed.

**success cases**   Concrete examples of the impact of training that show how learning leads to results that the company finds worthwhile and the managers find credible.

**succession planning**   The process of identifying and tracking high-potential employees for advancement in a company.

**summative evaluation**   Evaluation of the extent that trainees have changed as a result of participating in a training program.

**support network**   A group of two or more trainees who agree to meet and discuss their progress in using learned capabilities on the job.

**survivor**   An employee remaining with a company after downsizing.

**sustainability**   The ability of a company to make a profit without sacrificing the resources of its employees, the community, or the environment.

**SWOT analysis**   An identification of a company's operating environment as well as an internal analysis of its strengths and weaknesses. SWOT is an acronym for Strengths, Weaknesses, Opportunities, and Threats.

**synchronous communication**   Communication in which trainers, experts, and learners interact with each other live and in real time in the same way that they would in face-to-face classroom instruction.

**tacit knowledge**   Personal knowledge that is based on individual experience and that is difficult to explain to others.

**talent management**   The process of attracting, retaining, developing, and motivating highly skilled employees and managers.

**task**   A statement of an employee's work activity in a specific job.

**task analysis**   Training analysis that involves identifying the tasks and knowledge, skills, and behaviors that need to be emphasized in training for employees to complete their tasks.

**task redefinition**   Changes in managers' and/or employees' roles and methods.

**team leader training**   Training that a team manager or facilitator receives.

**team training**   A training method that involves coordinating the performances of individuals who work together to achieve a common goal.

**telecommuting**   Working in a remote location (distant from a central office), where the employee has limited contact with peers but can communicate electronically (also called *teleworking*).

**teleconferencing** The synchronous exchange of audio, video, and/or text between two or more individuals or groups at two or more locations.

**temporary assignments** Job tryouts including employee exchanges and volunteer assignments in which employees take on a position to help them determine if they are interested in working in a new role.

**threats to validity** Factors that lead one to question either (1) the believability of a study's results or (2) the extent to which evaluation results are generalizable to other groups of trainees and situations.

**time series** An evaluation design in which training outcomes are collected at periodic intervals pre- and post-training.

**Total Quality Management (TQM)** A style of doing business that relies on the talents and capabilities of both labor and management to build and provide high-quality products and services and continuously improve them.

**traditional training methods** Training methods requiring an instructor or facilitator and involve face-to-face interaction between trainees.

**training** A company's planned effort to facilitate employees' learning of job-related competencies.

**training administration** Coordination of activities before, during, and after a training program.

**training context** The physical, intellectual, and emotional environment in which training occurs.

**training design process** A systematic approach to developing training programs. Its six steps include conducting needs assessment, ensuring employees' readiness for training, creating a learning environment, ensuring transfer of training, selecting training methods, and evaluating training programs.

**training effectiveness** The benefits that a company and its trainees receive from training.

**training evaluation** The process of collecting the outcomes needed to determine whether training has been effective.

**training outcomes (criteria)** Measures that a company and its trainer use to evaluate training programs.

**training site** The place where training is conducted.

**transfer** Giving an employee a different job assignment in a different area of the company.

**transfer of training** Trainees' applying to their jobs the learned capabilities gained in training.

**tuition reimbursement** The practice of reimbursing employees the costs for college and university courses and degree programs.

**Uniformed Services Employment and Reemployment Rights Act** An act that covers deployed employees' rights, such as guaranteeing jobs when they return, except under special circumstances.

**uniqueness** The extent to which employees are rare and specialized and not highly available in the labor market.

**upward feedback** An appraisal process involving the collection of subordinates' evaluations of managers' behaviors or skills.

**utility analysis** A cost-benefit analysis method that involves assessing the dollar value of training based on estimates of the difference in job performance between trained and untrained employees, the number of individuals trained, the length of time a training program is expected to influence performance, and the variability in job performance in the untrained group of employees.

**valence** The value that a person places on an outcome.

**values** Principles and virtues that symbolize the company's beliefs.

**verbal information** Names or labels, facts, and bodies of knowledge.

**verbal persuasion** Offering words of encouragement to convince others that they can learn.

**vicarious reinforcement** A situation in which a trainee sees an example of someone being reinforced for using certain behaviors.

**virtual classroom** Using a computer and the Internet to distribute instructor-led training to geographically dispersed employees.

**virtual expatriate** An employee assigned to work on an operation in another country without being located permanently in it.

**virtual reality** Computer-based technology that provides trainees with a three-dimensional learning experience in a simulated environment that responds to their behaviors and reactions.

**virtual team** A team that is separated by time, geographic distance, culture, and/or organizational boundaries and that relies almost exclusively on technology to interact and complete projects.

**virtual work arrangement** A work arrangement (including virtual teams as well as teleworking) in which location, organization structure, and employment relationship are not limiting factors.

**vision** The picture of the future that a company wants to achieve.

**Web 2.0** User-created social networking features on the Internet, including blogs, wikis, and Twitter.

**Web-based training** Training delivered on public or private computer networks and displayed by a web browser (also called Internet-based training).

**webcasting** Classroom instructions that are provided online through live broadcasts.

**whole practice** A training approach in which all tasks or objectives are practiced at the same time.

**wiki** A website that allows many users to create, edit, and update content and share knowledge.

**workforce analytics** The practice of using quantitative methods and scientific methods to analyze data from human resource databases, corporate financial statements, employee surveys and other data-sources to make evidence-based decisions and show that human resource practices (including training, development, and learning) influence important company metrics.

**Workforce Investment Act** A 1998 federal law that created a new, comprehensive work force investment system that is customer focused, that provides Americans with career management information and high-quality services, and that helps U.S. companies find skilled workers.

**working storage** The rehearsal and repetition of information, allowing it to be coded for memory.

**work life balance** Helping employees deal with the stresses, strains, and conflicts related to trying to balance work and non-work demands.

**work team** A group of employees with various skills who interact to assemble a product or produce a service.

# Name Index

# Company Index

# Subject Index